T0300810

CLOUDLAND JOURNAL
BOOK ONE

The First Year of Exploration
and Personal Discovery
in the Wilderness

TIM ERNST

CLOUDLAND.NET PUBLISHING
Cave Mountain, Arkansas
www.Cloudland.net

Printed and bound in the United States of America
Library of Congress Control Number: 2008908120
ISBN: 978–1882906–659

Most of the names in this book
have not been changed to protect the innocent.

Other books by Tim Ernst

Arkansas Landscapes picture book
Arkansas Waterfalls picture book
Buffalo River Dreams picture book
Arkansas Portfolio II picture book
Arkansas Wilderness picture book
Arkansas Spring picture book
Buffalo River Wilderness picture book
Wilderness Reflections picture book
Arkansas Portfolio picture book
Arkansas Nature Lover's guidebook
Arkansas Waterfalls guidebook
Arkansas Hiking Trails guidebook
Arkansas Dayhikes for Kids guidebook
Ozark Highlands Trail guidebook
Ouachita Trail guidebook
Buffalo River Hiking Trails guidebook
The Search For Haley

Autographed copies may be ordered direct from

www.Cloudland.net

CLOUDLAND.NET PUBLISHING
HC 33, 50–A
Pettigrew, Arkansas 72752 (Cave Mountain)
870–861–5536

Contents

Introduction

It is a beautiful day in the wilderness today, a textbook fall afternoon with blue skies, puffy white clouds, and crisp-clean cool air. The only sounds I hear are the music of the Buffalo River far below, and the screams from a pair of red-tailed hawks soaring nearby. I'm sitting out on the back deck of my cabin, feet propped up on the railing, and enjoying the day. The electricity to the cabin has been off for several hours so I am writing this by hand—that seems fitting since the beginning of the Journal was also written by hand!

It was more than ten years ago when I first put pencil to paper and started to write down my thoughts about this new life I was beginning in the wilderness. I wanted to keep a record of what went on out here, the good times and the bad. At first I wanted to keep a journal for an entire year, then perhaps publish it as a book to share with others. Then I decided to post my musings on my web page just in case anyone was interested. I soon discovered that a lot of people were indeed interested, and soon had a regular following of folks who logged on each week to see what this grizzled wilderness guy was up to.

Even though I was not much of a writer and had no formal training, the words came easy for me that first year—there were so many new and exciting things going on here that it was natural just to sit down and talk about them. I discovered that it was also an outlet for me to spill my guts when things were not going well—when you live alone in the wilderness there is only so much you can shout at the trees! When you are writing out your feelings it is a one-way conversation and often much easier to be truthful with yourself, and there is no one to be embarrassed in front of for being silly.

As the end of that first 12 months drew near I began to get e-mails from folks who did not want me to stop writing. Hundreds of e-mails in fact. I had no idea this Journal had impacted so many lives, but was thrilled and humbled and almost in disbelief. How did so many folks find it, and why keep reading? I've received many tales over the years from folks who spent hours each day reading the Journal *at work*—oops, sorry about that!

So I continued to write, and kept putting off publishing the book. I wrote more, and more. The years and the adventures rolled on. When the ten year mark arrived I decided it was time to finally produce a hard copy. No way to squeeze all of the text from those years into a single book (more than a quarter million words in the first year alone!), so I am going to try to make it a Trilogy. Book One contains the complete first year of the Journal (with a few edits). Other volumes will follow as I get to them. Turns out the online Journal is one of the oldest and longest-running of its kind on the Internet.

There are not any photos in this book for a couple of reasons. First, that was way back before the advent of "see photos now" digital cameras (1998–1999). And secondly, color photos would have made this first book *really* fat and expensive. To see photos that go along with the text you can visit the original Journal online at www.Cloudland.net.

One note about my situation during that first year—I actually lived and worked in Fayetteville, not at Cloudland. I had built the cabin the year before and was slowly finishing the inside and moving my stuff in, although I was not quite ready to make the move to fulltime wilderness living. I spent a great deal of time at the cabin during this first year of the Journal, and made a lot of discoveries, both in the wilderness and within myself.

The cabin was actually built in Montana from my design by a group of Amish craftsman, then moved to my property in Newton County and reconstructed by a local group of Amish workers. I've been refining it ever since.

I have just completed going back through the entire first year of the original Journal and doing a bit of light editing to make everything fit. It was the first time I read any of it since writing it all down ten years ago. All I can say is *WOW!* It was one incredible year, and I hope you enjoy tagging along with me as it all unfolds. Stay tuned for more to come...

Tim Ernst

The original Journal was written by hand in a loose-leaf notebook. On the first page, before I began to write any notes, was this:

This is the first entry in this Journal, and the first day of its life. It has taken nearly a year to get this Journal started. A journal and guest register have been on my list all that time, but it was my girlfriend, Leslie, who finally bought a notebook, gave it to me for my birthday, and said to use it, *now!* This Journal will serve as the official record of dates and facts, and the place for my notes. It will be a reflection of life here at Cloudland. I plan to write something in it most every day that I am here. Anything of interest that happens, or is seen or felt might be recorded here. Once a weather station is installed, I'll have a running log* of that information too. Birds. Wildlife. Strange visitors. The changing of the seasons. Parties. Great Food. Whatever. Fair warning to all who come to party or find love here—most names will not be changed to protect the innocent! This Journal will be uploaded, along with a few selected pictures, to the official Cloudland Home Page on the world wide web for all to see and read. Thanks for reading, and *enjoy!*

* Due to power outages I was not able to post this info for every month

MAY 1998

5/16/98

The sun rose into a clear sky early this morning, the first blue in a while. It has been hazy and cloudy all week as the result of smoke from a giant Mexican forest fire, and rather warm. A cool front swept away the smoke, and temps were in the 50's. Ever since I built this cabin, I have vowed to explore a new place in the wilderness from Cloudland each month. Today will be my first such venture. I have a lot of catching up to do! The bluff across Whitaker Creek is where I will head, and take a picture of the cabin, just to see and show what it looks like from over there.

I left my trusted guard dog Stable behind to guard the cabin and headed down the old historical trail to the river with water, "extractor" (snake bite kit), and camera in my daypack, and wearing long pants and long-sleeved shirt (welcome attire in the summer jungle). I took the Ladder Trail down to Whitaker Creek—the underbrush had *really* grown up already. (The "Ladder Trail" is the historical trail that connected the mouth of Whitaker Creek to the Cave Mountain Church and schoolhouse. Folks in the area along the Buffalo River used it quite often way back when. It takes its name from the fact that a ladder was required to make it up/down through the bluffline, which breaks down to only about 12 feet tall where the trail comes to it, which is right near my property. Above the ladder, the trail crosses my property on its way to the church. When I bought the property in 1992, the old ladder had rotted away, so I replaced it with a new one, which is still in use.) The sun was still low, and barely made it through the trees. It was rather dark. I was surprised at how much water there was flowing in Whitaker Creek. From up on the back deck at Cloudland before the trip down, the wind was still and I could hear the Buffalo River talking loudly, so I guess there was more water everywhere than I had thought. It was good to see all that water.

I crossed through two rock walls that were lining what was probably an old field on the other side of the creek. An old road trace left the area going uphill, so I followed it. Bill McNamara (a neighbor and a talented watercolor artist) had always told me that there were wagon wheel grooves cut into the bluffs above, but other locals have said that there is no such road between here and Lovell Hollow, far upstream. Sure enough, the road headed UP the hillside, even switchbacking at one point, and I had high hopes. About two-thirds of the way up to the bluff, the road landed on a level bench next to a large boulder, and disappeared. I didn't spend any time searching further, but headed straight up the steep hillside to the base of the bluff. It was an impressive bluffline, much larger than I had expected. Gosh darn it, how was I going to find a way up through it?

I turned to the right and followed the bluff around the point, then headed up the Whitaker Creek drainage. The trees were so full and thick that I really couldn't see out much. A squirrel up ahead jumped from his tree onto the bluff, then ran up the face of the bluff and out of sight. He was actually showing me a way up, and I thanked him. The bluff was broken up some, and there were dozens of Ozark columbine wildflowers growing on the face—the best patch that I had ever seen! After a bit of a struggle, I made my way up through the broken bluff and onto the top. There were no really open views, but I did manage to snap a picture through the trees of my cabin and Buffalo River Valley beyond.

Then I spotted a small but brilliantly colored tree with red leaves. I had seen this very tree last week through the telescope. It really stuck out with all of the green trees around it. Don't know why it turned red. I grabbed a leaf to make an ID, but I think it was a serviceberry.

I made my way around to the point overlooking the Buffalo River. It was quite a stunning view, and I could see both up and down the valley, although the view would be much better during leaf-off (after the leaves fall off the trees). This is a great spot to sit and welcome the sunrise, as I imagine Ozark pioneers and Indians have done in the past. There were a bunch of firepink wildflowers right there that must see the sunrise every day.

I turned around and made my way up the Whitaker drainage, still along the top of the bluffline. At one point, it looked like there was going to be another way down. As I scrambled down the steep incline, the land came to an abrupt end—it was another 30 to 40 foot drop. It looked like a waterfall area when there was a lot of runoff. Peering over the edge, I was greeted with an umbrella magnolia tree, growing up towards me. It was covered with *perfect* blossoms! The huge leaves formed a round backdrop to the flowers, which were all the way open and laying flat on the leaves. I thought about these trees for a moment, and decided that they must seek out scenic areas to live, and only those in the most scenic locations, like this one, are allowed to bloom.

As I continued along the bluff it finally broke up again and I found a way down. Under the bluff near there was an overhang guarding a sea of what looked to me like some sort of sorrel wildflower. I took a snapshot and hoped to ID them later. They had tiny pink flowers.

On the way down the steep hillside I made two decisions. One was that I would spend a great deal of time exploring this wonderful wilderness during the next year, make an effort to keep notes, and then put it all into a book. I don't really need an excuse to be in the woods anymore, but what the heck. And I decided that I would also make an effort to try to learn how to sketch. A pencil and pad are a lot lighter than a lot of bulky camera gear, not dependent on good light, and easier to put into a book if any are usable. Of course, a sketch takes a lot longer to produce (and also requires talent, something I lack)!

Before long I landed back at Whitaker Creek and stuck my head under—cold creek water is such a wonderful thing when you are hot and sweaty! I headed straight up the hillside, and soon found myself back at the ladder. A shooting star wildflower, one of the last of a very good season for them, met me at the top of the ladder. As I looked up, I could see spiderworts dotting the hillside, all lit up by the still early morning sun.

It was a great first hike but I was glad to get back to Cloudland, take off my boots, sit back in the swing, and gaze across my kingdom...

The main project for the day was to attempt a complicated wiring project downstairs in the basement. It took me over four hours, but I actually managed to get two sets of three-way lights and switches wired together, and they all worked! It is amazing what you can learn out of a book.

My girlfriend was going to come out to the cabin for the weekend, but her car gave up and she got delayed. I made up some Cloudland Appetizers to take to the "First Annual Buffalo Bash" at friends Dean and Bonnie LaGrone's property, which is located down across Boxley Valley and up on Walker Mountain (a ten mile drive). Just in case the Greek invention of mine didn't work out, I also packed up a case of cold Arkansas Ale.

It is a steep haul up to the LaGrone's, but it is a really nice piece of bench property—the views down into Boxley Valley are good, but would be really great if they would just cut out all of those big trees! We all sat around the fire and had beer, bratwurst (very good), burgers, and a fine time. Roy and Norma Senyard, Dean and Bonnie, Bob and Dawna Robinson, and assorted others were there. Oh yea, the Greek rolls disappeared before I got one. My girlfriend at the time, Leslie Brashears, arrived from Fayetteville in time to enjoy.

Back at Cloudland after the party, Leslie read the first part of this Journal (written by hand in the journal book that she gave me). She said that I should concentrate on writing more and talking less. Hum. I didn't know how to take that, but at least that was one vote to continue writing in this Journal!

5/17/98 Stable and I got up early and went for a short walk. I noticed a number of tiny yellow flowers popping up—I think they were buttercups. Also saw several cicadas moving about. I was always fascinated as a kid with the empty shells of themselves that they shed and leave behind. Still am. I always get them confused with katydids, which are the bright green ones. The arrival of the cicadas marks the beginning of summer to me. I have many fond memories of going to sleep to their songs on hot summer nights in my youth.

Leslie and I had Cloudland Coffee and a Cloudland Omelet in bed (do you see a trend in naming foods here). After a nap we headed up the hill for a walk, visiting Bob Chester's garden along the way (he has an old cabin nearby but is only there a day or two at a time—his residence is in Ft. Smith). We hiked across the East Meadow towards a group of rare wild yellow lady-slipper orchids. We noticed how huge the umbrella magnolia leaves were, and how they grew in wet areas—must need a lot of water to feed those giant leaves. I looked and looked and couldn't find the lady-slippers anywhere. I knew they wouldn't be yellow anymore, but I couldn't believe that I couldn't find the plants. It was really becoming a jungle out there. I pulled up a small sassafras plant and held the root to my noise as we walked along, enjoying every deep breath of the sweet aroma. Leslie did not like the fragrance at all.

My brother, Terry, his wife Marsha (she is responsible for the animal slippers and beanie babies that populate the cabin), and my mom came by in the afternoon. They brought a case of fine wine from my sister (birthday present). Terry and Marsha went on back to Illinois, and Leslie fixed spaghetti and salad for lunch. We lingered on as long as we could, enjoying the afternoon to the fullest (some fun stuff went on up in the loft while mom and Stable enjoyed the back deck), then we left Cloudland behind and headed back into town.

5/20/98 I arrived just before dark and it seemed almost as hot as it was in town—getting hot a little too early for me this year! The cabin was nice and cool though, about 15 degrees cooler than outside. I spent the evening planning the next day's projects, and enjoying a new stereo.

5/21/98 I awoke to the sound of raindrops on the tin roof—rain, yea! My excitement was short lived, as I realized that the rain was only heavy dew running off of the roof. Bob and I planned an early hike to go see the lady-slippers and showy orchids, so I got my boots on and headed out. An orange ball broke through the haze and filled the woods with streaks of brilliant glowing light. Before I reached the gate, the streaks had turned to yellow and then to white—sunrise was complete.

There is a patch of wild bergamot (a wild mint that you can make tea from—used to make Earl Gray tea, my favorite) on both sides of the road as you leave my property and enter the Faddis Meadow. There was an orange butterfly on almost every plant—I counted almost 60 of them! It was an amazing sight, and they seemed to quiver in the new light. This is one of those scenes that you could never photograph very well, but that I would like to be able to sketch (it would have to be in color). As I walked on by, all of the butterflies took to the air at once, filling the morning sky with more yellow streaks.

When I got to Bob's cabin—and this is a *first*—he was still in bed! We headed down the hill, past the old orchard (only one old apple tree left now). He took me to the showy orchids, which live at the base of a large ash tree, right next to the creek. Their blooms had faded, but Bob said it was a great year for them. We both walked past the lady-slippers without seeing them. Now I felt a little better about missing them before (Bob couldn't find them either). We did eventually find them (just before the end of the old road, marked with three rocks). Their blooms had faded as well. I did manage to get a good picture of them a couple of weeks before, and it can be found on page 100 in the new ***Buffalo River Wilderness*** picture book.

I spent much of the day working on more wiring in the basement. After many hours of work, the power flow didn't go as expected. It was HOT outside, nearing 90 degrees. The basement remained a cool 68 degrees. I got frustrated and gave in to the wires and the heat and sat down and had an Arkansas Ale.

The shadows were growing long so I headed up the hill to Bob's place to check on a door he had called about (he went back to town). A black bear had wrecked the outside of his place the week before, and he wanted me to check that the door was all closed up. It was like an oven inside his place, but I sat down anyway and read the Jasper paper. There was an article about a twelve-year old boy from Jasper that was becoming a great elk photographer.

I heard something out on the back deck. Certainly it couldn't have been the bear. I was about the only one around who hadn't seen him yet. I thought it must have been Eddy Silcott or Billy Woods dropping by. I went outside, down the deck steps, and peeked around the corner. Son of a gun, there was a tall and *very* black bear, standing up on his back legs, leaning against the cabin. Damn! He turned and looked at me with one of those "What do you want?" looks. He had the most luxurious black coat that I had ever seen—deep black, shiny, and lustrous. He was a very healthy bear, and looked a bit out of place standing there against the cabin wall looking at me. Oh yea, that's right, there was a big black bear, 24 feet away, looking right at me, and he was hungry!

My reaction was to take a step or two towards him, yell at the top of my lungs, and wave my arms like crazy. He got the message, turned and bounded off of the deck. I ran around the other side of the cabin to see if I could get a glimpse of his hind end disappearing in the woods, but instead I found him stopped right in the middle of the yard, looking back at me. I ran at him, making as much noise as I could, and he turned and headed down the hill towards the woods. He stopped again when he got to the woods, and looked my way. I really wanted him to associate this cabin with something negative, and I figured that a screaming maniac coming at him would do the trick, so I ran after him once again, and he lumbered into the steep woods and out of sight.

One note—bears look much smaller on the ground as they are running away from you than they do when they are standing up close staring at you.

As I walked back to the cabin I realized that I was still clutching the newspaper and must have been waving it at the bear the whole time. I sat down outside on Bob's deck to note the event in his journal, when I looked up and saw Mr. Bear again, coming out of the woods in my direction. I got up and chased him back into the woods. About five minutes later there was a tremendous crash out in the woods nearby, like a big tree had fallen over. It was getting dusky dark by then, and I decided that I had better hike back to Cloudland while I could still see. At that time of day, there is still plenty of light around you, but it drops off quickly and the woods become *very* dark. I wondered if the bear would follow me. I made it through Bob's fields OK, but felt a bit uncomfortable as I entered the dark woods of Cloudland. You must realize that in this situation, each squirrel that crashes through the brush (and there were many of them doing this) triggers an active imagination. It was a long walk home, and I was very glad to see the logs at Cloudland, glowing warm in the late evening light.

5/22/98 I got up early and sat on the porch swing and greeted the day. The summer bugs were very loud, and you could tell that it was going to be a hot day. I headed into town to do a TV interview, wired part of my mom's house that had gone bad, and then returned to Cloudland about dark. Bob had returned for the weekend. He had placed two coolers full of food on his deck railing, just daring Mr. Bear to return. I'll bet that he does return again within a week. So far, Mr. Bear has stayed on the north side of the ridge between Bob's place and Cloudland. While it is kind of nice knowing that he is in the neighborhood (Mr. Bear), I hope that he stays on that side of the ridge. I don't really have room for a bear rug at my place just yet.

I put up one of my fly rods on the wall over the picture window. It has always been my intent to only put stuff up on the walls that is both decorative *and* functional. The cross-country skis, snowshoes, fly rods, and gun can and will be taken off of the wall and used. I guess that I will have to put up a picture or two someday, but that will be OK. The only photo that I have put up so far is in the guest bathroom and it fits just great.

5/23/98 I must have been dreaming. I awoke to the sound of music. The woods were alive with the music of raindrops—yea!!! These raindrops were real, and I jumped up out of bed and ran into the morning to greet them. The shower didn't last too long, but it was as good as any in a fancy hotel. The summer bugs turned up the volume. I sat in the swing with a Starbucks mocha and a toasted bagel. Over the roar of the summer bugs, I could hear a dozen or more different kinds of birds singing in the distance—I think that they enjoyed the brief shower too.

It was cool this morning, with a light breeze filling the air. Jim Brickman turned down low on the stereo was a perfect complement to the bugs, birds and breeze. *Nothing* can match the relaxing atmosphere of an early morning at Cloudland!

Being Memorial Day weekend I fired up the grill and made myself the First Official Memorial Day Weekend Cookout: grilled apple-chicken sausage, green peppers, onions, and yellow squash; iced Arkansas Ale; and homemade Cloudland oatmeal chocolate chip cookies. *Very* good.

After I finished off the cookies I sat out on the deck and read a while, soaking up the cool breezes. Just as light rain began to fall, three hawks appeared in the canyon out back. I swear they weren't looking for food, but were simply playing in the wind, as happy for the rain as I. At some point, for an unknown reason, the summer bugs all stopped. Their sound was replaced with dozens and dozens of bird songs, coming from all directions, from close by and from far away across the valley. I need to learn some bird sound ID's!

After a much-needed nap I got busy and put together am oak trim around the kitchen bar. Like most things on this building project, it took me a lot longer to finish than I had expected. And I used every single power tool in the place. It is done, for now.

Later in the evening I went on the most amazing little walk, and I never really even left the area! After a second session at the BBQ, I headed out into the evening breeze, up the hill to do my usual loop to the Faddis place, over through the East Meadow, and back through the woods. It had stayed near 70 degrees all day, a welcome relief. The sun was very low, breaking through the clouds. The wind was tossing clumps of daisies around in the Faddis Meadow, painting a moving picture of color. The orange butterflies were back on the wild mint, and the glowing sun really lit them up. The connection road over to the East Meadow was lined with daisies along both sides and down the middle. I felt like I was walking into a painting as the graceful curves of this lane led me to the East Meadow.

As I stepped out into the open I looked up and saw three deer at the far end of the meadow. They saw me too. After a few seconds of nervousness, they went back to feeding in the lush green grass. This field, too, was dotted with clumps of white and yellow daisies, the rest being rich green something or other, about knee high. The colors of the entire scene grew richer with each step, as the setting sun cast "Ozarkglow" across it all. The deer moved about cautiously, twitching their tails and spending as much time watching me as they did feeding. Their fur was so bright brown and clean-looking, which is typical of this time of year. They let me get pretty close to them, too close probably, before they bounded off into the deep woods. I sat there in the grass at the upper end of the meadow until the last rays of light faded. On my way back, the clouds up high lit up brightly and lighted the path home.

5/24/98 I was out wandering around in the woods when the sun, once again a big orange ball, popped up over the hill and began to burn off the morning haze. It was clear skies above it all, and something told me that the cool high of 70 degrees from the day before would be long-gone. I sat on the back deck swing and watched the sunlight fill each little valley below, one at a time.

Today was a day for the little swifts, who dart about and dance in the air, devouring gobs of insects (I'm not really sure if they are swifts, I just call them that). These little birds were getting brave, and flew closer and closer to the cabin, sometimes even swooping down over the lower deck and almost under the porch. Way to go guys, eat them mosquitoes all up! Later, a couple of buzzards flew in closer too, and circled inside the open space, then landed on a snag. (The open space below the cabin is a meadow I cut out to act as a fire break, but also to open up the view.) A pileated woodpecker flew through this space today too. And I saw several bluebirds hanging around—I wondered if any of them were refugees from Bob's, tossed out into the wilds when his bear smashed their houses last week. I sure am glad that I cut all of those trees out of the way below the cabin, because the opening has really attracted a lot birds.

Bob said that he saw a pair of scarlet tanagers today. This is one bright bird that really stands out in the forest. Last year at about this same time, as I was just creating the opening below the cabin, a single scarlet tanager would sit in the snag out front for an hour or more. It was the first that I had ever seen, and I remember digging through the bird book back home to see what it was. There are at least two bird ID books at the cabin now, and I wish someone would use them and add to the "Cloudland Life List," which is located on the bookshelf. There is also a list of animals and trees and flowers that I've have seen here.

Leslie decided not to come out this weekend (a trend), so I had the place to myself (and all of the food that I brought out). I forced myself to eat a hearty plate of Cloudland Hash, and then drank a small pot of Cloudland Coffee. I don't really like coffee, but do make it when my girlfriend is here. I probably shouldn't have drank this pot by myself (it has a lot of booze in it). After a pot of this wonderful stuff, all I could do was sit out on the deck and watch the birds until it got too hot, then I laid around the cabin all day, enjoying the peace and quiet. When I sobered up a bit, I did climb up the big ladder (23 feet tall) and removed the insulation from the power vents in the ridgetop, and did some staining where some of the outside rails needed it.

But mostly I just laid around. It was near 90 degrees outside, 72 degrees on the main floor inside, and 65 degrees in the basement. I hiked over to Bob's near dark and had a glass of wine with he and Tom Triplet. The no-see-ums ate me up, so I didn't stay too long, but did have a nice hike back in the cooling twilight air.

5/25/98 The summer bugs must have been screaming for water all of this time, because at 4:30 this morning a big storm rolled through, dumped a lot of water, and I haven't heard a peep out of the bugs since. It was one of those classic summer thunderstorms, with lots of swirling winds, a sky full of lightning, thunder that bellows and rolls on forever, and hard rain. The temp dropped into the upper 50's, and Stable even crawled into his fuzzy bed for the first time in a couple of weeks.

I slept in late, and when I did get up, was greeted by a classic Cloudland vista. There were cloud banks hanging low, hiding the Buffalo River, and extending up into every side canyon. I sat out on the deck in awe. The scene changed dramatically every few minutes as the clouds moved back and forth—they were like solid light, moving and defining each ridge, separating the canyons from one another. At one point the clouds lifted right up to and engulfed the cabin.

Cloudland is where the clouds live and play. It is where sunlight comes to rest. Where the rain becomes sweet, and where the wind perfects its music. It is the place where birds vacation and find mates. It is a spa where one comes to renew the soul. You don't have to *do* anything here—you just have to *be* here. And enjoy. And as I found out while having my breakfast among the clouds this morning, Cloudland is also a place where when you drop your toasted bagel that is smothered with butter and raspberry preserves, it will land upright! What a place. If I ever tire of this place, if I ever say that I don't want to come here, if I say that it doesn't matter, then please light a match to my feet and scatter my ashes with the clouds.

The clouds opened up and it rained really hard for a couple of hours. I was forced to retreat to the couch, where I spent my time aboard ship with John Muir in Alaska. I even got a nap or two in. Then the sun broke through, and I got up and finished building the walls in the basement. Ray Scott and his girl-friend, Susan, came by to get his red vest that he had left at the cabin during an April photography workshop, then Stable and I headed home.

5/30/98 When I arrived this morning the first thing that I saw was a pair of red-tailed hawks sitting in the tree at the edge of the opening in the back. They both took off towards Hawksbill Crag, then circled back to see who had disturbed their Saturday morning sunbath. It was very cool in the cabin, but heating up rapidly outside, and the summer bugs were loud. This was going to be a work day, and it proved both very constructive, as well as quite long.

The first thing that I did was solve the problem with the extra log arm that sticks out from one of the back deck posts. One of the Amish kids installed this log arm there last summer—it sticks out and goes nowhere with no apparent reason to be. Most folks who visit ask what it is for, and so I have had to repeat that the Amish boy did it just for laughs over and over again. It isn't really structurally sound enough to hold anything, nor have I wanted to take it down. Now it is the proud resting place for a colorful windsock, showing a field of flowers and butterflies, with blue, yellow, purple and red streamers. It actually adds a great deal of class, color and motion to the place. While I had already bought the windsock when I ran into my ex-mother-in-law, Mary Jo Grisham, in Harrison Thursday night (haven't seen her in ten years), she is the one who first got me interested in such things. The butterflies are for my own mom. The sock is an accurate wind direction indicator too.

Speaking of the wind, installing the new weather station that I had just received (finally) was the big project first on my list. It will record the wind speed and direction, inside and outside temperatures and humidity (highs and lows), rainfall, windchill, dew point, and barometric pressure, plus it stores everything. Two of the cables weren't going to be long enough, and they were out of extension cables at the store, but I hooked everything up anyway, and set up the computer console in the loft bathroom (this was the only place where all of the cables would reach). The temp/humidity sensor and rain gauge locations were easy to establish, but the wind gauge was going to be tough. It was supposed to be mounted at least four feet above the roof line. I ended up selecting a location where the loft roof line breaks from the great room roof line. It was a tough spot to reach, and the metal roof was heating up rapidly. I managed to get everything set up without falling off of the roof, but realized that I would have to climb back up later and install a taller post—the gauge was only just above the roof line, and it probably would not give a good reading.

While I was up on the hot tin roof a red-tailed hawk paid a visit. He came in close, down low, and circled three times, making eye contact all the while. The tail feathers were quite colorful when backlit by the sun. This is one animal that really lives up to its descriptive name—it really *does* have a *red* tail (unlike redbud trees that are purple or firepink wildflowers that are bright red). The reason that he came by, except to say hi, was to show me his lunch—he was holding a rather large snake in his talons. This was a very smart hawk, who doesn't really have to hunt to survive. Next to one of the many snake trails in the woods, he had erected a sign. Whenever he gets hungry, he just goes to his sign and waits for a customer. I was glad that he came by to show off his lunch to me.

There was another wonderful creature nearby that I discovered—a luna moth sleeping on the side of the cabin, near the carport light. It was almost as large as my hand, and neon green color. It stayed there all day, oblivious to the noise that I was making above. This wonderful creature must have some great story behind it somewhere in history. It is so striking, and so large for a moth! I think perhaps the species migrated here from the moon, when the cheese all ran out (hence the name "luna" moth).

Another big project for the day was to replace all of the three-quarter-inch hot water lines with half-inch water lines. The smaller lines would be more efficient. I should have installed them in the first place. I was really dreading this job because it took Ken Eastin and I so long to put the lines in the first time, and I had to unhook all of the pipes before I could even begin this time. *Wow*, Ken and I must have been drinking a lot that day or something when we first put the pipes in, because replacing all of them this time was a snap—total time was less than two hours (it took us a couple of days last time). I now feel much better about the water situation, and get hot water a lot quicker at the taps. One odd note: I realized that the water in the hot water tank was still warm, even though it had been over five days since I had shut it off, and the basement was a constant 65 degrees—I've got a great hot water heater!

The next project was the loft closet. This was my main goal of the weekend, to put up shelves in the closet. Before I could do so, I had to run the wind gauge wire through the closet walls, cut out a hole in the bathroom wall for a built-in hamper in the closet, and install the new water pipe in this same closet wall, plus install cedar paneling on the closet walls.

It was kind of weird cutting a large hole in the aspen wall of the bathroom for the hamper (the interior walls of the cabin are covered with 1 x 6 inch aspen lumber from Colorado—beautiful), but after I did it and tried out the new convenience, I wondered why all bathrooms weren't so equipped—what a great idea! Hampers are too small and a pain to get into, and I just don't like a bucket of dirty clothes out in plain view in the bathroom, so it is only logical to me to toss the dirty clothes into the closet, where I have plenty of room.

Putting up the cedar was pretty easy, and *wow*, what a great smell! Finally I got to the shelves, which were more trouble to put up than I had expected, but now look and work great. It was good to get so many things done.

During the day I took frequent TV breaks. (I had decided that there is so much going on outside that can be seen from the back deck—as much entertainment as you would find on any TV screen—that I would call this view my TV—"Tim's View." I intentionally designed the cabin so that there would be no spot to put in a real TV, which would force one to seek entertainment elsewhere, like on the back deck.)

Boy, there sure was a lot going on outside! It was hot and hazy, but the soaring birds loved it. At one point, I could see seven different levels of soaring birds—some down in the canyons, some level with me, and many more high above. I could see buzzards miles away that were just specks. There were mostly buzzards, although there were also a lot of hawks out. One red-tailed hawk came in really close—the middle of the opening below the cabin seemed to be at the edge of his flight pattern, so close that I could really look into his eyes. I love doing that—makes me feel part of it all, like I am connected and interacting with these birds.

One hawk came in close several times but I couldn't figure out what species it was. It wasn't shaped or colored like a red-tailed hawk at all, and I couldn't find him in my bird books. I need some bird watcher at Cloudland to help ID. I had a telescope set up all day, but I realized that it was best suited for viewing stationary objects, like Hawksbill Crag, the river, or a distant tree. I really need a good pair of binocs for viewing birds. My little ones are actually pretty good, but a real pair would be ideal. Darn, sounds like another purchase.

While there wasn't too much traffic to the Crag on this hot day (I was keeping an eye on it through the tele), there was one young couple that caught my attention. She was wearing a tank top, hiking boots and cutoffs—very nice legs. I would consider it quite a compliment to be admired from over a half-mile away. Anyway, while they were sitting there talking, she reached into her daypack and pulled out a book and started looking through it. Upon close inspection with the tele, I realized that it was one of my guidebooks! It made me feel good that I helped this couple get to the wonderful spot that they were at and obviously were enjoying very much.

I normally don't like hot summer days, but the changing panorama in front of me was great, the wind was blowing, and I was utilizing my new favorite seat—an outdoor bar stool and table that I had just bought from Wal Mart. This seat is really comfortable, it swivels, and is high enough to get me up to see over the log rails that surround the deck.

One buzzard that came in close was easy to single out because he had a single main wing feather out of place and sticking straight up. It was interesting to see how the buzzards and hawks all soar together, not really paying much attention to each other. I guess they really aren't direct competitors, since the buzzards only eat dead stuff and the hawks normally enjoy the thrill of the hunt and the capture of live prey. All in all it was a great TV day!

I worked hard all day (except for the TV time), and only had a salad to eat—rather unusual for me. Also drank a gallon of sun tea. I worked until 11pm, took a shower and crawled into bed. The quarter moon lit up the canyon with an eerie glow. There was a lot of haze around too. Around midnight

I heard something—it was loud and deep with a regular beat. I went out on the loft deck and saw red lights coming at me from across the river. It was a big helicopter, and it was flying just about cabin level and moving slow. I couldn't see it plainly because of the trees, so I went down to the back deck. Soon the chopper was right over the open spot below the cabin, and as it passed, a spotlight came on and lit up the cabin. This was really weird! It was one of those big, twin-rotor choppers. It never stopped, and within a few seconds it turned off the spotlight. I could see how someone could mistake this for a UFO! I ran down to the lowest deck and watched it fly up Whitaker Valley. Now picture this—the eerie moonlight, the haze, and this giant helicopter hovering over the valley with Hawksbill Crag in its spotlight! This was really bizarre!

5/31/98 A whippoorwill outside my window woke me up at 5:20am. Don't recall hearing one early like this before, as they are usually night birds (it was still nighttime outside I guess). I had a big breakfast of Cloudland Hash, then hiked to Bob's. On the way I discovered that a frog had taken up residence in a mud hole that had been created by the recent rains in my road. There seemed like a new batch of wild mint near the gate—there was tons of it growing in the same spot as the wild bergamot. I soon realized that this new mint *was* the bergamot, without its floppy head. I need to make some tea out of this stuff, or perhaps mint juleps.

The mint was spreading but the daisies in the Faddis Meadow were dull and shrivelled up—they had been so bright and cheery just a week ago. I don't think it was because they got burned up (after all, they are a summer flower), but I guess the heavy rains that we had were too much for them. Bob's place was OK—no sign of my bear friend. There was an article on cicadas in the Jasper paper that I tore out. It did a pretty good job of explaining the little critters, and why there are so many of them this year.

There are several different kinds of cicadas. They all live in the ground, dormant for many years, then all of the same species emerge from the ground and crawl up into trees at about the same time. They only live above ground for a short time, to breed, lay eggs, then they die. And they shed their shells first thing. Two of the species are the 13 year variety and the 17 year variety. We are one of the few places in the country that have both species, and this year, for the first time in over 200 years, they both came out together. So there were actually *twice* the normal number of cicadas out there in the woods, making all kinds of racket. This noise is what I have been referring to as "summer bugs," although tree frogs and a few other assorted critters have also contributed. I heard a story on the local *Ozarks At Large* radio program (Fayetteville's NPR station, KUAF), that scientists and photographers from all over were in the Ozarks studying and photographing what in some locations was literally thousands and even millions of the cicadas coming out in the same location.

The blackberry bushes were filled with green berries so it looks like it will be a great cobbler season. Where is that recipe?

When I returned from the hike to Bob's I took up my place on the back deck and watched the show. That speckled hawk that I can't ID came by close in again. I realized that I now have room for 24 people to sit on the decks, in six different types of seats (log rockers, log rocking bench, log porch swing, high-back plastic chairs, swivel bar chairs, and the picnic table). My new hammock would make seven, but it isn't put up yet (once it is up, I probably won't get *any* work done!).

A three-inch walking stick hiked up the tree trunk that is growing out of the lower deck. I wonder if this is going to be one of the big years for walking sticks too?

The wind blew hard all day, with the new weather station operating fine (from the bathroom). I discovered that when the wind reaches 23mph, it sends the big BBQ grill sailing across the deck, crashing into the railing. I had to move it back and set the wheel lock, which took care of it for now.

I laid on the couch and read for several hours. I wanted to finish John Muir's account of his 1881 trip to Alaska by boat. I'm a slow reader, and was interrupted by several naps. I finally finished with Muir and got myself to work again. I baked bread, put up a pair of fly rods in a new location over the loft staircase, drilled holes and strung wire and put the weather station in its permanent location on the wall below the thermostat. The temperature/humidity wires reached OK, but the wind and rain wires did not. I decided to try ordinary telephone cable as an extension, and it worked just fine. Now that the rain gauge is up and running, I want it to *rain!*

Every time that you drill a hole you create a pile of sawdust—especially with a paddle bit, which makes a large hole. So I spent a lot of time with the central vac in hand cleaning up all of my little sawdust piles. This central vac system is a *great* product.

At 10:40pm I called the weather service in Fayetteville to get the barometric pressure reading so that I could calibrate my new weather station (I hadn't thought about calling until this late). We had a discussion about what factor to use for my higher elevation at Cloudland. With that set, I shut the cabin down for the night (still hot and muggy outside), and Stable and I went for a short walk. The stars were incredible—no haze at all tonight—and the moon was small enough to allow the stars to shine, yet cast enough light to view the hills and canyons all around me.

While I didn't get to spend nearly enough time at Cloudland in May, it has been a wonderful month here, full of wonder and work and Mother Nature, and even a big bear. I look forward to many more Mays here at Cloudland.

JUNE 1998

6/1/98 Yellow sunlight filtering through the trees woke me. Where I sleep, the way that my side of the bed is pointed, all that I have to do is open my eyes to view the sunrise. What a wonderful way to start the day! Of course, it is tough to sleep in. I could tell even before looking at the new weather station that a sweep of high pressure had passed through during the night—confirmed by the gauge. The sky was clear blue, the sunshine white, and all the trees were green—no more haze!

I had a lot of Journal writing to do so I gathered up my stuff and had breakfast on the back deck, then stayed there all morning, writing, watching, listening, and doing my best to concentrate on the Journal as the spectacle of nature proceeded out in front of me. Yesterday was mostly soaring birds, but to-day the open space was filled with all kinds—a scarlet tanager, neon red w/black wings, spent some time hopping from tree to tree. Later, a bright bluebird sat in the dogwood tree below. After close inspection, I realized that it was an Indigo bunting! Beth Motherwell had left **Stokes Beginner's Guide to Birds** here, and it is proving to be a great asset to me. Later, a downy woodpecker spent some time in the oak trees right next to me. And the hawks were out in full force.

It was obvious that one pair of hawks hunted together—they each soared at different altitudes, but usually followed the same pattern. Once in a while they would dive and swoop, generally play around with each other for a few minutes, screaming all the while. Let me tell you, it was very difficult for me to write with a pair of binocs on the table next to me! I took a lot of breaks to watch and to study. The wind was blowing, and it was a most pleasant morning.

The highlight of the morning had to be the noise that I heard in the woods below. I got up and went to the rail and saw a deer creeping through the brush. She was headed right for the open spot right in front—I just sat back and en-joyed. She eased her way into the opening and began to munch on some very large leaves of a plant that was growing close to the ground. She would bite off a few leaves and then lift her head up and look around as she ate, always looking for danger. She worked her way right through the middle of the opening, then slid into the woods below and out of sight. It was a joy seeing this deer, not only to be able to witness her in "her" world going about her business (you seldom get to see this with deer in the wild), but because this was the very first deer ever seen from the cabin. She never saw me, nor was the least bit disturbed by the cabin. It was mid-morning.

Soon after the deer left, the pair of hawks came in very close. They normally fly with feet and legs tucked up tight against their bodies to cut wind drag, but one of this pair was flying in "landing gear down" position. I don't know why. He never made an attempt to land. Looked kind of funny.

Tree frogs seemed to have replaced the cicadas as the loudest of the "sum-mer bugs" noise. I don't normally like summertime in Arkansas, but I think that this one will be different—I'll try to watch as much "TV" as I can. Time to wash dishes, pack up and head back into town.

6/2/98 It was very late when I got here, and I nearly hit a doe and fawn on the way—thank goodness for anti-lock brakes! It was a clear night, and a half moon lit up the canyons, but still allowed enough darkness for the stars to twinkle. I installed the hamper door in the loft bathroom—a proud moment for the builder—then hit the sack.

6/3/98 I hit the ground running early. It was warm, and the cabin didn't cool down much during the night. Opening and closing the windows was beginning to be a pain. They are such good quality, and seal so well that they always stick, and it takes a bit of muscle to open them. One problem is that the little ridge on them is just not enough surface to grip to open—it takes two hands. I must get some handles!

The first order of business was to get the new, taller wind pole put up. I got a 10 foot electric conduit that I think will be strong enough to hold up. I figured out a way to simply bolt it to the existing wood post already in place, which seemed to make it very strong indeed. And I ran the wire down inside the pipe for protection. I drilled a hole through the log wall into the loft closet, and ran the wire there and down into the basement to the main computer plug. I discovered that plain telephone wire works just fine for the extra wire length needed. I also found out quickly that the extra five feet in height on the wind pole made a big difference—the wind was indeed a lot slower at roof level, and I will get a much more accurate reading at five foot above the roof level.

The day flew by and I got a ton of chores done. Good thing, because early in the afternoon I got a call saying the first set of proofs for the new *Buffalo River Wilderness* picture book were in, so I literally dropped everything and sped home. One of the things that I got done before I left was to install a full-length "tick inspection" mirror in each bathroom—very important this time of the year!

6/4/98 A beautiful wood nymph met me at the cabin door upon my arrival this evening, and she had a plate full of fresh grilled chicken and veggies. My girlfriend doesn't cook much, but when she does, it is certainly worth the wait. It was the perfect end to a very hectic day in town of working the new proofs with John Coghlan and Milancy McNamara.

As Leslie was pulling the last bird off of the grill, a thunder bolt landed in the valley just upstream with a loud crack that shook the cabin. I glanced at the barometer, which had dropped steeply, and realized that a real storm was upon us—oh boy! I love storms, especially summer thunderstorms. The wind blew and the lightning cracked. As we crawled into bed, it started to pour, and then the light show really got underway. What followed was one of the most amazing and intense electrical storms that I had ever seen. It was a powerful storm, and moved right over and through the cabin area. From our perch in the loft you could see a long way up the Whitaker Creek Valley towards the Buffalo Fire Tower (about five miles away). Each flash lit up a different area of the scene. Sometimes the flash would throw one ridge in shadow, sometimes another, and it was happening in quick succession, kind of like a giant strobe light going off, only it was moving around. The rain blew in so hard that I had to close all of the windows—it even blew under the porch roof and into the living room! It was an incredible storm, and I enjoyed every second of it. There were a few scary moments as we could hear trees and branches crashing. I was anxious to see how the weather station performed. In all other storms here it was frustrating because I never knew how hard the wind was blowing—now I would be able to know for sure.

6/5/98 It was a gray dawn, and we were engulfed in a foggy cloud. I ran downstairs to check the particulars—1.67 inches of rain and 53 mph winds—a good beginning speed record. A few chairs and a table were blown across the porch, but all else seemed OK. I brought Leslie a Cloudland breakfast in bed.

Later as she was driving away, she honked her horn and stopped the car. Uh oh. There was a large hickory tree down across the road. I managed to get enough of it out of the way for her to pass. She soon stopped and honked again. This was a bigger tree, and I had to go get the chainsaw out and do a little work. It was very cool outside, in the 50's, and it felt great to work with the saw. No more big trees down, but lots of limbs, and you could see many other trees down in the woods. I guess 53 mph winds can do some damage!

The fog was clearing when I got back to the cabin, and I soon realized that there were a number of trees down around the opening as well. The tops had blown out of several of the trees at the edge of the opening, including one entire big tree near the corner. The top was blown out of the maple right in front of the porch—this is the tree that is so brilliant on page 112 of the ***Buffalo River Wilderness*** picture book. The river was really running too, and very muddy.

I put up my new snowshoes on the wall overlooking the kitchen, ate a quick lunch, and headed back to civilization to visit my brother's grave—it had been 28 years since he was killed him in a car accident in Missouri.

I arrived back at Cloudland late, near midnight, under the moon and stars. I had left the windows open all day, and it was downright cold in the cabin—61 degrees inside, 53 degrees outside (and this is June?). The heavy quilt on the log bed felt great. Now, if I only had a warm body to curl up with...

6/6/98 Sunshine, breezy, 50 degrees. I sat out on the porch and wrote and had breakfast, all bundled up with sweatshirt and comforter. I just now realized that there are no soaring birds about, but lots of little ones flittering here and there. And there was one strange bird call close by that I'd never heard before. Then a grey bird flew across the scene—it had a funny hump in its back. Lots of folks on the Crag today—must have been some groups—they all looked about college age, all with the same type of dress—the standard boots, shorts and t-shirt.

The highlight of the day was when a bright blue Indigo bunting came by, perched on the dogwood tree (it too was damaged by the storm, ripping off one of the main branches, creating a nice perch), and sang and sang for 15 minutes. I was able to get the spotting scope on him and observed him for a while—you don't get to watch many birds this way because they are always moving around. It felt like a fall day outside, and never got higher than the 60's.

I am really glad that I opened up the area down below—it has really created a wildlife playground and feeding area, and I doubt that I would be seeing many of the birds and other wildlife without the open space.

I walked down and looked at the storm damage, which included one larger hollow tree that just twisted and buckled and fell. The top of the tree right at the corner post is also gone, and the big tree next to it was completely blown over—this was a really big tree, but the root ball was not too big—no wonder it blew over (and it took others with it). I was really surprised at how everything was growing up so thick and lush down in this opening. I was told by some know-it-all that nothing but arid species like cacti and blackberries would grow there (he said that all of the soil had been removed since I cut down all of the trees). What is growing is hickory, oak, dogwood, and dozens of other species. I don't think there was much soil lost at all. The only places that are not covered with vegetation are the two spots where I've had brush fires. I think it will be a battle to keep the forest cut back! So much for meddling nosy experts.

I spent the day doing more wiring in the basement, and finally have seen about the end to it (I hope). Also got an outdoor outlet put on the lower deck. No visitors all day. The nighttime air was quite pleasant, and a three-quarter moon lit everything up. I think that I found a good spot to put up the hammock on the lower deck, but I need two screw hooks to set it up—next visit. I brought out a chair and sat in the moonlight and listened to barred owls up and down the valley talk to each other.

6/7/98 Wow, what a spectacular morning at Cloudland! The pre-dawn revealed oceans of fog below. As the sun rose and lit up the fog banks, they began to move about, like the tide rolling in and out. Looking up the Buffalo River, each holler was well defined by the fog, and the black ridgetops that were sunlit on the upper end disappeared into the fog below. As the fog warmed up, it moved around, sometimes covering up the ridges, sometimes backing off and revealing two or three ridges that were hidden before. It was a terrific view from everywhere in the cabin. Sure am glad that I cut out that view! Fifty degrees outside. Time to take my hot chocolate and breakfast out to the deck, bundle up, and enjoy the show.

The fog burned off in a hurry and was all gone by 7:30am. There must be someone camped near the mouth of Boen Gulf, as there is a cloud of blue smoke hanging in that area of the valley. Out across the Buffalo River comes the lonely cries of a mourning dove. And a rooster—first time that I have heard this guy. Must belong to the neighbors across the canyon (a mile away), and is sleeping late. Time for a morning hike.

The highlight of this walk around was an orange butterfly. As I turned and walked down a lane covered with trees (kind of like walking through a tunnel), this butterfly joined me, and began to fly alongside. You know butterflies—they don't exactly fly in a straight line or follow any predictable pattern. They just sort of fly up and down, left and right, round and round, wherever life happens to take them. Well, this one did the same thing, only he did it within a few feet of me, and pretty much stayed right alongside the whole time. I walked and walked, and we conversed on the glories of the world, the problems (and solutions—butterflies are very smart), and about life at Cloudland in general. Butterflies usually don't make friends, but I considered this one mine. He stayed right with me for a couple of hundred yards, until we got to the end of the tunnel, then we bid farewell and he floated on up into the treetops. I felt like a very lucky traveler this morning!

I also discovered that some of Bob's corn in his garden had been flattened by the heavy winds. And it looked like something awful might happen to some of his sweet peas on the vines, as well as several onions, so I brought them along with me. The peas didn't last too long—these were the sweetest things that I have ever eaten out of a garden! Crisp too. I visited the new cabin that the Woods brothers are building nearby, and found that they had made progress. The outside is nearly complete. It appears that the log rocking chair that I gave them as a cabin warming gift was now living elsewhere—I wonder which brother took it home. There was a heavy dew, and I returned to my cabin with soaked shoes, socks and jeans (the wheat in the North Meadow was thigh-high).

After a nap I hiked on over to the Crag. There was a couple there doing what couples do on a sunny summer day in the wilderness—they were all laid out on the Crag reading thick novels. I'm not sure if they even noticed that I had been there. I found a cucumber tree on the way back. The locals call them "cowcumber" trees. Their little cucumber fruit was strewn all over the ground.

I didn't get too much work done but did entertain some friends/relatives of Bob's that he brought by. They were from Oregon, Michigan and Missouri. I did spend some time filling recent holes I had made in the cabin walls (electric wire holes, vacuum exhaust pipe, weather station cord holes, etc.). I filled them with foam, and insulated the new half-inch hot water pipe. Then I made two wonderful Cloudland pizzas. That night there was just a little moonlight, but *lots* of wind.

6/8/98 A howling wind woke me, with dark, dreary clouds moving about. The wind was whipping at 20-30mph. I love wind, and got up and wandered around outside. It is amazing to me how much wind the leaves can take without ripping out of their sockets. My Indigo bunting friend was singing in the meadow (I'm calling my open space the "meadow" from now on). I grabbed the spotting scope and studied him. He was perched on the tip-top of a bare stick of some small tree, and was just singing his little heart out. In between songs, he was all puffed up, kind of like a blue tennis ball with head and tail. Some of his feathers were ruffled and out of place. I can't get over just how much of themselves these birds put into their singing—they use their entire bodies, which is how they can make such loud music with their relatively small bodies I guess.

6/10/98 It was hot and windy when I arrived back at Cloudland in mid-afternoon. The air was full of soaring birds—more than I have ever seen here before! They filled the canyons as far as you could see in all directions. And they were having a good time too, riding the waves and cutting across the currents. Several of them were using the meadow to display their talents.

I hooked up the hammock to the tree in the lower deck and a rail post—it was perfect, except that it put too much pressure on the rail, so I unhooked it and set up the green metal stand. I was forced to try it out for awhile and can report that it works just fine.

The wind had topped out at 55mph the night before (.6" of rain), but I couldn't see any damage from trees being blown down. This is the highest recorded wind so far at Cloudland. The wind kept up all day. I worked inside, putting up insulation and setting up the bookshelf. What a difference a bookshelf makes! Nighttime brought more wind—45mph—and lots of rain. Plus, another electrical storm. I saw one bolt that hit over near Professor Dave Stahle's cabin that must have been a mile or more tall, straight up. I must say that I'm a little surprised that the power stayed on all the time. It seems to go out for a minute or shorter every few days, no matter what the weather is doing, but it stays on during bad weather (yea!). I discovered two leaks in the south wall of the living room—one from one of the stationary windows. Just a few drops that were blown through the logs, but enough to worry about. Time to call the Amish! I went to bed around midnight, and it was very still and quiet outside.

6/11/98 I was literally blown awake at 5:30am as a cold rain hit me in the face—time to get up and close all the windows. The wind the night before moved the grill across the deck and ripped off its cover, but everything else was fine on the deck this morning. The strong winds made the light rain feel worse.

Since I just love cloudy, gloomy, windy days, it seemed like a perfect time to go on a hike. The rain was really just spitting, so I didn't bother to take a rain jacket—it was plenty warm, in the 70's. *Wow*, I wasn't the only one who was out wandering around—I saw more wildlife in this one little hike than I've seen here in a long time!

I think that I felt him coming long before I ever saw him. Then out of the corner of my eye I saw these unusual fuzzy posts moving through the thick brush. They looked so out of place! It was the velvet antlers of a huge whitetail buck, and he was moving right towards me, just sort of browsing on the tender leaves low to the ground. On a buck this size, even now, when the antlers aren't fully grown yet, what you see first, and what dominates your view, is that impressive set of antlers. At this stage, they are still just growing, and doing so very rapidly, and the expanding bone is covered with a thick, hairy covering, or "velvet" as it is called. It looks like you could just reach out and break one off. Hardly. Anyway, this guy finally did notice me, and froze (I had done so already). He stood there big and bold and majestic, like he belonged on a stamp or a postcard. And those antlers were huge! The main branches were laid nearly flat against his head (a sign of an older, more mature buck in his prime), and swung out wide to the side, then curved up and branched out. I counted five points on each side, and it was obvious that he wasn't done growing—will probably end up as a 12 or 14 point buck. Very impressive!

When I was much younger and used to bowhunt every day for five months every year, I dreamed about a buck like this one. Now I couldn't dream of ever killing him. He was so big that he looked more like a big mule deer instead of a little whitetail. He was a trophy for sure. Since it was obvious that he had lived through many hunting seasons, I suspect that he will remain a wild trophy for some time—he is a lot smarter than any hunter. Guys like this are one in a million, and know where to go hide when opening day comes around.

Only once before had I ever seen a whitetail buck like this one. It was in the bowhunting days of my youth. I used to spend the first hour of daylight creeping, crawling, inching my way through the overgrown fields and woodlands where I used to hunt outside of Fayetteville. If you stood there and watched me, I could cross the field in front of you, but you would never see me move—that's how slow I hunted—it's called "still hunting," and really lives up to its name. The idea is to move so slowly that your movements are not noticed by the game, and so you can literally creep up on them. Many times I would walk up on a deer that was bedded down in the tall grass.

Anyway, there was this one magnificent buck where I used to hunt, and I snuck up on him several times, but every time that I did, he would instantly see me at the same time that I saw him. Sometimes we were very close to each other, within spitting distance, and my heart would pound like a big bass drum. The problem with hunting with a bow is that once you see your game, you have to draw the arrow back before you can fire, and you have to do so with some precision. Well, this old fine buck wouldn't ever give me that opportunity, so I never got a shot at him—he was always hidden so well that I was just too close to do anything when I spotted him. Before I could even think about drawing back the arrow, he would jump up and disappear into the woods in a flash. I know that he must have spent a lot of time laughing at me. If he ever dozed off for just a minute at the wrong time, or perhaps spent a little too long daydreaming about that young doe of his fancy, I would have gotten him. Thinking back, just knowing that he was out there, year after year, testing my skill, pushing me to the limit every day, made me a better hunter, and it would have been a shame if I ever did get him. I would much rather have spent my time pitting my skills against his rather than looking at his stuffed head on the wall.

The buck standing right in front of me today was just as smart, cunning, lucky, and magnificent as that one. Without the tension of me being in the "hunting" mode, I was able to just stand there and really enjoy this creature. Our eyes were locked onto each other for what seemed like an eternity. I felt like we were on more equal terms, both living in and enjoying the Buffalo River wilderness, and out for a morning stroll. It used to be that a buck's gaze would strike terror in me, but now I felt friendship. We were brothers of the woods instead of enemies. After all of my hunting days and killing several dozen fine whitetail bucks, and now not having the need or desire to do so anymore, I felt a great deal of respect and admiration for this animal. This buck would have normally bounded off in a flash, but instead he simply flipped his tail, turned and walked away. I think that he felt some sort of kinship with me as well. Or it could have just been that he knew what date it was, and that I didn't have a weapon in my hands!

Later I saw a bobcat cross the lane in front of me. I've seen a lot of bobcats, so this was no big deal, although I had never seen one at Cloudland before. And this guy was a little different—he had white socks on all four feet! He didn't stick around long—these cats are very shy, and normally only out at night. I also jumped up two wild turkey hens—they ran off into the woods. It should be time for them to be sitting on a nest somewhere.

When I got to the edge of another meadow I paused for a moment before crossing into it. Don't know why I did, but I do know that it is always a good idea to do this, just to take a look around and see what might be in the meadow. Well, there was nothing there, so I went on, but then I saw motion to my left and stopped in my tracks. Another deer. This one was a doe. She walked cautiously out into the field, and right behind her came a tiny fawn, its spots beaming. This little guy was a bundle of joy and bounded left and right and was just having a ball. It didn't walk or even run like its momma, but rather kicked up its back legs and landed on its front ones, with the back legs going high up into the air. I could swear there was a smile on its face. Not a care in the world, and an entire wildflower meadow to romp around in. Momma never saw me, but I could tell she knew something was amiss, so she hurried junior along and they exited the far side of the meadow. The guy standing there at the edge of the meadow had a big grin on his face. Like I said, I love "weather." It just seems to bring out the best in nature.

6/12/98 The sun rose bright and early to a cloudless sky and a wind-filled day. Stable and I got up to mill around for a few minutes outside, then went back to bed—a new mini-blind that I put up next to my bed may be the death of me, as all I had to do was pull it dark and roll over and go back to sleep! Before the blinds were there, the sun was hitting me in the face and I had no choice but to get myself out of bed and enjoy the best part of the day. When I finally got up for good, I spent some time on the porch, watching the wind twisting and thrashing all the trees at high speed. It was a strikingly clear day, a contrast to the gloomy clouds of yesterday. There was not a single bird in sight anywhere—they have probably been blown to the ground! It is going to be a hot summer day to be sure, but with all the wind, I suspect that it will be quite tolerable here at Cloudland. I should have put up a windmill instead of bringing in electricity—I'll bet that it would work here. Of course, it would have to stick up above the treeline to be most effective, and it could be seen from Hawksbill Crag, so it probably wouldn't be a good idea. However, if I ever go broke and can't afford the electricity bill anymore, and have one last pot of cash hidden away (I wish), then I could put up a windmill and cut the power cord.

Bob called in the afternoon to invite me to come talk with a Game & Fish guy who was coming by to see about the bear. So I hustled on over the hill. Bob was there with Eddy and some friends from Iowa who were spending the week at Bob's cabin. The Game & Fish guy showed up right on time, to the very second. We walked around and talked about the bear, and problem bears in general. You could tell that he gets a lot of calls about bears that are not really that much of a problem. You could also tell that he perked right up when he realized that this bear was beginning to be a real problem, and a problem that we really needed to take care of. He kept saying "we really do need to get this bear's attention," and "we really do need to find this bear in October when we could legally kill him." He said that the chances of trapping him were slim, and that we would probably attract other bears to the trap instead, and then they would become problem bears too. And he said that every bear that he had trapped and relocated had always returned, sometimes traveling 75 miles in a day to get back home. He issued Bob some special rubber shotgun shells made in Italy, and they cost $45 a box of 25! They were very lightweight, with no recoil. Eddy shot one at the BBQ grill, and it didn't even leave a mark. Eddy left Bob a single shot 12 gauge shotgun. The folks from Iowa, who were staying in the cabin, were not amused. The guy gave me a ride down to my cabin, and we talked about the bear some more. I got the feeling that he would like to see this bear destroyed, but he didn't want to know about it. I got the message. He was very nice, great PR skills, and you could tell that he loved his job, which was mostly working with the elk in Boxley Valley. By the way, the very first thing that he noticed when he walked into the cabin was a flint knife with the bone handle that I had stuck into one of the logs. I like it too.

Ken and his wife Terry were scheduled to show up at 6pm to begin the weekend of festivities at the cabin. They were late. I was making Cloudland Pizza, and it was late too. They finally showed up at around 7, having taken the "short cut" between Fallsville and Cave Mountain Road (FR#1410—there were six downed trees across the road). They looked like they had been dragged through the brush behind their jeep when they arrived! Terry headed for the shower, and Ken headed for the jeep, with a big grin on his face. He opened the back door and screamed "Happy Birthday!" He had brought a wonderful old black farm bell. I'm not sure if he realized it or not, but I was secretly wanting to buy this exact thing—it was wonderful! We quickly got a ladder and installed it on the overhanging log at the end of the carport, right next to the rain gauge. I had to step in and keep the Amish boys from cutting this very log off flush with the roof—I just knew I would need it for something. Anyway, the bell looked and worked great. *Thanks* Ken and Terry!

Cloudland Pizza is just the same old stuff that I seem to make everything out of here, but these two decreed that it was the best homemade pizza that they had ever tasted. Of course, it could have been all the beer too. After dinner and dark, we hung out on the lower deck, in and out of the hammock, and watched the most incredible electrical storm move across the sky in front of us. It began over near the fire tower, then slowly moved to our left, and finally settled in out in front of us. It was one of those cloud banks that was full of lightning—almost all of the strikes were contained within the thunderhead (which stretched all the way back to near the fire tower). Each bolt lit up the thunderhead from within, making a lot of bright colors. And since there were always several bolts going off at the same time, the thunderhead was really lit up. The funny thing about these types of thunderstorms is that there is never any sound—it was completely quiet. Very strange. (I saw one in Kansas once at 3am as I was driving to Wyoming, and one down at Lost Maples State Park in Texas. They are always quite amazing.) Every once in a while, a lightning bolt would escape from the thunderhead and shoot across the sky. It was a very impressive show, and we sat there for what seemed like hours watching it. We learned the next day that what we were looking at was most likely a thunderstorm that was actually *south* of Ft. Smith! No wonder we never heard anything.

6/13/98 BUSHWHACKER PARTY #1. Ken and Terry mostly laid around all day outside (I was afraid to look and see what this young love-crazed couple was doing), and I mostly laid around all day on the couch—it was very hot. Terry finally came in and made up a terrific watermelon bowl—with lots of fancy carving. I made up a few appetizers out of the same stuff that the pizza was made out of. Terry and Bob Robinson and I went up and raided Bob Chester's garden—what we brought back looked like something out of a farm life design book. We also gathered a lot of wild bergamot mint leaves, and Terry made up the most incredible sweet tea! I couldn't stop drinking it. It was very hot outside, and I turned on the AC, which made the inside really comfortable.

Guests filtered in all afternoon, and precisely at 4pm, I fired up the blender. The first bushwhackers at Cloudland were consumed in a hurry. It was a great crew: Ken/Terry Eastin, Bob/Dawna Robinson, Luke Collins & Mary Wright (brought all of the marinated chicken!), Jim McDaniel & Susie Crisp (they left their own wonderful cabin over near Richland Creek to come, and brought a hummingbird feeder that looks more like a work of art), Norma Meadors & Roy Senyard (they brought all the veggies), The Wildman (Carl Ownbey) & Mary Chodrick, Hete (Dennis Heter), and Scott Crook. Scott blew out a tire on the way in and was not a very happy camper! We all had a grand time, feasted on kabobs and bushwhackers and other delicacies and listened and danced to wild music long into the night. Norma was especially entertaining (as always), and she got everyone (well, most) out on the dance floor more than once. Let's see, what was that song, something like "In them old, cotton fields back home..."

6/14/98 I was awakened at 4:30am by a big blow and got up to close all the windows (I made everyone sleep outside on the deck or downstairs in the basement—most were on the deck). The rain was blowing in at 40 mph. I knew some folks were scurrying around down on the deck. Upon investigating, I discovered Scott off of the deck, down on the hillside with a flashlight. The wind had blown away his sleeping bag, pad and pillow! He swears the lower deck acts like a wind tunnel and that the wind was considerably more than 40 mph—I would agree. Terry got up and worried about her car windows—it was pouring down. She headed out the front door, turning on the porch light, and realized that there was an old griz passed out in the swing—it was Hete, and he was a grumbling. Terry came back in, but I volunteered to go close the windows. When I passed the old griz, he snapped at me.

I must tell ya, this storm was a very strange thing indeed. It was pouring buckets, blowing at 40 mph+, and when you looked out the back into the valley, it was all lit up by the moon! Boy, it was really weird. The rain didn't last long, and soon all was calm again and back to normal. Later I got up and fixed Cloudland Hash and Terry cooked blueberry pancakes for everyone. Soon the crowd thinned out and I was left with only myself and a few dirty dishes. The only major "party event" that happened was that there were several cups of Bushwhackers spilled on the floor—no big deal except that at Cloudland any liquid on the main floor goes right on through down into the basement! I was afraid to look.

6/19/98 I arrived at the cabin late in the afternoon and it was rather hot, and very hazy. This was the longest that I had been away in quite some time, but I had business in town all week. The cabin was about 10 degrees cooler than it was outside. There were lots of birds fluttering about, singing and playing. I spent some time on the deck enjoying the view, and peering through the binocs. A huge red-tail hawk came soaring by, and I mean a really big one. It just had the faintest of red in its tail. I got a good look at it through the binocs, and followed it for several minutes as it flew back and forth, playing in the wind. This guy looked like an immature eagle—it was that big, and had those kinds of markings. The leading edge of its wings looked like airplane wings, very thick and rounded. Duh, I guess that is where they got the idea for airplane wings from! The buzzards were following along the bluffline too, back and forth, back and forth. Every once in a while one of them would swing over into the meadow airspace, just to check on me to see what I was up to. Leslie arrived with a car full of recreational toys, a kayak and two bikes. She would be heading out the next day for two weeks in the Appalachian Mountain area and the East Coast. We grilled some apple/chicken sausage and veggies. I'm not sure if I spend a lot of time out on the deck grilling because of the terrific food or the view. It was a calm night, and we turned in early.

6/20/98 The morning was a lazy one, and I got up and fixed Cloudland Coffee and Hash and returned to the loft with Leslie. She was leaving for a two-week trip later in the day, so I would not see her for a while. (As it turned out, this would probably be the last time that she visited Cloudland, since we soon ended our relationship.)

After she left I decided to get in a little play time myself, so I headed out for a hike. One thing that I realized is that no matter how many times you pass the same place, you are bound to see something new and different. There is just so much going on in the woods, especially this time of year. One of my favorite spots along the lane towards Bob's cabin is one such place. The ground was covered with new hickory nuts. I looked up and saw three large shagbark hickory trees that I hadn't noticed before—it is going to be a great year for nut trees. The bark of one of the trees was nearly smooth, almost no "shag" at all. And just beyond I noticed a section of old fence that was stretched between two trees, and had grown into their bark. This fence was within a few inches of the lane, but I had not noticed it before.

Bob's was fine—no sign of Mr. Bear. I walked on over to the Woods cabin, through the North Meadow. *Wow, what a meadow!* The winter wheat was really tall and looking fine, but the meadow was also full of wildflowers, all swaying in the breeze. Most of the flowers were the bright yellow black-eyed Susans, but there were lots of others too—in fact, I could see eight different species in one small area. This is what I want my little meadow to look like—mostly wildflowers, with tall grasses. There was a black cat standing guard too.

On the way back up over the ridge I spotted a barred owl perched near the Faddis cabin. And right in the middle of the day too! He kept a close watch on me as I passed underneath. After a quick visit to the Crag (no people), I scooted on back to the cabin. As I came into the lower end of the meadow I saw an Indigo bunting in the low brush. He seemed to be quite anxious about me being there, but would not fly away. Then a wren appeared in the same brush. They both fluttered about squawking, as though they were protecting a nest. That would be quite normal, but I have never seen two different species protecting the same nest! Perhaps they were very close neighbors. I didn't want to bother them any more, so I went on without further investigation. There were several buntings in the low brush of the meadow.

After a couple of naps and some computer work I headed out for another hike. The shadows were getting longer, and the day cooler. The big buck was lurking around my gate, and he eased off just to the edge of my sight as I approached. He knows when deer season is. His rack is still very impressive, and getting more so every week.

As I got down to Bob's I saw the bear again—he was coming out of the log smokehouse, and left in a hurry. He had ripped the door to the smokehouse open, and had been feasting on four large steel garbage cans of birdseed. He was attempting to haul one can full of shucked corn out the door when I scared him off. Bob says that this bear is very polite, and usually takes his food outdoors to eat—he doesn't want to make a mess. Hah! He has been making a mess everywhere that he goes! Upon further investigation I found that he had been at the cabin too. He ripped off the screen of the front porch door and tried to get in—the wood door stopped him, and then he tore off several boards of the bathroom door (this is where he had entered twice before, but the door had been boarded up), but failed to gain entry. Guess the birdseed was calling him.

I figured the bear might return so I got the 12 gauge shotgun that was on the bed, loaded it with the special rubber slug from Italy, and sat on the deck and read the local paper (I find more interesting information in this paper than I do in any of the big ones). Sure enough, within ten minutes, I heard something coming down the hillside behind the smokehouse in the leaves. I took up a position at the corner of the cabin and waited for him to enter the yard. It was just about dark by this time. My heart began to race, and I wondered exactly what impact the rubber bullet might have—was it going to scare the bear off for good, or would it just piss him off and bring him charging at me? Certainly the cabin would be no refuge—the bear had already proved that he could get in at any time. The shotgun was only a single shot, but I had two other shells in my pocket just in case. Yeah, right, a second rubber bullet is going to help out a lot with a charging, mad bear! I waited. The sound got closer. All of a sudden, a dark mass entered the yard. Here he comes! A big doe and a tiny, spotted fawn stepped into the yard. What a beautiful sight. Life renewing itself, and in such a precious creature. Few things in the world are as wonderful to see as a new fawn. They made their way across the lawn and into the woods. I felt honored to have seen them. I put the shotgun away, closed up the cabin, and headed back to Cloudland, just as the last twinges of light faded from the forest.

6/21/98, First day of summer began like a bowl of Rice Krispies—snap, crackle, *POP!* A big storm was rolling in, and the pre-dawn light showed a lot of big black clouds. It was still dark enough for the lightning strikes to light up the countryside, and it was an impressive show. Then the clouds opened up and released their precious cargo. It rained about a half inch in 30 minutes, then let up. It had stopped completely by sunrise. I've never seen a sky like this one before—dark clouds overhead stretched all the way to the horizon to the south and west, but to the east the black line stopped just short of the horizon, and there was a narrow break, which was bright orange. Soon the sun made a quick appearance, then rose into the blackness. I rolled over and returned to my dreams.

Later in the morning I was jarred awake again by loud cracks—this time the thunder and lightning was right down on top of me, and making a strange metallic noise. The clock beside the bed was not working, although there was power to everything else. I went downstairs and found the breaker tripped.

When I reset it I realized that it was 10:30am! Wow, I hadn't slept in that long here at Cloudland before! Don't know why that one breaker had tripped—it only fed the loft outlets.

I sat on the porch watching the morning show—it was still very dark out, with black clouds swirling around, and a few fog clouds down in the valley. Then the clouds opened up once again, and I could see the large raindrops coming all the way across the valley. A cloud formed around the mountaintop across the way, and soon it began to boil over and spill down into Whitaker Creek Valley, moving rapidly. A large fog bank had formed in the Buffalo River Valley, and soon this fog was racing up Whitaker Creek. As the two fog banks collided, clouds of mist and mystery shot up in all directions, some up to and through the cabin, others far up into Whitaker Creek. This stuff was having a great time playing at Cloudland.

I hiked on over to Bob's to check on the bear and found Bob and Tom Triplet there, cleaning up the mess from the night before. It seemed that not only will Bob no longer sleep in his own cabin anymore, but he is afraid to even be there by himself—not a good thing. Something has to be done, this is insane. Wildlife is one thing, but a bear that keeps you from living at your own cabin is quite something else.

Bob and Trip came by the cabin for a bowl of ice cream, worked in the main garden some, then headed back to town. Right after they left another amazing lightning storm rolled through. I spent an hour on the deck mesmerized by the show. This one was far up the Buffalo River Valley, sending bolts into Bowers Hollow, Terrapin Branch, and the main river areas. Most of the bolts were really tall, vertical ones. But several entered the valley and really branched out, booming thunder all the time. I tried in vain to capture some of this with the little point and shoot camera, but it never was quick enough (my real camera was safely tucked away in a closet back in town). So I gave up and decided to try to make a little sketch—it looks more like something a first grader would do. This one particular bolt is one of the neatest ones that I have ever seen, and it just spread out right there in the valley in front of me. The rain total was almost an inch for the day.

I hiked up to Bob's and decided to hang around for a while and see if the bear returned. Sure enough he did, but I was ready for him with the rubber bullets in the 12 gauge shotgun. He came around the corner of the cabin, and I blasted his behind with a rubber slug. He sort of grunted, and ran off into the yard. He stopped, and turned back to look at me. By this time I had reloaded, and so I blasted his behind again. He got a little peeved and took off running, this time at a good clip, and quickly disappeared into the woods. I hoped that he had gotten the message—to connect a pain in his butt with being at Bob's cabin—and would not return. Only time would tell.

6/22/98 I didn't sleep much during the night. That was probably a good thing, because I was awake at 5:30am when the sky lit up with an incredible display of brilliant color. I got up and spent a couple of hours on the deck, enjoying the view, then packed up and headed back to town.

6/23/98 Another hot summer day in the mountains, although it was quite cool and pleasant on the back deck at Cloudland. Roy and Norma stopped by to spend the night. We all sat out on the deck after dark and pondered why there weren't as many lightning bugs these days as there were when we all were kids. Pesticides was the answer. You used to be able to run through fields and catch as many as your jar could hold in a matter of minutes, then spend hours wandering around in the dark with only your bug lantern to show the way. I told them of the practical joke that I helped play on the ladies of one of my high school trail crews many years ago. The girls had all left (three boys, three girls) to hike down the trail from our base camp to a telephone a couple of miles away downstream along the Little Missouri River. The boys and I spent an hour catching lightning bugs. We put all of them inside the girls' tent. Wow, you should have seen that tent light up! It reminded me of one of those thunderheads with all of the lightning going on inside, just like we had witnessed at Cloudland a week or two ago. When the girls returned, they spent an eternity catching fireflies and releasing them outdoors. That was all pretty funny, but this continued every night for a week, as it took them that long to get all the bugs out! I was proud to be the originator of that joke.

By the time I had finished telling my little story the meadow below us was filled with fireflies—they were everywhere, and seemed as thick as they were in our youths. Man, they really lit up the meadow. Most of them were flying down low, close to the ground. But every once in a while, one would venture up high, close to our altitude, and would send its bright light streaking across the dark sky. Had we three been a little less sober we probably would have been down in the meadow with the fireflies, filling a mason jar. The stars were late coming out, but were glorious. The moon was in a dark phase.

6/24/98 I had a dentist appointment in town so I left the cabin at 5:30am, leaving behind a loaf of fresh bread baking for Roy and Norma. I heard later that it was eaten in its entirety.

6/26/98 It was quite hot but breezy when I arrived in mid-afternoon, about 8 degrees cooler than in town. The soaring birds were out in full force, riding the currents and playing like crazy, pretending to be working at finding food all the while. I knew better. If I only had wings, you know where I would be—out there with the buzzards, riding the currents, swooping up and down, crisscrossing the valley, playing tag with the wind. Can't think of any other creature that I would rather be than a soaring bird (preferably a hawk, not a buzzard!).

I spent an hour or two reading more adventures of John Muir in Alaska. Every time that I read him, I get to feeling very lazy—some of his feats were quite amazing. As far as his stamina, energy and obsession with exploring everything in sight right away, I would create a class with him, Bob Marshall, and Eric Ryback. There are a few others, but these three come to mind. I would also add Terry Keefe, Eddy Silcott and Terry Fredrick from this neighborhood to that list. And I never realized until today that Muir wrote an entire book (it must have been a very short one) about a little dog, Stickeen. Their travels together were quite exciting, and reminded me to some extent of my own dog Yukon (my beloved springer-spaniel who passed away a year ago), who is at this very moment probably sitting down next to the river, teaching a beaver how to swim correctly. Oops, I get to go take a swig of Yukon Jack in his honor...

After the usual grilled dinner I headed out for a short hike. It wasn't nearly as cool or breezy in the woods as it was on the back deck, but the workout felt great. As I entered the Faddis Meadow, the wind picked up again, and I started singing a song to the wind—can't remember a single word to it now, but I remember it was quite good. I also remember that I thought that I should stick to taking pictures and selling guidebooks and not get into music.

There is a wooded hillside that slopes up to my left on the way to Bob's place. It is heavily wooded with hickory, oaks, and a few large dogwood. But the understory is rather clean, and there seems to always be some type of natural carpet covering the forest floor. Back in late April and May, herds of mayapples popped up, eventually producing a hillside of white and yellow flowers, easily visible from the walking lane below (you often have to look hard to see these delicate flowers that bloom under the low mayapple leaves). Just as they began to fade away, tiny yellow wildflowers took over, covering the floor much closer to the ground. They are gone now, and the lush carpet is poison ivy and Virginia creeper, all of it rich shades of deep green. In the fall, this carpet will turn yellow and gold and crimson. I've always wanted to photograph this hillside, and will make it a point to do so come October.

I hiked across to the East Meadow and inspected the sweet corn, green beans and yellow squash coming up. The squash and beans were ready to eat, but my veggie bin was full. Bob and his good friend, Benny Stovall, were coming later in the weekend, so I left it all for them. In the dried earth where no crops were planted, there were only a couple sets of animal tracks—a doe and fawn, probably ones that I have seen a time or two before. It was so funny, because the doe's track was a pretty good-sized track, and next to it were these tiny, tiny impressions from the fawn's hooves. They give you an idea of just how small and delicate a young fawn can be. The upper end of the meadow was waist-high with tiny white and yellow wildflowers. These are the ones that grow tall on the stock, and bunch up, perhaps 15-20 little flowers in each bunch. They look all white from a distance, but when you look close, you can see the yellow centers. I suppose this is all really a weed, but it sure makes you feel good to walk through a tall sea of them, all waving in the late evening light.

As I sat on the deck later and made plans for a quick trip to the Wyoming mountains I looked at the incredible view right out in front and wondered why I wanted to leave it for a hot drive across the plains. It was warmer outside than in, but with the steady breeze it was very comfortable, and I lingered there until the last rays of light left the hilltops across the way. I determined that there were about eight "points" that I could see from the cabin in the Buffalo River Valley in front. At some point this year, most likely after the leaves are off, I want to hike up on top of each of those points, all eight of them, in one day, and return to the cabin. I suspect that I will gradually have to work up to them, and each trip will get a little easier, because I will know the route on all of the first ones. Perhaps that is something that I will do every New Year's Day from now on. Also, I decided that I wanted to continue the hikes to the river during each full moon, at least for the rest of the year, and plunge my body into the waters, even in the winter. It will be a fun year!

As dark slowly creeped in the lightning bugs emerged. First, just a few, then eventually an entire meadow full of them. I had spent so much time watching them that I forgot about the stars—when I looked up, I was nearly knocked down by the number and brightness of them—they were everywhere, and contrasted against the black sky.

6/27/98 Cool and cloudy with a nice breeze at daybreak, low 70's. It was cold out on the deck with all of the wind, and I had to put a long-sleeve shirt on. This is all that I ask for in Arkansas in the summer—to be chilled by the morning air!

I drove on over to Bob's and picked up a wheelbarrow, then spent a couple of hours filling it with clay dirt from various spots near my cabin, and dumping them at the corner of the cabin where water was collecting. I'd hoped to be able to divert the water away from the foundation, to stop it from seeping down and getting into the same corner of the basement. The pond of water was twelve feet from the foundation to begin with, but it somehow has been making its way down to and through the basement wall, six feet underground. It was hot and sweaty work, but I sure did need it.

When I returned the wheelbarrow I went on over to check on the progress of the new Woods cabin and found four of the Woods boys hard at work putting up drywall. On their way in this morning they had seen a cinnamon bear in the North Meadow. It was probably the same bear that had been seen at Bob's on and off the last three years. They said it was a pretty big boy. Darn it, I might have to go bear hunting again. I had hoped that all of that nonsense was over. Let's hope the bear stays away from the cabin.

Bob came by and brought the season's first red tomatoes from his garden (well, they will be red when they turn). He had been out doing maintenance on his section of the hiking trail early in the day. He will be heading to Nova Scotia in a week for 16 days of bus touring. His garden is about overrun with weeds right now, and it should be about gone by the time he gets back. His neighbor at Cloudland sure does need to learn how to pick weeds!

It was a lazy afternoon and I managed a couple of naps and several chapters in the big Muir book. It is amazing that when Muir was a young man (1860's), you could just take off walking, and ramble around the countryside for days, weeks and even months, camping wherever you wished, working now and then for cash, but mostly just spending time exploring the wilderness that was still all around. He wandered up into Canada once, and stayed there for a couple of years. I remember one funny story about when he was staying at a home for months, and one day when the owners were away, a bird got into the house, and the family cat pounced on it. Well, Muir never liked to see any living thing harmed, so he chased the cat around the house, finally catching it, and ended up choking the cat to death trying to get it to release the bird. The famed world renowned naturalist, choking a house cat to death. Muir was going to be a physician, until one day a classmate at his University got him interested in some plant. That one incident on the school steps changed the world.

I went rambling myself in the early evening and ended up at the old community of Ryker, right where the old post office stood. This is the exact same spot where the Cloudland mailbox stands today. I had no mail, but I did stand there in the road and read the newspaper from Springdale that was in Bob's box. There were a lot of small horse flies out, but not much other wildlife that I could detect. Except for a lot of squirrels. I made the loop from the cabin up past the Faddis house, past the goat man's field (which was filled with new big hay bales), and on out to the main road to the mailboxes. Then I dropped on down the hill and picked up the trail to Hawksbill Crag. The Crag was a stunning place this evening as always, and not a soul in sight. Then it was back along the bluffline, past the "cowcumber" tree, and finally to Cloudland. A nice leisurely loop. After all of the pizza that I baked up and ate, I should have made this loop about a dozen times!

The nighttime was breezy and cool and I sat/laid out on the porch swing, watching night fall, the stars and fireflies come out, and listening to **The Pickin' Post** and **The Folk Sampler** on KUAF radio through the window. (I am always amused when the national syndicated **Folk Sampler** advertises that it is coming to you from "the foothills of the Ozarks in Siloam Springs, Arkansas." I didn't know that there were any hills in Siloam Springs. Come to think of it, there is one *big* hill there, and it was always at the end of the triathlons that I used to run—that hill really killed me!) The breeze was gusting, and creating many songs of its own, as the trees and branches swayed back and forth, with tree frogs and cicadas joining in now and then. Often the radio music matched the night sounds perfectly, and actually complemented all of the natural sounds.

The **Folk Sampler's** theme this night was about lost loves. Some of the songs really struck home. This music about love, combined with the swirling winds, swept me away to my high school days of summer love. My sweetheart and I used to spend hours and hours several nights a week in June, July and August, laying out in the middle of a hay field that belonged to a friend of mine. After all of the magical time of physical discovery was over, we would talk and talk and study the heavens and generally solve all of the problems of the world, and plan out our adventurous lives ahead. This young lady was a year older than me, and a great deal smarter, in fact, near genius level. I never could understand why she wanted to spend time with me, just a local hayseed, but when we were together, the sparks flew, both mentally as well as physically. My mind has never worked so well as when I was outside, under the stars with her. She probably never knew it, but her influence had a great deal to do with me becoming a nature photographer and environmentalist. She is now a doctor of something and a professor at Cornell University in New York. A far cry from an Arkansas summer night with a hayseed. Looking back on that summer, I think that we both learned a lot from each other, about the natural world, and about ourselves. I often wonder what she would think of me now. I'm still just a hayseed, but a much more traveled one.

The moon, though just a sliver, was shining very bright, almost blinding in the black sky. I put the telescope on it and could see the rest of the moon hiding alongside it.

6/28/98 The phone rang at 12:30am but no one was there. I laid there for an hour or two, wide awake, enjoying the breezes coming in through the windows. At 4:30am Stable woke me up, apparently anxious to go outside. I got up and obliged, and spent fifteen minutes wandering around under the bright stars. I have always loved being outside at night in the summer Ozarks. The temperature seems about right. Knowing I would be tired at sunrise, I closed the miniblinds at my bedside window. The next thing I knew it was 8:30an—boy, those blinds really do work! I got up to close all of the cabin windows, and eat more pizza. The steady breeze continued, and soaring birds were out in full force.

I feel a little like *Doogie Howser, M.D.*, as it is late at night, and I am sitting here at the computer typing in my Journal for the day. Actually, he had a great idea, one that many folks should do every day. While I do enjoy the physical act of writing in the Journal with a pencil, it takes me a very long time to write, and I literally get writer's cramps. I find it much easier to spend time at the keyboard, and end up putting a lot more down. Plus, at least most of the words are spelled correctly with a spell-checker—maybe not the right words (like bare instead of bear), but spelled correctly.

The day was another lazy one and I spent most of it indoors, reading and writing and eating and laying around enjoying the cabin. While eating a late lunch on the deck a single cloud across the way caught my attention. It was a small cloud at first, and about the only one in a clear blue sky. When I noticed it again a few minutes later, it was much larger. This peaked my interest, and I began to watch it continuously. Son of a gun, it was growing. Slowly, but it was increasing in size, mostly staying put and not moving around, just billowing up. It got larger and larger. At first, I couldn't figure out exactly what was going on. Then it appeared to be raining underneath it—not the really noticeable streaks of water that you sometimes see, but the air was distorted enough to know that something was going on. And gradually, the cloud got smaller. And smaller. And smaller. It almost disappeared. Then it started getting big again. It got larger, then smaller, then larger and smaller again, several times in an hour. I guess what was happening was a micro-scene of how clouds are formed and rain happens. First, the sun hitting a humid hillside extracts the moisture from it as vapor, which eventually gathers together and forms a cloud, then builds larger and larger, until the moisture content is so heavy that it can no longer be suspended in the air, and then it releases it, as rain. When the cloud gets small enough again, the process starts all over. Probably not really what happens, but it sounds good to me that way.

Late in the afternoon I got out the spotting scope and looked around my world a little. Over towards the fire tower, on the last ridge before the one that the tower is on, there was the crown of a tree that stuck up above all the others around it, in an area that had been logged some time ago. The tree had died recently, and all the leaves were brown. I wonder what killed it? Some day I shall hike down to Whitaker Creek, follow it upstream and around the corner, then climb out and up to this logged area and see if I can find the tree. It will make a fine hike.

I also spotted a bunch of shiner minnows down in the river with the scope. They were just below the little falls that you can see from the deck. Every time that they rolled over to catch some little morsel of food tossed to them by the rushing water, the sun glinted off of their broad side, creating a little flash of light. This is where they get their common name from. I was a little surprised that I could see this from way up at the cabin. Of course, I had the tele set on 45x. It was time for a trip down to the river.

After putting on my usual summer jungle wear of long pants, long-sleeve shirt, gaiters, and floppy hat, I headed off down the hill. It was hot, bright and breezy and a lot of the low growing vegetation was showing signs of burning up. When I descended the ladder I plunged into another world. It was darker, very still—not a wisp of air—and everything was lush, lush, lush. I may have said this before, but man, it really was a jungle. There were a number of huge, giant trees (oaks, gums) that rose up through the thick tangle of branches and smaller trees, and disappeared out of sight. At one point I thought I heard rain, but realized that it was only cowcumber fruit raining down from a large cucumber magnolia tree. The forest floor was covered with a thick carpet of Virginia creeper and poison ivy, and I seldom ever saw the old trail that I was following steeply down the hillside.

A couple of benches down I came across a lot of storm damage—about a dozen very large trees had been blown down. This was probably the same storm that took out the ones in my meadow. I was actually a little glad to see them because someone had noted that the trees down at my place were probably the result of my having cleared the meadow, giving the wind a direct path to attack the trees. Well, these were mature, healthy trees, right in the middle of a thick forest, and they were blown over, so I felt better. Boy, that was some wind— some of these guys were monsters! And two of them were on top of each other, right across the trail. On their way down, one of them realized that the trail was there, and turned and twisted just a little until it crashed down on the trail with big branches protecting the corridor—there was a space under the tree to pass through without much trouble at all. Thanks Mr. Tree.

I heard a weird bird call. One that I think I had heard before, but I had no idea what made it. I milled around a little, and finally saw what looked like a blue jay making the sound. As dark as it was, I couldn't tell if it was actually blue or not—looked all grey to me. But with a strange call. I must consult my bird lady.

Also along the trail there were these blue wildflowers, some of them on stalks six feet tall! I have not been able to find them in the wildflower book, but will continue to investigate.

Whitaker Creek had some water in it but it wasn't running, just sitting there quietly, reflecting the jungle that was gleaning life from it. The Buffalo River was running a little, but the fish, crawdads and other life in the water really stirred it up a lot. It was a jungle getting to the river, but once there, the immediate river course was open and easy to traverse. I put my fanny pack down on the gravel bar and headed upstream. I just wanted to look around a little, but realized that I needed sandals to explore very much. It was obvious that I would have to jump in, so I located a deep enough slough right next to the gravel bar, and after getting into my Ozark swimwear and waving off several crawdads, eased into the water. I was surprised to discover that the water was quite warm. I used to be able to jump into the water in the middle of the winter and love it, but now in my old age, prefer warmer waters. But this was heaven! My desire to just cool off quickly became one to actually swim, so I got up and headed downstream to find a real swimming hole.

The very next hole was just perfect—6-8 feet deep and very long, perhaps 200 yards or more. There was a little rushing water at the head feeding it, boulders lining the western side, and a narrow gravel bar along the eastern side. The bottom was a little slimy, but the water was clear and warm, and I had a blast. I took up a position just below the inlet, and soon dozens of fish gathered. Guys learn fast to protect themselves in such circumstances when biting fish are about. Most of these fish were sunfish, but there were also a couple of little smallmouth bass milling about. I had caught several pretty good smallmouth with my fly rod in this pool a couple of years ago.

This hole of water was right in front of the main camp spot in the area so it might not be the best place for a weekend skinny dip with a young lady. There are no doubt dozens and dozens of other such fine swimming holes on this stretch of the river, and I vowed to seek them out on my next visit. I also wanted to bring a mask and snorkel. I like to spend time in the riffles, just laying there in the shallows with my snorkel sticking out for air. When you first get there and lay down, all of the fish scurry away to cover and hide. But before long the river will get back to its normal life, and the colorful fish of every size and shape will gather around the oxygen-filled water, darting about and grabbing whatever morsels the water brings them. At least, that is what they are supposed to be doing. I think they are just playing half the time—really looks like fun! The water itself is an incredible silver whirlwind, dancing about and singing a tune. I never tire of this scene, and you can find them in any stream in the Ozarks that has running water in it. My favorite place used to be Richland Creek, but I have a feeling that name is about to change.

The hike up the hillside back to the cabin was not all that bad, and the trail was easier to find. It is too bad that the forest service will not allow us to open up the corridor to this historical trail. Perhaps with enough use it will get beat back so that folks can follow it. The trail really does have a great deal of historical significance, and I would hate for it to disappear. I'll work on it.

I huffed and puffed and sweated all the way up the hillside. But it felt great. I need to do this a couple of times a day. Stable was waiting for me upon my return. He is not one of those dogs that begs to go, and then scowls at you when you return after not having taken him—he knows what kind of hikes I go on, and is glad to be left behind to guard the castle. As long as I leave him enough treats.

Since I had a healthy hike I had a healthy dinner too of a fresh salad and glass of red wine. I rid the cabin of sweets a couple of weeks ago, but was now craving them. Couldn't find anything to munch on. When you live in the mountains, far from civilization, you learn to do with whatever you have. So I invented a new dessert—Clouds in a Cup. It consists of a heaping cup full of Reddi-Wip (left here by my girlfriend—I know she had other ideas for it) and fresh blackberries, with Baileys Irish Cream poured over it. Wow, beats a candy bar any day!

Lots of stars out tonight shimmering against a black sky. The moon sliver is low and out of sight behind the trees.

6/29/98 Very still outside, cool, a little hazy. The sounds of a hundred birds can be heard, small and large, near and far, like a woodland symphony welcoming a brand new week. Reluctantly I left my little wilderness world and headed back to civilization.

June rain was 3.3 inches, low 49 degrees, high 90 degrees, wind 55mph

JULY 1998

7/1/98 The moon was only half full but it lit up the forest quite nicely. The view off the deck was a little eerie. You could look way up the Buffalo River valley and see faint fog banks beginning to build. There were a few fireflies out, but not very many. It was cool, in the upper 60's. I checked on Bob's on the way in, but no sign of bear activity. I'm still worried that the cinnamon bear will put in an appearance. Since Bob will be gone for over two weeks, and I'll be gone much of that time as well, the bear could have easy pickin's.

7/2/98 The eastern sky glowed as early as 5am, got really brilliant, then faded a few minutes before the sun rose over the ridge. The scene out back was as wonderful as any I had ever seen here. The valleys were filled with seas of fog, each layer turning gold as the first rays of sun touched them. The fog banks began to move with the warm sunshine, and within 30 minutes were completely gone. I don't know why this scene still amazes me—I've seen it dozens of times before already this year, but it is just too incredible to ignore. I hope that it never becomes ordinary to me. I guess that may be one indication of the quality of life—when remarkable things cease to stir the soul, when they pass unnoticed, when you no longer gasp at a glorious sunrise, pause at a thunderous waterfall to soak up the spray, listen to the call of a distant owl, strain your neck to follow the path of a red-tailed hawk soaring overhead, or sit quietly in awe in a field of wildflowers—when these things are ignored, then life has taken a turn for the worse, and perhaps it is time to remove yourself from whatever you are doing, wherever you are, and head to the wilderness with nothing to do but exist and recharge the batteries.

I decided to head on up the hill to check out the garden and was surprised to find that Stable, my loyal cabin dog, was anxious to go with me. This dog only moves when there is food on the horizon. He is rather old, so I allow him to lay about the cabin as he pleases. But today he not only hit the trail, but actually kept up with me, and even went out in front some! I couldn't believe it. Don't know what had got into him. He sometimes gets hyper when a storm is approaching, but it was nothing but clear blue skies out. There was an interesting patch of Virginia creeper that had been eaten up by some bugs. It seemed like there was more of the leaves eaten than were left—made some really interesting patterns in the leaves. I will try to remember to take one home and see what it would look like on the copy machine.

We made it to the garden and found lots of tomatoes about to ripen, green beans, bell peppers, new potatoes, and a few onions, all ready for the picking. The corn was coming along nicely. I put Stable inside the Faddis cabin, and I went down to Bob's to check on things. As I approached, I heard noises coming from the cabin. It sounded like someone was there, and was working on something. But as I got closer, there was no vehicle in the driveway. Damn, not another bear! I approached cautiously, peeking around every corner, but never saw anything. And nothing had been disturbed. Everything was OK. I have no idea what the noises were, unless they were manufactured in my head by my still active bear mind.

I swiped Bob's John Muir book as it has more of the mainstream writings in it than the one that I have been reading. These are very large books, and I thought how funny it was that I was carrying this big Muir book through the woods on a hot summer day—me, a guy who has barely read a dozen books in his life. On the way back up the hill, I heard a thud up on the hillside in the woods. A few seconds later I saw the maker of the thud—it was a huge hickory nut that had fallen out of the tree, and was bumping and bouncing its way down the steep hillside, crashing through stands of Virginia creeper and poison ivy along the way. It stopped just short of the path that I was on. One big nut— glad I wasn't standing under the tree when it fell!

As Stable and I crossed the Faddis Meadow on our way back to the cabin I noticed a tall thunderhead off in the distance. I didn't make the connection at the time, but that thunderhead was just the beginning of a much larger storm system, which had to have been what made Stable so active—he is a great weather dog. Two hours later, I was shaken from my nap on the couch by continuous rolls of thunder. I got up to a very dark, green sky all around, and lots and lots of thunder and lightning. Then it began to rain, and a heavy fog rolled in. This wasn't a real violent thunderstorm that is typical of summer ones here, except for all of the thunder and lightning, but rather a very nice rain shower that was badly needed. I sat out on the deck and watched the lightning bolts for awhile, then retreated to the computer when it began to rain. For the first time that I remember, the power went off while I was typing, and I would have lost a great deal of unsaved work, had it not been for the backup power system that I had installed on this computer—it just beeped to let me know that the power had been interrupted, then continued on as though nothing had happened. The power was only off for a few seconds in the cabin, but that would have shut down the computer for sure, and I would have lost all that I had typed. Money well spent!

OK, the shower continues, it is very cool, I have a heavy John Muir book on the table, it must be time to go lay down and read for the rest of the afternoon. Life at Cloudland can sometimes just be rather tough.

Lori Spencer from the Ozark Natural Science Center came by for a visit and to check out the trail to the Crag for an upcoming Elderhostel hike. She is the director of programs for the Center, but more importantly, a butterfly expert. In fact, she is working on an Arkansas Butterfly ID book. She tells me that there are 127 different species of butterflies in Arkansas! Good grief. I was just pulling some Cloudland Pizza out of the oven as she drove up, and we spent some time on the back deck devouring it. As darkness fell, I turned on the front porch light to attract some moths (also a speciality of hers) to see what we had living around here. Below are a few notes from Lori.

10:00pm. Tim's porch light—insects identified Catacola moth—biggest one at the light so far, Limacodidae-detailed green moth family, 12 different geometrid moths, Weevils, ladybugs, May beetles, Ant lion-looks just like a damselfly, but flies at night, and if you look closely at the base of the wings and the long antennae, you can tell immediately it's an ant lion. Have you ever seen the larvae's sand pits? These are what the adults turn out to be. The wings on this one were mottled with a charcoal gray color. It's not quite calling time for the silk moths like the Luna, Cecropia, and Polyphemus. "Calling time" means that's when they release their pheromones to attract mates. Silk moths only live for about a week, just long enough to mate and breed. In fact, they don't even have any mouthparts--no time to eat. Silk moths "call" each other between midnight and three, usually, so we'll have to check later to find any. Five in the morning will be a good time to do a "deck check" and see if any have spent the night. I can't get all the moths to species, but I'm seeing at least twenty different kinds in various sizes. Most moths rest with their wings open straight out--one of the ways you can tell them apart from butterflies. Obviously, most moths are nocturnal, butterflies the opposite. But some of these smaller moths are resting with their wings over their bodies as if they were roofs, like butterflies do. I'm hoping for a dobson fly or a few click beetles, but mainly for some silk moths.—Lori Spencer

7/3/98 I was tired and went to bed before the midnight calling began, and I think Lori did too. I was awakened by a pair of screech owls at about 4am—they seemed to be right outside of the guest bedroom window, but Lori later said she never heard them, so I guess she was fast asleep. Neither of us got up to check the lights just before dawn, although there were still a few moths hanging around when I finally did get up. We hiked on over to the Crag as it got warm in a hurry. With Lori the butterfly expert along, I began to notice that there were all kinds of butterflies everywhere, mostly traveling in singles, fluttering and flapping to and fro with no particular route in mind. Lori identified almost all of them, although the names were foreign to me. She is one of those people who can spout out multitudes of scientific and common names like she is talking regular English, and most of it goes right over my head.

Just before she left for civilization I spotted a pair of butterflies in the front "yard" of the cabin. She grabbed her net, and before I could even tell what color they were, she had swooped *both* of them up in the net and was examining them. She made it look so easy—I'm sure if I tried to do such a thing, I would not only smash the butterflies (if I ever got close enough to them), but would probably wind up smashing my head with the net pole too. Anyway, she ID'd them right away (Pipevine swallowtails), and discovered that they were a pair—one male and one female. When I first saw them, they were flying in formation, and looked so graceful, kind of like a pair of dolphins in the sea. It was obvious that they were true mates.

After a nap or two and some Muir reading I headed out for another hike, this time to the Crag and then out to the mailboxes and loop back via the road. Along the way I passed three folks from Oklahoma who were enjoying the rocks to the west of the Crag. It was getting hot. Hey, it must be July in the Ozarks! But there was a nice, cool breeze blowing, and I took up residence in the back porch swing, letting the breezes rock me to sleep. Could it be that I have returned to my childhood, always wanting to nap? Actually, I don't think that I napped very much as a child, I think that I spent most of my first few years running wild in the woods around my house. Perhaps I was reclaiming my lost youth. What the heck, I am still a child, a child of the wilderness!

My gentle nap was broken by the ringing of the bell in front of the cabin, and I realized that Roy and Norma had arrived for the weekend. It didn't take long to convince them that it was time to head down the hill to the swimming hole. This would prove to be one of the best hikes to date here at Cloudland.

We all bundled up in long pants and shirts, boots, daypack laden with water and swim masks, then were sprayed with bug dope—yuk, I wonder if it wouldn't almost be of lessor evil to be covered with bugs rather than with this foul smelling stuff! As we headed down the hill, Norma remarked "I just love the smell of the heat from the forest floor." An interesting observation.

As we dropped below the ladder the same sense of a tropical jungle came to mind. All was dense and lush and dark. Some of the trees were just *huge!* I don't know why this continues to excite me every time that I see them, but it does. We determined that the largest one was a red oak, towering way up out of sight. Next to it was a six foot tall blue wildflower, which I still haven't looked up the identity of yet. The trail was very easy to follow, even through the thickest of underbrush. The more traffic it sees, the more this will come true. Roy kept pointing out that the big trees were all old growth. I sometimes feel that way myself, but hope that in my old growth years I don't spread out quite as large as these fellows! Towards the bottom we came across some golden seal plants that I had spotted before (I've heard the roots were going for $40 a pound). And near them, we found a trail that had been cut out and flagged by horse folks. It came across one of the homestead areas, crossed our trail, and went on down to Whitaker Creek. But it ended there. Some day I must follow it backwards and see where it goes.

We reached the Buffalo River, stripped off (well, not everything, after all, there was a lady present), and jumped in. The water was super warm and felt great. We made it to the big swimming hole, donned our swim masks, and disappeared underwater. Few things in life are more interesting to me than peering into the lives of fishes. This is the first time that I really got to take a look around underwater in this hole. It is over 100 yards long, most of it being about six feet deep in the middle. On the far side is a row of boulders and small cliffs that line the pool. We three spent an hour or more exploring around, then made our way downstream to another interesting pool, where we spied several good-sized smallmouth bass hiding under a big rock.

Back at the main pool Norma and I found a cave of sorts, or at least a place where you can swim down under a big boulder and come up on the other side. There were a lot of fish hanging around at the bottom of these big rocks too, wondering what all these other big fish with funny eyes were doing invading their space. At the head of this pool is where the water comes in, warmed by the shallow pools upstream. You can lay there in the foot-deep whitewater and the little fishes will come crowd around you. It is wonderful to lay there and have the warm water wash all over you.

Roy and Norma retreated to a flat rock upstream and relaxed while I took off upstream with mask and snorkel in hand—I wanted to see if there were other great swimming holes nearby. The rocks underwater were very slippery, and my sandals were of no help. I sloshed my way upstream, as big black thunderheads loomed on down the valley. Once in a while thunder could be heard. Hey, it was the 4th of July weekend, so I expected it to rain at some point.

Most of the river was shallow, but I did find one deep pool that allowed me to put on the mask and dive into. This pool was quite different from the main one, and had a point or two that were deeper than it, although it was much shorter. There were two main boulders out in the middle—that's where the deeper water was. As soon as you got underwater a couple of feet, the temperature got cold in a hurry. In fact, it was so cold at the bottom of these boulders, that I could hardly stand to be down there—must be spring fed. I had a grand time exploring this little pool, chasing the fishes around, and seeing what was in all of the dark recesses. I tried to cover every inch, seeing all that there was to see. As I worked my way upstream the water got shallow and was rushing. I kept my head underwater and sort of pushed my body along. There were fishes of all colors, sizes and shapes darting about. It was an amazing color show. This is what I had come to see, and was content to lay here in the shallows with my head in the water for a long time. Just then the sun came out from behind a cloud, and I was blinded by a million tiny silver sparkles—holy smokes, I had just discovered the most incredible diamond mine! The view before me was quite indescribable, and was one of the most amazing things that I had ever seen. The sunlight had turned each tiny air bubble that was forced down into the shallow by the rushing water into liquid silver. And the sunlight was creating shadows and silver slivers on the bottom from the patterns of water on the surface, but the real gems were a million times more than that—tiny air bubbles lined every rock and the floor of the pool and when the sun hit them, they simply exploded with brightness! It was just unbelievable. And add to all of this the hundreds of fishes that were flashing about. This is my world. My wilderness. My playground. This could not be created on film. It was Mother Nature at her finest. And no scene in the ocean could top it.

I don't know how long I laid there mesmerized, but I eventually got up, quite stunned at what I had just been watching, and tried to stumble my way even further upstream. Just a short distance away was another pool, a little longer than the first. I had a good long swim there, and it was a fine pool, but it contained little of the gems like before. The river began to turn back to the left, the thunder increased in intensity and volume, so I turned back and headed downstream. Instead of tromping through the shallow waters, I was determined to stay head down and swim my way as far as I could. I was able to stay in the water most of the way back, and had a grand time playing with the fishes.

At one point I was laying in water about two feet deep, at the edge of a ledge that made the water about two inches deep upstream. This shallow flat was filled with rushing water, and it seemed like every square inch of space was taken up with silver minnows, schools of a hundred at a time. Since I was in the deeper water, they didn't seem to pay any attention to me, and danced back and forth in time with the water. I was quite entertained. Then I was shocked back into reality by the loud crack from the clouds now looming above. I got turned around and crawled through the shallow water to where Roy and Norma were reading the paper.

Roy, a ex-marine, was getting a little concerned about the impending storm, but I smiled with each new boom, and Norma got up and headed for the big pool to swim a few laps. Norma is one of those city-slicker girls that you would expect to be running for cover when the first cloud appears, but she is quite the outdoors woman, and was relishing the thought of hiking in the rain.

I put on my hiking clothes and headed up the hill, making it to the top without stopping a single time—I was trying to get into shape for an upcoming trip to the high country in Wyoming. The trail was very easy to follow. It was quite warm, and I collapsed on the front porch of the cabin completely drenched. I sat in the swing, trying to regain my composure, and listened to the thunder. Soon the sky opened up and it began to pour. I had just missed getting caught in it. What I also missed was a terrific experience of hiking in an Ozark summer thunderstorm. I kind of knew that, and almost took off back down the hill, but my attention was taken up by the fact that the power was off.

It poured and poured and I just knew Roy would be moaning. Before long they appeared at the cabin, both completely drenched, but both absolutely bubbling over with excitement and glee. They were like two little kids playing in a mud puddle. Roy was grinning from ear to ear, and kept talking nonstop about how it was the greatest thing that he had ever done. They had just started up the hill when the sky opened up. In a dense forest like this one, you can hear the rain hitting the treetops high above, but it takes a while before the rain can make its way down through all of the canopy and to the forest floor. When it finally did hit the ground, Roy described it as "...the dancing flora on the forest floor..." It really is a terrific treat to hike in the rain when it is warm.

I told them that there would be no showers available since the electricity was off (and therefore no water pressure pump), but they just shouted with glee and began to strip off all their clothes and headed for the rain pouring off of the rain gutters. Boy, now why didn't I think of that? Of course, they were all hot and sweaty from the hike up, and I had cooled down—the thought of the cold rain was not appealing to me, but they sure did have a ball!

Being the gentleman that I am, I sat on the back porch while Norma, 'a-la-natural', bathed in the front of the cabin. It was still raining, and the scene out the back was tremendous. There were those dark clouds overhead, still booming and spilling buckets of water, but just a little ways out it was perfectly clear and the sun was shining. And then it happened—a brilliant rainbow appeared in the valley. It arched down to the river where we had just been swimming. This is the first ever rainbow that I had seen at Cloudland! I ran to the van to get my little camera (it must have been quite some rainbow, because I never even noticed Norma in the buff just a few feet away—perhaps I have been in the woods too long!). I shot a few pictures of the rainbow, and got a wood carving of a waving bear in the foreground (it is one of the railing corner posts). Rainbows are tough to take pictures of, especially with a bear watching.

Roy joined me on the deck and soon the rain quit and the rainbow disappeared. But the steam banks began to pop up all over the valley. They would grow and move back and forth, up and down, then disappear. The sun would light up one of them, and it would dance and sway around. Roy was especially excited about the show, although I had seen it many times before (was still spectacular to me too!). He lit up a cigar, popped open a beer, and kicked back in the chair to enjoy the show. Norma soon joined us, and I felt a little out of place, since I still stunk from my hot ascent, and they had been freshly bathed in rain water. The power was still off. Birds began to appear in the meadow. My friend bunting came and sat in his place and began to sing. Then a scarlet tanager flew through. The birds were putting on quite a show themselves.

You could tell that Roy and Norma were about to burst with excitement, yet they were so relaxed that they could hardly keep from sliding out of their chairs. Norma finally spoke and summed up their current state of being—she said that the day had been "*satisfactory*, in a Nero Wolf kind of way." I agreed.

I was telling them about this huge walking stick that Lori and I had seen on the limb right out in front the day before. Upon further inspection, we discovered that it was still right there, only inches away from us, and completely unnoticed. It was over six inches long, rather large for this time of year.

Before long the bell rang, and Hete appeared, with a beer and cantaloupe in hand. He was not in a good mood, but wouldn't explain. We tried to ignore him and continued with our "satisfactory" day. It was soon time to fire up the grill, and we all got busy preparing dinner. As it turned out it was nearly 9pm before we all sat down to a dinner of BBQ chicken with all the fixin's. It was a fine meal, and was good to have a table full.

Out came another cigar, along with the moon, and we spent some time examining the moon with the telescope. Don't know if all the beer had anything to do with it or not, but the craters on the moon were especially clear and detailed this night, and the moon itself was very bright silver. And I swear, we may have even been sober, but there was a bright light making its way across the sky in front of us. It was nearly as bright as the moon. As I ran to get the telescope, the light quickly faded, then disappeared altogether. Satellites do not light up like this thing did! Nor do airplanes. And neither would just disappear. I'm not saying that it was a craft full of little green men, but it certainly was a UFO, the first ever sighted at Cloudland.

7/4/98 There were only a few clouds hanging around in the valley this morning. Roy and I had breakfast on the deck, and Norma caught up on her beauty rest (it is obvious that she has been quite successful doing this). There was a very nice breeze blowing through, and lots of birds about. The little Indigo bunting made an appearance, and spent ten minutes in his usual place, singing and praising the glory of the day. And then the scarlet tanager flew through. This guy is rather shy, and always tends to stay out a little ways, but close enough to give us a great view of his brilliant red body.

When Norma got up Roy was ready to go hiking. Norma wasn't. We all enjoyed the morning breezes a while longer. No firecrackers anywhere, although we did hear Bob fire up his lawn mower, which sounded quite out of place here in the middle of the wilderness. Before long Roy and Norma headed out for a hike to the Crag. They returned a while later, refreshed by the hike, but needing to get back to town, and left.

I took up my proper holiday spot on the couch, under the ceiling fan, with the John Muir book. I read his ***Thousand Mile Walk To The Gulf*** book, then managed a good long nap. No one was stirring on the mountain. I was awakened by two birds who flew into the west windows. I went out and checked on them, and could not find either body, so I figured they were OK and flew off.

I went downstairs in the basement to check on something and discovered that I had a growing problem down there, literally. Two of the steel doors had mildew growing on the base of them. So did some of the stuff that was up against the north wall. I moved everything away from the wall in both rooms, and realized that there was indeed a crack in the concrete where the floor met the wall. I would have to get some crack-fixing stuff, and get something done about that soon. I already had the waterproof paint to go over it, but you've got to fill in the cracks first. I hoped that all of this would fix the problem, otherwise I would have to put in a dehumidifier.

It was nearing 90 degrees outside but I felt that I had lounged around like a lizard long enough, so I headed out the door for a hike to the Crag, then out to the trailhead, and back. As I left the cabin and bushwhacked down the hillside to the informal trail to the Crag, I realized that when you hike without a trail in thick brush like this was, you really don't get much of a chance to look around while you are hiking—your attention is focused on the unstable and mostly hidden ground that you are stepping on. I do a great deal of bushwhacking around, and prefer to wander around that way most of the time, but hiking on a proper trail is really the way to go. You don't have to worry about where you are walking much at all, and can spend your moving time looking at everything around you instead of at your feet. It was pleasant in the cool of the woods.

There was a young couple at the Crag, enjoying the day, and each other. I excused myself for interrupting their solitude, and stepped out to the edge to take a look around. I will never tire of the Crag. We struck up a conversation, and I just had to laugh when I was asked if "I had been hiking long." With the outfit that I was wearing, I took it to mean how long in general, not this day.

I had on a pair of very long shorts that hung to the knees, a clean white t-shirt that was tucked in, no water whatsoever, and white tennis shoes. It must have been the tennis shoes that prompted the question. I was lectured on the proper attire for hiking in the Ozarks—I bit my tongue, thanked them for their advice, then hiked on. As I left, I heard the girl telling the guy about how the Buffalo River was right below them, and that the beginning of it was just to their right—good description, but the wrong river.

Up the trail a ways I passed this odd beech tree. It had a wonderful personality, and had been hollowed out a great deal over time. On one side there were three uniquely-shaped holes. I have always wanted to photograph this tree, but can't figure out a good way to do it, since the image would be very tall and skinny. I guess I will just have to shoot it, then crop out the distracting woods on either side, making instead of an 8 x 10 inch print, a 2 x 10 inch print. Just beyond the beech, I heard another one of a dozen squirrels scampering about. Although this one was a little different. I looked up and saw a huge squirrel running through the leaves at the base of a small bluff that I had never seen before. That was no squirrel, it was a woodchuck! A woodchuck, what in the world was he doing down here in the woods? He saw me and hesitated a moment, then disappeared into a hole at the base of the bluff.

I followed the trail out to the trailhead, then turned right on the road and followed it back towards the cabin. Along the way I saw the old owl again. Roy and Norma had said that they saw what looked like an owl perched on a big bale of hay in the field right next to this spot. It must have a nest nearby or something. I found a large feather on the ground near this spot, and it was half white and half black. Don't know what it came from. I also found that there were a few blackberries on the vines nearby that were screaming to be picked. Always wanting to help out, I gathered a cup full and continued on.

As I entered the Faddis Meadow I saw a pair of goldfinches playing in an apple tree—the male was brilliant yellow with striking black wings. I always used to call these birds wild parakeets—good thing that I have a bird ID book.

It is great to hike in the summer, but it is wonderful to take a cool shower at Cloudland upon your return! Sometimes I think that I built this cabin just so that I could take showers at the end of hikes. Of course, the couch makes a great reading spot. And the back deck a splendid breakfast nook. And the loft bed a fine spot for nighttime storms...

For dinner I grilled the usual fresh veggies and chicken/apple sausage and inhaled a pitcher of strawberry daiquiris. The daiquiris were spiked with the cup full of blackberries that I had picked during the hike—they must have been fermenting on the vine, as this pitcher really knocked me for a loop! Of course, it could have been the rum too. The wind died down, and the no-see-ums came out in full force, so I retreated to the couch to begin another John Muir book, this one his *My First Summer In The Sierra*. He mentions "Cloudland" several times in the early chapters, and I must do some more digging to find out exactly what he is talking about. I had never heard the term Cloudland before I named my place, except for the campground in Colorado up near Mt. Evans.

At one point I took a break from the Sierra and sat out on the deck, star gazing, and enjoying the moonlight. The moon was a little past half full, and I think is the perfect size for the view from Cloudland. It was bright enough to light up the ridges and valleys, but not so bright that it destroyed your night vision. Boy, I really wish that I could have sketched the night scene—there must have been twenty shades of grey, all the way from pure black in the deep hollows to the brilliant silver of the moon. It was spectacular.

This wonderful scene was interrupted by an idiot who was camping at the Crag. He had built a campfire right out on the Crag, and had it stoked up pretty big. He set off a few firecrackers too. Ahhh, the silence of the wilderness!

At some point during the weekend I realized that my young girlfriend was not too interested in me any longer, or in being at Cloudland (this was just another in a long string of weekends I spent alone). I guess she was on the same wavelength, as she had never even called or wrote once all the while she had been gone on her trip. So I decided it was time to end the relationship. I will keep many wonderful thoughts of her tucked into my head. Funny, she never once wrote a single word in this Journal, even though it was she who bought the original notebook and encouraged me to write in it. It is time to move on, in hopes that someone who wants to share the wonders of Cloudland will appear. I really do hate to waste all that is here on just me!

7/5/98 John Muir kept me awake long past midnight, and since I had the blinds closed, I never saw the beginning of the day. Stable got me up after 8am, telling me that he had urgent business outside. I needed to get some business of my own done, as I had a lot of work to do before I left the cabin and headed home at mid-day. It was very still outside, not a whisper of wind, and getting hotter by the minute. There were lots of birds playing about as I dined on toasted bagels and Starbucks mocha on the back deck. From across the way, came a sorrowful, mournful howling from a dog. Roy and I had heard the same howling the morning before, but could not agree as to where it had come from. The howling this morning was quite clear, and easy to tell where it was coming from. The poor dog only howled twice, then was silent. A vision of a mangled dog flashed through my head, lying at the base of the bluff. Hurt in the fall, he could not move, and could only muster enough energy for two cries for help each morning. I had to do something. I had to go see if I could help.

Within minutes I was clothed in my summer bushwhacking attire of long pants, long-sleeved shirt, boots and a bandanna. In my daypack I had some water, a turkey sandwich, a couple of Worther's candies, and my 9mm pistol, just in case the poor fellow was beyond help. There was an urgency in my step, and I had fallen twice before I ever got to the ladder. I had to slow down, or I might end up in the same position as this dog, only my cries for help would probably not ever be heard by anyone. It was a quick trip to the bottom anyway, and soon I was across Whitaker Creek and heading up the other side. I wanted to find the log road that left the old field and climbed up the hillside, but the brush was just too thick, and I was unable to find it. I was reminded that I really should have been wearing a headnet, as the spiderwebs were everywhere, and most of them ended up in my face.

Before long I found a beautiful rock wall that I had never seen before. It was quite wide and sturdy. I put it on my mental map of things to explore later in the year, when I could see farther, and when there weren't so many spiderwebs out! I climbed over the wall and continued up the hill. Son of a gun, right on the other side of the wall was the road that I had been looking for—I was glad to find it. Up, up and away it took me, but all too soon it ended, just like before, although I did manage to push the end of it up another bench. It was a steep last two benches up to the bluffline, but I made it OK.

My plan was to follow along the bottom of the bluff, reaching out to the steep slopes below with my eyes, looking for any sign of the dog. I rounded the point, and began to search carefully, as this was the area where I thought the howling had come from. I called, and whistled, just in case he would respond to a human sound. About ten minutes into the search, he cried out—again, two long, moaning cries for help. He was close, but not in the immediate vicinity, so I hustled along the bluffline, around a little point, then stopped and called out again. He answered, and sounded very close, perhaps just on the next point. I scrambled along the bluffline, falling a time or two in my haste.

As I got around to the nose of this little ridge I slowed down, called and listened. Nothing. He had to be right here somewhere. I sat down on a rock and called some more. Still nothing. Had he used up his last breath crying out to me and could call out no more? Time seemed to be very important now. I scrambled and clawed and stumbled about, but no pup. I went back up to the bluffline and continued along it for some ways, until I figured I was out of the range of where his cries had come from. I doubled back, lower this time, just in case he had rolled down the steep slope. Nothing. I climbed back up to the bluffline, and rested under an overhang (this is the same one where I had found the wood sorrel back in May—the delicate flowers were all gone, and the little plants were about dried up, although there was a small pool of water in the back, catching a few drips that were running down the wall).

In a few days I would be hiking at 11,000 feet, well above timberline, probably sitting next to a snowbank, in the Wind River Mountains in Wyoming. It would be in the 20's at night, maybe even lower, with an average humidity of 20% or less, and a snow shower or two every day. What a contrast to my present resting place, with its jungle vegetation, heat and humidity. I love them both. I hated to leave the jungle, but was really looking forward to the mountains.

I rested and waited, calling and whistling, but only silence. Not even a breeze to stir things up. I really wanted to find this dog, and find him alive, but feared I was too late. I just had to look some more. I got up and scoured the steep hillside once again. I whistled, and called, then listened. A cry rang out from behind a giant boulder near the base of the bluff, and as I approached

51

it, a little beagle dog stood there, smiling and wagging his tail. He was alive, and in good shape—hurrah! He turned and disappeared behind the boulder. I followed. Near the back of the boulder I found a more somber scene. Another small beagle dog, with a smile on his face, but a badly torn up body, lay in the leaves. Apparently the two were traveling together, as is often the case with these beagle dogs. It appeared that the second one had indeed fallen off of the bluff. He probably got confused during the big storm on Friday and simply couldn't stop. Somehow the other dog got down the bluff and found him, and was so loyal that he would not leave his side. He didn't look too good, and with broken legs he obviously could not walk. I was surprised that he had lived so long in this condition, with nothing to eat or drink. They hadn't had anything to eat in a while anyway, and the healthy pup was nothing but skin and bones.

The healthy pup cowered over to the side, and let me deal with the hurt pup. I could not see anything that I could do, he was just so badly hurt. I gave him a drink of water, and then fed him my turkey sandwich, which he gulped almost without chewing. Then I gave each of them a piece of my hard candy. I sat with the injured pup for a half-hour, holding him as best I could, and told him of my own brave dog Yukon, how he used to run these very hills with such great enthusiasm, and how he is buried not far away, on the banks of the Buffalo River, overlooking a fine swimming hole. He looked up at me with eyes of great understanding, comforted in knowing that when he left this earth in this beautiful valley he would not be alone. He seemed quite peaceful, and at rest. Then he breathed his last in my arms. I never had to use my firearm, and was thankful for that.

I spent some time preparing a proper grave in the rubble at the base of the bluff, laid him in it, then covered him up with a nice pile of moss-covered stones. During leaf-off he would have a great view of the valley.

I turned my attention to the other pup and decided to try to get him to follow me back to the cabin, where I would feed him and take him to a neighbor that I thought he belonged to (neither dog had a collar). He would not leave his buddy at first, but I did manage to get him down off of the hill, and he followed me to the base of the valley, me slipping and sliding all the way, and he just moseying along. When we reached Whitaker Creek, it was flowing some, and I stopped at a little hole of water and splashed myself. The beagle came gingerly over and drank for about two minutes—he was quite dry! We rested a while, and I gave him the temporary name of Whitaker Sam.

Before long we had climbed out of the valley and were standing at the base of the ladder at the bluff. I was completely soaked from head to toe with sweat, and out of breath. Sam had a smile on his face, and breathing normally. Rub it in little beagle dog! It took some doing, but he finally allowed me to grab a hold of him and carry him up the ladder. He followed me to the front steps of the cabin, and I went inside and got a bowl of dog food and set it out by the outside faucet with a bowl of water. He would not approach at first, but once I left and went inside, he was seen emptying both. My soaking clothes were on the front porch, and I stood there naked under the ceiling fans, trying to cool off. Sam finished his dinner, then curled up in the shade at the base of a hickory tree.

I showered, cleaned up the cabin, spent some time at the computer, loaded everyone up including Whitaker Sam, and reluctantly headed for home. I would be leaving for the high country tomorrow, and had to give a slide program at the Ozark Natural Science Center near Eureka Springs tonight. Spending the summer at Cloudland was a lot nicer than I had ever expected, and I looked forward to getting back and exploring more of the jungle. But first, I had to enjoy my second home in the mountains for a few days, clear out my lungs, and rest my crippled arm. Along the way home I stopped and left Sam at his house—the kids were very glad to see him, but sad to hear of his buddy's accident.

7/13/98 Wow, I can't believe that I have been away so long! The trip into the high country in the Wind River Mountains of Wyoming was quite spectacular, as always, and it went by very fast. The Wildman and I made the drive in record time (less than 18 hours), stopping only three times for gas and the other essentials. We only spent a few minutes in town, then headed up to the trailhead. We got there so early, we decided to go ahead and hike in and spend the night in the mountains instead of acclimating at the trailhead. Carl did very well with his heavier-than-expected pack. Both of our packs weighed in at 40 pounds—I always have a scale handy so that no one can stretch the truth.

The next day we continued up to and over a high pass. Since Carl was a little slower than me, I gave him a head start, while I stayed in my little tent and recovered from the drive out. When I finally did get up, I was shocked at how easily I handled the altitude, and the steep climb with the full pack. I guess my little trips down into my Ozark jungle and back UP the hill to the cabin had kept me in much better shape than I had thought. Anyway, I raced up to the pass, expecting to pass the old Wildman at every corner, but he was nowhere to be found on the trail. I thought that he must have made a wrong turn or something, because he could not have stayed that far in front of me. Son of a gun, when I got to the top of the pass, there he was, keeled over right in the middle of the trail, with his backpack still strapped on, and engulfed with a swarm of mosquitoes. My first thought was that he had a heart attack, and died right there on the trail with one of the most incredible views of the high country as his last scene. That would have been one of the two ways that he would like to go (the other being hanged as a rapist at age 99). Upon closer inspection, I found him to be in deep sleep, sawing logs like he had a bridge to build. He, too, felt great and scampered up the hillside, which exhausted him, and he quickly collapsed into sleep when he got to the top. Apparently this took a great deal out of him, as he really never recovered from that climb.

The days in the high country were gorgeous—blue skies, a few puffy clouds, a cool breeze, and a high in the low 70's. The nights were clear and cool, dropping down into the upper 30's only once, with a bright full moon shining across the snow-capped mountains. There had been a great deal of snow in the high country, and with the warm weather of the past couple of weeks, the snow melt created near flood conditions in all of the now raging streams and rivers. The Wildman recovered enough to grab the fly rod the very first afternoon and fill his time with thrashing trout. We bent down the barbs on the hooks of his flies that not only allows the fish to be released a lot easier, and unharmed, but also saves the flies—he fished almost the entire time and only used two flies, only changing once to a different color. Most flies with barbs on the hooks would get torn up after a few fights, and the fish end up in much worse condition. We had camped next to a small snowbank, and happy hour began any time after noon each day, with the snow providing the basis for our patented Whiskey Sours. These were actually invented by the then ten-year-old son of Luke Collins. We all were on a hiking trip into the Sawtooth Mountains in Idaho, and he gathered up a cup full of snow, sprinkled a little lemonade powder on it, poured some Wild Turkey over it, and handed it over to his dad. The Turkey melted the snow, and presto, instant Whiskey Sour! It is now my standard mountain cocktail, and the Wildman and I enjoyed a number of them on our little trip.

We only ate trout once, four unfortunate souls that happened to have grown up in a little secret lake that I knew about a couple of miles from our campsite. No one ever fishes this little hole, but I have always found it to be full of 12-14 inch trout, which is larger than most of the rest up there (certainly there are much larger ones in the bigger lakes, but they take too much effort to catch— these are always willing to jump into the frying pan). We filled the trout with butter, fresh lemon juice and seasonings, wrapped them in foil, and baked them in the campfire coals. They were simply wonderful, better than any gourmet restaurant. Funny thing though, both of us had very strange dreams that night, totally unrelated, but the most bizarre that either of us could remember having in a long time. Perhaps the fish getting back at us?

While I made a number of hikes around the area, I only had one really big day of hiking. The Wildman stayed behind and fished, and I went out to take a look at all of the trail work that my volunteer crews had done during the period between 1990 and 1994. We had built five log bridges, plus scores of turnpikes, boulder steps, waterbars, and new trail reroutes. It was of great comfort to me to find all of this work still in excellent shape and working fine. My hike was a fabulous one, full of exhilarating views and new discovery. I had worked in this very same valley for five summers, and yet found several new things, like a thundering waterfall on the main river. The river was so wild and thrashing, that I had to hike over two miles out of my way in order to find a safe crossing.

I visited all of my old haunts and rambled cross-country across hillsides and meadows with ease. The deep snow at higher elevations kept me from making a big loop that I had wanted to do, and so after hiking about 15 miles—all of the trail that I could reach that wasn't snowbound—I returned to camp in early afternoon, just in time for a nice rain shower, and happy hour.

We reluctantly bid the high country farewell and raced back across the desert of Kansas and Oklahoma, making another record 17 hour drive! The humidity socked us in the face, but I knew that I would soon be back out at Cloudland, where nothing so far has dampened my spirits.

Boy, I didn't mean to get off on that Western trip, but it was very nice. So was my return to Cloudland. It had just rained, and everything was fresh and green and plump and actually kind of cool. It had reached 91 degrees the week before outside, and 81 for a high inside. I unloaded a couple of granite boulders that I borrowed from a Wyoming field, set up a new water cooler, and left on a hike, happy that the cabin was no worse for my having been gone an entire week. I walked up to the big goat meadow, and was met there by three whitetail does grazing in the twilight. Funny, I only saw one animal in Wyoming, a big mule deer doe near camp. My favorite hickory trees had showered the path with nuts, making it nearly impossible to walk without bending over and picking up a few nuts to toss at nearby trees. There were hundreds and hundreds of hickory nuts on the ground. Euel Gibbons could make Grape Nuts for years from this harvest. ("Tastes like *wild* Hickory Nuts...")

I ended up at the Crag, sat down and marveled at the exquisite view laid out before me. It was quite a dramatic change from the stunning views of the high country, but I felt even more relaxed here in my own backyard jungle. It was very quiet, and still, no breeze at all. As darkness fell the volume of the summer bugs increased to a high pitch—cicadas, tree frogs, barred owls—they all got in the act. It got dark in a hurry, and really loud. The sky began to dance with stars of all sizes and colors—the sky was really dark, and the bright lights stuck out. The light shows in the high country were wonderful, but a bright moon was always shining, so we never got to see many stars, at least not as bright and clear as this sky was. I must have been tired, because I retreated to a tree away from the Crag a little and fell sound asleep. Thank goodness there were no biting bugs out, or they would have eaten me alive. Hard to believe that I could go to sleep with the deafening sound of the summer creatures all about.

I don't remember what I was dreaming, or if I was at all, but all of a sudden I awoke, in a daze, and it took me a minute to figure out exactly where I was. Yes, I remember, the Ozarks jungle, the black night, a million bugs screaming in my ear. But it was very bright out, and there was hardly any sound at all. I struggled to my feet, still a little stove-up from all the hiking in Wyoming, and walked out onto the Crag and was blinded by the bright moon rising over the far ridge—it was nighttime daylight, and the moonbeams lit up all the hills and valleys just like sunrise. But what was really strange, was that there was no sound at all—it's as if the night bugs had been hushed by the brilliance of the moonlight, like they had paused in their continuous pursuit of high-pitched chatter to pay homage to the moon. This silence must have been what woke me up. I sat there on the Crag, in the moonlight, mesmerized by it all.

Then a barred owl broke the silence from across the way, calling to anyone who would listen. One of these days I will have to learn how to call them so that I can carry on an intelligent conversation with these forest friends of mine. It seemed like this owl was the main spokesman for all the critters, for soon after his calls, the forest woke up again, and all the bugs and frogs started screaming at the top of their lungs. It was kind of neat, the pause in the verbal action, like everyone was sitting back and staring at the spectacle of the rising moon as I had been doing. Wouldn't you just love to be a wild critter for a day, just to see what they are all about, what they think, and do and say to each other? Wow, what a gift that would be. Perhaps all of these bugs and critters are people who have gone before us, and we will indeed end up as a cicada or a tree frog or an owl. If so, I would pause and gaze at the rising moon just as they had done.

I made my way back to the cabin in the moonlight—as fine a hike as anyone could ever want. And the cabin looked as grand as any in the Rocky Mountains. My faithful guard dog Stable was waiting for me, or actually he was waiting to get out the door to pee. It was late, so I quickly drifted off to sleep inside, but with the summer bugs still ringing in my ears.

7/14/98 Daylight found the cabin engulfed in a fog bank—hey, it's CLOUD-LAND! I was very tired and closed the blinds, but moved on over to the other side of the bed where I could gaze at the view from time to time. It was 8am before the fog had retreated enough for a really good view, which brought me out of the bed and out onto the back porch—*wow*, what an incredible view! The sea of fog laid down on all the streams in the valleys, and stretched as far as you could see in all directions, with the ridges sticking up above it all. It took nearly an hour for the sun to burn everything off. It was very still, cool, and quiet. Only a few small birds were about, including my friend Mr. Bunting, singing from his dogwood tree perch.

7/16/98 I spent a great deal of my time back in town typing in the first month of this Journal (late May and early June) so that I could upload it to the web page—this first part had been hand-written because I didn't have the computer at the cabin yet. While there is a certain satisfaction in writing in the Journal with a pencil, I find it very slow, which means that I won't write as much, and there are many more misspelled and misplaced words. It took a long time to type all of the back pages in, but now everything is on the computer, with multiple copies (in case the cabin burns down).

I arrived on Cave Mountain late in the evening, after dark, and went by to check on Bob's cabin. Everything was OK, but I discovered that his gardens had been raided by his caretaker Benny earlier in the week. I had planned to use some of the produce from the gardens for a feed at Cloudland on Saturday.

The moon hadn't shown up yet, and I spent some time on the lower deck in the hammock, gazing at the incredible sky full of a zillion stars. It was dead still out, not a wisp of air moving. The summer bugs were as loud as I had ever heard them. Man, how did the pioneers and Indians ever get any sleep?

I set up a dehumidifier down in the basement that I bought at Lowes—it is really getting bad down there. I have all of the items needed to coat the concrete walls, but am still not sure if this is going to solve the problem. I have been waiting for them to dry out completely before I do the coating, but we seem to get just enough rain now and then to keep the seep alive, if that is what is happening at all—I won't know for sure until I get everything coated.

7/17/98 I slept in late but did manage to get up, stumble out of bed and make it for breakfast of a blueberry bagel and Starbucks mocha out on the deck before the morning show was over. It was dead still once again, and no clouds in the valley. The shadows from the early, low light in the valleys was fine, and it seemed like there were more little birds flying around—some even daring to land on the tree growing out of the lower deck. There are so many birds around in the meadow now, I just can't imagine how many there will be once I get any bird feeders up.

I hiked up to visit Bob's gardens to see what was left and found a bunch of near-ripe tomatoes that I could use for the feed tomorrow. Eggplants were about ready (I need to learn how to cook them), and the field corn was way up over my head. Bob will use this stand of corn to make corn meal out of later in the fall (he gives most of it away). Then I went over to the garden in the East Meadow and didn't find much—tons of sweet corn, but it was still a week or so away. Looks like Benny had picked tomatoes a plenty. There were a few yellow squash ready. And the watermelons that Benny planted were coming along, but no actual melons yet—must be an August thing. There were lots of deer prints in the garden.

Benny had mowed the connecting road between the two gardens and out across the East Meadow, which made the walking a lot nicer. There were a ton of spiderwebs out across the way though. I have received at least two dozen phone calls lately about hikers wanting to do the Ozark Highlands Trail, and the discussion has always ended up with "Be sure to bring a headnet for the spiderwebs." Most people never think of that, but in the woods a headnet works wonders. Come to think of it, I *forgot* to bring mine!

It is quite pleasant back at the cabin. I cut and pulled some weeds in the front, sent a few e-mails, and did some Journal work. It is clear blue outside, with no wind—I suspect that it is going to be hot today, which means I will be forced down to the river later for a swim. But for now have to decide between more work, reading another John Muir book, or a nap. Hum.

Well, I did them all. Followed Muir high up into the Sierras, worked a little, managed to sneak in a nap on the couch, and went hiking several times. I found two different types of fungi that were interesting. First, a small but bright, lime green mushroom in the prefect mushroom shape was poking up from the middle of the trail—I'd never seen one that color before. Then I found a most unusual shelf fungi. It was rather large, about eight inches across, and growing right out of the ground, with the shelf about an inch above the ground. What was really strange about it was the fact that there were about a dozen shafts of grass growing right up through the shelf—these were the regular wide grass shafts (for lack of a better word), and didn't seem to be the least bit bothered by its location. I could not figure out if the grass had grown up through the fungi (the fungi shelf was very hard), or the fungi had grown around the grass.

There were also several brilliant red trees in the forest along the trail to the Crag. The leaves were as gorgeous as any in the fall. On one tree, all of the leaves had turned. On another, only three or four leaves at the end of a branch were red. Then I found several small copies of the trees near the ground, and they were completely turned. I could not identify the tree—there are a couple zillion species out here, and I can ID maybe a dozen or two. It's funny, how in the fall all of the experts weigh in with all of their scientific glop about what makes trees turn and when. And here we have some of the most brilliant color of the year, right in the middle of summer—I wonder how that fits into their scheme?

Many of the larger persimmon trees have dropped a lot of their fruit—about large marble size, and colored bright green, or deep green or deep purple. I've not seen this before, but then this is the first summer that I have really paid much attention to what was going on in the Ozarks. I bit into one of them and it was quite dry, not at all edible. Can't figure out why they are dropping them now, unless they need more rain. Also saw a lot more small hickory nuts on the ground, and lots of acorns. One of my favorite hickory trees, growing big and tall right out in the open, was full of *big* hickory nuts. It had dropped a lot of smaller ones a couple of weeks ago—perhaps this is just to rid the tree of some fruit before going on with the good stuff. Boy, when this baby drops its full load, I would like to be sitting under it with a strong umbrella! From out on the Crag, you can look down onto the tops of many big trees, and you can spot a few that are hickories—their same large nuts really stick out.

On the way back from a hike out to the mailbox I brought back a bucket of tomatoes and white and yellow onions from the garden. Had a bunch of the tiny tomatoes with my giant salad that was dinner. The salad was perfect, and I felt great, having put in a lot of exercise today with not too much to eat. Then I got into this wonderful stuff that I bought at SAMS yesterday—had to go take another hike after pigging out (Viennese wafers filled with cream of hazelnut and cocoa).

It is dead still outside at dark, and no clouds at all. In a few minutes the sky will be filled with spots of light, all straining to light up the dark forest.

7/18/98 A little bird landed on the gutter overhead while I was sitting out on the back deck having breakfast and enjoying the morning. All I could see was his tail feathers, which were sticking out over the gutter. This little guy was there for nearly 15 minutes, bouncing up and down and moving back and forth. I never got to see any more of him than just these tail feathers, and I never really figured out what kind of bird it was. But it was fun trying to converse with these living tail feathers.

I spent a couple of hours cleaning up the cabin, getting ready for the arrival of guests for the first ever "Cloudland Erection Party." This was the first anniversary of when the logs were erected (actually, it was begun on the 17th, and lasted until late in the day on the 18th last year). I wanted to keep the numbers small for this party, so only invited eight people. Keeping the numbers under ten seems about right to me. The humidifier was working very well, and I had to empty the water container about every six hours—boy, it was sucking a great deal of water out of the air! The basement wall was beginning to dry out.

Roy was the first to show up (Norma had to go to Ft. Smith to deal with plans for her daughter's wedding, and would be late getting here), quickly followed by The Wildman and Mary Chodrick, Bob and Dawna Robinson, and then Dean and Bonnie LaGrone (with their two dogs Mocha and Cocoa). Everyone brought a ton of food and booze with them, along with great spirits.

It was getting hot so several of us loaded up and headed down the hill for the swimming hole. Roy and Dawna stayed behind to guard the cabin, and the booze. The trail down to the river is getting worn in pretty good, and was fairly easy to follow. Only one of the dogs made it down the bluff, the other returning to home base. Lots of spiderwebs across the trail—I should have let someone else lead. The Wildman and Mary got a little behind, and ended up wandering off of the trail and bushwhacking through a thick stand of briars before finding the water. Just as we were about to reach the river, and I knew that I should have never opened my mouth, but I talked about how I had not seen a single snake all summer—really, not a single one, anywhere. And, of course, within minutes, as we reached the river, there was Mr. Snake, right at the edge of the water. It was a banded water snake, harmless and rather small, and it quickly swam off. But my streak had been broken. That happens a lot when you mention some streak. Hey, you know what, I have never won a million dollars before!

We all jumped into the warm water with shouts of glee. This is one of the things that can be enjoyed, even looked forward to, here in the Ozarks in the summertime. If more people had this wonderful swimming hole at their disposal, more people would love summer in Arkansas! Of course, this hole is available to everyone (hundreds of other holes around the state too)—they just have to make the effort to get to them. Dean talked about several great holes on the Buffalo River in Boxley Valley, just downstream a few miles—these holes are a lot easier to get to, reached merely by walking across a pasture—but they are much more "public" than our little swimming hole, and you never know who, or how many other swimmers will be there.

I had urgent business back up at the cabin (needed to start making up some appetizers, and the bread dough in the bread machine was about to be ready), so I bid farewell and hurried back up the hill, making it all the way up without stopping. Roy hiked up to the garden to gather cherry tomatoes for dinner, Dawna was out on the back deck enjoying the view, the solitude and a good book. I put the Beatles on the stereo and went to cooking.

While taking a break down on the river the swimmers had an unusual experience. They were all sitting off to the side, drying off on a flat rock that is slightly slanted towards the river, and ends down in the water. There is a good view upstream from there. Anyway, they were all laying around enjoying the day, when they heard splashing upstream. A doe deer had stepped into the shallow river upstream, and was slowly crossing, keeping an eye on the funny-looking critters that were sunning themselves on the rock downstream. She was almost across when out stepped another figure behind her—a spotted fawn. Wow, what a great scene. Where was I with my camera!? As the fawn stepped into the river, it slipped, and went down, thrashing and splashing and making all kinds of commotion. Mom just looked back and smirked, and motioned to get on with it junior. The fawn regained its composure, then sort of hopped across the shallow water until it reached mom. After checking that her baby was OK, they both continued on across the dry river bank and into the woods, leaving their stunned viewers with big smiles on their faces.

The swimmers returned to the cabin, all sweaty, but proclaiming that it was not all that big of a climb up from the river (yea, right, only after they were handed a cold beer and told that they could indeed take quick showers). Norma arrived, and everyone fell into the familiar tone of party life. I passed out the hot appetizers and made pitchers of bushwhackers. The well-oiled party machine hit a snag when my gas grill sputtered and ran out of propane, just as the corn was about to be grilled. Ah-ha said Roy, gas is no good, you need charcoal! No problem I said, I have a spare bottle. Sure enough, the spare was full of propane, but the fittings were not the same, so we were out of gas. And we had salmon filets to grill! Dean and Bonnie raided Bob's cabin and came back with a sack of charcoal briquets, so they set up a makeshift grill out in front and everything got back to normal.

Roy and The Wildman grilled the salmon to perfection, and we all enjoyed a splendid feast fitting of the first annual Cloudland Erection Party. The menu included the salmon, corn on the cob, broccoli/tomato dish, wild rice dish, special salad a 'la Bonnie, bread sticks, wine, and a wonderful cheesecake for dessert. Typical of the dinners at Cloudland. But it was the company that really made the meal, and the celebration. Friends like these are hard to find, and I have been blessed with quite a few of them. I plan to keep feeding them good food and drink for a long time to come!

Milancy McNamara, the business manager of the famous artist William McNamara (they both live a few miles from here), dropped by after dinner to look at the third set of proofs from the new **Buffalo River Wilderness** picture book. The book is a collection of my photographs and Billy's paintings. Milancy and I sat on the office floor and worked through the proofs, while The Wildman tested the range of his personal cannon (a .44 magnum revolver) off of the back deck (it was rather loud!).

Everyone else ate cheesecake. Once all the cheesecake was gone the party wound down and everyone actually got to bed before midnight. The stars were out and dancing their spectacular dance as usual. So were the no-see-ums. Dean and Bonnie were driven into the cabin by early morning by the pesky little bug-gers. Before that happened though, one of their dogs got all excited by a "large, lumbering creature" that was stirring about in the woods next to the cabin. Perhaps it was the cinnamon bear checking things out, the smell of grilled salmon being too much to ignore. If it was him, he never made a formal appearance.

7/19/98 I got up soon after sunrise to make coffee and wandered out to the back deck with my own little vial of Starbucks mocha. Bob and Dawna were already up, perched in the high deck chairs, with their legs dangling over the log railing, chattering like a couple of squirrels. This is one of the best things about Cloudland—it creates a space, if you will, for couples, friends and soon-to-be either, to gather and converse in a comfortable and perhaps even stimulating environment. I noted that they were up early (after a big party), and they re-called that I had said that the best hour of the day was between 6am-7am, and they didn't want to miss a single second.

They related the following story about a minor wildlife struggle they had just witnessed. A bee and an ant had a minor war. It seems the bee had a hole in the tree right in front of the deck, and was buzzing about. One of those large carpenter ants climbed up and was trying to get into the hole—there was prob-ably some sweet sap or something running out of it that he was interested in, although, it doesn't take all that much for an ant to become a pest. Anyway, the ant kept trying to get into the hole, and the bee kept dive-bombing him and shooing him away. Finally, it looked like the bee had lost interest, and the ant made it to the opening of the hole. It seemed like he turned around just for an instant to be recognized by all who were watching that he had indeed reached his goal, and then the bee returned and knocked him right off of the tree and sent him into space. Score one for the bee.

I sat back and enjoyed the new day as well, and one by one the rest of the cabin came alive and ended up on the back deck too. Before long, the deck looked like some big lodge deck, with most all of the seats filled with people, all bubbling over with stories and conversation and contentment. This continued long into the morning—a fine way to begin the day!

Roy and Norma spent the night in the basement bedroom and mentioned that a ceiling fan might be good down there—Roy got a little warm, and when questioned, I found out that he only got warm because he was zipped up in his sleeping bag! It was 69 degrees in the basement. But it brought up the point that I really do need to get that bedroom finished off and a real bed put in. That way guests could sleep under a sheet instead of having to cover up with a thick sleeping bag. I need to get on with that project.

Dean and Bonnie bid farewell and headed off to visit their own property over on Walker Mountain. Bob and Dawna went out for a hike. Some friends from Ozone came by to see the cabin. It was Decoration Day at Cave Mountain Church, and they had come over for the celebration. They were all Sparks peo-ple, and one of the most interesting of the old homestead sites down along the Buffalo River belonged to their ancestors—a cabin with two stone chimneys. There were a lot of little kids in tow, which is typical of the mountain families around here. Nice folks. The Wildman and Mary headed back to town.

The rest of us packed up and headed down to the swimming hole once again, leaving Dawna behind with her books. She had a few other visitors during the afternoon, including Willie Faddis, the guy that I bought the land for Cloudland from (he is a chicken farmer in Gravette, and grew up at the Faddis cabin). One of the Woods boys came by, Danny and his daughter. Bob bought his additional 80 acres from the Woods boys and their dad. Danny was there on that dreary winter day when I sat down with all of them and made the deal for Bob to buy their land. They are super people, and we are fortunate that they continue to be involved in the land here. Dawna got to spend some time talking to all these folks, and apparently learned a great deal of the history of the area from them (she was gone when I got back to the cabin, and learned of all this only by her note).

Down at the river the water seemed a little cooler than usual, perhaps because it was still morning, and it hadn't had a chance to warm up enough. Still, it felt terrific, and we swam and dove and played in the big hole. Roy called me over to look at a swarm of bluegills fighting over a spot on the river. As we watched through our swim masks, there were indeed dozens of bluegill and other small fish fighting and playing and generally making a big fuss over a small spot of the river bottom, about four feet down. It seemed like it might be a nest, but there was no clear fish in charge. As we watched in amazement, a *giant* smallmouth bass swam over and immediately chased everyone else away—it was clearly her nest, and she must have been scared off when Roy came by, and the others took advantage and were attacking with vengeance. As we watched, the old girl did her best job of keeping all the others away, but they kept nudging in. The rocks below her were all cleaned off, and she seemed intent on guarding her nest.

On another part of the river, much shallower, I had noticed seven or eight piles of stones that looked a lot like the ones the bass was guarding. It appeared that these stones had been piled up there, one at a time, and some of the piles were six inches tall and about two feet in diameter. I assumed that they were places that fish had built, then laid eggs in. Although none of these locations were being guarded. Roy noted that there were many tiny minnows swarming around one of them—new fish from the nest perhaps? I would have loved to seen the fish building these nests!

We waded/swam/floated downstream, visiting several other pools and stretches of the river. There is one large flat boulder that is laid out in the middle of one pool. I found this rock many years ago, right after I bought Cloudland, and have often camped on top of it—it is covered with a thick layer of moss.

Anyway, none of the pools were as deep or as nice as our main pool, although I did have a great time exploring around the edges of each and every one of them. In the last one, as I was creeping around the boulders at the edge, just underwater with my mask, I came across two small bluegills, staring right back at me. I got a little closer and examined their brilliant blue masks—boy, these guys were brightly colored! They parted and let me pass, but they seemed to be guarding the entrance to something. Sure enough, way back in the shadows, up against a wall of rock, there was a much larger bluegill—this one was a large as my hand! She was very wide as well, and seemed to be guarding a nest. She stared at me and dared me to approach closer. Somehow I knew that she really meant business, so I stopped my progress, and just sat there and watched. Her eyes were digging holes in me. She was hovering about two inches above the cleaned-off pebbles below, only having to twitch a side fin once in a while to stay in place. While I was there, several little fish approached, and she quickly darted at them and chased them off. This was one mean little momma! I thanked her for the show, backed off, and went on with my exploration.

After taking a few pictures back up at the main swimming hole (I used Norma as a subject for some "right way and wrong way to photograph people" pictures that I had to do for a TV show next week), Bob left, and Roy, Norma and I laid back on the sunning rock, now in shade, and soaked up the afternoon. Norma got out a Nero Wolf book, and read it out loud. It was a great little book, but her voice was quite soothing—Roy's snores soon mingled with the sounds of the gurgling water, the birds, the wind, and Norma's Nero Wolf. It was a wonderful hour of relaxation! All too soon I headed back up the hill to begin making pizzas for supper, leaving Roy and Norma to commune with nature alone. I made it back up the hill to the cabin in 18 minutes. Lordy, I was HOT. Even after a cold shower, I had to lay down on the bed with the ceiling fan going full blast for ten minutes before I really cooled down. This is one of the coolest spots in the cabin—I made sure of that when I built the place by putting the big fan down low, right over the bed—I have to sleep cool at night!

I met Roy and Norma at the front door with a frosted mug of cold beer—they looked like hell, exhausted and soaked from the climb—not nearly as exhilarated as at the end of their last climb up during the big rainstorm. After showers they got back to normal. We all feasted on Cloudland Pizza. I hit the couch while Norma cleaned up my mess in the kitchen, then the young couple departed and left me with the quiet sounds of the evening.

There is always a little depression that sets in after an all-too-short weekend with good friends. And I must say that the normal regimen of having to spend hours cleaning up after such a party simply does not happen at Cloudland—the messes are almost always cleared away and cleaned up by my group of friends before they leave. Gosh, they bring booze and food and great conversation and wonderful personalities, and they even clean up! What more could one ask for? I value, no, I treasure my friends.

It was an early evening for me. I sat out in the hammock and watched the stars come out, read a little, then retired.

7/20/98 There was a thin haze in the air at dawn, the yellow sun stirring up the breeze a little. I sat on the deck and finished the pizza for breakfast, while birds flew hither and yawn (I've always wanted to say that), and squirrels barked and gathered nuts. I rigged up the dehumidifier so that it would run all the time, draining into a floor drain in the basement (instead of it shutting off every time the water bucket was full). Then I wrote in the Journal, gathered up the laundry and trash, bid Cloudland farewell, and headed back into the oven of civilization. I would soon return.

7/21/98 The evening sun was filtering through the forest with a rich orange glow, calling to me to get out and explore. I stopped the van even before I reached the cabin and went for a hike. You can head out in any direction here, and follow old roads, trails, or just amble through the open woods or meadows and have a great hike.

Some of the woods are rather thick at this time of year, but it always amazes me how some of the forested areas have almost no underbrush whatsoever. These remind me of the pictures that I have seen of the old wilderness parks of Europe, the ones that have been set aside for hundreds of years. I suspect this is what the Ozarks used to look like all over, with giant white oak trees that towered a hundred feet or more in the air, their heavy canopies blocking out the sun so that underbrush couldn't grow. Now I find the open underbrush to be in groves of maple trees. It is quite a sight to come over a rise and look down onto an open bench below, a maple bench of fairy-tale forest.

I was tired, and didn't get a single thing accomplished once I got to the cabin, except for some sitting on the back deck and admiring the nighttime sky. Guess the city swelter wore me out.

7/22/98 I woke up early and got a wild hare to run on down to the river for an early morning swim. It was hazy out, and the sun barely shown through. The forest was still asleep as I stumbled on down the steep hillside. And the water was rather chilly! I plunged into the big swimming hole and did a few laps, having a conversation or two with the fishes along the way. One thing about skinny-dipping when you are a guy—it is not always a good idea to do so when there are pesky little fishes around. Think about it.

The hike back up the hill actually felt pretty good, although I was drenched when I arrived back at the cabin. I took a cold shower and fixed a little early lunch. There was some wonderful smoked ham leftover from the weekend, but it needed a little something extra. I thought about all the sweet corn in Bob's East garden. He was still out of town. So I hiked on up the hill and swiped a couple of fresh ears. Lots of tomatoes on the vines too.

I learned all about cooking and eating sweet corn at an early age from my grandpa, who had one of the largest sweet corn farms in Minnesota. I used to spend most of the month of August there, just as the corn was getting ripe. We had corn at least two meals a day, and I never got tired of it! To this day, I still eat my corn the same way that he showed me how to when I was about six or seven years old. The rest of you can do what you like, but there is only one best way to eat fresh corn on the cob. There are lots of great ways to cook it, but only one way to eat it. The quickest way to cook it is simply to boil it, and only for about four minutes—any longer and you just ruin the tenderness and cook out the flavor. Then you cut the corn off of the cob. I know, I know, how could I do such a thing. But I promise you, you will not only get *more* of the corn this way, but it will be a lot *sweeter* than if you bite it off of the cob. Plus, it is a lot less messy to eat, especially if you are a hairy guy like me. Once cut off, I put butter, pepper, salt, and a dash of thyme on it. *Nothing* in this world is so good!!!

I'm not sure if I have written this elsewhere in this Journal before, but since I was talking about my grandpa, I will put it down here. He is the one responsible for my desire all of my life to own and live in a log cabin in the wilderness. The very first time that I remember going to the farm in Minnesota was actually in the winter. Just my mom and I drove up. In these northern farm houses, there was always an area where you put on or took off all of your heavy clothes and boots. I remember sitting down to take my shoes off and seeing two things on the wall opposite me. One was a double-barrel shotgun. The other was this most incredible painting, an image that immediately had a major impact on my perception of the world, and implanted not only my desire to have a log cabin, but also created the impression of what "wilderness" would come to mean to me. The watercolor showed a trail leading to a log cabin at the edge of a lake, with smoke coming out of the chimney and a warm glow from the fireplace seen through the windows, and in the background was a snow-capped mountain, and a waterfall pouring into the far end of the lake, the entire scene being lit by a full moon. The moon, a waterfall, a hiking trail, the log cabin—does this sound like me or what! I was mesmerized by the painting, and I always ran to see it as soon as I would arrive each summer. I have no idea who did the painting, but have seen many similar ones that were done by Thomas Kinkade.

Years later when both of my mom's parents died, she asked me if there was anything of theirs that I wanted—*the painting, of course!* It isn't really all that much, and was in a cheap frame, but it is the only thing that hangs in my bedroom at home, and it is the very first thing that I see when I wake up. I have never brought it out to Cloudland, well, I guess because Cloudland *is* that painting. Anyway, ever since that winter day way back in 1960, I have wanted to live in a log cabin. Thanks grandpa!

A couple of years ago while watching a rerun of **The Waltons** on TV, my mouth dropped open when I spotted the very same painting on John Boy's bedroom wall—really, the exact same painting. It appeared in dozens of episodes. I even taped one segment of the show just to stop the frame and compare the two. I guess it was depression era art.

After my sweet meal of corn and ham I spent the day down in the basement, putting up peg boards and organizing tools, and installing a water filter on the main waterline. While the well water is seldom ever dingy, once in a while it is, and it has been staining the inside of the dishwasher, although the dishes are always fine. I suspect some of this might be leftover clay residue in the lines from when the waterline was broken last fall.

7/23/98 Hot, hot, and muggy. There was a great cloudburst in town during the day, which dropped the temperature down to 70 degrees, but when I arrived back at Cloudland late in the day, there didn't appear to have been any rainfall at all. The rain gauge confirmed this. We've had less than two inches of rain this month. Actually, I would like for the rain to hold off a little longer, at least until I can get the basement wall painted with the waterproof covering. The dehumidifier has been doing a great job, and it is not only quite dry down there, but the noisy machine has actually been shutting itself off now and then because it has been lowering the humidity. Since it warms up the basement too, this is good news. It has raised the temp down there by three or four degrees.

For the first time in a long while I got out my guitar and spent an hour playing. One of my problems out here has always been that I have been unable to find a comfortable spot to play. I sat just about everywhere and still couldn't find a good place, one that lets me sit upright and supports my back, while allowing free movement of the guitar. The only place that I have found is sitting on the carpeted floor in the loft, leaning up against the log wall. The music sounded pretty good, although the sounds coming from the strummer were less than desirable. My fingers wore down in a hurry—I really need to trade this wonderful steel-stringed instrument in for a classical one with the softer strings. The thin steel strings really dig into my tender fingers. Of course, if I would play an hour or three a day, the fingers would soon get in good shape. I really hate to get rid of this guitar, although I have barely ever played it. The thing is really a piece of fine art, with its maple back and sides being as fine an example of man's crafting of Mother Nature as I have ever seen. I should just set it in a stand in the middle of the great room for all to admire.

After my fingers gave out I landed in the hammock on the lower deck, and spent some time gazing at the stars and listening to the music of the night. There was a light haze in the air, so the stars were muted, but still a delight. There was also quite a bit of heat lightning going on somewhere, but it must have been a long ways off because there weren't really flashes of light, but it was rather like the entire sky twinkled just a little every now and then.

7/24/98 For the first time in a long while it was cooler outside than in at daybreak. There was no sunrise, just a gradual lightening of the forms outside, as the greys and blacks turned to shades of green and lighter greys. It was hazy, and there appeared to be some low clouds hanging around. Hardly any breeze at all. In fact, July has been rather calm, with the high wind only being 17mph.

Mr. Bunting was waiting for me, perched in his normal location in the dogwood tree right where the branch was broken off by the storm, his blueness standing out against all of the green background of the trees. It sounded like he wanted me to know that I should leave the singing to the professionals, such as himself. He sang and sang and sang. I noticed, for the first time, that there was a group of bright yellow wildflowers down in the right-hand corner of the meadow. They were pretty big, and I needed to go down and see what kind they were. All of a sudden, one of the flowers got up and moved about ten feet. What? It moved again. I went to get the binocs, and what I found was the most brilliantly colored goldfinch that I had ever seen. His yellow body was as richly yellow as the wildflowers, and his coal black head and wing tips looked really weird. Come to think of it, the wildflowers also had some coal black parts. He was a perfect wildflower, with his colors just rearranged a little. Or were the wildflowers the goldfinch? He was playing in the flowers, and seemed to be eating seeds from them. He would sit on one for several minutes, then fly to another. I would like to get the bunting and the goldfinch together on the same branch some day and take their picture (add a scarlet tanager too!).

While I was concentrating on the birds out in the meadow a hummingbird came by, inspected the tree in the deck very closely, working his way around and up the trunk, then he came in under the porch, hovering close to the rocking chair that has a pad on it. I wondered why he choose that particular chair to look at, but then I realized that there was a floral pattern on the pad—smart little bird! I have been hesitating to put up the great hummer feeder that Jim and Susie gave me last month, mainly because I didn't know how to anchor it to keep it from being blown to bits by the high winds. But now that the high winds have been reduced to calm breezes, I must make up some sugar solution and hang it.

While it never felt like there were birds everywhere this morning there was a constant parade of different kinds of birds, each waiting their turn to make an appearance. Several chickadees made a big racket nearby. I've always thought that their noises are nothing more than laughter. A pileated woodpecker came screaming through, always loud, always annoying, but always a welcome guest. I counted at least fourteen bird calls that I could not identify, nor see the birds that made them.

Looking at the telescope, and after watching the way that guests try to aim it, I realized that folks have all but ruined the screw plate. When the tele is on the tripod (which is most of the time), and someone wants to point it at something, they don't try to move the tripod head like you are supposed to do, they always just grab the telescope and try to move it. This doesn't work. What it does do is tear up the tripod attachment on the base of the telescope. Now the scope won't mount to the tripod. I guess if I ever get it fixed, I will have to put some sort of sign on it.

There is a large tree across the way on the Boen Gulf hillside that appears to be turning yellow. I remember a tree in that general area as being the first to turn green back in March or April. I wonder if it is the same tree? I will keep an eye on it.

I hiked up to raid both gardens, filled my basket with cherry tomatoes, regular tomatoes, green peppers, squash, and sweet corn. The garden in the East Meadow had been visited by deer, and they were taking a toll on the melon crop. About a dozen of the young melons were either partially or completely eaten. The only tracks in the dirt were deer tracks. Some of the melons were all eaten except for part of the shell—they had scraped them clean! Others only had a bite or two out of them. And I found one shell in the middle of the corn patch—carried there over twenty feet. Last year Bob had said that all of his cantaloupe were eaten by the bear—I guess he must have found the tracks—but I wonder if the deer were not to blame for that as well? Deer are such wonderful critters to see in the wild, so gentle, and personable and beautiful. But they can get rather destructive to crops for sure. I guess it is their garden too!

Lunch was made up of the fruits of my raiding, and I gorged myself until I couldn't move. All I could do was sit out on the deck and watch the soaring birds, which numbered in the dozens. They were all playing in the air, swooping and turning and diving, and coming in very close to the deck. Eventually eight or nine of them landed in the dead snag at the edge of the meadow. It was hot. I got to thinking about that snag. I've seen the buzzards there, doves, hawks, jays, cardinals, and scarlet tanagers. It seems to attract everyone who flies by. Kind of like the only bench in a park I guess. I'll bet there have been some wonderful stories told by the perchers. If only that tree could talk!

I spent some time down in the basement washing the bottom of the cement wall with a solution of muric acid and water. Not sure if it did any good. I do know that it made the wall all wet again! Things are looking a lot better down there in the tool/junk room, especially since I put up peg boards and hooks. Now I seem obsessed with wanting to go hang something every time that I walk in there. I also decided that I would buy and put up an outside storage shed, not too large, to hold any tools that are strictly outdoor tools—like chainsaw and fuel, shovel, pry bar, etc.—which would free up more space in the tool room.

As I was emptying the acid bucket outside I looked up and noticed green swirling clouds overhead, and to the west, *black* clouds! Just then a bolt of lightning hit nearby and rattled the deck. Oh boy, a storm! For some reason, instead of running out into the storm like I am prone to do, I choose instead to come inside and sit down and experience this storm at the computer, which is what I am doing now. I can hear the storm cell moving closer, and it has begun to rain. Flashes of light are all around. *Boom!* There goes a big bolt of thunder off to my right, and it was only two seconds after the lightning bolt. Wow, here comes the rain for real—it is pouring, and blowing as hard as I have ever seen it pour here. Wow, Beagle hill has completely disappeared, and I can hardly see even the end of the lower deck through the blowing rain. Thirty-six mph says the gauge. Wasn't I just talking about no wind this month? *CRASH!!!* Another strong bolt hit somewhere nearby. I was holding onto the cabin walls when that one hit and the entire cabin really shook, like a truck slammed into the front of the place. The bolts are coming about every ten seconds now. The trees that I can barely see outside are twisting and thrashing about, and there are numerous branches with leaves attached flying by. And now, hail, about pea size, is thumping the metal roof. More rain, and wind, and lightning, and *thunder!* Man, is it loud with the windows open. I have to close them because the rain is blowing in.

As quickly as the cell hit it is now moving off. The black clouds are now visible over the valley to the east, and Mossville is about to get pounded. You can hear the thunder echo up and down the various valleys. It is still flashing. The rain has all but stopped. I can see far up Whitaker Creek that steam clouds are beginning to form in the valley—they are slowly rising up to the sky. There is still heavy rain in the Buffalo River Valley upstream, and black clouds overhead. I can see up that way about five miles to Curtis Cemetery. There is clear sky a long ways off under the black. The temperature dropped 15 degrees in about five minutes. It smells wonderful outside—Mr. Clean has just come by, and he wasn't using Pine Sol!

Large steam clouds are forming just off Whitaker Point out back, and on up the Buffalo River Valley. They are moving fast the opposite direction of the storm, working their way up Whitaker Creek, and boiling up over the point and across the meadow. I just ran around and opened all of the windows—I try to do that whenever the temperature is lower outside than in (closing them when it is hotter outside—this helps cool down the cabin and keep it that way). The remnants of the storm are blowing through the cabin now, moving papers around and sweeping the cabin air clean.

I can hear more thunder off to the west—another cell approaching! It has begun to rain again now, only slower. And while there is a great deal of thunder building, with flashes every few seconds, the lower sky is light, and I can see all the way to Buffalo Fire Tower. Perhaps I need to get out and play in this storm. But soon the rain stopped, and all was calm. I sat back on the deck and spent an hour watching the best ever show of steam/fog/clouds down in the valleys. They were building up in the main Buffalo River valley, then were racing up each and every hollow, no matter how big. It was a very active fog playground. And the battery in my camera was dead. All I could do was sit and enjoy. Oh darn.

Eventually all of the fog went away and the sky broke up a little, but still remained mostly cloudy. I decided to hike out to the mail box and get Bob's paper, and see what I could find on the ground.

Storms blow all kinds of neat stuff on the ground. Stuff that you would never see otherwise. There were all kinds of green leaves and branches on the ground, plus a number of brilliant orange and red leaves, turning a few months too soon. I discovered that the orange trees that I had seen a week or two ago were young cowcumber trees. And today I spotted a very strange object on the ground under one of them. At first I thought it was a young, naked bird blown out of its nest. Or perhaps it was a mouse that hadn't survived the blow. It was a mass of slick red and grey, with a couple of orange eyes popping out. Son of a gun, it was the fruit from the cowcumber tree! But it looked nothing like the cucumber fruit of just a few weeks ago. There were actually several "eyes," which were seeds popping out. A strange looking mass of color. And later, under what looked like a hickory tree, were red cucumber fruits—they looked just like the cowcumber fruit that I had seen before, only they were red instead of green, and had fallen from a hickory tree—I need to go back and confirm whether I am going nuts, or they really did come from the hickory tree.

As I walked through the Faddis Meadow the air was filled with grasshoppers. Not everyone realizes that they not only hop quite well, but they also fly, and these guys were doing a lot of flying.

A wild turkey hen burst into the air with a great deal of commotion. I have seen this lady in the same spot several times, so she must be guarding a nest in the area. Few things in nature are as startling than a big old turkey taking to the air. It is a wonder how they can get off of the ground with all that mass. I guess that is one reason why they make so much noise—it takes a lot of wing flapping to get enough lift!

There were a ton of new small persimmons on the ground, dark purple as well as bright green, plus lots of hickory nuts—many much larger now. It is a wonderful fruit and nut year! Although, I noticed that all of the blackberries had vanished. I was sort of waiting them out, until the fruit got just right, only snatching a handful or two every now and then. Now they were all gone. I think they did all get ripe, and then were all eaten by birds before I could get a hold of them (or by Mr. Bear).

No vehicles had come in since the rain, but it looked like Eddy Silcott had gone over to his place. I should go down and see what all he has done, although I hesitate to do so until invited. I think he is still mainly clearing and cleaning and getting ready to build a cabin. He found his property in a novel way. He couldn't find anything for sale to buy, so he went down to the courthouse in Jasper, looked up all the property owners in the area, and called many of them to see if they would sell any land to him. Sure enough, he found a guy living in Colorado (I think that is where he was from) that sold him a very nice parcel that borders the wilderness area and Dug Hollow. There was an old homeplace there and some open fields. He tore down the home place, and has cleaned up the fields (lots of old junk cars). It will be one terrific place once he gets something built.

I got the newspapers, left them at Bob's, and strolled back to Cloudland just as the sun was setting. The clouds really lit up with some great color—vibrant oranges and reds and yellows, and some muted, more delicate colors as well. There were dozens of bats out patrolling, and it was a wonderful sight to see them silhouetted against those colorful clouds. Go bats, go bats, eat them bugs! Everything had been scrubbed clean by the rains, and smelled great. All was well on my little mountaintop world.

7/25/98 It was nearly 6:30am before the sun rose above the ridge—I was out on the back deck just waiting for it. There was a cool breeze blowing, it was 71 degrees, and it was a little chilly as I sipped on my Starbucks mocha. There were a few clouds down in the valley, but most had worn themselves out playing the day before. After getting some more work done in the basement, I was going to return to town for a short visit with my brother and his wife who were down from St. Louis for the weekend. Then it would be back to Cloudland for more of my fix.

As I was driving off I noticed some sort of track in the fresh dirt that I had piled up and smoothed down in the low area next to the entrance staircase. I paid it no mind, but noted that it must be fresh, as the hard rain of the day before beat everything down there—I had been watching the water patterns during the rain to see how my little mound of dirt was doing. Anyway, when I got back to the cabin later in the day, I looked at the track. Son of a gun—it was *A BEAR TRACK!* And within two feet of the front porch step. The rest of the area is surrounded by rocks, so this was the only place that one could have made a track. It appeared that the bear had been up on the porch, probably on Friday night or early Saturday, and stepped off into this dirt. It wasn't all that large, 4 1/2" across by 5" long, probably a yearling bear, or even a large cub. This is the very first time that any bear sign has ever been found on the south side of the ridge that divides my place with Bob's place. That ridge has always served as some sort of boundary line. No more. We have live bears at Cloudland! I found it funny that the bear track was right at the foot of one of the carved wooded bears at the end of the porch deck railing. Now I find myself spending more time looking out the front window.

After lots of grilled veggies for dinner, and a few hours of following Muir through Alaska, I retired to the porch swing to greet and enjoy all that the nighttime had to offer. It was rather warm for me—78 degrees—but the wind was blowing 10-12mph, and it was very comfortable. Before it got completely dark, I had a feathered visitor. A large barred owl swooped up out of nowhere and landed on the lower branch of the tree that grows out of the lower deck. He knew exactly where he was. He peered at me with those huge eyes, swayed his head back and forth a couple of times, then launched himself up and over the cabin and out of sight. I felt graced by his visit.

I must have fallen asleep in the swing and was awakened by a large crash around 11pm. It took me a minute to figure out where I was. There was a big thunderstorm passing out in front of my view, and it was full of lightning. The wind kicked up to nearly 30mph. Lots of flashes and booms. But it never rained a drop. It passed by slowly, then the sky opened up with its brilliant display of a million tiny lights. Up Whitaker Creek a ways I heard the lonely call of a barred owl, perhaps the one that I had seen. No one answered.

7/26/98 Late sunrise, mostly clear, nice breeze blowing. I slept in and eventually laid around on the back deck watching the morning fade away, then got some computer work done. Later in the morning a friend, Kevin Myatt, who is one of the editors of the newspaper in Batesville stopped by. He had been in Eureka Springs for a press club convention. While he is much too modest to make anything of it, he won first place for one of his articles that he had written during the year, and placed second for another. Batesville is not a mecca for hikers, but many of his articles are about hiking, since that is one of the main things that he does during his free time.

While we were out on the back deck the soaring birds put on quite a show.

There were about a dozen buzzards circling in one group, and there was a red-tailed hawk with them. This hawk stayed pretty much in formation with them for nearly twenty minutes, and would move right along when the formation moved. The buzzards didn't seem to pay him much mind. Later, two red-tailed hawks came in close by, riding the currents coming up out of the valley. The smaller one was really giving the larger one a lot of grief—kind of like when you see smaller birds picking on a crow or something. But these were both the same kind of hawks. Perhaps the smaller one was a female, and there was something going on there that we weren't privy to.

After Kevin left I finished up my travels with John Muir up in Alaska. He was really quite something, and I am glad that I have finally been able to spend some time reading his books.

Soon it was time to go hiking and I headed up the hill to see what the afternoon would show me. One of the first things that I found was a tiny, miniature feather. It was not more than 1/4 inch long, but almost as wide, very fluffy, with half of it almost pure white, and the outer half being bright red. It must have come from the breast of a scarlet tanager or something like that. Later I discovered that the red fruit that I had talked about being from a hickory tree was actually a cowcumber tree—duh. There are two of these trees growing together just inside Bob's property line along the road.

In the spot where all of the wild bergamot was growing there were now these wonderful, delicate purple wildflowers, standing nearly six feet tall. And like the wild mint before, they too were covered with the same orange butterflies, one assigned to each bunch of flowers on a stalk. These stately wildflowers were actually ironweed. We seem to have a lot of very beautiful "weeds" out there at this time of the year!

When I got to the garden in the East Meadow I confirmed what I had said about the deer eating the melons. I got to thinking that perhaps a bear had eaten the melons before the heavy rain on Friday, and then his tracks were washed away. But there were at least two melons that had been eaten since I had been there on Friday, and the only tracks around were deer tracks. Guilty!

It was a most pleasant walk in the evening breeze. I found dozens and dozens of leaves on bushes and small trees and even some poison ivy that were turning bright oranges, yellows and reds. One entire tree was engulfed with a poison ivy vine that was brilliant red. If these guys can hold off long enough, I think that we may be in for a spectacular fall color season. Some of the brightest leaves were sassafras leaves. Two of them were huge.

I gathered some of the colored leaves, along with a bit of the fruit that I picked up along the way, and took a picture of them. Hickory nuts, persimmon fruit, cucumber magnolia fruit, plus six or eight types of leaves, showing their fall color in the middle of summer.

Back at the cabin I did a little more reading, worked on a design for a mug for our volunteer trail building club, answered some e-mail, and made a few phone calls. While this cabin is basically right in the middle of wilderness, I am

72

still able to stay in contact with the rest of the world, which is critical for me right now. It seems to me to be the perfect match of wild and civilization—just enough civilization, and an amount that I can control. I got a bunch of e-mails this weekend, which I prefer now over a phone call or letter anytime. Well, I take that back. No communication can beat a great love letter. An e-mailed one is fine, but there is just something about that little extra human touch.

I hate to sound like a broken record, but the evening breeze was nice and cool, and darkness found me napping in the porch swing. While the fireflies seem to have died out quite a bit, the stars were as brilliant as I had ever seen them out here. I truly love moonlight, but when it is hiding like it is now, the stars really shine. My barred owl friend didn't pay a visit (at least not while I was awake), but he did strike up a conversation across the way. Not one, but two females answered him (I should be so lucky), and soon the valley echoed with a conference call of love.

7/27/98 I was wide awake at 4am, so I got up, cooked up a hearty Cloudland Hash breakfast, and enjoyed the pre-dawn light from the back deck. I decided to get in a little hiking, and see what the sunrise would look like from Beagle Point, so I put on my summer hiking garb, and headed down the ladder trail (I decided to name the hill across the way after the little beagle dog that died there). It was just light enough to see, and soon got very light, as the entire morning sky overhead began to glow. There were a lot of spiderwebs out as usual, but this time I remembered to bring my headnet, so I kept up a steady pace, not having to be constantly pulling fat spiders out of my eyes and mouth. It was still pretty cool, and the wind was blowing, and the ascent up to the bluffline was not too bad. I rounded the point and found the scramble up the bluff that the squirrel had showed me back in May. That little squirrel will save me a great deal of time as the years go by—the next place to climb up to this bluff is several hundred tough yards further on along the bluff.

The eastern skyline was still glowing pink when I reached the lookout point. Probably another twenty minutes until sunrise. I settled back against a moss-covered rock and got comfortable. I couldn't see my cabin, which was hidden behind the trees, but I could see a lot of the Buffalo River Valley spread out before me. At first, there wasn't much noise, just the sound of the wind in the trees. Then as sunrise got nearer, birds began to wake up and fill the valley with singing and laughter. I could see many of them shifting positions across the way, winging it from one part of the hillside to another. The music intensified, and reached a fever pitch as the sun peaked over the opposite hillside. Then, for just a moment, the earth stood completely still. There was a hush. A little blue wildflower, growing on top of the rock next to me, opened its eyes and yawned. The beginning of another new day in the wilderness. I was honored to be able to share it. The music struck up again, and the summer bug section joined in. I've never understood why people say they want to "escape to the peace and quiet of the wilderness." Hey, it is *loud* out here!

It was Monday morning, and anyone who knows me knows that I love Mondays the best. This day was certainly no exception. The perfect beginning to a glorious week.

Once I got back down to the bottom of the bluff I just sort of drifted on down the steep hillside, not really following any particular route (there really is no good way down this hill, and as long as you continue *down*, you will reach the bottom). I came down the east side of the hill, and wound up at the main Buffalo River, near one of the swimming holes that is upstream from our normal one. Hey, it was summer, and there was a swimming hole in front of me, so I was obliged to strip off and jump in. *Yikes*, it was cold! If the early hike up the steep hillside, and the incredible view of the sunrise didn't wake me up, this little plunge sure did.

I didn't linger in the water long and soon was up on a flat rock drying off. As I sat there, I watched several little bass and bluegill hunting along the shoreline for breakfast. Within seconds after anything hit the water, two or three little fish exploded on the scene. Several of those large carpenter ants that happened to wander by my seat ended up as fish food. It was interesting to see how the bass and perch hunted differently. The bass would patrol the shoreline, always moving, always turning and looking in every direction. While the little bluegill perch mostly stayed in the same spot, with their eyes focused on a certain area of the water surface. It seemed to me that both got their fair share of food, but the bass had to expend more energy to get theirs. Come to think of it, when you compare the two fish, the bass are long and sleek, while the perch are quite short and dumpy. Hum, I wonder, do I more resemble a bass or a perch?

By the time the morning breezes had dried me off the sun had finally found its way to the bottom of the canyon, and I could feel things beginning to heat up. I got dressed and headed back up to the cabin. For some reason, I had a bit of a tough time keeping my pace up the hill—perhaps it was the hash weighing me down. Then the afterburners kicked in and I scampered up the last, and toughest, of the steep benches. Those chairs on the back deck are a delight to the eye, and to the tired and sweating body.

A fierce storm swept through the area in the afternoon, with 41mph winds and .67 inches of much-needed rain. No real damage anywhere, except that my BBQ grill took an unscheduled trip across the back deck.

7/30/98 After giving a program to a group of gifted and talented kids at the Ozark Natural Science Center, one of the students came up to me with a painting that she had done there during the week. It was a painting of a photograph of mine, taken from my **Wilderness Reflections** picture book, and was a close up of two spiderwort wildflowers. She was quite proud of it, although not nearly as proud as the guy who took the photograph! I don't relate much to kids, even though I am still one myself in many ways. I grew up in a hurry (then retreated), was the youngest in the family, and have never been around kids much. I have trouble "teaching" anyone anything. But I do revel on the few occasions when something that I do or say strikes pay dirt in a young mind—their eyes and souls light up, and you know that you have made a connection.

It was late when I arrived back at Cloudland, near midnight, and all was calm and cool. A quarter moon lightly lit up a hazy view out back. Not too many bugs singing. There was one distant barred owl calling out to anyone who would listen. Only the bright stars were poking through the haze. I spent an hour working down in the basement, then retired.

7/31/98 There was an odd feeling about me when I awoke. Looking around, I found that I was not alone, and was being watched. A red-tailed hawk, perched on a limb just outside my window, was staring in my direction. What a beautiful beast! He was sitting there, proud and majestic, searching for some sign of life, with a look on his face of "When are you going to get up and do something?" I did, he flew off.

The haze had lifted somewhat, and the sky was full of low-hanging clouds, a dark and dreary day—just my kind of day! It was rather cool. I quickly sucked down my Starbucks mocha and a toasted bagel, then put on my walking shoes and headed out to see what I could find. There wasn't too much going on, and the forest was very still, although there was a slight breeze. It was perfect walking weather, in the low 70's. After dodging a number of giant hickory nuts that had come down in the last storm, I checked in on Bob's and found everything to be OK. He had a visitor spend the night, but the guy had already left. Bob had come back from his long bus trip to the Northeast, but I don't know if he ever made it out to his cabin this week or not. He is leaving early next week for a tour of Wyoming and Montana. Ever since he retired, he has been very busy!

I went over towards the East Meadow. As I try to do before stepping into any open space in the woods, I hesitated a moment and crept to the edge of the opening to look into it and see what was going on. So many times in the past I have stepped hastily into a field, and got to see the fleeing rears of deer, or turkey, or some other wildlife that I could have viewed undisturbed had I only stopped before entering. Anyway, sure enough, clear across this ten-acre meadow on the other side, I saw something dark and low moving in the tall grass. Could it be? *YES*, it was a bear!

There was no way that this bear could have seen or heard me, and at first he appeared to be undisturbed, simply moving about in the grass, minding his own business. Then, all of a sudden, he stopped, and stood straight up on his hind legs, and looked right at me from across the field. His big ears stood straight up, and his paws were bent in front of his coal black body just like some of the bears that you see on TV. I noticed that the wind had picked up a little, and it was blowing my scent right over to him. He stood there for a minute, then landed back on all fours, turned the other direction and began to walk away slowly. He must not have realized that I was a human, nor felt any threat, because he didn't run, but merely continued with his lazy exploration of the meadow. So I decided to watch him as long as I could.

The bear gradually worked his way around the outside of the meadow. He ignored the garden full of tasty treats only a couple of hundred feet out into the center. It was tough to follow his every step, because the grass was so tall, and he was down on all fours. Every once in a while, he would stand back up again, looking my direction. Those big ears always looked so funny sticking straight up. I knew that the size of the ears was how you could tell how big a bear was—the smaller the ears appeared, the larger the bear was. You see, bears' ears don't grow much, especially in relation to how their head grows. So if the ears look small, the head is large, but if the ears look big, the head must be small. This bear was not a cub, but was small compared to the big one that I had seen at Bob's cabin. I figured that he was about two years old, typical of many black bears seen in the Ozarks.

Rounding the far end of the meadow the bear continued his rounds and began to head my way. I took up a position in the trees, close enough to be able to watch him, yet far enough away I thought to keep from being seen. The wind was still blowing, although not as much as before. The bear began to get pretty close, and I was able to get a good look at him. He didn't seem to be feeding on anything, just nosing around here and there, trying to see all that was there. Don't know why he never went into the middle of the meadow—he stayed within 50 feet of the edge all the time. He would sniff something on the ground, then snort it out. From time to time he would test the wind, pointing his brown nose high into the air, swinging it from side to side, then once satisfied, he would go back to sniffing the ground.

The bear was now within 100 feet of me, and my heart was pounding. I clung to the hickory tree that I was leaning up against and using for some cover. Man, this guy was *black,* as black as deep inside a cave when your light goes out. Then he stood up on his hind legs, and looked right at me. He was as tall as me, and his eyes burned a hole right through me. I held fast. He sniffed the air again, knowing that something was there, but couldn't quite identify it. Suddenly it hit him that he was in the wrong place. In a flash he turned and hit the ground running, bounded across the meadow, and in just a few seconds had run all the way to the far end and disappeared into the thick woods. I think that my heart had stopped those few seconds, but started beating again, and I breathed a heavy sigh. I was extremely happy to have been blessed with such a long time of visual excitement, but at the same time was thankful that the bear didn't make a bluff charge, like they are prone to do. I probably would have fainted.

The hunter instinct in me wanted to see more of this bear, and I wanted to follow him, but hesitated to go into that thick brush. I opted to take up a stand on a hill overlooking a spot where the thick brush gave way to more open woods—this was actually my property line. Bob's property had been logged just before he bought it five years ago (selective logged—there were still lots of trees standing), and there was a definite line there where the logged part was growing up with thick underbrush, and my part where the trees were larger and there was no underbrush.

I hadn't been on my stand more than a minute when the bear appeared about halfway down the hillside. I have always been a lucky hunter, but was a little surprised when the bear actually did what I had expected him to do. He didn't seem to be concerned, and he was just moseying along on a general downward path, sniffing and pawing the ground. He pulled up a couple of big rocks, rolled them over, and got real excited. He must have found a good nest of ants, and he spent several minutes vacuuming them up. Next he found a rotten log, which he tore into and dug up for another several minutes. They find a lot of grub worms and other assorted bugs in rotten logs.

About this time the breeze came up again, and he stopped and looked my way for the first time since appearing in the open woods. He sniffed the air, then turned and ran down the hill. Darn wind! I was really getting into watching this bear, so I decided to follow and see if I could find him. The last that I saw him, he had gone over a steep hillside. This hillside dropped down in a series of near-vertical benches, broken up by the 100' bluffline that circles the mountain.

I got to the point where I saw him last, peered over the edge, but could not see any sign of Mr. Bear. I knew that he was down there somewhere. I made my way down the first bench—it was *very* steep, and I pretty much had to go from tree to tree, hanging on for dear life, and trying not to make much noise. No bear in sight. At one point I heard him on the bench below, but the underbrush in this area was so thick that I could never see him. He was moving around slowly, perhaps had even forgot all about me and was back to his foraging. I strained to see any movement through the brush, but nothing. I stood there, frozen to my tree, for about ten minutes, until I could no longer hear him.

I walked across the level bench, over to the edge of the next dropoff where I thought I last heard him, and peered over. Still no bear. I worked my way down that bench, making a lot of racket as I slipped and slid my way down. This part of the hillside was actually the top of the 100' bluff, although it was broken up by many ledges here, and it seemed possible to work my way down through some of it. While I couldn't hear or see the bear, I did pick up his tracks, or rather a trail of disturbed leaves here and there and bent over poison ivy and Virginia creeper plants, all pointing his direction. More than once, a hickory nut must have fallen and crashed onto the forest floor, which made me jump and my heart race.

Following his trail down through the steep, broken bluffline, I ended up at a point on a ledge where I could not easily go down, the next ledge being about six feet below. There didn't seem to be any way off of the ledge but down. His trail seemed to go to the edge, and I figured that he had jumped over it. I wasn't sure what I would find down there, or if I would be able to go down any further, but I had come this far, so what the heck, I grabbed onto a small tree for support and scooted over the edge, landing on firm ground below.

Just then I realized two things. First, it was obvious that my bear had not landed on this ground—no leaves were disturbed. Which meant that the bear was still above me. *Oh NO!* Terror swept into my brain, and I broke out into

77

an instant sweat. A second later I caught a blur of black out of the corner of my eye—it was the bear, up on the ledge right above, and he was coming *at ME!* (No kidding.) I really didn't have time to think, or to react—what could I do anyway, he had me, I was caught. A stupid kid playing a man's game. No wait, I did react, and fell to the ground. The bear came flying off of the ledge, and hit the ground next to me with a loud thud.

For an instant we were eye to eye, not two feet apart, his fur touching my leg. My heart really did stop this time I'm sure. What plans did he have for me? I knew that black bears did not attack humans as a general rule, but this one had been pursued, and was put into a survival situation. I could imagine his claws ripping into me, his teeth sinking into my chest. I hoped that he would go for my head first, so it would end quickly without much pain. A calm came over me for a moment, and I could smell the bear (they really stink—imagine wearing a heavy black fur coat all summer in this heat with no bath!). Then as fast as he had appeared, he disappeared over the ledge below, leaving me in a pile of shock and dismay.

When I finally did begin breathing again, and blood was restored to my extremities, I realized that I had just been blessed. I couldn't imagine being any closer to nature. I can't imagine being more in fear of my life. Perhaps one day if I slip and fall over the edge of a big bluff, and know that the end awaits me at the bottom, I will know more fear. But otherwise, this takes the cake. If I would have had a keyboard with me at the time, the pages would be filled with a hundred phrases of thanks, relief, curses, and of admiration for the bear. What a magnificent creature.

Looking back I realized that he must have been just as terrified as me, and the only reason that he came over the ledge at me was because that was the only way out, or at least the easiest way (the only other way being to go straight up the hill where he had just come from, and he knew that danger was up there as well—the ledge that he was on was blocked at both ends). I just simply was in the way, and got in front of him. He must have been crouched under the little overhang nearby, and I didn't see him at first, until he came rushing out to go over the edge.

I know what you are thinking now, did I follow him further? You bet! The next ledge was too high for me, but I was able to find a way down through it, and I got down through the one below too, which was at the bottom of the bluff system. I don't know if the bear knew that this part of the bluff was broken like it was, and that he could get down it or not, or if it was just dumb luck on his part. The bluffline on both sides for hundreds of yards is solid bluff, and the bear would have been killed trying to go over the edge (actually, it is over a mile in one direction before there is a break in the bluffline). I really do think that it was luck, because I don't think that this bear was from this area, and had been pushed out of his home territory and into this one by a larger male. Of course, since he had been at my cabin a week ago, which is located about a quarter mile from this spot, he probably had enough time to look around the country.

When I got down to the wide bench at the bottom of the bluff I continued to follow his disturbed-leaf-and-bent-poison-ivy trail. I had an idea that this bear ran all the way to the bottom and never looked back. His trail led down the five very tall and extremely steep benches to the river, where I gave up the hunt. I figured that I would not see him again. I really just wanted an excuse to go to the river, and being exhausted and completely soaked with sweat (it was now getting kind of hot), I jumped into a nearby pool with all of my clothes on, even my shoes and socks. I lay there in the water, floating on my back, thankful to be alive. Then the sun broke through and created a million sparkling diamonds on and in the water.

The climb out of the canyon was a tough one, the river water in my clothes being replaced with sweat. When I got back to the bluffline, I followed it around to the left. Even though this part of the bluff was almost directly under my cabin, I had only been to it once. Wow, it was really impressive! It is perhaps the tallest of the bluffs in the area, and painted with orange streaks and green lichen. I found a couple of large overhangs that were large enough to camp under. Both were east-facing overhangs, and probably not used extensively by the Indians. Under one of them I found a near perfectly square rock, smooth on top. I turned it over to see if it had been used as a grind stone (I've always heard that the Indians often turned them over to keep from being spotted), but the bottom was smooth too, and probably had only recently fallen from the ceiling. There were several phoebe nests, but I never saw any of the birds. Phoebes are small birds that build nests of mud under protected overhangs like these.

After all of the climbing, chasing, and nearly being eaten alive, I was really glad to see the ladder, which meant the protection and comfort of my cabin was only a few minutes away. I spent a long time in the shower, then took a cool nap under the fan. Then I got up and painted one of my basement walls with waterproofing paint. I've been trying to do this for a month! Billy Woods and his family stopped by—they were out for a weekend of work on their cabin. Later, after a dinner of Caesar salad, I hiked on over to see what progress they had made. A cold front had moved through and it was most pleasant outside.

The Woods place is looking very nice indeed. I stayed until dark, then wandered on back to my cabin. It's funny, but for some reason the sounds in the night woods didn't strike terror in me the way that they always have in the past. Perhaps coming face to face with those terrors, and surviving, has allowed me to calm my fears a little. Thanks Mr. Bear.

Back at the cabin I listened to blues on the radio and swung myself to sleep in the porch swing. It was cloudy, and the stars never did come out. It was a very cool evening, and had been a wonderful July.

July rain was 2.9 inches, low 67 degrees, high 94 degrees, wind 41mph

AUGUST 1998

8/1/98 It was in the upper 60's when I awoke at daylight, and a cool breeze was blowing in from the east. There was a crispness in the air like a fall day. Was I still asleep and dreaming—was this really August in Arkansas? You bet. It was an absolutely gorgeous day in the Ozarks, one of those days that calls out for you to get up, get out, and be a part of it. It seemed like every muscle in my body was sore from all of the climbing up and down through the steep hillsides yesterday, so I spent the first hour of this day on the back deck, soaking up the early fall weather.

Down below in the meadow I saw a butterfly going from flower stalk to stalk. Then I saw another, and another. Soon I realized that I had been watching them for 30 minutes or more. There were three different types of butterflies out. One kind was mostly yellow with some black, like a monarch. These guys were really getting after it, whipping about wildly, fluttering up and down, flapping their wings with great abandon, not spending much time on any flower. Going in crazy directions. It was almost tiring to watch a single one, trying to keep up with it. Another group was mostly dark, with a few light spots. These guys were much slower and more deliberate with their flight, and would spend several minutes on each flower. They spent a lot of time sailing through the air, coasting, getting a great deal of flight out of each wing flap. Then there was a blue butterfly, only one. He seemed to visit the flowers that the others missed. He was kind of in-between the other two speeds, covering a lot of ground, yet getting a lot accomplished. He is the one that I most related to.

I have known many yellow butterfly people in my life, the ones that are very hyper, always busy and needing to be somewhere else. That's it, the yellow butterfly people are always looking for greener pastures in life, or sweeter flowers, and are never happy where they are. The dark butterfly people that I have known are quite the opposite, not willing to move from their spot, in physical or philosophical terms. They really aren't all that happy where they are either, but aren't willing to change. And then there are the few blue butterfly types. I consider myself one of those. We are the types that are very happy in life, and like to sit back and enjoy things as they are, yet are also interested in getting out and exploring some of the rest of the world around us. If it rains, we are joyful to sit there and let it rain on us. If the sun comes out, we want to soak up every ray. If the wind blows, we'll go where it takes us, or let it cool our skin.

As I was deep in meditation about these butterflies, up higher in the meadow air, at about my eye level, a streak of bright yellow flashed by. It was a goldfinch. My attention turned to him for a while. Most birds that fly through the meadow do so pretty much in a straight pattern, flapping their wings as needed to maintain their course. But the goldfinch's flight is more like a roller coaster. He flaps his wings a few times to get him going, which sends him up in the air, in a graceful arch, slowly peaking and heading back down to earth. Then he flaps several more times and is propelled back up into the arch again, and repeats as necessary to make it across the meadow. I wonder which way takes more energy?

The soaring birds came out and played on the wind currents. Several of them landed in the dead snag, and I spent some time studying them with the telescope. These guys really are ugly, their heads completely bare of any feathers, and made up of red, wrinkled skin, with two gaping nostril holes and yellow beaks. If they only had some feathers! I wonder, is this what I am going to look like in a few years?

It was still very hazy, which I didn't mind, because it separated the ridges and valleys way out in the distance, and gave the scene more personality, as if it needed it. Mid morning and still no sun. Still fall-like temps and feeling in the air. I just couldn't believe how great it was outside. I stretched my sore muscles a little, put on my summer hiking gear (the long pants had dried out some overnight from being soaked the day before), and headed down the ladder trail for a walk to the river.

The forest seemed to appreciate the cool temps and breezes as much as I did, for it seemed to be singing a quiet lullaby. The air was sweet, the ground soft. I didn't follow the ladder trail all the way down, but rather just sort of wandered across the benches and down the steep slopes until I had landed at Whitaker Creek, now almost dry. In each little pool there were many water strider bugs (those spiders with long legs that "stride" or skim across the top of the water), and dozens of tiny fish of all colors. I followed the creek downstream, past an old homesite chimney, to the river.

The water level in the Buffalo River had been steadily dropping all summer, and now was just barely moving. Although it was still moving, all the pools were constantly being refreshed with new water. The shallows were teaming with schools of fish. It was still very cool, in the low 70's, and instead of jumping in for a swim, I opted to sit or actually lay out on the rock gravel bar and observed a little while. I laid there for probably an hour, watching the fishes going about their daily routines, and listening to the gurgling of the water and the sounds of the forest. All was at peace on the Buffalo River.

For some reason I got an urge to read, and so I left the water world behind and climbed the steep hill, this time following the ladder trail as far up as the ladder at the base of the bluff. Here I turned and followed the base of the bluff towards Hawksbill Crag. The next place to get up through the bluffline was beyond the Crag. I had been this way many times, and it is a pleasant and interesting hike. You really get a wonderful view of the towering bluff overhead. I got a little taste of it the day before as I had followed the bluff from the other direction. You don't really notice when you are below the Crag—there aren't piles of beer cans and trash like there is below other bluffs, like White Rock (another favorite spot of mine)—you really have to be on the lookout for the Crag.

Someone told me last year that the "throat" of the Crag had collapsed and fallen, their proof being one of Neil Compton's pictures from the 70's and one of my more recent ones. No way. It must have just been different lighting. There doesn't appear to be any recent breakdown of any significance when you are standing at the base of the Crag, which is where any breakdown would have ended up. The Crag has evolved into a half-arch form, and an arch is the most stable of all geological shapes. This is why caves don't "cave in" all the time—they have already done so, and have achieved this very stable arched ceiling. If given the choice of spending a major earthquake inside an arched-ceiling cave or in downtown New York, I would take the cave every time.

A little ways beyond the Crag I found the break in the bluffline and climbed out up to the trail, which I followed on out to the trailhead on the main road. I collected Bob's newspapers (the objects of my hike), and headed back to the cabin, stopping at the garden to pick up a few tomatoes and onions for lunch. It was early afternoon when I got to Cloudland, and it was still in the low 70's. Man, I just love summers in the Ozarks!

I made a big bowl of salad and sat out on the back porch and munched and read an entire week's worth of papers. One of the papers was the **Newton County Times**, and on the front page was a picture of a dead bear with the caption "Nuisance Bear." The bear had surprised a resident of the community of Deer (the bear was feasting on her apple trees), and when it made a charge, the resident's husband shot the bear.

I must stop here for a moment and confess something. Up until I built this cabin I had *written* more books than I had read. Really. I have always been a terrible reader, guess I just never had the patience or something. I could literally count the number of complete books that I had read on my two hands. Reading just simply didn't interest me. I've always been told that there is no way that one can be an interesting person without being a reader, so I guess that explains a lot about me. Anyway, the John Muir books have grabbed me and pulled me out of the dark and into the light of reading. I have now read all of his stuff that has been published in book form, including all eight of his wilderness discovery books, plus over 900 pages of his letters and various essays. Most all of this material is contained in two huge volumes. I had just finished the second of these books and returned it to Bob's the night before. The other one belongs here at Cloudland. I have a lot of interesting books, as you can see from the titles on my new bookshelves here at the cabin, I just don't know what is inside them.

After I finished the papers I fell back in the swing and took a long nap, the gentle breezes keeping this baby asleep (you can see how tough life really is here at Cloudland). I awoke to the sound of a hummingbird floating near my head. I really must get that hummingbird feeder put up! Feeling quite lazy, I did manage to get out of the swing, cut off the ends of a log rail spindle that I had an extra of laying around, and mounted it to the last log post on the west end of the back porch. The Amish had installed a similar spindle at the opposite end of the porch, which is where I have the butterfly windsock hanging from. I mixed up the suggested sugar and water combination, boiled it, placed it into the feeder, and hung the feeder from the end of the spindle. Yea, I finally did it!

Now the hummers will have more to do here than just look at sleeping bodies. It will take a little while for them to find this little oasis, and none came by the rest of the day.

With that little task completed a strange desire came over me—I wanted to read some more! I couldn't believe it. Walking over to the bookshelf, Neil Compton's *The Battle For The Buffalo River* jumped out at me. I have known Neil for a long time—he is sort of a god to me (and, of course, to many thousands of others), and was just out at Cloudland back in April. He had given me an autographed copy of this huge book back in 1992 when it first came out, but me not being a reader, I had never sat down to read it. While being about as thick as each of Muir's two books, the pages must be a lot thicker, because this one was less than 500 pages—a giant nonetheless to me! So I thought that I would sit out on the back deck on this cool August afternoon and see what Neil had to say. Any one of my past girlfriends would have fainted to see me with a book of this size in my hands, especially when there were trails to hike, rivers to fish and mountains to climb all within my reach.

It was about 4pm when I started the book, and I was sitting in one of the high swivel bar stools that I had on the deck, my feet propped up on the railing, with all of the Buffalo River wilderness spread out before me. Wow, this was some interesting stuff! I relished his words, devoured every page, and anxiously awaited the outcome of each new section. I knew many of the characters in the book, and was surprised to learn of some of the goings-on that they were involved in back in the 1960's. I didn't know about the shootings on the river, how stupid the State of Arkansas was, plus dozens of other major events that happened during the struggle.

I really wish that I had been "of age" while all of this was going on—it must have been a grand battle, and I would have loved to have been in the middle of it. I was in the single digits age wise back then, and had never even heard of the Buffalo River or the fight to save it. Towards the end of the war, I was in high school, and did float the river during spring breaks. But I never knew enough to get involved. Don't know if I would have back then anyway—I was just another teenager who hadn't discovered the real outside world yet. The dates did take me back to some fine times on the Buffalo River, and during the long sweet summers that followed.

The hours passed and the pages kept turning, slowly. I moved into one of the log rockers (one with a thick pad!). Then into the swing. I strained to read each word as the light faded. I got up and turned on the porch light, then quickly returned to the saga. More hours passed. My only nourishment during all this time was a single beer and a handful of pretzels and peanuts.

8/2/98 The no-see-um bugs eventually came out and drove me into the cabin, where I took up residence inside on the couch without missing a beat. More hours passed. Finally, the Buffalo National River became a reality, and I had come to the end of the book. Wow, what a struggle, what incredible people had been involved, what a great feat of courage and honor Neil and all the others had done! I was impressed, and more than ever proud to know them. It was 3am. I'd been reading for 11 straight hours (I'm a slow reader).

Neil Compton wrote the foreword to my new ***Buffalo River Wilderness*** picture book. He is one wonderful writer, and the Ozarks have never had anyone write about them with such passion. After finally reading his work of art, and now having the complete picture of the struggle to save the river, I must write Neil a letter, a thank you note from one of the multitudes of regular folks who will be enjoying the fruits of his labor for many decades to come.

When I tried to get up my legs were stiff as boards, and I hobbled up to the loft and fell into bed. My body was exhausted, but my mind was racing. Images of the history to save the Buffalo River kept running through my mind. While I think that I did fall asleep in a hurry, those images continued all night. Many of the scenes were from the book, others were made up by my brain. I saw Neil Compton, Orval Faubus, John Heuston, The Hedges, Chief Justice William O. Douglas, the bad guys Trimble and Tudor and the local rednecks who fought the Park and played nasty tricks in favor of the dams, and I saw Ken Smith. I knew that I must have been dreaming because Ken spoke to me—he hasn't said a word to me in over 15 years, even though I always extend a hand to him with words of praise every time that I see him—he just ignores me and walks away— I've never figured out why.

When daylight came I rolled over, closed the blinds, and continued with the saga. Finally, at 9am, I had enough, and got up to a still glorious morning. The birds were singing, the butterflies were making their rounds, and the air was pretty clean—not hardly any haze at all. And it was still cool! After breakfast on the deck, I fired up the computer to do some writing. I felt like music, so I turned on the radio and immediately heard some wonderful sounds. It was an ***Ozarks At Large*** program on KUAF, but it was this incredible music. My little wire FM antenna is always acting up, and this morning it was playing with my mind. I could not find a location to put it where the signal would be clear—the only way that I could get a good signal was if I stood next to the receiver, holding the wire straight up in the air. I was fascinated with this music, so I stood there, holding the wire up, and listened with eyes closed. Anyone walking in on this scene would doubt my sanity, as if they don't already. Finally I figured out that I could hang the wire from the log coat rack, so I dragged it over. If you ever come to Cloudland and see the coat rack over next to the stereo, you will know why.

The radio segment was with Mike Shirkey, who does the ***Pickin' Post*** with folk music on Saturday nights. The guest artist played several songs, and I soaked them all up, then finally, at the end of the set, they gave his name—Steve Fisher. I must go out and try to find his CD!

I plugged in a CD and went back to the computer, where I wrote for several hours. It was so cool outside, I opened all of the windows in my office. From the computer station I can look out one of my windows that faces east, another one that looks out over the main Buffalo River valley, and I can see all the way to Curtis Cemetery, and the third window that has a view all the way up Whitaker Creek, and I can just see the Buffalo Fire Tower five and a half miles away. It's a pretty fair view, and is a wonder that I ever get anything done.

It is noon now, still cool and cloudy bright outside, though beginning to heat up. It's time for me to get off of my fanny and go downstairs and put a second coat of waterproofer on the basement wall. Then I plan to build a long and narrow deck along the east end of the cabin—this will be my wood-stacking area, and will keep the firewood out of most of the weather. That fall weather yesterday and this morning has got me thinking about the wonderful cool and crisp days ahead (well, they are two or three months ahead, but what the heck), and the need to better organize my wood chopping and storing area.

It got hot this afternoon, at least for a fat boy doing some manual labor. I put the second coat of paint on the basement wall, then spent a couple of hours building that long, narrow deck, and stacking some split wood up on it. At one point during the afternoon, my break on the upper deck was interrupted by some sort of grey matter down in the meadow that flashed across the corner of my vision. I didn't get to see what it was, or if I had ever actually even seen anything. I went back to work.

I was making all kinds of racket outside, sawing boards and screwing them in with the power drill, and bouncing lumber off of the deck. During my next break, right after I had sat down with my cold Diet Dr. Pepper, I looked down and saw a grey fox rolling in the ashes of the brush pile burn area down in the meadow. When I creeped over to get the binocs, I must have made a noise, because the fox jumped up to attention, staring my way. I froze, and we gazed at each other for several minutes. He was sitting upright, with his tail wrapped around his feet—as fine a little fox as I have ever seen! And about the longest view that I ever had of one in the wild. They are usually moving pretty fast when I see them.

Before long he turned away and moved slowly into the thick underbrush. I could see his fur through the weeds every now and then. I went back to work. Twenty minutes later, I looked up and there the fox was again, back in the same bare spot of dirt and ash. He wasn't rolling this time, but had his nose to the ground (in between looks my direction), and seemed to be looking for something. Satisfied, he wandered off, checking me over his shoulder several times before he went out of sight down the hill.

My work done for the day, I put on a pot of rice and cooled myself down in the shower. Neil's book was still tugging at me, and I once again drifted back to the young and carefree days of my youth in the early 70's. Gosh, there was so much discovery then, many fond memories of friends and situations. (It was kind of like the summer of 1998.) I put on an old Bread album (CD) on the stereo, sat down with my veggies and rice, my memories, and the golden rays of sunlight creeping up the mountains outside. Absolutely satisfactory!

After dinner I fired up the computer and worked on my accumulating e-mail, and wrote in the Journal. It's a good thing that I was alone, because every other song it seems pulled me away from the computer, out into the middle of the great room, where a sing-a-long ensued—it was not a pretty sound I assure you, but it felt great. I hadn't heard this music in a long time. *I Wanna Make It With You. If. Guitar Man.* Good stuff Maynard.

Once all of the computer stuff was done I shut down the music and wandered around preparing the cabin for sleep. Something took me outside for a moment, where I discovered a wonderful sight that seems to happen a lot out here at Cloudland. It was a half-moon, maybe just over half, and it was lighting up all of the wilderness just enough to see all of the ridges and valleys. The moon was in the southern sky, making a low arch, just like the sun does in the wintertime. I must study this moon path stuff, because you would think that it would be right overhead in the summer. But it isn't.

Anyway, it was splendid outside, in the mid-70's with the wind blowing, and quite delightful. I sat out on the lower deck for some time, gazing into the moonlit hollows, and listening to the night sounds. While Bread was mighty fine music, this music was every bit as good.

While the night sky was rather bright because of the moon, and the stars weren't out too much, I knew that next week would be the peak of some great meteor showers, so I tried to figure out what and where would be the best time to view them. After the full moon on Friday this coming week, the moon would rise later and later each day, so by the following weekend, it wouldn't come up until well after midnight—this would keep the night sky plenty black for several hours, and make for great meteor watching. There will be a day-after-full-moon party out here this coming weekend, and I guess I need to have a meteor shower watch party the following weekend. I've heard that the best viewing will be in the northeast sky, but my view is mostly southern, from east to west. So I thought about another place nearby to go watch. No problem—the East Meadow has a terrific view to the north, and I bet that would work. I needed to make sure of this, so I got a wild hare and decided to hike up there this moonlit night and see what I could see.

While not nearly as bright as during a full moon it was still pretty bright along the path to the East Meadow. Of course, the shadows in the deep woods were *very* black, but I didn't want to use a flashlight because it would ruin my night vision. I reached the East Meadow without any big monsters jumping out and getting me, and I walked into another world up there. Oh, man, it was just so cool in the meadow! The moonlight gave everything soft edges, and I could see forever across the meadow. There were a few flashes on the horizon, and it looked like a thunderhead was out there somewhere, teasing me. I strained to see if there were any animals out there feeding or moondipping, but the grass was so tall, waist deep on me, that any deer out there would be almost completely hidden. And any bears prowling about would be below that level too, unless they were standing up on their hind legs like the one was the last time that I was in this meadow.

No question, this meadow would be the perfect vantage point to view the meteor showers. In fact, I don't think that any of my soon-to-be-invited guests had ever been to this meadow, especially at night, so it would be a nice trip for them. I tromped down some of the grass and weeds, and made a place to lie down. The ground was warm, the breezes were cool, and I lay there for an hour gazing at the Big Dipper and North Star in the bright sky. I think I even fell asleep for a few minutes—it was one comfortable spot, and I could see why deer and other animals choose meadows like this one to nap. Wouldn't it be funny if someone drove into this meadow, expecting to find deer out feeding, only to see a human jump up from the weeds and bound off into the woods?

The trip back down to the cabin was rather uneventful, just another glorious walk in the summertime night woods. The thunderhead flashed every now and then, showing more of the forest than the moonlight did. I wasn't ready to test the waterproofed basement wall, but would be thankful if it rained. The wind was blowing so hard that I didn't need to turn on the ceiling fan above my head. It felt great.

8/3/98 Another fall morning in August! You know, it was only 71 degrees this morning when I got up, but it just "felt" like a fall day. There must be something in the chemical makeup of the air in the fall, and this morning, that makes one feel this way. I look forward to the real thing come October. The wind was blowing, and I never saw a single bird while having my breakfast on the deck. It rained some, and was heavy overcast, but it didn't last long. It felt like rain though, and I suspect that it will rain some on and off all day. The radio says that it is going to be between 95 and 100 degrees in town today, and tomorrow, and the next day.

A light rain began to fall just as I was leaving for town. Stopped by and gathered a few tomatoes for mom—it was great to stand out in the open and soak up the cool moisture.

8/5/98 The rain on Monday must have been a good one—we got nearly an inch! Winds to 23mph.

I escaped from town and arrived back at Cloudland in the late evening. It felt so terrific out here that I put off unloading the van and immediately headed out for a walk. It seemed that just about everywhere that I went, whether it be forest or meadow, I saw wildlife. Lots of squirrels and birds in the woods, and deer after deer after deer in the meadows. The younger deer, now void of all spots, were romping and playing and really having a grand time. Moms were always more sedate, but I could tell that they were enjoying being out in the cool evening air as well. It was quiet, and peaceful outside.

As I walked through the East Meadow (this has become my favorite meadow), I began to feel a little strange, like I was being watched. There were still some deer lingering at the edges, but it wasn't them. I stopped and searched all over, but couldn't locate anyone. Then, all of sudden, there it was. Huge, silent, looming right over my shoulder—the moon had just broken through some clouds and was shining bright in the evening sky. Two days from full, yet still an impressive sight. A friend, out to keep an eye on this city slicker rediscovering the wilderness.

At Bob's cabin, Benny and Mildred had arrived for a short stay. They have done a considerable amount of the restoration work to Bob's old cabin, and still do most of the work around the place. Although they don't get out here often enough. It seems then the time they spend here is all spent working. I need to soak up a little of their habits!

After a short visit I strolled into the dark, taking a detour back through the East Meadow once more. It was a little overcast now, very thin, which only spread out the moon beams, making the light softer. A meadow in very soft moonlight is a wonderful place indeed, and it took me nearly an hour just to cross it (this is one of many places that calls for a lovely young lady to be holding hands and sharing the moonlight with). The nighttime bugs came out and began singing, and kept me company the rest of the way to the cabin. I unloaded the van and spent another hour out on the back deck, my feet propped up and my hands around a glass of wine. There was enough moonlight to illuminate the valleys below, and I could see a cloud bank forming in the bottom. It was good to be home again.

8/6/98 In the middle of the night, around 2am I think, my outside alarm went off. It does that every now and then, mostly because of deer moving through, so I didn't pay too much attention to it. A few minutes later, I heard a thud on the front deck—damn, somebody, or something, was out there. I got up, stumbled down the staircase, and peered out the front-door window. I could see the front yard, driveway and woods, all illuminated by the hazy moonlight, but the porch was in shadow, and dark. I turned the porch light on. Nothing. I must have imagined the noise. Or perhaps a bird had flown into the window.

I shut off the light to save my night vision. As long as I was up, I thought that I might as well go out and water the wildflowers, saving my precious well water. I unlocked the big front door, and stepped out. Thump, thump, thud, thud—my heart stopped and I almost lost my wildflower fluid—there was a bear on the porch with me! He must have been off to one side and out of sight when I had turned the light on. He dashed across the porch and down the steps, then across the driveway and into the woods. It happened that fast, and then was over. I was now fully awake. The porch swing was swaying back and forth—he must have been over in that corner of the deck and hit the swing as he went past. Either that or he was sitting in the swing enjoying the view when I had disturbed him. Holy smokes! Can't a guy go out and pee in the middle of the night without being scared to death anymore?

It took me quite a while to go back to sleep, in fact I'm not sure if I ever did. Visions of teeth and claws kept going through my head. I gave up the sleep part and got up early, before sunrise, ate a quick breakfast and decided to get some work done. By the time the sun came up I had already put together a storage shed that I bought in town. This will be the home to my chain saws and outdoor tools.

It was in the 60's, and felt great to wear a pair of jeans and a long-sleeved shirt. There were broken clouds in the sky, and no breeze. I found fresh bear tracks at the base of the front porch steps, right next to the track that had been made a couple of weeks ago (I had covered the old track up with a pan to show people)—these new tracks were much larger than the old one. In all of the excitement during the bear incident, I never really got a feel for how big the bear was, but looking at the tracks, I realized that I should have fainted when he came across the porch—this was one big bear. I retreated to the other side of the cabin to enjoy the view.

The new hummingbird feeder was already seeing a great deal of use—the little critters had drained about half of it in less than a week. It didn't take them long to find it this morning, and I spent some time watching and listening to all of the fuss. When Jim and Susie gave the feeder to me, they warned that the little hummers might get a little aggressive—boy, were they right! These little guys have trouble getting along! They hiss and snarl, and spend most of their time chasing each other away from the feeder (I may have to put up another feeder). As I am now inside writing this, one of them has come over to the window next to the computer three different times, as if trying to figure out what the heck I am doing. Perhaps he wants me to come out and play!

The butterflies are going nuts this morning too. I decided to spend some time trying to identify some of them. I went down to the lower deck with the binocs and ID book. Good grief, there were over a hundred of them out this morning. They were everywhere, feeding on the wild yellow sunflowers (woodland or hairy, I haven't figured out which yet) that have now crowded into the meadow below. Come to think of it, the sunflowers are everywhere. They stand about 4-6 feet tall.

With ID book and note pad in hand, and binocs around my neck, I walked down and spent about 30 minutes wandering through my little meadow wonderland. The butterflies have no sense of fear, and never even batted an eyelid (do they have these?) when I was next to them. It was peaceful and exciting at the same time.

The bright yellow butterflies are Eastern tiger swallowtails, and these are the largest of the bunch, many as big as my hand. They were more sedate today, spending most of their time munching on the flowers. Next in line both in number and size are the Spicebush swallowtails, black and blue in color. Often there were both kinds feeding on the same stalk of wildflowers, and they didn't seem to even notice each other. There appeared to be a lot of pairs out too—they stuck together as they went from flower to flower.

The other main butterfly was an orange and rust colored one, pretty large, but I couldn't ID it. These were the friendliest ones, and one even sat on my outreached hand for a few seconds. Then there were several others, smaller, that

I can't ID either. Guess I will have to get Lori, the pro butterfly guru, back out here to help. Later, back inside the cabin, I found the name of the larger orange butterflies in an unusual place. I was looking through a National Geographic book for some reason (**America's Wild Woodlands**), in the chapter that included some of the Ozarks, and son of a gun, right there was a close up picture of this very butterfly. Great spangled fritillary butterfly. I looked it up in the ID book, but it didn't look the same. Right below the picture in the National Geographic book is a picture taken by Tim Ernst. Hum.

Benny and Mildred came by and told me of their bear problems. A large bear had been into two of the three gardens overnight. In the Faddis garden, he ate every single ear of special corn that Bob was growing. The bear had broken down most of the stalks too. Funny thing though, he left the sweet corn alone. And the tomatoes. They must not like tomatoes. Too bad, since everyone who has tomato plants has too many, that would be the perfect job for these problem bears—to eat all the extra tomatoes! The bear also tore down a large martin house at the Faddis cabin. This is the first time that a bear has been to the Faddis cabin area (since Bob has owned it). Not a good sign. I took them out to the front porch to show them the fresh bear tracks of my own—and we agreed that it must have been the same bear. Not a good sign either.

After they left I hiked on up to see the bear damage firsthand. The East Meadow garden, the place where I had just had my little wonderful stroll the night before, was torn up pretty bad. The bear had gotten into the tall corn and actually got down on the ground and rolled—knocked down three rows of corn—and then ate all of the ears. There were still lots of ears left, but this guy was on a rampage. The tracks were big, very big. I'll bet this was the cinnamon bear that Billy had seen in the North Meadow last month. And the same bear that was on my front porch—yikes!

The cinnamon bear is the only bear that had been seen at Bob's place before this summer. He had been there off and on over the last three years, tearing down bird houses, getting into the birdseed, and messing up the front porch of Bob's cabin. And last summer he ate all of the cantaloupe. (I had wondered about this before, but now realize that it must have been him.) For some reason, this bear has laid low this summer, perhaps because the big black bear that I had been seeing had run him off or something.

After being in the garden for about ten minutes I noticed some movement up the hill when I started to leave—it was a turkey hen! She made a lot of noise as she flew off. As I approached the spot where she had been, an entire flock of them jarred me with their flapping wings and loud commotion. There were eight more of them, although these were smaller than the first one. All of them had been right there in the middle of the meadow the whole time that I was in the garden. The grass and weeds were so tall that I never saw them.

As I wandered through the woods towards the Faddis garden the black clouds overhead opened up and it began to pour. No thunder, just lots of wonderful rain! I stood under a big oak for a few minutes to stay dry, then went on out into the woods, where I got soaked in a flash—didn't seem to mind—it was quite refreshing! I started singing that B.J. Thomas song (*Raindrops keep falling on my heard...*). The shower soon ended. The Faddis garden was just as torn up as the other one had been, only nearly every stalk was down on the ground. And that poor martin house. I don't know if there were any birds in it this year, but there were last year.

Martins are funny. Bob has always said that they would only build nests in a house if there were people around. He has had this house at the Faddis cabin for several years, but only once had any birds in it. That was last summer, when the Woods boys were restoring the Faddis cabin—they were there every day! Plus all of my Amish crew was coming and going. And now this summer, there is no one at the Faddis cabin, and the birds did not come. Bob needs more guests at the Faddis cabin, especially during martin nesting time.

On the way back to my cabin I found several places where the bear had walked right down my dirt road—they were the same large tracks as the ones in the gardens, and in my front yard.

After a nap and a pile of junk food I decided to go back up to the East Meadow and hang out a while and see if the bear came back for more corn. I can hardly believe this myself, but I took two books with me! Wow, this place has really gotten to me—I'm reading books in the middle of the day. I spread myself out in the upper end of the meadow, propped my feet up and started reading, stopping every page to scan the meadow slowly for any movement. It was overcast, and threatening rain at any moment. I could hear rumblings off in the distance.

I got through the first book pretty quickly—**Selected Poems by Edgar A. Guest**. I have no idea where this book came from (printed in 1940), but it was on my bookshelf, and was short, so I brought it along. It was OK, but nothing that I would quote. The second book was **Epic Trips Of The West** by Tom Stienstra. I'm going to write a book kind of like this one some day, and wanted to see what his was like. The first story was about his search for a Bigfoot creature in northern California during a hike that he took with forest service officials. He said that the Hupa Indians call Bigfoot "Ohmahah," which means "Wild Man of the Woods." Seemed timely for me to be reading this story because it will be the "real" Wildman's 77th birthday tomorrow, and I was sitting there in the weeds waiting for my own type of Bigfoot. Once I finished that story (he never found the large fellow, but did see some evidence of one), I began to read another one in his book about a hike along the John Muir trail in California.

About halfway through this short story I looked up to scan the meadow for the 100th time, and saw some movement at the far end. I got out the binocs, and right there at the edge of the meadow, stood the largest black bear that I had ever seen. Holy cow, this guy was *huge!* And sure enough, just like everyone had said, he was cinnamon color—most likely the same bear that I had seen on my front porch only a few hours before. That color happens in about 30% of black bears. His ears sure were small. He was very hesitant to come into the

91

meadow—perhaps he smelled me, or where I had been walking. Or maybe it was just his natural caution, which was why he had grown to be so big.

He disappeared back into the thick woods, then emerged again about a hundred feet away. Then he disappeared again, but soon came out at the original point, and headed straight over to the garden. He walked right into the corn and began munching. I saw one stalk go down, then another, then another. You know, I knew that I had wanted to see this bear in the daylight, but now that I was watching him, I had no idea what to do next. I felt kind of funny just letting him tear up the garden, but did I really want to go out across the open meadow and charge this bear, screaming like an idiot? Sure I did. And that is exactly what happened.

I got up and walked towards him. At first he didn't see me. I got pretty close, and he still didn't see me. So I started yelling—he immediately stopped what he was doing, stood up on his hind legs, and looked right at me. Holy smokes, what was I doing? Was I insane? I screamed louder and moved toward him. Just then I remembered that I had brought the shotgun with the rubber bullets that the Game and Fish had issued us, which I had carried down the hill. He dropped back down on all fours and turned away. I popped him in the rear with a rubber slug. He didn't stick around for a second one, and tore across the meadow and into the woods. Whew. I took a deep breath and put another rubber bullet into the shotgun, hoping that I would not need it. I wondered what that rubber bullet would do to an angry, charging bear? Duh, perhaps it would be better if I didn't find out. I walked back up the hill, gathered up my stuff, and high-tailed it back to the cabin. It was beginning to get dusky dark when I arrived. I felt good that I was able to hit him with some rubber, and hoped that it got his attention (like it apparently had done for the other big bear that was bothering Bob's cabin—he has not been back since I shot him with rubber bullets in June).

It was exciting seeing a bear that big, especially so close. As I was sitting out on the back deck telling my story to someone on the phone, I looked down and saw not one, but two grey foxes. I guess the one that was there the other day liked the place, and brought the Mrs. back for a visit. They snuck into a certain clump of weeds and never came out. I should go down there and check to see if they are making a den or something. I need to find out more about foxes. It is nice to be talking to someone on the phone and just casually interrupt the conversation and say "By the way, two foxes just came by for a visit, and they are sitting right here in front of me." I never saw them again this night. Boy, this day sure has been full of wildlife! Butterflies and foxes and bears, oh my.

As I was stepping out of the shower later a barred owl struck up a conversation right out in front of the cabin. I sat out on my loft deck and listened, but I never saw anything. I don't know if there were two or three of them, or just one, but there was a lot of hooting and hollering going on, and it all seemed to be coming from just one tree. Man, they sure can make some funny noises!

I just remembered—when I was out looking for bear tracks around the cabin, I found a set of deer prints that came right up next to the cabin—like the deer was looking into the window. I wonder if they do that? If I ever turned around in my easy chair and saw a deer staring at me I would probably pass out, or start laughing out loud.

It's late now, after ten, and the sky has cleared and the moon is shining bright. Tomorrow is the full moon, so it is big. There aren't any fog banks down in the valleys, but there is one about halfway up the mountainside across the way, hovering over the Buffalo River. The moon has it so lit up that it is bright white, and looks really strange and out of place in the middle of all the dark mountains. I'm heading to bed now, and hoping that the alarm doesn't go off! It has been another spectacular day at Cloudland. Simply "satisfactory."

8/7/98 No alarms, no bears on the front porch. I awoke to the soft cooing of mourning doves in the meadow. While I was having my mocha on the back deck, the doves seemed to be working in pairs. One would call out, while its mate would fly about here and there doing something, then they would reunite on the same limb. There were two pairs working the meadow.

The hummers were out in full force too. Five of them were at the feeder at one time, or were trying to get to the feeder anyway. At one point, there was this one hummer who would sit on a tree branch nearby. Every time that another hummer came close to the feeder, he would fly over and chase it off. Come on buddy, there is plenty for everyone! They have been using the protected corridor of the back porch as a fighting alley.

I never saw any foxes this morning. But I now spend a great deal of time looking down in the meadow for them when I am out on the deck. There weren't many butterflies out this morning either. But there was one big, bright yellow one that was flying about twenty feet up in a tree—its brilliant yellow body really contrasted against the dull green of the tree. Wonder why it was up so high?

The morning began very cool, in the upper 60's, with hazy skies and a low cloud cover. But now, at 10am, the clouds are breaking up, the sun is out, and it is warming up in a hurry. Think I'm going to go for a hike.

I did hike up to check out the gardens, just to see if Mr. Bear had been back, and everything looked OK. The spiderwebs were out in full force today, and I was covered from head to toe with them in just a few minutes. I ended up getting a dead branch and holding it out in front of me as I walked. I only had to eat two or three spiders.

When I went out on the back deck to eat my rice and veggie lunch, there was no wind, so I turned on one of the ceiling fans out there to help keep me cool. A large butterfly came up and flew near the rotating blades of the fan—I thought for sure they would cut him up, but he avoided them. He landed on the ceiling near the fan, and just sat there for a moment, looking everything over. Then he swooped down below the fan, and made a number of attempts to fly right through the blades, stopping and dropping back just before hitting them. This was really strange behavior. After about a dozen tries, he made a final charge and flew *right through* the fan blades without getting hit! I couldn't believe it! Satisfied with his feat, the butterfly went merrily on his way.

There were a couple of soaring birds out but no sign of the bickering hummers. I spent some time at the computer, cleaned the cabin up a little, then headed to town (stopping to raid the garden for tomatoes for my mom on the way out). The Wildman is having a 77th birthday dinner at his house tonight that I am going in for. I will be back out soon though, as I have guests coming out for the full-moon party this weekend.

The full moon was beaming when I arrived back at the cabin, where I found Roy and Norma soaking it all up. At one point Roy asked me to turn off the spotlight outside, and I told him that the only spotlight on was the moon—it was very bright.

8/8/98 It was cool at dawn, with a light breeze. A few small clouds were chasing each other around in the valley below, and the hummers were chasing each other around up on the back deck at Cloudland. Norma read in an ID book that the first hummer that finds a feeding station becomes its guardian, often waiting on a nearby branch, and running off any other hummers that come to get a drink. This was easy to see. We never could figure out which type of hummers we had here, although one species fit our description exactly, but the book only showed them living along the west coast. Perhaps we have become a "California" type of place here.

Bob and Dawna Robinson rolled in from Ft. Smith, and we all went on a hike to visit the bear damage at the gardens, then down to Bob's place, and on to the Woods cabin, where Billy Woods and his family were slaving away, trying to get the place finished in time for hunting season in November. Their cabin is looking very nice indeed. We found a good-sized pile of bear scat, which was mostly undigested wheat hulls, confirming Billy's notion that the bear was spending a lot of time in the North Meadow, which is planted with wheat. The bear must be watching those TV commercials about eating whole wheat to help prevent cancer.

Spiderwebs were in great quantity all along our route, but I was glad to have Norma leading the way and eating most of the spiders that I normally get to catch. Near Bob's cabin we discovered that the pawpaw trees there had some green fruit on them—this was the first time that I had ever seen fruit on these young trees. As they ripen, they will get rather fragrant, adding to the pleasure along my hiking route past them. On the way back to the cabin we found more bear tracks in the road, although they were not fresh. In fact, there wasn't any fresh bear sign, so I hoped that the rubber bullet worked on this latest monster marauding bear.

Black clouds were building up in the afternoon and we decided to stick around the cabin and do a little work. We spent a couple of hours wiping every square inch of the logs inside with damp cloths—getting rid of a great deal of dust and soot from a winter of fireplace fires. The logs began to glow once again. It was a little like a beehive in the cabin, with everyone running around or climbing up and down ladders, working like crazy. Roy noticed that the fireplace mantle was not entirely level, and I told him that was the way that I had designed it. Who could argue?

The black clouds did open up and pour down for a short time and we all got to see a good lightning show as well. Many of the bolts were hitting in sight, within five miles. The back deck is a great place to watch the progress of an approaching storm. Just as the raindrops dried up, Hete showed up. He had spent the last couple of days showing property to a couple from California who flew in to buy some Ozark property. Like an increasing number of others, they want to escape the rat race and relocate to the backwoods. We went on another hike to show Hete the bear damage. It was funny how the bear had taken the corn cobs, and instead of just chomping them whole, had eaten the corn off of the cob, just like most people do.

We had an early Dawna-made lasagna dinner (early for us—the usual Saturday night dinner is around 8 or 9pm, but we finished up by 7), then packed up and headed on over to the Crag along the blufftop trail (our goal was to witness the moonrise from the Crag). It was a wonderful little stroll, and we found the Crag deserted when we arrived. The sun had already gone down, and darkness was advancing. There was a thunderhead over in the eastern sky, lighting up orange every few minutes with a giant thunderbolt. We passed the time discussing our favorite movies, and trying to get the attention of some barred owls that were talking across the way—none of us were good at owl talk. As it got cooler the warmth that the Crag had soaked up during the day felt good.

Someone looked up and noticed a glow in the eastern sky—"What is that?" Right on cue, a brilliant fiery ball appeared behind the trees at the top of the ridge, and the full moon began its rapid rise into the summer sky. The forest around us that had been brimming with the conversations of birds and bugs, immediately grew silent. So did we. We all sat there on the sandstone outcropping in awe at the moon, its color, its size, and its speed of advance. Wow, this was an incredible moonrise! And to make things even better, the moon soon disappeared into a cloud bank, then emerged again, giving us a second moonrise. We couldn't have asked for a better sight.

As the moon climbed higher into the night sky a few stars popped out here and there, and we began to see satellites and jets passing overhead. The major topic was trying to figure out the exact departure and arrival cities of the jets. And we found a couple of shooting stars, one streaking across half of the sky. The stars were giving us a preview of the meteor showers that we all would gather next weekend to watch. The moon eventually lit up the sky so much that we could hardly see many stars, so we packed up and hiked back to Cloudland.

8/9/98 It was a bright, but red/orange sun that greeted the day. We all slept in a little, except for Bob and Dawna, who slept out on the back deck (Hete slept in the front porch swing, guarding against any bear attacks). This back deck area has really become the main gathering place at the cabin, no matter what time of day. I wonder if it will continue to be the main place once it gets colder? It was a little cool this morning, and felt great.

After a lazy morning we all packed up and headed down the ladder trail towards the river. Along the way we discovered another grove of young pawpaw trees, growing right next to the trail. No fruit on these guys yet, but it is only a matter of time. We did a little trail maintenance, removing some dead falls and branches that blocked the trail, as well as rocks that were in the way. With all of the use this summer, this trail has turned into a pretty nice corridor through the woods, although the original trail route is still *very* steep, but it is the best way to get up and down the hillside.

The river had gone down some but the main swimming hole was still intact and a wonderful place to lounge away the day. The water was cooler than normal. Much of the river is spring fed, and as the water levels drop, the cold spring water contributes a larger percentage of the water, with the warmer runoff being less, so the overall water temperature drops. Sounds kind of strange, that the water gets colder as the level decreases, but that's the way it is. Dawna and Hete had not been to the swimming hole before. Unlike our last trip here, Norma forgot her Nero Wolfe book and so didn't read to everyone. The fish were kind of looking forward to it.

The hike back up was a little warm but everyone arrived in good shape. After cool showers and clean clothes, we all settled in on the back deck, and after a beer or two, things got pretty quiet. Almost everyone was napping at the same time, and it looked rather strange to see all of these bodies in chairs lined up along the railing. The afternoon was cool, as it had been all weekend, with just a little breeze, and a few hummers darting around. We watched the colorful goldfinches and butterflies working the meadow, but never saw the foxes.

The subject of hummingbird feeders came up again. It seems that the liquid with the red dye in it is very bad for the little hummers, and you should always make up your own solution of sugar water. Hete said that he had read somewhere that you had to boil the sugar and water together, or the hummers would get the runs. We all agreed that someone very low on the totem pole must have had the job of figuring that one out.

Bob and Dawna left to go back to the rat race and the rest of us lounged away the afternoon (Norma took a short hike). Before long it was time for Cloudland Pizza! We sat out on the back deck, gathered around the glass-topped table, and made four pizzas disappear in a flash. After cleanup, Roy, Norma and Hete headed back to town as well.

Near dark I laced up my walking shoes and went for a stroll. The plant-smells in the night air were just wonderful. And for some reason, there were no spiderwebs out. It was cloudy, so no stars were visible. I returned to the cabin well after dark, and crawled into bed. It had been another wonderful weekend of conversation, food and wilderness.

8/10/98 Sometime during the night the breezes quit and the sky opened up and it poured for about five minutes. Then the water stopped and the wind picked up again. My dreams were hardly even interrupted. The breezes continued for the rest of the night and into the new day. Laying in that wonderful bed in the loft as daylight filters in to light up the logs and aspen boards, and as the breezes gently flow through, it is difficult to get up. So I didn't, at least for awhile. It took a flannel shirt to brave the morning on the back deck, a textbook morning of cool breezes, soft sunshine and singing birds all around.

8/12/98 I returned from town to a freshly washed forest—it didn't rain too much, but just enough to scrub everything clean. The sky was clear, and after I unloaded the van, I hiked up the hill and around to the East Meadow to see what the stars were up to. It was very dark out, and the moon wasn't due up for another couple of hours. So I laid down in the tall grass and searched for shooting stars.

Barred owls seemed to be out in full force, calling from several different directions. They were the only sound. Well, I guess the nighttime summer bugs were out too, but I sort of ignored them. The sky was black, and the stars were twinkling like crazy. The East Meadow is so open, the sky seemed to just wrap around me, and I felt like I was right up in it. I read somewhere that for every shooting star you witness, you will be blessed with a spot of good luck. Since I have spent many nights in my life doing nothing but looking for shooting stars, I guess that would explain all of the great fortune that I have had. There were only three stars that streaked across the black sky, and satisfied that would be enough to carry me through the night and next day, I got up and made my way back through the darkness.

The starlight had just enough power to show me the way through the meadows, but in the woods it was black, coal black, and I had to use a small flashlight to find my way (something I almost never use). I heard a sound in the leaves up ahead, and pointed the light in that direction—a raccoon! No, it was too slender, and only had a short tail—hey, it was a bobcat! He turned back to look at me with those big eyes, then sauntered off through the woods, not really too interested in worrying about me. They look so funny with that bobbed tail. I guess one of the shooting stars already paid off—seeing a bobcat is a wonderful thing indeed!

Back at the cabin the night sky drew me out once again and I spent an hour or so down on the back deck, laying in the hammock, sipping a glass or two of red wine, and gazing up at the stars. The owls were busy on this side of the hill too, although they were all far off, and their hoots echoed through the canyons. I never saw another shooting star, but did enjoy the owls, and the Milky Way.

8/13/98 As it got light I rolled over to find myself engulfed in clouds. I couldn't tell if they were really clouds hanging low, or fog banks rising up. I had to get up and go out on the back deck to investigate. It was dead still outside, no breeze, no sounds at all. This fog was different from most—it seemed to be a lot finer. At first, all I could see was white. Soon, Beagle Point across the way showed up, then the next ridge, and the next. One by one a ghostly image would appear, then gradually get darker and more defined. The fog wasn't rising, or sinking—it was just disappearing. Every now and then the silence would be broken by the drumming of a woodpecker far away. The sound would come across the fog bank, then roll past and up into the next valley.

After a couple of hours the fog banks were still hanging around some, and the sky was overcast. A soft rain began to fall. I couldn't tell if it was really rain, or just moisture from the fog. A very tiny bird landed in the top of the snag at the edge of the bluff. I got out the telescope, cranked it all the way up to 45x, and the bird was still tiny. There are usually giant turkey vultures resting on this snag, and this bird was about as big as one of their feet. He kept looking nervously in all directions, singing every now and then—and was answered by another one off in the woods.

He flew on over and perched in a dogwood tree nearby, and would fly up and grab a bug, then land again in the same spot. While I could count the feathers on his chest with the tele, I couldn't figure out what bird he was—a very nondescript brown and grey sort of fellow. Actually, he was probably a she, but I call everything "he" until the gender is known.

The hummers were out too, although they were mad, and kept flying past my nose. I finally realized that they had nothing to eat—I took down their feeder last night to clean it, and hadn't put it back up yet. So I cooked up a little sugar water for them. It only took three minutes for the hummers to begin to feed after I hung it up.

I usually listen to NPR news in the morning, and after the news the KUAF radio station plays classical music the rest of the morning. I have never liked classical music, probably because I have never really been exposed to it. I keep it on as more background music than anything else. Although I am beginning to notice that this stuff really does go with the atmosphere out here at Cloudland. And while I do like some of it now, I still can't name any of it. I have a lot to learn in life. Good thing that I am just a young whippersnapper with plenty of time and desire to learn.

It stayed cloudy most of the day, with one heavy downpour and several other periods of light rain. Nice and cool. And still, very still all day. I heard on the radio that it was 90 degrees in Fayetteville. I got up and looked, and it was 69 degrees here at the time.

A bright burst of yellow streaked across the meadow and broke the visual silence. It was one of those "flying sunflowers" as I have come to call them, a goldfinch. He went down into the wildflowers, then flew back up onto a branch. I put the scope on him, and he was almost entirely yellow, only a few patches of black on his head and wings.

A lawyer from Little Rock called and wanted to know if I would testify in a civil suit against a company that built a golf course and messed up a pristine mountain stream. I would be an expert witness as to the value of that clear, wild water, and what it meant for it to be destroyed. Hum.

Later in the day I was awakened from a nap on the couch by an eerie feeling. Couldn't quite place it. When I looked over my shoulder, I knew what the deal was. Holy smokes! I felt like I had just walked into a grand cathedral! The clouds that had the mountain socked in all day were parting, and golden sunlight was filling the valley below. Rising steam clouds were everywhere, many backlit with rays punching holes through them. In the main valley, the clouds cast a shadow on the hillside they were floating next to. And up in the sky, oh my goodness, pure white thunderheads were stacked a mile high, and were crowded together in the back of that grand cathedral, listening to the sermon. I sat out on the deck with my jaw dropped for 30 minutes. And they say that you have to go to a fancy church and give money to a preacher in order to worship. They don't really know what The Almighty is.

After the incredible show out back I munched on a salad for dinner, then laced up my shoes and went for a hike. The stillness of the day continued in the woods. Not much was going on anywhere. Not even any bugs out. Well, there was this one pesky horse fly, but I liquefied him before he could do any damage. I wandered around a bit, and ended up heading towards the East Meadow just as the sun dipped below the trees. Things always seem to happen there. Like I always do, I slowed down and creeped to the edge of the meadow, trying to see if anyone was home. Son of a gun, there he was—black and cinnamon fur, and walking right down the path towards me! It was an old coon dog, thin as a dime. I just love those old hound dogs—they are always so friendly and happy to see ya. He seemed to be enjoying his walk too, and the cool day. We conversed a little, then he continued on his way.

Looked like the deer had been back in the garden, as there were several more melons eaten. No bear sign though. Lots of bats flying around, seemed like more than normal. I hoped they were getting fat on no-see-ums.

As I was about to leave the meadow a coyote down off in Dug Hollow started yipping. "Yip, yip, yip." It echoed through the hollow. These guys really have a high pitch voice. "Yip, yip." He was a long way off. "Yip." Then one answered that was very close, just off in the woods a few hundreds yards probably. The same high-pitched "yip, yip." I hadn't heard a coyote out here in some time, since last February I think. I love to hear them howling, or whatever that is they do after the yip. "Yip, yip. Hooowwl."

On the way back I stopped and picked some of the purple iron weed and wild sunflowers for the kitchen table that were growing in the power line right of way. They add a little color to the inside of the cabin, and make the place a tad more homey. I never know when a wonderful young lady will step out of the woods and knock on the front door, so I always want to be prepared with a handful of wildflowers nearby to hand her. Yippieeeeeee.

The starlight out back was just enough to illuminate Beagle Point. The rest of the canyon was engulfed in a fog bank that had settled in. Starlight is so soft, almost not there. Out in the open, you can see, but just barely. In the woods, forget it—dark as dark can be. I remember once trying to hike three miles back to my car at night with nothing but starlight to guide me. This was back in 1975 when I worked as a tour guide at Blanchard Cave. I had just delivered a church group to a wilderness campsite on the Sylamore Creek (I was the official forest service leader, and was even in uniform). It took a lot longer to get the group to camp because one of them was crippled, and the going was slow. Anyway, it was dark when I left their camp. I was not at all prepared for night travel, and didn't have a flashlight (nor a pack or any sleeping gear). I set off in the darkness confident that I could "smell" my way back to the car. Yea, right.

It was tough going, but I was able to feel my way along an old logging road for about half a mile, running into many trees in the process. When you hike in the dark through the woods, it is always a good idea to put your hands out in front of your face to keep any branches from poking you in the eyes. I soon realized that I would never make it up the mountain to my car, so I decided to lay down on the ground, curl up, and spend the night right where I was (I was wearing a short-sleeved shirt and long pants—I had nothing more). It typically got down into the low 50's at night, sometimes even lower, so I was not too comfortable. In the middle of the night I managed to gather up some small sticks and started a fire, then curled up next to it. I would sleep an hour or so, then would wake up, shivering, and would feel around and gather up enough sticks to get a small fire going again. Then I could curl up and sleep a little more, until the fire went out. It was a very long night, but I survived, and hiked out and made it into work at Blanchard Cave on time. Love that starlight!

8/14/98 Very hazy at daylight, 67 degrees, no wind. Only a few butterflies and that flying sunflower were stirring. The thick haze continued all morning. Another wonderful, cool August day in the Ozarks!

Bob and Dawna arrived at the cabin in the early evening, followed by Hete, Roy and Norma, and Mary and The Wildman. We all hung out on the back deck, sipping various delights, and waiting for the stars to come out. About 10pm we packed up and headed for the East Meadow. It was fabulous out, and the stars spread out across the wide open sky, gently illuminating the meadow with soft starlight. As soon as we got there a brilliant star streaked across the sky. To celebrate, we popped open a bottle of champagne and passed it around.

As the hours passed we saw many more shooting stars, drained several bottles of champagne, and generally enjoyed a delightful night under the blanket of shimmering lights. This was all part of the Perseid Meteor Shower that happens each year. We were not showered with hundreds of shooting stars per hour as some of us had seen in previous years, but there was enough of the amazing streaks to keep us happy. Even the owls enjoyed the show, hooting their approval off in the distance. All too soon, folks began to cool down, and we packed up and returned to the cabin. We should have all brought sleeping bags and slept out in the meadow, enjoying the stars all night. Mark that down for next year.

8/15/98 By sunrise the back deck was a buzz with conversation and sleepy guests enjoying the morning. The hummers were up too, providing a great deal of entertainment for all. There were many goldfinches down in the meadow, darting back and forth. The butterflies were out too, awing us all with their size and brilliant colors. One butterfly was entirely lime-green in color, looking a bit out of place. And Roy surprised everyone with a plate piled high with fresh baked blueberry biscuits, which disappeared in a hurry.

At first light everything was engulfed in fog. Gradually the scene before us changed, the fog moved around and lifted and retreated, and all of the ridges and valleys appeared, one by one. Another textbook morning at Cloudland.

Before noon everyone left except Roy, Norma and me (the only one with a valid excuse for leaving was Bob—he had to fly to Hawaii the next morning). The three of us left out for a short hike that lasted several hours. We hiked up the power line right of way, and discovered a *giant* mint plant, actually three of them. These plants were about five feet tall, and full of pale blooms. *These can't be mints!* But the square stems and very minty scent from the crushed leaves proved them to be just that. Wow, what a cup of tea you could make from these!

We dropped by the Woods cabin to check on their progress, then hiked on over to Eddy Silcott's land. He has really done a wonderful job of cleaning up this plot of hillside that had been carved out of the deep woods long ago. All of it was neatly mowed, and while he hasn't built anything to live in there yet, the cabin site is placed at the top of the bare bench land with a nice view out over Dug Hollow. There were several huge cowcumber trees there, each heavy with colorful fruit.

On the way back we admired a wonderful umbrella magnolia tree near the Woods cabin. This tree was growing right next to an old spring. Some of the branches hung right down next to the ground, and we were able to get a close-up look at the magnificent leaves. We also found a perfect black-eyed Susan wildflower in the North Meadow (well, I guess they are *all* perfect, but this one was especially so), then headed back to Cloudland.

All along our route we found pairs of butterflies chasing each other. It was difficult to tell if it was love, or aggression, or both. This was evident in the meadow below the back deck too. All day the butterflies were chasing each other, sometimes swirling round and round, up and up, often getting as high as the tree tops before either disappearing into the trees, or breaking away from each other and floating back down to the ground. It was always butterflies of the same species that were chasing each other, lending weight to the love theory. Once in a while there would be three of them chasing each other at the same time—hum.

It was a lazy afternoon. Roy decided to try out the new futon that I had installed in the office—he wasn't available for comment for a couple of hours, so it must have been OK. Norma read out on the back deck. It was a cool afternoon, with a light breeze.

Before long the second round of weekend guests began to arrive: Dean and Bonnie LaGrone, Hete, Beth Motherwell, Bob Chester, and Larry and Carrie Davis (Carrie was very well endowed and wearing a loose halter top, something that got Bob Chester's attention). The cabin was alive with chatter again. We marinated chicken, baked brownies, shucked sweet corn, and had a drink or two. It would prove to be another classic Cloudland feast, with everyone filling plate after plate (grilled chicken, sweet corn, Cloudland rice, fresh bread, Caesar salad). When it was all said and done, the biggest pile of corn cobs was on Norma's plate. Then it was time for dessert! Hete prepared banana splits (which we continued to consume the next day for breakfast and lunch and late afternoon snacks). Nuts, whipped cream, cherries, chocolate bits, French Vanilla ice cream, and oh yes, bananas.

Then someone put on a little dance music. The more the dancers danced and laughed and sweated, the more music they wanted. And the louder it got. I must say that from my seat in the office, it looked like we had some pretty darn good dancers out on the floor. And, shock of all shocks, I couldn't believe my eyes when *Bob Chester* got out on the dance floor! Now I have seen everything here (Was it Beth, or Carrie's *hooters* that got him out there?). I was eventually dragged out there myself, although I looked a little out of place because I had already put on my meteor watching clothes. Finally, the music died down, and all of us but Roy and Norma headed out for the meteor fields again (they stayed behind to create their own sparks).

The sky was even darker than the night before and therefore the stars brighter. It didn't take long for the stars to give us a grand show, and we saw more shooting stars in a given time period as well. No champagne though. It was another fine night in the meadow.

8/16/98 Larry and Carrie got up at sunrise, making some great coffee, and soon the back deck once again filled with conversation and hummers. It was a carbon copy of the morning before, with the fog doing its thing and providing breathtaking scenery. Beth, the resident bird expert, helped ID many birds, including the hummers, which she determined to be immature and female Ruby-throated ones. In fact, it is possible that most of them are from the same brood. We saw many more goldfinches, and one hawk that we think is a sharp-shinned hawk. Hete had heard screech owls and yellow-billed cuckoos the night before.

Breakfast was made up of odds and ends, including fresh baked muffins by Roy, and pastries from Carrie. Then Beth brought in a cold watermelon. As she was preparing to cut it open in front of the waiting mouths, she told how it had been specially selected the day before at the Farmer's Market in Fayetteville by the very farmer who grew it. There were a few groans as it rolled in half— overripe and inedible. Darn! It would later become bait in the wild hog trap at Williams Woods Nature Preserve.

Norma and Beth worked on a crossword puzzle. Norma and Roy were going to go home early just so that she could get the Sunday paper and work the puzzle, but Bob Chester had acquired said paper from Danny Woods who drove to Harrison to get it, and so Norma was able to stay at Cloudland for most of the day. It took them awhile, but finally they got the last word, and the puzzle was complete! I could not believe some of the words these folks knew.

The rest of the day was full of reluctant good-byes, and visits from other friends and neighbors. Oh yes, we had several rounds of banana splits too! The highlight of the afternoon was when a visitor messed up the telescope, causing it to later crash down onto the lower deck—a $500 telescope ruined. Also, I discovered that the screen on the deck door had been pushed in. All of this being normal wear and tear by guests—I guess that you just have to expect such things when folks visit. I must say, though, that my water conservation program and especially the "men pee outside" policy has been working, as the well has not run dry since a big party back in February. The conservation policies will continue.

There were a total of 31 guests and visitors to the cabin over the weekend. At times you could hardly make it across the front porch because there were so many coolers and pairs of shoes (no shoes allowed in the cabin).

The following poem was left at the cabin by one of my guests:

MORNING IN CLOUDLAND

I cannot see beyond my cabin door.
The river far below is in a shroud of ghostly fog,
wet fingers touch, explore the pines and rocks;
my home is in a cloud.

A bluebird in dripping pines awakes to shake her feathers,
to greet another dawn with carols;
here's the sun, and morning breaks,
and with the warmth, the heavy mist is gone.

A graceful blue-gray crane flies slowly to her treetop nest against a rocky ledge.
And I, like her, am perched high,
with a view of peaceful hills and trees,
at heaven's edge.

After everyone had left it was nice to walk into a clean kitchen—thanks to Beth and Norma. I had a dinner of leftover rice and cheese, and a fresh ear of corn. I had bought a gadget that cut the kernels off of the cob, and it worked flawlessly. Now I could enjoy corn the way my grandpa had taught me without having to work too hard at it.

After dinner everything was quiet and still outside, and having been cooped up in the cabin all day, I decided to go for a hike. With no particular agenda in mind, I put on my long pants and boots just in case I got into some heavy brush. I left the cabin and just sort of rambled through the woods, going wherever my interest took me.

Before long I found myself in the middle of a big flat area in the Dug Hollow drainage. I've been to this area many times before, and have always been amazed at how large and flat it is—what a perfect campsite, and I wondered if entire tribes of Indians had ever camped there before. It was in the Buffalo River wilderness, and heavily forested, but there wasn't much underbrush and you could see a long ways in all directions.

Out in the middle of the flat was a giant red oak tree, leaning at about a twenty degree angle. It really stuck out against all of the other trees. And it was really big—my arms around it barely made it halfway around the trunk. I decided that this tree was a lot like me—a bit abnormal and skewed just a little in the mainstream of life. I had become the butt of many jokes by my guests over the weekend, and so I was feeling a little out of place. But, just like this tree, I would struggle to remain firmly rooted in my landscape, and continue to grow and enjoy life.

The sun had gone down below the trees and the light in the forest was even with no shadows. This is the best light to be able to see the most detail, and I enjoyed wandering around looking at all there was to see. I had not been to this part of the wilderness in quite a while. The serene beauty of it all kept drawing me further and further into the wilderness. I dropped down through the bluffline at the only point for over a mile in either direction that a horse or mule could go down—this was actually part of a historical trail that connected the communities of Ryker and Mossville. The trail was no longer visible, but it was obvious that animals of all kinds were still using the break in the bluff.

I kept easing down the slope, exploring my back yard in the dim light. There was no breeze, no birds, no sound at all. And hardly any spiderwebs, which was nice. Before long I found myself at the bottom of the hill where Dug Hollow meets the Buffalo River. It was almost dry there, but a short walk upstream brought me to a big, deep pool. I knew this pool, and had been there many times. Bats played in the air above, and I lingered there until faint stars begin to show themselves. Stars? Oops.

Stars in the sky meant that the woods would be *dark*. I didn't have a flashlight, and the moon wouldn't be up until 2 or 3am, and even then the quarter moon wouldn't provide any illumination in the deep woods. It was a tough, steep climb back out to the cabin, and I doubted that I would have had an enjoyable trip in the dark. So I decided to make due where I was, and spend the night in the woods. In the back of my mind, while I was wandering further and further away and towards nighttime, I must have been thinking about that overnight stay on the ground in the woods back in the 1970's. I did want to move away from the river though, where it would be the coldest and buggiest. And I wanted to be next to my best friend.

I scrambled up the hillside to the level bench above and into the dark woods.

It was an easy, level walk to my destination, but it was very slow going, as I had to literally feel my way through the forest. The ground was soft at first, then got kind of rocky. That was good—I wanted to be in the rocks. It was tougher walking though, and I stumbled a time or two. The ground rose up some, then dipped down into a small ravine. Yes, that is what I wanted! In the bottom of this little ravine there was a bit of running water—water from a spring far up on the hillside. I got down on all fours, and sucked up the cold water from the gurgling liquid. I didn't bring a water bottle, so this was wonderful.

After I had my fill I stayed down on all fours, and crept up the opposite creek bank, which was a little steeper, but not too high. Once back on level ground, I searched with my hands and feet. It has to be here, somewhere close by. I couldn't see a thing. Then I found it, a pile of moss-covered rocks. I burst into tears. I had found my best friend in life, the grave of my faithful springer spaniel, Yukon. He and I had spent a thousand more times the amount of time in the woods together than anyone else I ever knew. I wanted to spend the night here, and converse with my old buddy, knowing that I would be safe and warm and happy.

The night was a long one, and very noisy—lots of summer bugs and owls and whippoorwills screaming. I didn't have any matches to start a fire, but I did bring a headnet, which proved to be invaluable as the bugs got a little pesky. I never really slept for long periods of time, but I did manage a bit of sleep now and then, in-between tossing and rolling and trying to get comfortable. The temperature couldn't have dropped below 60, but twice I did have to stand up and jog in place in order to warm up. But mostly I just laid there on the ground, curled up next to Yukon.

I did use a bit of wisdom garnered from John Muir's writings of more than a hundred years ago to help keep warm. I stuffed my shirt with dried leaves. Yep, natural insulation. It felt kind of strange, and was a little noisy when I rolled over, which I did quite a bit, but it seemed to work. The only real problem was that along with the dead leaves came a number of bugs, and I spent some time digging and scratching as the night wore on.

Once during the night all of the bugs got really quiet. That's not a good sign. It is a sure sign that something is approaching. Within moments I heard a rustling in the leaves. It got closer and closer. Try as I might, I couldn't figure out what it was. But it was larger than a squirrel. Closer and closer. It was coming down the hillside on a line right toward us. Finally, not wanting to get stepped on by a deer or a fox or a coyote (the subject of bears never came up in my mind—yea, right), I stood up and screamed. Probably scared the poor thing to death, whatever it was. It left the area in a hurry, making all kinds of racket in the process. All in all it wasn't a bad night, although I would have liked to have had a hooded sweatshirt and a bottle of water with me.

8/17/98 As daylight creeped into the forest I got up, stretched a little, bid Yukon a fond farewell, and headed up the steep hillside. I was a little chilled at first, and stiff, but that soon left me as the work of climbing warmed everything up. There were lots of spiderwebs out this time, and I kept the headnet on. While I was a little hungry, I wasn't empty enough to want bugs for breakfast. Man, it only seemed like minutes, but there I was, standing on top of the bluff and walking on the level towards the cabin.

As I sat out on the back deck sipping my Starbucks mocha the orange ball rose above the opposite hillside and flooded the valleys with sunshine—no fog at all, but it was hazy. Birds of all colors and sizes and sounds played in the meadow below, in the sky above, and out in the forest. The hummers were out in full force. And a breeze was bouncing around. It was nice to be home. It was great to spend the night with my old friend.

8/19/98 The sky was full of hummers soon after sunrise. It was very still out, no fog, but lots of haze. There were at least a dozen hummers buzzing around the back deck feeder. Often, there would be three of them feeding, with several others in a holding pattern above—reminded me of the Denver airport.

Lots of goldfinches out too. You can always tell when one of them is on a wild sunflower—the bird is so heavy that the flower swings back and forth. They would fly from flower to flower, feeding and playing and getting some good exercise. Then, without warning, one would fly up and over the treeline at the edge of the meadow, and head out into the grand canyon, getting smaller and smaller visually, then disappear completely. I have no idea where they are going, or why. They kind of sneak up the hillside through the trees, so they never make a grand entrance, but their exit is always interesting.

8/20/98 An orange ball hung in the hazy evening sky as I made my way to Cloudland. Several deer played in the meadows. I found a pleasant surprise in my mailbox—my very own copy of the **Newton County Times**, with a label showing a year's worth of them to come.

The sky grew black and the stars came out—more stars than I had seen out here in a long time. The Milky Way shone brightly. The air was dead still. And so were the night bugs. It was really quiet. I sat in the log swing sipping wine and listening to the stereo, then moved to the hammock on the lower deck—much better view of the night sky from there. And the night bugs came out in full force—I no longer needed the stereo for my music.

The city was beginning to drive me nuts, especially now with all of the U of A students and faculty returning for the fall semester, so escaping to Cloudland was more important than ever. And it was so much *cooler!* I could breathe easy once again.

8/21/98 One of the outside alarms went off at about 2:30am. I got up and looked around a little, but never saw anything. I hoped that it was just a deer or something, and not another bear sniffing around. I went out onto the lower back deck, the one with the good view of the sky, and was nearly knocked down by the brightness of the dark sky (does that make sense?). What can you do but stand there and stare up into the heavens in awe.

I didn't pay too much attention to the sunrise, only rolling over to escape the light and going back to sleep. I didn't realize that right outside my window was one of the most incredible views ever! I happened to glance down into the valley, and saw a solid cloud bank hugging the river bottom, blue sky above, and no haze in the air at all. It hadn't been like this in a while. I jumped up and landed down on the back deck in a hurry. Wow, what a sight! These were real clouds down there, not just the fog or mist. And it all was still thick and tight, even an hour after sunrise. The ridges on the east side of the canyon were silhouetted and black, while the ones on the west side were lit by the full glory of the morning sun. It was a great contrast, with the sea of clouds between them. The temp was a cool 66 degrees.

Before long the clouds began to move as the rays warmed them. They were awake and dancing to the tune of the sun! This went on for about fifteen minutes. Then, all of a sudden, the clouds began to disappear. Within ten minutes they were all gone, and only a faint haze remained. I guess the temperature or humidity reached just the right spot. Or the clouds had urgent business, and were beamed elsewhere. Either way, it was an impressive sight.

The meadow below was filled with busy goldfinches, perhaps 25 or 30 of them, and it seemed like every bush and wild sunflower was moving, though there was no breeze at all. In contrast there were no butterflies to be seen, and only one pair of hummers. The hummers were probably all elsewhere looking for food—they had drained the feeder the day before, and I had just hung up a new batch. I guess they lost hope when it went dry and flew elsewhere. The pair that was there this morning seemed more interested in each other than in eating anyway.

I spent most of the morning working on our hiking club's newsletter. At one point the silence was shattered when one of my outdoor alarms screamed. Someone was coming down the road. She looked really funny, waddling right down the middle of the road—a wild turkey hen! She was all by herself. I went out to join her for a short stroll, and was amazed at how much of the forest floor was turning colors. The poison ivy is just beautiful right now—red and orange and gold. Mostly bright red. It covers the ground and climbs the hillside, spreading brilliant color.

Lunch was had out on the back deck in the porch swing. The hummingbird feeder is just three feet away from the swing. About halfway through my rice and veggies, a tiny hummer landed on the feeder and began to feed. I just sat there, motionless. This little guy really sucked a lot of juice. When I raised my arm to load another fork full, he jumped up and flew away. But he came right back. And this time, he wasn't interested in the sugar water—he wanted to see what I was all about. At first, he was two or three feet away from me, hovering in the air staring me right in the face. He would jerk over about a foot, then hover and stare some more. He made a series of these moves, each time moving just a little to the right, and getting in a little closer. By the time he had made a complete revolution around me, he was only a foot from my face! It was really strange being watched so closely by such a noisy wild creature. I was hoping that my ears didn't look like flowers. Wow, could you imagine what life would be like if hummers were blood suckers? Yikes! All of a sudden, an adult hummer came flying up and crashed into the little one that was watching me, and they both flew off. None returned for about ten minutes. Then everyone in the whole forest showed up—it was business as usual at the feeder, with a dozen or more of the little guys feeding and chasing and bouncing off of each other.

By mid-afternoon it was hot outside, with a good breeze, and lots of speedy butterflies. They weren't really feeding, but rather flying frantically from one side of the meadow to another. I wondered if they had eaten all of their food in the flowers and were looking for more? Is that possible? I dunno. They looked like butterflies on a mission of some sort.

And the soaring birds were out in full force too, playing in the wind currents. Someone said that the sun warmed the air in the open space, and created updrafts, which is one reason why the soaring birds come in so close. Today they came so close and fast that you could actually hear them rushing by.

After a nap, more work at the computer, and some salad for dinner, I went on out for another ramble in the woods. This time I wouldn't be leaving the top of the mountain. I worked my way around through the woods and up to the East Meadow. As I was walking through the upper end of it, I saw a flash of black. Oh no, another darn bear!!! Yep. When I first saw him, he was milling around at the edge of the garden. Then he disappeared below the brushline. I crept a little closer, and found him rolling in the dirt! The dirt was rather dry, and he was really kicking up a cloud of dust. I'll bet that this bear was at my cabin early this morning and was what had set off the alarm. This guy was coal black, and pretty big—he had small ears. I hadn't seen him before. His coat was shining brightly in the evening sun. A very deep black.

The wind was blowing from me towards the bear so I knew that I would soon be discovered. I bent down and settled into the brush, trying to stay out of sight. Sure enough, before long he stopped his rolling, stuck his big nose into the air sniffing, then stood up on his hind legs, and looked straight at me. I was about a hundred feet away. Having a tiny hummingbird staring at me from close range was one thing, but having this giant mammal doing it from even a hundred feet away was something altogether different. The hair on my neck stood straight up, and a chill went down my spine. I hoped that he could see me well enough to realize that I was not a giant corn cob. In a flash he was down on all fours and bounded off across the meadow and into the woods. It only took him about three seconds to reach the woods! I breathed a big sigh of relief.

The bear had been in the garden for a while, and had knocked down and eaten most of the remaining corn. I wondered why they don't have a lot of bears in Iowa? It didn't appear that he had bothered any of the melons, a couple of which were getting rather large.

I continued my hike and made it to Bob's cabin, just to check on things and to see if the bear had been there—he hadn't. I discovered a peach tree along the way—found fresh pits on the path, and looked up to find a tree full of them. They weren't quite ripe enough to eat yet, but you can bet that I will keep my eye on them. The pawpaw fruit is beginning to get fragrant, and it is wonderful to walk past them.

I made my way back to the East Meadow and sat down against a young dogwood tree in the upper end. I could see most of the meadow from that spot, and wanted to see if the bear would come back for more corn, or more dirt. The sun had already gone down below the treeline, and it would soon be getting dark. There weren't any bugs out, which surprised me a little, and there was a light breeze blowing. Lots of bats were out though, dancing all over the sky, and would eat over a thousand insects each before going back to bed. I sat in the meadow until I could see the first star come out. *Star light, star bright, first star I see tonight. I wish I may, I might, have the wish I wish tonight...* My wish was that I wouldn't be eaten by the bear on the way back through the dark woods to the cabin. It was a very pleasant little "sit" in the meadow. The bear never came back, nor ate me on the way home.

Back at the cabin it was time for me to begin a new book, so I sat down and opened another fat one, the 800+ page **Comanche Moon**, a novel that set up the early years of **Lonesome Dove**, which is my all-time favorite mini-series. The people in that series are so real, and the actors so perfect for their roles. The Wildman gave me the new book.

The novel quickly sucked me in, and before long it was midnight. Since much of the book is about Indians, and their customs and beliefs, I got to thinking, thinking about the bear in the East Meadow. I decided that I wanted to soak up as much of the bear's spirit as I could, so I packed some stuff up and headed back to the East Meadow to spend the night.

8/22/98 The sky and clouds were breathtaking, dark and bright at the same time. It was the dark of the moon, so the darkness would continue all night. The view was spectacular. I laid back on my pad in the tall grass and stared at the universe. Before long a number of meteors shot across the sky, followed by more, and more. It was a much better shower than we had either night last weekend, partly because there was no haze and the sky was clearer. Each one was awesome!

I didn't really expect to see the bear in the meadow this night, in fact it would be better if I *didn't* see him in the dark, but being there, right in the middle of his feeding grounds, put me closer to his spirit (can a living thing have a spirit—sure it can, I've got lots of spirit, and I'll bet that you do too). The starlight lit up the meadow enough that I probably could have seen a big black bear, but I tried not to look.

The air was sweet, and cool, and the screech and barred owls and whip-poowills were out in full force. So were the night bugs, singing loudly. I laid on my back and tried to sleep, but it was tough, with all of the night music and the stars. Before I knew it, I woke up to bright sunshine in my eyes, and was covered with dew. Guess I did get to sleep after all, since it had been light for over an hour. No sign of Mr. Bear, although I did feel a little closer to him.

I spent most of the day back at the cabin, laying on the couch or out in the swing, reading about Gus and Woodrow and Clara and Maggie and Buffalo Hump. Love this stuff. My only break was to watch the hummers fighting at the feeder. There was one ten minute period—I actually timed it—where there were three hummers at the feeder, chasing each other off, and none of them ever got a single drink in all that time. And all three of them had their own feeding station. I don't understand them—why would they spend so much time bothering with each other and not eating a thing themselves? Most things in nature make sense, but these hummers sure don't to me.

It was sunny and hot outside with a steady breeze. No one came by the cabin all day. Not even any wild turkeys. Lots of soaring birds out.

Long about suppertime I downed a bowl of salad, then decided to head back up to the East Meadow and do a little bear watching. I took the book, of course. Down in the tall grass on my pad, I would read a page, scan the meadow for movement, then read another page. An hour went by. Then two. Just me and the book and the meadow.

As the sun turned gold and began to dip below the treeline, the shadows grew and stretched across the meadow. The colors at first were brilliant reds and oranges, then softened gradually with the progress of the shadows. Once the sun was gone, the horizon glowed pink and orange and yellow. The meadow glowed with the same colors, though much more muted. I absolutely *love* this time of day!

I caught some movement out of the corner of my eye, over at the far end of the meadow. It wasn't black. It was a deer. A very large buck stepped into the meadow, and was looking nervously in my direction—I'm sure he could smell me—the wind was swirling around. I got out the binocs and looked him over good. He had a very impressive rack, still in velvet. I counted ten points, and the tines were very tall. His rack was very tall too, sticking way up there. This was not the monster buck that I had seen a couple of times before, but a trophy none the less. Another buck stepped out behind him. This one was an eight pointer, but his antlers were bare, no velvet at all—a little early in the season for that to have happened. Both deer stomped and froze and flicked their tails, then repeated, each time coming a step further into the meadow.

A third buck stepped out behind them, and this guy was the largest of all, another trophy rack, still in velvet. He too had ten points, but the rack was much taller than the first one, and the tines were more impressive too. Still not the big monster from before, but probably larger than any buck besides him that I had ever seen in the wild in Arkansas. Wow, three big bucks in the same meadow, right there in front of me, all nervous. They came a little closer, and were near the melon patch—I'll bet these guys were the ones doing all of the melon eating! But they were more interested in me this day than in melons. They came closer, and closer, each stomping, and freezing and flicking their tail. They were looking right at me, but since I was so hidden in the tall grass, they couldn't quite make me out clearly. They strained their necks to see. "Who are you? What are you? And what are you doing in our meadow?" My heart pounded—I think they could probably hear it. I began to sweat. There sure was a lot of wildlife looking at me this weekend.

The breeze must have blown directly from me to them, because all of a sudden all three of the deer jumped up and landed facing the opposite direction, and within seconds disappeared into the woods. A spooked deer can cover more ground in a second than any other wildlife that I have ever seen. It took me a while to recover and to get back into my book again. I had decided to spend a second night in the meadow, so I brought my sleeping stuff with me, and a bottle of water (sitting next to my bottle of wine!). The stars came out, and the hoot owls, and I lay back and began another night of star gazing, soaking up more bear spirits.

8/23/98 I must have been in deep sleep, because I couldn't figure out what had woke me up at first. Then I remembered—it was a wolf howl. What? We don't have any wolves in the Ozarks. I must have been dreaming and got the wolf howl from the book. Then a second howl nearly knocked me back against the pad—this was no dream, and the sound was close, probably right at the edge of the meadow. But was it a wolf, or just a coyote? It was a howl and not a yip, but coyotes howl too. I was still half asleep, and couldn't think and process the sound very clearly. Then there was a third howl—I was sitting up and looking right across the meadow towards the sound this time. A wolf? A coyote? My brain was still scrambled. It sounded exactly like a wolf howl, and they don't sound anything like a coyote. But then, it didn't, not exactly. I shivered at the possibility—not that I would be afraid of a wolf, because that wouldn't be any cause for concern—but because it would be an incredible happening! But I wasn't sure, and there were no more howls. Whatever it was just wanted to wake me up and let me know that it was out there, then it wandered off.

It took me a *long* time to get back to sleep—over a dozen shooting stars worth of time, whatever that was. The night sky was simply incredible.

I got up at first light this time, covered again with dew, and hiked back to the cabin. The wind was blowing pretty good, and I had to steady myself to keep the log swing from blowing around too hard. I was more than halfway through the book, and read on steadily, almost all day. There were lots of soaring birds out again, including several red-tailed hawks. And lots of hummers making all kinds of noise. I no longer consider them to be very smart birds—they waste so much energy fighting each other when there is plenty for all.

By late afternoon I finished the book—I've never read so much in my entire life as I have this summer—four giant books! I guess the air out here at Cloudland is having a positive effect on me. The wind continued to blow. I ate another salad, then returned to my meadow bear-spotting post. And I took another book along, a much smaller one this time, and read a few chapters as the evening shadows turned into darkness. No bear, no deer, only owls and whippoorwills. And a few mosquitoes.

Once the first stars came out I packed up and headed back to the cabin. Heter was bringing by two folks from out-of-state to drink a beer on my back deck, so I felt obliged to join them. Hete has quickly become known as a crack real estate seller, and people from many states are flying in to have him show them property. He has been showing a lot of property.

This couple (actually brother and sister) was looking for the perfect spot for a get-a-way home for their family. They were high class and well-groomed, and wanted Hete to introduce them to some writers. I was the only one that he could think of on short notice, and I'm not really much of a writer, but I had a good view and cold beer. Their family owned an island somewhere, and a house in Florida, and no telling how many others. They were typical of many folks these days wanting to get away from the rat race and relocate in the Ozarks. Very impressive people these two were, delightful company, and I hoped they found a good spot here. We all saw two shooting stars from the deck.

After a long weekend of reading and bear-spirit gathering I was worn out and retired early, this time to my own bed in the loft. I laid on the side of the bed next to one of the windows where I could see the night sky. The outside alarm went off three times—probably was the bear coming to see why I wasn't up in his meadow. I thought that I heard heavy footsteps on the deck a couple of times, but didn't bother to get up and investigate.

8/24/98 Daylight came early today—clear, no haze or fog, nice breeze blowing. I didn't have any more Starbucks mocha at the cabin, and it is still too warm for hot chocolate, so I sat out on the back deck and sipped ice cold water for break-fast. The butterflies had returned, and were busy milking the wild sunflowers again—a great sight to see. In the past, there have been great numbers of three or four different varieties in the meadow below, but today there were probably a dozen different species, and they were scattered all over the meadow, staying close to the ground because of the wind.

The wind may have kept the hummers grounded too because there were hardly any of them out at all. But there were lots and lots of soaring birds riding the wind currents. I guess having a warm day with lots of wind is like the carnival coming to town for the soaring birds!

I spent the rest of the morning at the computer writing the Journal, working on the OHTA newsletter, answering e-mail. All too soon it was time to leave, and I reluctantly shut everything down and headed back to the hot, noisy and crowded place they call civilization.

8/28/98 There was a great deal of activity down in the meadow when I returned to the cabin. Mostly from flying sunflowers chasing each other. Man, they can really get up some speed as they scream through the tall flowers and low bushes! And I don't know if they were running into the plants, or it was from the wake of their passing air current, but the flowers and bushes were really swaying back and forth. The air was dead still—no breeze at all.

There were also other species of birds chasing each other (females perhaps?). And two squirrels that were making quite a ruckus. I've not seen too many squirrels out here around the cabin. I wonder if they were scared away from all of the construction commotion last summer? One of these two seemed to have romantic intentions on his mind. Later, I saw one of the squirrels dangling from the bottom of a large, horizontal tree limb, hanging on for dear life. I always laugh when walking through the woods and a squirrel hits the ground with a big thud in front of me, having missed a limb and fallen out of a tree above. They always look rather surprised and embarrassed as they scurry off in the leaves. How come it is when a wild animal or bug falls a great distance (relative to their body size) that they never get injured? Is it simply because their body weight is so light that the impact is less? Heck, when a human falls a few feet lots of things smash.

The day was cloudy but the air was clear. There were a number of trees already turning fall colors down along the river—probably sweet gums. I saw a number of other trees on my drive in that were turning brilliant colors—lots of black gums and dogwoods. I'll bet that I heard twenty people say this week that we were going to have a horrible fall, and no color at all. I love to hear people say that, because they are almost always wrong. I think we are going to have a fantastic fall! And the trees that are turning now are already showing some great colors. I prefer to put my stock in the trees instead of people who don't know what they are talking about.

Just before sunset the clouds began to break up. Bright sunshine flooded the valleys below, and lit up the hillsides. Several different tiny birds took turns perching on the old dead snag at the edge of the meadow where the soaring birds usually have their meetings.

There weren't any hummers out—they had drained the feeder and had gone off to seek other nourishment. I filled it immediately, and I'm sure they will return soon.

The blues show on KUAF is now bouncing off the cabin walls, and soft warm light is filtering in through the trees from the setting sun. And *wow*, there is one heck of a light show going on up in the sky outside—a ton of brightly-colored clouds against blue sky—first pink, then orange, then blood red. Just another typical Cloudland sunset.

After the show died down, a friend from Little Rock arrived—Janice Rogers. She claims to have read every word of this Journal (How could any human endure such torture?), but this was her first visit to the cabin. I had been installing a new zip drive into my Mac when she arrived, and I met her at the front door with a small flashlight in my mouth, and told her that I would begin my hosting duties as soon as I had put all of the computer guts back, and cleaned up my mess. After the proper spirits were poured, we conversed for a number of hours (way past my bedtime), and watched an absolute black sky sparkle with a million diamonds.

8/29/98 I rolled over to see an orange ball through the trees rise in the eastern sky. By the time I made it out onto the back deck, both the sun and Janice had been up for a while. A number of birds and butterflies were up too, making their rounds through the wildflowers and celebrating the morning.

We had toasted blueberry bagels and pasta salad and tea and all kinds of stuff all day long. The birds really put on a show, and we spent hours and hours studying their fun through the binocs. There were a lot of soaring birds out, including many hawks—as many as five overhead at the same time. Most of the hawks were red-tailed, but there were a couple of Cooper's hawks out too. In fact, we would see these hawks off and on all weekend.

A nighthawk danced up high in the sky and looked a little out of place in the middle of the day. And a pair of pileated woodpeckers flew through the meadow, in formation. One of them veered off and landed on the snag, then quickly followed the other one up towards the Crag.

There were a number of yellow butterflies that came swooping down from high in the trees. Some of them would drop like a rock until just before they got down into the brush, then they would level off and begin to explore the sunflowers. Others would come out of the treetops and zigzag in wide streaks on down to the flowers. They were quick, and not as large or brilliant as the tiger swallowtails that dominated the sunflower patches. But it was interesting to watch their fall. I looked them up in the ID book and discovered that they were cloudless sulphur butterflies (and an e-mail to my butterfly expert, Lori Spencer from the Ozark Natural Science Center confirmed this).

There were lots of butterflies of all kinds working the meadow all day. The tiger swallowtails seemed larger than usual—as big as my hand. I think they are really getting some good grub out of those wild sunflowers, and are growing to monster size.

The hummers did return, but only one or two at a time. And there were almost no fights at the feeder. I guess the rest of them found greener pastures. There was one pair of them that landed on a dead twig right out in front of our perch. Janice and I both had our binocs trained on them. The tiny birds scooted along the branch towards each other, then leaned forward and touched the tips of their long beaks, and held them there for a few seconds—a hummer kiss! It was a delightful moment at Cloudland.

We spent most of the day with the binocs in hand—more time looking through magnified glass than I had ever spent before. And while I know that my little armored Bushnell binocs aren't the greatest, they did a great job. We got to be included visually in many remarkable moments of acrobatics and glee up in the sky. Before we knew it, we looked up and it was 4pm. Good grief, it felt like we had just sat down for morning coffee!

4pm on a hot summer Saturday afternoon? Must be time to go swimming! We packed up and headed down the ladder trail. The river was the lowest that it has been all summer—hardly even flowing at all. But the good old swimming hole was still deep, long, and the water was just about perfect. The sun had gone down enough so that the pool was completely shaded. I swam a little, then laid back in the water against a warm rock, while Janice explored the water world. The water temperature was the most perfect temperature—just delightful!

When we were up at the cabin we had noticed a number of trees down along the river that had begun to turn fall colors. The only ones that we could find were beeches—that's right, beeches turning to crimson and red and in August! That was a little strange. The root system of one of the beeches that was growing right in the stream bank didn't have much soil around its base—we thought that perhaps the trees weren't getting enough water, and were turning color as a cry for help. I'll bet they survive and continue to provide a great deal of pleasure in the wilderness for a long time to come.

The upper, shallow pool, felt more like a bathtub rather than a pristine mountain stream. And it felt great! While we were in that pool, one of the smaller hawks flew down the stream towards us, then landed in a leaning tree just ahead. It sat there for about five minutes, and I was able to move over and get some binocs out of Janice's daypack and give him a good look-see. Nice bird. I hadn't seen too many hawks flying low along the river before.

There was a boulder out in the middle of the pool that had obviously been the resting spot for a great blue heron or some other large bird—there was a huge blob of white at the top of the boulder, and it had run all the way down the face of the large rock. He must have been using the rock as a fishing dock.

It was another splendid visit to the river and all too soon we headed out of the valley and up the hill. Sometimes this steep old historical trail is a real tough climb, but other times it isn't too bad. Both of us noted later that we hadn't broke a sweat until we reached the bluffline. When I looked at the weather station, I saw that the humidity was only 40%. Nice and dry, yea!

Janice kept saying that she was a novice when it came to hiking, but she seemed as comfortable out in the woods as anyone, and I never bothered to worry about her. She is the vice-president of TAOWN—Todays Arkansas Outdoor Womens Network. This is one great group of women, mainly from the Central Arkansas area, but they have members in other parts of the state as well, and I suspect their numbers will grow steadily. They do all kinds of outdoor recreation things, like hiking, canoeing, hunting, fishing, and on and on.

Norma and Roy arrived at the cabin later and I made Cloudland pizza—a double batch. It took a long time to do the pizza, and we set a new record by eating very late. We stayed up and enjoyed the night air for another hour or two. There was a screech owl making his weird noise out on the other side of the meadow below. And a few falling stars even lit up the sky.

"Come look at this!" I heard from the back deck. It was a great one. The nearly-half-moon was setting, and if you stood down on the steps or out by the waving bear you could get a clear look at it. It was a huge moon, deep gold in color, moving rapidly down into the trees. Everything was dead still and quiet for a few seconds. We all held our breaths. Then it was gone. A great moonset!

8/30/98 A coyote woke me up with a single long yip. The sun wasn't up yet, but it was light outside. Another long yip. Not quite a howl. The coyote was either down on the bench below the cabin and back to the north some, or across the valley somewhere—it was hard to tell exactly where. That's all there was—two long yips. Then silence. I rolled over and went back to sleep. Nice doggie.

Soon the cabin below came to life and the back deck became active with conversation, laughter, hummers, and coffee. I heard Norma in the kitchen and wondered why she was up so early (she sleeps late when we let her). It was almost 9:30! I guess it is OK for the host to sleep in once in a while.

It was a little breezy and simply wonderful outside all morning. Soaring birds were out all over the place. Although sometimes they would disappear and the sky would be clear. Then a few minutes later there would be six buzzards flying out in front of us. And these guys were having a great time. They were riding the warming air currents like amusement rides. It was amazing how all they had to do was bend their wings down a little, sometimes just curling their wings inward, and they would change direction, or gain elevation. And they were doing a lot of dive-bombing, both down into the air, and at each other—looked more like eagles than buzzards.

Still no large numbers of hummers out. Those that were here seemed to spend most of their time sitting in the trees, instead of at the feeder. We noticed that they always perched on dead branches, sometimes very small ones. It had to be a dead branch or twig. I wonder why?

The afternoon temperature began to rise, the river called out, and soon we were on the trail down to the swimming hole. As we approached the river bank, a flock of ducks flew up right in front of us and disappeared into the woods. First time for seeing ducks down there. And the gravel bar (actually it is full of stones, larger than gravel, but I didn't know what to call it) was covered with small sycamore trees—a hundred of them or more. They were sprouting up everywhere! These little trees are funny looking—they are only a foot or two tall, but their leaves are as large as any in a mature tree.

The water wasn't as warm as it had been the day before, but it was a wonderful swim just the same. Norma and Janice explored downstream and Roy and I guarded the deep pool. Lots of minnow schools and small bass around.

Realizing that I had been growing a bit wide at the mid-section I carried a regular backpack down to the river, loaded with a couple of tents and other stuff for weight. I have decided that I am going to make at least one trip down to the river every day with the loaded backpack—a couple of times when I am here all day—in hopes of shedding some of the built-up Cloudland pizza and desserts. It was hot. I nearly died. But at least the humidity was low, and I never even got soaked on the way up. The gauge said 28% humidity—man, that was low!

On the way up Norma and Janice grabbed a limb from one of the small trees above the bluff that was turning brilliant red. No one knew what kind of tree it was, and I was determined to figure it out using our tree ID book. Norma keyed it out in the book—it was a black gum tree. This is normally the very first tree to turn in the fall, usually in late September. I guess it is going to be an early fall in the Ozarks this year.

We spent another couple of hours out on the back deck recovering from the hike up, keying the tree branch, and enjoying the evening light that was slowly creeping into the valleys below. Oh yea, the beer was *very* cold! Before long my weekend guests cleaned up the kitchen, loaded their trucks, and headed back to civilization in a cloud of dust.

The low sun was producing red streaks in the forest so I put my walking shoes back on and went on my usual Sunday evening ramble. I worked my way up the hill to the edge of the East Meadow, passing a dozen more of the black gum trees that were in full fall dress. The tall grass was glowing. I crept into the meadow, and found the three big bucks stomping around in the watermelon patch. They hadn't seen me, and the wind was still. I sat down in the grass, slowly, and watched them. These were obviously the same three bucks that I had seen here before. They were the watermelon raiders all right, and they were cleaning up the patch right in front of me. I didn't have a real good view, sitting down on the ground in the tall grass, but I could see those huge racks on two of them bobbing up and down, still in velvet. Then the wind picked up a little, and they scented me and immediately turned away and bounded off. I will never get used to watching whitetail deer in the wild. Especially ones with such impressive racks as these.

I examined the watermelon patch, or what was left of it. The only melons still there were a couple that were covered with fencing. There seemed to be fresh deer tracks on every other square inch of soil in the garden (although they didn't go into the corn patch area—the bear did leave a few stalks, even some with corn on them).

On the way over to the Faddis place I passed a section of pawpaw trees—the fragrance was very sweet. I had shorts on, tennis shoes and no socks, and while I could see the trees off in the bushes, the underbrush was so thick that I didn't venture over to them to inspect the fruit. I was delighted to find this patch of pawpaws on *my* property—hadn't found any before. The patch was near the peach tree, which had no peaches left on it at all. I'd return for the pawpaws another day.

The new ***Buffalo River Wilderness*** picture book of mine and William McNamara's work that has been overseas at the printer is finished. I made arrangements to drop off some copy transparencies and the book pages at Milancy McNamara's house tomorrow—it was strange having a local phone conversation tonight with someone out here (both Milancy and Bill live near Cloudland). That is sure one fine book, and I look forward to doing a little book promotion touring this fall and winter.

The hour is late. The night air is terrific. I'm going to go out and visit with the moon some, then shut down another fine weekend at Cloudland.

8/31/98 It was a very still and quiet morning when I rolled out of bed at sunrise. The little meadow below was filled with goldfinches, but they were mostly feeding on the wildflowers, and not flying around too much. There were a lot of them, perhaps the most that I have ever seen out here before. One hummer came over and hovered right in my face, then flew off. None at the feeder. I guess they are still mad at me. The woodpeckers were out in full force, and their drummings could be heard coming from every distant hillside. This is somehow a comforting sound.

Then I heard it. Oh my God, it was so clear, and loud, and there was no question where it came from or who made it. The sound echoed across the entire wilderness. A *wolf*. I don't care that the Game and Fish Commission says there are none in Arkansas—they have been very wrong in the past. This was a wolf. No question about it. I know what a wolf sounds like. He let out an incredible howl, and kept at it, changing pitch and adjusting volume. It was beautiful music. And he was right across the valley, over on Beagle Point. The sound was crystal clear. And loud! Wow, I was stunned and overjoyed and breathless. It was perhaps the most important moment at Cloudland so far. A wolf is the ultimate sign of true wilderness. A wolf is the heart and soul of wilderness. A wolf is something very, very special.

After what seemed like a full minute a couple of coyotes up on a hill overlooking Whitaker Creek opened up with yips and yells and howls of their own, answering the wolf. It was like a baby crying during an opera. The wolf immediately stopped, and I never heard another word from him again. Damn coyotes.

Wow, what an incredible start to the week (today is Monday). And a great end to a wonderful August at Cloudland. In the past I have always shied away from Arkansas during the summer, spending my time escaping the heat in the mountains in the West. But now I have not only survived the hot and humid summer here, but have really *enjoyed* it. I will continue to visit the high mountains in Colorado, Wyoming and Montana during the summer, but I won't be running *away* from Arkansas—I like it here, I *love* it here, I will always call it my home, and now I genuinely look forward to next summer at Cloudland!

August rain was 1.3 inches, low 66 degrees, high 93 degrees, wind 23mph

SEPTEMBER 1998

9/1/98 It was very black in the shadows but quite light in the moonlit areas when I arrived at the cabin late. A light breeze was blowing, and the summer bugs were singing proudly. I was exhausted from a long day in the city, and all I could do was collapse into the hammock out on the lower deck and drift off with the moon. Several hours later, a barred owl woke me—he was somewhere very close, and was trying to get my attention. It was darker than I had remembered it being when I went to sleep. Oh yea, the moon. I got up and looked to the west—there it was, a pure white three-quarter moon dropping behind the distant hilltop. Thanks Mr. Owl, for alerting me to this incredible sight!

9/2/98 I finished the night up in the loft and slept in late. A weird sound woke me up—this time it was no hoot owl. I got up and ran outside and found a small, noisy helicopter hovering right over the meadow! It was so low that the prop wash was moving the wild sunflowers around. I studied the pilot through the binocs, and saw that it was a woman, and it looked like she was smiling. I waved. She waved back, hovered another moment, then turned away and flew off down into the valley. She followed the river upstream, remaining just barely above tree level. I sat down and watched her through the binocs until she disappeared around the bend four miles away. Only then did I realize that I was stark naked! I wondered if she had been smiling in approval at what she had seen, or laughing hysterically?

This was going to be a day to work on the new ***Buffalo River Wilderness*** slide show. Picking the slides was easy—I am going to use all of the images in the new picture book. But the tough part was going to be selecting the music to go along with them. The images will be wonderful, but it will take the right music to make the show a great one. I want tears from the audience. The music has to be right.

I spent most of the day and long into the night plowing through dozens of CD's, listening to each note, trying to come up with four or five perfect pieces of music. The ones that struck me got played over and over and over again, and I was often seen dancing and humming and tapping my feet to the rhythm. Every now and then I would stand next to the window and let the music flow over and through me while I soaked up the view outside. I took a couple of breaks during the day when Bob and Benny dropped by for a visit, and then when Milancy and I went over some of the details of the upcoming book tour and slide show schedule. Billy McNamara will be with me for many of the programs, but I will be doing most of them myself. I look forward to having him along when possible—he is one great artist!

9/3/98 Sometime in the early morning hours I turned off the stereo and wandered down onto the lower deck. *Wow!* The moonlit wilderness in front of me was nothing short of incredible. I'm not sure what it is exactly, but moonlight is just very special. It has a certain quality of light about it, unlike anything else you will ever see. It was quiet, with a slight breeze, and an owl or two hooting off in the distance. The night sky was very bright—I could hardly see any stars. But while I sat there in the hammock for thirty minutes, I saw three shooting stars! These guys must have been *really* bright to show up in such a light sky! I firmly believe that the more time that you spend out in the moonlight the happier you will be. I spend a lot of time in the moonlight.

After a few hours of rest I went down and greeted the new day from my usual spot out on the back deck. It was clear out, and the delicate orange sunlight bathed the tops of all the ridges, then turned yellow and finally white as it made its way down into the deepest valleys. There were a few hummers out, and lots of butterflies. The radio said that it was going to be between 95 and 100 degrees in town today—I just had to laugh.

Once my Starbucks mocha and yogurt were gone I cranked up the stereo and continued my search for the perfect music. I had found four of the five songs that I wanted the night before, but still needed one more. I put all of the selected CD's together and listened to the order over and over, assembling certain images and title slides fading into one another in my mind. Yes, the music was coming along, and this was going to be one terrific slide show! That fifth song was going to be an illusive one. Several were picked, but just didn't work out right. I typed up and printed out the title slides, and listened to more CD's (I've collected about 140 of them over the years). Still no perfect song for the number three slot—I had the first, second, fourth and last songs matched up.

Then I caught a movement out of the corner of my eye—it was the shadow of a butterfly on one of my office mini-blinds. He flew back and forth. I believe he was trying to tell me that it was time to put away the music for now and come out and play. Hey, it's not a good idea to argue with a butterfly! So I shut down the computer and put on my walking shoes, then slipped away into the forest. You can do that at Cloudland, anytime that you want.

9/5/98 The moon was just above the ridgetop at sunset, climbing rapidly into the sky. It was sort of a pale orange, not too bright, but very moon-like just the same. It was *huge!* A harvest moon perhaps—one day away from full. I sat in the back porch swing, sipped a little wine, and watched as the wilderness dimmed, then lit up once again with the moonlight. It was warm, in fact it had been the warmest day of the entire year (95 degrees), but the wind was blowing at 15-20 mph, and it felt nothing short of wonderful.

Moonlight conjures up thoughts of romance and adventure. Well, there was no romance to be found this weekend at Cloudland, but I sure could create some adventure. At least a little Cloudland adventure. I laced up my hiking boots and headed out into the night for a hike. The first thing that I noticed as I made my way through the woods was that there were *no* spiderwebs! What a pleasure it was to walk without eating spiders all along the way.

The wind hadn't penetrated the woods, and there weren't any critters out that I could detect, which made it very quiet out. The shadows created by the bright moon were filled in somewhat with reflected moonlight, so it was easy to wander around without a flashlight. It was sort of like those old movies that were filmed in the middle of the day with a very dark filter on to make it look like nighttime. It was nice walking, but it was clearly nighttime. And there was always a sense that something big and mean would step out from behind a tree at any moment.

As I passed the bear cutout that I had installed along the road several months ago to welcome visitors, my heart skipped a beat and I broke out in a cold sweat—even though I had driven past it a hundred times, and walked within several feet of it dozens of times, even many times in the dark, the sight of a bear outline jolted me. Calm down son, no real bears out tonight.

Beyond the bear I walked out into the open Faddis Meadow and was met with the cooling wind and bright moonlight. Walking, standing, sitting in the tall grass, it didn't matter—it was absolutely incredible being out in the moonlight and the wind. Don't know exactly why. I have always enjoyed being out on summer nights ever since I was a little kid. I felt very much at home.

I walked out into a patch of very tall weeds—they were like giant queen Anne's lace—white bunches of tiny flowers on tall stalks. I wouldn't dream of walking through this thick, prickly mess during the heat of the day, but in the cool moonlight it seemed magical. The stalks were nearly six feet tall, and I got lost in the sea of blowing weeds. Looking up, I noticed a bright object that shown through the bright sky right next to the moon—it was Jupiter, and was about the only thing showing anywhere near the moon.

I left the Faddis Meadow and headed over towards the East Meadow. The tunnel of trees that connected them became rather spooky—the trees were so thick that no moonlight penetrated to the ground. But there was enough reflected light that I could see the path easily. Ahead I could see an open patch, and it was really lit up. I thought about all kinds of different things that might be in that opening—a big bear or mountain lion that would come after me, chase me deeper into the woods, and feast on my bloody bones. Or perhaps a beautiful wood nymph would appear, take me in her arms, and allow me the ultimate commune with nature. While lost in this mental haze, I stepped into a depression in the path, stumbled, and fell flat on my face in the dirt. So much for the lovely wood nymph.

While I twist or pop my ankle a lot the pain is normally eased by simply walking it out. So I continued along the dark tunnel, through the bright opening (no bears or nymphs), towards the East Meadow. The pain in my ankle grew, and shot up my leg to my knee—not normal. By this time it was just as close to continue on as it would have been to turn back, so I kept going.

Soon I entered the East Meadow—it was like walking back into bright sunshine! Hard to believe that it could be *so* bright in the middle of the night. The wind picked up again, and I walked into the moonlight. As I moved on,

I saw flashes of white in the meadow ahead—deer! I forgot all about sneaking up on the garden to see if anything was there, and I spooked them. Probably the three bucks that I had seen there before. I could see their white tails waving high in the night sky, bounding towards the woods, then they disappeared. I sat down in the weeds, actually I guess I laid down in them, and soaked up all the moonlight that I could.

My ankle began to throb so I got up and continued my hike. I left the bright meadow and eased into the dark woods. While I had a flashlight in my pocket, I vowed not to use it unless I really had to—I wanted to experience the woods in the moonlight. This stretch of the woods was rather dark, not too much moonlight to bounce around and light things up. All I needed was another misstep and my ankle would be really messed up. I slowed down. Instead of walking through the woods, I went from tree to tree, using them as friendly handholds, a helping hand in the night.

When you move through the woods at this slow pace you not only appreciate them more, but you get to know the individual trees. You feel their bark and branches, and sometimes, you know that they are smiling. I wrapped my arms around an old oak that was smiling—he had enjoyed thousands of moonlit nights, weathered countless severe storms, been the home to flying squirrels and woodpeckers and snakes, and had seen many loggers cut down his buddies. This night the wind produced sweet music in his high branches, and I knew that he must be dancing inside.

I moved on, carefully, and came to a broken bluffline. It was only about six feet tall, but quite solid, and covered with moss and small ferns. The rock still contained the heat of the day—like a living, breathing being. This dude was firmly anchored to the earth, solid, and nothing would ever move it. Yet the moss gave it a soft personality.

The wind picked up and the entire forest began to sing. The areas of light and dark moved and danced about and created a thousand patterns on the forest floor. I sat at the base of another old oak and took in the show. The trees were silhouetted against the bright moon. In daylight you never really see trees silhouetted—there is always some green or brown or red or whatever. Only in the moonlight can you see natural silhouettes. You can study the shape and form of the trunk, the branches, the individual leaves. I like silhouettes.

Looking up, I noticed a large blob in one of the trees. It began to move. It was moving down the tree. It got to the ground and started coming at me, making a lot of noise—oh my gosh, it was a bear! My heart pounded. I was trapped. He got closer and closer. In a flash he was right in front of me, about to crash into me. Just then an ant crawled up my leg and bit me, and I woke up. The moonlight had lulled me to sleep, and one of my greatest fears had invaded my dreams. Lordy, I was glad to be awake, and in the company of friendly trees instead of a charging bear!

My ankle had stiffened and was really throbbing now. That, along with all of the bears running around in my mind, pushed me on towards the cabin.

I left my forest wonderland behind and followed the road home. The warm glow of my cabin logs lit up by an outside light was the perfect balance to the moonlight, creating a very welcome scene. I imagined what this same scene would look like under a blanket of fresh snow—I'll have to photograph that this winter if it ever snows during a full moon.

Now it was time to get back to work. I had more CD's to listen to, and really needed to choose the final song for the slide show. Then it hit me—I knew exactly what song I wanted—I couldn't believe that I didn't remember it before. I heard this song a couple of years ago, and immediately noted then that it would be in one of my slide shows some day. I dug through my pile of CD's and found it. Yes, that would work! I put all of the chosen songs together in the CD six pack on my stereo, and listened to the sequence over and over, for two hours. I turned up the volume, and played the dissolving images in my mind. After listening to over 75 CD's, I finally had my show.

9/9/98 The sky was pitch black and a million stars were out when I returned to Cloudland. I know that I keep saying this, but the sky was as wonderful as I had ever seen it, and the stars went on forever. The temp was in the upper 50's, the wind was blowing a little, and it was *fall!*

After unloading the van of all my slide show putting together stuff I happened to look out the back window of the cabin and saw a tall white object. I went outside and discovered the big pine tree in the meadow was being lit up by a bright light—it must be the moon! But the hilltop where the moon had been rising was black. I walked around the east deck and son of a gun, there it was, a three-quarter moon rising into the night sky. But it was in the wrong place! It was in the same spot where the sun rises this time of year, but just a week ago it rose at the other end of the ridge, about where the sun rises in December. I wish someone would come out here and explain all of the moon's movements to me. The sun has a predictable path that it follows, but sometimes the moon just seems to jump around wherever it pleases. Perhaps that is one reason why I relate so much to the moon—I kind of jump around some too. Anyway, it was a lovely moonrise, and soon the valleys were lit up just like after sunrise, with the shadows creating all kinds of patterns.

I sat out on the deck a while enjoying the night spectacle. There were hardly any summer bugs out at all—perhaps they had already crawled into the ground. Or maybe they were just sitting there staring at the whole scene like I was, soaking it all in.

Later, after I went to bed, several owls woke up and began hooting back and forth. And even later, a coyote started yipping and howling. I love to hear them. Another one answered him. Then another. There were at least three of them in different areas of the wilderness that were singing to each other. For me, it was like stereo with a center speaker—the original surround sound! This went on for several minutes, and it was music indeed. All too soon they stopped, and the forest was quiet again.

The cool night sent me deep under the quilt. I always sleep better when it is cool.

9/10/98 A loud bang shook me awake—fall must be near, because an acorn had slammed into the metal roof. When the oak and hickory trees decide to release their fat fruit, it really gets loud at the cabin. You don't notice it too much down in the lower levels, because the logs and roof insulate the sound so well. But up in the loft, with all of the windows open, the sound is very loud, and startling. The lady that I am looking for to share my loft will need to be a sound sleeper.

Temps in the 50's, a light breeze, clear blue skies, it was heaven at Cloudland. Summer has been absolutely wonderful out here—way beyond my greatest expectations. But fall is going to be ten times better, if that is possible. I could not imagine being in a better place.

There was a noticeable absence of butterflies and hummingbirds (the feeder wasn't even empty—guess they have already flown elsewhere). But there were lots of goldfinches still around, and they were really enjoying themselves playing in the upper airspace above the meadow.

As I sat in the swing nibbling on hashbrowns and cheese the grey fox appeared down below. He obviously saw me, and in fact was giving me a good look-see, but didn't seem to be too concerned. He went into a brush pile and never came out. I remained glued on that spot, but no more fox. He must have a den there, but I have been hesitant to go investigate for fear of disturbing him. This is in the same spot as I had seen him twice before, right near the burn spot where he has been rolling—there are always fresh tracks there. I'm very glad to have him as my neighbor.

It is absolutely beautiful here right now. And there are more and more trees turning already. There are a number of smaller trees turning red along the top of the bluffline that I can see winding off in the distance, and there are even several splotches of red and orange trees above the bluff. Along the river too there are more trees turning. I suspect that some of them are turning because of a lack of water. But I think it is going to be one terrific fall color display this year. You will probably hear me say that a lot. Or all of the leaves will turn brown and drop off. One or the other.

I got a glass of wine and plopped down on the hammock to rest a little before going to bed (sounds strange to rest before going to bed, but sometimes you just have to). The moon was up, a breeze was blowing, and there was almost no sound at all. The moon was shining brightly through the trees, creating dozens of silver starbursts (or I guess they should be called moonbursts). This was amazing, and unlike anything that you would see from the sun. And because the wind was blowing the limbs and leaves around, the moonbursts were dancing all over the place (I swear that was the only glass of wine that I had all night!). I was mesmerized until I dozed off. Then the deck woke me up when I fell out of the hammock. Duh.

9/11/98 I missed the sunrise again but crawled out of bed in time to enjoy a good part of the morning. I walked out onto the back deck, and scanned the meadow below for any signs of the fox—none. As I hobbled down the stairs to the lower deck on my way to water the flowers, I startled some deer that were at the edge of the meadow. Darn, I was so concerned with finding the fox, I completely missed seeing the deer! They took off across the meadow towards the woods, their white flags waving in the morning sunshine. I didn't see a third one, but these two were both big bucks, and probably two of the ones that I had been seeing in the East Meadow. I'll bet the third one was close by, standing in the shadows saying "I told you guys not to go into that meadow!"

I was forced to eat my bowl of fresh peaches, yogurt and Grape Nuts out on the deck, scanning the meadow for any movement. As soon as I sat down, the fox appeared. At last, I was able to get a good look at him with the binocs. What a beautiful animal—mostly grey along the top, but rust-colored all along the underside, up the neck, and around the back of its head and ears. The face and tail were black. From reading the description that Gretchen Huey wrote in the Ozark Natural Science Center newsletter, this was indeed a grey fox—no white tip on the tail like red foxes have.

The fox wandered around the left side of the meadow and went over to where the deer were when I first saw them. At one point it stopped and stretched out and yawned. Another time it went jumping after a butterfly. When it got to the edge of the meadow it turned around and circled back. I was watching all of this through the binocs. As it walked through a small opening it passed within a foot of another fox who was lying in the dirt—wow, two of them again! I was a little startled to see the second one—he was looking right at me.

This second fox was larger, probably the male, with a lustrous grey coat on top also, and lots of rusty-red underneath, with a red chest, but no red ears. OK, I had a good ID on both of them and could now tell them apart. The guy has black ears, and the lady's are red. The guy stayed put in the dirt while the lady walked around some more. Then she went back into the bush where I had first spotted her, and disappeared. The guy put his head down onto his outstretched arms, closed his eyes and appeared to snooze and soak up the morning sunshine. He seemed to be pretty relaxed.

While I was watching the fox a red squirrel jumped up onto a nearby branch—the closest that a squirrel had ever been to the cabin—and began to bark and cuss me out loudly. I put the binocs on him too and studied every hair. His tail was incredible—it was wider than his body, and over half-again as long as his body—it really stuck high up in the air. And he was waving it as he barked. It was backlit by the sun, and the red and grey hairs shown brightly. Come to think of it, this little squirrel looked a lot like the foxes down below, complete with a rusty underbelly and neck. No red ears though—he looked more like the male fox. I swear the gray coat was the same color too. This was the first red squirrel that I had seen at the cabin—most squirrels in the woods seem to be grey squirrels.

The fox down below woke up and glanced my way to see what all the ruckus was about, then went back to dozing. The squirrel continued to bark. A red-tailed hawk showed up and screamed a little too as he rode the warming air currents up and out of sight. It seemed that everything out this morning except the deer had a red theme to it. I eventually finished my peaches, got up and went inside—neither the squirrel or the fox seemed to care. As I am typing this, I can still see the fox down below, sunning himself in the meadow. The squirrel has moved on to more important things. I am pretty sure now that there is a fox den in the meadow, and I think I know exactly where it is—one of these days I will venture down and make sure, but I don't want to scare them off just yet, so I'll wait a little longer for confirmation.

The wind is picking up and it is getting warmer outside. There are a few clouds rolling in. Another butterfly shadow just raced across my mini-blinds—must be time to get up and do something. I think I'll go take a hike.

It was a short hike, just out to the mailbox and back, but along the way I began to get very weak, even a little shaky, and was having trouble walking. Being way out in the country you tend to make your own diagnosis, so I decided that I was having chocolate withdrawals. Pretty serious condition. Especially when I began to think about the fact that I didn't know of a single thing in the cabin that could remedy my condition. I got weaker, but my pace quickened as I approached my cabin. I raced the last few yards, tore off my shoes, and burst into the kitchen. No ice cream. Nothing in the fridge. The cabinets were completely bare of all sweets. I opened one last cabinet door, and a package of Reese's Peanut Butter Chips jumped out and screamed *eat me!* I did. Whew, that was a close call.

After my small feast I just had to go down and see if I could find a fox den. Boy, the little buggers sure had the meadow beat down in a number of places. I never did find any sign of a den, but I did discover what they were now using the burn spot for—a cat box!

Many of the smaller trees and bushes are now showing signs of stress from the lack of water, and lots of them are dying out. Only time will tell if this is just temporary or if it is really killing them. I suspect that if we get some rain soon, they will survive, but if the dryness lasts several more weeks, I'll bet that we get a lot of dead trees. Several times during the day large, dark and threatening clouds gathered, but then moved on, without depositing any water.

Friday night has now become my main pizza night so I whipped up a batch of dough and stuck it in the oven to rise. A new friend from Benton was stopping by later for a quick visit, and I hoped that she would help keep me from killing myself by eating all four pizzas (which I have been known to do—they are small, but still more than any one human should eat in a sitting).

I wandered out to the back deck to listen to some Leo Kottke on KUAF radio (**Ozark Outdoors** then **The New Blues Show**) and soak up a little spectacular scenery. There were lots of puffy clouds hanging around, and the sun was getting low and shining below all of them, putting on quite a nice light show. Since I have been seeing so much of the foxes down in the meadow, I now spend most of my time scanning the meadow looking for them and ignoring the main view. Sure enough, right on cue, the little lady fox appeared out of the brush, sauntered on over to the burn spot, and squatted. Not very ladylike. I did get a good look at her glorious salt and pepper coat though. Her face was streaked white and black, and the red from her belly and chest wrapped around the back of her ears. A terrific-looking lady.

The sunset was rather marvelous. Not much happened though until after the sun dipped below the ridgetop far away and behind the trees. The western sky lit up like a giant forest fire was raging below it. Nice rays. The wind was blowing pretty good, and it felt great out. The Blues on KUAF, a terrific sunset, Cloudland Pizza, cold Arkansas Ale, and a wonderful young woods maiden on the way—what more could a guy ask for on a Friday night? Life continues to be a struggle out here, but I manage.

By the time Jenny had arrived, one of the pizzas was already gone. Oops. The sky was growing dark and the stars were coming out. While sipping a glass or two of wine on the back deck (she brought a wonderful bottle of merlot), we saw a couple of shooting stars—one of them disappeared behind a cloud. Hum. The valley below began to glow, and we eased around the corner of the cabin and watched a gorgeous orange moon climb into the night sky, lightening up the valley along the way.

I fired up the projectors and the sound system and the first official presentation of the new **Buffalo River Wilderness** slide show was made. I routed the soundtrack through the cabin stereo, and it sounded pretty darn good. The images were nice too, dissolving into one another on my big new screen. I could see that the audience was going to have a problem telling which images were paintings and which were photographs. McNamara's watercolors often look so real. I'd have to work on that.

Before long the bottle of merlot was empty and the wilderness was very bright, so we decided to take off on a hike. We made our way through the woods up to the East Meadow, and lingered there a while soaking up the moonlight. The moon was only half-full, but it was still very bright—bright enough to see animals moving about in the meadow. Well, actually, we really didn't see any animals there, but it was bright enough for us to have seen some if any were there. Perhaps if we had a little more merlot we would have seen something.

Jenny suggested we do a rain dance, so we spent some time doing just that. It was sort of a combination moon dance and rain dance, right out there in the middle of the meadow. I wonder how many critters were watching us? Some of them probably had ID books and were trying to key us out and decide what in the heck we were. "One of them has a bare head and the other all of those curves. And blue eyes all around. They must be just migrating through."

After we had danced enough to please the rain gods we migrated through the dark tree tunnel on over to the Faddis Meadow, then eased down the road and back to the cabin. We saw several more shooting stars along the way. And more clouds moved in. At one point the clouds covered the moon, leaving only a faint glow in the woods. It was enough light for us to find the way home. Good thing that I had Jenny along for protection, or the bears might have gotten me. It was 3am when we arrived and time to call it a day.

9/12/98 We missed sunrise (two days in a row for me!), but did manage to make it down to the back deck in time for coffee and blueberry biscuits. The main goal of the day was to see a fox—no one but me had ever seen a fox here before, and I was beginning to wonder if they were a figment of my imagination. Well, I guess I could always prove their existence by scooping up a pile of fox poop. The more we looked though, the less fox we saw.

The sun was out and there were clouds racing each other across the sky. The wind was blowing and it was quite cool. The little meadow of mine down below the deck had turned from a wild sunflower meadow to a sea of goldenrod in just one week. The sunflowers died out and the goldenrod flourished.

There were a lot of finches out playing, both in the meadow as well as up in the wind currents. We wondered how the little guys could be so accurate with their flight in such a strong wind. Guess they know how to fly. Lots of leaves were flying by too, some green, and others red and gold and orange. They were blowing across the meadow in front of us, and a few of them were even rising up into the air. The finches were teaching the leaves how to have fun.

The music of the wind filtered through the trees all morning, sometimes reaching a high pitch. It looked like rain, though didn't smell like it, and nothing fell. Some rain would be most welcome. All too soon Jenny had to attend to wild grape gathering and fishing chores—she bid Cloudland farewell and headed out. We had been e-mail pals for a while, but had never met, so it was good to spend some time with her in the flesh.

The wind picked up and the clouds got thicker. I was forced onto the couch for a nap. I'm not sure if it was the sound of my outside alarm or the smell of rain that woke me up. I quickly ran out into the front and welcomed both a rain shower and Erna Hassebrock, a friend from Hot Springs. She had e-mailed ahead and wanted to know what kind of homemade cookies were needed at Cloudland, so I was especially glad to see her! Hey, I'm always glad to see Erna. Let's see, she brought me two wonderful bluebird houses on her first visit, two great bear lamps on her second visit, and lots of edible goodies on her third.

Besides five bags of great cookies, Erna had brought another surprise—the most wonderful, heavy flannel Cloudland sheets!!! They have a cloud and star pattern against a blue background—stars and clouds and blue—what a combination! (very thick and made in Germany) I wanted to frame one of the pillow cases and hang it up on the wall. Come to think of it, there are four pillow cases, so you just might see one of them on the wall out here. Erna chatted a while, took a few pictures, then left. She needs to come back more often.

Oh yea, the *rain!* It never really rained hard, but it did rain for several hours—a light rain, and blowing a lot. The temp dropped and I had to go around and close up the windows—I consider this to be one of the first signs that fall is coming, having to close the windows to keep the cool air *out* I've been opening the windows during the night all summer to allow the cool air *in*. I look forward to the days when I can just leave the windows open all the time. It looked like our little rain dance up in the meadow last night worked.

One of the odd things about the weather today was that it all blew in from the east—the weather normally comes in from the southwest here. While this wouldn't normally be a problem, it sure did mess up my routine of where I stood to water the flowers—a constant and predictable wind is vital to the chore! There were a lot of clouds moving rapidly across the sky during the day—this was a big front, and I only wish that it had a little more water in it, but I'll take what I can get. The rain was wonderful.

The afternoon found me back to work on the slide show, cleaning slides and repositioning some of them. And I ate a few cookies. *Prairie Home Companion* was on the radio, playing more Leo Kottke. It's funny how you won't pay too much attention to something, or someone, like Leo Kottke, and then all of a sudden it/he will be everywhere. I went to my first Leo Kottke concert with my high school sweetheart way back in the 70's. I've had his CD's for a long time, but seldom listen to them. In the past two days I have heard him on the radio twice, and he is going to be playing in Eureka Springs in two weeks. Guess I will have to dig out those CD's.

The light rain and winds continued into the evening, when the gray day faded away into dark. I munched on leftover pizza (always great the second day), ate a few cookies, and sat out on the back deck and wondered how much longer this year I would be able to sit out there to eat and hang out—the winter winds make it rather chilly, although I am now used to sitting out there, so perhaps I will brave the cold and enjoy the view more often.

The Pickin' Post show on the radio was sounding good, as it always does. Mike Shirkey sure does a great job of putting together some nice music. I have been sitting here at the computer working on the Journal, and every now and then I have had to jump up and go sit in the middle of the great room to listen to a song. I've never heard any of these cuts before. While I really do like folk music, I just never listen to it enough. Mike talked about what a great thing it is to go see live music. Cloudland is a virgin in that department—no live music has ever been played here before (my own sour notes on my beautiful maple guitar don't count). I know a few friends who are musicians. There needs to be some live music at Cloudland.

The long, soaking rain continued. I sat out on the back swing and nursed a bit of Wild Turkey liqueur and ate some cookies. The raindrops were soothing and peaceful, the breeze refreshing. There were no other sounds. The sky was dark. Most storms of the past have been accompanied by thunder and lightning, but none were around this day. A fire would have felt good tonight. OK, OK, enough work, enough cookies, enough great music. Time to crawl under the quilt and drift away with the raindrops.

9/13/98 Two of the windows next to my bed in the loft open up onto the tin roof of the back porch. The steady rain all night falling on that tin provided great music to sleep and dream by. You could just hear life coming down from the clouds, giving everyone a well-deserved drink. It was tough to get out of bed in the morning. Over an inch of rain had fallen, and it was still coming down. The cloudy, misty fog filled the valleys and swirled around back and forth, creating new scenes every few minutes. It was chilly out, and the rain was blowing in onto the deck furniture, so I opted to stay inside and enjoy the views through the windows. There are eight windows facing the great view to the south, including the picture window and the big sliding glass door. There is a great view from just about every spot in the cabin. Hum, who would have designed such a place? I'll take full credit.

This long, soaking rain couldn't have come at a better time for the wilderness. The river below is as low as I have ever seen it, and the stress on the forest has been evident. The river won't really come up too much, but the vegetation certainly is smiling this morning. I am still predicting a splendid fall in the Ozarks.

The rain and wind and fog continued most of the day, ending up at about two inches worth of wonderful water. As I left the cabin and headed to a meeting in town, it felt like it just might keep right on raining for days.

9/17/98 And boy did it ever rain! It didn't stop raining for five days! And all of it was slow, soaking, perfect rainfall. The weather station collected 5.4 inches of rain, and a top wind of 27mph. There were lots of branches down all over, and the road into the cabin was covered with leaves—it looked just like fall!

I returned to the cabin late at night, grabbed a glass of wine and headed for the back porch swing. The night sky was very black—the moon wouldn't show itself for another week. The sky was clear, the week-long storm having cleared out all clouds and haze. The stars twinkled with renewed vigor. It was still, and there were a few night bugs out. But there was something out there that I hadn't expected. Something there that hasn't been around for a very long time. Something wonderful, and welcome and joyous—the sound of the river! Oh the glorious voice of that long, winding friend! It takes a fair amount of water to create enough river music to reach all the way up to the cabin, and it was certainly doing it tonight. A hushed sound. Soft and inviting. It matched the gentle starlight perfectly.

In the dim glow of the night I could see a fog bank developing down on top of the river. I had a feeling that it would be one terrific sunrise and morning. But the night wasn't through yet. One shooting star after another streaked across the southern sky. It was like they had all been sitting around and holding out for a clear night, waiting for a chance to sparkle, not wanting to waste their brilliance behind the clouds. I wondered how many other late night viewers were out and taking in such an astrological show. I know one group of folks that was still up late in my neighborhood—the owls. More of them than I had heard in a long time. I couldn't quite tell if they were all welcoming me back, singing the praises of the rainfall, or shouting out loud with glee at the shooting stars. No matter which—I was glad to have them as company.

9/18/98 The outside alarm screamed and woke me from my dreams at 5:30am. I had recently adjusted the sensitivity of it so that it would only trip when something large moved in front of it, like a human, deer, or a bear. It was still dark out. I sat up and listened, expecting to hear the thud of a bear on the front porch at any moment. Then I turned my head and looked out the window to the east—there it was, delicate, thin, almost parallel to the ridgeline—a tiny glowing crescent moon! The moon, it is large enough, I'll bet it set off the alarm! It was one of those sights that leaves you breathless for a moment.

The view to the south out one of the other windows was blank—nothing but fog. I thought that was a little strange, because it was clear all the way to the moon to the east. So I laid there and studied the moon. There was a very gentle breeze moving through the loft, the soft glow of the orange rising sliver, and absolutely no sound at all, except for gentle drops of dew falling from the roof. How could one do anything but be lulled to sleep? How could one not stay up and soak it all in?

A couple of hours later the moon had long since faded into heavy fog, and the sun had failed to show up for work. The dew kept falling. I forced myself up and hurried down to the back deck to see what was going on. I could just barely see two pine trees rising from the fog, and not much else. There were birds singing everywhere, though I couldn't see any of them. A blue jay's cries rang out in the distance, and I could tell that he was moving, as they often do when they cry out. I strained my eyes to look through the fog down into the meadow, but couldn't see any wildlife.

As I made my way down the steps to the lower deck to water the flowers I heard the brush moving. There was a flash of grey. Darn, I had startled a fox! A few moments later I could see grey moving across the meadow. I hurried back up to my meadow-viewing post and studied the ground and the brush through the binocs, but couldn't see anything. I wondered why I was so concerned about seeing the fox again, since I knew what it was, and exactly what they looked like. But there is just something about having wildlife so close that makes you want to stop and see. I want to study every hair on them again, watch their movements, see what they are doing, gaze into their eyes. An old Native American medicine man once said that looking deep into the eyes of a fox would bring you good luck, just like watching shooting stars. Much of my life is based on luck, so I need as much as I can get.

The sun didn't show up until after 8am—it had grown lazy and was sleeping late. It would be working double time to burn off all of the fog.

Today would be full of mixed emotions for me. It was one year ago that my most trusted friend in all the world died in my arms. We had spent the night in the woods after a short hike to explore an area near here. Even though it was still kind of warm out, I built a campfire and stayed up late, discussing the problems of the world with my two dogs Yukon and Stable. I remember the fire reflecting in Yukon's eyes as he looked over at me. He was trying to tell me good-bye then, but I didn't get it. Sometime during the night he curled up right next to me. I could feel his warmth.

In the morning it was obvious that something was wrong. *Very* wrong. Yukon wouldn't wake up. He lay there, breathing heavily, with his eyes closed tightly. I knew that I had to get him to the vet. We all loaded up and headed for town. He was limp, like a bag of flour, when I carried him in. It didn't take but a minute for the doctor to say that it was no use—kidney failure. He said it would be best to put him to sleep. I held Yukon, rubbed his paws, and felt life slip from his body. It was the most difficult thing that I had ever done in my life. In a moment, it was all over. The impact of that moment would stay with me for a very long time.

For thirteen years Yukon had followed me, led me, explored with me everywhere that I went. He loved to run in the woods, to play with logs, and to swim. The guy actually had webbed feet. He was a springer spaniel. And a rather handsome one at that. I could never wear him out. He would forgo food and attention as long as he could be in the woods.

I remember one trip when he and I took off for a hike on a warm February day. After a couple of hours, the sky turned dark, and a cold rain began to fall. I was totally unprepared, wearing only shorts and a t-shirt. We crawled into a low narrow overhang and got out of the direct rain. It was a pretty nice place to hide and watch the woods dance in the rain. Before long cold and stiffness crept in. Our little spot was still dry, but without moving to heat ourselves up, we both began to shiver. The rain poured on. Yukon kept looking at me with those big brown eyes. I didn't know what to tell him—his master was an idiot. I know that he would have stayed there with me all day, until we both froze to death if it came to that. He was always willing to do whatever, whenever, as long as I was for it. I finally had enough, and dashed out into the frigid downpour, and ran up the trail. About halfway up the hill, as I was about to give up hope of ever being found alive, I turned and looked at Yukon. He was smiling, probably laughing inside, and having a great time. He lifted my spirits, and I immediately began to enjoy myself too—even though it was pouring rain on me in the middle of the winter and I was freezing!

I drove from the vet's office back out to Cloudland, loaded Yukon into my backpack, and headed down the hill towards the river with a shovel and pick in hand. It was a hot day. Yukon loved the river, and I took him down to one of his favorite swimming holes. I found a level spot overlooking this great hole of water, and right next to the flowing waters of a spring. There were lots of moss-covered rocks there. The spring waters poured over a ledge and right into the Buffalo River. Yukon would be happy here. I dug a deep hole, carefully laid him in, and covered him with dirt and rocks.

I'm not sure why the death of this dog has affected me so, more so than even the death of my own family members. I guess we had shared so many things in the wilds, more than with anyone else in my life. He was not my first dog, but was the one that was with me the longest.

He was a great trail companion. He went along on countless hikes with me for thirteen years, had hiked over three thousand miles, and had been with me on most every trail construction project. He used to carry a whisky bottle in his little pack on OHTA hikes, so everyone loved to see him come down the trail. He contributed a great deal to my time in the woods, and to my life. I remember taking a break one day after hiking 60 miles in three days—we were both worn out. A group of small blue butterflies landed on his head. And while I know his foot pads were smoking, he gave me a look of eagerness and encouragement to go the next mile that I've never received from any human. Once, while building a trail near Memphis, I looked back to see that he had carefully "retrieved" every single branch and log that I had just cleared out of the trail and thrown down the hillside, and he put them all right back on the trail. I knew he was just trying to help. And one day, while I was building another trail, lost in the sound of music from my walkman radio, I saw him out of the corner of my eye come running up, barking, to a spot that I was about to back into. I turned to see him lunge at a large rattlesnake that was coiled within my next step. Before I could react, the snake bit him three times in the face (Yukon survived, the snake did not). He had literally laid down his own life to save mine—what more could you ever ask of your best friend. You will be missed Pal.

There is a bottle of Yukon Jack on the mantle here at Cloudland. I bought it the day he died, a year ago today. I went over to the Wildman's house that night, and we toasted my trusted friend. It is Cloudland policy that any time Yukon is talked about here, that everyone present takes a swig from the Yukon Jack bottle in his honor. I'm going to go down to the river and visit Yukon here in a few minutes—I'll be passing that bottle around a lot today.

And later today, Neil Compton, the man who led the fight to save the Buffalo River so many years ago, will visit Cloudland to hike and feast and spend the night. I'm going to force him to watch the new ***Buffalo River Wilderness*** slide show. I had better go find that fox and gaze into her eyes for luck.

Not long after I left the cabin I looked up and saw a hawk coming through the trees right at me. He veered away as soon as he saw me, and I got a good look at him. He was a red-tailed hawk, with a beautiful red tail, and a bit husky. Husky? This dude was *fat!* That's all that I can say. Must have been feeding on a few field mice in the meadow.

I headed down the steep hill towards the bluffline. The fog was still very heavy, and when I would look over the edge down to the next bench below, I couldn't see to the far end of the bench—and it was quite spooky looking. I made my way down through the first spot in the bluffline that I knew about. All of a sudden my hair stood on end—I realized that I was at the point where the bear and I had a close encounter of the scary kind back in July. I looked around very carefully as I inched down the slope. No sign of any bear today.

Once below the bluffline I angled over to the right some, then landed on a wide and level bench. I didn't recall being here before. It was a magical place, especially with all of the fog. There were dozens of *huge* trees, towering overhead. They were so tall that they actually disappeared up into the fog. Sweet gums and red oaks. Man they were big, and there were so many of them. Surely this wasn't a virgin forest. Pretty much everything in the Ozarks had been logged at one time or another. I know what happened. When they first logged this bench, probably way back in the 1800's, they only took the largest trees out and left the rest. These giants of today were some of those that they left, probably over a hundred years old now. It all reminded me of the coastal redwood groves in northern California. There is one hiking trail there that I have frequented, and the fog lays in thick every morning, just like it was here today. Wonderful, wonderful. Eat your heart out John Muir!

As I stepped down onto the next bench my feet slipped out from under me and I landed on my butt. Those sorts of things take the breath out of you not only because of the landing, but because it is such a surprise and you wonder what the heck just happened. I knew what happened as soon as I hit—hickory nuts. The ground was *covered* with hickory nuts! They acted just like a floor full of marbles, and I got caught trying to walk on them. Boy, the hickory nuts are having one great year! It was a good thing that there were no witnesses.

The fog began to lift a little as I continued down the hill. I visited the old Sparks homesite. This is where there are two stone chimneys—one was at the opposite end of the cabin from the other. The stones are all that are left. One of their descendents is Clyde Sparks, and he was the rock mason that did all of the fine work on my cabin (along with Billy Woods). Clyde is an unusual character. He is a craftsman, and does wonderful work. I only hired him to build one rock retaining wall, and I liked it so much that I kept him working for quite a while, ending up with the fireplace inside the cabin. The only problem with Clyde was that right in the middle of a big job, he would fail to show up the next day to work. No warning. His tools were left scattered all over the place. He would stay gone for several weeks, then again without warning would show up and continue his work. I have been told over and over again by folks out here that this is simply the pace of life out here, and is especially the case for rock masons. He does fine work, when he works.

I came to a little creek that was full of moss-covered rocks. The water was running pretty good, cold and clear. I followed this spring water on down the hill until I came to Yukon's grave, which is located right next to the flowing water. I sat down and talked with him a little while. Boy, he sure did have a nice view of the river! And it was running pretty good too, making a nice rushing sound. As I always do when I visit Yukon, I placed a new rock on his grave. This particular rock was about half covered with lush moss, and had a bright red dogwood leaf on it. And I left him a treat.

Down in the big pool of water on the river there was a beaver working. I could see him through the trees, and he did seem just as busy as a little beaver, swimming back and forth. I went down for a closer look, and found him swimming towards me with a gnawed stick in his mouth. He brought it over to the river bank just upstream, left it there, then disappeared under water. I took this as a sign that he wanted to add this beaver stick to Yukon's grave, so I picked it up and marched it right up the hill and planted it in the middle of the rocks.

I bid my friend farewell and walked downstream alongside the river on the bench above it. It was a wonderful day, and all of the fog had lifted. When I got to Dug Hollow, I was really surprised to find it bone dry. I thought there would be something flowing in it after five inches of rain. I worked my way up into that drainage, gaining altitude as I went. The vegetation was very thick, and I was thankful that I had on long pants and a long-sleeved shirt. There were hardly any spiders out, and I was enjoying rambling on up the hillside.

Then I smelled something. It wasn't a pleasant odor. I looked around a little trying to follow the smell, and finally spotted the source. Right in the middle of one of the benches in the thick brush was the remains of *a bear!* Wow, I had never found anything like this in the woods before. Well, actually there wasn't too much left, just a few rib bones, several claws, some parts of the skeleton, and the skull. Alright, the skull! And there was black hair everywhere, scattered around in a twenty foot radius. I collected what I could, searched around the area some more, but didn't find anything else interesting, so I headed on up the hill once again.

I wondered what happened to this bear? Did he fall off of the bluff during a storm in the middle of the night like the beagle dog did? Was he shot by someone? Did the coyotes get him? Disease? Or did he simply die of old age? The skull looked pretty old to me, but I really have no idea about such things. Hum. One less bear.

As I climbed, the hill got really steep—kind of hand-over-fist climbing from one tree to another. Then I smelled something else. This odor was sweet, very sweet. It smelled like pawpaws! And sure enough, the ground around me was littered with overripe pawpaw fruit, each eaten to a different degree by one critter or another. I reached down and picked up one that was only half eaten, and bit into it. *Very tasty!* There were still a number of them up in the trees, so I decided to take a few home with me. It is one of those rites of passage to shake a pawpaw out of a tree and catch it before it hits the ground, then devour it on the spot. I obliged. I've wrestled with a bear, built a log cabin, made love to a beautiful maiden under a full moon (I haven't done that one lately—I need to get back into practice), and now have caught and ate a pawpaw. Perhaps one of these days I will become a full fledged wilderness man.

I continued up the slope and made it to the base of the big bluff. As I walked along I came across another fragrant smell. This one was very light, and sweet, like wildflowers. I couldn't figure out what it was, but it lingered all along the base of the bluffline.

Eventually I came to the spot that I call "Magnolia Canyon." This is a wonderful little spot where there is a split in the bluff, and you can walk right though it. In fact, the canyon is thirty feet wide! On the right the bluff is about 40 feet tall—this rock is really just a giant slab that has broken off from the bluff. The main bluff on the left is probably 80 feet tall. The floor of the little canyon is covered with moss-covered rocks and a few tall umbrella magnolia trees, but it is pretty much open besides that. The magnolias shoot up and spread out, creating a roof over the canyon. Hardly any sun can penetrate their wide leaves, and I'll bet the sun is blocked by the tall bluff on the south side in the winter, preventing any sun from reaching the canyon floor at all. There is one giant tree guarding the entrance—I couldn't tell what kind it was.

Towards the end of the canyon there is a split in the big rock slab on the right. You can go down into this crack and stand at the bottom of a 40 foot chimney. I wondered who else in history had stood in that very same spot and pondered the same thing. You can also climb up and out the other side. The main canyon itself is about 150-200 feet long. It is always cool, and shaded, and mossy, and just marvelous. I go there sometimes and just sit and think. It is a little world all to itself, isolated from everything else, even from the sun.

Further along the bluffline I came to a spot where magnolia trees had shed all of their leaves, and the forest floor was covered with a smooth carpet of soft, giant leaves. The stress of the drought caused them to save themselves and drop their leaves and go dormant to conserve energy. There were some beech trees that did this same thing too—this was really strange, because they don't lose their leaves in the fall, but rather hold onto them until the new spring leaves push them out. It has been an interesting year in the wilderness so far!

I made it on over to the base of a waterfall and found it actually running some. Not a great roar, but a decent little waterfall. In the spring the waterfall is splendid, and the bowl below it is filled with flowering magnolias, and there are lots of wild azaleas above in full bloom. It's another magical place. The side of one rock slab there, perhaps 15 feet tall, was covered with the thickest, brightest, most luxurious carpet of green moss that I had ever seen. What a great place it would be to lie down on and take a nap if it was only level. All of this lushness was juxtaposed with dried-up maidenhair ferns along the base of the bluff.

Once I had climbed up through the bluff via a natural rock staircase next to the waterfall, I noticed that the entire forest had changed. Below the bluff it was a jungle, literally. Lots of big trees, thick underbrush, pawpaws, moss, and just *thick* woods. Above the bluffline the woods were more open, with less underbrush, and it seemed drier. I wonder why?

The East Meadow was covered with yellow—the goldenrod had moved in, and it all was blowing back and forth like a sea of wheat. And standing right out in the middle were three deer—I had remembered to stop before entering the meadow and take a look for any sign of wildlife. And there they were, not really feeding, but just roaming around. It was a mom and twin fawns. Well, they were hardly fawns any more, since they were nearly as large as she was. But they still had their spots! That was really odd. It is very late to still have spots! They soon caught wind of me and bounded off into the woods.

When I got back to the cabin the phone was ringing. I hurried in and was talking on the phone when I noticed a *huge* hawk sitting in the snag on the other side of my little meadow. Hawks don't normally sit in that tree. He was as large as an eagle, and I wondered if it was a young one. I got to the binocs, but didn't get to look very long before he took off. He certainly wasn't a red-tail hawk. He soared around for a little while, then wandered off. A smaller Cooper's hawk came around too and rode the wind currents a little. And lots of buzzards showed up. As I sat down to watch it all I discovered that there were dozens of soaring birds all over the place. It was getting warm. Well, it felt warm to me anyway, and I had to turn on the outside fan. Wait a minute, how could it be warm? I looked at the temp and it was only 75 degrees—but the humidity was 93%. That would explain all of the blue haze in the air too.

Neil Compton was on the way out, and while it was going to be great to visit with him, I was also looking forward to the two ladies that he was bringing with him, not to mention all of the wonderful food that I knew they were going to cook (I was told not to worry about providing any food, and not to eat too much before they got here—these kind of guests always have a standing invitation at Cloudland!).

Neil and his ladies showed up right on time. Neil Compton, a living legend, his friend Kay Richardson, and Beth Motherwell, whose Leica binocs I have coveted for a long time. Within minutes we had unloaded several coolers of food and drink and treats, and were all lounging out on the back deck.

This was the very first time that I had ever sat down with Neil and had time to really converse. He knows more about the Ozarks than anyone alive. Probably more than all the dead ones too. He is a living encyclopedia, and it was marvelous to sit there and absorb all of it coming out of him. There were many personal stories of the old days, historical tales of the pioneers who lived around Cloudland, geology, biology, zoology. He went on and on.

During a lull in the conversation I got out the first copy of the new **Buffalo River Wilderness** picture book. Neil latched onto it like a magnet, and clutched it in his lap. We all gathered around and looked through it, page by page. The images brought out more stories and facts from Neil. This was one of the main reasons that I wanted Neil to come out and spend some time here—I wanted to be standing right next to him, with unlimited time, when he looked through this new book. I wanted to see his reactions to the images and the words, and to hear the stories that I knew they would entice out of him. I value his opinions a great deal, and hung on every word. It was a wonderful experience for me.

By the end of the book it was time to get to work on dinner, and the ladies sped off to the kitchen. I left Neil alone, and noticed that he picked the book back up and quickly turned to the foreword, which he had written. He carefully read every line, words that he had written months before. Then he went through the introduction that I had written. The Buffalo River is sacred ground, and Neil is the God. I wondered if I had done it justice with the new book, scared to death that I might have fallen well short of his expectations. I brought out a bottle of wine and some goodies and set them on the deck table. Neil was silent, still buried in the book. Was he disappointed, was he mad, did I screw up this most important picture book? I sat down, sipped my wine, pondered my immediate future, and held my breath. Finally Neil closed the book, got up and walked over towards me—there was a serious look on his face. Then a wide, warm smile appeared, he handed the book to me, and as he shook my hand he said that it was the most beautiful thing that had ever been done on the Buffalo. My soul soared. I breathed again, and handed him a glass of wine.

We all gathered 'round the wine bottle' and talked about wildlife. Neil told of his first visit to Hawksbill Crag back in the early 1970's. They collected a pile of unknown scat, and had it analyzed later by someone who knew what they were doing. It turned out to be cougar scat. There aren't supposed to be any cougars in the Ozarks. Neil had the proof.

Dinner was remarkable, as I knew it would be. I won't go through all of the particulars—there were too many to list—but I will say that the ladies put on quite a spread! And we had fresh pecan pie for dessert—worth a long hike in itself. Milancy McNamara dropped by just as the last slice was served (on her plate).

While Milancy and Beth and Kay and Neil talked, I rearranged the furniture and set up the slide show. The lights went out and the music came up. I was worried about the slide show too—concerned whether Milancy would like the way that I portrayed Bill's paintings. Unlike the book, which she had a lot of input on, she wasn't involved in the slide show production at all. When the music ended and the lights came on again, there was smile on her face. Whew, two in a row. The program is good, but I will have to tweak it as time goes on to get it perfect.

I began a new tradition at Cloudland. I am going to make a log floor lamp, and will have everyone sign the lamp shade. While I don't have the lamp built yet, I did have the shade, and got everyone to sign it—Neil first. So now all who visit will leave their mark, which will be in lights for many moons to come.

Beth and Milancy cornered each other in the kitchen, and Kay and Neil and I moved out onto the back deck. It was completely dark outside, but the stars were out and we talked astronomy and listened to the cicadas and to the owls. Neil soon retired, and Kay and I talked on. She lives on Beaver Lake, and has a great dock where she spends lots of time by herself and with friends.

Beth and Milancy moved to the couch, but continued the non-stop, involved conversation. Then it happened—the second time in as many months— a flash of light. At first I thought it was just in my mind, but Kay saw the very same thing—a flash of light that seemed to come from within the cabin. Neither Beth nor Milancy saw anything, but that wasn't surprising since they were so involved. This same flash of light happened back in July, but that time we all were sitting around in the living room, and everyone saw it. It seemed to come from within the cabin then too. It was weird, really weird, and we couldn't come up with an explanation. Hum.

Later I served the official Cloudland after-dinner drink (well, actually there are several of them, but this one is actually called a "Cloudland"). It is two parts Bailey's Irish Cream (chilled), and one part Frangelico liqueur—um, um good!

After Milancy left, a chorus of coyotes sang out—from at least three different areas in the wilderness. They talked back and forth for several minutes, then fell silent again. We all retired around midnight.

9/19/98 Sometime in the early light Beth snuck out from her basement bedroom and headed down to the river, her trusty fishing rod in hand. She is a country girl through and through and loves to fish. I wish that I would have gone with her because it sounded like she had a great time. She caught a number of smallmouth bass and perch, got a visit up close from a beaver, and did a little skinny-dipping (well, she said that she went skinny-dipping—my telescope was still in the shop so I couldn't report that first hand).

Neil and Kay were up early too, lounging on the back deck with their coffee and the morning sounds. Neil hit the ground running, and began talking once again of the natural diversity of the Ozarks, his eyes wide and sparkling. He talked about how the ice age and the deep valleys of the Buffalo River combined to produce beech trees, and how the trees weren't found in other, less deep drainages like the King's River, just a few miles away. He talked about the band of sugar maples that spread across the Ozarks (he had recognized some individual trees and groves of maples pictured in the new book). Cloudland is located right in the middle of that band of maples.

We talked a lot about the early logging in the area, how they used cables to get the big white oak logs out of the deep valleys—you can find a few pieces of these very cables down in the bottom of Whitaker Creek. And he talked about how the repeal of prohibition in 1933 actually helped destroy some of the great white oak stands of the Ozarks—the wood was prized for the whiskey barrels that bourbon is aged in (they char the inside of the barrels first). So a lot of the virgin timber of the Ozarks was cut up and shipped over to the distilleries in Kentucky. A lot of it also went to the Fulbright Mill in Fayetteville (Senator Fulbright became one of the greatest national politicians from Arkansas).

Kay slaved over the stove again, and produced piles of homemade biscuits and gravy and jam, peppered ham, and eggs. We feasted. Beth returned from the river with the stories of her exploits, and we all enjoyed the morning. Then Neil got really wound up. I've always known him as a most serious gentleman—after all, he had been going toe-to-toe with lots of big thugs in the battle to save the Buffalo River, not to mention all of the big shots in the Corps of Engineers that were trying to dam the river, and all of the politicians. Neil was a lot larger and more important in life than any of them ever were, which is in part why we have the Buffalo National River instead of a bunch of crummy lakes. Anyway, Neil kept us rolling on the deck with some very amusing stories, the topper being his rendition of a famous speech in the Arkansas legislature many years ago by a Johnson County politician. I will try to procure the text of that speech at some point, but am not sure if it is fit to print in this Journal. It is one of the funniest things that I have ever heard. Of course, I'm sure that the way Neil recited it had a lot to do with that.

Out in the meadow there were a number of birds and butterflies playing. The goldfinches were pairing up—instead of seeing three or four brilliant yellow males flying together, now there were pairs of one yellow one (male) and one dull one (female). I don't know when their mating season is, but love seems to be in the air right now in the goldfinch species. At one point there were two different species of woodpeckers in the old dead snag at the same time. A Cooper's hawk came by, and several red-tailed hawks.

Neil had a new set of expensive hearing aids. They sang a lot, which drove him crazy. A high-pitched whine that everyone could hear—they needed a little adjustment. To me they sounded like birds singing off in the distance, so I didn't mind. Hey, what a good idea—adjust all hearing aids so that they sound like birds singing—and issue them to everyone in the world! We would all go through the day singing.

Once when Beth was in the cabin I came in and announced that a fox had crept up onto the deck and ran off with her Leica binocs—everyone ran towards the deck just for a second, then realized that it was only a ploy on my part to explain the disappearance of her binocs (which I would have swiped if I could have come up with a believable story!).

The day was growing warm and it was time to pack up and get ready to go. We all went down onto the lower deck to take a few pictures. Neil and I were lined up against the logs acting like good models when I caught some movement out of the corner of my eye. In a flash a big hawk swooped down, grabbed a chipmunk off of a log, and raced away above the meadow. He didn't have a good hold on the chipmunk, and it struggled in the hawk's claws. The hawk soared out over the Whitaker Valley, and the chipmunk's struggling caused the hawk to veer off course a time or two. Once the hawk gained full control it made a wide arch and returned to the meadow, swooping right in front of us, then circling overhead—he just wanted to show off his catch. It was a fitting end to a marvelous visit—one that I will long remember.

I had to leave the cabin as well and drive down to Lake Catherine below Hot Springs to give the first official ***Buffalo River Wilderness*** slide show to the Arkansas Canoe Club group gathered there. It was very hot and humid, and nearly 200 folks packed into the Exhibit Hall to see the show. The music is a major part of this slide show, and my stereo was messing up as I set everything up. I got very nervous. Finally it seemed to be working. The lights went dark, and I cranked up the music. Two notes into the very dramatic beginning, the stereo went dead—*crap!* After a few anxious moments, I got the sound back on again, and it worked fine. I doubt that anyone noticed. I still didn't know how this new program would be received by the masses, so I held my breath once again. As the first credit slide came up, there was a thunderous applause, followed by laughter, then more applause. It was so loud, that no one even heard the music. Then another image appeared on the screen, the place got deathly quiet, and the music took over again. You see, I always sit through the credits at the end of a movie, and it always has irked me how everyone jumps up and leaves when they start rolling. Hey, some of the most interesting music comes during those credits, and once in a while, like in my slide show, there is more on the screen. It is just my little way of making a point.

I think the show went over pretty well. I was relieved. You never know if the outside world will see and appreciate the same beauty that you do. And I always want to produce something that the audience will like—that is the entire reason why I do these shows (and to sell books). The show is off and running.

It was nearly 3am when I returned to the cabin. It had been a very long and productive day. The sky was black, the stars were out, the bugs and owls were singing, and the loft bed felt great.

9/20/98 I slept in and missed most of the great morning light. When I finally did make it out to the back deck with my mocha, it was getting warm, but there was a breeze blowing. There were groups of living things out this morning. Dozens and dozens of those cloudless sulphur butterflies dropping out of the tops of the trees again. They were so funny. When they would first appear, high up in the air, they would fall like rocks—like rocks tumbling out of control. Just before they hit the ground, their wings would straighten out and they would, well, float like a butterfly, and go merrily along their way. They are yellow, greenish yellow.

And three times during the morning a flock of blue jays would appear above the cabin, normally 15-20 birds and spread out, and fly across above the meadow and head towards the opposite hillside. I haven't seen many blue jays here, but have heard them sounding their loud alarms.

My own alarm went off, and I had a visitor. It was Lori Johnson, from Dallas, who had been camping in the area and stopped by to see if Cloudland was real. I invited her to sit a spell and see what birds we could spot. I swear this is true—within five minutes of her arrival, that "big hawk" that I had seen sitting on the snag two days before appeared over the woods to the left, and swept across the top of the meadow in front of us, not making a sound, then disappeared over the woods to the right. A single white puffy breast feather floated in the air. Lori gasped, then ran through the cabin to her car. When she came back, she had a pair of Leica binocs around her neck. She was another bird expert—yea! And, of course, I immediately coveted her binocs too. What she said next I could not believe—"the big hawk" was none other than a golden eagle! Oh my Gosh, a *golden eagle* at Cloudland! I was thunderstruck. So was she. We looked him up in the bird book and sure enough, it was the same as the "big hawk" that was sitting in the snag two days before.

Eagles don't normally spend the summer in Arkansas—they come down from the north for the milder winters. However, there have been pairs of bald eagles moving in lately as year-round residents, but they are still very rare. I had

141

never seen one in Arkansas other than in the winter before. My friends Dean and Bonnie had told me that they have been seeing a golden eagle in the valley this summer—this must be the very same one.

After the eagle went by I noticed an odd absence of anything moving around, except for the butterflies. All of the birds in the meadow and surrounding woods were silent, and unseen. I wonder if they had seen or sensed the eagle and hid? We searched the skyline, the valley, the forest all around, but no sign of the eagle. At about the time that we settled back into our chairs and got comfortable, there he came again. This time he approached from the right, flew right over the meadow again, and disappeared. It was over in a few seconds. We both had our binocs trained on him. He looked straight ahead, but just before he disappeared, he looked down and glanced at us. Neither time did he ever flap a wing. Needless to say, we spent most of the next hour scouring the sky with our binocs, but we never did see him again. I guess he had just flown up from Boxley Valley, and took a quick tour of Cloudland and Hawksbill Crag, then returned home. The bald eagles do that too in the winter, although I usually get to watch them soaring around for a lot longer. No matter, I was thrilled and proud to have seen a golden eagle at Cloudland!

Lori soon left and headed back to Dallas, not sure how she would explain our sighting to her birding friends. As her car disappeared I remembered that I forgot to get her to sign the lamp shade! Then I wondered—were both Lori and the golden eagle merely a dream and wishful thinking on my part?

Alone again on the deck I kept an eye out for the eagle. It was tough watching though, because I was still obsessed with the foxes, the foxes that still had not shown themselves for anyone to see but me. Most of the time that Neil was here, I kept my eyes glued down on the meadow, looking for any grey movement. Several times this morning while I was scanning the meadow for the foxes, a shadow would move across the ground—the eagle had returned! Nope, it was usually just a turkey buzzard. Although there were a number of red-tailed hawks playing about too, and they were fascinating to watch soaring around and riding the air currents.

As the day lingered on the soaring birds took a break. The sky opened up and it poured for about a half hour—what a wonderful and pleasant time that was! I had noticed that the forest, once getting near to being all dried up, was now quite green and healthy looking. All of the rain last week had put a halt to the progress of the fall color change, and in some cases even seemed to reverse it. All we need now is a shower every now and then to keep the trees happy, then a cold snap in October with a little frost, and the wilderness will transform into a brilliant wonderland of color. The official start of autumn is three days away—I look forward to being a part of it all.

9/22/98 There were five copperhead snakes crawling across the road as I was driving in today. They must be migrating or something, or the rain drove them out of their dens. I haven't seen a single snake in the woods all summer (only

142

one water snake in the river)! There was a big storm the day before, and I had to stop and remove 13 big branches that were across the road. The rain gauge showed another 1.5 inches of rain, with 29mph winds.

There was a lot of life down in the meadow when I plopped myself down for the afternoon view. I startled a fox, and it made its way across the meadow and out of sight. I could follow its progress by all of the goldfinches that it disturbed as it passed—lots and lots of bright, yellow males that must have been feeding down in the brush. There were hawks and buzzards and other birds and butterflies all out enjoying the afternoon too. Then a red-headed woodpecker appeared and flew out from the meadow and headed into the deep canyon. I watched him through the binocs—he kept flying and flying and flying, getting smaller and smaller. Lordy, it was a mile or more in the direction that he was flying before he would find solid ground. It was easy to follow him because his white feathers really stuck out against the dark green of the distant forest. I kept watching, until he finally just disappeared. Then a second one took off flying in the same direction, but soon flew some to the right and headed towards Beagle Point. I watched through the binocs. It took him forever to get there, over a half mile of flight, but he did finally drop down and disappeared into the trees.

I took these two birds as a sign, and decided that I must follow them. So I stuffed a few things into my daypack, including my sleeping bag, and pointed my boots down the hillside. It felt right to be heading into the wilderness on the last day of summer, with plans to spend the night and awake to a new season—fall was to be officially here at 2:30am the next day.

When I reached the bottom I was really surprised to find Whitaker Creek flowing, and doing so at what looked like a normal springtime level. The water was clear and gorgeous. That last 1.5 inches of rain must be running off instead of being soaked up. And the main Buffalo River was the same—lots and lots of water, rushing by with a passion. Summer was indeed gone.

I headed upstream following along beside the river. Wow, what an incredible hike! I knew that there was some neat stuff down here, but the sights along the river were much nicer that I had planned on. There were lots of big boulders in the middle of the river, moving water surrounding them. I had hiked this stretch of river once before back in July, but there wasn't too much water, and I was face down in it anyway, paying more attention to the little fishes and sparkling diamonds than to the surrounding landscape. Looking around, it looked more like Richland Creek than the Buffalo River (Richland is probably the most scenic watercourse in Arkansas).

There was no trail, and so the going was pretty thick and tough. A bear helped out some though—a large rotten log blocking the way had been ripped up by a bear recently, allowing easy passage. I knew that there was an old pioneer road going the same direction, but it was off of the river some, up a bench or two, and I wanted to stay down along the river.

I came to a large flat-topped rock slab, sticking out nearly to the river's edge, and decided to climb up onto it and see what was there. The face of it was covered with moss, and there was an easy stair-step climb up on one side. It did take a little effort though. After all, I was carrying a pack full of gear. The top of the rock was wonderful—covered with thick, soft moss and lichens. And there was a great view of the river from on top. I felt a little foolish when I looked around and discovered that the top of the rock also led right out the back side onto level ground—I didn't have to climb up at all!

Further upstream there was another giant rock slab, and this one stuck right out into the middle of the river. I had to investigate. Most of this rock was bare, but the view from it was incredible—you could see a long ways up and down stream, and the river hugged it on three sides as it flowed past. I hadn't hiked/swam up this far in July, but probably would have found a terrific swimming hole if I had—the water around the boulder appeared to be very deep, perhaps even deep enough to jump off of the rock into! The surface of the rock was a little uneven, and there wasn't really a good spot worthy of sleeping on, so it wouldn't make a good camp spot. I did spend some time enjoying the view, then moved on.

Next I walked through a large and long grove of beech trees, the very type of trees that Neil Compton had talked about. They were everywhere! And some of them were pretty good sized, although many of the larger ones had lost their tops and were rotting down the middle—typical of big beeches. I didn't see a single carved name, thank goodness. Several of the beeches had lost all of their leaves during the dry stress of the end of the summer, and the ground was carpeted with them. I'm sure that I noted this once before, but since I don't get to note too many things, I will do so again. Beech trees don't lose their leaves in the fall like most of the other trees do. They just turn brown and stay on the branches until the new leaves in the spring push them out. Many a fine winter hike has been enhanced by walking through a grove of young beeches on a cool sunny day, especially when the wind blows them around a little and creates some rustling music to go along with the golden sunshine.

Many of the beeches had been gnawed on by beavers. They didn't really chew into the tree much, but rather seemed to be scraping off the bark. One tree looked like it had been the target of beavers several times before, each time they chewed a little more, but it was still alive. So I had hope for all of the rest. I guess the beavers were eating the bark.

At one point there was a large pile of smaller boulders, all covered with moss and lichens and leaves. It appeared to have spilled out of a small valley up above. Don't know exactly what caused it, or when.

Several times I passed through small groves of pawpaw trees, and I was forced to linger in the heavy fragrance. Funny though, while the ripe fruit was evident from the smell, I could never find any of the fruit, either in the trees or along the ground. Perhaps the critters had beaten me to all of the fruit, and only the smell from the juices remained. Kind of reminded me of a beautiful young lady standing there wearing cutoffs and a t-shirt, smiling at me, lifting my spirits. Then her boyfriend walks up.

As I got further upstream the land leveled out and the valley opened up. The ground underfoot became very soft, and my boots sunk in an inch or two. Part of it was the thick mass of leaves, the rest was sand. You could take off your shoes and run around in this stuff all day! It felt wonderful hiking through it.

The dogwood trees were already showing off their bright red berries. Plump and tasty looking. Many of the trees had lost their leaves, leaving behind naked branches covered with the red berries. One such tree that hung out over the river gathered in the glorious sunshine and it was almost blinding to look at.

And one entire hillside was covered with lush ferns. After seeing all of the dead ferns in Dug Hollow last week, it was nice to see these guys all green and happy. In fact, the forest in general looked very good and healthy up close.

I finally reached the general area that I wanted to hike to—the mouth of Boen Gulf. Actually I wasn't sure exactly where it was, but I knew that I was across from the mouth because the hillside had opened up across the way. Much to my surprise, the river was flowing so much that I could not find a dry crossing. I did manage to hop from rock to rock to rock, and only got my feet wet a couple of times. If my backpack had been heavier, I would have had to take off my boots and wade, something I just hate to do.

I thought that I was still downstream from the mouth of Boen Gulf, since I hadn't seen it, but I was mistaken. I found the stream and followed it downstream to the river. It played a trick on me, and had entered the Buffalo River hidden behind a giant rock slab. Boen Gulf was also flowing clear, though not as much volume as Whitaker Creek.

Hum, that big rock slab looked mighty inviting. I made my way out to and up on it, and sat down. This guy had been in the river a very long time, and had seen many floods. The top was polished smooth—it looked like limestone, but I felt sure that it was sandstone. There were a few cracks that were filled with dark moss, but otherwise it was all smooth stone, and mostly level.

The river rushed along around all four sides of the rock, whitewater on one side. Upstream there was more white water, as the river tumbled and gushed and fought to get around other boulders out in the middle of the river, splashing and making all kinds of noise. Just downstream, the river relaxed and flowed into a long, wide quiet pool of green.

Since I had arrived at my intended location I decided that the correct wilderness protocol would be a little skinny-dip, followed by an afternoon nap. My new found friend the rock was going to be my headquarters for the rest of my trip. I stripped off my sweaty clothes and slipped down off of the rock into the crystal clear water. Then there was a bloodcurdling cry that echoed up and down the valley. A wildcat scream? A bear? Some woods nymph being attacked? Nope, it was just me—that wonderful water was *very cold!!!*

It was a refreshing dip to say the least, but I couldn't take it too long, and soon was up back on the rock, basking in the warm sunshine. The last hours of summer drifted by in a hurry. I really do think that if everyone in the world would spend an afternoon laying on a rock beside a mountain stream, letting their troubles and frustrations and personal problems flow downstream and away, then the world would be a much nicer place indeed. Thoreau said that "In *wildness* is the preservation of the world." He was so right.

One of the few problems that I have ever had in my life is an allergy that no one seems to be able to diagnose, or treat in any way. It has usually happened towards the end of the summer, as I was returning to Arkansas from a summer up in the mountains of the west. I had always dismissed it as my bodies' way to protesting leaving the mountains. But it is real, and the symptoms are really annoying, both to me as well as others around me. I get this horrible cough, that comes from deep down inside, and it persists for weeks and even months. Nothing that I have ever taken has had any effect on it. And a really strange thing is that talking on the telephone seems to make it worse. Anyway, this cough has been creeping into me this past week. But after only a few hours out in the wilderness at Cloudland, it has completely disappeared. Hum. Perhaps it is all in my head, and I simply am growing allergic to city life. Anyway, it was a relief to be away from that terrible cough!

As the afternoon moved on into evening I spent some time exploring around the area, and found several good future campsites. The east side of the river was rocky, but the west side was mostly that soft earth. I always have to laugh when people call up and ask if there "is any place to camp along the trail?" In pretty much all of the Ozarks, I think that you can find a place to camp just about anywhere that you care to. In fact, the more I got to thinking about that on this trip, the more funny that question was. I decided that in the Upper Buffalo Wilderness alone, if you set up your tent in a different place every night, out of sight from your last night's camp, that you could camp in a different place every single night for the rest of your life and never even come close to a previous site. Hum, that would be a nice thing to try to prove. I was looking for group campsites today though because I was bringing in a small group of fellow backpackers this coming weekend to camp near here.

As it got dark I got back out onto my smooth rock in the middle of the river and settled in for the night. I munched on my dinner sandwich some, although I was not all that hungry (mark that down—I am *always* hungry!). I laid back and watched the sky turn from blue to grey to black. The air was at first filled with little birds and an occasional hawk or buzzard soaring around, then the bats came out and danced all over, and finally the bats were replaced with a thousand stars. I couldn't see all that much of the sky from my rock home since the hills rose up sharply on two sides, but I did have a good view downstream to the north, and up to the south (that sounded a little strange didn't it?).

Most of the time when I sleep out in the woods I have trouble getting to sleep because I am always listening for bears or wolves or bigfoot or some other monster to sneak up and kill me. And, of course, most of those times all of the noises are made by squirrels or deer or something else just as harmless (I've only been attacked by a bigfoot once). But on this night, all of the sounds of the forest were muted by the rushing of the whitewater at my side, and it didn't take very long for me to be lulled into deep sleep. It was comforting to know that when I awoke, it would be autumn!

The autumnal equinox was going to happen sometime in the early morning. This is when the sun is directly above the equator. From then until March 20th the sun would be in the southern hemisphere, when it would once again pass directly over the equator and be up in our neck of the woods for another six months.

I swear that the big rock slab that I was sleeping on shook when it happened. I was startled awake by a loud crash, and I was certain that another slab of rock had plunged into the river. It was very dark, only a little bit of starlight, and I didn't have a flashlight. Then I realized what it was, and it happened again. There was a beaver in the calm pool downstream from my rock, and he wasn't at all happy that I was napping in his living room. While I couldn't actually see anything in the dark, I knew what he was up to. He was slamming his broad tail against the surface of the water just to see if I would jump. I did. Then he would swim around a little, and do it again. This went on for an hour. He finally decided that I wasn't going to give up my rock nest, nor was any threat to him, so he went about his business of chewing up beech trees and chasing beaver.

9/23/98 By first light my smooth rock bed had begun to suck the warmth right out of me, and I was getting rather chilled. I snuggled deeper into the bag until there was just a tiny peep hole for me to look out of. Even through that little peep hole I could see the forest and river coming to life as birds played in the trees and fish fed on the surface of the water. Sunlight streamed through the forest to the valley floor below. It took a while for the warm light to find my little frigid rock though. There are very few finer scenes anywhere in the world than awakening to a wilderness river at your feet. Now, if I were a real mountain man, I would have crawled out of that sleeping bag and jumped right in. There is a little sanity left in me. Just a little.

I laid in my bag and finished my dinner sandwich, then ate two homemade biscuits (left by Kay last weekend). By then I was all warmed up and ready to emerge from my cocoon and greet the day. Nope, still didn't jump in. But I did splash myself some and wash my face. Not jumping in seemed like a very smart thing—that water was still cold!

I quickly packed my small camp up, looked around and made sure that there were no traces of my stay, and hopped across the river and headed back to Cloudland. This time I did follow the old pioneer road, and while it was grown up with trees and brush, it was a lot easier walking than down beside the river (though not nearly as scenic). There were more of those ladies in their cutoffs along the way—very refreshing.

Soon I was standing at the base of my little hill, and I leaned into it and started climbing. Boy, I had really gotten out of shape! I had to stop several times on the way up and blow. Guess there had been too much ice cream and too many cookies within reach this summer! There were lots of spiderwebs across the trail, so I had a few of them to snack on. As I topped out at the edge of the meadow, a cool breeze swept across and made the climb all worth it.

The afternoon was sunny and breezy, and I spent most of it lounging around out on the back deck, making sure that the swing was still suitable for guests. The foxes were both out, and I spent nearly an hour watching them. The red-eared lady was moving about a lot, circling around where the male was laying in the dirt. I could only see his head, and he was watching her every step. She was really intent on doing something, then I finally realized that she was chasing and catching grasshoppers! Then the guy got up and joined her, and they both made their way around the meadow.

Right in the middle of all this a wolf let out a piercing howl from across the way. Gosh, what an incredible sound! I quickly put my binocs back on the foxes, and they were both frozen and looking towards the sound, their ears standing up and pointing. There was only one howl, no more. The foxes remained frozen for a few more seconds, then turned and looked at each other, and then instantly jumped up and disappeared. I mean they were gone in a second! I didn't see where they went. I have seen these foxes before when coyotes yip and howl, and while they do pay attention to them, they have never really stopped what they were doing, and never have disappeared. I guess that wolves like to eat foxes, and these two guys knew it. I can't believe that I heard the wolf again. It was marvelous. This time he was not up on Beagle Point like before, but rather across the Buffalo River to the east, up on that hillside somewhere.

About a half hour later the foxes did appear again in the meadow, but they weren't nearly as carefree and playful as they had been before. After studying them more through the binocs, I did realize that the male had red ears too, although not nearly as bright as the female's ears were. When he looked at you straight on, he looked mostly grey, much like a coyote face.

And then another wildlife treat happened—a red-shouldered hawk flew through my little meadow. The first thing that I noticed was his tail, which was fanned out, revealing many white bands that ran through it. And sure enough, the top of his shoulders, all the way across the back of his neck, was covered with rusty-colored feathers. He never flapped a single time, just coasted through and then was out of sight in a few seconds, but I got a good look at him through the binocs. I never saw him again all day. Both of my birding gurus, Beth Motherwell and Lori Johnson, have told me that I am likely to begin seeing many different hawks this fall as they migrate through. Looks like it will become tougher and tougher to get any work done out here!

After a dinner of rice and cheese I took off for an evening walk. I visited the East Meadow and found that Benny had bush-hogged it, leaving one dense stand of goldenrod. There were a couple of pumpkins getting larger in the garden. The sun had dipped below the trees, and there was a cool breeze blowing, which made for a perfect walk through the meadow. On my way over to check on Bob's cabin, I discovered another grove of pawpaw's—sweet fragrance, but no fruit. Man, that girl is really making the rounds!

On the way back down the hill towards my cabin the woods are really open, and you can see far into them. What I saw this night were lots of squirrels moving about, jumping from tree to tree and running up and down the trunks.

When I landed back in the deck swing I got a close up look at what the squirrels were up to. I put the binocs on a nearby squirrel and followed him for a while. He was stretched out, hanging by his hind feet, and had grabbed a fresh hickory hut. He hung there and twirled the nut in his front paws, knocking off bits and pieces as he went—you could hear the scraps drop out of the trees and hit the ground. When he was satisfied that his nut was completely smooth and round (I guess), he swung back and scurried down the tree. Once he got onto the ground, he raced here and there, looking for the perfect place to bury the nut. I'm not sure why they spend so much time searching for just the right spot, or how in the world they ever find it come winter, but they do manage quite well. I wonder how many hickory nuts go uneaten and remain in the ground each year? Come to think of it, those are the ones that grow up and become hickory trees—way to go squirrels!

Squirrels gathering nuts and hiding them in the dirt—is there a better sign of fall?

It was getting dark, and once the squirrel had found his perfect spot and buried his nut, then climbed back onto the tree for another one, I turned my attention to the sky. A tiny sliver of moon appeared in the grey sky. But it shown brightly, and really made the statement that *less is more*. As the evening wore on, the sky turned black, and the moon changed to a bright silver, then to orange as it sank into the western sky.

It had been a fine autumn day. I crawled under the covers early.

9/24/98 With more than a full nights rest in me I got up early, before sunrise, slurped down my mocha drink, put on my backpack, and headed down the steep trail towards the river. The climb up the day before had told me that I really needed to do something to get back into shape, so this was my little fitness hike with the full backpack (well, it weighed about 30 pounds). It was a wonderful little hike down the mountainside in the cool morning air. When I arrived at the river, it was singing and dancing and enjoying the new season. I located the swim mask and snorkel that I had stashed behind a tree all summer, and loaded it in my pack. I knew that while there may still be a plunge or two into the ol' swimming hole this fall, that I probably would not be in the water long enough to do any exploring with the mask.

And I found a single cardinal wildflower along the river bank. These brilliant red guys usually grow right in the middle of the dry river beds in the late summer, and were mostly underwater now or washed away all together. This lone survivor stood as a reminder of the warm waters of summer.

There were also bunches of these wonderful blue wildflowers with yellow centers growing along the bank. I have looked them up in the wildflower book before, and the only thing that come close is Asiatic dayflower. I question the

149

ID because it says that they only last one day, and I have seen these same flowers in the same locations many times. At any rate, they were wonderful, and my favorite color too!

On the way back up the hill I started making up another song—"Buffalo River Blues, I got the Buffalo River Blues. Blue skies, bluebirds, wild blue berries..." Probably won't make it to the top-10.

I did make it up to the top of the hill though, but I had to stop and blow three times, always for less than ten seconds. If I could only stay with my promise of doing this every day, I would feel and look a lot better. I will try to do it again, and keep it up.

The sun was peeking out from behind a few clouds when I reached the cabin, and another cool breeze came along with it. It must be humid, because I was drenched. The forest floor was dry, but the small sycamore trees along the river bank and the wildflowers were wet from dew.

All too soon it has come time for me to leave Cloudland for a little while, and go back to civilization to visit with my mom. I shall return tonight or tomorrow. It will be interesting to see if my cough returns during this short trip into town.

I almost always take one last look from the back deck before I leave the cabin. When I did so, I saw not one but two pairs of hawks and vultures flying together. They were circling in formation, one pair down low in the valley, and the other pair up high. The lower pair nearly crashed into one another once. Very strange. Neither of the hawks were red-tailed hawks, nor red-shouldered, and they were large so not Cooper's—I have no idea what they were. I need Beth or Lori or someone to just move in out here to help ID birds!

One of the hawks came soaring over close by, and I could see that he was carrying something in his talons. In fact, he even juggled it a time or two. He sort of swooped up and flung it into the air, then reached up and grabbed it. It didn't look like a body of any kind, but rather was round, and about the size of a hickory nut. A hickory nut? Is that possible? Right in the middle of all this he flew down and landed in the top of one of the trees at the edge of the meadow. He seemed to be adjusting the nut some, then took off in flight again. Wow, I'm glad that I walked out onto the deck for one last look!

9/25/98 It is Friday afternoon, pizza is in the oven, a cold Arkansas Ale in a frosted mug is in my hand, and the evening light is just spectacular—must be another weekend brewing at Cloudland!

The wind is blowing a steady 10-15mph, and it is very hazy out. Some of the ridges are silhouetted, defined only by their fuzzy tree-lined ridgetops, while others are lit up by the sun, and every big oak and hickory tree is visible. Just across the way, over on Beagle Point, there are three smaller "draws." The right-hand side of each one is lit up, while the left-hand side is in the shade, although you can still see the individual trees there. Everything is smoky. All of that smoke and the low light gives the landscape a very surreal feeling. There aren't any birds out—not even a single one that I can see. And my fox buddies are nowhere to be found. I guess they all know that there are a number of guests coming out for the weekend, and they have gone into hiding. That's OK with me—I feel like doing that sometimes myself.

The forest out here has responded to the rain last week in a very unusual way. I swear that the trees that had begun to turn colors are now back to their normal summer green. Is that possible? I know that some of the leaves simply turned color and dropped off, but the woods just look a lot more green than they did two weeks ago, and there is not nearly as much color. In fact, there really isn't much color at all. Although I did see some sumac bushes the other day that were brilliant red, which is typical for them at this time of the year. Fall is going to be glorious, no matter when it hits or how brilliant it is.

Time to go cut up the pizza, pour another Arkansas Ale, and tune in to **Ozarks At Large** and **The New Blues Show** on KUAF. Tomorrow I will be leading a group of OHTA members down to the river and up into the heart of the wilderness for an overnight trip. I look forward to each and every step.

I had two sets of folks coming out for the weekend. About a dozen backpackers for my hike, and several friends that were just coming out to spend the weekend—Rob, Sharon, Patsy, and Cindy, who arrived at about the same time that I finished my pizza. The wind kicked up, and blew like crazy.

As Patsy and I were out on the back deck conversing I noticed something hit the oak tree right in front of me, but it was dark and I couldn't see what it was. A few minutes later it happened again. I went inside and got a flashlight—son of a gun, it was a flying squirrel! He had literally "flown" from a tree about twenty feet away. He looked down on all of us with these two giant eyes that took up nearly half of his head, and he was clinging to a big acorn that was stuck in his mouth. My friend Scott Crook, who has a number of flying squirrels as pets, showed me last year how flying squirrels will eat a hole in an acorn, dig out the little grub that is living in most of them, then discard the nut. It turns out that flying squirrels are about as common in the Ozarks as any other variety, but since they are nocturnal, we seldom ever see any.

The wind continued to blow, but since it was a little warm, it felt great. We all stayed up and gabbed through more blues on the radio, jazz, and on into early morning. Then they all spread out on the lower deck and let the wind and stars put them to sleep.

9/26/98 I got up pretty early, shouldered my "fitness" backpack, and headed down the ladder trail to the river for my morning hike. On the way down I realized that the steepness of the trail, and the weight of the filled pack, were taking a toll on my knee. I really don't mind the climb up at all, in fact rather look forward to it (because I know it is helping burn off some fat), but the descent is a real killer. So I decided that this might be my last fitness hike down this steep trail with a loaded pack. I would have to figure out some other hike with the pack that I could do from the cabin.

The river was relatively quiet when I arrived. The water level had dropped dramatically in two days, but it still filled the valley with hushed humming. I turned around and headed back up the trail, taking off at a pretty good clip at first. When I hit the first steep bench, my pace slowed significantly. I leaned into the hill. It felt great. The second steep bench was tougher, and my breathing got kind of loud. By the time I reached the third steep bench, I was whipped. This one is always a killer for me. And the footing is bad. I sucked it up and plowed on, creeping up the mountainside. Sweat began dripping onto the ground. I thought about pausing to catch my breath, but wanted to make it without stopping. Another few steps. Damn, I need to stop and blow. Keep going. Keep going. Heck, I can just stop for a minute, who cares? I do. I wasn't doing this for anyone but me. And it did matter if I made it to the top without stopping. I had to keep going.

The fourth and final tough bench appeared. The little stretch of trail between them isn't quite as steep, so I "rested" as I walked across it. Up, up and away. My eyes were glued to the ground at my feet. Every fraction of an inch is important, so I made sure that I didn't step any higher than necessary, which sometimes meant veering off course a few inches to miss a rock in the way. The sweat was really pouring off now, and I was sucking wind like there wasn't much left. At last, the ladder! But I wasn't finished. My pack felt like it weighed 100 pounds as I climbed to the top of the bluff. One foot after the other. I can make it. Just as I reached the edge of my property, sunshine hit me in the face, and also illuminated a stretch of purple aster wildflowers that were swaying in the wind. A breeze, yes, the breeze felt great!!!

The rest of the cabin was awake when I finally dragged myself in, and we all sat down to a wonderful egg casserole. It is always so great when my guests bring a lot of food and spread it around.

When I ended my hike I had noticed a footprint in the mud near the front porch, but was too ravished to investigate. After cleaning up my plate I went out to see what it was—*another bear track!* This one was a print from a back foot. It looked like the bear had stood there and put his paws up on the front railing. He probably had come up last night and just wanted to listen to the blues show, and stood up to hear better. Nice bear.

Breakfast revived me, and I slipped into a pair of coveralls, grabbed a few tools out of the Rubbermaid shed, and went to work on a short stretch of trail that I had been wanting to build between the cabin and the ladder trail. I dug and chopped and sawed and moved rocks. Then I made a couple of passes with a McLeod (a special trail-building and fire-fighting tool), and the trail was nearly complete (well, as complete as I was going to make it this morning). This was the very first trail work that I had done at Cloudland. It only took me an hour, but will make the short trip from the cabin to the ladder trail a lot easier.

Soon the backpackers arrived and both the parking lot and the cabin were crowded. I weighed my pack (my real one for the trip, not the fitness one), and it topped out at 13 pounds. How nice! Everyone else's looked a lot *bigger.* Sometimes I like to be a minimalist backpacker, and this was one of those times. I had everything that I needed though, and didn't feel like I was "doing without" anything. So what the heck. I had spent the night in the woods this summer already with much less. Well, actually with nothing. There were a few smirks from the group.

The contents of my pack: daypack, pile sleeping bag, bivy sack, water bottle, water pump, 16ozs. wine, pizza, rain jacket, bandanna, camera, two apples, three breakfast bars, gum, flashlight, comb, lighter, toothbrush and paste, Kleenex, headnet, map. I was wearing shorts, long pants, long-sleeved shirt, hat, socks and gaiters.

We lost one hiker after only 15 minutes—his knees just couldn't handle the steep trail. The rest of us went on, but slowly, as a couple of others lagged behind. Before long we were all standing on the wonderful giant rock slab that I had visited a few days before. Several of the group hurriedly peeled off a few clothes, stood on the edge of the rock, and jumped in. The water was great! And pretty deep too. After a few seconds of debate, we decided to camp across the river on a sand and gravel bar. Within minutes everyone was exploring our new swimming hole. It was about eight feet deep, and you could see all the way to the bottom easily. One odd thing was that there were hardly any fish in the pool at all. I don't know why.

The gravel bar was rather interesting to me. The size of the rock/gravel/sandbar got smaller as you got further away from the river. The bank was lined with softball-sized polished rocks of all shapes. A little further up the slope the rocks were baseball, then golf ball sized. Then large gravel, still all polished and smooth. Then coarse sand. And finally, right up next to the edge of the forest, very fine sand. This fine sand strip is where most everyone set up their camps. Who needed a sleeping pad in this soft stuff. I didn't have any camp to set up.

Once we all cooled off a bit we took off for an exploratory trip upstream. One of the first things that some of the group noticed was that there were several areas of "stinging nettles" along the route—they were wearing shorts. Ouch! I hate those things. And you don't really know that you have gotten yourself into them until it is too late because there is a delay before the tiny stickers begin to itch—and by then you have walked through a lot of them, so you know the pain will continue for awhile. I had on long pants, so didn't pay them too much attention. Or did I really go out of my way to take the group through more patches of them? Hum.

The river down below was spectacular. Lots of emerald green pools with big boulders, and water rushing from pool to pool. And there were dozens of big beech trees, most of them in good shape and not rotten.

We headed up a steep hill, away from the river, topped out on a small ridge and dropped down into Hubbard Hollow. Wow!, what a great place! I had always heard about it, but this was my first visit. The place was magical. There were *giant* moss-covered boulders strewn about everywhere. When the water is really up, there would be hundreds of waterfalls. Like the siren of the sea, we were drawn up into the beauty, climbing up and up into the hillside. The scenery just got better and better. Every side drainage in this area of the Buffalo River has some incredible stuff in it, but this one is so special because it is a lot steeper than the others, so all of the neat stuff is compacted. And tougher to get to, too. That's good—this place would never get too many visitors.

Once while off to myself, I got into a silly predicament that could have gotten serious. I tried to get across the face of a moss-covered bluff, but ended up slipping and falling. I managed to grab a grapevine that saved me temporarily. There I was, dangling on the side of the bluff, with no footholds, hanging onto this grapevine that went way up into a big tree. After several anxious minutes of looking around to see what I could do to escape, I decided that there was none. All I could do was let go of the vine and hope for the best. As I let go and began to fall, I rolled to my left against the face of the bluff. That took me away from the worst part of the fall, and I was able to get a foothold and get myself under control again. Good thing no one was around to witness this. I managed to escape with most of my pride and my rump intact.

Before we were able to see all of the hollow, stomachs began to growl, so we turned around and headed back to camp. It was a very nice, easy stroll through the beech groves and along the river.

Leftover pizza (guess who's?), sandwiches, rice and broccoli, Mexican tortillas, freeze-dried dinners—there was a little bit of everything spread out on our rock slab table as nine hungry hikers chowed down. Our overnight hikes are limited to ten hikers. I always over-book, but assume some are going to cancel. Twelve signed up. Two cancelled. One had to turn back.

Dawna and I found a plant on the gravel bar that was covered with what seemed like wild peas or green beans (I have looked and looked but couldn't find anything in my ID books about it). We ate a number of them, and while a little crunchy raw, we thought that they would be pretty good if steamed. It was a wilderness gravel bar salad.

One of our group, Mike Anderson, must have been a beaver in a previous life. After dinner he jumped up and gathered firewood, and gathered firewood, and gathered firewood. We all laid down in the gravel around a marvelous campfire and talked long into the night. The crescent moon hung high over the river at first, but dipped below the trees and out of sight while the conversation was still in high gear. Roy had hiked into our campsite while we were out exploring and left a two-way radio behind. He returned to the cabin where a party was going on in my absence. The radio was to keep up with an important football game going on back in town (Roy was one of the cancellations, but he was kind enough to bring in the radio, then returned to the cabin). We got frequent updates, but really couldn't believe the score (Arkansas was beating Alabama badly).

At some point in the evening we had a good lesson about fire rings. *Do NOT build them!* I'm not sure why this stupid practice is so deeply ingrained in our American psyche, but the first thing that everyone wants to do is build a fire ring. They are stupid because they don't really contain a fire in the first place, they leave blackened and scarred stones behind to mar the landscape, and coals hidden under the stones often will get blown around by winds and cause forest fires long after the camper has left (even after "drowning" the rest of the fire). They are a waste of time, a fire hazard, and a scar on the landscape. And they aren't even necessary in the first place. So please, Smokey Bear says don't play with matches, I say don't build fire rings! Thank you. Now, back to the river.

Our little busy beaver kept getting up and hunting more firewood. He returned one time very excited—*Want to see some glowing bugs?* These things were incredible. They were actually isopods, sort of relatives of roly-polies (I could not figure out how to spell this!). And when you flashed a flashlight on them they looked perfectly normal. But when the light was out, they glowed like a firefly with a broken switch. And they lined the riverbank as far as you could see. There was probably two or three hundred years of woods' experience represented in the astonished faces gathered there, but none of us had ever seen anything like it.

With temperatures in the low 70's or upper 60's the campfire really felt great. Is there a better gathering spot in all the world than a campfire beside a river? Conversations went round and round. Stars came out. It must have been after midnight before we finally called it a night. I was the only one not sleeping on the gravel bar—I wanted the big rock. So I headed across the river and through the woods in the dark, much to some of the other hikers' amazement. What, me hiking through the woods in the dark—that's just what you do at Cloudland, and you *love it!* I did.

I found a nice depression in the big rock slab that just fit my body and spread out the blanket. I had taken some ribbing from the group because I had not carried in a sleeping pad. Heck, I backpacked for ten or fifteen years before I ever used one. I do normally carry one, but didn't really feel the need to pack it in this time. All you have to do is get it in your mind that the rock is "firm" instead of "hard" and you will be OK. At least for one night.

The campfire across the way still flickered and glowed. One by one flashlights went out, and I was left all alone with the river and a million stars. The night sky never ceases to amaze me, and this was one very clear night. I laid there and stared. There went a shooting star. Then another. And another. I remembered back to a personality test that I took during training with the forest service back in 1973. One of the questions was *When was the last time that you spent five minutes looking for falling stars?* For me it had been the night before. I passed the test.

OK, it is late, I've seen falling stars before, let's get a little shut-eye. Just one more falling star and I'll close my eyes. Five minutes. Ten minutes. No more falling stars. Now it was driving me crazy. I had to see just one more. The sky remained silent and still. I was wide awake now. I got up and went over and sat on the edge of the big rock, which was about twelve feet above the water. Oh my—all of the night sky was reflected in the still pool below. And the edges of

155

both sides of the river were lined with those glowing roly-polies. It looked a little like flying up the coast and seeing all of these lights of cities down below. This is one of those scenes in Nature that is very spectacular, but is impossible to photograph. It can be made up on canvas with a brush I guess, but not on film. So I was forced to simply sit there and enjoy. Then, as I was looking deep into the water, an incredibly brilliant star shot across the sky, lighting up the reflection in the water. I held my breath. It was beautiful. I turned around and saw the tail still glowing. Then it was all dark again. OK, I was ready for sleep.

9/27/98 The gravel bar across the way was up and moving at first light. I stayed over on my little perch and had breakfast, pumped some water, and sat and stared into the pool. Eventually everyone packed up, made their slippery way across the river, and we were on our way out. We passed several fragrant paw-paw patches, but none of us could locate any fruit—it was that darn lady in cutoffs again. (After my last little story about this, I got an e-mail picture of a lovely lady in a bikini sitting on a rock in the Buffalo River—she wanted me to recognize her if I saw her in the woods and not think her one of the elusive ladies in cutoffs.)

When we got to Whitaker Creek there was an incredible display of Asiatic day-flowers growing in the creekbed—it must have been ten feet wide and contained 60-80 little bright blue and yellow wildflowers. And on the other side someone spotted an orchid growing right in the middle of the trail (not in bloom at this time of the year, but I'm going to look for it come April).

Oh yea, and we had this little hill to climb up. Hey, a piece of cake for me—I had just made it the day before with a full backpack that was much heavier than the daypack that I had on. I fell in behind a couple of hikers with very large packs on their backs. I knew they would fall by the wayside soon. Up and up we went. One of them peeled off in the middle of the first steep bench. It was getting hot and muggy, and there was no breeze. I broke out in a heavy sweat. The other guy ahead of me seemed to pick up speed. I leaned into the hillside, but couldn't keep up. Surely he would run out of steam soon. Nope. He just kept right on going, and my pace slowed to a crawl. I made it up to the ladder without stopping, but Bob Robinson was already there and breathing normally. It does pay to be in good shape! I'd be there one of these days.

Bob stayed behind to help get packs and people up the ladder. I pushed on to the cabin to see if it was still standing—we could tell from the radio transmissions the night before that there was a major party going on in my absence. That was the first time that I hadn't been in on a party at my own cabin. When I arrived everything looked OK, and breakfast was in the oven. There was a great deal of food and beer and water consumed in the next couple of hours. All of the hikers made it out alive, although two of them on their very first backpack trip were questionable. (Not a good idea to go on a "difficult" rated backpack trip as your first hiking experience, especially when there is no trail! We all live and learn. Some lessons are tougher than others.)

For the first time that I can remember every single seat on the back deck was occupied, even the swing and the log glider. I either need to get more chairs or have fewer guests. No, it was just right. It was getting hot, and there was no breeze at all, except for the two ceiling fans overhead. And there wasn't a single bird anywhere to be seen. Not even any buzzards. I guess all of the racket from the many conversations kept everyone away.

Soon all good-byes were finished and the cabin and I were alone again. It was nap time!

The evening light lit up the canyons as I munched on the last of my pizza. It was dead still. No birds. No squirrels. No bugs. It was kind of eerie. As I was talking on the phone to my mom, I moved on over to the railing and looked down into the woods. Right there, sitting on a limb, was a *huge* black hawk. He looked up at me a little sheepishly, like he had been caught at something, then spun around and lumbered off through the woods. It was a roughed-legged hawk. He was dark, and big.

Later on after the sun went down, but before it was completely dark, one of my little fox friends returned and paced back and forth in the meadow down below. I was kind of surprised that it had returned so quickly after all the noise died down. And this was the first time that I had seen a fox in dusky-dark conditions. It was dark enough out so that I couldn't see any color—never knew if it was the guy or the girl fox. But it was great to see it.

The nighttime air is cool now, it is still, and a band of night bugs are out. Think I'll go lounge around, converse with them and soak up the moonlight.

Speaking of the moon, I had a great view of it from my bed in the loft as it hung low in the western sky, then it dipped below the ridge and out of sight. The lower it got, the more orange it became. The moon was lit from the right, and a little below. During a recent **Earth and Sky** show on the radio I learned that whenever the moon is lit from the right, it is waxing, or getting larger (more of the moon lit up every night). When lit from the left, it is waning, or getting smaller each day. I will keep an eye on it during this cycle to make sure that they are correct.

9/28/98 The sun broke over the hillside with a brilliant yellow glow. The valleys and ridges were covered with a fine mist—not really haze or smoke, but mist. As I sat on the back deck with my mocha, I saw a giant bird soaring way up the main valley. While it was over a mile away, I could still see it pretty good through the binocs. The wings were flat, meaning that it was not a buzzard (they have a "V" shape to their wings when flying). Since it was so large, it had to be an eagle, probably the golden eagle that we had seen before. I watched him for about a minute, and he never flapped his wings a single time. He soared on into the Boen Gulf drainage and disappeared. I've never seen a soaring bird out so early here before. I wonder what he was up to?

I had decided that I would make a pilgrimage down to the river this morning to photograph the bouquet of Asiatic day-flowers in the creekbed that we had seen the day before. I knew that the sun needed to find them for a little while before they would "wake" up and pose, so I wasn't in a big hurry. I packed up my fanny pack with the big camera, film, and a few accessories, got my big tripod (12 pounds worth) and headed down the trail. It was pretty easy going, although there were a lot of spiderwebs out. When I reached the flowers, they were still asleep and covered with dew—the sun had not gotten to them yet. I dropped my stuff there and went on over to the main river.

There was a little mist rising from the cool water. The river was pretty low now, but still flowing more so than July or August levels. I laid down on Norma's Reading Rock beside one of the pools and drifted off. About a half hour later the sun poked through the trees and woke me up. I had a strange feeling that something was watching me. As my eyes got accustomed to the brightness of the blue sky overhead, I saw my spy—it was the eagle, up high and just coasting downstream. He was looking right down at me, but soon soared out of sight. I suspect that if I had woken up 30 seconds later I would have never seen him.

That was kind of exhilarating, being studied by a golden eagle. And the sun made things rather warm. So I walked downstream to the big pool, stripped off my clothes, and jumped in for one last swim of the season. The water was cool, but not cold. I swam a couple of laps, then got out and returned to the flat rock to let the sun dry me off.

Back at the flower garden the sun still hadn't done much good so I went off to wander around in the woods some. I examined the stone chimney at the old homesite nearby—I wondered if they built the chimney first or the cabin? When there is snow on the ground, you can see this chimney through the telescope on my back deck. I also wondered if the people who lived here spent as much time down by the river enjoying it as I had done this summer? It was a splendid location for a homesite.

Whitaker Creek was flowing a little—the water was clear and cold. I laid down beside it and sucked up some of the crystal water. Just then a batch of coyotes let out some yips and howls way up the valley—the sound echoed off of the steep forest walls and spilled out into the main canyon. I was full of wonder this morning, and wondered if they were calling out to each other, laughing at some joke, or moaning for a full moon.

I wandered down the creekbed and found an odd-looking caterpillar. I had seen this type before, but have been unable to find anything like it in the ID books. This one was resting on a sweet gum leaf that had already turned a nice shade of red and fallen to the ground. It was time for me to get working, so I set up the camera and shot 36 macro pictures of the little guy and the leaf. The scene looked great through the viewfinder, but I never know if it will turn out OK until I get the film processed.

It was obvious that the sun was not going to illuminate the flower garden the way that I had seen it yesterday—must have imagined the even light in my mind. Our brains have a way of making things look better than they really are sometimes, which is one reason why many of the pictures that we take just don't turn out the way we remembered the scene—our brain made the scene look perfect, when in reality it wasn't.

Anyway, I found one flower that was lit up just right, so I set up my camera rig and shot a few pictures. Then I shot a few more. And a few more. Another roll of 36 was soon used up, and I bid my flower garden and the creekbed farewell and headed up the hill to the cabin. About halfway up I adjusted the heavy fanny pack to the front, which helped throw some of the weight into the hillside, making it easier to climb. I did stop and rest for a minute or two a couple of times, as much to take in the wonderful forest around me as to catch my breath. It was hot, and humid, but I didn't mind the exercise, especially after all of that pizza!

I am back at the cabin now, have showered and snacked and cleaned up and cooled down. Since I have a lot of work to do in town this week, I may not be back out here to Cloudland until the end of the week, which will be in October. For me October signals the beginning of fall. And I have been thinking back this morning to the summertime just ending, and all of the great and wonderful things and people that have happened and visited here. It has been a summer beyond my wildest dreams. I have met many wonderful people—interesting and funny and talented and, well, just plain good people. I have been honored that they, many of you, have taken the time out of their busy lives to stop by and share this place with me. I have been loved, challenged, and made sport of (not enough of the loving though). We have had tremendous feasts, a lot of fine wine, and mouth-watering desserts. I have learned a great deal about our Ozarks history, about the people and plants and animals that call this area home, and have become friends with foxes and deer and falling stars. Summer is always the worst season of the year for me—as great as this past one has been, I look forward with glee to the seasons to come. I hope that you will come along and share it all with me. Thanks for reading.

9/30/98 I did get to spend part of another day at Cloudland in September after all. It was dark with a light rain falling when I arrived. That typical fall crispness was in the air, and the temperature had dropped down into the low 60's. The cabin was warm, but quickly cooled down with all of the windows open. I had to put on a long-sleeved shirt to sit out on the back deck. The rain didn't last too long, and finally gave way to moonlight. The clouds were high and broken, and the moon and a few stars broke through them to light up the night. Cloud banks gathered low in the valleys, then were blown around by the wind. They seemed to be searching out something, perhaps another season. Good-bye summer. You were one grand wilderness lullaby!

September rain was 7.3 inches, low 59 degrees, high 95 degrees, wind 30mph

OCTOBER 1998

10/1/98 Hello *fall!* Glad to see ya again. It was very misty as light crept into my loft retreat. I rolled over expecting to see a sea of clouds down in the valley, but all of the fog banks had escaped to some unknown location during the night. I have found that even though I might be tired and still sleepy at daylight, I will often jump up out of bed and race to the fridge (to get my mandatory Starbucks mocha) and then take my place on the back deck just to be there to soak up the early morning. This is not really like me at all, but I find myself doing it more and more out here at Cloudland. Must be the atmosphere.

There really wasn't all that much going on outside, not even any birds flying around, but it was cool and damp and cloudy and I loved it. I strapped on my backpack and headed out for a fitness hike. I went down my new little trail and then along the top of the bluffline to the Crag.

Not too far from the cabin I found some fresh bear sign—he had dug into the ground and torn up a bee nest. You could see a lot of the honeycomb scattered along the ground, and some that was still in the dirt. It must have been rather fresh, perhaps just that morning or the night before, because many of the bees were flying around in a daze and trying to figure out what had happened. Bears are a lot like me—they love the sweet stuff!

I stepped out onto the Crag for just a moment to survey the progress of fall up in the valley (it hadn't progressed much—everything was still pretty much green), then continued on. I really needed to get my heart rate up, and walking on the level wasn't having much impact. I passed beech trees, and limbs and trees that had been tossed across the trail by recent storms, and cruised through the forest on automatic pilot.

I must have been deep in some thought and not paying any attention whatsoever, but when the trail got steep, I looked up and didn't have a clue where I was. I had apparently hiked for a few minutes, crossed a small creek, then hiked some more, without even knowing it—wow, that is automatic pilot! The climb that followed, though small, felt great, and I finally got my heart pounding a little. I came out on the main gravel road, then hiked back to the cabin on my "long driveway," for a total hike of about four miles in just over an hour.

There weren't any birds, bugs or spiderwebs out this morning, but there were a *ton* of squirrels out! I counted 43 of them on my little hike. Good grief! And almost all of them were running along the ground, or jumping from tree to tree. I guess the cooler temps gave them some sense of urgency that winter was on the way and they had better get to burying some nuts. I can't remember ever seeing so many squirrels. They were everywhere. A funny thing about them was that there were more of them along the road than along the trail.

There was one spectacular persimmon tree up in the Faddis Meadow—it looked more like an apple tree, with its branches loaded with nearly-ripe fruit and hanging towards the ground. The leaves were green, but the persimmons were all colors, from green to orange and red. I wouldn't normally think of a persimmon tree as being a great-looking tree, but this one sure was. If it only weren't for all of those darn seeds!

The misty day lingered on, but it never did rain. Stayed plenty cool though. And there were never any soaring birds out at all—guess there weren't any thermals to ride. But there were lots of flickers out. I saw five around the meadow at one time. And another red-headed woodpecker, which flew off and away just like the others had done. And there was this one little red chipmunk down in the meadow. He was running about just like the squirrels. As I watched him through the binocs I wondered why so many of the animals here had rust-colored fur or feathers: foxes, squirrels, hawks, and now chipmunks. (Seems like I've said that before, but thought it bears repeating. Oops, I shouldn't use that word.) A couple of owls hooted at each other around 3pm.

There wasn't a sunset, but soon after it got dark the clouds cleared out and a nice moon, over half full, lit up the wilderness. It was so bright in fact that you could see the river from the deck, reflecting the moonlight from.

I had to go around and close all of the windows and put on long pants—must be fall! I almost lit a fire in the fireplace, but decided to leave that for some official ceremony later—the first fire of the season and all that. There will probably be a toast involved.

10/2/98 I awoke early to the sound of children playing—wait a minute, not at Cloudland. I soon realized that it was just a squirrel, chattering away in one of his dozen or so different voices. They have more sounds than about any other animal that I know of.

It was in the 50's with a strong breeze blowing. It was a grey, overcast day, the kind that I like! It looked like someone unrolled a roll of cotton across the sky, and that it might snow any minute.

I suited up in my overalls, grabbed my log-splitting axe, and went down into the meadow to chop up a little firewood. I rather enjoy this chore, and the colder, the better. The meadow is full of downed tree parts, many of which have been cut up but not split. We did a lot of splitting last winter, and hauled much of it up to the cabin and burned it. But there is still a lot of split wood that needs to be hauled up. I said that I love the splitting part, but don't relish the hauling part at all! The plan was for my weekend guests over the winter last year to pitch in and help haul the wood up, but that almost never happened—we all were too busy enjoying the novelty of the cabin. I am going to get a group of folks out here next weekend to form a human chain up the hillside, and then we will toss the split wood up, which will make it a lot easier. So I will be spending some time this weekend getting the wood ready to be tossed up.

Just as I finished up an hour of splitting it began to rain. Not too hard, although the wind made it seem so. I sat in my easy chair on the deck and let my bare feet get soaked. The forest is still mostly green, and not showing any signs of turning color. Although much of the forest is getting a lighter shade of green, and looks more like spring green—this is a little odd. It looks like everything is about ready to turn yellow or something, but I doubt that will be the case. I guess the forest doesn't quite know what to think about all of the dry that we had in August and early September followed by so much rain, or what to do now. Sometimes, when we have a really wet fall, the colors aren't so good. I prefer a dry fall, followed by some good rain at the last minute, but I will take what I can get.

The black gums are beginning to turn red again (they already did so three weeks ago, but got knocked back by the rain). I think that the forest is all assembling its color machine at the border, just waiting for the right moment. Then it will burst forth with all its got and create a splendid fall color show. I continue to read all this scientific stuff about why the leaves turn color, but not much of it really makes any sense. Instead of trying to calculate all of the factors that they say go into all this, I prefer to simply get out as much as possible and enjoy whatever comes along.

Well, a cold rain came along this evening. The temp dropped into the 50's, strong winds whipped up (30mph gusts), and the rain turned frigid. Although it wasn't a hard rain, it hit you in the face hard since the wind was blowing. Only a trace measured on the electronic rain gauge. I spent most of the evening on the couch reading and listening to the blues on KUAF radio. Since all of the windows were shut, I was oblivious to the storm raging outside. This cabin is so airtight, that the 30mph winds could not be heard at all, even with the radio turned off. It got chilly inside, and I almost lit the fire. I keep thinking about that big toast.

More signs of fall showed up as I prepared for bed. The standard soap here is Dr. Bronner's liquid soap (biodegradable). All summer the flavor has been peppermint, because it leaves you really refreshed and cool. It was not fun tonight to step out of the shower into a cold bathroom with peppermint all over me! It is time to switch to the eucalyptus flavor, which leaves the body warmed but still refreshed. Also, I had tweaked the hot water heater down to a low temp for the summer—now the hottest water in the shower is not warm enough. And finally, when I crawled into the bed, the crisp cotton sheets of summer were just a little, well, cold. I needed the *flannel* sheets from Germany that were stashed in the closet! So fall has indeed arrived at Cloudland.

The winds blew and blew all night, and I could hear their tunes in the trees now and then. The nearly-full moon was obscured by the heavy cloud cover. I don't think that there were any owls out hooting tonight.

10/3/98 I did *not* get up at first light this morning, but rather simply rolled over and sunk deeper under the covers. I really need to get a comforter for the loft bed. I have a wonderful down comforter, but it is normally too hot. The quilt is not quite warm enough. Actually, the loft is probably the coldest right now that it will ever be. Once I get the fireplace going, it will be warmer in the loft, and the quilt will probably be warm enough. So should I fork out some bucks for a new comforter to cover with just a week or two a year? Probably not. I'm cheap you know.

When I did finally get up it was misting outside and blowing hard. A cloud bank hovered just above the ridgetops. It was very clear below the clouds and I could see that the forest looked another shade lighter in color—perhaps it is getting ready to pop. The weather reminded me of October in Canada. Most people would look out and say *Yuk!* But I just love this kind of weather. I don't really have a destination this morning, but I am going to strap on boots, grab my rain coat, and take off into the woods and see where the wind blows me.

When I went outside I realized that it wasn't nearly as cold as it looked. It was a little damp out, and misting just a little. I walked slowly and deliberately rather than taking off on a fitness hike. The moisture in the air and on the ground really made the colors of the forest come to life. The greens of the mosses and the browns of the leaves on the forest floor were *so* much richer than normal. And at my slowed down pace, I could afford to take close looks at anything and everything that caught my eye.

One thing I saw pretty soon was a little wilderness drama that would take a hundred years to play out. There was slab of rock next to the trail, about ten or twelve feet square and five feet tall. A serviceberry tree had rooted itself in the cracks on the top of the rock, and was growing rapidly. It had pushed a chunk of the big rock over the edge as it grew, and this chunk landed against a small beech tree. (I guess that I could call it a son of a beech, but I'll stick with just small). The chunk was still laying on the big rock, and the serviceberry was still growing and pushing on the rock chunk. Meanwhile, the beech tree had embraced the rock chunk and was growing "arms" on both sides to hold the rock in place and keep it from falling.

The serviceberry tree will continue to grow and push the rock against the beech. I wonder who will win? Probably what will happen is that the serviceberry tree will eventually cease growing, or will find the rock too tough to push, and will simply grow in another direction. Then, after maybe a hundred years, the beech will die, after having cradled this rock slab almost its entire life, and the rock will fall to the ground. A hundred years to move the rock slab a couple of feet—that is a microsecond in geological time. But is great to be here at this moment and be witness to it. Can you think of any specific events like this one going on along your favorite trail?

My pace slowed more as I came to a lush carpet of thick mosses and lichens. The green was *so* rich! A lot of people think that the type of film that I shoot makes the colors in my images richer, more intense, and exaggerated. Not true! I simply shoot my pictures when the light is good and the natural richness of the colors show themselves, like the mosses and leaves today. Many people stay indoors or put their cameras away when it is wet outside—I pack extra film!

A little further along the trail I came across a bunch of weeds that normally get in my way. But today they were covered with bright, yellow trumpet flowers. I had never seen them before, even though I had just hiked this same trail two days ago. They were gorgeous, and the yellow too was very rich in this light. They were growing right out of another carpet of moss, the kind of moss that reminds me of a miniature pine forest. When you get down on your hands and knees you can see that the moss is made up of thousands of individual "trees." What is this stuff called? I must look it up. Anyway, the next time that I am bothered by a bunch of nondescript weeds, I must give them a little leeway because they just might burst out into yellow flowers someday!

I was having such a grand time inching my way down the trail that it took me over an hour to arrive at the Crag. There was no one else there. I sat down and took a good long look. The mist had stopped, and the clouds were lifting some. There still weren't any soaring birds around, but there were a couple of crows that flew up the valley from the Buffalo River. I sat and watched them as they flew towards me, then overhead, and continued up the valley. It was odd that they had to flap constantly—they weren't soaring at all, and had to fight for every foot of air travel. I wondered if it was just a lack of air currents to ride, or if crows are just not built to do that. Perhaps a little of both.

There were several squirrels barking way off down in the valley, and up on the other hillside. They usually do this when there is someone or something approaching, so there must have been deer or other critters roaming about.

As I was leaving the Crag a chipmunk jumped up on a log and "chipped" at me. Then he got down and ran over to the base of a big rock. His backside was red just like the one at the cabin. He turned and looked at me once more, then disappeared. I got down on all fours and looked deep into the entrance to his castle. There were two bright orange mushrooms growing right in the middle of the entrance. Boy, this guy had it made. Not only was the roof of his house covered with 100 tons of rock, but he had his breakfast growing right at the front door!

When I was a kid I used to spend a lot of time in the woods around my house turning over rocks. I was always fascinated with all that I found under them. There were a lot of bugs—beetles and spiders and such—plus always a million ants—some with those giant white eggs—and once in a while a scorpion. But the prize was always a snake—I loved finding snakes under rocks! Sometimes I would just find an empty passageway where the snake had been. And I always wondered, how in the world could a snake crawl under a rock and live without the rock crushing him? I still wonder a lot.

Along the blufftop trail there is a line of rock slabs that are carefully placed on top of the bluff, far enough apart to leave room for viewing and exploring. Out in front of one of the rock slabs, a large pine tree that was growing on top of the big bluff has blown over. The rock slab behind caught it, and some of the roots remained in the ground. The tree has continued to grow, diverting its growth up. The root-ball is very large, and you can walk around the entire thing—but be careful, you do get within a foot of the edge of the bluff! It is a neat sight, and one that would look great as a sketch—it is difficult to photograph, and the details of what is going on don't really show up too well.

I heard a cry from high up in a red oak tree. A large hawk had spotted me coming down the trail towards his tree, and was not at all happy to see me. He screamed again. I stopped and tried to get a fix on him—I didn't have my binocs with me, but probably need to start carrying them. He screamed again, and this time was getting mad at me. I never saw him where he sat, but did see him get up and fly off—he lumbered through the thick woods at a very slow pace, then flew down out of sight. I guess he was just hanging out and didn't want me to disturb him.

I found several more walnut trees along the road that I had not noticed before—their walnuts were all over the road. I picked up several and tossed them at a nearby tree. I hit the tree three out of five times. Batter out!

It occurred to me that I hadn't seen hardly any squirrels this morning. I wondered where they were. As luck would have it, I decided to count how many I saw in a minute period, and just as I started counting, they came out of the woodwork—five squirrels in one minute! They were just waiting for me to begin counting I guess.

From Doc's I went down to visit the Woods boys, who were at work in their new cabin. New floor, rock steps out front, and a rock skirt all the way around the base of the cabin. And they almost had a complete kitchen in—man, they had done a lot of work since I had been there. Billy and Danny Woods were there working. Good old boys both.

Neither one of them said anything about my overalls. Come to think of it, it is nice to be around people who don't question your dress. I wore the same overalls that I had on hiking today in town yesterday, and got funny looks and comments everywhere that I went—mostly from people that I knew. What's the big deal about wearing overalls? I have two pairs. In cool weather they actually make pretty darn good hiking attire—lots of places to put stuff, free and open and unrestrictive, and you don't have to wear a belt. The only two problems that I find with them are that they are tough to get off when you need to "go" and it is really cold, especially if you have on a jacket or something over them (this is much more of a problem with women than with men); and when it is warm out, the fabric is just too darn hot. I need to find a pair that is made of some other type of material, something that breathes better. That reminds me of one time when I was cross-country skiing in Colorado at about 20 below zero, wearing overalls, and I had to go and didn't have any toilet paper. I won't go into the details, but will tell you that snow makes great toilet paper!

From their cabin I dropped down into Dug Hollow, and walked along the top of the bluff there. It is really thick and rough, and not nearly as easy walking as over on the other side of the hill in Whitaker Creek. In fact, I couldn't even follow right on top of the bluff because it was so thick. As I made my way through the brush, I got the feeling that I was following someone, or something. There weren't any tracks or broken limbs or anything, it was just a feeling that I had. I guess there could have been some disturbed leaves, but I didn't really notice. I continued to bushwhack through. The canyon below was getting narrow, and I was about to level out with the creek, where I could go down below the bluff.

Then a movement caught my eye, something black. Oh darn. It was a bear! He was across the canyon a couple of hundred feet in the thick brush on the other side, and was ripping apart a rotten log. He hadn't seen me, so I sat down and watched. Wish I had my pair of binocs! He would reach out and break off a section of the log, then nose around and paw at it for a minute, flip his nose in the air and lick his chops, then reach out and dig up another piece. I guess he was eating ants. Bears love ants. You would think it would take so much effort just to get a mouthful though. Then he abruptly stopped, sniffed the air, turned around and looked my direction, and in a flash was gone. He must have caught my scent. Most of the time you just simply don't pay any attention to the wind, but wildlife lives or dies by the wind, and if you are upwind from them, they will scent you and flee. Even after all of the bears that I have seen and been around out here this summer, my heart was pounding like crazy. I was really glad to have seen this bear, but was even gladder that he was on the *other* side of the canyon!

Once I composed myself I got down to the creek and headed downstream. There were a few pools of water, but the stream was not running, only dripping a bit here and there. This little section is quite wonderful when the water is flowing well—lots of tumbling waterfalls and pools. But when the creek is mostly dry like today you can hop around and get to places that you ordinarily wouldn't be able to if there was water. I wandered around a little while under a large overhang, then continued on downstream, away from the bear's log.

As I was approaching one of the main waterfalls I found a big red oak tree that had been hit by lightening. A strip of bark and wood about three inches wide was blown off of one side, all the way down to the ground. Some of the strips had been thrown fifty feet away! Wow, that must have been one blast! And the tree looked like it was just fine. I have seen lots of trees that have been hit like this, and they seem to live normal lives. Some people do that too, although you just have to wonder.

I made my way up the hillside and onto the big flat area by the skewed oak. There were hickory nuts all over the ground, but I was careful not to get rolled by any of them like I had done before. They were bright green and rather large. There were also a number of acorns on the ground that had holes eaten out of them—more flying squirrels in the area.

The sun broke through and it began to warm up. I was also walking uphill some. I realized that I had not run into a single spiderweb—guess it was all of the blowing rain from the night before that kept them inside.

I crossed the East Meadow (two pumpkins looking very nice in the garden), and headed down into the woods for the final leg home. The woods were open, and the sun created many shadows on the forest floor. Just before I reached the cabin, I ran into one big spiderweb—I had to pick it out of my beard and hair (no jokes please), and off of my face and neck. Only one spiderweb all morning, but it was a big one. When I got inside the cabin I realized that my little ramble had lasted over four hours!

I plopped down on the back with a tall glass of diet Dr. Pepper and a Caesar salad (you would think that with all this diet food and exercise that I would be really thin—not!). There were lots of orange butterflies cruising about. I had seen many of them in the meadows that I had just walked through too. They didn't seem to be going anywhere like butterflies usually do, they were just out cruising. One of them got caught in a little wind current out over the meadow, and just sort of hung there, not flapping its wings at all, like it was enjoying riding the current. I didn't know that butterflies ever did that. Wish I could.

Surprise, surprise, when my outside alarm went off, who should show up but Leslie, my old flame from spring and early summer. She hadn't been to the cabin since June. While I have always wanted to get this Journal going, she was the one that finally went out and bought one and gave it to me in May and said "Write!" Anyway, she was going to hike down to the river and just wanted to stop by and say hi. I pointed her in the right direction, wished her luck, and went back to my lunch.

It got warmer, the wind picked up, and the soaring birds really came out. Mostly just vultures at first. They were doing some incredibly acrobatic things. Although they were often more like big bombers than swift jets, and sometimes missed their mark or veered off course—a big, awkward bird like that can't exactly turn on a dime, but they try.

There were eight of them in the old snag at one time—a record I think. And this one kept trying to land on the very tip-top point. He made at least four passes, each time fanning his tail and spreading his wings and stretching his feet and claws out to grab the tree. Then he would hit the tree and tumble and keep on flying. The others just looked up and snickered. But on the fifth try, he was successful. Once he got his perch on top, it was tough for him to keep it, as he kept losing his balance—he had to flap his wings to steady himself. I guess it is kind of like that in life too—people have a hard time making it to the top, and once they get there, have to keep flapping their wings in order to stay on top.

I watched these guys through the binocs for twenty minutes. They were all pruning and cleaning themselves. It was funny to see such a big, ugly bird reach down under its wings with that beak and red skin. And out of nowhere would come these white fluffy down feathers—big ones, but still white and fluffy— and they would drift off into space.

There were two or three little Cooper's Hawks out playing in the wind too. And later, one big, red-tailed hawk entered the canyon and soared all the way to the other end without flapping a wing. His brilliant tail was backlit by the sun when he was up high, and it was spectacular.

Before long I ended up on the couch for a little nap. Then I heard footsteps on the front deck—another bear? No, just Leslie returning from the river. I escorted her to the back deck with a cold beer, and we sat and talked for a while. It was tough for me to concentrate because there were all of these darn hawks flying around everywhere! I spent half of the conversation with the binocs stuck in my face. She went on up the road (it was great to see her again), and I returned to my nap. The nap didn't last long though, as the buzzer for the bread machine went off, and I had to get up and make pizza.

While I was wolfing down the pizza the evening light in the canyons and on the ridgetops started getting really nice. There were still some clouds in the sky, but it was mostly clear. Each and every little canyon was defined by the low light. Man, the light was magnificent tonight! It felt like hiking light, so I put down the pizza and put on my walking shoes.

Just as I stepped off of the front porch, a breakfast cereal came back to haunt me—snap, crackle, *pop!* My darn ankle snapped again, and sent me reeling across the yard. Anytime that it makes that much noise when I "roll over on it" I am in for trouble. Sharp pain shot up my leg. The only way that I know to keep it from swelling up and getting really nasty, is to walk it out. Good thing that I had my walking shoes on.

I took the low bench out from the cabin towards the Faddis place, then cut uphill into the Faddis Meadow, limping along and wincing with each step. This is a great walking route, and I plan to open up a trail here some day—one that will connect my cabin with the Faddis cabin, and run along this great level bench that is full of big trees. And in the winter you can see out into the Whitaker Creek drainage.

The meadow was being hit by the low angle of the sun and looked really nice. The persimmon tree with all of the big fat fruit on it was glowing just like a Christmas tree. And there was one dogwood tree that had lost its leaves that was full of bright red berries—they really lit up in the sunlight.

As I eased along the lane between the Faddis Meadow and the East Meadow I jumped a deer. I saw the white "flag" of the tail moving ahead. I just kept right on moving, assuming that the deer had gone off into the woods, but then it appeared again. I couldn't really see anything more than the white flash and the body moving—the brush was very thick. I continued. Then it must have let me get really close because I heard and felt the hooves hit the ground as it bounded off—this time into the woods for sure.

I crept out into the edge of the meadow and surveyed the scene, but no deer. If it was a buck, it probably would never go through an open area like this one after it had been spooked anyway. There was a slight breeze, pink clouds in the sky, and strands of orange light across the meadow. A very tranquil scene, and I rather enjoyed moving slowly through it. My ankle was feeling better.

As I approached the far end of the meadow there was a crash in the brush to my right, then a flash of flesh. A big whitetail buck bounded out of the woods and into the meadow. He stopped about a hundred yards away, right in the middle of the little patch of goldenrod that had not been mowed down. I held my breath. No, I think my heart stopped completely. It was one of the big bucks that I had seen before in this very meadow. His huge antlers were now fully hardened and magnificent. What an incredible creature! His eyes burned deep in me. And while my heart was stopped and I was holding my breath and this giant buck was staring right at me—I noticed the near-full moon in the blue sky just above him, and it was just as pink as the clouds. How could you imagine a more wonderful scene? While it has taken me several minutes to write about this, I'm sure our encounter didn't last more than a second or two. Big bucks just don't stand out in the open like that very often, especially in the fall, and never for more than an instant. He vanished. Blood returned to my brain. I had to sit down—my knees were weak. First the bear, then Leslie, and now this! Lordy, I do love Cloudland.

While I was sitting there I noticed how *yellow* the goldenrod really was. The only way that I could describe it at the time was as "pure yellow." And before this summer, I didn't even know what goldenrod was, or at least never appreciated it. And now I was sitting in a patch of it smiling like I'd just won the lottery. In a way I had.

Once I got back to the cabin and the light show outside faded, I remembered that my beloved Razorbacks were playing a big football game tonight, and it was on TV. Please don't hold this against me, and this was the very first time that it has ever happened, but I got in my van and raced over to Bob's cabin, turned on his satellite TV, and watched the Hogs win one of the most exciting games of the decade (we beat Kentucky 27-20).

Oh yea, back to wilderness. The moon shone brightly and lit up everything there was to see. Well, for a little while. Then a thick cloud cover moved in and the light faded, dimmed, then went out entirely. It was dark outside! And tomorrow night is the full moon. The moon was still lit from the right.

It is late, nearly midnight, and another wonderful day at Cloudland is about to end. Last weekend there were 15 people here. Today I was alone most of the time. I will take it as it comes, and do my best to enjoy it all.

10/4/98 During the night I rolled over several times and gazed out the window. The cloud cover had gotten thinner, and the big moon, though still not visible, lit up all of the fog and haze, and I felt like I was inside a light bulb—it was pretty bright out, but kind of eerie.

I got up early and had my mocha and blueberry biscuits out on the back deck. The wind was blowing, and the fog had totally engulfed the cabin—a true Cloudland condition. It retreated just a little, and revealed the ghostly outlines of the trees around the far edge of the meadow. Every now and then I could see the silhouette of a bird flying through the fog.

There is a clock on the mantle here that not only tells time, but also shows the phase of the moon. There is an image of the full moon sitting on the top of the clock, and a black cover that rotates around the image, showing more or less of the moon as its phases move on. The cover is completely around the back of the image today, and the small, full moon is beaming out across my little cabin. Today the actual moon will rise at about the same time the sun is setting—it always does this on the day of the full moon. The day before, yesterday, the moon was up about 50 minutes before the sunset, which is why I saw it up in the sky above the big buck before sunset. Tomorrow, the moon will rise about 50 minutes after the sun has set, rising into a dark sky. This is predictable behavior, and happens just like this every 28 days. (Actually, I'm sure it is not exactly 50 minutes, but that is about what it seems like to me.) So you can pretty much tell if the moon is full or not by the time it rises. One factor that does throw that off some is your relative position in the countryside—if you are down in a valley, the moon will rise later because of it being blocked by a hill. Since Cloudland is located near the top of the ridge, the moon pretty much rises when it is supposed to. Although it still wanders back and forth all over the eastern horizon. In case you couldn't tell by now, I am very lunar.

Before I returned to town I had to go out and ramble around some in the fog. I just wanted to get out and work my ankle a little—it has swelled up some during the night. So I opted for the level bench to the west of the cabin. It was level, and easy hiking.

The fog was really thick and the wind was blowing, but it was on the warm side. I inched my way along the bench, taking the fog deep within my lungs, closing my eyes and letting the wind wash my face. There were a number of very large trees along the way, often rising up and out of sight in the fog. And there were a couple of big "N" trees—trees that were knocked down and bent over in their youth by a falling tree, then continued to grow, creating an N shape in their trunk. The N in both of these trees was low enough to the ground that you could hop up on the horizontal part and sit there, which I did in one.

While I was sitting in the tree admiring the forest a squirrel started barking just down below the lower edge of the bench. He was disturbed. Then a flash of grey—a doe deer slipped up the hill and onto my little bench world. She was in a hurry, but did not seem to be frightened. When she got to the level part of the bench, she stopped, looked around some, then began to feed on the acorns on the ground. She would munch a little, then flip her tail up and glance around in all directions, sniffing the air. Convinced that she was alone, she would go back to browsing. The squirrel barked again, and she swung her head around and looked in his direction. She fed closer to me, one step at a time. The wind was right, so she could not smell me. I hung on to the tree trunk and tried to remain still and quiet.

She fed right on around me, once coming within ten feet of my tree, then wandered on up to the next bench and out of sight. She never saw or scented me. I guess my scent was carried up and away from the ground. The "N" tree afforded me a front row seat without being discovered.

As I was crawling down out of the tree an owl began to speak. He was on the same bench as me, to the west some, and his speech was crisp and clear despite all of the fog. I studied his voice. There were always eight distinct sounds, in pairs, seven "hoots" and the final one a "haaawwww. " So it was "hoot, hoot... hoot, hoot... hoot, hoot...hoot, haaawww" in quick order. This guy was a barred owl, very common in the Ozark forests, and a frequent visitor to Cloudland.

There have been great horned and screech owls around, but most of the hoots that we have heard all summer have been barred owls.

He eventually flew off and I decided it was time to return to the cabin. A couple of wildlife encounters was enough to sustain me until I returned in a couple of days. The humidity outside was 97%, but it was 99% inside the cabin—guess I shouldn't have left the windows open! The fog remained thick and wet and the wind continued to blow as I bid farewell and headed to town.

10/9/98 There were lots of limbs down across the road and I knew a storm had blown through. A quick check of the weather station showed that it had rained 3.5 inches on Monday the 5th, and the winds got up to 31 mph. It was in the low 50's when I arrived, and felt great—hey, it must be fall!

After unloading the van and tuning into P.J. Robowski and her ***New Blues show*** on KUAF radio, I decided it was time—time for the first fire of the season. There had been a basket full of kindling and small logs next to the fireplace all summer, just in case, so I quickly emptied it and fired up a match. There wasn't a great deal of fanfare with this first fire like I had anticipated, but I did toss back a single toast to the fire out of the bottle of Yukon Jack that rests on the mantle (this is the bottle that is raised in honor of my dear old friend Yukon whenever his name is brought up). The firelight was warm and cheery bouncing off of the log walls, the whiskey grand, and I sat back into the overstuffed leather recliner and gave thanks for it all.

Before I knew it my friend, Jenny, from Benton had arrived. She came bearing gifts of a bear t-shirt, and Ansel Adams wall calendar, and a fine bottle of merlot. The merlot didn't last too long, but the conversation did, and soon we were into a bottle of homemade muscadine wine left by Benny.

It had been a year since John Denver had died, and I wanted to remember him all weekend, so I put on the first of many Denver CD's, and we listened with fondness and sang those tunes of our youth. John Denver is responsible a great deal for my being so nature-oriented. I'm sure that I would have been so without his influence, but his music brought an entire generation and more back to the woods, and helped bring a nature-way of thinking into the mainstream. This acceptance of hiking and nature-study by the public has allowed me to pursue my love of the outdoors and make a living at it. His music will live on forever, and will bounce off the walls at Cloudland for many moons to come. Another toast went out to John Denver.

10/10/98 The horizon glowed early, like an approaching forest fire. Clouds crowded into the valley below. We got up, bundled up, and had a breakfast of coffee and blueberry biscuits outside as the new day was born. Sunshine crept ever so slowly into the wilderness below. Each minute brought a new scene, and soon the forest was alive with light, song and laughter. It was quite chilly out, especially with a breeze blowing, but it didn't seem to matter—the view warmed the soul.

I reluctantly went inside and fired up the computer to do a few electronic chores, while Jenny kept watch for new delights outside. A few minutes later I glanced up and saw her frantically waving her arms and jumping up and down. With that much excitement it had to be something pretty good. And sure enough, it was. I had wanted this to happen for months now, if for nothing else to prove that I was not crazy. Right there in front of us, down in the meadow, stood a beautiful grey fox, one of my buddies. No one but me had ever seen either fox there before, and someone else seeing one of them finally proved their existence. He just stood there for a few moments looking up, broadside to us and out in the open. Then he slinked off into the brush, and eased on down the hill and out of sight. I never tire of seeing him.

Once my electronic chores were done Jenny and I put on our hiking shoes and headed down into the meadow to look around a little. Before we could explore much, visitors arrived, and we climbed back up to meet them. It was Beth Motherwell and some friends from the University, Alex and Hanna and Judith. They had come out to do a little mushroom hunting—they were experts on the subject, and Jenny and I joined them for a hike out towards the Crag.

It is funny how you can spend so much time walking through the woods and not always notice the little things, like mushrooms. With a little close inspection, we found many of them, and the scientific names were called out with ease (they all looked the same to me!). While examining one tiny, orange mushroom, we discovered tiny grapes covering the ground. Jenny called them Possum Grapes. It didn't seem like they were large enough to eat, but she says they make great jam.

We arrived at the Crag to find it deserted, and took in the view. Unfortunately I had to get back to the cabin, so Jenny and I bid farewell and hustled back down the trail. I was to meet William McNamara, the painter, and his business manager, Milancy, and we were going to sign all of the copies of the books that I had brought out.

Bill McNamara lives in a tiny cabin several miles away, and while he spends a great deal of time walking the hills around Cloudland, he had never been here before. For someone so talented and famous he is easygoing and friendly.

Jenny made a wonderful pot of chili and some cheese dip, then we turned our attention to the books. The new **Buffalo River Wilderness** books were individually boxed (about four pounds of wonderful Buffalo River scenes each), and Jenny and Milancy unboxed them all while Bill and I sat down at the large Amish table and signed them. It took us a few minutes to get it all organized, but once we did, the autograph machine rolled on, and we plowed through the large pile of books in no time (well, I really shouldn't say "plow"—I scribbled my usual signature, while Bill was very careful and deliberate with his—kind of the way he paints).

Once all of the books were signed and safely boxed back up again, we munched on chili and chips and dip and Arkansas Ale. Then Jenny had to leave and return to civilization. I was grateful for her visit, for all of her wonderful gifts, for the chili, and for the fact that she got to see the fox! Bill and Milancy soon headed up the hill too, and I was left with all of the books, the chili, and a bunch of soaring birds that had come out to play in the warming air currents.

Guests for the Bushwhacker Party #2 began to arrive. Scott and Carolyn Crook, Dean and Bonnie LaGrone, Jim McDaniel, Susie Crisp (Jim and Susie brought me a pair of wonderful black bear pull chains for ceiling fans—they always bring great gifts for the cabin), The Wildman, Mary Chodrick, and Bob and Dawna Robinson. We lounged around on the deck and admired the view, tossed back pitcher after pitcher of Bushwhackers, and *cooked*—another Cloudland feast was at hand!

Jambalaya, Cloudland pizza rolls, spaghetti, Caesar salad, grilled brats, rice, pineapple upside-down cake, and chocolate heaven cake were but a few of the delights covering the bar. Needless to say, we all pigged out.

The Wildman began to mix Wild Turkey with the Bushwhackers. It was a good thing that I had everyone sign the lamp shade early in the evening.

John Denver and The Beatles gave way to Led Zeppelin as the night went on. Then everyone really got mentally impaired, and Scott and I got out our guitars and the first ever live music was played at Cloudland. Well, calling it music is a bit of a stretch, but there was noise coming from the guitars, and folks were singing.

Jim and Susie had to leave and return to their own version of Cloudland over near Richland Creek. Then everyone else began to turn in, and the cabin shut down well before midnight for the first time in history (for a major party). We had started drinking very early in the afternoon, and we had some heavy-duty work to do in the morning, so the early hour seemed about right.

10/11/98 A textbook Cloudland morning greeted everyone at sunrise—a thick bank of pure white clouds hung low in the valley, and black ridges stuck their heads above. The clouds began to move around as the rising sun warmed them. We had blueberry biscuits, coffee, OJ, bacon, Cloudland Hash, and fresh waffles made by Carolyn.

Someone noted that they didn't know what was more beautiful—the white clouds or the green hills or the blue sky. The Wildman, who wasn't saying much, thought that the hills didn't look quite as large as normal.

Scott got up and proclaimed that my roof leaked. What? How could my roof leak, it hadn't even rained during the night? He was sleeping out on the deck under a section of roof that had its rain gutter ripped off by high winds some time ago. As the night drew on, dew formed on the roof, then ran down the roof and splattered onto Scott. His wife kept hearing water drops. Scott nearly got soaked before he woke up and realized what was happening. The last time that Scott slept out at Cloudland, the high winds blew his sleeping bag right off of him and down into the woods below—he was out at 4am looking for it with a flashlight. Now the rain soaked him. I wonder what will happen on his next visit?

A flying squirrel had devoured several acorns on top of the grill during the night. I thought it was fitting for this to happen near Scott and Carolyn, since they have five of them as pets in their living room at home.

We all had one big job this morning—to move as much of the split wood down in the meadow as we could up the hill to the cabin (firewood for the winter). I *love* to split wood, especially when it is cold, but I don't relish having to carry it up the steep slope from the meadow to the cabin (many trees were cleared to create the meadow, and they have been cut up into firewood). So I devised a plan to invite a bunch of good friends out, feed them and get them drunk, then make them work it all off the next day. Hey, it worked!

We formed a human chain up the steep hillside and tossed the sticks of wood from one person to another. Many of the logs were heavy, and the word "hickory" was shouted out as the logs moved up the hillside (hickory is a lot heavier than oak). Within an hour we had most of the wood moved up and in place on top of my new wood deck beside the east wall of the cabin.

While we were searching the meadow for split logs we found bunches of long, yellow ladybugs with black spots. I'd not seen these critters before—they were more elongated than round like normal ladybugs. They were beautiful, and flew up in flocks every time that we disturbed a weed that they were on. The fox never returned, and I wondered if he would after all of the disturbance in the meadow. Of course, since we took away most of the downed logs, it would be easier for them to get around!

It was time for the next chore. This one was not at Cloudland, but rather over at Dean and Bonnie's property up on Walker Mountain. They are slowly developing their wonderful spot of heaven, and have this nice pavilion there that is the center of social activity. Well, during the storm last week, a giant hickory tree decided to get a closer look at the pavilion, and it came crashing down right on top of the pavilion, and was left hanging. It would take a monumental effort to get it cut out safely, but we were just the crew to do it. So we all loaded up and headed over to Dean and Bonnie's.

The giant hickory was impressive, but even more impressive was the fact that the pavilion had withstood the blow, and was still standing, although it was leaning under the stress. Dean used my big extension ladder and climbed up and cut off chunks of the tree, while the rest of the men in the group pulled the logs out of the way of danger as they came crashing down.

It was kind of a funny scene. Dean was doing all of the work, especially all of the dangerous stuff. The guys were all standing around giving their opinions on how to do the job the best. And the women were all wincing and pleading and playing the parts of wives off in the distance. It was a dangerous job, but Dean managed to get the huge hickory cut off and saved the pavilion, although it may never be the same.

With the heavy drama over we returned to Cloudland, and feasted on leftover Jambalaya, chili and cake. Everyone helped me load up all of the signed books back into my van, then we reluctantly bid farewell to the cabin and headed back to civilization to the OHTA club meeting. It was another fine weekend in the wilderness.

By the way, the forest was still rather green for the most part, and not showing signs of fall yet. There were a few black gums and a sweet gum here and there turning.

10/12/98 Dean returned to Cloudland to bring back the large ladder that he had used to cut out the hickory. On the way out, he reported seeing a large black bear up near the gate. This same guy has been seen in the vicinity of the Faddis cabin several times this past month. He is probably the same one who left his footprints by my front porch.

10/13/98 The black sky was filled with a million stars that sparkled like diamonds when I stopped to unlock and open the gate to Cloudland near midnight. The human eye can only see about five to six thousand stars at any one time, but a million is what it really seems like.

As I was swinging the gate open a pair of spots of fire came bounding towards me—eyes lit up by the headlights. It was a bobcat, frisky from the cool temps, out playing and welcoming me home. He didn't stick around long, and before I knew it all I could see was a short tail disappearing in the darkness.

10/14/98 There were thin clouds in the early morning sky, and they were dark purple—a color that I didn't remember ever seeing in the sky before. Within a span of ten minutes, they turned from the purple to orange to salmon and then to yellow, an incredible light show that covered the eastern skyline and kept my eyes open as I fought back sleep. The sunrise has now moved from the left side of the window next to my bed, across it and now to the right side. Before long, it will rise out of sight, and I will have to lean out to view it. Or just move the bed a little.

I rolled back over and napped a little, then my outside alarm went off—the Amish are coming, the Amish are coming! I jumped up and scrambled to dress as their black trucks came to rest in front of the cabin. The crew of Amish builders who built my cabin were coming back to do a few fix-up things. Their community of nearly 150 folks is near the town of Berryville, about an hour's drive north of here.

They spent the day staining most of the log deck rails and posts that had begun to fade in the harsh summer sunshine. They also installed a brace under a sagging deck staircase, put up a new section of log railing in the carport, drilled holes in a pair of long log segments that I am going to make floor lamps out of, fixed my front door that was sticking, and did a bunch of other little chores. Most of the time they speak a very form of Pennsylvania Dutch (a form of German), but when you approach them, they automatically switch into English, then return to their language as you walk away. While they were here for three months building the cabin last summer, they tried to teach me a few words, but

I was unable to pick any of it up. Every now and then they will say something to each other when you are standing right next to them—you know then that they are talking about you, or saying something that you aren't supposed to hear. That is OK, except when they start laughing and looking at you.

During their lunch hour the four boys took off down the trail and hiked to the Crag. "We made it in nine minutes!" they said on their return. Sure enough they were only gone twenty minutes, and were covered with sweat and short of breath. I had never seen any of them break a sweat before. I guess this hiking stuff is pretty good for you.

After lunch one of them spotted a small rattlesnake in the woods. They all dropped what they were doing and rushed to the scene. By the time I got there the poor little snake had been smashed by a dozen rocks. Amish don't like snakes.

The light was getting low and beginning to shift color as they drove away. I put on my hiking shoes and headed up the trail through the woods. It was perfect hiking weather! Temps in the high 60's, a light breeze, and a little sunshine. I wanted to go have a look around the Faddis cabin to see what the bear had been up to. There is one apple tree there, and it is full of red apples right now. Bears love apples. But there didn't seem to be any bear sign around the tree—even apples that had been on the ground weren't disturbed. I felt obligated to eat a few, and while they were very hard and kind of small, they were tasty.

I moved on down to the pond nearby, which was about half full of dingy water. The far side of the pond bank was covered with fresh bear tracks. You could see where the bear walked one direction, took a drink, then turned around and walked back the other way. One of the bear tracks had a raccoon track right in the middle of it. And there were lots of deer tracks too. I'll bet all of the area wildlife come to this pond to drink, especially during dry periods.

Up on top of the pond bank the bear had knocked down the tall weeds and brush, like he had been rolling around up there or something. And over on the side, a *giant* pile of bear scat! Really big. I offer the following description only because so many people ask me what bear scat looks like. Well, it looks just like a big pile of people scat! Really. Only it will have persimmon seeds in it (like this pile did), or some other seeds, depending on what the bear has been eating. I have seen bear scat that looked just like a cow pie, some that looked like a mound of berry preserves (the fruit had been processed, but in a different way), and some that was compacted wheat hulls. But this pile looked just like a 400 pound man had done it. I thought it a little odd that the tracks were not all that large, but the scat was—I guess scat is a better indication of the size of an animal than its tracks! I would estimate this bear to be between 400-500 pounds. This agrees with the size bear that has been seen near the Faddis cabin by four different people in the last month.

The lower section of the meadow below the Faddis cabin and next to the pond had been cleared and terraced for Bob to use as a garden. Low water levels in the pond has prevented Bob from using it as such (he had planned on a gravity-fed irrigation system). The meadow was grown up with chest-high weeds, all having flowering heads. It was kind of nice looking. And down on the ground there were hundreds of yellow and orange mushrooms growing—wish my mushroom experts were here today! The mushrooms were all growing in groups, like space was at a premium. There were groups of 20-30 mushrooms all growing on top of each other. Mushrooms must like each other a lot.

The pond was rimmed with small black gum trees, and they had all turned an odd color—sort of a dark purple/red color. There was a red oak on one end of the lower meadow, and its leaves had all turned a bright, light orange. And on the far side of the meadow, there was a larger black gum tree, nearly 40 feet tall. This gum was one of the most brilliantly colored trees that I have ever seen! From the sunlit side, the leaves were deep blood red color, and shiny, and really stood out in the middle of the green forest behind. From the backlit side, the leaves caught fire and blazed away against the blue sky. It was one spectacular tree! As bright as any maple could ever want to be.

There were several other trees in the meadow that Bob had left when he had the spot cleared out. Directly under the canopy of the trees there were no weeds growing at all. And there were lots and lots of bear trails that crisscrossed through the tall weeds of the meadow. Lots of bear activity. I wonder if the bear ever looks up and notices the brilliant leaves?

I returned to the apple tree for another snack, then made my way on over to the East Meadow, just as the sun slipped down below the treeline. I had expected to see a deer or two in the meadow, but nothing. There were plenty of tracks in the garden though. And there were three orange pumpkins still on the vine there. It must be getting close to Halloween. The sumac bushes along the trail had turned dark red, and there were lots of colorful sassafras trees too, all a most wonderful salmon color (kind of like part of the sunrise color).

I returned to the apple tree once again, then went on down to check on Bob's cabin. The well pump there was doing funny things, so I shut it off. Bob has several large maple trees there in his front yard that shelter his little circle drive. One of the maple trees was flaming red from top to bottom, and the others were touched with red along the edges. On the way back from his cabin I found lots of walnuts on the ground—it was easy to see where they got the name "black" walnut—once the green fruit hits the ground, they turn completely black all over (and get soft inside).

It was nearly dark as I made my way through the Faddis Meadow once more, then down my lane and back to the cabin. The wind began to pick up. As I was about to end my little hike I realized that I had not seen a single animal of any kind on my hike. No bears, no deer, no foxes, not even a squirrel! It was only a couple of weeks ago when I had seen 43 squirrels on a single hike. Where was everyone? I had no idea. Then an animal did present itself—a bat came flying by, very low to the ground. He made several passes, and circled me once. Thank goodness. I was about to think that all wildlife had deserted me.

It felt like a salad and homemade wine night so I sat out on the deck and munched and drank as the day ended. The wine caused me to get out the guitar and play a few Jim Croce, John Denver and Beatles tunes. For some reason they always sound a lot better after a fine bottle of wine. Hum. As I made my way up into the loft, the wind began to blow really hard, and I was glad to be snug in my little log cabin.

10/15/98 The wind pounded away all night, but it remained clear outside and so no bad weather. A band of coyotes howled and yipped loud enough to be heard over the wind, and invited me to get up out of bed and greet the day. I did. The wind let up, and another gorgeous wilderness day began.

The forest is still basically green today, but there are more and more red trees showing up. I have this feeling that the forest is going to pop before too long, perhaps sometime next week. It is impossible for anyone to predict the peak of fall color, especially because it will happen in different places at different times. It does seem to happen in the Buffalo River area a little before the rest of the Ozarks though. So probably next week this area will be great, then the following weekend and the week after that across the forest. But the hiking is nothing short of wonderful right now, and will continue so for a long time, so my advice to everyone is to *get out* as soon as you can and as often as you can!

Just as I was getting ready to leave to head into town, I took one last look out the back. Two hawks came speeding by. They weren't red-tailed, but I'm not sure what they were. They were beautiful though, and chased each other back and forth in the airspace just above the meadow, often swooping down and nearly touching the trees next to the cabin. I watched them through the binocs. Every now and then one of them would look my way, and I was thrilled. The trees seemed to be turning by the minute—fall could pop at just about any time now. What a wonderful time to be in the Ozarks!!!

10/16/98 A weird light entered my mind as I awoke and rolled over and gazed out the window. I'm not quite sure how to describe it, but there were dark clouds hanging around, some mist, and a great deal of wind. It was dark light, if that is possible. I stepped out onto the back deck and looked up—there were not one, not two, but *eleven* soaring birds up in the clouds, flying in place, or actually just hanging there in place, not moving much, riding the high wind coming out of the South.

The hillside opposite was showing more and more signs of fall color. I got out the binocs and studied the trees. There were some really bright red ones, and lots of green ones too. I counted several patches of trees, and it averaged out to about 15% of the trees had turned color. And they weren't all at the top of the hill, or at the bottom, but rather scattered from top to bottom—that is a good sign. In a normal year, the trees in the lower elevations will turn first, then the color will work its way up the hillside. By the time the color reaches the top, the lower trees have already lost their leaves. The view is always a lot more spectacular when the color is more even like it appears to be happening this year.

Bill and Milancy came by in the morning and we spent several hours taking pictures of Bill and I for a magazine cover and article. Few things are as distasteful to me as getting my picture taken. Perhaps that is one reason why they never turn out well! The wind was blowing hard, gusting up to 30mph, and the sun kept popping out from behind the clouds, both conditions disrupting the picture session. We did get to take a short hike to a spot in the woods for a few pictures, and the woods were wonderful.

Soon after Bill and Milancy left the sky opened up and it began to rain. After working long into the night, then having my picture taken all day, I was rather tired, and the combination of my exhaustion, classical music playing on the radio, and the raindrops on the tin roof, sent me onto the couch for a long nap. It had to rank up there with one of the best naps that I have ever taken!

When I finally awoke, the rain had stopped and the wind had died down to a whisper. I grabbed a quick meal, then put on my boots and headed out for an afternoon walk. Everything was wet, and the moisture brought out some incredible color in the forest. Deep greens, browns, and many shades of reds, oranges and yellows. And the earthy smell of it all was heavenly.

As I passed through the Faddis Meadow, a red squirrel dashed across in front of me through the bright green grass. I stopped and knelt down to watch a while. He was one busy little dude, and ran back and forth from the base of a large hickory tree, where he had no trouble finding hickory nuts that covered the ground, out into the meadow, where he carefully dug a hole in some secret spot and buried the nut. The sun popped out during all of this, and lit up his tail. That brilliant red tail and the green grass was quite a sight.

I wandered down near the pond and found new bear tracks and a fresh pile of scat, all done since the rain, so I must have just missed seeing the bear. In fact the scat was steaming. There were lots of persimmon seeds in it again, but also a lot of smaller seeds and some type of grain—guess this guy had been grazing in a nearby meadow.

There were many more apples on the ground under the apple tree than before, and the sweet smell of them was heavy in the air. I resisted the temptation to reach and eat. It didn't appear that anyone had been there to feed on them (like deer or bears). I don't really understand this at all—what a great food source for the wildlife, and it is just rotting on the ground.

A deciduous holly tree nearby was loaded with red berries and the limbs were drooping under the weight. Soon all of the leaves would be gone, and this single tree will look like a highly decorated Christmas tree, especially when it gets dusted with a little snow next month.

The path leading to the East Meadow appeared much like a Monet painting—the gracefully curving path was lined on both sides with delicate purple wildflowers, bright yellow goldenrod, and layers of multi-colored sumac bushes, sassafras, dogwood and black gum. It was one spectacular sight to behold! I wish that I could paint. Although I don't know how anyone could capture the glory and depth of color of this scene. Walking through it was pure pleasure.

And there was a light, sweet fragrance in the air too.

The path from the East Meadow on over towards Bob's cabin goes through the deep woods. And the woods this day were as colorful and brilliant as the previous path had been. There were layers and layers of color—bright red black gums up high, and yellow hickory trees and red dogwoods, all three colors mixing and contrasting. These last two little stretches of blazing color are perfect examples of the fall color in the Ozarks. The overall view is still mostly green, but when you get out into the woods up close and personal, you can see some incredible color. It is always like this, every fall here, and no matter how dull the scene might appear, you can always get out and find great color. So I just have to laugh when folks comment about how disappointing the color is or was—they literally can't see the color for the trees.

When I returned to the cabin there was a large hawk circling overhead, looking down on the blue tin roof. There seemed to be a lot more hawks out today than buzzards.

I swear that the trees across the way had turned brighter during my little nap and hike. In fact there were a number of large trees that had turned bright orange that were green in the morning. I did another unofficial count, and found nearly 25% of the trees on this hillside had turned color. So fall was marching on, and in a hurry! However, the hillside on the south side of the valley was still mostly green. So fall is popping, but much more so on certain hillsides. Or perhaps it is only happening at Cloudland. I know there are a lot of folks out there waiting for the peak of the color before they get out, but my advice is to get out *now*, today, and then every other day that you can—you will have some terrific hiking no matter what.

Roy Clinton and some friends dropped by for a short visit—they had just been on a hike to the Crag. Before they left, they had two signed copies of my new book in their hands, and there was $120 on the bar. Hey, I like doing business at Cloudland.

I installed a new wind chime that Scott and Carolyn had brought out. It now hangs from the front porch, out of the direct wind. I figured that if I put it up on the back deck, the strong and constant wind would drive me crazy, or break the chimes, or both. So I'm going to try it in front and see how it does.

The wind blew and it rained and lightning lit up the dark night. The wind peaked at 41mph. The rain totaled 1.5 inches for the day. I shut down the cabin and crawled into bed to the sound of the wind pounding outside.

10/17/98 Things had calmed down during the night, but by daylight the wind had resumed its relentless attack on my little hillside, and the clouds hung low. Through the mist I could see several soaring birds dancing and playing in the wind. It was warm, 70 degrees, and for the first time in a long while, the main Buffalo River was running muddy—they must had gotten more rain upstream, and it must have been hard.

The wind continues to blow hard, and the mist swirls, and I can just barely see the dim glow of orange and red and yellow trees across the way on Beagle Point. I must leave my little heaven this morning, to go to another part of the forest and lead a hike up to Hare Mountain, the tallest point on the Ozark Highlands Trail. It will be a great hike, and my little world at Cloudland will be waiting for me on my return, with new colors and smells and sights and sounds to enjoy.

A storm did roll through later in the day, as recorded by my weather station. The wind got up to 40mph, with .6 inch rain. Ann McCutchan from Austin, Texas came out and spent the night at the cabin (she is the sister of a friend of mine). She left behind a new book for the library, plus most of a bottle of good Vodka (in the freezer, where all good vodka should be stored). Guests like her are *always* welcome!

10/20/98 There was a deer hunter cloaked in orange sitting under the apple tree at the Faddis cabin when I arrived back at Cloudland. It was muzzle-loader season all week. A couple of hunters are staying at Bob's for the hunt, one of them being Benny, the maker of the homemade wine that I have been drinking, which I found out was wild blackberry wine—great stuff. Right now is muzzle-loader deer season. A "muzzle-loader" is a primitive weapon, the kind that Daniel Boone and the rest of our pioneers used. These rifles use black powder and a round ball, which is loaded through the front of the muzzle by hand, one piece at a time. They are a lot of fun to shoot, although the sky fills with black smoke and it takes a few seconds before you can see anything!

The cabin was snug and warm as always, and a welcome sight. It appeared that the rain over the weekend really knocked back the advance of the color in the forest. There was more color in the hills, but only slightly more than I had seen on Saturday. Rain will do that. No problem—we've got lots of time for color, but almost always need more rain. Although the Buffalo River was running pretty good, and the hushed roar of it could be heard from down below.

I unloaded another thousand pounds of picture books from the van into the basement, one box at a time, then moved a dozen arm loads of split firewood from the downstairs stash up to the wood rack on the upper deck, just outside the sliding glass door. It was probably cold enough for a fire in the fireplace, but all that work warmed me up so much that I never lit one.

Then I unpacked my new toy, uh, er, tool. A new pair of binocs! I had come to the conclusion that I just simply couldn't afford the thousand dollars for a pair of Leica binocs (or didn't really deserve such a fine instrument), but still wanted something a little larger than the compact Bushnels that I had been using. While standing at the counter of a friend's gun shop yesterday, a pair of fine Nikon 8 x 40 binocs jumped up and shouted at me—they fit my hands and face perfectly (actually about the same size as the Leicas), and I had just enough money in my pocket, so I bought them. Wow, after a few seconds, I fell in love. They are wonderful, and I can understand why the Leica folks enjoy theirs so much—the size is just perfect. In reality, there probably isn't any noticeable difference in the optical quality between the two brands—these Nikons are very good, and I know optical quality, and am most picky. Mine are armored, nitrogen-filled and waterproof. And they seem to gather light very well.

Across the way there were a number of trees that were bright yellow. I got to noticing that many of the trees on the west end of Beagle Point were orange, while the ones on the east end were yellow. After a careful look with the new binocs I found that the yellow ones were hickories—I'd never seen such pure and bright yellow in a hickory tree before! I would say that there is color in about 35% of the trees now. That rain sure did slow things down. In a week or two the color will be at its peak.

As the evening grew dim, I got hungry, and cooked up a pan full of my famous Banff Pasta. I discovered this recipe in a cafe in Banff, Canada back in 1995, and it is simply wonderful (and I hadn't had it in a while, so it tasted extra great!). While I was chowing down the outside alarm went off, and I looked out and saw a deer walking down the lane towards the cabin. She was rather nervous, and eventually trotted off into the woods and out of sight. That alarm goes off at about the same time during the night, and is probably deer wandering by (they are nocturnal and follow a pattern much of their lives). I noticed that as the deer made her way through the woods several squirrels sat up and started making their alarm calls. Once the doe passed on, the squirrels went back to gathering nuts.

One of the hunters got a deer up near the Faddis cabin during the day. I have mixed feelings about this, and won't get into the politics of hunting right now. I'll just say that I come down squarely on the fence—I both support hunting (I used to hunt, but don't any longer), and treasure the wildlife that I see roaming around at Cloudland. Anyway, Bob said that the hunters had seen the big bear (now named the Faddis Bear) five times during the day, and had shot at it, but never hit it. Bears are legal game with muzzle-loaders right now. Score one for the bear. Benny had seen the bear up close, and it was laying right in the middle of that large area of hickory nuts that I had seen the fox squirrel in the other day. I wonder how many hickory nuts it takes to fill up a bear?

I spent the rest of the evening building two log floor lamps. They are my invention, and contain a built-in round table, and are topped with a little fox. They will become the home for the lamp shades that I have been getting visitors to sign. After spending a couple of hours sawing, gluing, screwing, and wiring up the lamps, I was feeling pretty good (the wine helped I'm sure). Then I pulled on a cord that I had run up through one of the lamps, and pulled the cord right out of the lamp—a big mistake. And I was unable to get it put back through the tiny hole, so I gave up for the night.

A new pair of binocs, two new lamps, and I put my new flannel sheets on the bed! I spread out the thick, luxurious sheets and crawled into bed. Something was missing though, and I realized that since the cabin is so air tight, that I couldn't hear the river. So I opened up the window next to the bed, and drifted off to the sound of the Buffalo River.

I had a strange dream during the night. I went out in front of the cabin and was nearly run over by several different bears, including one giant one that looked more like a grizzly than a black bear. In fact this big bear stood up on his hind legs and his head towered over the front of the cabin. Then a couple of wolves came by, plus two giant foxes that were the size of horses! I escaped the stampede by running into the cabin and closing the door. But I watched them all from the back deck with my new binocs. Who wants to interpret?

10/21/98 Keeping track of the cloud bank this morning turned into a full-time job. When I first awoke and rolled over and looked out the window, the cloud bank was several hundred feet below me, hovering over the river. As the morning progressed, the clouds gradually lifted and moved back and forth and hung around for three hours. The clouds were only in the Buffalo Valley though, and were not up in the Whitaker Valley at all. Although there was one time when the clouds pushed their way into part of the Whitaker, but then quickly receded. I took a few pictures with the snapshot camera.

And it is a *spectacular* fall day outside—blue skies, trees turning, temps in the low 60's. Just another textbook October day in the Ozarks. I tried to sit out on the deck and take it all in, but that just didn't work. Time for a hike!

I strolled alongside a stand of maple trees. They had not yet started to turn color, but the sight of this stand is always striking because there is almost no underbrush—you can see far into the forest. And with each day that passes you can see even further, even in the rest of the forest. Trees are losing many leaves each day, which opens up the view. But the really neat thing today were the dozens and dozens of small black gum trees that were growing along one side of the maple stand—and every one of them was brilliantly colored! Red, purple, orange, yellow. Some little trees had all of those colors on the same branch! I really have a new respect for black gum trees now—they are just marvelous. I didn't notice any large parental black gums around.

The path was covered with freshly fallen leaves. Some were red or another fall color, and many were just brown. I look forward to the day when a majority of the leaves come off of the trees on the same day, like it did last year (I call this "leaf-fall"). It doesn't always happen every year, but I have been part of maybe 15 or 20 of them before, and each one was pure magic. Last year it happened very late, on November 15th. I'll keep a watch for ya.

Beyond the maples and black gums I came into yellow light. A stand of hickory trees was towering over me, yellow sun beaming down through their big leaves. This is the best year for hickories in a long time for sure.

The sun was creating quite a spectacle with the dogwood berries too. Many of the dogwoods had big clumps of the bright red berry clusters which made their branches sag. And when the sun hit the berries, red light splashed off in all directions. The birds are going to get fat this winter.

I made my way up to the apple tree at the Faddis cabin, and came away with several of them in my pocket, and one in my mouth. Very sweet. Nearby I

183

discovered a second deciduous holly tree, and it too was covered with red clusters of berries.

The persimmon tree was still loaded down with fruit, but much of it had already fallen to the ground. The bear had been eating them I know, because of the seeds in his scat. I looked up and found one persimmon that had landed in the fork of the tree, about six feet off of the ground. I had seen this little guy before, right after he had landed there. He was smooth and polished and bright persimmon color then. But time and the sun had aged him rapidly, and now he was all wrinkled up and dull looking. If you know anything about persimmons, you know that he was now ready to eat, and probably would be quite tasty. But I felt like he was put there for some special reason, spared being tossed to the ground to rot, perhaps to watch over the rest of the fruit. This tree is right next to the road into my cabin, so I left him there to watch over my coming and goings too.

When I returned to the cabin the valley was filled with soaring birds—mostly turkey vultures. Some of them were flying close, but many more were way up both the main Buffalo River valley as well as Whitaker Creek. With my new binocs I could see them working the air currents miles away.

And a bunch of wasps had gathered as well. I did not look forward to seeing them. Last fall, during a brief two-day swarm, thousands and thousands of them got into the cabin. They were seeking a place to spend the winter I guess. I never noticed them much except on warm days when things would get sunny in the cabin—they would quite literally come out of the woodwork and fly around. Then one day I let off a few of those bug bombs. When I returned the next day, the floor was covered with dead wasps. I counted out a section of them, then multiplied it all out, and decided that I had killed something like 5,000 wasps. That was before I had any furniture, a nice floor, or any carpeting in the cabin. I hoped the swarm wasn't as bad this year.

The afternoon sun was getting very warm. I laid down in the porch swing and became a little lethargic. Then a red-tailed hawk appeared overhead, which sent me running for the binocs. I got a good look at him, and could nearly count his feathers as he played back and forth in the wind currents. He was soon joined by another hawk, and they began to crisscross the sky above the meadow, getting lower and lower with each pass. One of them would swoop down like he was going to grab something, then pull up at the last minute and turn away. The other one began to scream and make all kinds of noise. The second one joined in. They flew closer and closer to the cabin, and I swear I could see them looking right at me when they screamed.

Pretty soon a grey squirrel landed on the deck and came running towards me. He didn't say anything at first, but then he jumped up onto the deck railing and started chattering away. He inched closer and closer to me, his tail twitching with each sound, then would turn around and run to the other end of the rail section, chattering and squawking all the while. Then he would turn around and work his way right back to me. What the heck was going on?

Then I felt a thump below, and I began to get a little worried. Another thump, and the deck shook. I looked over and saw that the squirrel had vanished. So had the hawks. More thuds. And more shaking. Then at the opposite end of the deck, where the stairs lead down to the lower deck, a black bear appeared. Uh oh. He swung around and headed my direction, lumbering across the deck. What the heck was I supposed to do now? The only way off of the deck was through the door into the cabin, which was between us. He was right in front of the door, and closing fast. I screamed at the top of my lungs, and waved my hands, but he just kept coming, like he was deaf. Oh, well, he did look up and smirk. Damn, now I *was* in trouble! The only thing left for me was to play dead, and since I was already laying in the swing, that was easy. I put my hands over the back of my neck, with the fingers interlaced, and tucked into the fetal position.

I felt the deck shake, another couple of thumps, and the swing moved. I began to hear heavy breathing. I was about to pee in my pants! I held my breath. The bear was standing right next to me, and he reached out and licked my face with his wet, coarse tongue. *Yuk!* I opened my eyes and stared into the biggest and deepest wild eyes that I had ever seen. Then, and this is the most incredible part of this story, the bear spoke, in a very human-like voice, although very deep—"It is time for you to get up from your nap now and get back to work!" The next thing I remember I was in space, falling, and then I hit the deck, hard—I had fallen out of the swing, which woke me up. I jumped up and looked around—no bear, no squirrel, but there was a pair of red-tailed hawks circling above. Hum. What was that I had for lunch?

After another helping of my Banff Pasta for dinner, I put my boots back on again and went for a hike. The sun was about to go down, and a light breeze was blowing. It was a more relaxing hike than most, partly because I did not need to be real quiet or sneaky or creep up along the edge of the meadows—any deer that were in the area had long since been scared out of their normal and easygoing life style by the hunters, so I wasn't going to see any strolling about. They would pretty much be on high alert now until on into December. So I got to wander around not really paying any attention to how much noise I was making, or which way the wind was blowing.

The colors in the small sumacs, sassafras and goldenrod were outshone only by the bands of pink clouds that stretched across the evening sky. The sun had gone down by the time I reached the Faddis Meadow, but the sky glowed with incredible brightness. It was cool out, but that light warmed the soul.

The weatherman had predicted cloudy skies all day, and more at night, with rain. Of course, it was clear and sunny all day, and there were a million stars out soon after dark. I got out the telescope and tried to spot the moons of Jupiter—we did this during the last bushwhacker party, but I wasn't sure if we were really seeing moons or just the effects of the booze. But sure enough, there they were, bright and clear, four moons. And they had moved. When we saw them before there was three on one side and one on the other, but tonight there were two on each side. I zoomed the tele up to 45x and could see them very well. They appear to be tiny stars, but are actually moons circling the planet, just like ours. I could even see them with my new binocs, which are only 8x (tiny moons).

It was getting a brisk outside, and they are predicting temps down in the low 30's, maybe even frost. I have set an alarm on the weather station to go off when the outside temp reaches 32 degrees so that I can be up and part of the first frost of the season! I think I'll go build a fire in the fireplace.

10/22/98 Well, it never got too cold—only down to 44, but it felt *wonderful* when I crawled out of bed and was greeted by the crisp morning, the bright sunshine, and a clear blue sky. They just don't make days any finer. However, I didn't get to enjoy too much of it, as I had business in town, and left early. I noticed on the drive home that once I left the Buffalo drainage there simply wasn't any color at all—lots of green hills. There were a few trees turning now and then, but not much.

There was a tiny sliver of a moon in the western sky when I returned just after dark. And it was lit from the right—which means? That it is getting larger! So we will have another full moon in about two weeks. It was already 42 degrees, so it was bound to be a little colder this night. The special Cloudland flannel sheets felt great.

10/23/98 I got up early for once, even beat the sun up, and the sky over yonder was glowing orange. It looked like another textbook fall day in the Ozarks—clear blue skies and lots of sunshine.

I heated up some water and had the first hot chocolate of the season as I sat out on the back deck and watched the sun streak across the hills in front. It was chilly, but not frosty out—it only made it down to 39 degrees—the coldest so far. While we can often get much wilder weather out here at Cloudland, the temperatures always seem to be milder here than in town—cooler in the summer and warmer in the winter.

It was going to be a busy day here so I didn't get to lounge around too long. I did a little computer work and some housecleaning, then greeted Hete and several folks from the **Arkansas Times Health and Fitness** magazine. Hete was going to take them on a hike deep into the wilderness, and was using the cabin as a jumping off point. Judy, Kelly and Rusty followed Hete down the ladder trail, and I bid them farewell. Then the TV producer showed up.

Fred McClure, the producer of **Arklahoma Outdoors** for KFSM TV5 in Ft. Smith/Fayetteville, was out doing a story on the new book. Just for the record, this was the very first time that a TV camera graced the inside of Cloudland. I suspect there will be more.

We went back out to the Faddis cabin and hiked down to the Crag, then he shot some footage of my hiking around and taking pictures. The light was great, and the view spectacular. The Crag was all lit up, and the sun was still streaking across the hillside in front of us, revealing some great color. Once he got done with me, a couple of hawks began to fly back and forth just above the trees across the way—right on cue!

Once Fred got finished filming the hawks playing in the wind currents, Billy and Milancy showed up. Bill set up his pad and began to paint in some outlines of the land forms up Whitaker Creek, while the TV camera rolled. The lighting was really good. I even got out my camera and shot 30 pictures of the TV man taking pictures of Billy painting pictures. Good thing no one was there taking pictures of me...

We all returned to the cabin for a beer and some more TV footage. This TV life is tough you know. Get up and go hiking and then sit on the deck and drink beer while the hawks soar overhead. No one said that it would be easy living here at Cloudland.

After my company left I got down to some serious napping, although this time there were no bears licking me in the face. I did look up once to find three red-tailed hawks circling. I watched them with the new binocs for a long time, and I never could tell if they were hunting or just having a good time. Probably some of both. I had never noticed before how they will twist their tail feathers to steady themselves. I think when they twist them to the right, then they bank to the left. Or is it the other way around? Anyway, it was great to watch.

Before long I heard huffing and puffing coming from down below. No, not another bear, but Hete and the crew was topping out from their hike. I met them with a cold beer each, and we all sat out and admired the view while they told the tales of their hike down and over and up into Hubbard Hollow and back. Actually, they really didn't look too much the worse for wear, and they seemed to have had a terrific hike and didn't mind the hill too much.

A few minutes after they left the bread machine rang and out came a wonderful loaf of steaming bread. The first slice is always the best, and mine was smothered with honey and butter—um, um, *good!* As good as the bread was, I could see that the forest was looking mighty good too, so I cut off another hunk, strapped on my boots, and headed out for a hike.

It was dead still out, and the low sun sent orange beams deep into the woods. Since it was still muzzle-loader season, and I figured the wildlife might be a little spooked, I wasn't all that quiet as I lumbered along. That was a mistake. As I popped up over the hill and into the East Meadow, I disturbed four turkey hens that must have been feeding, and they went scurrying towards the opposite end of the meadow. They didn't get up and fly, just ran along, weaving left and right.

There was also a deer standing right in the middle of the meadow, and she saw me and got spooked too. Darn—why didn't I creep up to the edge of the meadow like I should have? I guess there hadn't been any hunters in this meadow in a while.

The sun was just dropping below the trees when I stepped into the Faddis Meadow. I looked around a little, then headed towards my lane. Then I remembered that I had wanted to check on my little wrinkled-up persimmon in the fork of the tree, so I turned around and went back a few feet to the tree. There he was all right, still perched right there taking in the view.

Then a movement caught my eye. Son of a gun, there was the Faddis Bear, right out in the middle of the bright green grass just beyond the Faddis cabin. He was a ways off, and there wasn't any breeze. I just stood there and watched. He wasn't really moving, just staying in place and shuffling around some. I realized that I was so far away, that I could easily move closer without him taking note of me. But I had to move slow, and quiet.

There was a woodpecker up in the top of a big hickory tree making a lot of noise, and he, the branches, and all of the nuts, were all silhouetted against the bright western sky. Off in the woods to the right there were several squirrels running up and down trees and along the ground and making all kinds of racket. The bear was the quietest thing out there!

I stood beside a small tree for a few minutes. The bear appeared to be *grazing* in the grass! There weren't any fruit or nut trees nearby, so I couldn't figure out what else he was munching on. His body would stay still, but his head would go up and down and swing back and forth. A grazing bear, now there is one I haven't seen before. Then he laid down in the grass—just plopped right down and went on chewing. He was facing away from me. I thought that I would move still closer.

The cabin hid my advance as I crept along in the grass towards it. I could not see what the bear was doing, so I took it slow. Just as I was approaching the corner of the cabin, I peered around and saw the bear, just on the other side of the cabin. He was up and moving, but still hadn't detected me. He was about 100 feet away from me. He moved slowly, swung his head to the right and looked my direction, then up in the tree at the woodpecker, then glanced over towards the squirrels. He was a pretty large bear, and I think the same one that I had seen twice before—once rolling in the garden back in August (or September?), and then once down in Dug Hollow several weeks ago. Pure jet black glossy fur. And a brown nose. And very small ears.

He ambled up the hillside some, and found a hickory tree. It was so funny to see this big furry bear right in front of me and hear him crunching on hickory nuts. I don't know, there was just something special about that moment—I think it may be one of the most remarkable wildlife encounters that I have ever had. And one of the longest. Unless you are in a blind and specifically watching for wildlife, wildlife sightings are usually short, ending with the critter dashing off, no matter if it is a bear or a deer or a fox. And I had been watching this bear for over twenty minutes. One thing that I learned a long time ago is that you can sneak up on game if you will only move when they are moving—they are usually making a lot of noise and can't hear you making noise. It works.

The light was getting dim and I had halted my creeping. The bear continued up the rise, walked up the road some, then headed on over into the brush on the other side of the road. He did stop once in order to settle the point about whether the bear does it in the woods or not, then walked on out of sight.

Two more things about this bear sighting. When the bear was broadside to me, and he was either down grazing or picking up a nut, his outline looked just like a grizzly bear, complete with the hump on his shoulder and all. Obviously he was not a griz, but it looked just like one. And the other thing is that the entire time the bear was in view, I was never nervous or heart-pounding excited or shaking or anything like that. That must be a first for me—I always get a little shaky when I see large wild game, even if it is a deer that is basically harmless. I don't know, there is just something about being out there in the forest with a wild critter. Perhaps I was feeling more like a wild beast myself today, or maybe I could feel some sort of kinship with this bear. He is the only one that we have had out on the mountain this summer that was not a trouble maker. He stayed around and has been sighted a lot, but has never gotten into anything. Just hanging out and eating nuts and berries and grazing a little. And swimming in the little pond down below. Yea, that is it, me and the bear are some sort of wilderness soul mates. Wow, how lucky can you get?

I walked on over to where he had been grazing and found several places where he had pawed around and dug up the grass—looking for some juicy grubs I guess. There was some sort of other plant growing there too, and I bet maybe this is what he was chewing on.

It was getting very dim so I headed on back to the cabin. Just as I was getting ready to leave the meadow, a layer of clouds up high lit up with an incredible pink color. I stopped and looked and took a deep breath. The sun had gone down below the trees 30 minutes before, yet the most spectacular color was just now happening—a note for outdoor photographers—don't quit shooting just because the sun goes down!

As I walked through the forest I had to turn around and walk backwards—it looked like the woods were on fire as the brilliant light from the clouds shown through the canopy. It was *amazing*. I had to go, but I had to stay and watch. I sat down at the base of a tree until the last glow faded. Wonderful.

When I returned to the cabin I did a little grazing myself on fresh wheat bread washed down with apple cider. I spent the rest of the evening working on the Journal, answering e-mail, and listening to the blues on KUAF. I glanced over once just in time to see a field mouse poking his head into the open deck door. You should have seen me move! I jumped up and chased him not only out of the cabin, but across the deck and *off* the end of the deck! Then I wondered if he only wanted to listen to the blues too.

I just walked outside again into the crisp night air, and the only sound to be heard was the hushed music of the river below. It is very dark, and the clouds are creeping in. 52 degrees. I'm going to shut down the computer, build a fire, dig out the maple guitar, and see if some muscadine wine can make me sound like John Denver. I must still be dreaming.

10/24/98 It was a little chilly at first light, but cool temps were perfect for my little daily chore now of splitting a few sticks of wood. This is a ritual that not only becomes vital now, but has always been a chore that I have truly enjoyed. There is just something about picking up an axe and watching the log split as the sun breaks over the hill. And when it is chilly out, it becomes exercise that warms the body and soul instead of just being a daily chore. I try to split enough wood to last the day and following night. Of course, right now it is more exercise since I'm not really using the fireplace all day. But I am getting enough of a supply split that I can roll over and stay in bed on some mornings if I want, and still have plenty to burn.

It was clear and another great fall day in the Ozarks. I put on my overalls and boots and headed out for a hike and a little more work. I had noticed that some poachers had been driving on one of my old roads, a road that I don't want people to drive on. So I wanted to build a little rock wall there to discourage their use. The entrance to this road is in a corner of the East Meadow, and I enjoyed spending some time there hauling rocks and building the wall. I didn't see any wildlife while there, but did get to take frequent breaks in order to scan the meadow for any movement.

Once my little rock wall was complete (at least enough for now—I will add rocks every time I visit the area for awhile), I hiked on over to the Faddis Meadow to pick a few nuts. As I was approaching the edge of the meadow, I was startled by a covey of birds that burst into the air from a few feet away. I had hoped for a covey of quail, but they turned out to be robins.

My goal this morning was to fill a five-gallon bucket with hickory nuts to give to Scott and Carolyn who have five pet flying squirrels. They will need lots of nuts to feed them during the winter. They normally like acorns, but there are hardly any of them this year, and there happens to be lots of hickory nuts.

My first five minutes under the big hickory tree were a bit disappointing— the squirrels and the bear had really taken a toll on the nuts, and the bottom of my bucket wasn't even covered. But I persisted, and scooted around on the ground with my yellow bucket and picked up all the nuts that I could find. Once I got all of them under this one tree, I moved on to another one, and found many more nuts. The sun was up, a light breeze was blowing, the birds were singing, and I had a great time there on the ground picking nuts.

My bucket began to fill up rapidly. Then a flock of cedar waxwings descended on me. I have always loved these little birds, although I normally only see them in the winter, and wondered what they were doing here now. They were up in the trees, in the bushes, and all over the ground around me. I felt a little like St. Frances of Assisi with all the birds around me. There were many robins out too. I spent some time watching the birds but never could figure out just exactly what they were eating—surely it couldn't be the hickory nuts. But there weren't any berries on the trees. I could see one of the deciduous holly trees nearby, which was loaded with red berries, but the birds weren't interested in them. So I continued to pick up my nuts and enjoy the birds and sunshine.

Several people came by and said hi, and I asked them not to tell anyone that they had seen me rolling on the ground picking up nuts. It got warmer, and I shed a layer or two. I kept picking. Before I knew it my bucket was full—hurray! But there were still nuts on the ground. I foraged around in Bob's shed and found another five-gallon bucket, and began to fill it up as well. I was really getting into this nut gathering stuff. I just couldn't stop. I went from tree to tree, and realized that while they were all hickory trees, they were not all the same species—some of the nuts were small, others were large. Some had thick skins, others had very thin skins. In fact what I found out was that the ones with thick skins had the smallest nuts, while the one with thin skins had big nuts. Hum—I wonder if that is true of men too?

As I gathered the nuts my mind wandered off onto the subject of bears. I kept looking around for movement—bears or deer or hikers—but never saw any. But I did come across a pile or two of bear scat. And I got to thinking about how these nut or fruit bearing trees were so smart. Some trees have their seeds scattered by the wind, like maple trees who have those little wings on their seeds. But fruit and nut trees have their seeds buried deep within tasty morsels, which attract bears and deer and coyotes and other critters that eat them. The seeds are almost never digested, so they end up being expelled in the scat of the animal. These seeds will grow into new trees, spreading their distribution far and wide—wherever the critter happens to roam.

I also realized that I was competing with the bears and squirrels and whatever else that eats hickory nuts for food.

Much to my surprise I soon had the second bucket full! Wow, ten gallons of hickory nuts! It was a great feeling of fulfillment. I got up and walked back to the cabin—it was 1pm—I had been picking nuts for over four hours!

It was such a wonderful day outside I decided to go back out for another hike. I put some bread dough in the machine to cook while I was gone (I was going to a party over at the LaGrone's later, and was going to make up a batch of Cloudland appetizers to take). Then I hiked on over to Hawksbill Crag to see how many other hikers were there.

There were lots of folks coming and going, and I ended up spending an hour there just hanging out and talking to them and laying around on the rocks. I met a young lady who was alone and taking pictures there. She seemed to know what she was doing, and was getting some really good pictures. Being the shy type, and not wanting to become known as someone who preys on lovely ladies visiting the Crag, I resisted the temptation to talk with her at great length, and left the area and headed back home. Along the way, I came across more hickory nuts. I had now become obsessed with gathering nuts, and since I just happened to have a plastic bag in my pocket, I spent the next hour on the forest floor filling the bag. These were the best nuts of the day by far, and I really enjoyed gathering them. Hum, it appears that I have now become someone who enjoys gathering nuts instead of talking with beautiful young ladies—oops, I must reverse that right away!

On the way back to the cabin I met a group of men who had just hiked from the Kapark Trailhead, across Beagle Point (they called it Berrywest Point), down to the Buffalo River, and up the ladder trail. One of the guys had grown up down along the river, and we talked a bit about his experiences. He confirmed a story I had heard about a man who died down below, and had to be carried up the ladder trail and out to the church. He said that they had made a pine box to carry and bury him in. It was in 1935. I hope that some day I will be able to go down the trail with this guy or someone else who lived down along the river and could point out lots of interesting things. Someone really needs to write all of this up some day before all of the old-timers are gone.

The men were Arnold Sparks ("Sparkie"—the one who lived down below), Richard Sparks, Wesley Sparks, and Tim Sparks (who lives in Oregon). They are all related to Clyde Sparks, my rock mason, who I have talked about before. I started to make some comment about him disappearing from my job for weeks on end, and they all laughed and said that it sounded just like Clyde!

All of this nut gathering and visiting made me a little late, and I rushed around fixing my appetizers and getting ready for the party. I loaded up and drove on over to Walker Mountain and arrived just in time for the start of dinner. My appetizers disappeared quickly, but I did get to eat one myself this time. There were lots and lots of people at the party. Dean and Bonnie always have a great crowd of wonderful friends. I always feel out of place at parties, being single, when almost everyone else has a partner, so I didn't stay too long, and soon returned to Cloudland. Also I had a splitting headache that had been with me all day. When I crawled into bed, I slammed my head back against the log headboard, which didn't help matters any. As I was lying there in my misery, a gorgeous crescent moon that was hanging low in the western sky broke through the clouds, and the pain subsided.

Roy and Norma arrived from the party and took up residence for the night in the guest bedroom. I remember waking up several times during the night and hearing the wind blowing hard and the wind chimes out front making music.

10/25/98 The sun came up an hour early today, my headache was gone, and I made a pot of Cloudland coffee and fired up the computer to do some quiet work so as not to disturb my guests. They soon got up too, and we wandered around out on the decks for a little while, enjoying the sunshine and a very warm morning. There were already people out on the Crag too.

10/26/98 I couldn't sleep and got up at 3am and wandered out onto the lower deck. The night sky was beautiful, of course, with a bright moon. I tried to find Jupiter and see how many moons were out, but I could not locate it. Sometimes when I get restless like this I feel like I am wasting my time trying to sleep, and I get up and do some work. So I decided to spend some time unboxing more books. I really got into that, unboxing books down in the basement in the middle of the night, and before dawn I had a couple of hundred books unboxed and hauled upstairs and ready for McNamara to sign. Then I went to bed for a couple of hours and woke up quite refreshed!

Billy came by around noon and we spent a couple of hours signing and boxing the books back up. Then we spent an hour sitting on the deck with beers in hand, discussing the wilderness and the pioneers who used to live down below. It continues to amaze me how much this guy knows about the area, but then I guess he has lived here for over twenty years, so he has had a bit of time to learn everything! There were lots of soaring birds flying around and playing in the wind, and it was a warm afternoon.

Later my good friend from Little Rock, Nancy Williams, came by and brought two of her friends out for a visit (Eaton and Dutha). They all were staying in a cabin near Eureka Springs, and had been hiking the Lost Valley and Hawksbill Crag trails today. These two ladies were from Louisiana, and weren't used to all of our hills! They were glad to have comfortable seats to spend some time in. They were delightful company all three, and they even brought out dinner—prime beef for the grill! Nancy always brings something wonderful when she visits.

Nancy and her husband are champion skeet shooters. In fact they spend two or three months a year driving around in a big motor home going to shooting events. Nancy has been on the All-American shooting team for some time. Her husband is at least as good, and they both have a room full of trophies.

Anyway, the filets were terrific, and so was the rest of the meal and conversation. One of the ladies and her husband own the Louisiana Hot Sauce company, and I just happened to have a bottle on the shelf. I love the stuff because it is not nearly as spicy hot as Tobasco sauce.

When the wine was empty my guests headed on up the lane back towards Eureka. I knew that the next three weeks were going to be one hectic mess (looking forward to it!), so I turned in early and got a good night's sleep.

10/27/98 I got up early, split a little wood, then wandered up to the Faddis cabin with an empty bucket. My friends' flying squirrels had loved the hickory nuts I had brought them so much that I decided to gather up another load for them. I was greeted by the morning sun at the Faddis Meadow, and by about a dozen red squirrels. These little guys were jumping everywhere. I'll bet there are thousands of nuts buried in this meadow.

I got down on my rear and began to search for nuts. There was a fresh crop that had fallen since I had been there last so it was no problem finding nuts to collect. I have discovered that I really do like to gather nuts this way. It is one of those things that you can do without really putting any mental effort into it, which means that you can either concentrate on working through something else in your mind, or let it wander, which is what I did.

The squirrels, after running off and hiding when I first appeared, soon returned and went right on about their business around me like I wasn't even there. I felt like part of the family. The warming morning sunshine, those bright red fuzzy tails jumping around, and the abundance of fresh nuts all kept me well entertained. Life in the country is good.

Right in the middle of all this bliss I looked up and was startled into reality—there was a black bear about 150 feet away looking right square at me. It was my old friend no doubt, but I was immediately shaken by his presence. He sniffed the air, flipping his nose up and down. He didn't have to stand up on his hind feet to see me, he knew who I was. I expected him to flee at any moment. But he didn't. Once we exchanged glances, he began to graze on hickory nuts that were all around him. There are several hickory trees around the Faddis cabin, and his was about two trees away.

I really didn't know what else to do but sit there and be quiet, although he knew that I was there anyway. It was all very strange. I noticed that the squirrels had all run off, but were returning. The bear would rub his nose in the ground, grab a nut or two, then lift his head and chomp on the nut. Hickory nuts being crushed make a lot of noise. Every now and then he would look over in my direction while chomping. It was as if he was trying to tell me that he could do the very same thing with my bones if he had a mind to. *Chomp, chomp, chomp. Gulp.* (the gulp was me) I felt about an inch tall. Then I thought, heck, I was gathering nuts when he walked up on me and that didn't seem to bother him, so I might as well go back to doing what I was there to do. And I did, but I kept one eye peeled in his direction. It was about this time that I realized that I was nothing more than a link in the food chain, and I was competing for *his* dinner! Yikes!!! But he really didn't seem to mind. I guess there were plenty of nuts for all of us. Mr. Bear slowly moved on up the slope, walked across the road to a new tree, then disappeared down below the rise. *Chomp, chomp, chomp.* I could hear him long after he disappeared.

This bear has been different from all the others that I have seen this summer. I generally don't like bears prowling around, mainly because they do quite a bit of damage to property and people. But this guy has not touched a single thing that did not belong to him. I continued to see him as my friend, and this latest encounter has left me glad that he is around.

Boy, I got to tell you, none of the stuff that I did during my trip into town even remotely compared to my experience with the bear. And ya know, no one that I saw could relate to it, so I never even mentioned it. I guess a lot of experiences that one has out in the wilderness are like that—very special indeed but tough to relate to others who haven't been there. So you just go around with a smile on your face all day, and warm fuzzies in your heart.

The moon was awaiting me once again when I returned, and I lingered for a while in the moonlight before crawling between the flannel sheets.

10/28/98 Several members of the *Trailside* crew showed up at the cabin bright and early, and the Director of Tourism for the State of Arkansas, Joe Rice, was with them. *Trailside* is a series on PBS that documents great outdoor adventures around the country. They were here to do an episode about Arkansas, and the best place to begin was—where else, but Cloudland! The director and the camera man were French Canadian, and they spent a lot of time speaking

French. Their English was very good. Joe had never been to Cloudland before, and was quite impressed. He wanted to call **Southern Living** magazine and get them to do a photo spread. Hum. We'll see.

The field producer was from Florida, and she was a delight to work with. We quickly decided that the opening of the show would be shot at—guess where—the front of the cabin! Hey, Cloudland would be in pictures! Then I took them out to Hawksbill Crag and they were knocked over by the incredible beauty. The color had been advancing well, and it was all quite spectacular.

My Amish crew had also showed up this morning, and they were going to spend the day spraying another coat of clear protective finish on the outside of the cabin. And this stuff was laced with some special bug dope that would help keep the wasps out, which were really becoming more of a problem.

I took the **Trailside** crew on down into Boxley Valley to look at a couple of other sites, then on to Steel Creek. We found some good shooting locations, and fleshed out the "script" a little (their host would be working from a script, I would not). The host of the program, Ray Browning, wasn't present, and would be flying into Harrison later that night, and I would meet him then next morning. The crew went on to scout other sites, and I returned to the cabin.

10/29/98 Soon after daylight five vehicles from the **Trailside** crew showed up at my front door. *Wow*, what a production! A sound man from Oregon was added, along with a guy who always carried a very large backpack. When I asked what was in it, they just told me *everything*. It felt like it.

They shot the opening scene right at the front of the cabin. The series host, Ray, drives up in a Chevy (the program is partially funded by Chevrolet), then gets out, puts his backpack on, and walks around the side of the cabin, where he finds me on the back deck, looking through the telescope—a very believable shot. My first scene went very well, and they only shot it twice. In the next scene, I was to give Ray an overview of our two-day hike, both on the map, as well as show him the route as best I could from the back deck of the cabin. Well, for some reason, I got hung up on the word "Boxley" in Boxley Valley, and we had to shoot the scene 17 times. The crew was very patient, and it helped me a lot to have just seen Ray mess up about a dozen takes in the opening shot. The sun was going in and out of the clouds, and it was spitting rain, but I finally did get the shot right, and we all were happy. Then they shot the exact same scene over about a dozen other times from other angles. This would become norm—we would spend a lot of time getting the main scene down just right, then we would do it over and over and over while they shot it from different angles. In the final production, they will use cuts from several different angles, making it look like it was all one take. Oh yea.

We packed up and hiked on over to Hawksbill Crag. The view and the wilderness was about as spectacular as I had ever seen it! It was just amazing, and we had no trouble coming up with something to say and getting the lines right. While we were filming, and I was talking about how I thought HAWKsbill

Crag got its name because there were always hawks flying around, there were several hawks flying around doing wonderful things. I don't think they were able to get them in the scene, but they really added an element of beauty to the entire situation.

I had to give a program in Tulsa, so as soon as my scene was finished I ran up the hill to my van, then sped off to town, leaving the crew to gawk at the beauty on their own. It was about 2am when I made it back to the cabin. It would be a very short night. I was one tired puppy.

10/30/98 I needed a full pot of coffee to get me going (and I don't really even drink coffee—mine was spiked a little with Baileys Irish Cream), and I drove down and met the TV crew in Boxley. We shot and hiked and shot and hiked all morning and all afternoon. Some of it was stupid, some of it was very good. The host, Ray, is not only a talented athlete (five-time champion of the Iron Man Tri-Athlete competition in Hawaii), but he is a darn nice guy, and a pleasure to work with. We got along well, and I hope that is seen on screen. In fact the entire crew was very nice, and that, combined with their obvious talents, made for a very enjoyable experience overall for me.

We shot a scene at a gorgeous pool down on the main Buffalo River just as the sun peeked through the fog, then shot some in the pastures nearby, then climbed up the hill to another part of the trail and shot more, then back down to the river, then up on another hillside for a visit to a giant sinkhole, then over to the Beaver Jim Villines Homestead near the Ponca Bridge.

The highlight of the day for me was when we were trying to get a scene right, and I was having trouble. Then a group of people walked up, and the field producer made them all stand back and be quiet. Oh lord, now I had an audience to watch me screw up. I took a deep breath, a swallow of water, and we nailed the scene. Right after, one of the group asked who I was, and it turned out that they had several of my books, one of them in hand, and I got to do an autograph right there in the woods. I felt like somebody.

Anyway, the day was a very long one, but it ended well with a shoot at the base of Roark Bluff. I drove back to the cabin and spent a couple of hours doing chores, then hit the sack.

10/31/98 I was up early once again, but did get a good night's sleep, and drove on down the mountain to Roark Bluff, where I set up "camp" and got a fire going for breakfast. The first shot of the day was of me waking up and crawling out of the tent, while Ray handed me a plate full of pancakes and Canadian bacon. The backdrop of the towering Roark Bluff was very dramatic. Ask me about the pancakes sometime.

Next I took the crew *up* on top of Roark Bluff for some shooting. You must realize that most of a production like this one is staged—it just has to be that way. But I wish the cameras could have been rolling when they all stepped out to look at that view for the first time. Now this crew is made up of very talented

196

folks who make their living filming in the most wonderful outdoor scenery in the world. And they were completely blown away by Roark Bluff and the view from up there. Ray lives high up in the Rockies, and even he couldn't believe how gorgeous it was. Hey, "it is just Arkansas" I told them.

Once we finished the shots at the viewpoint, the director wanted to shoot us walking along the top of the bluff off in the distance, which required us to bushwhack about 1/3 mile to get to a good location. It was just Ray and I and our backpacks—the crew stayed behind. Well, there was no trail, and we were both wearing shorts, and the greenbriers were murder. By the time we reached a clear spot, our legs were shredded and bloody. Ray was not too happy with the director. We were talking back and forth as we hiked, bitching and moaning, and communicating every now and then with the director via walkie-talkies. What we didn't realize was that both of the mikes that we were wearing were transmitting everything that we said back to the headsets of the director, cameraman and field producer. Oops! Oh well, we were the ones being cut up.

You won't see any blood until the very last scene that has me in it. Ray and I walk over to Twin Falls (the one at Camp Orr), which wasn't running very much, but was the only waterfall that I could think of along the trail that was running at the time. You might be able to see all of the scratches on our legs. The rest of the hiking part of the show was shot before we got all scratched up.

We didn't finish up until late in the afternoon. I bid the crew a fond farewell and drove like a madman back to the cabin. My mom's birthday party had begun at noon, and I had missed most of it. I arrived to a nearly empty cabin— everyone was out hiking! (*The TV show turned out pretty good and eventually aired hundreds of times over several years on PBS stations across the country.*)

The birthday party went very well, and it was great to see my mom enjoying herself at the cabin, along with all of her kids. My brother, Terry, and his wife, Marsha, and my sister, Dorcas Cecil, and her husband, Richard (his mom is Jeanne Cecil, who lives in Harrison), all came down from Illinois, along with my niece, Sarah, and nephew, Matt. The Cecils brought a case of fine wine, which we were forced to sample throughout the night (some of it survived and will fill slots in the wine rack if I ever get it put up). There was also a great deal of wonderful food. Scott and Carolyn and Luke and Mary came over from Fayetteville to join in the party. Terry and Marsha and Luke and Mary and Scott and Carolyn were spending the night, but mom and the rest of the crew had to drive back to Fayetteville and Harrison.

It was a long week for me, and so I hit the hay early once again. Oh yea, I guess it was not only Halloween, but also the end of October. What a *terrific* month I have had at Cloudland! None finer anywhere. The fall colors turned out to be wonderful, as bright as any I had seen in a while. And while I never got to shoot any pictures, I did get to spend a lot of time out in the woods enjoying the colors and the great weather. Marvelous. Just marvelous!

October rain was 5.4 inches, low 39 degrees, high 74 degrees, wind 40mph

NOVEMBER 1998

11/1/98 I was exhausted from a long week and was looking forward to sleeping in, but I heard footsteps and conversation from down below early, so I gave in and got up and joined my guests. It was a little cool outside, but everyone was enjoying the view and the crisp air and didn't mind. Before long there was talk of a breakfast feast. Soon the smell of bacon filled the air, and we all moved inside and piled our plates with bacon, Luke's special French Toast, fresh fried taters, muffins, and other goodies. I knew that Hete and Roy and Norma were staying up at the Faddis cabin over the weekend and doing a little hiking, but I never could get them on the phone to come down and help us take care of the food. I began to get a little worried when Mary walked up and found no one awake, but Roy's truck in the drive, just as it had been the day before.

Just as we all cried out that we had had enough and could hold no more, Roy was spotted walking past the window. Good, at least he would come in and help with the leftovers. When we opened the door, Roy looked a little funny, and was covered with sweat. He was smiling, and said that he had been out on a little hike. Yes, he sure had. In fact he had been out hiking all day on Saturday, got lost over near Bowers Hollow, spent the night curled up next to a log, and only this morning was able to get his bearings and hike out.

He had a space blanket in his pack, and rain gear. He didn't have any matches. Once it got dark he found a big log and laid up against it all night. At first light he continued to find his way out by using a compass, which never did him any good, and only wore him out more and got him in deeper trouble. Roy finally realized that the compass was useless. He sat down and thought for a minute. He could hear water down below—a stream. He knew that all streams in the area flowed downhill and into the Buffalo River. All he had to do was follow the stream to the river, then turn left and go downstream until he crossed Whitaker Creek, which was the first large stream that he would come to. He had been there many times before. From that point all he had to do was follow the trail up the hill to the cabin. While it took him a couple of hours to do this, it was really just that simple. He found the river, then the trail, then the French Toast on my dining table. Good going Roy!

I got really lost and in trouble once in the woods way up north in Canada. I won't go into all of the details, but I will say that I had relied on a compass and a map drawn by a native Indian. The map was wrong, and so the compass was of no use. But I trusted it with my life, and it wasn't until a stroke of luck happened that I abandoned the compass and found my way out. I was within a few feet of dying in that flat wilderness, all because of a stupid compass. I've not carried one ever since. That was in 1979.

It was going to be a very long week ahead for me, and so after the excitement of Roy's self-rescue died down and everyone left, I packed a few things up and bid my log cabin farewell.

11/4/98 Dawn came early, although it was very cloudy out, and in fact I couldn't see a thing outside my windows. There was a TV crew coming up from Channel 7 in Little Rock to do some filming of Billy and I about the new book, so I did all I could to shoo away the clouds. By 9am the fog had lifted some, and the glorious wilderness stretched out in front of me for many miles. And a new friend had begun to appear—just across the way, over on Beagle Point, several trees had lost their leaves, and I could see part of the sandstone bluff there. The bluff is nearly 80 feet tall, but is completely hidden when the leaves are on the trees. It is the same bluff that Hawksbill Crag is made of, and runs throughout the entire wilderness, causing streams to leap into the air as beautiful waterfalls. It was good to see the bluff, and the view.

As soon as the TV crew left I had to pack up once again and head back to town, a much too short visit to Cloudland—they all are too short. I had another program in Russellville the next day, then another up in Springfield. Both of these shows were to packed houses too. People were turned away from the one at the Nature Center in Springfield—they took 200 reservations and then cut everyone else off. That is one gorgeous Nature Center that they have there, and the people of Missouri should be proud of it. And the people were nice, and rather quiet, but they didn't buy very many books (the Director of the Center was very nice and most helpful, and I would like to convince her to move to Cloudland!). On the other hand, the crowd in Russellville was loud and chatty and bought a record number of books for one of my shows—34. I enjoyed both shows, all four shows during the week in fact.

11/7/98 It seemed like it had been ages since I had been to the cabin when I rolled up at noon today. The road was again covered with leaves, and it was raining lightly, and chilly out. The cabin was a welcome sight, and while it was cool inside too, it was much warmer than it was outside. In what would become a daily ritual for me this winter, and one that I dearly love, I filled the fireplace with wood and got a crackling fire going in no time. It would take several hours and even a day before the heat warmed the logs, but the sight of the flames in my very own fireplace warmed my heart instantly. The wind was howling outside, but I was all snug and warm and safe and secure in my log castle.

There was still lots of fall color left, but I could tell it was past peak, and many trees had already dropped their leaves. The bluff over yonder on Beagle Point was showing itself even more now.

It was nasty outside—temp about 40, winds gusting into the 20mph's, and blowing rain. *Cold!* And the windchill factor was down in the low 20's. This is a new factor that I will be reporting on (wind chill)—I just can't wait to see what the weather station registers when it is in the 20's outside with a 40mph wind!

Hum, nasty weather, lots of fall color, and me not having been outside for a long time—I decided to forgo my book chores for a while and go on a hike! This new book has been pretty much taking over my life, which is fine, since that is what I do. But I need time in the wilderness. So I put on my boots and some rain gear and drifted into the forest. The ground was covered with bright yellow maple leaves, freshly blown from their branches. Quite by accident, I had built my cabin right in the middle of that band of maple trees that streaks across the area, which means that I can take off hiking in any direction and walk through maple trees! And they were really nice today, with all of that yellow.

I hiked on up to the East Meadow—gosh, I hadn't been there in two weeks? As I strolled across the meadow I found three big doe deer bedded down right out in the middle of the meadow. They saw me immediately, of course, but didn't bother to get up and run. They did keep their eyes glued on me, and I froze in place at first. It was a stand-off. But my light coat was not nearly as warm as theirs, and I had to get moving again or really become frozen. I took a step, expecting them to bolt. Nothing. They just kept staring. Then another step. Still nothing. What the heck, I'll just walk on and enjoy the day. I did. They followed my every movement, but never budged an inch.

There seems to be a pattern developing here. Deer stay in their beds while I pass. Bears keep on munching nuts right alongside me without distress. What is going on here? Have these wild animals seen me enough to become comfortable with me and not afraid? Do they know it is me, or would they do this for other humans? I hope that is not the case—some humans carry guns, and arrows and other stuff, and have visions of meat on the table. Me, I just want to see these wild critters in their own living rooms and watch them at play. I continue to be amazed at my acceptance by these wild creatures, and revel in their beauty.

The next stretch of forest didn't have any maple trees in it, and the leaves on the ground were mostly brown, although many of the trees above were yellow—lots of hickories. Hum, I wonder if my friend the bear is about? I worked my way on down the hillside near the top of the bluffline, then just wandered around a little. The wind wasn't blowing nearly as much on this side of the hill, but the rain did pick up a little.

I noticed some fresh diggings up ahead. There have been several holes or dens in the dirt on this hillside, and I have been trying to figure out if they were fox dens or something else. One in particular I had walked past many times in the last two months, and it always looked like fresh traffic at the door. Today I could tell that someone else had been there. The hole had been enlarged, and a lot of dirt had been dug out. The den was now about three feet in diameter, and it went back in about that far too. I got down on my knees and looked into the hole. Aha!!! I figured out who's den it was, and what had happened. Apparently a bear had done the enlarging, and laying in the back of the hole was what was left of the shell of an armadillo! The bear had scooped out the den, and the armadillo too—possum on the half shell! I don't like armadillos. I had never seen any of them up in the Ozarks until about 15 years ago. They have been migrating up from Texas, and I wish they would go back. They can do quite a bit of damage to a forest, and I have seen them destroy sections of hiking trails with all of their digging (I wish we could control their diggings, then maybe we could get them to build a few trails). I guess they do look pretty good sunning themselves beside the highway though.

The rain came down harder, and it was getting cold, but I was really enjoying being out and gliding around through the woods—kind of set free after a week of being cooped up inside auditoriums with crowds of people. I went on down to Hawksbill Crag and found a splendid view. Man, it was *gorgeous!* There was still lots and lots of brilliant color in the trees down below. A lot of bright orange that I hadn't seen before. I could see many trees with no leaves too. The wind whistled and the rain hitting the trees produced a delightful lullaby.

I had more "maple hiking" to do. Instead of following the trail back to the cabin, I went uphill to the first bench. That band of maples lives on this bench, and I wanted to spend more time walking through those wonderful trees. The ground was covered with the same yellow leaves at first, then a few red ones were mixed in, and eventually they were all red leaves. There were a few places where the underbrush was thick, and I got pretty wet, but most of the hike was through open maple forest. And this band of maples led me right to my cabin.

The cabin was warm and inviting and a joy to return to. I checked the weather station, and the windchill had been down to 15 degrees during my hike. I stripped off my wet clothes and hung them on my new wooden clothes dryer. I had bought it at the end of last winter, and never got a chance to use it. It is one of those cheap things that you can buy at Wal-Mart, but it seemed to be just perfect, and my clothes were all dried out in no time. Of course, I did stoke the fire a bit and spent some time right in front of it drying myself out too. I also have one of those boot dryers out here. I've used one for many years, and they work just great, but have never known anyone else who had one. I can't figure that one out. You put your boots on it and plug it in, and slightly warm air goes up into the boots—it takes 12-15 hours to dry out a leather boot, but it does so without any damage to the leather.

Before I left on my hike I put some mix in my bread machine, and so the cabin was filled with the aroma of fresh baking sourdough bread when I got back. Life is tough up in the mountains.

After I devoured half of the warm bread, plus a bowl of my special veggie soup and rice (with Louisiana Hot Sauce, of course), and a glass or two of homemade wild blackberry wine, I laid back on the couch and took a well-deserved nap. When I woke up it was dark outside. It was a fine nap. And no one needed one more than me!

As the evening drew on my supply of firewood ran out. I had built a firewood stash next to the cabin so that I could go out in the middle of a rainy night and get dry wood, and me stay dry, and this was the first time that I put the system to the test—it worked great! I have a spotlight right above the firewood area, tools in the shed right there, and the entire area under cover of the cabin roof overhang high above. I can even split wood and stay dry during a driving rainstorm.

I loaded up the indoor wood stash, filled the fireplace with a couple of large logs, and crawled between the Cloudland sheets, happy and warm and snug in my little log cabin. This was the first time in a long while that I had gone to bed with a big fire going downstairs, and I had forgot about the show on the ceiling. All of the log rails, log perlins and fan blades created a pattern of a hundred shadows on the light-colored aspen ceiling. The shadows danced and played to the rhythm of the fire. Who needs to count sheep with all of this going on?

11/8/98 I woke up in a fog, and while it wasn't quite as thick as it had been the night before, it completely engulfed the cabin. I could only see a few feet away from the cabin, where the branches of a few maple trees poked their way in, and their leaves were glowing orange. It was dead still out—not a wisp of wind at all. It was eerie, and wonderful and exciting all at the same time.

The big log that I had put in the fireplace burned all night, and was still flickering when I got up. In the past, I had filled the fireplace with smaller, split wood, which burned out within a few hours, and it was normal for me to have to get up two or three times during the night to keep the fire going. My fireplace is a great one, but is designed to burn hot, to keep a good flame going which keeps the glass burned off and clear. Even shut all the way down, the fire burns at nearly full blast. Now I use one big log instead of smaller ones, and it will often burn all night.

I sat in the big overstuffed leather chair that is next to the fireplace and sipped some hot chocolate and frozen cool whip. It was a little chilly in the cabin, but nice and toasty around the fire. I have found that it feels great to stand in front of the fireplace and get my backside very warm, then go sit in the chair, which warms up the leather, which in turn warms you up again.

But it was glorious outside—fog and great color. I had to make a choice—to stay in my leather chair and fireplace world, or go out and hike in the fog? It was an easy call. I put on my dry hiking boots and disappeared into the fog. Since the wind wasn't blowing, it felt kind of warm out, or at least not nearly as cold as the day before, although it was 39 degrees. The branches were covered with red and yellow maple leaves, and the thick fog blended the color together into a mystic colorful soup. It was very quiet out, and even my boots were silent against the wet carpet of leaves. There weren't any critters out either—no squirrels in the trees or on the ground, no deer in the meadows, and no bears munching hickory nuts. It was a pleasant stroll through the woods.

The forest looked as though someone had taken buckets of red, yellow, orange, and green paints, mixed them all together just a tad so that one color streaked into the next, then splashed the entire batch through the woods. I walked through the greatest masterpiece ever created. And I'll bet most people stayed home today because the weather was "cold and miserable out." Ha! Give me a day like this and I will live forever.

As I got back to the cabin the fog was lifting, and I could see the lower half of the wilderness, all the way down to the river. But I couldn't see any of the tops of the hills, which were still up in the fog bank. It is funny how sometimes you are above the ceiling here, with the fog bank down in the valley, and the hills poking up through it, and sometimes you are right below the ceiling, like it was today, with all the wilderness below the fog.

I sat in the leather chair and worked on books and answered e-mail and wrote in the Journal, then I got up and split a little more wood. I just love to do that when it is chilly out. Next I brought in the big extension ladder, carefully extended it 23 feet up to the main ceiling beam in the living room, and gingerly crawled up with screwdriver and insulation in hand. I had to remove the grill to the big power exhaust vent there and fill the space with insulation. Otherwise, there is a free-flow of warm air through the space and out the roof. This is great in summer, but not in the winter. I will have to crawl back up in the spring and remove the insulation. I used the step ladder to do the same procedure to the power vent up in the loft.

As I was returning the large extension ladder to its resting place outside, an incredible burst of sunlight spilled out from the clouds and lit up a dozen parts of the wilderness, creating a magical light show. *Wow!* Without the sun, the overall view is OK color-wise, but not real brilliant. There is still a great deal of color, but many of the trees have lost their leaves. When the sun hits the forest, all of the color that remains really packs a punch! And you can still see lots of green trees, so there is more color to come. We are past the peak now though.

That light show was a fitting end to my short visit. I will not be able to return to the cabin for a week, which seems like an eternity to me right now.

11/13/98 Just after I passed through my gate a very fat raccoon ran into the road ahead and led me on down the hill towards the cabin. It had been very foggy all the way from town, but the sky was clear at Cloudland, and the stars were out in full force. The weather station revealed that there was one a big storm a few days before, with winds up to 46mph and some rain. The low temp so far this fall has only been 36 degrees, can't believe that we haven't had a freeze yet.

A bright star that I think was Jupiter was in full view (OK, I know, it is a planet not a star), so I went inside to get the telescope to see how many moons were out. By the time I got back out onto the deck, less than a minute, the fog bank had caught up with me, and all of the stars disappeared. Wow, it really moved in fast, and was very thick. At one point I looked up to the ceiling and couldn't believe that it was foggy *inside* the cabin! That was some thick fog!!!

While it was only in the low 50's outside, it was rather chilly in the cabin, so I made a big fire, and even turned the heat pump on (first time this year) just to get the logs warmed up a bit. I filled my glass with wild berry wine, and autographed about 100 books.

11/14/98 An orange glow penetrated the loft at first light. I rolled over and realized that I was surrounded by bright yellow and orange maple trees just outside my windows, the colors all smeared into one by the heavy fog that was still here. It was downright beautiful! And there was no way that I could lay in bed—I had to get up and get out and see what was going on. The fire had almost gone out. I put on a new terry cloth bathrobe robe, blue suede slippers, grabbed a Starbucks mocha from the fridge and went out onto the back deck to enjoy the show.

The fog was moving around a lot. First it surrounded the cabin completely, with only the closest trees in view. Then silhouettes of the next layer of trees would show up. Soon the fog had settled and I could see all the way across the valley to the ridgetops that were sticking up out of the fog. There was another layer of fog above the ridges too, so the cabin was suspended right in the middle of two layers of fog. And then the sun broke through. It lit up the narrow fins of the ridgetops, which were still covered with colored trees. It all created another surreal scene at Cloudland. Within minutes the sun had risen up into the upper fog bank and the sunshine disappeared.

I realized that I needed to get off of my deck and out into the woods and try to take a picture or two. After all, I was a nature photographer, was expected to take lots and lots of colorful pictures in the fall, but I hadn't even loaded a single roll of film yet this fall. So I jumped up, put on some work clothes, grabbed an apple, shouldered my heavy camera pack and picked up my tripod and took off towards Hawksbill Crag.

The Crag hung out over a sea of white, out there in the air all by itself. I quickly set up my camera gear and started shooting. The fog was on the move, but I think that I got a few good shots. I don't normally like to shoot the Crag without hikers standing on it (for scale), but The Ozark Society wanted a new picture of the Crag for their new membership brochure, and they didn't want any people on it. So I shot away. Then I heard voices, but they weren't coming down the trail. They were coming from up above, from the direction of the Faddis cabin. A group of five folks stepped out onto the Crag, which was still hanging out over the fog bank. My camera motor went into high gear, but only for a couple of pictures, then I got to the end of the roll.

As I quickly put in a new roll of film, one of the group called out my name. Oops, I got caught. It was Mike Mills, former Director of Tourism for Arkansas and owner of the Buffalo Outdoor Center down in Ponca. He was going to take his hot air balloon crew up for a fun ride this morning, but the fog kept them grounded, so he decided to bring them up to the Crag. I shot a few more pictures, we all soaked up the view, then I led them on over to the cabin for a quick tour. Then I realized that all of the Tourism Directors for the State of Arkansas for the past 25 years had been at my cabin in the last two weeks (well, that is only two guys, but I thought it was significant).

Once they were on their way I decided to head back out again to see if I could find a few pictures. I had wanted to drop down into Whitaker Creek, then work my way upstream into the headwaters of this most scenic drainage. To my horror, I discovered that I only had two rolls of film left—72 pictures. I had shot about 100 pictures at the Crag. I would normally shoot three or four rolls of film for each good scene that I might find, so going out on a major shoot with only two rolls was not very good. What I decided to do was hike and explore and look around until I found one single scene, then shoot all of my film there. And even when I ran out of film, the hike would be a splendid one.

So I went back to the Crag, then made my way along the top of the bluffline to where I could get down through it, then I slipped and slid on down the hillside to the bottom, where I found Whitaker Creek running pretty good. I made my way upstream. The fog had all lifted, but it was still overcast, just exactly what I wanted. I passed by a number of wonderful scenes—white water rushing over moss-covered rocks, lots of bright green ferns, and a few deep pools of emerald water.

Then I came across one scene that I thought might fit the bill for my remaining film. There were several small maple trees growing right next to the stream, and their leaves were brilliant yellow. I guess their time had come, because it looked like about half of their leaves had dropped off recently, and they blanketed the green rocks in and along the stream below. And there was some white water in the stream. So I stopped and set up my equipment. The right spot to take the picture was at a difficult location for my tripod—I had to secure it on top of a slick boulder that was at a 45 degree angle. I could get the camera in position OK, but when it was just right, there was no place for me to stand and look through it. It must have taken me ten minutes to get set up the way I wanted it. And then horror struck—just as I was loading the film, the sun broke through the clouds above. This scene was basically worthless with the sunshine on it. I fired off a few quick pictures, then laid down against the rock to wait out the sun, hoping for a cloud or two to drift by.

After about an hour of waiting, no clouds. I got a little frustrated—this was a very nice scene indeed. And I knew that it wouldn't do any good to proceed to find a different scene, because I couldn't shoot any of them as long as the sun was out. I could see a lot of blue sky. I waited. Finally, a thin layer of clouds drifted by, and while the shadows were never completely eliminated, I did manage to shoot my two rolls of film. Not a masterpiece, but an OK snapshot.

From the creek I decided to head straight up the hillside and see what I could find. This was one *steep* hillside, about as steep as it could get without being bluffline. I made it up to the bottom of the main bluffline, where I found some really gorgeous trees in full fall dress. This was the same bluffline that runs through the entire wilderness, and that the Crag is made of. The trees were beeches, bright yellow and orange, more yellow maples, and a lot of really yellow oak trees too. I found one rather perfect red oak tree leaf that was the most pure yellow that I had ever seen. I've never seen oaks like this before. It was a glorious walk below the bluffline, then I found a break in the bluff and had another fine walk along a level bench up above. I tried to forget that the sun was out and ruining my pictures. But then, what the heck, I was out of film anyway. So I really enjoyed this walk through the yellow woods. Then I came upon a tiny red maple tree, about a foot tall, that was bright red, and in great contrast to all of the yellow.

I was really surprised to see so much color. When looking at the long views, more than half of the trees were bare. But up close and personal walking through the woods there was a tremendous burst of color everywhere that you looked. I sat down to take a break, and was joined by a fat grey squirrel in the tree next to me. He was in a small maple tree, and really looked out of place running past all of those yellow leaves.

After my short conversation with the squirrel I hiked on and picked up the Hawksbill Crag Trail and headed towards the cabin. When I reached the Crag there was no one there. I sat down to rest and to enjoy the sunshine. I was immediately surrounded by a herd of ladybugs—they were everywhere! Bright orange ones with black spots. And a hawk or two soared low, down along the treetops in the valley.

I hiked up to the Faddis cabin and through the meadow there. No more hickory nuts. No persimmons. But the deciduous holly tree was looking mighty fine. And I ran into a flock of bluebirds—the first that I had seen up here in a long while. They were busy jumping back and forth among the hickory tree branches. Their orange breasts shown brightly against their own blue feathers and the blue sky above.

Oh, I forgot to tell ya before that the wasps had gotten rather thick in the cabin, especially since the fireplace had warmed all of the logs up. I set off a bunch of smoke bombs in the cabin before my hike. When I returned I found hundreds and even thousands of dead wasps on the floor. You could hardly walk without crunching one. Unfortunately there were also hundreds of dead lady-bugs too—I guess they run with the wasps. I got out the vacuum and sucked them all up. Then I collapsed out on the deck, weary and sore from my little hike. The camera gear weighs about 42 pounds, and I realized that I had really gotten out of shape during my marathon book tour. Lots of sitting in the car and driving, and a ton of bad junk food on the go had taken their toll. It was a great hike, but I was glad to be sitting down on my deck!

Today was the first day of deer season, but I didn't hear too many shots. As I sat there recovering from the hike, and waiting for a pot of red beans and rice to boil, my brain wandered back to the days of my youth, to my very first deer season when I was seven years old. My dad had been a world class swimmer when he was young (really—at one time he held the world record in the breast stroke, was an All-American for three years in college, and was ranked number one for the Olympic Team). He won the very first race that he ever swam—it was a five mile swim in the Meramec River outside of St. Louis. I still have a copy of the half-page newspaper article about his feat. I swam competitively from age five through my first year in college, then I discovered cameras and left the Razorback swim team that I was on. I was never the athlete that my dad was, but swimming was good to me, and taught me a great deal about discipline.

Anyway, his heart muscle was a tremendous one, but a lifetime working behind a desk took its toll, and he had a heart attack at a young age. He survived that one, and several others, but was unable to really get out and enjoy the woods like I know he wanted to. He had been an outdoorsman growing up, and wanted his boys to follow. The special relationship that I have with the outdoors began on that first hunt with my dad some 36 years ago. Because of his heart, he mainly stayed around our deer camp and cooked and generally kept things running while all of the hunters were out in the field. I went to a Catholic school, and several of us boys were excused each deer season to go hunt. I got to go out and run around in the woods for a full week, and loved every minute of it!

There was one time during that very first hunt so long ago that my dad took me out into the woods and taught me a thing or two. I've never told this story to anyone before. It would be the only time that my dad would spend time with me out in the woods (because of his heart condition), and somehow we both knew that it was special. We didn't carry our guns. He took me down a small hill into a little ravine near camp, where there was a small waterfall that ran over moss-covered rocks. We sat down at the base of the biggest tree that I had ever seen. He told me that I was big enough to carry a gun now, but that it was also up to me to care for it, use it responsibly, and never cause any undue harm to anyone or anything with it. Legal game during legal seasons for food and self-defense were the only living things that my gun was to be pointed at. That was all pretty basic. But he also talked about the forest, and the land, the rocks and trees and birds and the earth in general. He pointed up to the big tree above us and said that it would be up to me too to be responsible and use the trees and the land wisely, that if I cared for them, that they would care for me in return.

He said that all he ever expected from me was to be kind to others and to be the very best person that I could be, to work hard and to always be honest and fair. That was quite a load for a seven year old, and much of it would never hit home for many years to come, but I think he knew that he might not be around long enough for another talk, so he might as well cover as much as he could right then and there. I'm sure that I strayed from these principles many times while growing up, but seeing him stick to them throughout his life continued to steer me back in the right direction.

My dad did live many more years, but we never did have another talk, except for a short one on the day that he died, seventeen years later. I had just sold my studio photography business to become a nature photographer full time. It was a big risk for me to give up a steady income for an uncertain freelance career. He was recovering from yet another heart attack, and we spent about ten minutes talking about life, only our second real talk ever. He told me that he supported my decision to become a nature photographer, and he reminded me of our little walk in the woods so long ago, and that all he ever expected was for me to do the very best that I could, no matter what I was doing. He died several hours later. I have always tried to live up to his standards. As I sat out on the back deck today, looking at one of the most beautiful places on earth, I thought about my dad. And how lucky I had been in life, not only to have all of the things that I do, but that I had him as a father. He was the greatest man that I will ever meet, and I am proud to bear his name.

So you see, to all of you who don't like the sport of hunting much, there is often a great deal more to hunting than just killing animals. I don't hunt anymore, but am thankful that my dad gave me a gun, and the road map for life that went with it.

It is late at night now, and I have just completed a marathon book signing session with Billy McNamara. The sunset was incredible—a high layer of clouds lit up bright pink and orange against a blue sky. And you almost had to wear sunglasses inside the cabin just before sunset because all of the maple trees outside were glowing brightly. It was a good move for me to have built this little cabin right in the middle of a maple grove.

The half-ton of books is now loaded back into the van for delivery to Barnes and Noble and for me to sell at the upcoming programs. I'm headed back to town in a few minutes for I have to get up early, unload all of the books, load up all of my program equipment, then drive to the Arts Center in Leslie, Arkansas to give a program. It will be a long day, but I will enjoy getting to meet the people of Leslie. After I give a small program in Fayetteville on Monday, McNamara will join me for the largest show of the season at the NWA Community College in Rogers. It will be the 1,000th program that I have given since I started doing this back in 1981. I wish that my dad could be there to see it—I would hope that he would approve of the route that I have taken in life. It all started with that first hunting trip and the walk with him in the woods.

11/17/98 I couldn't stand it any longer. Just about everyone that I talked to had been out or was going out to see the meteor shower, one that was supposed to be the best in many decades. Couldn't see too much from town, so I decided that I must be a part of it all, and made a quick trip out to Cloudland.

It was nearly midnight when I pulled into the East Meadow and shut off the engine. I got lucky—crystal clear skies! I spread a ground cloth out on top of the wet grass (dew had already begun to form), then crawled into my sleeping bag, putting myself in a perfect position for star gazing. And it didn't take long for the first shooting star to streak across the black sky above. Fabulous. Then there was another. And another. The regular stars were bright and twinkling, but the shooting stars were just spectacular as they spread silver dust in the heavens. It seemed like many of them were closer than the normal variety. Perhaps the sky was just clearer. And something else was that there were many very tiny ones that could be seen, not just the blazing ones.

There were a dozen, then two, then three. Sometimes I could even see two shooting stars at the same time. It was a grand show indeed. Although I had missed the real peak of the shower—it was supposed to have been at 2pm—great for watching in Tokyo, but a little bright in the middle of the day in the United States! But what I saw was like a peak to me—many more than I had ever seen before. Brilliant, just wonderful.

I began to drift in and out of sleep—after you had seen a hundred stars, how many could one mind take? A lot more I'm sure. But I was dead tired, and didn't last nearly long enough. I crawled down into the summer sleeping bag and pulled the top over my head for warmth—it had gotten a wee bit chilly.

Sometime later in the night a barred owl let out a scream near the edge of the meadow, and I must have jumped a foot off of the ground. Where was I? Shooting stars, oh yea, right. As I rolled over another one reflected in my eyes. My mind drifted into space as I forced myself to stay awake. No problem—the cold that had crept into my bones was keeping me awake, and I began to shiver. That was it for me. I bid farewell to the sky and returned to the cabin, crawled in between the flannel sheets under the down comforter, and conked out.

11/18/98 Something woke me from within—that seems to happen a lot out at Cloudland. It was light, no, *bright* outside. Must be time to get up. I did, then quickly discovered why I needed to be up. *Leaf fall* was happening!!! There is usually one day in the fall when a majority of the leaves in the forest drop from their lofty perches to the ground. It is always after the peak of the color, but seldom ever this late in the year. Last year it was on November 15th, and that seemed about two or three weeks late. Maybe we are beginning a new trend.

I had sat through many leaf falls while deer hunting, and knew that they are one of the greatest natural phenomenon there is. I grabbed a Starbucks mocha out of the fridge, put on some warm clothes, and my boots, and headed out into the chilly morning air. I walked hurriedly out into the middle of the bench to the west, and plopped right down at the base of a big red oak tree.

The sun was out, and I had stepped right into a magical wonderland of motion and music. There were leaves coming down from *everywhere!* And there was no wind, so they all just gently rocked back and forth in the air until each gently landed with a gentle hush. When I closed my eyes, it sounded like a rainstorm, and the sounds were many, varied, and went deep back into the woods. Wow, I live for this! Once you sit through one, and you have to sit there quietly, with absolutely nothing else to do or think about, then you will be hooked for life. Few things are as wonderful as this treat.

It was cold, but the sun warmed things up nicely, and before long, I had shed the first layer and was laying down in the leaves, staring at a 100 "leaf meteors" rushing down towards me at probably 1/10mph. It was a pretty nice pace of life. Every now and then a leaf would land on my nose—it's a big target you know. I closed my eyes and imagined that they were giant snow flakes. That is what they reminded me of, although the leaves landed with a little more force than do snowflakes. Of course, if you listen very close, you can hear a snowflake hitting the ground too. At least you can here at Cloudland. I'm hoping for many concerts out here this winter!

After an hour of bliss I had to get up and rejoin civilization to give another program or two, but I would be back soon.

11/20/98 The road was covered with leaves—solid. I had locked the gate because it was deer season and many folks do a lot of driving during that time, exploring new roads. I didn't want a lot of this kind of traffic on my wet road, so mine were the first tracks. The cabin was a little chilly, so I built a fire and turned on the heat pump for a little extra kick. There was a thin haze outside, and the stars were blurry. And the wind was blowing. Two days before it had blown up to 36mph (this was the leaf-fall day), and we got 1/2 inch of rain. The low temp was still 36 degrees—the middle of November and no frost yet!

The fire was great, and the cabin was a warm and welcome place, and old friend. After unloading some of the van cargo, I plopped down in the big leather chair with a glass of wine and soaked up the fireglow. It was great to be back, and for a couple of unhurried days too. I had work to do, but except for a trip into Jasper in the morning, had no time schedule for the weekend—just the way it should be.

Oh yea, I almost forgot, the fireplace messed up. It wouldn't draw, and every bit of smoke from the burning paper came pouring out of the front. It seemed like the flue was stopped up, but I had no idea what it could have been. So I just closed the doors and forgot about it. The fireplace had never done this before. Ten minutes later there was a roaring fire going! Never found out what the problem was. Later in the evening the wind picked up, my glass got empty, and I retired to the loft.

11/21/98 Several of the maple trees on the east side of the cabin still had yellow leaves on them, and the early sunshine really lit them up. I sat out on the back deck and sipped my Starbucks. The scene out front had changed dramatically from just the weekend before, heck, even from two days before. Most of the trees had dropped their leaves, and the overall color of the forest had changed from yellow and orange to brown. But it was a nice shade of brown, and I rather liked it. And the bluff just across the way over on Beagle Point was really visible. It is a pretty nice bluff that remains hidden all during leaf-on.

I lingered for a few minutes, then left my Cloudland heaven and made a quick trip into the library in Harrison. I would be giving a program there in December, and wanted to drop off seven books that I was donating to the library. It was a very nice little place I must say. I have been speaking at some pretty nice places all over the region, several that I had never seen before.

Before long I was back at the cabin with vacuum cleaner in hand, sucking up hordes of dead wasps. Those bombs that I had set off a week earlier were still working. There weren't any live wasps, but there were lots of dead and dying ones. I also worked some on my bread maker, which had not worked the last two times that I tried to use it. I beat on it a little, then ran through the cycle with nothing but water, and then finally put a batch of sourdough mix into it.

From the back deck I could see the main Buffalo River way upstream—the sun was hitting it just right, and there was a clear shot, more or less, to the silver sparkles of the water. I could even see side streams tumbling down the hillside towards the river. And Whitaker Creek was up and running—it splits up into several tributaries just before joining with the main river, and the sun was glinting off of each path. When there is snow on the ground, you can see the old chimney down there next to the creek. There weren't any soaring birds out at all. In fact, I hadn't seen any in a while.

I put up a new bird feeder that Erna from Hot Springs gave me when I was down there doing a program. This one is for the winter birds—it's natural log with balls of peanut butter and fat rolled together and attached. It was up all weekend, but no one visited it—could have been all of the strong wind, or it may just take a few days for them to find it.

After a few more indoor chores were completed, I decided to go on a hike. Just as I had laced up and headed down the trail, someone yelled up from below. It was Bob and Dawna, which I had expected to stop by and spend the night, but I wasn't planning on running into them in the woods first. They had been on an OHTA hike earlier in the day, and just decided to bushwhack all the way from Hawk Hollow to the cabin instead of hiking back with the group. They had a long and interesting trip. One of the "highlights" they told me about was a tornado area that they had hiked/crawled through. It was somewhere upstream from Bowers Hollow, but they didn't know where for sure. And it was fresh—probably just a couple of weeks old. They saw lots of twisted trees and ones that had been snapped off ten feet high and tossed about in all directions. Sounded like a tornado alright!

The main thing that spurred them on was the knowledge that if they had to spend the night in the woods, that they would end up in the Cloudland Journal like had happened to Roy! They are a great couple together, and I know that they had one terrific hike. Adventure is one thing. Getting to do it with your favorite companion is even better.

A little later Norma showed up—she had led the hike, and was coming by to see if they made it out alive, and to get a sip of wine and a bit of dinner. Also Dottie and Steve Hobbs dropped by. Another nice couple—a product of our little hiking club entirely (they met each other through the club and got married last year). Steve and Dottie had to leave, the four of us popped open a bottle or two or three of some special Hawaiian wine that Bob had brought from a recent trip. And we fired up the grill and put on some wonderful filets that Nancy Williams had left a couple of weeks ago. Meat and spuds and salad and homemade bread (the machine did work!), and fine wine and even home-made cheesecake (Dawna)! Good food, great company, a crackling fire and nice music. Sounds like just another typical evening at Cloudland.

Norma returned to town, and the three of us did a little star gazing through the tele. We found Jupiter, but could only see a couple of its moons hugging close below. The moon sliver was the star of the night—the part that was lit up by the sun was its usual brilliant silver, but you could also see the outline of the dark part, and I swear it had a color all of its own—kind of a dark muddy brown. Bob and Dawna forgot to bring their sleeping bags (they have always slept out on the deck), so they were forced to spend the night in the spare bedroom—no sympathy from the host.

11/22/98 It was about 2:30am when I got up to feed the fire. Man, the wind was howling outside, although it wasn't too noisy in the cabin. In fact, you could hardly hear the wind. But the wind chimes in the front were playing lots and lots of music. I couldn't go back to sleep, so I decided to get up and take a short stroll in the wind. The pitch and volume changed constantly, and the wind made music in the trees. It was kind of weird because the stars were out and so bright, but there was all of this wind. The trees swaying back and forth in the wind made the stars really twinkle. I sat down at the base of a tree and turned my face into the wind. It felt great, but I got chilled quickly, and soon got up and returned to my warm little nest in the loft. My brief wandering did the trick, and I was fast asleep in no time.

The mice were running down on the main floor before sunup, so I got up and joined them out on the deck—it was a brisk morning, and the wind was still blowing. The predawn sky was really nice—lots of color. Then the horizon went pale, and the sun popped up, but it was way over to the right of the ridge from where it had been rising. Man, I really have been away from the cabin for awhile—the sun was rising in a different spot!

Dawna cooked up some blueberry biscuits, and we all put on hiking duds and headed out the door. We walked on over to the East Meadow (saw three deer in the thick cover just below the east end of the meadow), then out an old road and down to the big flat with the leaning red oak tree. There was no wind on this side of the hill, and the sun was warming things up nicely. We made our way down the old trail through the break in the bluff, through the little magnolia canyon, and on over to a waterfall which was running pretty good. Lots of moss-covered rocks around too.

Next we visited more waterfalls up in Dug Hollow, which were running great too. It seems to me to be getting harder to climb around in there these days—I wonder if my appearance on the cover of ***Active Years*** magazine is having anything to do with it? I smashed my little finger trying to get up one spot. The creek water was very cold, and cleaned up the wound nicely. But it hurt. I'm becoming a wimp too.

Once while we were standing there admiring the falls, a hawk came swooping down to say hi. I hadn't been seeing too many hawks out here in a while.

As we were approaching the Woods deer hunting cabin we spooked two deer that were nearly within sight of the cabin. No one was home. But there were a bunch of tired dogs, and one momma, that had two darling little puppies with her. One of them was so fat that when he rolled over to get his belly rubbed, he couldn't roll back over on his own! We stopped off and had a good chat with Bob (he fed us dried apples and peanuts). While we were there one of the Woods boys drove up and showed us a nice little buck that he had in the back of his pickup—deer season can be quite bloody. They had harvested a number of deer during the week, including several in the immediate Cloudland area. I don't think that they got any of the big ones that had visited me, and no one had even seen the big monster that I had seen a couple of times—he is probably long since checked into a hotel in the tropics for the winter.

We headed back to the cabin and we ran into Janis Rogers from Little Rock on the road. She had stopped by to pick up some guidebooks for her TAOWN club. Their officers are going to have a little retreat at Cloudland in February. Hey, I'll do anything to get some nice ladies out here!

The sunlight on the far slopes was good, and we set up the tele and scoured the hillsides for sign of the tornado damage that Bob and Dawna had hiked through the day before. It was a long way off, but son of a gun, there it was—dozens of trees that had been peeled clean and snapped off and it all looked like a big mess, even from four miles away.

Everyone left, and it was time for me to dig into my chores. I put up a section of rain gutter that prevents rain from getting onto the main deck (where Scott sleeps), sucked up many more wasps with the vacuum, and finally put up a nice wine rack! This dude is big—holds 126 bottles of wine. It is down in the basement in the tool room. I loaded up all of the wine bottles that have been donated this past year, and even tried to categorize them. I ended up with 9 bottles of merlot (love it), 14 different cabernet sauvignons, plus many other miscellaneous wines like pear, peach, Big Daddy (screw top), red muscadine, and three bottles of champagne—52 bottles in all. Far short of capacity though. I'll have to get to work on that.

The afternoon was sunny and very windy. And also rather crowded. There seemed to be a steady stream of visitors. I could hardly get a nap in. Neil Compton came by with his daughter, Ellen Shipley, and her husband, Curtis, and their son. Curtis Cemetery, which is visible on a hilltop about 5.5 miles up the valley from cabin, was named for Curtis's family long ago. A number of his relatives are buried there. It was good to see Neil again, and especially in such good spirits (isn't he always?). I took this opportunity to ask him how the Crag got its name. He proclaimed that "I named it." And I'm sure that he did. But why Hawksbill? He said that while it didn't really look like a hawk's bill, he thought that it was OK, especially since there were so many hawks flying around. That was almost the exact same thing that I told the PBS TV crew while we were standing on the Crag and on camera. Good. Then Neil said that it really looked more like an eagle's bill than a hawk's, but that there weren't any eagles around. Of course, there are eagles around now, thanks in part to the chicken industry. Hawksbill still sounds better, and I'm glad that's the name. You always learn something from a visit with Neil Compton.

Billy Bisswanger from the Pack Rat and a couple of buddies stopped by. Billy is quickly becoming famous as the guy who is dangling from the bottom of Hawksbill Crag on the last page of the new *Buffalo River Wilderness* picture book. It took a great deal of work on his part to get that picture taken. I just stood there and pushed the button.

Mary McCutchan from Kansas City came by too, along with Melba Conklin and another friend. They were staying in a small log cabin down in Boxley Valley, and had been out doing trail maintenance all day. Nice weather for it.

Once they all left I brewed up a big pot of Cloudland soup, and drank a little more wine and munched on dried apples. And I hauled a lot of firewood up the steps too. Looks like that will be happening a lot this winter. The wind continued to pound the cabin, although you really couldn't tell it from inside.

One of the questions that everyone keeps asking me on these book tours is what will my next project be. I have always told them that selling all of the books and putting out the **Cloudland Journal** book next fall were my two main priorities for the near future. I will also be doing several photo workshops, filming two different hiking videos, and beginning work on filming several scenic videos. All of that will be great fun, and a lot work. But there has been another project bouncing around in the back of my head for some time now. And at least three different people have been urging me to consider doing it. While I had thought about it a lot, I had never really been too serious about it. Today, while napping on the couch, I woke up with the realization that I **did** need to do this new book project. And so I started running through everything in my mind, and now think that I might be able to make a go of it.

I just heard a thump or a thud outside. The wind had taken the gas grill and tossed it up against the east railing. The gusts were over 41mph, with pretty steady winds in the 30's. I just can't wait to see the windchill reading when it does that at 10 degrees! It is a bright sky outside tonight too, and the stars are winking and dancing to the music of the wind. Orion is rising over the eastern hillside. It's time for me to go to bed.

11/23/98 The wind howled all night, but it was the howl of a dog that woke me just after daylight. It was a very grey day outside, and the wind had quit. We had heard a lonely dog the day before, but weren't sure exactly where it was coming from—it sounded too close to be from over on Beagle Point. I got up and sipped my Starbucks mocha out on the back deck, and listened. Sure enough, he barked again, and it still sounded very close, perhaps just down below the bluffline in front of the cabin. I had to get back to town to a meeting, and didn't have time to go wandering off in the wilderness looking for lost deer dogs, but I decided to go ahead and see if the guy was close by.

I slipped down the ladder trail and made my way around the base of the big bluff. Man, this chunk of rock is very impressive, and probably 75 feet thick. The rock face is covered with multi-colored lichens, except for a spot here and there where fresh rock had broken off. And there was a great deal of that rock lying on the forest floor below the bluff. In fact, there was an entire rock garden! Boulders of all shapes and sizes filled the level area, and I had to climb hand over fist in a few spots. Most of these boulders were covered with the same lichens as the bluff face, but some of them were clean—recent arrivals I presume.

But there was no dog to be found. As I was on my way back to the ladder, the dog wailed away again, and this time I could pinpoint the location—he was over on Beagle Point for sure. I really didn't have the time, nor was I dressed for a hike, but I just felt like it was my duty to make a rescue attempt. So I headed straight down the hillside, splashing across Whitaker Creek, which was running pretty good, and then up the opposite hillside. As I crossed the flat I began to see bare ground—it looked like a flock of turkeys had been scratching up every leaf in sight. And even though I halfway expected it, I was literally knocked to the ground with surprise when the largest flock of turkeys took off into the air all around me—it sounded like a 747 taking off! I counted over 20 birds, and am sure that I missed at least that many. The ground was nearly bare as far as I could see in all directions—that was one large flock!

I decided to try to cut some time out and go straight up the hill instead of finding my way around the front end like I usually do. This was somewhat of a mistake, because the hillside was just about vertical! And with all of the fresh leaves on the ground, the going was slow, and tough. I literally had to go from one tree hand-hold to another.

It must have taken me 20 or 30 minutes to make it up the slope, but I eventually arrived at the base of the bluff, huffing and puffing and scratched up a bit. The dog barked again, and I found him within a few seconds. Son of a gun, there were two dogs, both black, and they had fallen about halfway down the bluff and had come to rest on a ledge, and were unable to go back up or jump down. This was the very same spot on the bluff that the squirrel had showed me way back in May. I knew that I could get up to them, but wasn't sure how I was going to get them off of the ledge.

They were quite happy to see me to say the least, and were very friendly. There was one male and one female. When I saw the name on their collars, I knew that I had done the right thing. There is a creek nearby that is shown on maps as "Edgemon Creek." McNamara has some paintings that I put in the new picture book from there, and he spells the name "Edgmon," without the e. And that is the way that I left the spelling, even though all of the maps show it with an e. Well it just so happened that these dogs were owned by Marty and Lawton Edgmon—the name in the book was spelled correctly!

Oh yea, back to the dogs. I managed to get them back up the bluff to the top by lifting them up to another ledge, and then another. Once on top, they both took off running further up the hill. I followed. I had never been up on top before. And it was wonderful up there. The hillside leveled off into a wide open bench, and there were many piles of rocks. In fact, the rock piles went on as far as I could see. Someone had cleared this parcel as a field once upon a time, but there were nothing but big trees everywhere now, and the rocks. A little further up the ridge there was a wonderful rock wall, perhaps 200 feet long, and four or five feet tall. It was covered with nice green lichen. A great rock wall. I never did find a homesite, but I'll bet there is an old chimney nearby somewhere.

One of the dogs started barking wildly, and I went over to investigate. He had treed a squirrel. I must say that this was one dumb squirrel, because after a couple of minutes the squirrel came down the tree and started running across the ground. Well, the little black dog tore off after him, and nearly caught him. At one point the dog did get a mouthful of squirrel tail. But the squirrel did jump into a small tree and disappeared into a hole. Lucky squirrel. I pulled the dog away from the tree and headed him on up the ridge. I didn't have time to walk out all the way to the road with them, but I thought that if I could get them headed in the right direction, they would do it on their own. And then I would call the owners and let them know where to find them. Both dogs bounded off up the ridge, and I headed back down the hillside.

I found a deer trail, and followed it down through a split in the bluffline. And then I came across a big chunk of blue styrofoam—it must have been blown there overnight in the big wind (it was just sitting on top of the ground, with no leaves on it). Some building is missing part of a panel of insulation. I continued down the steep slope. About halfway down, I looked up and saw both dogs tearing down the hill, right on past me, and then they disappeared once again down below. I knew where they were headed—they could hear Whitaker Creek, and they were thirsty!

Once I got to the bottom I found both dogs sitting in the creek, lapping up the cold water. Another old dog joined them, but I had to take my hat off. I hadn't had any water in a while either. When I looked up I realized that we were right in the middle of a very scenic spot—there were many boulders all over the place, both in the water and on the bench next to the creek, and all of them were covered with a thick carpet of bright green moss. A really nice place. There must be some springs feeding the creek here in order for the moss to be here.

After our drinks we continued across the creek and up the opposite hillside, up towards the ladder trail. The dogs only followed me for the first bench, then took off along the bench, barking like crazy—they must have jumped a deer. I knew that I would not be able to follow them. My rescue attempt had been interrupted. The best that I could do was hope they gave up soon and backtracked and followed my scent up the hillside.

I lingered a while at the ladder, and called out to them, but only heard a faint bark way down in the bottom. All I could do was go back to the cabin. I called the owner and talked to his wife. I gave her as much information as I could. After I packed up the van and locked the cabin door, I went back down to the ladder, just in case. No dogs. Oh well, I did feel much better about them. At least they weren't stranded on the ledge, where they most certainly would have starved to death. Now they might be able to find their way out, or be rescued by their owners. I hope so. They were a couple of nice dogs.

On the way back I ran into Benny and a friend who were hunting. They had shot a deer in the East Meadow the evening before, but hadn't been able to find it. A good hunter will always spend a great deal of time looking for wounded game, and they had spent a couple of hours the night before, and a lot of time again this morning looking for the deer. They only found one tiny spot of blood. There is a good possibility that this deer was not wounded very bad and would survive. You always hate to waste game.

I gave Benny four more empty wine bottles in hopes that he would return them filled with some homemade blackberry wine! As I thought about it on the way home, I decided that I needed to look into making my own wine—I have all of those empty slots in the wine rack, and I could develop a couple of Cloudland wines down in the basement. Yes, a great idea. I'll look into that.

11/27/98 The sunset was terrific. Or should I say that the "after" sunset was. There were lots of thin clouds up high, all scattered about, and they turned the most wonderful shade of pink after the sun went down. Against the blue sky they looked quite dreamy. It was warm outside, and the wind was blowing. A half moon was about straight up—lit from the right, so it was waning. And there was a bright star or planet next to it, just above and to the left.

As I sat out on the deck enjoying the evening, a campfire way down below began to flicker. Someone was camped at the old homesite on Whitaker Creek. It was one of those balmy nights when you really didn't need a campfire, but they do add so much atmosphere.

I went out for a quick trip around in the woods. As I headed back to the cabin I noticed that the planet (it was way too bright to be a star—must be Jupiter) was now directly over the moon. Hum. The moon and Jupiter were having a race across the sky.

After I ate a baked potato (covered with sour cream and cheese), I unloaded the car (more boxes of books), and sipped a glass of wine or two while soaking up the view—the moon was really lighting up the wilderness, and all of the main features could be easily seen, even Hawksbill Crag. I couldn't stand it any longer, so I laced up my boots and headed out for another hike.

Once again this phase of the moon proved to be just the right amount of light for hiking—I didn't even bother to bring along a flashlight. There was plenty of light to see where I was going, yet I couldn't see into the shadows (the light is so bright during a full moon that there is too much contrast between the light and dark areas, so the shadows are black—not good when there are bears and bigfoots lurking there). As soon as I left the cabin area, the wind died down and I wandered through a silent forest, with only the swooshing of my feet in the leaves making any noise.

I walked along the lane between the Faddis and East meadows, and was careful to avoid the low spot where I had sprained my ankle on my last moonlight hike there. It was very quiet and even a little eerie walking in silence through the moonlight. Then I came to the big East Meadow where there had been so much killing in the past couple of weeks (at least four deer have been shot here during the season, perhaps more). I looked around carefully, but didn't see anyone grazing. Orion was rising above the line of trees at the east end of the field. The night sky was spectacular as always, and I drifted out into the meadow.

A barred owl broke the silence, and I stopped to listen to his conversation. He hooted and cried, but no one answered (I still don't know how to answer!). It was such a wonderful night, I wanted to hang out there a while, so I stomped down a little spot in the tall grass and laid down. Somehow I feel more connected to the earth when I lay down in a meadow, or in a pile of leaves on the forest floor. You can really *feel* the land. The wilderness recharges my soul, scrapes away the layers of city dirt and grime. For me, being outdoors is a necessity. I laid there, under a blanket of stars, grasping the meadow, and gave thanks for how lucky I was to be there. There were even a couple of shooting stars out. All was quiet, and still, and warm, and the world was right.

I think that I fell asleep, but was awakened by a noise in the grass. Couldn't tell what it was, but it was getting louder, coming closer. I wanted to see whatever it was without spooking it, so I stayed put, but tried to roll my head over towards the noise just a bit. I saw them—two deer were working their way across the meadow right towards me. My heart began to thump a little. They were grazing some, but mostly just wandering around. They veered to my left, away from me. One of them was a little smaller—I could see them pretty well in the moonlight. The small one must have been this year's fawn—he began to hop around a little, and play in the moonlight. Mom wasn't so casual, but she did seem to be enjoying the night as well. I just laid there and tried not to move, or make any sound.

The owl cried out again, and both deer stopped and looked back in his direction. I wonder what deer think when they hear other animals talking? Deer seldom ever say anything, although I have heard a yearling cry out before—kind of like a "bleeeaaat." And, of course, when a deer discovers something odd in their world that they can't identify for sure, they will whistle really loud, and stomp their feet. I've had them do this while right in front of me—they just wanted to see if I would be startled and move at the shrill sound. I've never heard a buck snort, like you hear a lot of people talk about. I think folks often call the whistling that deer do snorting, and "snorting" is always used when talking about a buck (and it is usually a doe). Anyway, the deer didn't whistle, or detect me. They just grazed and played and wandered off to the other side of the meadow. Another blessing bestowed on me.

Even though it was warm out a chill began to creep into my body, so I got up and walked across the meadow. The deer must have still been at the edge of the meadow because as soon as I got up, I heard them snort (oops, I mean whistle), and saw a couple of white flags waving in the moonlight as they darted into the nearby woods.

I entered the woods at the opposite side of the meadow and began to work my way down the hill towards the cabin, through the maple grove. The woods were so open, and the moonlight so bright, that I didn't have to walk with my hands in front of my face—I could easily see any branches, although there weren't too many in the first place. There was a single lamp on in the cabin, and it glowed warmly in the night. Another great walk in the night, and another hiker glad to be home.

The planet had passed the moon and was sure to win the race to the horizon. I would have never thought that the stars moved faster than the moon. Well, actually it is the earth that is rotating faster than the moon is moving across the sky, but no matter. I continue to learn a lot of stuff out here.

The wind was blowing some, and the campfire down below was out. I filled up my wine glass, grabbed the guitar and found a comfortable spot on the back porch swing. I know. the sounds coming from my maple and spruce box were crude, but somehow they mingled with the night winds and sounded pretty OK. I sent Jim Croce, John Denver, and the Beatles out into the moonlight.

11/28/98 It was smoky, hazy outside at daylight. And very warm—in the mid 60's. I didn't even take the time to drink my mocha, but instead put on my walking shoes and headed into the woods for a morning stroll. There were lots of squirrels out, still burying nuts I guess. Although I wondered if they weren't digging nuts instead of burying them?

I was stunned to discover that there were both green and ripe *tomatoes* on the vines in the Faddis garden. Tomatoes? It was nearly December! There were also all sorts of greens still growing—I need to learn how to cook them.

There wasn't a soul at the Crag, but I could smell campfire smoke while on the way down. All of the trees were bare, and the wilderness was brown. The air was heavy with moisture, and it was a little damp out. I sat down on the exposed rock and pondered a while. A large bird appeared out of the haze, and floated across the way in front of me—an eagle! The first one of the fall season for me. This guy made quick work of his visit to the Whitaker Valley, and was out of sight within a minute. He took my breath away.

I made another discovery—I came across an old pioneer road—just the slightest trace of where a lane had once been. Daniel Boone was good at blazing new routes, but I am pretty good at locating old ones that have long since melted into the forest. I followed this one back towards the cabin, but it soon disappeared. It may have simply ended. I put it away in my head for another search some day.

As I approached the cabin I could see a light show beginning to happen. I grabbed my mocha and took a seat on the back deck. Way up the main Buffalo River valley the haze had parted and the sun was breaking through, lighting up the hillsides and part of the river. When the leaves are off, and the sun is just right, you can see the river three or four miles away from the cabin. Since the rest of the wilderness was still rather dark and hazy it was kind of like seeing the light at the end of a tunnel. And then the light began to move towards the cabin, a sweeping beam of light illuminating the forest as it went, leaving dark haze behind it. Finally it reached the cabin, and the world sparkled. Then within a few seconds the light moved on, and I was in the haze again. I sat back and smiled. Some moments out here are just special, and you can feel them all the way deep down inside. Well, OK, *lots* of moments out here are. That one burst of sunshine would be the only time that I would see the sun all day.

I put a CD on (***Nature Sounds of the Beatles***), worked on the Journal and answered e-mail. While I was in the middle of all that, the eagle swooped across the scene—I had a 180 degree view of him, but again for only a short time. He headed downstream towards Boxley Valley.

As I was looking at the weather station computer, I noticed that there had been a 41 mph wind here a few days ago. That is a pretty good batch of wind! I went outside to see if my rain gutter had held up, and it looked fine. Upon closer inspection though I discovered that one of the braces was missing—the wind had torn it completely off! But the gutter was fine. I'll have to put up a couple of more braces next time I am out.

And I noticed a spot of color over on Beagle Point. When I looked through the telescope I saw that large chunk of blue styrofoam that I had found during the dog rescue. I can't believe that I didn't cover it up when I was there! Now I will have to go do a styrofoam rescue (and I will carry it back). The bluffline over there really shows up great now, with no leaves on the trees and no sun. In fact, if there were dogs stranded on the bluff now, I could actually see them through the tele.

The humidity in the cabin is 61%, but it is 92% outside—the air is really saturated with moisture.

I've got to make a quick trip back into town to return a new car that I have been test driving, and get my mom some dinner, but I plan to return for another moon and planet race tonight (supposed to be cloudy for the next couple of days, so I may just have to imagine it—easy to do out at Cloudland!).

When I returned to the cabin I had a friend of mine in tow, Emily Johnson, along with a bottle of wine. We sat out on the back deck in the moonlight long into the night. There was no race, as the star/planet was already a long way from the moon. The wind was blowing like crazy, and the chimes out in front were making a lot of music. The wind finally chased us inside sometime after 2am.

11/29/98 The wind blew and howled all night, up into the 30's, but it was a warm wind. It was quite hazy at first light, and the wind was still blowing. We sat out on the deck and watched the forest come alive. Our blueberry biscuits were interrupted once by a black and white blur—a mature bald eagle cruised by right in front of us, headed out into the main canyon and played in the wind currents, then disappeared. Emily had only seen a couple of eagles before, so she was excited. I had only seen hundreds of eagles before, and I was very excited.

A guy that Emily works with stopped by to go hiking with us (Eric). He is a young whippersnapper, in college, and seems to know a lot about the outdoors. He had "done" Dug Hollow and Whitaker Creek, and wanted to go someplace a little more challenging. I smiled. We all laced up our boots and headed down the ladder trail towards Hubbard Hollow. It was a warm, wonderful day to be in the woods.

When we reached the old home place next to Whitaker Creek we discovered that the campfire that I had seen on Friday night had come from the chimney itself—actually a good place to build a fire. The campers had a couple of rock seats propped up in front of the chimney, and everything was clean. Although it looked like a herd of elk had bedded down there because there were many level spots in the leaves. We had seen two backpackers earlier coming up the ladder trail and past the cabin, but didn't talk to them. I think they had been down there for several days, and maybe moved their tents. They had also hung a bottomless tin tub in a tree, and had fashioned a bunch of trash and duct tape to use as a basketball. Some people come to the wilderness to shoot hoops. I just come to enjoy.

We headed upstream past some lovely green pools and a little white water. The river looked great, and sounded nice too. When we stopped to take a look at a chert cave, Emily stirred up about a thousand tiny flying bugs that were bedded down in the leaves. I don't know exactly what they were, but I'll bet they enjoyed getting out in the warm air.

Once we climbed hand-over-fist up a steep slope, we dropped down into Hubbard Hollow. This is one terrific little playground, chocked full of giant moss-covered boulders, caves, waterfalls, huge sycamore trees, and all kinds of neat stuff to explore. Eric really liked it. Me too. I didn't have my camera with me, but I did find a bunch of scenes that I want to come back to in the spring and photograph. This is one of those places that you could spend all day in, then come back the next day and find different things.

We exited out the top, over the big waterfall on the main bluffline. Then we just sort of drifted across several level benches, wandering through the open woods. It was a great way to hike, not really needing to follow a particular route, just flowing with the terrain. At one point we passed through an area that had obviously been hit hard by a tornado many years ago—there were dozens, perhaps hundreds, of dirt mounds, which were the remains of the root balls of trees that were ripped out of the ground by a tornado. And there were still many logs left, although it was obvious that the big old trees had come down a long time ago because they were almost entirely rotted out. And you could tell that it was a tornado instead of just straight-line winds because the logs had fallen in all directions, not in the same direction.

We intersected an old road at the very top of the ridge and followed it on out onto Beagle Point (this is the same road that comes from the Kaypark Trail head area). I was going to settle the mysterious road down through the bluff issue once and for all (Billy McNamara and others had told me of this road, but some of the locals denied that it existed. I had followed a part of it up from Whitaker Creek, but couldn't find where it went up through the bluffline.). The old road did exactly what an old timer told me it would do—veer off to the right side of the mountain and away from the Whitaker Creek drainage. We were getting close, I could feel it. Most of the time the road was easy to follow, but every now and then it disappeared below the pile of fresh leaves, and we had to look very close to figure the route out. It turns out that Emily also has a good nose for finding and following such things, and she led some. I enjoyed hiking with her a great deal.

Just as we were about to be lulled to sleep the road trace took a hard turn to the right and headed down the hill. Then another turn through some smaller broken bluffs. Then we lost it entirely. Darn, so close. I sniffed the air, then drifted over the edge of the hillside, and there it was—a major road trace that had been cut through the big bluff! It switchbacked down through the bluffline, through a couple of giant boulders. It was obvious there had been a great deal of work done on this dude. I had been looking for and wondering about this little spot since the very first day of this Journal back in May, and I was happy to have found it.

We climbed up onto one of the big rocks to take a break and celebrate our find. The back edge of the rock made a great back rest, but we had to be careful because the back side of the rock was completely vertical, and it was about 35 feet straight down! Nice rock.

I laid back in the warm afternoon sun, munching on sunflower seeds and chocolate-covered raisins, and wondered what it must have been like way back in the 1800's when they built this road. It was rather tough I imagined. Hard working folks with a zest for life. I could hear their laughter bouncing off of the big bluffline, and their cursing.

From the bluff the road headed down the hillside at a pretty good clip, and much of the route had been long since eroded out deeply. The downhill side was lined with lichen-covered rocks. It switchbacked a time or two, then went into a very soft, almost sandy soil section. We lost the road trace there. I know we must have walked over it three or four times, but it was just gone. Happy and content about finding the route through the bluff, we continued down the hill to Whitaker Creek.

It was time to make the climb back up to the cabin, a part of the hike that I was particularly looking forward to. I wanted to see what kind of stuff Eric was made of. He had done pretty good so far, but this hill was a little different. Young folks with his credentials shouldn't have too much trouble. Ha, ha. I leaned into the hill, and knowing that both of my hiking partners would probably pass me halfway up, I wanted to run out ahead and at least have a few minutes of glory. I think that the hill had grown some since my last trip up, because it was one tough bugger. Don't know exactly why, but I get real competitive when I hit this hill.

Try as I might, I just couldn't make it all the way up without stopping. And the first time that I stopped to take a blow, I turned around and was surprised to see them lagging a little behind, down on the bench below. That spurred me on, and so this old guy took off up the hill at a quicker pace. And, of course, that nearly killed me! But I kept going. Another stop. They were a little farther behind. Then another stop. They were out of sight. I was about to die, but I couldn't let them see me keel over, so I went on, pushing and lifting and trying with every fiber of my being to keep on going. And much to my surprise, I did keep moving, and finally made it to the ladder. I climbed up to the top, sat down, and drank a liter of water. Emily soon appeared and joined me. She was a little red faced, but not really out of breath—in great shape for sure (she is a pretty young whippersnapper too, and I mean that both ways). I thanked her for not embarrassing me by running off and leaving me.

Then Eric showed up, dragging just a little. He knew that he had climbed a hill in the Buffalo. I just smiled and went on up to the cabin. Bob Robinson had blown me away on this hill once, but today, it was still my mountain. I heard a country song the other day that said "A real man doesn't need to prove anything." I got to thinking about that quote on my way up the hill. And it is partly right. I'm a far cry from a real man, and while I really don't have anything to prove to anybody, I do have to continue to prove a few things to myself, including that I can keep going under stress. I think it helps my mind, not to mention my body, when I push myself just a little bit—gets a few of those cobwebs knocked out of my brain.

The wind was really screaming when we got to the cabin, up to 40mph, but it felt great, although a little chilly on our sweat-soaked bodies. We sat around a while recovering, then Eric loaded up and headed out. He took Emily with him. Story of my life. I won the mountain, but lost the woman. I think that I enjoy them both, mountains and women, equally well, and am happy to have either around for any amount of time.

Wow, I just realized that November is over! It has been one terrific month out here at Cloudland, filled with spectacular fall colors, lots of wildlife encounters, many wonderful hikes, and some great company. And it hasn't even frosted yet. I'm hoping for a cold winter with plenty of snow, but I'd take several more months just like this one. On to *WINTER!*

High wind of 41mph, low temp of 36 degrees

DECEMBER 1998

12/2-5/98 After a meeting in Fayetteville I drove out to the cabin to deliver some books. I was a zombie by then, no doubt, but the thought of getting to spend some time at Cloudland kept me going. It was warm and sunny, and after I unloaded all of the books, I couldn't help myself, and headed out into the woods for a short hike.

The leaves were so thick on the forest floor, and crunchy, and they smelled great. I didn't walk far, and sat down in the leaves and leaned up against a moss-covered rock. Sitting still at last. What a relief. But it was much more than a relief. I was in heaven, my own little brand of it. I laid back in the leaves and stared up into the blue sky. Leaves and rocks and trees and sky and sunshine. Why did I ever leave? Why do I ever leave? I rolled over and stuck my nose in the leaves, and took in their, well, their "leaf" smell. Nothing else smells like it. I closed my eyes and quickly drifted off into a deep sleep.

An hour or so later I woke up, and reluctantly walked back to the van and headed towards town.

The following day was a long one too, with a ton of book and picture business to take care of, but I got to spend a few hours with Emily in the evening that made it all worthwhile. Five entire hours of nothing but great conversation (plus a bit of good food, wine, and hot tubbing in the moonlight). She left at 1am, and I loaded up the van with more books, then drove back out to Cloudland. Everything seemed pretty damp, but warm. It didn't take me long to crash.

I was up by 6am and spent several hours unboxing books and signing them. It was a very grey, overcast day, with intermittent rain. I realized that my rain gauge wasn't working, so I went out into the rain and climbed up the ladder and fixed it. It seemed like about an inch of rain had fallen before I fixed it, so I'll add that to the total. The warm rain produced dozens of steam vents that danced about in the valleys below. Every few minutes I would look out the window and the scene was entirely different—the clouds were really on the move, getting bigger, then smaller, and moving back and forth all the while. And then the sun broke out, and lit up all of the clouds—it was a spectacular light show!

Back to Fayetteville I drove, unloaded the van of the program stuff, then loaded it again with books, then drove back out to Cloudland. It was after midnight when I arrived. I was getting a little tired, but the fact that I do love all of this book business was keeping me going with no problems. And I had lost eight pounds. That was hard for me to believe, especially since I had been eating so much junk food on the run.

The next morning I got to sleep in until daylight, then got up and loaded more books into the van. The wind was blowing like crazy, and it had topped out at 41 mph during the night. I had secured all of the chairs on the deck, and the gas grill, so nothing went for a walk. It remained very warm, in the 60's. As

I was leaving the cabin, I came across the Woods clan, all dressed in the orange hunting garb, working their deer dogs. It was the last weekend of deer season.

The cabin was snug and warm and a most welcome sight when I returned. Especially because I knew that I would get to stay here for two whole nights, and an entire day. I sat out on the back deck and sipped a glass of wine, surveying the wilderness that was lit by the moon, which had turned back to its normal white, and was dodging back and forth behind clouds.

All of a sudden, down below in the Buffalo River valley, a couple of miles upstream, a real fire flared up. Someone was camped down there, and they had built an incredible bond fire—the flames looked to be at least 20 feet tall to me. I think someone must have dumped a bunch of stove gas on it in order to get it started. The Indians had a saying—"Indian build small fire and sit close. White man build big fire and burn down forest." The giant flames were reduced to a flicker within a few minutes. Man, that was one big fire.

12/6/98 The wind howled all night, but somehow I managed to stay under the covers until almost 9am. It felt great. I had nowhere to go all day. While sipping my Starbucks mocha out on the deck, I decided that I really needed to get out and do a little hiking, so I planned to go back to Beagle Point and try to find the road connection that had eluded us last weekend. And I wanted to retrieve that piece of blue styrofoam that was still visible across the way.

It was very warm. I wanted to travel light, so I didn't take a pack. The wind was really blowing—gusts up into the low 40mph's, and a pretty steady 25-35mph. I wonder why the wind was in such a hurry?

Last week Emily used a hiking pole, which seemed to help with the really steep sections, so I took an old sassafras walking stick with me. I have gone through several phases in my hiking life of using walking sticks and not using them. When I walked across the United States back in 1980-81 (I actually only did half of the country), I used one and it was great. Most of the time that I am hiking I am also carrying a tripod in my hand, which means that I can't carry a walking stick, so I have gotten out of the habit of using one. But I would use one today.

And the stick did indeed help a lot, especially on the very steep ladder trail, which was covered with a heavy layer of leaves. It didn't take me long to reach the bottom, and soon I was down on all fours, getting a drink out of the rushing waters of Whitaker Creek. Lots of water. A flash of white caught my eye, and I was quite literally stunned when I looked to my right and discovered that I was face to face with a *cottonmouth snake!!!* What, in the middle of December?! Sure enough, there he was, with his big mouth wide open, pointing it right at me. They do this to scare you away. He was far enough away that I was not in danger of being struck, and he wasn't coiled up anyway. And he was so stiff from the cool nights that I don't think he could move very fast. But it was just so startling to see this snake in the middle of the winter (OK, it isn't officially winter yet, but almost). I did not see even a single poisonous snake all summer!

225

I reached over with my sassafras stick and flipped him into the water, just to see if he could swim. Oops.

I headed up the hillside and found the old road trace. It ran alongside that beautiful rock wall that I had discovered before. This one wasn't built all that great, but it was covered with thick moss, bright green. Kind of unusual for a rock wall up on the hillside. I followed the road up to where I had lost it before, then continued along the bench, searching for the connection. It was very difficult to see—the bench was level, and so there was no cut for the road. But if you looked very closely, you could see a faint line of rocks, and an area along the bench where there were no rocks—had to be the road. I followed it along the bench for over a quarter of a mile, and then ran right into the spot where we had lost it last week. At last, the final connection! Yea. I was thrilled.

I took the road up to the bluffline, then climbed up onto the "back rest" rock as I have named it and took a little nap. There was a pretty good waterfall coming off of the bluff, which made the perfect backdrop for my dreams. This is a really nice rock (this is the one that drops straight off the back side), and you can lean up against the far side of it to rest, your back supported by rock.

There is a witch hazel tree growing right out of this rock. We found it last week, but I never mentioned it in the Journal. Last week the tree was in full bloom, but the blooms had curled up somewhat today—they like bright sunshine. Normally, witch hazel bushes have this incredible fragrance with the bloom, and they only bloom on sunny days during the winter. But we had noticed last week that this tree, and another one that we had found, had no fragrance at all. Someone told me last year that there are actually two different varieties of witch hazels—one that was more of a bush that grew along stream banks and was *very* fragrant, and one that was more tree-like, and grew up on hillsides, and didn't have any fragrance. We were not sure if this was true or not, but it did seem like that was the case. At any rate, I love witch hazel trees, and this one was in the perfect spot for me to admire—I plan to climb up to this spot many times in the future and take naps.

From the bluff I climbed up a bench and made my away around Beagle Point to the main lookout area. Wow, it was a splendid view! I had never been to this spot during leafoff before, and was amazed. I sat on the bluff top and could see the Buffalo River way up into the drainage, but could also see downstream all the way to Boxley Valley, and even back up the Whitaker Creek drainage, and could see Hawksbill Crag.

It was still mostly overcast, but the sun had punched several holes in the clouds, and beams of light were dotting the wilderness, and dancing across the hillsides. It was like someone was upstairs above the clouds with a dozen big search lights, and was trying to spot something down below. I sat there mesmerized for a while. Clear blue skies are OK, but clouds often create magic.

I made my way around the bluffline to the spot where I could get down through (no dogs today), then found the chunk of styrofoam. I picked it up and half hiked/slid on down the steep slope all the way to Whitaker Creek. And man did I land at a gorgeous spot on the creek—it was wonderful! There was lots of water, and lots of moss-covered boulders. Not to mention several deep-green pools of calm water that were connected by small waterfalls. I hopped around from boulder to boulder, looking deep into the pools, and laid down next to the rushing water to see what it had to say (no big white cottonmouths here). The creek was glad to be so filled up with life-giving water. And it would probably be like this until late spring.

Then I spotted a rather odd thing in the pool up above. A whirlpool, right there in the middle of the pool. It was about six inches across, turning clockwise, and had a little tornado down under that stretched almost all the way to the bottom, a foot below. I sometimes see these at the base of a waterfall, but not right in the middle of a quiet pool like this one. If the styrofoam was just a little bigger, I might have jumped onto it and gone for a swim.

This little spot on Whitaker Creek was a very special, magical place for sure. I'll bet there are fifty of them on the creek—special places worth some time. And I'll bet that there are a thousand of them in the wilderness, and many more times that all throughout the Ozarks. You don't really need to visit a big-name attraction to find great beauty. It's all around, in just about every little hollow and along every stream or bluffline or ridgetop.

While I wanted to stay there all day, I had chores to do up at the cabin, so I pressed on. The hike up was OK, I was sucking wind pretty good, but made it to the top with only one stop. The exercise felt great.

There seemed to be a steady stream of visitors to the cabin all afternoon—I did get my chores done, but didn't have time for a nap with all the traffic. And once those clouds opened up and it poured for about thirty minutes—a half-inch. And the wind kept blowing and blowing, hard, all afternoon.

Just about sunset the glorious sunshine broke through the clouds and lit up the forest. I believe all of this weather was just Mother Nature's way of welcoming me back to the cabin. I really did enjoy it.

The sun has gone down now, my chores are done, there is a Cloudland Pizza in the oven (well, OK, four of them), and Emily has just showed up for the night. The wind is still blowing, but all is calm and well in my little Cloudland world inside.

After a little feast of veggie pizza and salad, we spent many hours in great conversation, only getting to nap a little before the sun came up. You know you are having a grand time when you turn to look at the clock to see if it is midnight yet and find that it is after 4am.

The temperature began to drop when the sun went down, and so we kept a fire going in the fireplace all night—it felt *wonderful!* It was getting cold at last. *Yippie!*

12/7/98 It was chilly and grey at daylight, although the sun did peak through the clouds now and then. A downy woodpecker came to visit the log diner out back—he didn't seem too concerned with the two faces staring at him from a

227

few feet away. I guess peanut butter and fat make a great snack. There weren't any other birds out, but a squirrel or two were busy gathering nuts. The wind had died down to nothing.

I had to return to town to sign some prints and go to meetings, while Emily stayed behind at the cabin and tried the couch on for size. As I walked to the van to drive away I could feel winter creeping in, and see it in the woods. At the same time, there was a warm feeling inside me—that felt really nice.

12/9/98 It was dark as I made my way back to the cabin. It had been cold in town, and I hoped that it had frozen at last at Cloudland. There was a definite chill in the air. The cabin was cool, but not cold, 54 degrees inside. And *yes*, it had been 29 degrees early in the morning outside! Yea, freezing weather! I quickly built a fire in the fireplace, which warmed the living room up in a hurry. It usually takes several hours to warm up all of the logs. Once they are warm, they will stay that way, and radiate the heat, for quite some time.

There were lots of stars out, but clouds were moving in. The wind was still. I was worn out from all of my town stuff, or maybe just from all of the past couple of months. While I had wanted to lay out on the back deck and gaze up at the night sky, I elected instead to go up into the loft and crawl under my new down comforter. That must have been the correct choice, because I was sound asleep in a matter of minutes (very unusual for me).

There are now two down comforters at Cloudland. One is a big, heavy one with a blue cover that was given to me fifteen years ago. It could easily keep you warm in the cabin way down below freezing. The new one is a very light one, actually called a down blanket, that my sister told me about. The light one is all that I really need, as the heavy one is just too hot for me most of the time. The heavy one will live in the guest room. Erna has ordered me the perfect comforter cover for the light one, one that will match the Cloudland sheets, but it has not gotten in yet. The new comforter worked very well! While the fireplace and the heat pump keep the cabin toasty most of the time, I feel that it should be just a tad cool inside in the wintertime—hey, it's a log cabin, and it needs to be cold! Better sleeping, better snuggling.

12/10/98 A grey, cold winter day greeted me at first light. Well, maybe it was second light—I slept in a little. But since the wind wasn't blowing, it wasn't all that cold out—in the low 30's. I stoked up the fire, made some hot chocolate, and generally lounged around in my heavy robe and slippers. Cabin life is really beginning to get to me (in a good way).

I had a lot of chores to do, but decided to get out and go on a little hike first. It smelled terrific outside, and the swoosh-crunch-swoosh-crunch of my footsteps through the leaves sounded great. Not a critter was stirring, except me, and an occasional downy woodpecker that came flittering by. Quite often when there is a weather change, wildlife stays put for a little while. Once the weather pattern has set in, then they feel more comfortable, and get out and play as normal. I especially love it right after a blanket of heavy snow has fallen—you can ease through the forest without making a sound, and you won't see another thing stirring. After several hours, then everyone else comes out.

I climbed up to the East Meadow and did find some others out—there were five deer in the middle, grazing on new, green grass. They heard me at once, stopped what they were doing, and all stared at me. There were two big does, and three yearlings. They seemed to be in very good health, and not all that scared of me, even though they had just survived a long deer season where dogs were chasing them and people were shooting at them all day. After a few minutes they went back to grazing, and I slipped around the other side of the meadow and down off into the woods. I tried to be quiet, but the leaves under foot were just too much, and the deer bounded off.

There were more deer in the Faddis Meadow—looked like three big does this time, and no yearlings. They saw me immediately too, and seemed a bit more afraid. Since I was walking on the road there wasn't much noise, and they let me pass without bolting. They did stand there and stare at me, warm bodies frozen in the chilly air.

Towards the end of the meadow I saw movement—another deer. This one was a buck, a six pointer. He didn't pay me the slightest bit of attention. His eyes were focused on the three does. It occurred to me that since this was the first really good cold snap this fall, that the rut might still be in full swing, and perhaps even now going full blast. The rut is when the bucks hear the call of the wild, and go out seeking to breed as many does as they can. I think this dude was about to get lucky—he had pretty good odds. It was funny to watch his jerky motions—kind of like a teenage boy out on the dance floor for the first time. I could see the steam coming from his nostrils. He was hot and bothered. I would have liked to have stuck around to watch how well he did, but I had work to do, and so left the soap opera behind and went back to the cabin.

It was a short hike, but I was glad to see the deer, stretch my legs a little, and soak up some of the forest. Back at the cabin I unloaded the van of a half-ton of books (it seems like my morning chore of splitting wood has turned into loading/unloading books—about the same amount of exercise, but not nearly as much fun!), then unboxed them, stuffed them with price sheets, and got everything lined up for a visit from Bill McNamara to autograph all of them.

While I waited for Bill to show up I put on a pot of veggie soup and rice—one of my standard winter meals. When it got done I loaded it up with Louisiana Hot Sauce, and went out on the back deck to eat. It was cold, so I had to bundle up a bit, but the hot soup helped a lot. There still were no birds out anywhere, soaring or otherwise. It was very quiet outside, with no movement.

The even light was just perfect to see all of the tornado damage that Bob and Dawna had found a couple of weeks before. It was several miles up the main river valley, but you could see it if you looked really hard. And when I got out the telescope, man, you could really see the hillside that the tornado had destroyed—the trees had been ripped up everywhere.

Billy showed up and we spent an hour dealing with the books, and talking about the history of the area, especially about the geology and about the Indians and early settlers. He knows so much about this area, and it is great to sit and chew the fat with him. I have learned though that I have to allow enough pauses in our conversation for him to sign his autograph—otherwise, he would talk and talk for hours without getting any books signed! After he had finished, and I was showing him the tornado damage through the telescope, I also showed him a rock shelter across the way that someone had built under one of the bluffs over there. Billy hadn't been there. What? There was a spot in this wilderness that Billy had not been to? I was really surprised, and elated, because I would make that a main priority of mine to beat him over there to it (I hadn't been there either, but then I hadn't been to very many places—yet).

Once Billy left I loaded up the van and headed out to Jasper, where I had a slide show at the library. There was a great turnout, and it was good to see and meet some of my Newton County neighbors. And I couldn't believe how wonderful the library there is—it had been converted from the country shop, which apparently had been in very poor shape. It shines with beauty now.

It was late when I got back to the cabin, and I was a bit tuckered. The stars were out, and I stoked up the fire for what surely would be a cold night.

12/11/98 Sometime during the night a blanket of clouds snuck in, which kept the temp from falling below freezing, but the wind had picked up a little, and the windchill had dipped down into the single digits by daylight. I really wanted to get out and go hiking, but I had work in town to do, so I loaded up the van with the last of the books, and left my cabin behind.

12/17/98 Wow, it was a week before I returned, and the cabin seemed like an old friend, although it was a bit chilly. I had given my last slide show of the season, in Harrison, and arrived at the cabin late. The sky was filled with a million stars—there were more of them, and brighter than I had seen in a long time. The Milky Way was splashed across the sky, and Orion was high overhead.

A roaring fire brought the cabin up to room temperature, and I spent an hour in the big leather chair next to the fireplace getting nice and toasty before retiring. It was good to be back. And this time I would be here for several days, although I would have to make one quick trip into town. Outside the wind howled, and it was even blowing in the front of the cabin, creating a lot of music from the wind chimes. The wind would howl and roar all night, up to 43mph. And the chimes played on and on.

12/18/98 The entire eastern horizon glowed bright red well before sunrise. Even the southern and western skies had color in them. But a bunch of clouds had snuck in during the night, and by the time the sun rose, the cloud bank had covered up the eastern sky. The wind was still blowing pretty good, but a lot less than during the night.

I loaded up the van with one more pile of books (Billy had signed a bunch of books for me and left them at Milancy's house, so I had to go by there and pick them up), and headed into town. I had planned to return before sunset, but it remained cloudy all day, and so I stayed in town and took care of business, and didn't return to the cabin again until about 7pm.

This is the time of the year when the sun reaches its southern most arch (on December 21st to be precise). I have figured out that at some point around this time the sun sets directly behind the Buffalo Fire Tower, as seen from my back deck. I was up here all that week last year, but it was cloudy all week, and I never got to prove my theory, or get any pictures. I was hoping for clear skies this year, but the first night didn't turn out that way.

The first thing that I did was to empty the ash from the fireplace. I was surprised to find a few glowing embers left. I dumped the lot out in front of the cabin on one of the parking spaces. The wind was blowing really hard, and the ashes blew everywhere. It was kind of raining a little, mostly misting.

Emily was coming out to spend the night and go hiking the next day so I tried to get the place tidied up as best I could. While I was in the kitchen putting away the clean dishes I could admire the reflection of the fire in the kitchen window. At one point I realized that I was looking at not only the fire in the fireplace, but also a fire that was a blazing outside—oh my god, I had set the woods on fire with the fireplace embers! Nothing spooks me more up here than a forest fire (living in a log cabin will do that to you, even though log homes really don't burn very well—they mostly just smolder).

I ran out the front door and around to the side of the cabin to get a fire rake, thinking that I could contain the fire. I soon realized that the wind was blowing *so* hard that raking would be useless. So I ran into the basement and found the garden hose, then raced out in front and hooked it up to the outdoor faucet. The wind was really whipping up the flames. In another minute the fire would be out of control. Even though it was raining lightly, only the tops of the leaves were wet—there was plenty of dry stuff underneath to feed any fire.

The water came squirting out full blast, and I was able to douse the flames before they got away from me. I stood there and poured water into the site for five minutes, stirring the leaves with a stick. Satisfied that I had put everything out, I shut off the water and walked back to the cabin. Only then did I realize that I forgot to put any shoes on—I was standing there in the cold and wet barefoot, but I never felt a thing. I had dodged a very large bullet that I had shot at myself.

Emily arrived a little while later and quickly prepared a Mexican feast (it was wonderful), and we pigged out on enchiladas and dark beer. Outside, it was damp and cold and nasty, but inside we were snug in our little log retreat, sitting in front of the big fire and talking up a storm. It had been a long, often frantic week for me, and I could find no better way to end it than spending time with Emily at Cloudland.

12/19/98 I don't really know why, but both of us were up and milling around at 4am. We both ended up on the couch, and spent more time conversing (I love to listen to people talk in the middle of the night—what they say is often more revealing than at any other time of the day). By daylight she had gone back to sleep. I covered her up with a quilt, and I put on my hiking boots and headed out the door. We were engulfed in a heavy fog, and the wind had died down. No finer hiking than in the fog!

It was very quiet out too, not even a whisper of sound. I love the smell and feel of fog, especially really heavy fog like this was—you can breathe deep and get the fog down into the bottom of your lungs. And the colors outside were *sooo* rich!

Within a couple hundred feet of the cabin I came across a stump that I had never noticed before. It was only about a foot tall, maybe less, and ten or twelve inches across, all that was left of a tree that was cut down many years ago. The stump was completely covered with lush, bright green moss—every square inch of it. And some of the stump had already rotted away—it wasn't completely round, but rather had several "canyons" of decay, the walls of which were also covered with the moss. I wondered how long the little stump had been there, and how long it would last? Since it was so close to the cabin, I vowed to check on it from time to time, and see how it was doing. And on the back side of the stump I discovered an entrance of some sort—couldn't figure out if it was the front door for a chipmunk, or a wren. No matter, someone had a mighty fine little green house.

Down the trail a ways there was a little cedar tree, all by itself, about two feet tall. It was covered with large dew or rain drops. And when I walked around the back side of this little tree all of the drops sparkled, like jewels. I didn't have or plan to have a Christmas tree at the cabin, and decided that I would make this little tree the official tree, and that I would leave it right were it was, still growing. Later, I would make up some kind of popcorn or cranberry strings that the birds might like, and drape them around my little tree. Christmas in the forest, with goodies for all. What better Christmas tree could anyone have? Maybe I will do this every year, perhaps even add a tree now and then. One of these days you will be walking through the woods and look up and see a hundred decorated cedar trees in the forest—you would then know that you were approaching Cloudland!

By the time I returned to the cabin Emily was up, and we had some Cloudland Coffee and toasted bagels. The fog had lifted somewhat, and opened up the view all around. The Buffalo River was really running pretty strong from the recent rains, and was making a lot of noise. The clouds were still hanging around, and you couldn't see the tops of the hills. The wind was blowing around some streaks of fog, and it looked like there were two dozen of them dancing. Some were even going in opposite directions, passing each other. The wind was really having a great time with it all.

It would be a cool and damp overcast day—perfect for hiking!

We walked on up to the East Meadow, and snuck into the edge of it. There weren't any deer about, so we moved on into the middle of the meadow. Then we startled a flock of turkeys—half of them ran, the others tried to fly, but it was slow going and they just barely got enough altitude to clear the trees. It is always funny to see something as awkward as a turkey try to fly. I guess they do it a lot better than I do though!

We strolled across the big flat, admired the giant leaning oak tree, then went down through the bluffline. The side of the walls in Magnolia Canyon were really bright green this morning. We found several large beech trees that had been split down one side, but they were still standing. I never have figured out how they get like that. There were also a couple of large oaks that were leaning out over the edge of the bluff, and looked like they could fall over soon.

The creek in Dug Hollow below was running pretty good. We made our way on over to the main waterfall area. There was a huge oak tree just downstream from the lower falls that had fallen over all the way across the creek to the opposite bluffline—it had broken in two places. I bet the noise was incredible. This log, probably four feet thick, would be there for a long time.

We walked over a trail that was covered with a carpet of moss, around the head of the other big falls in Dug Hollow, then made our way down through the broken bluffline and rubble into the bottom. Wow, the creek was creating waterfalls everywhere! And blue/green pools in between them. And all the boulders were covered with the same bright, lush, green moss. The moisture in the air, and the light, and being with my friend made every step a spectacular one. Dug Hollow is just wonderful. And one of 25 or 30 others in the area—each drainage has a lot of special places just like this one does. Marvelous. And there were lots of giant sycamore trees growing out of the bottom too.

We continued our ramble downstream, past one magical spot after another. Then the water disappeared, and everything was quiet and dead still—the creek disappeared underground. There was so much water coming down, I couldn't believe that it would disappear. In the summertime or during other low periods, sure, but not when it was running so well. Hum.

We left the creek and contoured over to the opposite hillside. I wanted to show her the new spring that we had discovered last year—one that Billy McNamara says was not there twenty years ago. It is one of the most beautiful springs in the area, or at least it is as it cascades down the hillside over moss-covered rocks. We walked right to it, and it was running full blast, and was a wonderful sight. As we stood there thinking about the spring, and the disappearing river, I decided that the two must be connected. My theory was that the creek had continued to carve out a route underground, and finally it just broke through the surface and created this spring. The spot where the river disappeared and this spring were at about the same elevation. Hum. By golly, I think we've got something there! This is a beautiful spring. And it has no name. I'll have to take care of that one day.

When we reached the Buffalo River we found a very wide river, and it was indeed running pretty good. Neither of us had brought any gear to wade across a wide river, or even our hiking poles or sticks. Yet we wanted to find and explore a cave, and it was across the river. So we took off garments and rolled up others, and plunged right in. The water was very cold, and it came up to my thigh. But fortunately the rocks were smooth and not slippery. I hadn't lost the feeling in my legs or feet, but they sure did hurt from the cold! Emily is a little shorter than me, and of course the water level was higher on her, but she made it across just fine. I like hiking with folks that can make it on their own (she had hiked the entire Ozark Highlands Trail by herself, so I figured she could handle a simple river crossing).

We found a beech-leaf carpet to sit down on and dry off, and had a snack. Our mission was to locate Tom Watson Bear Cave. I really had no idea where it was, only that it was on this side of the river, and somewhere nearby. The story goes that Tom Watson was chased into the cave by a bear. I don't know if he escaped or not, only that he was chased there. And there are lots of "writings" by folks from long ago on the walls. I have been told all of this by several different people, so I assume it all to be true. But I had never really paid enough attention to them to know exactly where this cave was. I did remember someone saying something about a bluffline coming down to the river, so we headed upstream to find one.

Before long we came to one of the most beautiful holes of water in the entire Buffalo River system—deep and wide and the most gorgeous color, flanked by a small bluff. And there was a waterfall pouring over the bluff and into the river at the upper end. This hole of water belongs to my dog Yukon, and his grave is located up above the waterfall. He sure found a nice place to rest!

There was another great hole of water just upstream, and lots and lots of color. The river is simply spectacular at this time of the year. Wonderful.

We explored every little nook and cranny of the nearby bluff, but couldn't locate any sizeable cave entrance. We did find another spring, and it too was flowing well. The drainage of Little Pine Hollow empties into the Buffalo River just upstream from this spring. Darned if this creek wasn't dry also. I never would have expected it.

We climbed up a bench and explored some more. We came across several more springs, all running full blast. Then there was another bluffline. This one felt right. There was a cave entrance in the limestone bluff nearby. Nope, it didn't go anywhere. Then there was another one. Not that one either. I could *feel* it! Nope. Nope. Another dead end. Then the bluffline gave out. Darn, I just knew it was here somewhere.

We came to Big Pine Hollow, and it also was dry! What was going on here? These creeks were big ones, and there was plenty of water on the ground, why were they all dry? And why were all of the springs flowing so well? Strange.

I was getting a little frustrated not being able to find the cave, but Emily seemed to be enjoying herself even though her guide didn't have a clue what he was doing. I knew that there was an old road coming down from the top in the next section of hillside, and so we decided to go have a look at it, and see if perhaps the cave was near it—I figured that it might be easy to spot from a road, since so many people knew about it.

The hillside was steep there right next to the river, but we made it across, and found a road down along the river, and followed it. Another road came down from above and joined it—this was the main road that I was looking for. We walked along it for a short distance, and then spotted a cave entrance above in the bluffline. We had figured that there must be a well-worn trail to the cave entrance, and so weren't too encouraged by this cave since there was no such trail. It was a low entrance, and some critter had piled a bunch of green leaves on the floor—not really a nest, but just a pile of leaves about two feet across.

I got out my light and went inside the cave. It was low, very low, and I was duck-walking, and even down on my hands and knees. There were surprisingly a lot of small cave formations—stalactites, stalagmites, flowstone, rimstone dams, and even a column or two (I used to work in a cave you know). I didn't think that this was the right cave, since I remember folks talking about the writings high up on the walls—there were no high walls in this little cave. But it was interesting, and Emily soon joined me. She immediately found a little bat—an Eastern pip. They are loners, and always hang by themselves (literally). This first one was blonde, and covered with fine water droplets. You don't want to shine your flashlight on a sleeping bat because the warmth might wake him up, which would really screw up his entire system, and the extra exertion of flying around trying to escape might actually kill him. Anyway, we found several of these little bats, and took care to avoid hitting or disturbing them.

The ceiling remained very low, and we found the end of several passages. Lots of neat dripstone. Other critters included crickets, spiders, and a bright orange cave salamander with black spots. It was also neat that you could look back and still see the small entrance, even several hundred feet into the cave.

There was one passage that went on, but we would have really had to have gotten down and crawled, so we decided that this was not our cave, and opted to turn around and look elsewhere. It was a very nice little cave none the less.

Once outside we discovered that the bluffline soon ended, and there were no other cave entrances. Darn. We had to have missed it—I doubted that it would have been any further downstream. We gave up, and would have to return again, hopefully armed with a little location information. It was fun looking, and we found some neat stuff anyway. So we reluctantly headed back, and had another safe but chilly river crossing.

Next we visited Yukon's grave, adding a nice little mossy rock like I always do. Then we checked on a leaning fireplace at an old homesite to see how much further it had leaned over since my last visit. There appeared to be several rocks from the top of the chimney that had fallen off recently—I doubt that this historical artifact will last much longer—it is really leaning.

At the old Sparks cabin, the one with two chimneys, Emily dug around and found all kinds of pottery and plate fragments. Another thing that I like about her is that she is not worried about getting her hands dirty. There is a rock near the chimneys where someone has laid out a bunch of artifacts from the cabin, including three of the four iron feet from the wood stove, and gobs of kitchenware fragments. We dug around in there and uncovered all sorts of things. This rock is sort of a monument to the folks who lived in the cabin.

It was getting late, so we headed *up* the hillside to a break in the bluff that I knew about. This is one of the steepest climbs in the area, but going straight up is the best way to do it. There are often places where you are going nearly straight up the dirt hillside, and there are no trees to grab onto to help you up—it really tests the tread pattern on your boots!

It had been clear down below all day—no fog, but still overcast. We could look up and see that the tops of the hills were still in the fog though. As we climbed up the hillside, we began to get into the fog—things became more and more hazy all the time. Or was it just the altitude?

We came to one of my favorite boulders in the area (also a nice resting place, and we both were blowing quite a bit). It has the most incredible pattern in it that I have ever seen in a rock—obviously formed when it was created. There are lots of sculptured shelves in the rock. And in one of them, we found a pile of fresh moss, built like a bird nest. Was it someone who forgot to fly south for the winter? Or perhaps it was a little pack rat nest or something.

There were several large overhangs in the main bluff, and we found more piles of green leaves and moss. Some of them were simply piled up on the floor, while others were stuffed into cracks and crevasses and shelves high up above. Hum—all of this leaf and moss gathering leads me to believe that it is going to be a *cold* winter! I sure do hope so, because I've got skis and snowshoes that need a little exercise. I do too.

We finally made it to the top, and were in the fog once again. It was an easy stroll back to the cabin. It never rained a drop all day, and stayed fairly warm. We never saw any wildlife, other than the turkeys and several woodpeckers, and a few tiny little wrens.

OK, I couldn't stand it any longer. I called Billy McNamara and asked him about the cave. Son of a gun, the cave that we were in was the right one—we needed to continue through the belly crawl, then the room would open up into a 15 foot tall room, which is where the writings were, and then it would continue on and finally emerge outside in a different location. I felt a little better since we actually did find the right cave, but a little miffed that we didn't go on further.

Emily had to return to town, so she packed up her things and bid farewell. It was a nice visit, and I enjoyed her company. I am a very lucky guy, and have many more things in my life than I ever expected, but nothing pleases me more than the companionship of a good friend.

I chopped a little firewood and hauled it up and inside. Then it was time to fix one of my favorite meals—Banff Pasta! I made a big pan of it, then ate the whole thing. A bit of wine too.

No sunset behind the fire tower again today—nothing but fog.

It wasn't until I had all the dishes washed that I sat back and relaxed and realized what day it was. The greatest man that I ever knew died on this day nineteen years ago. My dad. I turned up the stereo, and spent the rest of the evening singing and remembering, and crying. Tears of sadness because my dad was not here. Tears of joy because he was my dad, a great man.

I guess that I stoked up the fire a little much—I had to get up in the middle of the night and open up the windows and turn on the ceiling fan—it was *warm* in the cabin!

12/20/98 Fog, fog, and more fog. And it was thick—I could hardly even see the trees just outside the window. I stirred up the fire (it had cooled down a lot in the cabin), had a Starbucks mocha (I still love a cold drink in the morning—even in the winter), then headed out for a hike. It was wonderful hiking in the fog, as usual. And there was no wind. Everything was quiet.

I walked along the bench towards the Crag. Slowly. Quietly. I saw some movement above me—there were three deer at the top of the bench to my right. The fog was so thick that I could barely see them. They were silhouetted, all in a row and broadside, right where the hill breaks. And they were staring right down at me. They were the same black as all of the things around them—the trees and boulders—only shaped a little different. I guess you could say that they were deer-shaped. Ha, ha. I was already chilled, and wasn't prepared for a standoff, so I continued on my walk, easing along the path. They watched me intently, but never moved a muscle. They were still right there in the same spot when I got out of sight. Bet they think that I never saw them. Wonder how many others I missed?

The Crag looked mighty fine sticking out there in the fog. I sat down and gazed out into the blank air for a few minutes. I could hear several pileated woodpeckers flying around on the opposite hillside, and a couple of other birds, but could never see any of them because of the fog. It was a little strange.

I climbed up the hill, past the Faddis cabin, and eased on over to the East Meadow—there is always something hanging out there. And today was no exception. I walked across the first half of the meadow slowly, but not really creeping. As I got closer to the garden area, I saw movement, then I really slowed down to what I call my "movingstandstill." I have spent many hours and days doing this as a youngster while deer hunting. If you go slow enough, you can actually move forward without it appearing that you are moving at all. This is the only sure way to approach wildlife.

There were about a dozen turkeys, all hens I guess, and they were milling and scratching and clucking about like a bunch of chickens. The group moved together, sort of, but very slowly. I wanted to see how close I could get to them before they discovered me. I kept creeping, slowly, ever so slowly. They made more noise, and moved quickly back and forth. I got within about 30 feet of them, when one of them looked up and saw me twitch or something—even though I knew it was coming, the *roar* that they made when they all took to the air scared the beegeevees out of me! And it took my breath away. They flew off in all directions, and all I could do was fall to the ground with laughter.

There were chores to do so I got up off of the ground and returned to the cabin, then hauled wood and cleaned up dead wasps and unloaded boxes of books. I put on some cinnamon-raisin bread to cook, and built up a big fire. It was getting colder outside, and they were calling for snow. Snow would be great, but I had to leave in the morning, so I hoped it wouldn't snow too much today! Well, it never snowed a bit, and hardly even got near freezing. It just didn't feel like snow.

Later in the afternoon some friends from Harrison came by for a visit. Bud Grisham (my ex-father-in-law, or as he wrote on the lamp shade, "once a father-in-law, always a father-in-law"), his wife Carolyn, and their friends "Stovepipe" Lawrence and his wife (I have always known him as simply "Pipe"). It was their first visit to Cloudland, so I gave them the grand tour. And it was Cloudland today—you couldn't see a thing beyond the decks but clouds. I got divorced from Bud's daughter more than ten years ago, but he and I have stayed in touch. Now he is trying to fix me up with his wife's sister—hey, we could be brother-in-laws then!

We all enjoyed a slice or two of fresh bread topped with some of Bob's homemade apple butter (from the apple tree next to the Faddis cabin). Carolyn is an interior designer, and I might have to hire her to come straighten my place out one of these days.

Once again there was no sunset behind the fire tower—too much fog.

Later in the day, just as I was finishing up another pan of Banff Pasta, Benny and Clyde Simmons dropped by to pick up some books (Benny is my homemade wine connection, and I found out that Clyde is too—they are going to help me get started making my own Cloudland wine). They were out muzzle-loader hunting.

It is dark and damp outside, and the fireplace is growing dim. I have had a great couple of days out here at my little retreat, but I must get up early tomorrow and return to town for more book business (there are orders for over a hundred books on my answering machine from this weekend—lots to do tomorrow!). I am ever thankful for my friends, and for the wilderness. Both continue to give me much more than I deserve, but I will continue to soak it all up as long as I can.

12/21/98 For the third day in a row, I awoke to a cabin engulfed in a heavy fog. When I bought this property, there was a lot of fog also the first several times that I visited it—which is where the name came from. But soon the fog gave way to rain, and the skies really opened up and it rained pretty good for a little while. This rain washed away much of the fog, and by daylight everything from the cabin on down was clear. Well, almost. There were still a number of individual clouds and steam vents dancing around in the valley upstream.

I had heard a weather forecast that said the high for the day was going to be about 30 degrees, so I wondered if any of the wet stuff was freezing? When I finally did make it downstairs to the weather station, it was 50 degrees—that was pretty warm. I guess a cold front was headed our way, but it hadn't reached Cloudland yet.

12/22/98 It rained about a half-inch yesterday and the cold front did arrive. And man did it arrive! It got down to 7 degrees this morning, with a windchill of 1 degree above (must not have been much wind, or the windchill would have been a lot lower). And it had "snailed" some during the night—this is compacted pellets of snow, a cross between snow and hail. There were lots of pellets piled up in the road when I drove it just before sunset, and the temp was still in the teens, which was the high for the day.

The forest looked in somewhat of a state of shock with the sudden cold—nothing was stirring. I had wanted to get the sunset behind the Fire Tower, or see just exactly how close it was, but once again I was foiled as the skies were grey and cloudy.

It was 52 degrees inside the cabin, and it had only dipped down to 50 during the night. That's about what I have the heat pump set on, which should keep any water pipes from freezing. It was in the mid 50's down in the basement. (None of this is real exciting news to most, but this is the first real winter that the cabin has gone through, and I am anxious to see how all of the systems work and the place holds up to the cold. Last winter was so mild I really didn't get much of a chance to test anything.)

Within minutes I had a roaring fire going in the fireplace (I did empty the ashes again, but this time made sure there were *no* live coals!). As I warmed up my core a little, I got splattered on. Then it happened again. Uh oh. Was the roof leaking? But it wasn't raining, heck it was 15 degrees outside. The ceiling above me was dry. Where the heck was the stuff coming from—an invisible bird flying around inside the cabin pooping on me? Then I found it—there must have been some snail or frozen rain that had worked its way into the underside of the chimney top outside—the fire was melting it and it was running out from the top of the chimney inside the cabin, then splattering on the top of the rock fireplace. It didn't appear too serious, but I would need to check it out and maybe do a little caulking upstairs on the roof.

I did a few chores around the cabin, cooked dinner, then sat down and gazed into the fire for a few hours before retiring for the evening. The new down comforter upstairs was quickly becoming a very welcome accessory indeed—I snuggled down deep under it and drifted off.

12/23/98 It was another grey day at first light, but it was a lot warmer than I had expected, the temp having climbed into the upper teens during the night. And it was dead still outside. I got up, stoked the fire, and sipped a chilled Starbucks mocha while warming my rump. Then I unloaded a van full of books (this continues to replace chopping wood as my morning exercise here—won't last long). I got out the tele and had a look around the wilderness—the air was clear, and while there were black clouds scattered through the overcast sky, it was pretty light. In some places the hillsides were lit up as good as I had ever seen them, although there was no sun. The tornado area upstream really stuck out, and you could see each tree that had been ripped out of its socket and thrown down. You could follow the route of destruction from near the river, up the steep hillside, over the big bluff, then up and over the top of the ridge. Lot and lots of timber on the ground.

Everything was pretty much monotone in color—that winter brown, with patches of grey bluff here and there. There were lots of ice flows on some of the bluffs, like on the big bluffs just across the Buffalo River to the east—must be a lot of water coming off of that hillside. But the bluffline over on Beagle Point was clean—no ice at all. There was one pretty good chunk of ice just this side of the Crag. All was quiet, except for the hushed roar of the river.

Then a brilliant red cardinal flew up, took a swipe at the feeder, then flew off and landed on a nearby limb. I remember that a lady friend had told me to replace the stuff in the feeder or the birds wouldn't eat it, I hadn't gotten to it yet. So I did just that, as the cardinal sat in the tree and watched. There were several little birds lurking about as well, and beginning to make a little noise.

And then a hawk appeared. I rushed for the binocs, and followed him as he made his way across the valley in front. You could tell that the air was quite dead, because this guy had to work for each and every foot that he flew—his wings were flapping like crazy—no effortless soaring today!

I don't know, something about the morning struck me. There is a different sense of life here. A slower pace I guess. But that's not exactly it. You *feel* this place, the vastness of the scene, and the closeness of the wildness. And when the wind blows, you don't turn away, you lean your face into it and feel it touch your skin. You sit down on the log or the rock not because you are tired, but because you want to see what it's like—the texture, the hardness.

There was a slight breeze, and it was coming out of the west—very unusual. Perhaps another front moving in?

I spent the day in town, but did return in time for another sunset that never happened. Oh well, looks like I'm going to have to wait until next year to see if the sun really does set behind the fire tower.

There were still a few coals in the fireplace when I got in, and it didn't take long for the fireplace to come to life once again. And instead of books, I brought a van full of wood—*aspen* wood! Do you know what that means? An aspen wall is going up somewhere, and it is going to be in the soon-to-be new guest room downstairs. I brought out 60-1 x 6 inch boards, and stacked them downstairs. I hope to get them nailed up by New Years or soon after. I'll probably have to bring out another load, but they should give me a good start. I think I'll call that room the Aspen Room, and the one upstairs the Dogwood Room (dogwood tree right outside the window).

It got up into the low 20's today, and remains there tonight. No stars out, and no wind. Cabin temp 57.

Sometime during the night I woke up and rolled over to see a sky filled with a million stars—about as bright as they can get! It was good to see my old friends, I only wish the clear skies had come along a few hours earlier so that I could have seen the sunset. No matter, I was thankful for their company on this cold night.

12/24/98 *Sunshine* at Cloudland! Few things warm the heart on a chilly winter morning as much as bright sunshine does. As the yellow ball climbed into the sky, it cast a glow across the frozen hillsides, illuminating many features that had been hidden for a week. Way up the main valley I could see a giant icicle hanging from a bluff down next to the river, and shining like a beacon in the night. I'll bet it was 30 feet or more tall. No doubt it will continue to grow as long as the temps remain below freezing.

A little closer to home the sun lit up three smaller bits of ice that were clinging to the gutter on the back porch—they sparkled brighter than any jewels! And over on the right, a downy woodpecker was munching on the new peanut butter/fat balls in the feeder.

I guess that I had gotten used to being so warm under the down comforter in bed, because when I sat down at the computer to write this morning, it was so cold that I had to both turn on the heat pump to add a little warm air to the area, and cover up with a blanket while I typed. The fireplace does a great job of heating up the main room, kitchen and loft, but the outer rooms do tend to get a little chilly.

Usually when I am here on a cold day the fireplace is all the warmth that is needed, and it keeps the main room warmer than what the thermostat is set at, so the heat pump hardly ever comes on. When I am gone and there is no fire in the fireplace, then the heat pump takes over. The problem with all of this is that not only do the outer rooms get cool when I am here, but so does the basement, which doesn't get any benefit from the fireplace at all. If I turn the thermostat up so that the heat pump comes on when I am here (warming up the basement and outer rooms), then the main room gets a little too warm for my taste. I haven't figured out how to solve the problem yet, but continue to seek a solution. Generally speaking, guests who visit Cloudland in the winter can expect to wear a sweater—I like it in the 50's or low 60's in the cabin. Hey, it's wintertime! Of course, when there are a lot of guests here, the added hot air usually keeps things much warmer...

All of this talk of cold rooms is a mute point right now though because it's time to get out in the bright morning sunshine and chop a little wood—the perfect internal heater!

Yikes! While I was out with my wood the wind kicked up and frosted my, well, frosted a few of my exterior parts. Chopping was supposed to warm +me up, but I had to quit and seek out the fireplace. The wind had dropped the windchill to nine degrees below zero. Ouch! I suspect that this reading will just be the tip of the iceberg, so to speak, as winter progresses.

It was a spectacular, bright blue crisp day, with the temps easing up into the low 30's by the afternoon. I spent several periods of undetermined time laying out on a rock, soaking up the sun. Then my brother and mom came out, and we went up to a section of my property that has some small grown-up fields in it—we were after a Christmas tree for the home place (in town). There are a number of cedars growing in the thick brush, and we picked out a good one and felled it with an axe, then loaded it on top of my brother's jeep, and carted it off to mom's house in town to spend the rest of Christmas Eve.

12/25/98 It was late, or actually very early, in the wee hours of Christmas morning, when I arrived back at Cloudland. The cabin was a bit cool. I quickly built a fire, then stumbled up into the loft and crawled under the down comforter. Santa is a different character up here in the mountains, so instead of milk and cookies, I left him a plate of gourmet peanuts and a dark beer.

Christmas is a time for family and friends. I guess I consider the cabin a part of the family, and I feel drawn to it during holidays. It was great to visit with the family and friends in town (the food and drink weren't bad either), but I have just as many wilderness things that qualify for family status as well. I wanted to wake up at the cabin on Christmas morning—no matter if I only got to sleep a couple of hours before the sun topped out over the ridge and lit up the forest with brilliant rays of sun.

It was cold and very still out, and not a wisp of wind. The sunlight slowly worked its way down the ridges to the creeks and rivers below, the sky growing more blue as the morning progressed. Since I didn't have any stockings hung by the fire with care to check on, I wasn't in any hurry to leave my downy nest. I greeted the day, shouted out a hearty *Merry Christmas* to the cabin, then went back to sleep.

When I finally did emerge, I suited up and went out and split up a little wood for a few minutes, then carried it upstairs. The temperature was about perfect for this chore—not too cold, yet cool enough to keep from working up a sweat. But I was short on time, and soon was driving off once again for town—I couldn't miss a Christmas dinner could I?

More great time with family and friends, and another feast. So far I have been able to weather all of the holiday feeds and treats without gaining any weight. I have lost twelve pounds since Thanksgiving! And I really needed to, especially after all of those weeks and months of hectic travel and junk food.

The sun was getting low on the horizon when I returned to the cabin. And the color of the light was already beginning to turn. I quickly put on my boots and headed for the woods. (The sun was already to the right of the fire tower, so no chance of the picture that I wanted—not until next December.)

It was cold, and the wind was blowing, but the low sun felt great on my face. The tree shadows were about as long as they could get, and the forest floor in between was lit with yellow light. The hillsides of brown and grey trees began to glow yellow as well. From yellow to orange. Then burnt orange. The color of the far away view of the forest was unique to this time of day—I guess it is a kind of Alpenglow/Ozarkglow. Whatever it is, I rather like it. The ground and the hillsides glowed, then in an instant all was dull—the sun dipped below the far ridgetop. This special time of day only lasts a few minutes, and if you stop to do anything other than give it your total attention, you will miss everything. Like spotting shooting stars, I strive to be a part of as many evening light shows like this one as I can. The rare light on your face gives you good luck.

As I was walking back to the cabin in the twilight, I spooked an owl from a nearby tree—he only flew a short distance away, landing in a tree on the next bench below. I got a good look at him—a barred owl. Haven't heard one in a while, and I had wondered where my friends were keeping themselves. This guy looked back at me intently, but never flew again. I tipped my hat to him and eased my way on down the trail.

The cabin was a bit chilly—49 degrees in the main room. I cleaned out the fireplace and soon had a roaring blaze going. In 2 1/2 hours the temp had climbed up to 58 degrees, then leveled off. The temp sensor is about 20 feet from the fireplace, on the opposite wall. It was a lot warmer in the rest of the big room, but colder in the other rooms.

Two Christmas cards arrived in my mailbox out here this week—both from young ladies named Rogers (not related). They were the very first pieces of First Class mail to be delivered here.

As the fire warmed up the cabin I punched up the volume on the stereo, and put on a Grand Funk CD. I remembered listening to this very music way back in high school, during spring break visits to the Buffalo River. Gosh, that was some mighty fine music! I turned out all of the lights, and watched the dancing of the firelight on the walls.

At one point I noticed a bright square on the floor. I looked up and discovered a bright 1/3 moon shining down through one of the upper windows. The moon was helping to light up my little dance floor! I dragged the tele over and was able to stand in front of the warm fire and watch the silver moon from inside. Jupiter was out too, very close to the moon, and I counted four of its moons, although the base and drums were bouncing the tele around a little.

One of the things that I notice is that I drink a lot of cold water at this time of the year. While a jug of water at room temperature would probably be just fine (since the "room" temperature in the cabin is normally about cave temperature), the water cooler in the office is great because I can get a draw at any time that I like. I've always liked cold water, even in the winter.

As the night grew on, more CD's bounced off of the walls of the cabin. And the moon moved. Laying back in the big chair, I could bask in the glow of the fire and that of the moon at the same time.

I moved on to a CD that my friend, Vicki Buck (from Austin, Texas) got me several years ago—some really great music by varied artists, all recorded live for a radio station there. This CD sounds especially terrific on the sound system here. There were a number of songs that not only have wonderful music, but great lyrics as well. I tried and tried to listen to all of the words on a couple of them, but would always get distracted inside my brain before the song had finished. It is easy to sit back and let your mind wander out here.

Then I couldn't stand it any longer—the moonlight was calling me out for a visit. I put on my boots, down jacket, and wind jacket too, and headed out into the cold moonlight. It was a bright moon, just the way I like it. I brought along a pair of clear goggles to see if I could hike through the woods with them on. Yes, they worked great—no worry about limbs poking your eyes out. But I couldn't see nearly as good around the sides of my vision, which is important to me, especially at night in the woods, so I took off the goggles and went back to hiking with my hands out in front in questionable areas.

The trees, and their shadows, and the stars, and the moonlight were all magnificent! It was cold, but I headed uphill and quickly warmed up. The wind was blowing, and it really bit my face, which was uncovered. I went on up to the Faddis Meadow, where there were millions of stars out. I stopped and chatted with one of the big hickory trees next to the lane. When you looked up into the sky, each of the hundreds of silhouetted little branches pointed to a star. And the patterns of the shadows on the ground were amazing. This old tree had a great deal of character.

I realized that since no one was at the Faddis cabin, or down at Bob's, and there were no cars at the Crag Trailhead, that I was probably the only person on this part of the mountain tonight. I love crowds. I treasure time with close friends. But sometimes you find yourself alone, and I both need and cherish those times as well. I guess I have much more alone time than any other, and more than most people.

I slipped on down through the woods to the bench below the meadow, where the maple stand is. The forest there is all open underneath, and the moonlight/stars/trees were spectacular! It was like walking through another world down there, not really light out, but not really dark either. There was a great deal of detail in the shadows, but nothing sharp or focused. All of it was kind of in between.

The wind had died down a little, and I decided to lay back in the leaves and study the forest and the moonlight and the stars. I reached out and brought up a pile of leaves close to me on either side for a little extra warmth. I don't go to any church to worship. I feel like I *live* in a church, the Church of the Wilderness, and I sure could feel an Almighty Power all around me this night. I don't know, you just have to go out in the middle of the night in the winter and lay down in the leaves to know what I mean.

Then I heard footsteps. They were soft and muted, more like a rustling than footsteps. I strained to hear, yet kept very still. I rolled over just a little to get a good view—a family of deer came slipping through the trees, backlit by the moon. They were cautious, only moving one at a time, and just for a few feet, stopping in between each series of steps to look around in all directions, and listen, and reach down and grab a nut or something else to munch on every once in a while. They came down across the bench, and headed towards the lower bench. They never saw or scented me. I was watching them for maybe two or three minutes. That was a marvelous gift indeed! How much more could anyone ask for—the moonlight, trees, stars, and deer to boot!

The chill worked its way into my bones, and so I got up and headed back to the cabin. Everything was quiet as I walked down the lane, the moon at my back. As I got closer to the cabin an unknown shadow appeared ahead. It wasn't a deer. There was no movement. I am normally not spooked much on these night hikes, but this shadow was beginning to tug at me a little. What the heck was it? A chill ran down my back, and it wasn't from the cold. Well, I didn't think that there were any bears out and up above the bluffline at this time of the year, and certainly it wasn't a person, so I just decided to walk on and spook it up and see what it was. I got closer, and closer, and closer, and still it was motionless. The echo of my laughter echoed through the forest—it was nothing more than an old stump! I'll bet all the other critters out watching me had a good laugh too.

The wind chimes mixed with the night air called me back towards my log haven. Through the windows I could see the shadows of the flickering flames on the walls. It looked mighty inviting in there. And it was. Fine music, a warm fire, the moonlight, and another day at Cloudland drew to a close.

Merry Christmas to all, and Happy New Year. Let's hope it's a good one, without any tears...

12/26/98 Early orange glow in the eastern sky. Above were pink clouds against a blue sky. Slowly, the color faded, then the bright sun peeked out over the hill and through the trees, warming all that it touched. There were great contrasts out in the forest this morning—bright detail in the sunny parts, and coal black where no light had reached yet.

I had a Starbucks mocha, w/Grape Nuts and yogurt, stoked up the fire, then descended into the basement to get things ready for the work day. Scott Crook from Fayetteville showed up about mid-morning to help with the aspen. And he brought all of the tools—an air compressor, hose, nail gun), and lunch. What more could you ask for—all of that plus free labor to boot!

We spent the rest of the morning, and all afternoon putting up the aspen boards in the downstairs guest room. Wow, what an improvement! We were only able to get two main walls done, and half of a third, but it was already looking like a guest room instead of some cold space in the basement. It took 19 rows of the 1 x 6 inch boards to reach the ceiling on each wall. Neither of us are finish carpenters, but we do OK.

Scott also helped put up many of the other aspen walls here. (He and his wife, Carolyn, own the Pack Rat Outdoor Center in Fayetteville.)

I had wanted to do all of the walls with simple drywall and paint, then with an all-wood siding, but both plans had been vetoed by my many guests, so I decided to spring for the extra $$$ and do the aspen. It is wonderful stuff, light in color and in weight, and easy to work with. Once it is all up, I will spray it with a clear coating, and then that will be it—the natural color will shine on through, and it won't darken much through the years. Aspen is on all of the non-log walls in the cabin, and up on the ceiling. The porch ceilings are pine.

We worked pretty steadily through the day, with only one break for visitors (well, we did take a couple of other breaks, but only for pecan pie—via Scott's wife Carolyn—homemade pies are required for the carpenter work out here at the cabin). As we were getting to the last of the pile of boards, the western and southern skies lit up with an incredible light display of multi-colored clouds against a brilliant blue sky. It was wonderful.

Later, I made a big pan of Banff Pasta, and had some muscadine wine to go with it (a clash of cultures I know, but what the heck). The moon and stars were out shining brightly, and the wind was kicking up a bit, making the 30 degree temp feel rather chilly. It had climbed up into the low 40's during the day, and is supposed to get up into the 50's tomorrow.

One odd thing that I noticed today—we never saw a single living thing, except for a couple of visitors. No birds of any kind, no squirrels, no nothing. It was a gorgeous day out, as winter days with full sun are apt to be here, but I guess the wildlife was all inside recovering from all of the Christmas parties.

I think that I am the only person out here on the mountain again tonight—no one at the Faddis or Chester cabins, and the trailhead is empty. It is a great time of the year to be outside, or at least sitting in your warm and toasty cabin gazing out into the cold moonlight.

No wild music tonight—just a little folk Christmas music from Mike Shirkey's *Pickin' Post* on KUAF. The fire is hot, and it is 66 degrees in the cabin.

I've only got three or four things to do tomorrow—put up a bunch more aspen downstairs and clean up all of the mess, write the OHTA newsletter, and go hiking. And I might have to cut, split and stack a little wood too. And maybe go on a couple of hikes.

12/27/98 It was a grey morning, with windchills down in the low teens. I got up, just a little late, and got to work on the newsletter. By noon I had it finished, and sat down for a big salad for lunch. Sundays are always a big day for visitors, and there had already been a couple of groups by in the morning.

It was getting warmer outside, in the low 40's, but didn't look like it was going to get much higher. The sun would break through the clouds now and then, and send a stream of sunshine down into the forest. The wind had settled down some, and I was ready to get out and go hiking.

There wasn't much out moving but me—I couldn't even find a single squirrel. However, as I got closer to the Faddis Meadow, I began to see birds. All kinds of birds. Lots of little, nondescript brown and white ones, and lots of bright flashes of red and blue too—cardinals and blue jays. It was good to see some life stirring about. It was a glorious day, especially when the sun peeked through.

I discovered an entire herd of people down at Bob's cabin. Bob wasn't there, and no one knew who was staying in the cabin—there was a white truck in the driveway, and a fire in the wood stove. But I did know many of the others, who had just stopped by to say hi to Bob. It was the Dodson clan, a family that I had known long ago when I was in high school. I used to swim with several of their kids, and a couple of them were here today. I hadn't seen one of them since high school graduation, over 25 years ago.

I moved on down towards Dug Hollow. After leaving the North Meadow, I just kind of drifted down through the forest, with no specific route in mind. It was easy hiking, and I sort of swung side to side from tree to tree. Anyone watching me would have thought that I was nuts, or was just a big kid, but I had a good time. Trees and I speak the same language sometimes, and we were today. They were loving the bursts of sunshine too, and the warmer temps.

All of a sudden I stopped and looked around, a little confused. I was completely lost in a grove of beech trees—several dozen really big ones, and hundreds and hundreds of small ones. I had always come off of the hillside above to one side or the other and always missed this particular spot on the hill. The big trees went on and on and on. I bet there were 40 or 50 of them. Perhaps the largest stand of mature beeches that I had ever seen. Just one after another after another. And then all of those little ones—they were *everywhere!* And all of them still had their full complement of leaves, all golden and crunchy and beaming in the sunshine. They were so thick, and you really couldn't walk in any direction without brushing against the leaves on both sides. I've always loved beech trees, but this grove was really special. I will return here again.

From the beeches I dropped on down the hill and came to the top of a waterfall. Holy smokes, you should have seen the ice formations! I didn't expect any ice, especially since it had been above freezing now for a couple of days. I carefully made my way down through the bluff—there were a few frozen spots. Ice hanging from the bluff on both sides of the falls, ice piles up all around the base of the falls, and ice flows in many other places too. It was one gorgeous spot I'll tell ya. And it was about time I gave this waterfall a name, so I have decided to call it "Stairstep Falls," since there is a flight of "steps" going up the bluff on one side of the falls where it is possible to get through the bluff.

I hadn't planned on going by the Dug Hollow waterfalls, but if there was this much ice around, I had to go take a look and see what I could find up there. All along the bluffline between Stairstep Falls and the Dug Hollow falls area, there were ice flows and icicles everywhere. And they were all white, or clear, instead of the muddy ones that I had seen elsewhere. I'd never seen such a highly decorated bluffline before. Even where the bluff was covered with moss there were ice flows—and the pure white of the ice and rich green of the moss looked unusual together. I even found one spot where the ice flow was completely clear, and you could see the moss right through it—the ice was green!

And then I got to the falls area. And yes, there was tons of *ice!* I had never been to this area with ice on before, but had always heard how wonderful it was. And the stories were correct. No telling how heavy some of the ice was, and even though it was melting, I was surprised that I never saw or heard a single crash. You will often get ice falling on warm days like this, when it begins to melt and loosens its grip on the rock. It is also very dangerous to walk along the base of blufflines when there is lots of ice, especially on warm days. But no crashes today. I could see where many ice formations had fallen off though.

All of this bluffline was on the south side of the canyon, which was facing to the north. The sun never finds its way along this side of the canyon in the wintertime, which was why the ice was still there. The opposite side of the canyon wall had hardly any ice at all.

This Dug Hollow area is certainly one magical place when the ice is on. I'm coming back when there is even more ice, and bringing my real camera and lots of film! I did have my little point and shoot camera with me today, and took a few snapshots, but they don't show anything like what was really there.

I made it a point to hike back to the cabin via a different route than I had ever taken before, and I did see some new country. Unfortunately, most of it was country that had been logged several years ago, and was grown up with thick brush, most of it briars! The area was full of new little trees too, and I know will be back to normal before too long. There were lots of nearly-mature trees too (kind of like me). The locals who cut the timber out did so using the select method, and they only took a few trees here and there.

Once I got back to the cabin I sat down and did a final edit on the newsletter. From my seat at the computer I saw movement out of the corner of my eye. There was a person standing just a few feet away out on the deck. It was Dana, one of the Dodson crew. They had all hiked down to the Crag and several of them hiked on over to the cabin (at my earlier invite). Before long it was wall to wall folks, and we all had a good visit.

I knew most of the people from my high school days, but there were a few new faces, including Eve, a transplanted Arkansawyer now living in Virginia. She was telling me how the Ozarks just "felt" a lot different than the Blue Ridge. She said the woods there were sad. I think that our Ozark hills are much happier, and she could sense that. I hope to have a new Cloudland reader in the Blue Ridge (it would be great to compare the weather, fall color, etc.).

I could tell that Dana had been reading the on-line Cloudland Journal as she quoted a number of things from several months ago that happened out here. And she said that "Your Journal makes me lust for the mountains, and I am living vicariously through your writing." And her sister, Lee Ann, who was in my class in high school, wrote on my lamp shade "Cloudland is a beautiful dream, a place to remember and savor when one is so far away from home." She lives in Florida now. What wonderful things for them to say!

It was a nice visit, and I enjoyed seeing them all. Soon the cabin was all quiet again. I finished up the newsletter, then headed downstairs and worked some more on the aspen. I was able to use most of the scraps on two very short wall sections. The rest of the scraps will be used to start up the fireplace. I will bring out another load of aspen when I return later in the week—it will take 40 more eight footers and 12 ten footers to finish up the downstairs guest room, and to redo the upstairs guest room when I get the closet torn out.

The guest room has always felt cramped to me, and so I have decided to remove the closet. In explaining my decision to do so to Scott yesterday, I told him that no one brings hang-up clothes out here when they visit anyway. He added that I probably didn't have any friends that even owned hang-up clothes!

Before I knew it the grey skies had turned black, and I had to feel my way through the cabin to turn on a light upstairs. I hauled a few arm loads of wood up, but never got around to cutting or splitting any new stuff. The wood pile is getting rather small, and I'll probably have to cut up wood sometime this week. I hope it snows—few things in life are as enjoyable to me as cutting firewood in the falling snow. I guess if I lived where it snowed all the time, and I was *forced* out into the snow to cut firewood every day, I wouldn't like it so much. Until that happens, I'll continue to look forward to the snow, and the firewood chore. Sometimes the simplest pleasures are the best.

After listening to NPR this morning I realized that the planet that has been next to the moon this week is not Jupiter at all (not at this time of the year anyway), but Saturn. I swear that I saw several of Jupiter's moons the other night through the tele. But then I had downed a glass or two of that great dark beer, and Grand Funk was shaking the cabin a little. I'll bow to the experts. It is too cloudy to see anything tonight, although the moon is high overhead and showing through just a little. It is nearly half-full.

All of my chores are done, I've written the newsletter, updated the Journal, answered all of my e-mail, and downed a big bowl of veggie soup for dinner. Guess all there is left to do is sip a little wine, enjoy some music, and go to bed. I've got to get up very early in the morning, and get into my office in town before 8am, then get the newsletter to the printer. Monday is always the busiest day of the week for me, and I do *love* Mondays! Really. The more that I can get done in town, the sooner I can return to Cloudland.

12/29/98 The cabin was rather chilly when I crawled out from under the down comforter. My usual routine in the morning is to stoke up the fire, then stand in front of it sipping my chilled Starbucks mocha. There was no fire this morning, and I didn't know where to stand. There was no warm place to stand and sip the cold drink, so I went back upstairs and had my mocha in bed, under the warm covers.

It was actually rather warm outside—felt warmer than inside the cabin, although it wasn't. The temp was in the upper 30's, and the sun was out.

I worked down in the Aspen guest room some, using up the remainder of the scraps that were there on the "short" walls. It was looking pretty nice. I would have enough aspen to finish the walls and the front of the closet with me the next time that I came out. I wandered out onto the deck and was blown away by the terrific view of the main river far upstream. The sun was at just the right angle, and you could see the river shimmering and winding back and forth for several miles upstream. I don't remember ever seeing this much of the river before. Since it is lined with trees the entire way (well, except for where the tornado got it), it is difficult to see the water unless the sun is just right.

I bid the river and the sun good-bye and headed to town to finish processing the newsletter, and to get supplies for the upcoming New Year's Eve Party.

12/30/98 When I arrived back at the cabin after dark I discovered that I had missed a rather cold morning—it had gotten down to seven below zero wind-chill factor that morning, with the wind whipping up to 28mph. It was 49 degrees in the cabin. I cleaned out the fireplace, and got a big fire going. Then the phone began to ring.

Billy Woods called and said that he needed to receive a fax sometime during the weekend, and he knew that I had the only fax on the mountain, and wondered if I would receive it? This fax machine thing has turned into an important job in the community! Several other people called too. I think there were more calls this evening than any other day in Cloudland history.

It took me a while to unload the van—I had a ton of stuff, mostly food, for the upcoming party. I never know quite what to bring. There were going to be as many as 18 folks here for two days, and all of them had been assigned food, but I didn't want to run out, so I doubled up on a few things, and got other stuff, just in case. Plus, I had planned to be here for five days, and Emily was coming out later tonight and was going to stay for several days also. So I needed lots of food. And I had it. Oh yea, and there was lots of booze—just in case we got snowed in, or attacked by a herd of winter snakes (whiskey = snakebite medicine, you know).

The entire downstairs was a mess—sawdust and tools and scrap aspen everywhere. I dove into it, and within a couple of hours had everything looking, well, more like a basement and less like a construction zone. I even arranged the tool room a little, and the utility room. I've had a nice front-loading clothes washer in that room for six months, but have never purchased a dryer to go along with it, nor built a platform to put it all on, so the washer remains boxed up for now. It makes a good place to pile stuff on. Wow, the basement hadn't been this clean in a very long time. I prefer it this way.

Once all of the chores were done I got down to the serious business of enjoying the night with a roaring fire and some good music. And then there was all that food. Now it was quite tempting I must tell you—this skinny boy who had lost all of that weight during the holidays, now starving, sitting right next to a kitchen full of food for 18—mostly party food, junk food, the best kind for a hungry boy late at night. And I must say that I did graze a little. Well, I grazed a little too much I'm sure, but it was hardly noticed.

And then one more phone call came in. I would have rather it didn't. It was

Emily, and she had gotten sick on her way out to the cabin, and had to turn around and go home. She was really looking forward to several days off in a row, and spending some time in the woods, but now all she could do was go to bed and hope for the best. She sounded really miserable, and I felt bad for her, but there was nothing I could do short of offering my sympathy. She is one tough cookie, and would bounce back.

So there was somewhat of a gloom over the rest of the night, but the moon helped out a little. It helped a lot. Looking out the window, the forest was so bright that I kept thinking it must have snowed. Two days to the full moon.

I turned up the music, lit a lamp, and spread some paperwork out on the dining table and worked. The moon and the music and the fire and the cabin—not a bad work environment at all. I really do enjoy most of my work. Creating a good place to slave away helps. But enough of this work—the moon was out and I had some hiking to do!

So I bundled up and headed out into the bright night air. It was 29 degrees, and I put on my down coat and ear muffs. I have said many times that the best time to hike at night is during a half-moon—I was wrong! This night was the best time to hike!!! I couldn't believe how *bright* it was outside! Wonderful, just wonderful. It was cold out, but there was no wind, so I didn't have to hike hard to stay warm. I got to just wander around in the moonlight, enjoying it all.

One tree that I came across cast a shadow on the ground that looked just like a giant spider. Other shadows blended together to form what I call "moon art" on the forest floor. The shadows are impossible to photograph (since the moon moves, so do the shadows, and they change shape constantly), but I guess you could draw it if you were fast enough.

It was nearly midnight when I reached the Faddis cabin, and I was surprised to find a truck there. No lights on inside though. I didn't recognize the truck. I wondered if they knew there was someone lurking outside? If they saw me in the moonlight they would probably think I was a bear. Oops, not a good idea to lurk around the outside of cabins in the middle of the night in bear country.

I hiked on over to the East Meadow to see what I could find there. I was walking fast, and as I approached the edge of the meadow, I thought to myself that I had better slow down and take a look into the meadow first to see if there was anyone out there. Too late. Before I could slow down, there were flashes of white everywhere. Deer. Lots of deer. They had been grazing no doubt in the bright moonlight, and could easily see me approaching. They took off in all directions. Five, six, seven. I counted eight white tails. That's about all of the animal that I could see, except for a dark blur in front of the white.

Hiking in the moonlight has become about as normal to me as during the day. I used to be afraid of my own shadow. But now that I have danced with bears in the moonlight, the nighttime just doesn't seem so scary. But something was a little different this night. As I continued across the field, a chill ran down my back as I spotted a dark object out in the middle of the field. It wasn't moving. Neither was I at first. But it didn't look like anything really, so I walked on towards it. Nothing more than a pile of rolled up fence. Someone had placed it there recently because I don't remember it. Then there was another dark object off to the right. It turned out to be a small cedar tree. My mind was working overtime, and on minimum wage. I was glad to get out of the field and into the woods. That seemed a little odd to me. You would think that I would feel safer out in the open meadow where I could see everything. But the woods are my home, and where I feel the most comfortable.

And the deep woods were lit up more this night than I had remembered. I could see every twig and leaf. The forest floor was very smooth, like the wind had placed every leaf just so. As I walked down the hillside across the smooth leaves, I turned around and could see my tracks in the leaves.

As I approached the cabin the familiar glow of the logs welcomed me with a warm smile. It was toasty inside. A walk in the moonlight always makes me feel great. Too bad it was a walk alone. But I had my trees with me.

Up in the loft I stepped out onto the small deck there for a minute to listen to the river. It was singing a peppy tune. And I could see the big dipper and the north star from the deck—don't recall ever seeing them from that spot before.

A hot shower felt very good. As I settled back under the flannel sheets the cabin was very quiet. The fireplace flared up, and shadows danced across the ceiling. The dancing shadows sent me away in short order.

12/31/98 I was up before sunup, knowing that I had a full plate. The fire was going as I finished my mocha. Then a bright sun poked its head above the far ridge—clear blue skies today!

The first order of business was to install a couple of iron hangers at opposite corners of the upper back deck. Then put together and fill up two bird feeders that I had bought the day before. At last, bird feeders at Cloudland! I got the kind that are a combination of a tube feeder and platform feeder. They went together and up easily. Alright, I had feeders. Now all I needed was birds. I really expected for them to come flocking as soon as I backed away, but, of course, that didn't happen. Just as well—I had lots of other work to do.

Next on the list was to finish putting up the aspen in the lower guest room, now that I had a plentiful supply of it. I jumped right into it, sawing and measuring and using the nail gun as fast as I could. There were a lot of same-length boards to put up, so I was able to cut many of them in a row, then nail them up, and this process went pretty fast. I did have to pause now and then to gaze out the windows to see what was going on outside. The view is nice from this bedroom. It was getting warm outside.

The sawdust piled up and soon all of the boards were in place. Oh boy, an Aspen bedroom! It looked pretty darn nice. Of course, there was still a bare, *cold* cement floor, but I would take care of that later. And none of the trim was up, and the closet wasn't finished, but at least it looked more like a real guest room now. I liked it. After a lot of sweeping and vacuuming, the downstairs looked nice again. Very presentable to a crowd of party-goers.

Emily was going to spend the day down in the meadow in back getting parts of it ready for wildflower planting, but she was still sick, and sounded like she was getting worse when she called in the early afternoon. I wished her well. I felt a little helpless. But I know that when I get sick, the last thing that I want to see is another person—especially someone that I know. I just want to crawl into bed and stay there in the dark until I am well.

I continued with my chores. One of them was to clean out the fireplace and get the glass shining. My fireplace is designed to keep the glass generally clear of soot, which it does a pretty good job of—I hadn't cleaned it since last year, and you could still see through it well. But it was a little dingy, and so I used this special soot cleaner that my fireplace guy gave me—*wow*, it worked wonders! I soon had a nice clean fireplace with sparkling glass.

All during the day I kept my eyes glued to the bird feeders, expecting to see a flock at each one. Nothing. Not a single feather was spotted all day. I guess they all were being well-fed somewhere else. But I knew they were out there, and would find my little all-you-can-eat restaurants sooner or later.

Once the cabin was swept and vacuumed in its entirety, and everything put away, I sat down on the couch with a beer. Everything looked good. I was ready for company.

The first to show up was Hete. He had a big ham to cook. Not only did he cook it, but he injected it with some magical liquid stuff that made the cabin smell incredible. All of the other guests that showed up were greeted with this wonderful fragrance. And then they got to eat it.

Hete had a plan for a date. His first plan fell through though, so he went to plan B. That was looking pretty good, until the weather forecast turned sour. She backed out. I had invited someone for him just in case, so he was covered. Always have a plan C. (Of course, I didn't have a date at all!)

The fire was roaring, the ham was a cooking, and guests arrived throughout the evening, all bearing goodies for dinner. We had planned to eat late, after 8pm, but folks were showing up earlier than they expected, so we pushed dinner up a little. Carolyn became the official ham taster. We all wanted to know if it was done. She would have to check. And check she did—samples were passed around. And again. And again. Then I put out the official Cloudland appetizers. We had chips with three different kinds of dips. Dottie and Steve Hobbs provided the best—a homemade bean dip. As far as I could tell, all of the food got rave reviews.

The noise level in the cabin got slowly higher and higher as more folks showed up, more food was put out, and more bottles of spirits were opened. I didn't realize it when I started inviting folks, but this would turn out to be the largest crowd for a party at Cloudland. Fine with me!

When it was finally time for the main course, and we uncovered the ham that Carolyn had been in charge of, we discovered that there wasn't too much of it left! But there was plenty, along with smoked turkey, and side dishes as far as the eye could see. And we even had enough seats for everyone.

After the smoke cleared, there loomed two very large cheesecakes that Keiko Peterson had made. One was chocolate. I don't know what the other one was. But with all the food and booze, I could sense the crowd was already beginning to fade. What? It was only 9pm. No fading at this party. I wouldn't allow it. So I had a plan. "Bundle up everyone, we're going on a hike!"

The moon was nearly full and it was as bright as could be outside, but it was the middle of winter, and a little brisk. Some were skeptical. But hey, when at Cloudland, do as the Cloudlanders do. So nearly everyone followed me out the door and up the lane.

It was wonderful out, of course, but the cold slowed folks down a bit. I picked up the pace, hoping that would help warm everyone up. And it did. Before long, we all were joking and carrying on like it was the middle of summer. We took a short cut over to the East Meadow—couldn't find any critters out, or at least any willing to stick around while our little noisy bunch approached. It was really bright. Several in the group had been to the meadow during one of the meteor shower parties.

We headed on over to the Faddis cabin, and used it as sort of a warming hut. No fire inside, but it was warmer because the wind wasn't blowing. After a short tour of the cabin, we headed out into the moonlight once again. I wonder what all of the wildlife up in the trees thought about all of the wildlife down on the ground as we passed? Soon we were back at the cabin, and the group that returned was much more alive than the one that left. This would prove to be pivotal, and would keep everyone up well past midnight.

It was warm and toasty inside, and time for cheesecake! And then the music got louder. And the champagne bottles began to pop. There was dancing in the streets, or well, in the main room anyway. As the night wore on, the only folks who drifted off were the three that didn't go on the night hike. Hum.

Long about midnight we lined up the champagne bottles and aimed them at the top beam in the big room—it was 23 feet above, and the target of our corks. POP, pop, pop. Mine hit the beam just below the top one. The Wildman's went everywhere but missed the top beam. Then Bob Robinson popped his—and hit the top beam dead on! He also spilled some of his. At last, the top beam was reached (first time in Cloudland history). We will select a new and more difficult target the next time.

As the new day and year began the music got louder, and folks hit the dance floor. I have noticed that with my crowd of friends that while most of them do dance, they only do so in small groups—I've never seen everyone up dancing at the same time before. I put on some Grand Funk. Then Black Oak Arkansas. And, of course, the standard *"In Them Old, Cotton Fields Back Home."*

It was getting late, about 1:30am, and I decided it was time to put on some real music. When the very first chords of *"I Should Have Known Better"* sounded, everyone jumped up and hit the dance floor! I always enjoy watching people dance. That is about the only real time that you can see genuine affection between a couple. You can see the love in their eyes, and in their body motions.

It is just the two of them, dancing together, no matter how many others are out there with them. And there is intense pleasure, not only in listening to the music and moving their bodies, but in being with each other. A lovely sight. And everyone in the room was doing this, well, except for me. I had no one to dance with, but I was loving the music, so I slipped back into the shadows and danced away anyway. It was a fine group of friends. No better music ever made. I deemed the party a success.

And so now I have come to the end of the very first full calendar year at Cloudland. And what a trip it has been! The year that had begun with a very solemn and gloomy outlook for me, ended on a very high note. Heck, most of the entire year was one big high note! Cloudland is a treasure, a very special place to live, and to visit, and to think about for me. The quantity of the fine wilderness experiences that I have had out here were topped only by the quality of my friends. My only resolution for the New Year was to spend more time at Cloudland, and to make it an even better place for my friends to visit and enjoy. Thank *you* for being a part of it all, and for reading this Journal!

JANUARY 1999

1/1/99 There were bodies all over the cabin. Six or eight on the main level, six or eight in the basement, a couple out on the deck, and me in the loft. It was actually a pretty calm party, with no real casualties. The only one that came close was Carolyn. She is the one who got into the ham early, and the wine, and she spent most of the dancing part of the night laid back in the big leather chair next to the fireplace, sleeping. It is one thing to sleep through all of the dancing and the music, but one of the two big sub-woofer speakers was directly under her head, and it was really pumping out the base, and we couldn't believe that she wasn't rattled right out of her seat. She did say that she woke up once and looked over and saw Bob Robinson down on the floor flopping like a whale, and so she decided she didn't want to see any more and so went back to sleep. Bob way trying to do some dance where he danced across the floor on his belly—he wasn't very good at it, but did manage to polish the floor some.

My first recollection of the new year was an intense yellow light. The bright sunshine bounced around the room and looked pretty neat. The yellow only lasted for a few minutes, then it disappeared, and I knew it was time to get up. Carolyn was already up and making coffee. She was the breakfast cook, and before long there were many warm bodies milling about, and fresh waffles on the griddle.

It was cold and icy outside. It had started to sleet or something at about 6 in the morning, and everything was covered with a layer of ice. (The sun broke through the clouds for only a minute). I immediately checked on the bird feeders, and not only found them to be quite scenic with all of the ice on them, but there were *birds* on them!!! Yea, at last, feathered friends had returned to Cloudland. They were all goldfinches, and they seemed to be enjoying the seed, even though they had to break through the ice.

Back to the kitchen. Hete was giving a lesson about bananas, and how they will actually come apart in thirds. Scott had to check it out, and found Hete to be telling the truth. I noticed that Roy had positioned himself at the bar within easy reach of where the waffles were being stacked. There was always a waffle on his plate. Good thinking.

Everyone survived the night, although Luke and Mary did kind of get blown off of the deck when the ice storm began. No hangovers that I could detect, and lots of smiling faces. It was brought to my attention that one of the carved wooden bears down on the back deck was not the same—he had two long icicles hanging from his mouth. He was promptly named the "Saber Tooth Bear," and got a lot of pictures taken of him.

The big thing this morning was that Hete, Bob Robinson and the Wildman were all supposed to hike down to the river and go for a swim. Yea, right. The trail was covered with ice, and I don't think they had planned on it being so cold. They quizzed me about the pond up at Bob Chester's—was there enough water in it for a swim? Lordy, I wouldn't swim in that thing on a hot summer day. Yuk. But, by golly they wanted to take a dip, so they bundled up and headed up the hill towards the pond. Well, Bob was all ready to swim, Hete went along for moral support, and the Wildman stayed back at the cabin.

The two troopers hiked to the pond, then on down to Bob's cabin to see what he was up to. Bob called us and said that they were indeed going to go for a swim, and suggested that someone run up the hill to pull out the frozen bodies before hypothermia set in. Before anyone had mounted a rescue mission, Hete and Bob showed up at the cabin. They had decided to do the swim in the pond, but wanted some reinforcements first. The Wildman was ready to go by this time as well. I counted eleven folks heading up the hill to the pond—most of them to watch.

I can't give you a first-hand account of the plunge, but I do know that the mighty three did brave the muddy, icy waters of the pond, and emerged OK. The only problem was that Bob sat down on a frozen rock to dry off, and his left cheek froze in place (yikes!). The only complaint that I heard from the group came from the bystanders—it seems that the Wildman went in, in the buff! I'll bet none of those guys will be able to find it for a couple of days.

Scott and Luke and I attacked the closet in the main guest room—and I do mean attacked it. I knew that closet was a mistake as soon as I had finished it last year. It just made the room too small, and no one was using it anyway. So we tore it out. Stick by stick. And within fifteen minutes, there was a lot more room in the guest room! It looked *so* much better. I had the aspen board to put in place (I hadn't finished the walls inside the cabin yet, so it was bare studs with insulation), but needed some more insulation first, so we elected to leave the walls bare for now.

Before the swimmers had returned the kitchen crew had everything cleaned up, and a new wave of cooks arrived. Ken and Terry Eastin drove up from Fayetteville. They had to stay home to take care of the kids, but did bring out New Year's brunch, complete with black-eyed peas, greens and corn bread. By the time the swimmers returned, brunch was well on its way.

There was a big football game on TV, and Bob and Dawna headed back up to Bob's cabin to watch it before brunch was ready. They are die-hard Razorback fans. This was one time when a TV might have been a good idea at Cloudland, for a group to watch a football game, but since Bob had satellite TV at his cabin, it wasn't really needed. For now. Thank goodness.

We all dug into the brunch, even though we had just finished breakfast a short time earlier. It was great. During the feed there was an eye exam being administered. The weather station served as the chart, and it had to be read from the dining table. Most everyone could read the temp—it had been 31 degrees all day. We did notice that the wind gauge was not working, as it had been showing 0-mph all morning, and there was an obvious breeze. I went on over and changed the display to read the inside temp, and all of a sudden no one could read it but me. Hum. Before the group left, the outside temp clicked up one to 32, so it was working, the temp had just been hovering at 31 degrees.

The weather seemed to be getting worse, and the forecast called for it to get really bad. As soon as brunch was completed, Dottie and Steve cleaned up all the dishes, and everyone packed up and left, all en masse. Within fifteen minutes, the cabin was empty.

When Bob and Dawna returned to Cloudland after halftime, they were a little surprised to find everyone gone. There was plenty of brunch left though, so they had a plate, and then took off themselves. I found myself laying back in the leather chair in the middle of a suddenly very quiet cabin. That was OK with me—there was still lots of laughter bouncing around me.

Even though we had a big group, and the water system was taxed a great deal, we never ran out of water. One of these days I may even let the guys pee inside instead of having to brave the cold/heat in order to save water.

I didn't linger in the chair too long, as I soon got up and began to clean up the place a little. My guests left the place in very good condition, as they always do, but for some reason I felt like putting a real shine on the place. I spent a half hour polishing the map bar, and the rest of the kitchen, then vacuumed some, and generally got everything neat and tidy.

Then I returned to the chair. The temp stayed at 32 degrees, and it began to rain. I love to hike in the rain, when it is warm, and I really enjoy hiking in the snow. But when the temp is in the 30's and it is raining, well, that is about the most miserable conditions that I know of to be hiking in. So I stayed inside, and took a nap or two.

Emily called to check in and said that she was beginning to feel better (that was odd for someone to be sick *before* New Year's, and then feel better the next day—it is usually the other way around! I found out later she had been faking and was never really sick—she did not want to be seen with me at a party).

Today was the first of two full moons in January. I doubted that I would get to see it, as the weather continued outside. There was a lot of food left from the party and feast, so I munched my way through the rest of the afternoon and into the evening. The rain picked up, and not only was it coming down hard, but it began to thunder and lightning! Goodness, that doesn't happen too much in the middle of the winter.

I fired up the computer and started to answer some e-mail, and work a little on the Journal, and then the power began to flicker. The computer shut down. Darn. I lost this big e-mail that I had been working on. The power was only off for a few seconds, but long enough to mess up the computer. I got it up and running again, and retyped my e-mail. Then the power went down again. Darn, lost it once more. This power flickering thing would become a trend.

Then the power went out for good. No computer, no lights. I sat there in the dark and enjoyed the fire. It was raining a lot outside, and there were clouds forming and dancing around in the valley below. I wrote some by candlelight—it felt like I should be using a feather quill pen! Then I decided it was time to call it a night, so by 8:30pm I was on my way up the stairs to the loft. I figured the power would be back on again soon, as it has never been off for very long. I was tired anyway. There actually was a great deal of light around—coming from the lightning flashes outside. The rain was really coming down too.

Just as I was drifting off to sleep the phone rang downstairs in the guest room. I have telephones all over the cabin, but the one in the guest room is the only one that does not require electricity, and so is the only one that works when there is no power. I got up slowly and made my way down the steps in the dark and into the guest room. I was *so* glad that I answered the phone—it was Emily, she was feeling a lot better, and was on her way out to the cabin. There had been somewhat of a somber mood in the air ever since she first called and was sick two days before, but all of that was instantly swept away, and a big smile landed on me. Good thing the cabin was all cleaned up!

I thought for sure the power would be back on again before she arrived, but just in case, I ran around and gathered up all of the candles that I could find. Oh yea, I forgot to tell ya. Luke and Mary had given me this wonderful, long four-wick candle that sits on the mantle. We had it going full blast during the party, but one of the wicks burned a hole through the back of the candle and lots of wax poured out. It spilled onto the mantle, then down onto the face of the fireplace, and finally pooled up in the grindstone that is set into the hearth. Yikes, there was hot candle wax everywhere!

When Emily arrived she said that the paved roads were OK, but the dirt road from Red Star was covered with ice and rather slick.

1/2/99 The forecast was for heavy snow, but that didn't really happen. It did snow during the night, but only an inch or so. It was a winter wonderland outside just the same, and the feeders were full of birds. They were segregated though—goldfinches on the east feeder, and juncos on the west feeder.

The power was still off. I stoked up the fire, and had in fact kept it going strong all night, so the main rooms were pleasantly warm (it was so warm in fact that I had a window open next to the bed all night). I rummaged around and found a backpacking stove and we heated up some water for hot chocolate.

Bob Chester called and was OK—I'm sure it was about 80 degrees in his cabin. His little wood stove does a great job of heating it up. But he did have a problem—his bird feeders were all empty, he had mad birds flying around everywhere, and he was afraid to make the trek to the woodshed for the bird seed without someone else being around (he did that once and fell and really messed up his knee). We wanted to get out and go on a hike, so we volunteered to come on over and rescue his birds.

We bundled up and headed out into the snow. It was very nice, but rather cold. As we reached the edge of the East Meadow two things happened. First, a bitter north wind hit us right in the face; and secondly, a coyote dashed across the meadow right in front of us. He was in a big hurry to get away from us, and even though he raced across the widest part of the meadow, he never so much as paused once to look back at us—he didn't like us, and he wasn't about to stop and talk about it. He was a beautiful critter though, and I guess you could say that he was really "dashing through the snow." Sorry about that.

We made it to Bob's, and found him cheery and warm inside. We helped him fill his feeders, which the birds just loved, then sat around for a while in front of the wood stove listening to his stories. He made us some hot chocolate and coffee to drink, then topped it off with whipped cream—very nice.

From Bob's we headed up the hill and then down to the Crag. It was pretty nice walking, although the wind was still blowing, and it was a might chilly. From the Crag we made our way along the top of the bluff, admiring all of the big sandstone blocks and interesting trees along the way. I knew that all the rain would create some nice waterfalls, so we hiked on over to the double-decker waterfall at the far end of the bluff.

We climbed down one icy bluff to get a better view of the upper falls, and spent some time under the overhang. There were some interesting ice formations there, and the waterfall was really cooking. We also found an Indian grindstone, and then Emily spotted some petrified wood up in the ceiling. What, petrified wood? Yep, sure enough. I had heard someone else talk about it, but had never seen any myself. This had to be some of it. There was also a phoebe nest tucked away under the bluff. A nice spot to hang out, but the falls were a little noisy, and it was getting colder by the minute.

It didn't take us too long to get back to the cabin, and we had warmed up a bit by then, and so spent some time down in the lower meadow taking a look at what needed to be done in order to get the area ready for wildflowers. It was going to take a lot of work—digging up small trees and bushes and clearing out a bunch of other stuff, then scratching the ground a little and planting seed. The area was probably too large to do all at once, so we decided that we might open up several areas first this winter and spring, then do more as time permitted.

A big flock of geese flew past—heading due south. They were a few days late, but looked to be having a good time. Normally a flock is all either snow geese (all white) or Canadians, but this group was made up of at least three different types of geese—snows, Canadians, and a composite species—white with black wings (or it might have been the other way around).

It felt a little funny, but as we made it up onto the back deck we both sat there in the rocking chairs, just rocking and talking. Hey, that is no big deal usually, except that it was probably 20 degrees outside, with a windchill below zero! We had gotten warmed up during the hike and it seemed comfortable.

We didn't spend too much time inside, just long enough to get a little something to eat, and make plans for another hike. Soon we were driving off up the hill, with a big waterfall in mind. One of the main places that I've always wanted to hike to out here is the twin falls way up in the headwaters of Whitaker Creek. We tried to find it one day last spring, but didn't go up far enough. It only runs good when there is lots of water, and there certainly was plenty of that today, so that was the destination.

We parked up along the main road and headed cross-country down into a drainage that dumped into Whitaker Creek. The little creek was running nicely, and there was plenty of snow to walk through. There was also snow blowing through the forest, and it was chilly. We hit Whitaker Creek, and to cover all bases, we headed upstream first, knowing that there would be a good waterfall along the bluffline that we had passed through. The creek was wonderful, a series of little whitewater areas and green pools. And the ice hanging from the bluffs on both sides was spectacular.

Sure enough, we finally did come to a pretty good sized waterfall. While it was a very nice one, it wasn't the one that we were looking for. We took a few pictures, then turned around and headed downstream, with Emily leading the way. That is one thing that I like about her, the fact that she is just as comfortable out here in the middle of the woods as I am, and I trust her judgement to find good routes.

The creek was running through a rather mundane stretch of mostly level terrain, and while the hiking was easy, and it looked like Christmas in all directions, we weren't too optimistic about finding a big waterfall. Just when the creek was about to lull us to sleep, we heard it—lots of water noise. There it was, right out below us, a big waterfall plunging from the top of a horseshoe bend in the bluff. We were up above it, and made our way gingerly around the side—everything was covered with snow and ice.

It was the double falls for sure. In fact, there was so much water, there were actually three falls, a smaller one in between the two main ones. During normal water flow, there is only a single falls there.

Emily found a narrow route down through the icy bluff that was not totally frozen. One reason why it was not frozen was because there was water flowing there—it would be a wet descent, but looked OK, and we really wanted to get to the base of the falls. She went first, and soon landed down at creek level. We both had complete waterproof coverage so the water was no big deal, except that I didn't have any spare gloves, so I spent the rest of the trip with bare hands (she had a dry pair in her pack—smart lady).

The waterfall was marvelous to say the least. Tall and skinny, and plunging into a deep pool. All of it surrounded by ice-covered bluffs. It was a very cold spot, but the beauty of it all kept us warm down to our toes. I was glad to finally see this place. I first saw a picture of it in one of Neil Compton's early books, and have wanted to get here ever since.

As we made our way back up the wet and icy climb, and then up the steep and snowy slope back towards the car, I realized that I had now been to all three of the major mystery spots that I wanted to see near my cabin—the Bear Cave, the Pioneer Wagon Road through the bluff on Beagle Point, and now the Twin Falls. And even though I had basically lived here for over a year and a half, it wasn't until just the last month that I had made it to any of these three, and I found all of them while with Emily. There are still hundreds of great mysteries and beautiful places around here to explore and discover, but now I felt like I had a good start on them at last.

The power was still off when we got back to the cabin. The fireplace was going strong, but we were running out of wood. In fact, I had gotten to the bottom of the big pile on the wood rack next to the cabin downstairs. When I emerged from the cold with a handful of wood, Emily cried out "Oh no, now we are burning the furniture!" She was partly right. There were a bunch of left-over pieces of the log railing that I had stacked on the bottom of the wood pile, and they were actually made of the same logs as all of my log furniture. So sure enough, we had gotten desperate, and were now burning the furniture!

The lack of wood was a bit of a problem. So we bundled up once again and went down to the meadow and spent some time hauling up a few big chunks of wood, plus some stuff that I had already split up. That would be enough to last another day or two.

And then we had a brilliant idea—bring the BBQ grill from the deck into the living room and use the burner on the side of it to cook on! The propane bottle was about full. It would be so easy. We had a real cook-top once again.

The clothes drying rack came in really handy too. All of our clothes were wet from sweat, waterfall splashes or melting snow and ice. Soon the rack was covered and the clothes were drying.

We lit up all of the candles and cooked up a storm—Banff Pasta! And, of course, there was plenty of wine—still 45 or 50 bottles in the wine rack down-stairs. If you are going to get stranded in a cabin in the woods somewhere, make sure it is well stocked with wine!

We spent a delightful evening in front of the fire, and the power being off didn't bother us a bit. Outside the wind was howling, and it was cold. The wind gauge had freed itself sometime during the day and was working again—it was 18 below zero windchill. Good thing that we were camping out in a log cabin with a big fire.

1/3/99 It was another warm night and I had a window open partway, although I closed it sometime in the early morning hours. It was 6 degrees at first light, but the sun was out, and it seemed a lot warmer outside (it wasn't).

We used the BBQ grill once again, not only to heat water for coffee, but toasted/grilled bagels for breakfast. It worked pretty darn well—I may have to leave the grill in the living room all winter. Well, maybe not. Needless to say, the power was still off.

The fire felt really nice this morning, and so we hung out in front of it a bit longer than normal. We wanted to wait until the temp climbed up into double digits before heading out for a hike. When it reached 10 degrees we were still moving slow, but at least we were moving. By the time we were all bundled up and ready to go, it had reached a balmy 12 degrees.

We wanted to go see the waterfalls in Hawk Hollow, and then drop down and measure the height of Bowers Hollow Waterfall, so we drove to the Kapark Cemetery Trailhead and headed out. It was cold, but it didn't feel too bad, and the hiking down the old road trail was easy.

One stretch of the trail went through some recent tornado damage—the same tornado that made the mess that can be seen from the cabin. Wow, this storm knocked down some *huge* trees! And took up big piles of dirt in the root ball with it. And created many little ponds, which were now half filled with water and ice. Some of the ice was formed in many patterns. One of the giant trees was simply twisted and snapped off near the base—it was one powerful storm for sure. And like most tornadoes the trees were tossed about in many different directions (indicating that the wind was swirling, not just blowing in the same direction), and it only took out big trees, leaving little ones untouched.

Hawk Hollow was just incredible! Not only were all of the waterfalls running wildly, but the ice hanging from everything was gorgeous.

We hiked on over to look at the view of the river and the hollow from a large wild azalea patch. Getting close to the edge of the big bluff was a little tricky—everything was covered with a layer of ice, and then snow on top. But it was beautiful. The sun was out all day, but it was bitter cold in the shadows.

Next we went on down into Bowers Hollow. The south wall there was simply covered with ice flows. Emily is an ice climber, and I could see her drooling at the sight. Some of the ice was climbable, but most of it was not quite right for one reason or another. It all looked like just plain ice to me! *Spectacular.*

We finally made it to the big waterfall, and it was running as much as I had ever seen it before. Words cannot describe it. We both stood there, silent, and then sort of wandered around on our own, without any conversation. To call it a magical place would be an understatement. Besides the incredible waterfall, there were tons of ice hanging from the surrounding bluffs. And there was ice that had built up on everything that the waterfall splashed on. I worked my way around in back of the waterfall, and man, it was like another world back there. I'll bet there were a dozen different types of ice back there, from very delicate almost hoar frost ice, to piles of smooth ice balls, all frozen together. The trees were covered with ice. The ground was covered with ice. Any plants around were covered with ice. And the walls were covered with ice. There was lots of ice. But I found it quite easy to walk on, although I did remain cautious—didn't want to end up in the frigid pool below.

OK, it was time for the purpose of our visit (well, I guess just being awed by the beauty was purpose enough!). We climbed up through the north wall and made our way towards the top of the waterfall. Even though the sky was blue and the sun was shining brightly, the air was filled with a million glittering ice particles—not really snow, but ice I guess. Whatever it was, was certainly, well, I've run out of expletives. It was just great.

I used a rock at the end of my rope, and tossed it over the edge next to the top of the waterfall. I couldn't see the bottom of the falls from that point, but Emily could see it from her vantage point, and she helped me know when the rock was at the right location (we had to move the rope a time or two to get a free and clear run for the rope). Got it. We hauled the rope up, marked the location, and wound it up on a piece of bark.

While we were standing there taking in the beauty one last time, there was some movement up on the hillside. It was another coyote, and he was heading on down the hill in our direction. As he neared the waterfall he veered to his right and ran along the top edge of the bluffline. We wondered if he just came down to take a look at the waterfall too? He disappeared. A few minutes later he came trotting back, working his way up the hillside. A beautiful animal. Not the mangy type that you would think a coyote would be. This guy's fur was all fluffed out, and his tail was red, and there were streaks of color in his coat.

We soon followed him up the hill, back onto the trail, and headed out. It was getting late, and the sun was low in the sky, casting long shadows of the trees. Once we hit the top of our route we slowed down. The next mile of hiking was one of the most enjoyable that I can recall. There weren't any really spectacular views or objects. I don't know. It was just very pleasant, walking silently through the snow and ice, in the evening light, with someone that I enjoyed being with. The only sound was the swoosh-swoosh and occasional crunch of the snow. We did not speak, or gesture. We didn't have to. We both were just enjoying the walking motion, and the moment, of being in the silent woods. It was very nice.

It was a slippery drive back—the roads were still covered with ice and snow. The cabin was warm, and was glad to see us back. The power was still off. After two days of hiking it was time to get cleaned up. I heated some water, and Emily disappeared into the shower. When she emerged later there was a large smile on her face, and that look of "boy it is great to be *clean!*" So I heated up a bucket myself. It had been quite a while since I had bathed out of a bucket, but it wasn't all that bad, and felt really good.

Hey, the living without power was not all that bad after all! We fired up the BBQ grill again and cooked dinner. Thank goodness we had hauled up enough wood—that is a major item in powerless living. You can take a lot, and even enjoy yourself, if you are warm and toasty, like we were.

After dinner we dug out the dominoes. I've had a set around for many years, a nice bone one in a leather case. But I've never played dominoes in my life, so they were unused. We sat down at the dinner table next to the fireplace and played dominoes for several hours. There was a great deal of laughter, and I even learned how to play dominoes, well sort of. She beat me, of course, but was kind enough to let me stay close. When we finally put the game away, the score was 380 to 365.

1/4/99 It was sometime around 4am when I got up to feed the fire. As I stepped outside to water the flowers, an arctic blast hit me and crawled up under my robe. It was *cold!* And it was also very, very bright. The moon was incredible, as were the million twinkling stars. All of that moonlight reflecting off of the snow made it look like the middle of the day—no problem running through the woods if you wanted to.

The sun broke over the ridge and lit up the world with pure light. The sky was clear blue, and it looked cold out. The weather station showed a windchill of 19 below zero. Yikes! The cabin was pretty warm though. We had a leisurely breakfast of coffee and grilled bagels. Having that BBQ grill right in the middle of the living room had its advantages.

All too soon Emily had to pack up and leave. I did too. Since there wasn't any hot water, or much water at all, we sort of stacked up the dishes in the dishwasher to leave for another time when I could deal with them.

The backup battery in the weather station finally gave out, and the screen went blank just before I left. The temp in the basement was 42 degrees, but it was quite toasty in the main room. I filled the fireplace with oak, loaded up all the bad food and trash from the big party, then fired up the van and headed for town—I would be back later in the day to stoke up the fire.

I did return later in the evening, and rolled up to a very dark cabin. The temp on the van thermometer showed it was 9 degrees up at the Faddis cabin, but warmed up as I got near to Cloudland, ending up at 13 degrees. That sounds about right—my little cabin is always a warm and welcome sight, even in the dead of a dark winter night!

Much to my surprise there were flames in the fireplace. That last log that I put on was still burning after eight hours. There was really a pile of ash built up in there—I hadn't cleaned it out since before the party, and it had been burning constantly since (four days). I did my best to scoop out the dead stuff and leave the live coals—seven gallons of ash. Then I wrapped myself up and went down to the little meadow with my yellow maul, and a flashlight strapped to my hat. It was dark, and cold, *very cold*. But no wind, thank goodness. There wasn't a scrap of wood left up at the cabin so I had to do a little splitting and hauling.

Even though it was a bit nippy out, after a few minutes of wood work, I was dripping with sweat. Love that wood splitting stuff. Then as I was standing there, feeling pretty good about myself, and enjoying the crisp night air, a bright light startled me—had the cabin come to life? Nope, something much better—an incredible bright orange moon topped the far ridge to the north east—wow—it was one terrific sight! I know it really didn't, but I would almost swear that it got a little warmer out once the moon came up. I turned off my headlamp and went back to work.

My bones ached under the weight of the wood and the steepness of the hill as I moved my new wood from the meadow to the upper deck. It was tough work, but few things could have been better for me to have been doing.

As I was filling the fireplace with the new wood another wave of light swept through my brain—this time, it *was* the cabin that came to life—the power came back on. Yea! This was the first test of the cabin under extreme conditions, and all systems seemed to work pretty good. The basement still had a ways to go before it was cold enough to have frozen any water pipes. Of course, being here and keeping the fireplace going helped out a great deal. This was one of the worst power outages up here in a while. It used to be off for a week at a time, but the power company has been very good at keeping things running much better in recent years. I hope they continue. But if they don't, I'll just have to plan to be here and keep the fire going!

The heat pump quickly warmed up the basement, then added to the rest of the cabin, which had gotten a little chilly as the big log burned down. I turned on the stereo, flooding the place with music. The weather station had totally melted down, but I brought out a new backup battery, and got it set up and running again. I had lost all of my highs, lows and rainfall totals for December. Should have listed all of that stuff before the party.

I turned the computer on and downloaded about 35 e-mails. Many of them were from folks who wanted to know what the heck was going on since I had not made a post to the Journal in a long time. Sorry. I had a good excuse! I spent a couple of hours answering e-mail.

Then I took a break and wandered on over to stand in front of the fireplace. The cabin was full of light and music once again, but somehow it was lonely—I missed Emily. Being in the dark and silence with only candle light and her voice for the past few days had been much better. Oh well, moonlight and falling stars don't last long either, and you just have to learn to enjoy them to their fullest while they are there. I counted my blessings to have spent some great time with Emily, then shut the cabin down and went to bed.

1/7/99 The clouds were setting down low, right in the trees, as I drove in near dark. There were six deer grazing in the big field at the top of the ridge. Deer are funny about cars. You can drive right on past them and they won't hardly even notice. Now if you stop the car, then they perk up. And if the door opens, they are gone in a flash. But if you stop the car and just roll down the window, they will usually just stand there looking at you. These did a lot of looking as I drove by. They looked really neat all silhouetted there in the heavy fog. Someone should have taken a picture.

I stopped by Bob's cabin to pour some antifreeze into his sinks, and to get a bottle of cumin that he had left for me (for my veggie chili).

My own cabin was cold. It was cold outside too. And beginning to ice up. I had no wood. It was down to the meadow for me. I had left the yellow maul down there the other day, and now, of course, it was covered with ice. When I first looked up towards the cabin the fog was so thick that I couldn't even see it! I split several logs, and hauled them up the steep slope to the deck. When I went out the door at first I had on a number of layers. With each trip up the hill, a new layer was shed. I had to put a pretty good thump on some of the logs in order to get them to split. Hard wood. Heavy wood. *Really* heavy wood.

This new wood was tough to get going. The wood that I had been burning this year had all been split up for a year, and it was just about perfect for burning. This new stuff had been cut down and sectioned at the same time as all the rest, but it hadn't been split until tonight. I guess it was more like green wood instead of seasoned. Once it got going good and hot it really took off, and before long I was resting my bones and my mind next to a roaring fire. More than once during the evening I would slip when picking up a log, especially the heavy ones, and one end would land on the pine floor—oops. Another dent. More personality some say. I say another dent!

At first I sat there in the dark, with only the music of the fire to keep me company. My cabin has great acoustics—especially when you are listening to the crackling of oak in the fireplace on a cold winter night. Then I put a CD in, and the volume went up. I went right to the fireplace song. "Oak will burn as long and hot as a July afternoon..." Yep, that's what I wanted.

The music kept getting better, and louder. I sat back and thought about how good it all sounded. I could close my eyes and pick out all eight of the speakers—a different instrument or sound coming from each one. Now I may not have the best stereo system, but my Bose system sure beats the $25 Radio Shack speakers that I've had since I was in high school.

It was still early and I had a ton of work to do the next few days at the cabin, so I dug out some paperwork and spread it out on the dining room table. I sat down in the rigid chairs and went to work. When I first got this log furniture from the Amish, I thought that it really was rather uncomfortable. And now I'm sitting in the chair for hours on end playing dominoes. I guess the more I use these chairs, the more I like them. Anyway, the chair felt great tonight, and I actually got some work done. The dining table next to the fireplace and surrounded by eight speakers seemed like a better place to work tonight than over at the cold desk of mine in the corner. Too bad the computer wasn't on this table. It was over in that cold corner.

One of the big chores this weekend was to get the Journal updated. The power being off really messed up my schedule, and although I tried to write while in town this week, I just couldn't—had to do it out at the cabin. Writing in the Journal is a lot like going out on a date for me. I usually have to spend hours, sometimes days, putting off calling or starting to write. But then, once I get into it, all is well, and smooth, and fun. I was at the beginning of that date tonight—I could do a lot of other tasks, but I just couldn't get the Journal started. So I put it off until the next day. After all, the fire was waiting, and I had to go stand in front of it.

1/8/99 Heavy fog isolated individual trees, and they looked like dancers. Ballet dancers. Without the fog, trees usually blend into one another, and so do their personalities. But with fog, the graceful curves and stout trunks stand out from the others, and create individual trees, the dancers. There were a lot of dancers around the outside of the cabin as grey light slowly crept in.

The temp has actually gone up a notch or two during the night, and it was in the low 30's, and would slowly climb during the day. After my mocha by the fire I spent the day alternating between writing in the Journal (I finally got started!), and splitting and hauling fire wood. It's funny, but the more you split and haul the wood, the less you really need it. Ha!

It remained cloudy all day, only retreating once around noon to show me the river below. There were a number of big ice chunks clinging to the bluffs over on Beagle Point. And the temp climbed up into the high 30's, and there was just a hint of rain. It was quite comfortable working outside, but everything was wet, very wet.

By the end of the day I had four different stashes of wood—two outside, and two inside. I added a pile of split wood downstairs in the basement because there was ice moving in, and the lower deck near the big wood pile gets really slick when it is icy out. I figured that I had enough wood piled inside and just outside the deck door to last me well into the afternoon the next day.

Once I was satisfied with my wood supply I put on my jacket and headed out for a hike. The wind had begun to blow, and the temp was dropping. In fact it had already dropped eight degrees by the time I started on the hike, down to 30. I made my way on up to the Faddis cabin, where a strong north wind hit me in the face. Yep, some kind of storm coming in all right—the wind doesn't normally come from that direction.

I went on down to check on Bob's, and everything was OK. Then I wandered on over to the East Meadow by way of the lower trail. When the wind wasn't blowing there wasn't any sound at all. And no movement either. I saw one bluebird at Bob's, but that was the only critter out besides me. I crept into the East Meadow hoping to sneak up on a grazing deer in the fog, a flock of turkeys, or at least a bear or two. But nothing. There was just nothing out stirring. They must have known something that I didn't.

The rest of the hike went well, as I strolled on down through one of the maple groves and back to the cabin. It had been a tough day at the mill, and I was ready for a hot shower. Bathing out of a bucket is fine when you have to, but few things can replace a wonderful shower.

There was no real end to the daylight—it just got a little darker over a long period of time, and then a little darker, more grey and less white. And then, after a while, I noticed that it was finally dark outside. The fog was very heavy. I sat back down and worked on the Journal. And fed the fire. And munched on junk food. Well, actually I had a good dinner, then munched on junk food.

The temp headed right on down, and it was in the upper teens by 10pm. My wind gauge had frozen up again so I couldn't tell what the windchill was, but I'll bet it was easily down below zero. All of the decks were slick. The fog had drifted off somewhat, but was still hanging around I bet, up there in the darkness. I listened to some blues on the radio, fed the fire, had a little wine, and wrote and wrote.

1/9/99 Very cold outside at daylight. 12 degrees. And very bright—clear blue skies and lots of sunshine! I got up and milled around the fireplace a little. And I'm glad that I was up. Man, even though it was clear out, there were these clouds of brilliant glitter floating past. Must have been frozen moisture of some sort, but they were so tiny, and the only place that you could see them was when they were backlit by the sun. As it turned out the sun was right behind the eastern bird feeder, and so I got to sit and watch several juncos feeding, always surrounded by all of this floating glitter. It was amazing! Looking out across the main valley, I could see a number of these glitter clouds drifting by. They would swirl around a little, then gradually get smaller and smaller until they disappeared. A little bit of magical dust from heaven.

Across the way, up on top of Beagle Point, all of the trees were frozen. I couldn't tell if they were covered with ice, or with hoar frost, which is kind of frozen fog. Looking way up the valley, all of the high hilltops towards the Fire Tower were frozen too. It must have been an altitude thing, because nothing at my level was frozen. Beagle Point is a little higher than me.

OK, enough of this beauty stuff. I went to the office and fired up the computer. I was still behind on the Journal, and vowed not to get up from the keyboard until I was finished. And this forced imprisonment worked—by noon I had finally caught up. It was a lot of fun going back and recalling the days past. In some ways writing the Journal is a way for me to relive all of the great times, and laugh at myself once again at some of the silly things that I do out here. Since I seldom get to sit right down and write about the day's events when they are fresh in my mind, I take notes. Often a single word note will produce three or four paragraphs in the Journal. My problem is not so much trying to find something to write about, but cutting back of what to write about—as you know, things can get a little wordy here, just like this paragraph.

With my Journal up to date, and the sunshine calling my name, I bundled up and headed out for a hike. The temp was in the low 20's, but it was cold, at least at first. I dropped on down to the trail on the bench below and headed towards the Crag, with plans to emerge from the woods near my mailbox and get the paper, then stop by Bob's cabin and borrow a inch drill bit that I needed.

Before I was out of sight of the cabin I heard screaming. It was coming from above. Hawks! There really haven't been any/many hawks in the skies at Cloudland in quite some time. What I saw was three hawks, all circling in close formation above. They were squawking and screaming, and appeared to be playing some sort of game with each other rather than hunting. It was great to see them. I hoped that they would stick around. What kind of birdseed could I put out to attract hawks—mice?

For a sunny day the colors of the forest floor, the trees and the blue sky were very rich and satisfying (normally harsh sunshine is not good). It quickly turned into a very pleasant stroll through the woods.

I saw some ice up on the hillside. It was hanging over a small bluff opening that is located right next to my property corner. From a distance the whole thing reminded me of a big mouth open wide, with all of these giant, white teeth. I guess it was the hillside waking up and yawning. I even took a picture.

As I was returning to the trail I thought that I had spotted the biggest cardinal in the world—and it was really bright *red!* As I got closer I realized that it was nothing more than a red mitten that someone had dropped along the trail, and someone else had propped up on a limb to be found.

As I moved on past a rock formation a little bird jumped up from the rock and landed on a nearby limb. It was a nuthatch, and he didn't like me disturbing his morning routine. He soon calmed down, and flew down onto the rock, within three feet of me. I stood there and watched, very still. He would turn his head and look over at me, then turn back and dig his beak into a small crack in the rock. There was something down inside there that he really liked. Pretty soon he ignored me altogether, and spent his time eating. Nice little bird.

There was no one at the Crag, but the view was spectacular, as always. My hawk friends were nowhere in sight. Probably off chasing mice somewhere. I did get buzzed by a bluebird though. He swooped down and flew right past my ear, then landed in a tree. Boy, this little guy was really puffed up and twice as big as normal—a good indication that it really was a little chilly outside.

I followed the bluffline trail to a point where I could look down and see a large part of the bluff, and it was highly decorated with ice. The sun was warming up the rock, loosening the ice, and causing it to break loose and fall, or rather crash on the rocks down below. And *crash* it did—sounded more like dynamite going off when it hit! I took up a comfortable spot leaning against a boulder, and watched the spectacle for a few minutes. There were about three crashes per minute. It became a game to see if I could spot a chunk of ice falling before it made any noise and crashed—this was tougher than it seems. I think that the bluff won this game, because I was only able to spot every third one or so. Not a good place to be walking down below.

I eventually got back onto the main trail where I passed a couple of guys that were hiking in from the trailhead. We stopped and chatted for a moment, and I'm sure they wondered about me since there was no other car at the trailhead. When they asked me where I was going, I just said "Out to the mailbox to get the paper, then on over to a friend's cabin to borrow a drill bit." They looked at each other, laughed, and hiked on. Twas the truth.

I got my paper, then walked the road towards Bob's cabin. As I was passing the big green field owned by the Goat Man I saw a large hawk hovering in the air, way up at the far end of the field. The closer I got, the stranger the hawk looked—it was doing all sorts of crazy things, but staying in exactly the same spot. There was a power line that went across the field there, and so he must be sitting on a wire. But the wind must really be blowing, and he must be trying to keep his balance. As I walked on, I decided that it must have been a trash bag or something caught in the wire instead of a hawk—there were just too many crazy motions going on. Then I got right up next to the narrow part of the field, and sure enough, it was a very large hawk, struggling to keep his balance on the wire. There were many trees nearby that he could have hung out in, and I wasn't sure why he choose to stay on the bouncing wire.

Birds, birds and more birds. They were everywhere at Bob's cabin. On the ground, in the trees, at the feeders, and flying back and forth overhead. They really like his place. And his feeders. I got the drill bit, tossed the birds a few handfuls of ground corn, and continued on my hike.

270

As I topped the hill near the Faddis cabin I spotted a flock of turkeys on the far side of the meadow. They saw me immediately, although they did not run off or fly away. They did sort of wander in the other direction though, and eventually disappeared into the woods. As I walked along the lane I could see them in the woods, just waiting for me to leave so that they could resume their meadow munching.

When I was back in the woods a flicker came flying by and landed on a tree in front of me. What was the deal with birds flying past me today—I think I saw more birds on this hike than any other in a long time. Come to think of it, with the exception of the two hikers, I didn't see any living thing today except for birds—not even a single squirrel.

Back at the cabin the temp was 25 degrees, and there was no wind. If I didn't have so much work to do I would have simply laid out in the swing and napped all afternoon. But instead I was a good boy and put on my carpenter stuff and worked inside for the rest of the afternoon. Actually I worked inside and out on the deck—I set up my sawing station on the deck, which meant that I got to go outside a lot. And every time that I went out to cut a board, I was forced to take a minute or two and survey my little wilderness world from the edge of the deck. Very nice, all very nice.

I worked until after dark putting up paneling in the new guest room closet, and adding insulation to a couple of walls that needed it. Then it was time to do a little cooking. Since Bob had left me the jar of cumin, I felt compelled to cook this veggie chili recipe that I had. An hour later I sat down in front of the fireplace and pigged out on two big bowls of black beans, tomatoes, zucchini, yellow squash, onion, green and red bell peppers, plus various spices and toppings (sour cream and cheddar cheese), and of course, the cumin! I wish that I had two or three stomachs, because I ate until I was about to pop, but still wanted more. A new Cloudland standard meal was born.

After a hot shower and dish duty I sat back down by the fire with a little wine and some folk music on the radio. I was tired, and didn't last too long. I got up a time or two to wander outside and collect some firewood—it was *very* cold out, and the sky was filled with a million, no make that two million sparkling stars. Wow, I was dumbfounded at the stark beauty of all that black sky and all those sparkles. Had it not been so cold I could have stood there for hours, staring up.

1/10/99 At some point in the middle of the night (I had to get up three times to feed the fire), I looked out my window and saw a half-moon rising above the ridgetop across the valley. It was not really orange, or yellow, or white, it was some other color. And it lit up the loft with very soft light.

The room got light once again—pink light this time. I could see the eastern horizon reflected in the lamp next to the bed (the spot where the sun rises is still out of direct sight from my pillow). I leaned over and saw an incredible pink light show, then rolled over and went back to sleep. A few clouds had moved in during the night, and there wasn't a real sunrise—the pink light just turned to white. I slept in.

After my now normal winter breakfast of Starbucks mocha and hot Grape Nuts (45 seconds in the microwave with milk is great!), I went over to the computer and began writing again. I only had yesterday and this morning to catch up on. Two big things happened while I was writing. First, the damn power went off, and of course, I lost whatever I had written but not saved (which turned out not to be all that much—I tend to save often these days). It seems that the power company gets its kicks by flipping the switch off for a second or two at least a couple of times a day. And the second thing that happened did so because of the power failure. As I stood up to stomp and cuss at the power company, I looked out the window and saw a mature bald eagle flying by. Yippie! I grabbed the binocs and headed out the door. This guy was big, with pure white head and tail, and a bright yellow beak. And he didn't just fly by on his way somewhere else like they normally do. He was actually in a pattern, which included my little meadow. At his closest point he was actually flying inside the pine trees out in back and very close to the cabin. He never made a sound, but he did look over at me and winked during one pass. Well, maybe he didn't wink, but he did look right at me. I stood there motionless, and not breathing. Bald eagles still take my breath away, every time. After several passes he made his way on up the valley and out of sight. Thanks Mr. Eagle.

While I was writing the above paragraph the power went off again—I had not saved, so it is the second version. I will be at the office supply store at 8am tomorrow morning to buy a new backup battery!

Sometimes things just happen, you know, without any explanation. Well, I just put up on the main room wall of the cabin one of my most favorite photographs ever. It is a picture that I took back in 1995 when I was touring around the country, taking pictures for my **Wilderness Reflections** book. I consider it one of the best of the 40,000 images that I shot that year. Anyway, the image is of a spectacular scene in the Canadian Rockies. Well, this morning, I received an e-mail from a lady in Canada who had been reading the Journal. I've never received an e-mail from Canada at the cabin before, and now one came as soon as I put up a picture (I hadn't mentioned this picture in the Journal before now). Hum, I wonder how that happened?

I'm afraid to report that the remainder of the veggie chili disappeared around noontime. Then I could be seen out on the swing, dozing in the warm sunshine. The swing is set so that the winter sun, low in the southern sky, will shine on it most of the afternoon. In the summer, the sun doesn't get there because it is too high in the sky, and is blocked by the roof line. But wintertime sunny naps are encouraged out here at Cloudland, so I did my best to comply.

However, I never really got to go to sleep. Something kept tugging at me. I wasn't sure just exactly what it was. After I laid there 30 minutes I finally realized what it was—it was the river who was calling to me. I hadn't been down there yet this year. A mistake that I had to remedy!

Soon my boots were slipping and sliding down the leaf-covered trail. The ladder had just a little bit of ice left on it, as did the surrounding bluffs. The sun had melted most everything. It wasn't long before I was down at the river. Right where I emerged was the source of the river noise—the music maker that plays its tune all day long and sends it right on up to the cabin. I walked on over to the rapids and tipped my hat.

There is a nice rock bar here too. I was amazed at how many different colored rocks were there. At least four or five different shades of grey limestone. Plus red and orange and brown shades of sandstone. And some blue rock. And white. And even a black one or two. All of them smoothed down quite a bit by the churning of the waters. They aren't polished smooth and shiny, but rather had a matte finish.

I reached down and picked up one stone that was mostly black, but had an interesting white pattern in the center—bird poop. The water looked cold, and I was glad that I didn't really need to see anything on the other side today.

I turned around and headed back up the trail, then went over to Whitaker Creek. Oh my goodness—there were a million diamonds floating down the swift current towards me, then they all came together in a small rapids and melted together like liquid silver. The splash sent them all in separate ways again, only to reconvene again at the next rapid. The bright sunshine was really lighting up the river. In fact, the water sparkles were so bright that everything else in the scene—the rocks and trees and ground—were all black. Nothing but black and silver. It was marvelous.

I went over to the edge and bent down to get a drink—looking carefully this time for Mr. Cottonmouth. He wasn't around.

As I left the stream and began to work my way across the grown-up river bottom, I was stopped dead in my tracks. The most wonderful, fragrant, light and beautiful scent in the world came drifting by—a witch hazel bush in bloom! Oh, wow, it was heavenly. And strong. Probably the first burst of fragrance from this particular tree this winter.

I breathed deeply to take it all in. If I had the time, I would have gone up to the big backrest rock up along the far bluffline to see what that witch hazel tree was doing. Just another example of perfection in nature.

The trip up the hillside was pretty good—I took it slow and deliberate, without stopping. About halfway up I passed a hiker coming down from above. First time that I had seen a hiker not from my own party on this trail in a while. When I reached the top and plopped down in the swing, I was very wet with sweat, but not breathing all that hard. The sun and light breeze felt great. The temp was 45 degrees.

1/12/99 *Holy Kansas!* The wind blew 44mph at 12:45am this morning. It was dead still outside when I arrived after dark, but I noticed that some of my chairs from the deck were missing. After checking the weather station and finding the big reading, I went outside with a flashlight and found the chairs, two of them broken, down on the steep hillside to the east of the cabin—this is the spot where most of the stuff that gets blown off of the deck ends up. It must have been one big gust!

It was very warm out—54 degrees—but was actually colder inside the cabin—the logs hold heat out as good as they hold heat in. I opened up the doors and windows to let some warm air come in, kind of odd doing that in January. Everything was a little wet, although I don't think that it had rained—just very high humidity. The pavement was all wet too. And I saw dozens of groups of deer along the roadsides as I drove in.

The Buffalo River was singing a very loud tune, and must be running pretty good. Maybe there was some rainfall upstream.

There were two chores that I had for myself this night. The first was to drill holes in the wall and install oak pegs up in the loft on either side of the bed—to hang clothes and robes and stuff on. I used to have two log clothes hangers up there, but used both of them to make the floor lamps down in the main room out of. I have two more ordered from the Amish as replacements, but like the peg idea even better. I may make a couple of more lamps out of the new ones.

The other chore was to learn how to play a new board game that I just got. It is called Mancala, and is a very simple game to play. I like it because it is made up of 48 stones that you move around on a wooden board. You can actually use any items instead of the stones, like acorns, or marbles, or, well, anything. So I opened it up and sat down at the dining table and began to play, using my alter-ego as the other player. Son of a gun, while it was easy to play, I must not be very good at it, because I lost! Come to think of it, I guess that I won too. A fun game, that will become a classic at Cloudland.

1/13/99 A heavy fog set in this morning, and it was dead still, almost spooky outside. No birds at the feeders. Oops, I take that back. There is one little goldfinch sitting at the feeder just outside the office window. He isn't eating anything though—just sitting there on one of the perches enjoying the view. Well, there isn't any view because of the fog, but he must like that. It was still warm out early—54 degrees.

I will load up my faithful van for the very last time. My new car has arrived, and I'm picking it up tomorrow. My old buddy van, which just turned 180,000 miles, has been one of the best vehicles that I've ever owned, and I will be a little sad to see it go. It went with me on the 50,000 mile trip around the US back in 1995, and has been my tent for over 500 nights. It has only let me down once, when the serpentine belt broke (I was out here, before the cabin was built, and had to get a ride back into town). Otherwise, I've done literally nothing but put gas and oil in it. But it is time for me to move on before it falls apart. The new car will be four-wheel drive, smaller, but with a better stereo system (the van has a great stereo in it though—sometimes I used to just go out driving so that I could listen to music). I spend so much time driving that a good stereo is important. The new car has one of the 6 CD changers too (I have had one in my vehicles for the past 12 years, and couldn't live without one), and a Bose speaker system in it. I can't wait. Actually, the new car is just a cabin accessory— I even got the color to match—Green ("..Deep greens and blues are the colors I choose..." —James Taylor). Greens and blues are the cabin colors. So I leave the cabin today for the last time in my good old van. But will return on Friday driving my new Mercedes SUV, and with a beautiful young woman sitting next to me (please, don't wake me up, let me dream a while longer).

The cabin is vacuumed, the heavy fog is still here, and the temp has been dropping like a rock—34 degrees at 11am. I discovered that the high wind yesterday picked up one of my big bird feeders and moved it—there were three goldfinch on it, trying to eat, and it was tilted 25 degrees. Must be hungry!

1/15/99 We arrived well after dark, and the cabin was a little chilly, but it didn't take long for the fireplace to get blazing. It was crystal clear outside, and there were a million stars out. The moon was nowhere to be found, so the sky was black city. (By the way, my dream had come true, on both accounts.)

The second thing that I did was to hook up a backup battery power supply to the computer—those darn power outages won't mess me up now!

1/16/99 Daylight came early, and the bright sunshine filled the cabin with a cheery glow. I had to get up a couple of times during the night to feed the fire— most of the wood slabs in the pile are pine scraps from the cabin, and they burn up pretty fast. But they are *hot* when they burn! We made coffee, had a bagel or two, then loaded up the new SUV and headed on over to the Richland Creek Wilderness for a day of bushwhack hiking.

Richland has always been one of my favorite wild spots in all of Arkansas, but I hadn't been there in a while. It is one of the many great drainages that empties into the Buffalo River, so it is sort of related to Cloudland. We were going to hike down to Twin Falls and Richland Falls, but also wanted to find a pair of mill stones that I had been told about. Emily had a new pair of boots that she was trying out. Since we would be bushwhacking those boots would get a workout in short order. Us too.

The creek that we followed into the wilderness was very nice—lots of little waterfalls and blue-green pools and whitewater. And right next to one of the more scenic waterfalls, we found a pair of historical mill stones, about three feet in diameter, and 8-10 inches thick. These babies were very heavy, and had been carved out of solid sandstone. There was not a single sign of anything else man-made in the area where they were, so I suspect that they were from a mill that had been used back in the 1800's.

We continued on down the stream, and the scenery just got better and bet-ter. More waterfalls, interesting rock formations, and other neat stuff to explore. We finally made it to Twin Falls, and spent a little time there taking pictures. Then we went on over to Richland Falls on the main Richland Creek, then spent an hour or so laying out on a rock in the middle of the river and munching on lunch, and just generally taking it easy. One thing that we had noticed on the way in was that there was almost no sign of life in the water at all—only a few minnows here and there. No crawdads or fish of any size could be found.

I crept over to the side of the big rock to peer over the edge, and was met there by a little spider who was trying to get to the top of the rock for a view. When he discovered me he turned right around and jumped off of the rock right into the river, which was moving past at a pretty good clip. He scooted across the surface of the water and didn't stop until he reached the opposite bank. Good grief, I didn't realize that I was that scary looking!

The sunshine was wonderful, and so was the day. After we finished off a pile of Andes mints that I had smuggled in, we left the river behind and headed nearly straight up a rocky hillside to climb out. There were so many rocks/boulders strewn about the forest floor on this hillside that it would be possible to hike/climb all the way from the river up to the top of the hill without ever stepping on anything but rocks. And we mostly did just that—avoiding the deep leaves in between the rocks as much as we could. Emily's new boots were doing great, but she took a nasty tumble when one of the rocks gave out, and sent her shooting down the hillside (no fault of the boots—just unstable rocks).

We finally made it to the top, and the view up and down the river valley was nothing short of spectacular! The last time that I had been to this spot was several years ago. I had hiked here in the dark (about an hour) to get the sun rising up over the wilderness. When I got there I realized that it was going to be so foggy that there wouldn't be a sunrise at all. So I just sat down and admired all there was to see. About an hour later the sun broke through the fog, and I got a good picture that ended up in the *Buffalo River Wilderness* book. We enjoyed the view as well, then found an old logging road that took us all the way back to the Hill Cemetery Trailhead.

Emily wanted to do a little target shooting when we got back to the cabin, so we set up a target and loaded up the pistols. She had a neat old .22 pistol that must have been 100 years old, but in great shape. Remind me to never, ever argue with her—she turned out to be a killer marksman with that little gun! I got out my 9mm Glock and managed to actually hit the target a time or two.

Just as we were finishing up David McClinton from Fayetteville dropped by with his daughter and her friend. David had just begun operations to purchase a home and some acreage downstream a ways at Steele Creek—a very nice place. I had asked him to stop by and take a look at my driveway, and give me some suggestions how to fix it up. He did, and we decided that the best thing to do was to wait until summer, then stockpile a bunch of large, softball size rocks, then spread them on the bad parts of the road and build up a good base, one that would allow seeping water to flow through.

By the way, my new SUV got covered with mud, and scratched up a little on our trip to Richland (I'm hoping the scratches are in the mud and not the paint!). This is probably a good thing to have happen early—now I don't have to worry about getting the car dirty or scratched, and can enjoy driving it!

Once the sun went down, and we got all cleaned up and built a big fire in the fireplace, Emily fixed a wonderful dinner dish of Indian cuisine. Boy, this stuff was *very* good! And I picked out a good bottle or two of wine to go with it. We spent the rest of the evening playing Mancala—this simple little game tends to get addictive in a hurry.

1/17/99 It was foggy at daylight and the wind was howling like crazy. I was shocked to find that the temp was 52 degrees outside! We had a hurried breakfast of Cloudland Coffee and blueberry biscuits, then we put on our work clothes and went down to the little meadow to clean up some brush. We got stopped in our tracks on the way down by a *pair* of bald eagles that were circling overhead. There were flying in formation, a sort of roving circle, and gradually moved across the sky. I hadn't seen two eagles together in the air around Arkansas in a long time. It was a stirring sight.

We spent the morning, which was a very warm morning, getting one end of the meadow ready for wildflower planting. Emily attacked all of the little trees and brush that had sprouted up—cutting out about a hundred trees which were up to a couple of inches in diameter, most of them being those darn thorny locust trees—ouch! I split up some wood and moved some of the larger stuff around. There has already been a great deal of wood removed from this spot, but I made five or six more piles of the stuff—good thing, because I think we are still in for some cold weather this winter.

We only took one break all morning, and wandered on down to Whitaker Point. While we were standing there admiring the view a mature bald eagle came cruising up the valley—brilliant white head and tail! He looked like he was just cruising around the area, checking things out, and didn't seem to pay us much attention. What a stunning sight to see a bald eagle flying over an Arkansas wilderness!

While we were back up at the cabin chowing down on some lunch, the skies got dark, and it began to thunder and crash—a storm was upon us. Then the sky opened up and it started to rain—we ran down and grabbed all of our tools and managed to keep them from getting wet. We got out the rock game.

Just as it really began to pour we heard voices down in the basement—Roy and Norma had been out playing on the bluffs down below, and made a run for the cabin when the rain started. They hung around a little while, and when they realized that Emily and I weren't going to let them in on our Mancala game, they had me drive them back up to the Faddis cabin.

The rain continued, and we took advantage of the sound and the smells and the sights and took a good long Sunday afternoon nap. Sometimes you hike. Sometimes you work. Sometimes you nap. There is no priority at Cloudland.

The clock was against us, and once the sun came out and burned all of the clouds away, we too packed up our things and bid the cabin farewell and headed back to town. It was as fine a weekend as has ever been had at Cloudland. As I drove away, I just had to smile. I hit another mud hole too.

1/20/99 Bright sunshine, blue skies, and a warm 60 degrees. I came by the cabin in the middle of the day with a group of photographers that were part of a photo workshop that I was teaching at the Ozark Natural Science Center all week. We had been shooting waterfalls in a nearby area, and just stopped by the cabin to enjoy the view.

The wind had blown at 38mph the day before, and slammed one of my feeders up against a log post, breaking the bottom platform of the feeder. I set the feeder aside to be fixed during the next visit.

1/22/99 My workshop ended, and I arrived at the cabin late this Friday night. The fog was about as thick as I had ever seen it—I had to creep along at a couple of miles per hour in the car, even with fog lights on. It was about 40 degrees outside, but nice and warm in the cabin. I keep the heat pump set at 50 degrees when I am gone, but it was 56 degrees inside, so the logs were insulating well.

I was exhausted after a week of driving back and forth to the Science Center and teaching all day. In fact, I was even too tired (or lazy?) to build a fire in the fireplace. So I just sat down with a thick, dark beer, and a pretzel, gazed out into the fog, then retired for the night. I opened the window in the loft, and slid down deep under the down comforter and let the music of the Buffalo River sing me to sleep.

1/23/99 A bird called out towards the cabin, and I rolled over to see that all of the fog had been blown away by the howling winds during the night. It was about an hour before sunrise, but the woods were taking shape out there in the pre-dawn light. The sun never did come up, but everything was clear down below a layer of clouds, and I could see the river, and all of the valleys. The river was running pretty good after a six-tenths of an inch of rain that we got on Thursday night here.

It wasn't until I got up out of bed that I realized that everything was covered with a fine dusting of *snow*—YEA! It was 32 degrees. I put on my thick robe and blue slippers and built a roaring fire. Standing in front of a big fire in a log cabin with snow outside—that's what log cabins are made for.

One of my big chores for the day was to write my hiking club's newsletter, which I spent most of the morning doing. It was great not to have to worry about the power going out in mid-sentence.

The little birds were gathering outside, especially after I fixed the feeder that had been broken during the big storm. I also filled up the suet feeder, which was almost completely bare. I found that when I raised the blinds on the window that is in front of my computer, that the birds would react when I got up and walked around—they usually flew off. So I lowered the blinds, and just kept them open. I spent a lot of time staring out the windows and looking at the birds flying around, mostly goldfinch and juncos.

Once I got the newsletter about wrapped up, and a good dose of bird-watching done, it began to snow, just a little. I had to get out in it, so I laced up my boots, and put on my jacket and headed out. The snow in the forest out in front was really very nice, sort of looking like someone had flown over and emptied a shaker of powdered sugar all over. In fact, it was a great way to really see snow—there was so much more detail there, with the contrast between the white snow and the brown leaves. I rather enjoyed an amble through the trees and the leaves and the sugar.

And I got to thinking about building a trail from the cabin up to the East Meadow, since that is one of the main routes that I take. I would lay it out so that you hiked gradually up the hill, through the open woods, past a couple of lichen and moss-covered boulders, with views down to the bench below, then on to the side of the East Meadow, right at a spot where you can look out into the meadow and see any wildlife that might be feeding or lurking there. I didn't have any flagging tape with me, but made mental notes of where the path might be built once I got the urge.

There were no critters in the East Meadow when I got there, but the north wind sure was blowing! The temp, a balmy 32 degrees when I left the cabin, was probably more like ten or twelve degrees windchill as I crossed the meadow. Down in the woods the wind was OK. Most of the snow had melted on this side of the hill, or never fell in the first place. Or got blown away by the wind—that was probably it. I have sat down in the middle of the forest before during a heavy snowstorm, when the wind was blowing hard, and noticed that the snow never did land and pile up—it just kept blowing.

No birds in sight. But I could hear a constant hum of their singing off in the trees, just out there beyond my vision. I think they were trying to talk the wind into letting up some.

There was a car parked up near the Faddis cabin. I took the trail down to the Crag, and met a photographer with a big pack coming out. He had come from Fayetteville, where it had snowed a lot more during the night, and hoped to get a picture of the Crag in the snow. Not much snow here, but he seemed happy to be out and about.

The snow that was around was mainly on the branches and downed trees. All of the leaves were this wonderful glowing shade of brown, and it made a great background for the snowy branches and logs—the snow gave them all individual personalities. I didn't realize just how nice an old rotten log could be until I saw one outlined with snow. It seemed that wherever I hiked this morning, I found the snowy landscape just a little different.

One thing that was the same was the rich color of green in the mosses that covered boulders and rotten logs—the moisture in the air and the soft light made the greens just luscious.

There were a number of people down at the Crag. Then another group over on the bluff by the big-bent over pine tree. One group left, and was soon replaced. Good grief, there were lots of people out today! I saw five groups when I was there. I wandered on back to the cabin, and enjoyed the stroll.

It was most pleasant outside, although it was 32 degrees and overcast, with light snowy specks coming down every now and then. The clouds above hung just above the mountaintops, so you could see the river below and all of the hillsides in the wilderness. But it almost seemed warm.

I spent an hour or two down in my little meadow chopping and gathering and hauling firewood—it felt *great!* I loved it. Mark that down—freezing is a perfect temp to chop wood. I filled two of my log carriers with split oak. This stuff would burn well, and keep things dry for some time. Hauling it up the hill was the toughest part, and I could feel that my bones didn't like it. I was forced onto the porch swing to rest more than once.

After my hike and log chores I settled inside and cooked up a batch of veggie chili—um, that stuff really made the cabin smell good! I'm tweaking the recipe, and will post it on the Cloudland Recipe page soon. It will be a staple on cold winter days here.

I brewed a pot of coffee, and had a bit with some Bailey's in it, and sat out on the porch swing for a while, watching the fog come and go, and the birds sneaking around. The river was singing loudly, and I could tell that it was having a good time.

Near the end of the day a car came driving up. They left the main road when they saw the cabin and headed down a dead-end lane. I knew they weren't looking for me, so I strapped on my boots and went to investigate. They got to the dead end, and were trying to turn around when they saw me walking towards them. The engine revved up, and their tires spun—I guess they remembered that they had driven right past the NO TRESPASSING and PRIVATE PROPERTY signs, and were a little concerned about this hillbilly walking towards them. They seemed to be in a bit of a hurry to leave. Hah! They sped off, tearing up part of my road. (I don't encourage unannounced visitors.)

I followed their tracks up the road—they didn't act like normal visitors, and I wanted to make sure they went on their way, and didn't bother anything up at Bob's. I didn't find any further sign of them.

As I passed through the Faddis Meadow on my way back I found a flock of bluebirds. There were probably 20 of them, and they were playing and bouncing and chattering about like crazy. They hardly noticed my presence, or cared. I never could figure out just exactly what they were up to, but they did spend a lot of time down on the ground, although it didn't look like they were eating anything—just playing tag or something. It was great to see their brilliant blue coat and rust breast against the grey day.

It was so nice out, and still a bit of daylight left, so I walked towards the Crag. I was about halfway down the trail when I heard a coyote cry out. I stopped to listen. He called out again. Sounded nice in the winter woods. A few steps later he yelped a little louder. As I looked around at the soaked forest floor, and felt the breeze on my face, I realized that it just might be possible for me to creep through the quiet leaves, and against the wind, and sneak up on this little rascal. Hum, could that be possible? I snuck up on a bear in August, why not a coyote? Guess I would have to find out!

I headed off along the bench in the direction of the sound. I covered the first stretch of ground pretty quick, but then slowed down as I crept up over the edge of the bench up above. I stopped and listened. The light was fading. Since the breeze was in my face, he would not be able to scent me, and the leaves were indeed very quiet. But he had to keep sounding out or I wouldn't be able to find him. Then he cried out again. Sounded like we were on the same bench now, but he was still a little ways out there. I moved across the bench and made my way through a number of smaller broken bluff rocks. I stopped again to listen, and realized that the rocks around me looked pretty darn nice—almost glowing with all that green.

The coyote yelped again, and he was very close, but perhaps up on the next bench. I crept up the hillside. Very slow, stopping and scanning the forest from left to right and then back again, scanning with every step. I crouched low as I approached the edge of the bench, and got behind a boulder for cover. Then waited. And he cried out once again, and I knew he was very close.

I moved on just a few more feet, and then I saw him—right there on the same bench, about 150 yards away, and along the edge of the bench, just like me. He hadn't seen me, and was busy milling about his little area. He wasn't really all that close—way out there at the edge of my sight—but he was *within* my sight, and I had snuck up on him without him ever detecting me! His hind end went down into the leaves and he howled again, two short bursts.

That's when the hair on the back of my neck stood straight up—I spotted another coyote—out there near the first one—and he had his eyes focused right at me. No, he was *drilling* those eyes right through me! It was not a friendly look. I felt very, very small. Gulp. We stared at each other for what seemed like an eternity—I didn't want to turn away from his gaze—I knew he knew that I saw him and that he had seen me. I wasn't scared, but was a little startled.

Within a few seconds in the real world, coyote #2 turned away from me and flipped his nose at coyote #1, then they both turned and trotted off into the darkening forest. I took a deep breath—hadn't had one in a while. Hey, I wanted to sneak up on a coyote, and it was well worth the effort!

I scooted on back to the cabin as darkness crept in. The wind had died down and the temp was still very pleasant. I could have walked another hour or two but knew since it was cloudy there wouldn't be any moonlight to direct my travels. So I settled for another little visit to the porch swing.

The evening soon melted right into the darkness. I had some dinner, a little wine, and mostly hung out in the firelight. The wood that I had split and brought up burned even and long into the night.

1/24/99 I rolled over and thought that I was dreaming—what I saw reminded me of the flesh of a golden trout that I had caught and ate up in the wilds of Wyoming several years ago—the sky was the most incredible color of salmon, no, not quite salmon, but golden trout. It was amazing! Soon the cabin filled with yellow light, then it quickly turned to white. Time to get up!

After some coffee and hot grape nuts I spent a little while bringing up more firewood. The sun had warmed up the lower deck, and it was time for me to bring out the cutting tools and measure a little aspen. I put the big miter saw out on the deck, and stacked all of the aspen boards nearby. My job this day was to put up all of the aspen in the upstairs guest room, where we had ripped out the closet. I had never finished the walls inside the closet because I was going to put up cedar there.

I had to make two cuts with the circular saw down the walls where the new aspen boards would meet the old aspen—sawdust went everywhere! Fortunately I had moved everything back and covered up most things. But there was a lot of fine sawdust around. I spent a bunch of time with the vacuum.

The cuts went OK, and after I measured all of the spots where the boards were going, I discovered that I had exactly the right amount of wood—oops, that meant that I could not make a single mistake!

It only took me about two hours to cut all of the boards and get them nailed up. The sunshine hitting the lower deck was great, and I was forced to linger out there a little longer than normal to soak it all up.

There was a steady stream of hikers over on the Crag, and several of them made it over to near the cabin—a few even hiked up on past the cabin. A guy from Clarksville who had a log cabin from the same company as mine dropped by to see how mine was coming. We compared notes.

A couple stopped by that was looking for a way down the bluffline—he had been shooting pictures and lost his tripod over the bluff—something that I had done myself a time or two. I sent them down the ladder trail (he later e-mailed me to report that the tripod was found was still usable).

Once the aspen was all in place I headed on over to the Crag myself for an afternoon stroll. I came across four folks from Oklahoma that were headed to Whitaker Point. We chatted a few minutes. They told me that someone down at the Crag was telling everyone that there was a road down at the end of my trail that would take hikers back to the trailhead. That is true, but it is a mile and a half *longer* than just hiking back on the main trail. I passed another group. Good grief, everyone was out today. A picture in the **NW Arkansas Morning News** on Friday really sent the crowds out.

I spent some time at the Crag talking with various hikers, then headed up the hill and back to the cabin. I passed the folks from Oklahoma along the way. While they were down near the cabin a bald eagle came flying by. I told them it was just one of my pets, and was trained to fly past hikers with cameras.

As the day grew long, so did the shadows. The color of the sun on the trees grew yellow, then orange, then red, then in an instant, disappeared altogether. The sun had set. It was time for me to head back to town. Another fine weekend at Cloudland.

1/30/99 It was raining and foggy when I pulled into the carport at the cabin. As I was walking away from the truck one of my longtime dreams came to life—

a beautiful young woman walked right out of the fog towards me. It was my lady friend, Emily. She had arrived a little while before me, had built a roaring fire inside, and was out for a walk in the fog. Cloudland was made for living dreams. It was good to be home.

We both had been cooped up in town all week and wasted no time making the best of a drizzly, rainy, misty day—we put on our hiking boots and rain gear and headed out into the woods. I absolutely *love* hiking in this kind of weather! The thick fog lifted just enough for us to see all of the world out in front of us. We went down the ladder trail towards the river. Even though it was chilly outside, we soon had peeled off all layers but one—guess the humidity was making things warm all over.

The forest had an overall green cast to it. We stopped and studied the scene. Many of the trees were covered from top to bottom with a fine layer of lichens. I wondered if they would eventually kill the trees, but we decided not. I don't recall seeing this much lichen cover before, except perhaps in Hoh Rain Forest in the Olympics in Washington.

We left the trail and bushwhacked our way on over to Whitaker Creek, which was running pretty good and making all kinds of music. The soft light, the mist, and the fact that everything was pretty much soaked from an all-day rain, made the colors in the forest just incredible—*super* rich greens and browns. The greens this time were from the thick, lush moss that seemed to cover everything along the stream. Boulders and trees and sometimes even the forest floor. And the moss seemed to go on forever up the hillside.

The earth was soft underfoot. And even though there was no trail, the hiking was easy—we just sort of wandered along beside the stream, which was running wildly in places. There were lots of little waterfalls and short stretches of whitewater, all dumping into emerald pools before leaving the other end of the pools to create another waterfall. Many of the trees were covered with layers upon layers of miniature shelf lichens, all soft and green. Other trees were carpeted with moss all the way up, and were leaning out over the stream.

We heard water noise coming from the bluffline up to our right. There were several waterfalls coming right out of the bluff and pouring down the hillside. They were really pumping out a lot of water!

There were several beech forests along the way. Dozens of young beech trees, all growing close together, and all still with their leaves. And the leaves ranged from deep bronze in color to nearly white. From a distance some of the trees looked like dogwood trees in full bloom. There were many places where the branches and leaves from the trees touched each other, and we had to push back the branches just to get through. The light color of the leaves reflected what little light there was getting down into the forest, which made those areas much lighter.

Thunder rolled on up the valley. Oops. It hadn't really been raining much, but it did get very dark all of a sudden, and we knew we were about to get wet. We left the main Whitaker Creek and made our way up Lower Fork, a branch of the larger stream. I have no idea why it is called "Lower" Fork. More thunder. Darker skies.

Emily shrieked with delight—she had found a most unusual beech tree. I'm not quite sure how to describe it, but will say that there was a short, stubby branch growing out of the smooth main trunk, and it pointed down at a 45 degree angle, and there was a stream of rainwater flowing from its tip. Hum. When I asked Emily how I was going to describe this tree in the Journal, she said "Just say that it was a well-endowed beech tree!" OK, enough said.

It got darker. And louder. Then flashes of light. The hillside was really steep, and the sky opened up and it began to pour. Just then we came to a neat little stretch of the stream with three or four waterfalls and wonderful pools—I'd not been to this spot before. We were heading to a larger waterfall, where there just happened to be a good overhang to escape the rain, so we didn't linger at the smaller falls area, and pressed on up the hillside.

Soon the big falls came into view. This is the second largest waterfall that I know of in the area, and it was running pretty good. Not very wide, but very tall! We scampered up the slick rocks and took refuge under the bluff. It was pouring down all over. And cold. We didn't stay too long. It was a wonderful waterfall, with no name.

We made our way around the bluffline and back to the main creek, then crossed it and climbed up onto the next bench and eventually found the Hawksbill Crag Trail. We took the lower, more scenic route along the top of the bluff. It continued to rain pretty hard. I love walking in the rain. There was a good view out over the valley from this trail.

Something caught our eyes—three miniature C-130 aircraft were gliding across the valley below, plowing through the heavy rain. Hawks? Eagles? Buzzards? Nope. They were turkeys! Big and fat and quite graceful. They never flapped a wing, but rather glided on over and into the trees, then came to rest in the large branches of a red oak (with a clunk I imagine). They reminded me of those giant C-130 military aircraft that train over the skies of central Arkansas—and they usually fly in threes too.

There was no one at the Crag—no surprise—but the view was still stunning, as always. We hiked on through the rain. It let up some, then all but stopped. The only sounds were those of raindrops hitting the leaves. I closed my eyes and listened. Sounded kind of like steaks on the grill from a distance—the juices splattering into the hot coals.

The trees and smaller bushes were covered with big drops of fresh rain, all shimmering. It hadn't taken long for the black skies to lighten up—almost looked like the sun was going to come out. Emily said that the black clouds were so full of moisture that the light couldn't get through, but now that they had dumped their load there wasn't as much to block the sun.

Down below, steam vents were forming fog banks, and the fog clouds moved back and forth, growing and shrinking and dancing all over the place. Many clouds were born here today.

We walked on in silence towards the cabin. Neither of us had much on but poly-pro and rain gear, but we were plenty warm. It wasn't until we reached the cabin and began to take our boots off that we realized that we were both soaked to the bone from head to toe! Inside, the fire was putting out a lot of warmth, and soon we were standing between a full clothes drying rack and the fire, sipping on hot chocolate laced with Irish cream. It was a fine hike. And a warm fire. There were smiles all around.

After hot showers Emily spent an hour in the kitchen preparing a wonderful dish for dinner. I chopped a few of the veggies, and made a couple loaves of French bread. The mantle was utilized not only as a spot to place the bread dough to rise, but also as a place to put the plates to heat up before serving.

Soon all the lights were out, the candles lit, a good bottle of wine opened, and we feasted on Green and White Spicy Pasta and French bread smeared with fresh baked garlic. The fire danced and the rain continued on. We were warm and dry and snug and full. Just another typical day at Cloudland.

1/31/99 It rained off and on all night, although never very hard. It stayed about 40 degrees. We stoked up the fire and had a breakfast of Cloudland coffee and toasted bagels for breakfast. Some of the mist out in the valley was rising straight up into the air, while other clouds were blowing across from left to right.

There was a feature on Sunday *Ozarks At Large* about the Blue Moon, which was going to happen later in the day. A blue moon is a second full moon in the same month. They normally only happen once every two years and nine months, but it just so happens that not only was there a blue moon in January this year, but also one in March, with no full moon at all in February. Very strange. Anyway, I was glad to hear that others were planning to celebrate the Blue Moon too, as I try to do. The full moon always rises close to the same time as sunset, and we would be right there ready for it.

Emily had brought some of her art to work on, and while she set it up, I put on my hiking boots and headed out into the cool morning air. Once I got into the woods it was very still, and quiet—nothing moving at all. The rains had scrubbed the forest clean and wiped away all tracks in the road, vehicle and critter alike. As I walked I realized that there wasn't a single critter track to be found. The longer I hiked, the more anxious I got to see something. Nothing.

I did see the ground covered with black hickory nut hulls under each of the big hickory trees in the Faddis Meadow. I'd never noticed such a complete ground cover in years past—guess it was a really good year for hickory nuts.

There weren't any birds out at all, not even down at Bob's cabin. His bird feeders were vacant. It was kind of weird.

I walked up the road, searching the ground for a single track of anyone. Still nothing. When I returned to the Faddis Meadow the sky exploded with color, sound and movement—birds at last! In fact, a lot of birds. Bluebirds, cardinals, woodpeckers, and several that I couldn't identify. I don't really know what the difference was in this second visit, which was only about ten minutes after the first, but something had happened, and the birds were out. Perhaps I had spooked them when I first appeared, and they all flew off and hid. Then once they recognized me, came out and stayed out, unafraid when I returned. I dunno. It was good to see and hear them.

But still no tracks on the ground. It had begun to get to me. When I hit the woods I got down on my hands and knees and began to examine the ground very closely for any sign that a critter had passed since the rain. Then, finally, there it was. And I followed the track off of the road and into the forest. I just knew that I could catch up with the critter that had made the track—since the track was made on top of my own, it had to be less than twenty minutes old. I got down very close to the ground. My heart pounded. Son of a gun, I had successfully tracked down a snail! He was crawling along at perhaps .00001 miles per hour. Nothing out on the ground but a snail—I guess it was still wildlife.

Back at the cabin Emily was busy painting, and I sat down at the computer and wrote in the Journal. I don't remember ever being there with just one other person before and both of us busy doing something entirely different. It felt right. (And I must say that her painting was very good—I had never seen any of her work before, and was a little overwhelmed at how good it was.)

But soon the call of the outdoors was too much, and Emily put down her brushes and put on her work clothes and went down to the meadow and started cutting brush. It was cloudy and cool out, and the breeze had died down. I soon joined her, and we spent the next few hours cleaning up the meadow spot, and building a really big fire. I mean a BIG fire—all of the brush that she had been cutting out flamed up really well.

There was this very large tree that had been cut down and cut up that has always been just too big to split up. I was trying to figure out whether to try to burn the blocks, roll them down the hill, or what. We discovered a really neat split pattern in one of the giant wood blocks, and thought that it would make a great picture. A little later Emily rolled one of the big blocks over to the fire. It wasn't until an hour later that I realized this was the log with the neat pattern on it! Oh well, it appeared that it would never burn anyway, so I figured I would come back later and take a picture.

Then I decided to try to split one of the blocks. *Pop!* It split right open! It took me a couple of hours, but I did manage to split up most of the big blocks. Since the tree was dead before I cut it down, the wood was already well seasoned. It made one large pile of split wood. Now, if I could only figure out a way to get all of that heavy wood *up* the hill to the cabin!

It remained cool all day, and rained on and off.

Boy, by the end of the day, large parts of the meadow and the hillside leading up to the lower deck were in pretty good shape. We walked/climbed around and made up plans for various plants to go here and there—ferns, hostas, azaleas, ground cover, an herb garden, a couple of trails with stepping stones with herbs planted in between them, and generally figured out what the landscaping might look like. The steep slope and the meadow would become a nice garden area. There would even be plants under the decks, which were nothing but barren dirt piles now. I was getting excited at all of the prospects. I wanted my little corner of the world to blend in with the surroundings, but also be a showplace for others to enjoy.

We put up the tools and sat down and drew all of the plans up on paper. I didn't realize how much went into planning something like this. We even got out the tape measure and figured out the square footage. Good grief, there is going to be a lot of plants! I will need to sell a lot of books.

Then the fog rolled in. Thick fog. It engulfed the forest and the cabin and our imaginations. It was getting dark, but we just had to go out and walk in the fog a little. We headed up towards the East Meadow. There was no sound but the fog. The leaves were wet, and the forest was all in silhouette. We crept into the meadow, straining to see if any critters were lurking there. A very strange sound rang out at the far side of the meadow. It must have been a coyote, but it just sounded, I don't know, a little metallic or something, not like a regular coyote sound. We only heard it once, and never saw anything. There is always interesting stuff in the East Meadow.

We walked on in the fog and talked and listened and watched, enjoying the trees and bushes and grasses. Emily spotted my little wild peach tree. I showed her the deciduous holly, and a couple of pawpaw trees. It was nearly dark when we returned to the cabin. A nice hike.

There was no view of the blue moon rise because of the fog. I had planned a picnic on the Crag, but will just have to try again on March 31st. Only once in a Blue Moon I will have a picnic on the Crag with a beautiful woman...

Emily likes to wander around in the cabin barefoot, and she let a dying wasp get the best of her little toe—she came running out into the great room holding her foot. I got out my trusty "Extractor" kit that I always have around, sat her down on the couch and let it work its magic. The sting spot was easy to find. I applied the contraption and we both sat there and watched it work, while she winced in pain. Nothing. The pain got worse. No fluid got sucked out. I guess there wasn't enough. Or something. She hopped on back into her room, still in a great deal of pain. I ground the wasp into the floor.

We fired up the BBQ grill and tried out some veggie burger mix. Hey, it was pretty darn good! I was surprised, and went back for seconds. We spent the rest of the evening playing our new board game (the one with the stones that she always beats me at), hanging out in front of the fire, and sipping fine wines. Well, not all of them were fine. I opened a bottle of Arkansas wine that was supposed to be very good. And I must tell ya, and remember that I am a guy that drinks wine out of a box, but this stuff was *terrible!* I detected a hint of lighter fluid. I don't know much about good wine, but I knew that this was really bad. And I had three bottles of it. We decided to let it breathe, for about a week.

In honor of the Blue Moon (it was hovering about overhead somewhere no doubt), I put on a Cowboy Junkies CD and we danced to their **Blue Moon** song. Well, I can't really dance, but the music and the company were great.

A couple of years ago I bought a gorgeous maple guitar with the specific purpose of singing songs during full moons to beautiful women at my cabin. Having never learned how to play it, I sold it last week. I am already longing for another guitar, but vow not to buy one until I have enrolled in a class and make myself learn how to play.

We could see the big fire glowing down below from the back deck. There was a large dark spot in the middle of the coals—must have been that big block of wood that wouldn't burn, the one with that neat pattern on it. The coals continued to glow even though it was raining—it was a big pile of coals.

Good grief, January is over! It has been a wonderful month, but I wasn't able to spend nearly enough time at Cloudland. I must say though that what little time I did spend was put to good use—some of my finest moments here so far were at the cabin in January. I will remember them with great fondness. The month came in with a great freeze and no power, and went out with rain and fog and veggie burgers. And I got to track a snail. I can't wait for February!

FEBRUARY 1999

2/1/99 The alarm went off very early, and even though it was still dark out, it was obvious that there were clouds dancing around outside. The fog had lifted, which allowed about a dozen little clouds room to play around in the valleys. There was no sunrise. But there were lots of birds—several of them at each feeder. My poor feeders. They had really taken a beating in the wind the last couple of weeks. Both of them had been blown right off of their perches. I will look into moving them to new spots.

Emily and I had spent a nice weekend at the cabin, but we both had places to go and things to do, so we didn't get to enjoy much of the new day, or the new month. I stayed behind and did a few quick chores, and then got to thinking about my dad. It would have been his 86th birthday today, and he would have loved the cabin. Probably would not have been able to get him to leave. I vowed to live the entire month in his honor.

As I left the cabin and drove through Boxley Valley on my way to Jasper to access my new car, I passed three big bull elk in a hay field. Standing right next to them on the ground were two bald eagles having breakfast. Yep, it was going to be a great month.

2/4/99 It was late when I bounced on down the little road to the cabin, after dark. Remember the *Trailside* episode that was shot at the cabin back in October? It has been airing nationally this month, and there was a special showing of it on the Arkansas Educational Television Network, plus a live call-in segment at the studio in Conway with me and Tom Aston (the river guide for the show) and Joe David Rice, Director of Tourism for Arkansas. The show turned out pretty good, except for the acting of that trail guy from Cloudland. The first several opening scenes were shot at the cabin, and included a couple of scenes of us on the lower deck in back, looking out over the scenery.

We got a ton of phone calls during the show from all over the state, and had some fun with it all. The only problem that we had was that we all got plastered with *makeup—YUK!*

There was a big blow at the cabin the morning before—the weather station clocked the wind at 44mph at 12:38am. Both the bird feeders had been blown off of their posts, smashing the bottom of one. I put them back in place, and added a bit of feed. Oddly, none of the outdoor furniture had been upset. Perhaps I have finally figured out where to put everything to keep it in place.

The sky was clear at Cloudland, and I was in for a treat soon after I arrived. While I was out in the swing on the back deck trying to get the thought and feel of that makeup out of my system, there was a hush that came over the wilderness. I think the river even stopped roaring for a few seconds. Up on top of the ridge across the river a bright yellow moon peered through the winter treeline, casting brightness and joy as far as you could see. It was one terrific moonrise!

2/5/99 Sunrise! Blue skies, white light, no wind. Winter sunrises are always special. And when I went downstairs I found a couple of dozen birds at the feeders—the most that I had seen there. Even they seemed to enjoy the sunshine. It was a quick trip for me, and I was soon headed back to town.

2/6/99 Fog today, and warm, very warm. It was late morning when I arrived. The cabin was *cold!* At least compared to the outside temp. And it was a very sharp cold too. When I looked at the weather station I realized that it was 56 degrees inside—not very cold at all—but it was 64 degrees outside. The humidity was 96% outside and 57% inside. I opened up a couple of windows and the two doors on the main level, hoping to warm up the cabin a little. The wind was blowing pretty good. Within a few minutes I realized that I was not only letting in warm air, but a great deal of moisture as well—the floor became wet with the humidity, so much so that I could see tracks on the floor where I had walked!

It really felt warm outside and the breeze was nice. After unpacking the truck and putting things away, I got on my overalls and boots, grabbed a handful of tools, and headed down into the meadow below. The wind had blown most of the fog away. My job today was to build a trail down the hillside and into the meadow, then along the bench there so that one could visit all of the wildflowers that would be popping up this summer. The soil was great, and the rocks were loose, so the digging was not too bad.

There were lots of birds darting around in the trees nearby and some of them hung out at the feeders. Once while I was taking a break (when you take a break at Cloudland, you are most likely looking out at the view), a big redtailed hawk came soaring by. He was a beautiful bird, and was having a good time playing up in the wind currents. There was no sun to light up his red tail feathers, but the color glowed a little anyway. I only saw him for a few minutes, then he moved on up the valley.

Within a couple of hours I had the main part of the trail complete down to the flat area of the meadow. Then I cut out a narrow path along the level that went to the far end of the meadow, passing through the middle of the remains of the wild sunflowers from last summer. I had to walk it several times just to see how it worked—it passed the test just fine. Once the wildflowers get up it will be a nice little stroll down through the meadow. I may even put a picnic table over on the eastern edge where we can have a picnic in the wildflowers and look down at the river. One trail down, one more to go this weekend.

It took a long, hot shower to scrape off all of the mud, but I did succeed, then got to work on cleaning up the cabin—needed lots of vacuuming. Then I installed a big photograph up in the loft—polished river rocks in the Washington Cascades. It is one of the special digital prints that I have started getting made. Very nice. Like the other framed photographs in the cabin, this one is matted with white and framed in basic black.

It was cold in the cabin once again, at least compared to what it was outside. And the humidity was low again, 61%, vs. 97% outside. I opened the two doors and watched the humidity gauges. Within five minutes it was 76% humidity inside! I closed up the doors—another layer of humidly had formed on the floor.

The fog rolled back in again, and it began to rain. Light rain at first, then it got heavy for a little while. I uncovered the BBQ grill and cooked a couple of veggie burgers for an early dinner. Good grief, after eating two of them on these big buns, with cheese and salsa, I was one stuffed puppy! I could hardly move. It is at those times that I know I must get up and move. And with thick fog outside, and the temp still up in the 60's, I just had to get out and hike.

I put on a t-shirt and my rain jacket, and thin pants. It was raining lightly, and the wind was blowing pretty good—felt great. Couldn't find any critters out stirring—they must have all been blown away. It was getting dusky dark as I got to the Faddis cabin. Someone was there—a guy was outside getting a bucket of water from the hand-dug well. I walked right on by and he never noticed me. I didn't recognize him or his car.

I took the trail down towards the Crag, but then veered off and bush-whacked on down the hillside. It was quiet, and soft underfoot, and the rain had stopped. Still lots of wind.

The Crag was deserted, as I expected, but the view was stunning. The sky was getting a dark grey, and the hillside across the way was beginning to fade some. I turned towards home and picked up the pace. As I got near the cabin I looked up and saw the big silhouette looming above. I made my way on over to the new trail, and took it through the dried wild sunflowers—good grief, some of them were seven feet tall! The rest of the trail wound round through the meadow, then on up the hillside. Not a work of art, but very functional.

When I got to the top of the trail I spent a few minutes in the fading light figuring out a route for the little trail that I had to build the next day. This one would drop down from each end of the lower deck (the one next to the base-ment) and go below the big lower deck, then back up again to the other side. It would visit the ferns and other stuff under the deck that would be planted, the herb garden, azaleas and other stuff on the steep and rocky hillside.

I sat out on the back porch swing and listened to a barred owl calling out across the way on Beagle Point. Haven't heard many of them this winter. And then a big bat came cruising by. This guy was being tossed around a bit by the gusting winds, but did manage to keep himself on some sort of reasonable course (how can you really tell with a bat?). The wind eventually carried him up and away. The warm breezes rocked me into a little nap. When I awoke it was pitch black outside. And it had started raining again, and I was getting wet.

The computer was my home for a couple of hours as I worked on the Jour-nal, answered e-mail and listened to **The Pickin' Post** on the radio. A storm raged on outside, with winds up into the 30's, and even some lightning. It was a real summer thunderstorm! In February. The radio station got blasted, and went off of the air for a time. Then the power went off at the cabin—my backup battery performed great, and the computer hummed right on along.

As the evening drew on the storm got worse, a lot worse. Both of the bird feeders got blown off of their perches, and I had to get out into the raging rain and rescue them. Top wind of 36mph. Lots of flashes, and boom, boom!

Soon after I had crawled into bed and dozed off I was literally blown awake by a giant explosion somewhere near down in the valley. The cabin shook. So did I for a second—a chill ran down my spine. Then another big crash went off, at the same time as the bright flash. The cabin shook again, and there was another chill. I doubt that a louder noise had ever happened in this valley before. It rained hard. I opened the window a little, and drifted back to sleep to the sounds of the rain and the wind and the river.

Sometime during the night I was blasted awake once again by Mother Nature, but this time it was a bright light that woke me, not noise. I opened my eyes and was nearly blinded by the moon—it had already risen above the hillside, but had just broke through a clearing sky. I couldn't believe it—only a few short dreams ago it was pouring and booming and flashing, and now the sky was full of moonlight and stars. What a quick change! The moon was a welcome sight, but I had to roll over and get out of its way before I could go back to sleep. Oh yea, and the moon had lit up the new picture on the wall—those rocks look interesting in the moonlight.

2/7/99 The eastern horizon glowed orange and blue about 30 minutes before sunrise. It looked like a bright sunny day was near. But before the sun could get to the horizon a dense cloud bank drifted in and there was no sunrise. I went back to sleep and didn't wake up again until 9am. It was a very grey day outside, but the wind wasn't blowing much. 50 degrees, 1.7 inches of rain.

As I sat out on the back deck with my Starbucks mocha (had to wipe the rain off of the chair), a shaft of sunshine broke through the clouds. It slowly made its way across the wilderness below. It was like a spotlight, in reverse, coming down from the heavens. It searched the hills and valleys, back and forth, and seemed to be looking for something.

The river below was not only roaring but it had turned a different color. It wasn't exactly muddy, although I'll bet many area rivers and streams were this morning because of all the hard rain. It was more of a khaki color. I think that is partly because of the increased amount of ground-up rocks—tiny particles suspended in the raging water—that the fast moving river creates. The river could be seen way up the valley. I'll bet it was high enough to float.

Several more spotlights searched the wilderness, but mostly the sky remained dark gray. The weather forecast was for clear, sunny skies all day. A few little birds flew by and complained to me—their feeders were still in hiding from the storm. I put them up, and within two minutes they had customers. Lots of juncos out this morning.

I retreated to the cabin and wrote some and listened to *Ozarks At Large* on KUAF. I love this radio program, but don't always get to listen to it on Friday night. A little different version is aired on Sunday morning.

Right outside my window a male downy woodpecker landed on a branch and began to peck at it. He stayed there for awhile, and I soon got interested in what he was pecking at and got out the telescope to get a good look. At first he was peeling off the thin bark of the small branch that he was perched on. He wasn't eating the bark, just knocking it off. Then he stepped back and started digging into a small hole in the branch—there must have been some good stuff in there because he spent a long time digging and eating whatever he came out with. Every time that he would thrust his head and beak into the hole his entire body would shake and quiver. He stepped up and pecked a little more bark off of the branch (I never could figure out why he was doing this, unless he was starting a new hole, although he never did dig into the limb, just peeled off the bark). Then he stepped back two paces and started pecking into another small hole that he had been standing over. I guess this was his own private little feeding spot. He turned and looked me right in the eye, then flew off. This little bird has an intricate pattern of black and white all over, and just a single band of bright red across the back of his head.

Finally, all of my indoor chores were done, and I went back down below outside to dig. I wanted to build the little trail that would visit the ferns and other stuff that we are going to plant under the deck. The digging was easy, and before long I had half of the trail complete. As I worked a group of buzzards gathered. After close inspection I found that these were not the normal turkey vultures seen here, but black vultures instead—they had black feathers covering their heads instead of the red skin of the turkey ones. I dug on.

My work was interrupted a couple of times by screams from high above— hawks! At first there was only one, then two, and finally a third. They soared in a circle, climbing ever so slowly. It was great to see them back again.

The sun did come out around noon, and it didn't take long for blue sky to dominate. It got a little warm, but felt great. Of course, I was forced to sit down on the hillside and nap every now and then. I didn't eat lunch, but snacked several times. One of my favorite mid day snacks is Fuji apple slices and pimento cheese spread. Doesn't sound all that good, but for some reason these two flavors blend together quite well.

I was getting stereo river all day long—both the Buffalo River and Whitaker Creek were roaring. And all of that water really lit up when the sun came out. "Come down and visit. Come down and visit" echoed through the valley. I am weak. I dropped my digging tool and headed down the ladder trail.

The roar of the river grew louder and louder as I approached. Yikes, Whitaker Creek was *really* running—high and fast! It was clear, and wonderful. There were waterfalls and whitewater everywhere.

And then I walked right into the magic. Rain, warm temps, afternoon sunshine, February—could only mean one thing—*witch hazel in bloom!* The fragrance was overwhelming. Super sweet and delicate. I laid down in the leaves next to the raging stream in the sunshine and took the heavy air deep in my lungs. Oh gosh, nothing else in the world like this. Visions of dancing ladies and color and money and chocolate, lots of chocolate, all ran through my head. No, they don't smell like witch hazel, but the wonderful fragrance does trigger all of the pleasing cells in your brain, and all kinds of great stuff jumps out.

I didn't get to dream very long, and soon was headed back up the hillside to get back to work. All of these distractions! I wouldn't have it any other way.

I did get the little trail complete—looks and walks just fine. And got some more wood split, and lined part of the lower trail with rocks to define it a little. So I spent most of the day outside soaking up the sunshine, and the witch hazel, and listening to the hawks and the rivers.

Later in the afternoon clouds moved back in again, the breeze picked up, and it began to cool off some. With my work done I headed out for an evening walk. The woods were quiet, but I didn't see any critters out. As I was on my way back to the cabin the clouds behind me really lit up. In fact, there was one incredible light show! There were bands of yellow and orange and red, alternating with blue. It was wonderful. I had to stop and sit down just to take it all in. Within a few minutes it was all over and I was left there in the dark with another terrific memory. And no flashlight. But I did make it back to the cabin, quickly packed my things up and headed to town.

2/10/99 Dr. Neil Compton, the man who founded the Ozark Society and is credited with saving the Buffalo River from destruction and leading the fight to get it established as America's first National River, died this afternoon after a massive heart attack. He had just led a hike to a cave near Jasper a couple of days before. He was 86 years old, and still in pretty good health for his age, and very sharp mentally. No one person, nor group of people, have done more to protect and promote the Ozarks than Neil Compton. He is the sunshine that lights up the wilderness. And while he may have left us, his efforts will continue to light the way for generations to come. Thanks Neil, for all that you have given us. You will be missed.

2/12/99 It was bright and sunny as I returned to Cloudland. This would be a sweet and sour weekend for sure—the wilderness was shining in all its winter glory, and would be warm and inviting, but the lifeblood and spirit of the forest had been snuffed out with Neil's passing. None of the wilderness would have been protected without his efforts.

The weather station showed that a great wind had rumbled through the day after Neil died—53mph winds were recorded—the second highest ever since May. It had to be Neil letting me know that he was still around.

After a small chore at the cabin I put on my walking boots and headed down the ladder trail to the river. There wasn't going to be a public service for Neil at the river so I decided that I had to go down and have one for myself. It was warm and sunny, and the witch hazel were popping out all over the place along the river. And the river itself was an incredible teal color, running and playing and singing a peppy tune—it was a glorious day on the Buffalo!

I reached over and snapped off a sprig of bright red and yellow witch hazel, took its sweet smell deep into my lungs, then tossed it out into the river. This was Neil Compton's river for sure. His life would flow in every drop for eternity. I wanted the flower to ride with Neil on down stream a ways. I sat there and thought of my friend, of his life and energy, of all the people that he touched, of all the joy and happiness that he had given and would continue to give to millions of folks, and of the wilderness, of the wild critters and the flowers and the trees and the stones and the moss-covered boulders and the towering painted bluffs. A red-tailed hawk rode the wind currents high above, and screamed out his own tribute to Neil. I came down to the river not to mourn the loss of my friend, but to celebrate this great man's life and all that he had done. I think that everyone should do this in their own way and on their own time. February 10th will always be remembered at Cloudland, but so will August 1st, Neil's birthday. Good-bye Neil. Thanks for who you were. For the values that you stood for. And for what you left behind.

The hike back up the hillside was nearly painless, and silent, except for my heavy breathing. Once I got up the ladder and on top of the bluff I hiked on over to the Crag. Hawksbill Crag is not part of the Buffalo National River park, but Neil Compton certainly had a great deal to do with it being protected. He told me once that during his first trip there in the 1970's he found a pile of "the scat of a large cat," which he collected and sent off and had analyzed. It turned out to be that of a cougar. Neil was like a cougar, and he will live on in all of them. I have not seen one out here, but will look forward to the day when I come face to face with one. I won't be afraid—Neil will be inside. I sat there on the Crag and soaked up the end of the day.

It had gotten a little cool outside, and I had a good fire going in the fireplace when my Emily drove up just after dark. She had a big smile on her face—there was a Cloudland pizza that was in the oven! It was clear and dark outside, but with a million stars shining.

2/13/99 The sun broke over the hill early and lit up the wilderness. Still clear blue skies. The temp was in the low 30's. No birds. We stood in front of the fire and had toasted blueberry bagels and coffee, and a wonderful fresh fruit mixture of apples, peaches, pears, and mangos. The mangos were especially good! A bright flash of red flew past the window—a pileated woodpecker stopped by to see what we were having for breakfast. Then we suited up and drove away to a remote trailhead for a day of hiking. There were lots of hawks hanging out in the trees along the road.

We began our hike at the Boen Gulf Trailhead. The first thing that we found was a mud puddle with a big glob of frog eggs in it. Half of the glob was sticking up out of the water and was frozen, and the other half was OK. I wondered if the frozen guys would survive. We followed an old log road into the wilderness and down into the Boen Gulf drainage. We passed a small group of OHTA hikers that were setting up camp near the creek. They had gotten an early start and were going to spend the weekend exploring around the area. Our goal was to follow the creek all the way down to the Buffalo River, then figure out a different way back to the car.

The creek was flowing pretty good, as it tumbled over moss-covered boulders into quiet pools. We came to a witch hazel bush almost immediately. It was still pretty cool, but the yellow flowers were putting out some very nice fragrance. I reached over and snipped off a twig, and tossed it into the moving water. Another nod to Neil Compton. The more we walked, the more witch hazel we found. One tree after another after another. And they all seemed to be calling out to me to snip off part of them and send them off down the creek, all wanting to become a part of the Compton memorial. I tried to reassure them that their fragrant blooms and brilliant flowers and sturdy foothold at the creek's edge would be monuments in themselves. How can you tell if a tree understands? I think they did.

The hillside next to the stream was pretty steep, but the earth was soft from recent rains and our boots dug in and grabbed hold easily. At one point as we were hiking across a level bench with Emily in the lead, she quite literally walked right into a screech owl. Really. The little bird was perched at about head level in a small tree. She didn't see him. I'm sure the owl saw her coming, but refused to move, assuming that she would veer off. It wasn't until she walked into the little tree that the owl decided it was time to get the heck out of there. It was quite a sight from my perspective as the little tree that she was walking through came to life and there was all this commotion. The owl flew off and landed in another tree a few feet away, and looked at us with disbelief. We looked at the owl with the same expression I'm sure.

There were a number of giant boulders in the streambed, great slabs of rock that tumbled down from the bluff up above. One group of these boulders formed one of the most beautiful pools of turquoise water that I have ever seen in the Ozarks—it was spectacular! I don't know how deep it was, but certainly was way over my head, and it was about 40-50 feet in diameter, with a waterfall pouring into one end of it. And there was one big flat rock slab on the lower side that would make a perfect sunning area. Had it been a few degrees warmer we probably would have stripped off and jumped in. This is one terrific pool! I shall return and take a few pictures when things green up some.

As we continued downstream we passed through an area full of giant sycamore trees. We tried to reach around one of them, but couldn't, even with both of our wingspans—it had to be 12 feet around or more. And towering high above. The stream had gotten rather tame down below. And quiet. The hillsides above were carpeted with thick moss and ferns. One big rock slab had about five or six different kinds of ferns growing on it. And a number of dormant wildflowers too—couldn't figure out what kind they were.

Back down in the streambed I found a flat rock that was covered with an incredible pattern of lichens. The bright green ones were outlined with a black border, and were growing in between dozens of white lichens. It all looked like a patchwork quilt, or an aerial photograph of farm country, with the individual fields outlined. I didn't have my good camera with me, but I certainly will return and look for this rock again.

Emily found an alder bush. We had seen a number of these on our hikes this year, but just recently figured out exactly what they were. They are quite noticeable because the plant has both male and female parts, which look a little weird growing right next to each other on the same branch.

At one point the river went underground, only to surface again a few hundred yards downstream as a spring up on the left bank—it was spilling down the hillside over thick moss. We found a giant flat rock slab nearby that was sitting in the stream, and sunny, so we broke there for lunch. The rock itself was cold, but the sunshine helped. Emily had noticed that the portions of chocolate kisses (with almonds) weren't quite equal—I had packed lunch, and had put three in her bag, but somehow 20 of them ended up in mine—I moved some of mine into her bag to keep from being attacked.

After all of the kisses I laid there on the rock in the sunshine next to Emily, with hawks soaring overhead, and the sweet smell of witch hazel everywhere. Gosh, I couldn't think of a better place in the world to be. The temp was in the 50's, although it seemed even warmer.

There were a few more waterfalls and giant boulders and deep pools to explore, then Boen Gulf ended its run at the Buffalo River, which was running fast and loud. The banks were covered with witch hazel, and the fragrance was marvelous. Some of the bushes had flowers that were all yellow. Others the flowers were nearly all red. Most of them had red centers with yellow extensions. These were all "winter" witch hazel bushes/trees, as opposed to the "fall" witch hazel that blooms in Nov.-Dec., and does not have any fragrance.

We could have easily crossed the river and hiked on back to the cabin, but wanted to circle back and find a new route to the trailhead. So we bid farewell to Boen Gulf and headed up the river. We ran into Dean and Bonnie LaGrone from the OHTA group who had come down the creek behind us. It was a great weekend to be out. A friend of mine, Dave Stahle (one of the world's authorities on aging trees—called a dendrochronologist), had marked a giant beech tree on the map, so we wandered around some looking for it. While we never did find it, we did come across a *huge* grape vine—it was nearly a foot thick!

A little ways upstream we found a small drainage that was spilling down the steep hillside. We followed it *straight up* the hill past many waterfalls. We stopped often to admire the view. Yea, right. At least one of us had to stop and suck in a little air! We finally made it up to the top and walked through a small valley that had been the home to someone a long time ago—we found an old tin can and a few piles of rocks. It was obvious that the more level areas had been cleared of rocks and farmed. The steeper parts of the area were covered with rocks. It was a nice little hanging valley.

We topped out and headed over to the far side of the ridge. I hadn't been in this area before, but knew from the map where I wanted to go. My plan was to drop down the other side of the ridge and find several nice waterfalls that I had been to once before, then make our way back to the trailhead.

My plans soon got messed up. We realized that if we continued walking in the direction that I had set out for we would end up some place else. We made a correction and continued on. Then we came to an old log road. Something wasn't quite right. I got out the map and studied it. The hills and valleys weren't where they were supposed to be! How could that be? There was an old road marked on the map, but it wasn't going in the right direction. I looked around very puzzled. It just wasn't right. And then I asked Emily—and let me tell you that I had to dig way down and get the courage to ask her this—I asked her if she had a compass. A *compass?* I don't believe in them myself, so I never carry one. After her laughter died down some, she said that she didn't have a compass—a girl after my own heart. What in the world did I need a compass for anyway I thought out loud—there was the sun, right over there, and it was going down, so that must be SW. Duh. I was trying to make the sun be in the wrong place, because the terrain just didn't match where I thought we were. Then it hit me—the map was upside down! What an idiot.

We left the ridgetop, dropped on down the hill and came out right on top of the very waterfall that I was hoping to find. Dumb luck for sure. But I had a good laugh on the way down. It was a beautiful open forest with a smooth leaf-covered floor, and a gradually sloping hillside. We were on auto-pilot and enjoying the afternoon and our smooth route. All of a sudden I heard a gasp, and looked over just in time to see Emily collapse to the ground—she had tripped on a grape vine and landed right square on her knees. I just had to laugh.

The waterfall was gorgeous. It was tall and running wildly, although it appeared right out of a very small drainage—the water was pouring over the main bluffline, and it was quite a fall. The top of the falls was lined with thick moss and lichens, and azaleas. We carefully made our way along the bluffline, threading through the thick stands of azaleas—this place will be quite spectacular in early May when they are in bloom! Then we came to a second falls—very nice as well. And then we came to the creek, right on our level, and a third waterfall. We made our way down through the bluffline and spent some time photographing this falls and the previous one. They both were guarded with azalea bushes, and a few magnolias. I've taken pictures here before, but not when everything was in bloom—this year for sure! This waterfall area does not have a name, but something will pop up one of these years no doubt. We decided that we should call them something very negative like Boring Falls or Rattlesnake Falls or some other term that wouldn't attract a lot of traffic.

From the waterfall area we bushwhacked on up the hillside and found the old log road that we had taken in, and followed it back to the trailhead. There were several other mud puddles with frog eggs in them, and the one that had been frozen had thawed and seemed to be OK. We also found a couple of old bicycles that had been given shallow graves. It was a great hike—I would be back soon, and often.

We were famished when we arrived back at the cabin and spent about 30 minutes attacking all visible food. Then we retired to the back deck—it looked like it was going to be one terrific sunset, and we were not disappointed. We sat there and sipped wine as the cloud patterns danced around and changed colors. The only sounds were that of the river far below, and the creaking of my friend's rocking chair. A female downy woodpecker came by to visit, and bravely munched on the peanut butter mixture in the feeder in front of us.

Inside there were two loaves of 12-grain French bread rising on the mantle. They would come in handy later.

The clouds turned pink, then burnt-orange, then brilliant red, all against bands of blue sky. The color lasted a long time. It got a little chilly, and I passed out comforters. We gazed on until the last wisp of color faded. It was a very peaceful time.

Sunset watching can sure take a lot out of you though, so we got back into the kitchen and prepared a Saturday night feast—Banff Pasta, fresh bread with baked garlic, salad, and a bottle of merlot. A roaring fire, some good blues music on KUAF, and a game or two of Mancala and we were all set. Just another typically wonderful day at Cloudland.

2/14/99 We had already been up for an hour or so by the time the sun peeked up over the ridgetop (hey, it was Valentine's Day, what can I say—and Cloudland is one of the more romantic places in the world if I do say so myself). It was a clear day again, and cold—about 30 degrees. We had blueberry biscuits and Cloudland Coffee, then laced up our hiking boots and headed out.

We drove on over and hiked into Sweden Falls Natural Area. The bluffline there is very nice, but the waterfall is quite impressive! It is one of the taller waterfalls in the region. And since the bluff is so high, it blocks out the sun at this time of the year, and there were a number of ice formations there. We took a few pictures and wandered around and enjoyed the lush moss-covered boulders. This is an unusual area because it is sort of land locked the Natural Area, which is protected and owned by the State of Arkansas, is completely surrounded by private property, and has no legal access. The folks who live nearby are very nice though, and will usually grant access if you are nice to them. It is one splendid area, although not very large.

We hiked down into another unique little area nearby—Hole In Rock Falls. This spot too is on private property, and there are many cattle grazing in pastures nearby. But it is a very unusual feature, a lot like the Glory Hole, where the water comes pouring down through a hole in the roof of an overhang. Only this spot is much smaller than the Glory Hole, but the water does form a nice waterfall just below the hole, which is interesting.

The sky was blue and without a single cloud when we got back to the cabin. After munching on leftover pizza we decided to play lizards for a little while, and spent a couple of hours sprawled out on the lower deck, soaking up the warm sunshine. When the wind wasn't blowing it got downright warm. We spent a little time down in the little meadow making final plans for clearing and wildflower seed placement, then packed up and headed back to town.

Time seems to fly by when I am out at Cloudland, but then again that time is usually well spent, as it was this weekend. I got to spend some quality time with my lady friend, and say good-by to Neil. I think I will return again soon!

2/18/99 Snow greeted me on my return to Cloudland. And it was blowing pretty hard. The trees, which were covered on one side only with the white stuff, looked magnificent! The snow was nearly silver. It was possible to look in one direction through the woods and see all brown trees—their bare bark—with a snow-covered forest floor, and then look the other direction and see nothing but snow, snow, snow. And it was still coming down. At first, very fine snow, then the snow dust grew into some pretty good-sized flakes, then back down to dust again.

The weather station showed the winds at 41mph on the 15th.

A fire was quickly roaring in my cabin, and then I realized that there wasn't much firewood at the cabin. It was about an hour before dark. I had a lot of prep work still to do in the meadow before I could sow some wildflower seeds I had bought in town, but it would be perfect if I could get the seed out and then let it get snowed on. But it didn't look like I would have the time to get it done, so I played with the split wood piles that dotted the meadow.

I spent a couple of hours moving the piles of wood out of the main meadow area and up onto the base of the hillside, where they would be out of the way, and closer to the cabin. A lot of the wood made it up to the cabin as well. And I got to playing with the rocks in the meadow too. There are lots of rocks there. Some of them highly colored with lichen, and others freshly cut from larger rocks somewhere up the hill. At first I just piled them up here and there, but then I used them to outline yet another little trail that I wanted to develop.

The snow was coming down very fine, but steady. No wind at all. There was the typical low ceiling of clouds hugging some of the hilltops and extending down into the valley way off. But there were also cloud banks forming and moving around in the valleys, just like when it rains. Were these snow banks, or clouds or what? It was very quiet out, and the entire scene was very serene. If you listened real close, you could hear the snow hitting the ground.

Since it was so warm, about 34 degrees, the snow was melting on the ground as fast as it was falling, so there wasn't much of an accumulation—only a half inch or so. But it was great to see snow at Cloudland. And that scene out in the wilderness was wonderful.

I worked until I couldn't see to walk any more. I was a mess from head to toe. Hauling snow-covered wood around is not too clean. But I got an idea. I have always wanted a "mud room" out here, but just didn't work it into the design of the cabin. How about using the front part of the basement, by the outside door? Yep, I think that will work. Uh oh, I may have to get out the pencil and come up with a layout for walls and such. Or perhaps just put a different floor and some seats in that area and leave everything open like it is now. Right now the mud room is also the main entrance to the cabin, and not a very good place for muddy boots and filthy clothes.

It seemed like a chili night, so I warmed up some of my leftover veggie chili. I must say that this stuff is one of those foods that is not better the second time—needs to be fresh. As I sat down at the computer to write, all of my kitchen chores done for the night, I had a sudden flash of despair—I was stranded out here without a single piece of chocolate! How could I have overlooked that? Then I had a thought. There is a tupperware thing in the pantry, and I have been putting treats in there for a couple of months now. I didn't remember anything chocolate that would be in there—mostly just hard candy—but much to my surprise, I discovered Hershey's Kisses—half of the bag that we started on last week! Man, there was a lot of them—I had hit the motherload. And almonds too. Now, if it could just snow a foot tonight...

Sometime during the night I was up feeding the fire and looked out and found a million stars—no clouds at all. But the temp was still in the low 30's.

2/19/99 It was grey and dark and cloudy when the sun was supposed to come up. It wasn't snowing outside, but the ground was still covered with snow, so it was all white out. I hung around the fireplace for an hour or so waiting for the temp to reach 35 degrees. At first, it was so foggy out that I couldn't even see the trees at the edge of the meadow. Gradually the clouds lifted, and before long I could see Beagle Point, then the river, and finally, all of the wilderness. And the sun began to break through just a little. The temp hit 35 so I dressed up and went out to work in the meadow. The snow on the ground hung around for a while, but then all melted in a hurry.

I spent most of the morning moving wood and rocks and cutting all of the little trees and suckers that had begun to grow in the meadow. Then I got out the rake and cleared out about 30 or 40 spots down to bare earth—these would be the spots where I would plant wildflower seeds. There was too much space to rake everything, but these smaller areas would eventually spread out (I hoped) and cover up the entire meadow. At last the meadow was prepped and ready for seed.

But first I went up to Bob's to borrow some sand. Then I filled the back of the new truck with hay that Bob had stockpiled at the end of one of his gardens. I saw Eddy Silcott up there. He was just out looking around, and was headed over to try to find the old gay lady community of Sassafras at the end of Cave Mountain. I wished him well.

I mixed up the seed and sand and started "broadcasting" my precious seeds. It only took me about twenty minutes to get rid of the $150 worth of the seeds. Then I covered it all with a thin layer of the hay, just to keep it all from blowing away. The sun had come out and the sky was mostly clear, and thank goodness the wind wasn't blowing. Finally, I had the job complete. A hawk came soaring overhead, just to inspect my work, and to say hello.

A group of young ladies from the Today's Arkansas Outdoor Women's Network was coming out to spend the weekend, and have a planning session for their group for the rest of the year. So I spent a little time getting the cabin in shape, then I packed up my stuff and headed back into town.

2/21/99 It was a little chilly and mostly cloudy when I arrived back at the cabin around noon. My guests were all packed up and leaving. The cabin smelled like they had been cooking all weekend—marvelous fragrance! It didn't take long for the sun to burn off most of the clouds, but it remained cool all afternoon, in the 30's.

I spent a couple of hours in the afternoon building a wood frame for a darkroom that I had set up in one of the spare bathrooms in my house in Fayetteville—all of my tools are now at the cabin, so I am forced to do all of my woodworking at the cabin. What a delight! The sun felt great, and I worked down on the back deck. I used the lumber that we ripped out of the guest room closet on New Year's Day—had to remove a few nails first, but the boards were just fine.

Once my little chore was done I had to take a nap on the couch. The sunlight bounced all around the log walls. It was a good nap. When I woke up I realized that the shadows were getting long, so I put on my walking shoes and headed out for a hike. The light was wonderful by the time I reached Hawksbill Crag. There were a couple of guys there who had me take a picture of them. They didn't want to be standing out on the Crag though for some reason, but I did get the Crag in the background, all lit up.

The woods were silent—nothing out stirring, not even the wind. The light grew orange as the shadows lengthened. I walked on up to the Faddis cabin and then over towards the East Meadow. I flushed up a woodcock or snipe just before I reached the meadow—couldn't tell which one it was. They both have a long beak. Don't remember seeing either one out here before.

No critters in the East Field either, although Benny had been out a few days before and plowed up the big garden there. It was now ready to plant some bear food in it. I wondered if we were going to have the major problems with the bears this new summer like we did last summer? I hoped that just one or two came around, and they would be friendly and non-destructive like my friend from the end of the summer was. I look forward to finding out.

The west side of the cabin was glowing when I got back—the sun was slipping down below the far ridge and putting on a splendid light display. I hauled up some firewood, then sat in the swing and watched as about a dozen bands of clouds lit up a bright orange.

I had some rice and veggies for dinner, then did a little computer work from a hike that I took early in the week. I am walking the entire length of the Ozark Highlands Trail, making notes and taking pictures of bad spots that need work. Then I transcribe my audio tape and make recommendations, like I did tonight. I'll be heading out to do another long stretch tomorrow. This is actual work for pay, funded by the highway department. I don't mind getting paid to hike once in a while!

As the evening drew on the stars came out, and so did the moon. Only it was about a third of a moon, and wasn't too bright. The temp dropped quickly, and soon was in the 20's. The fire felt great, and I took another nap on the couch while listening to some classical music on the radio. After a little more computer work I called it a night.

2/22/99 When I got up at 5am there were still lots of stars out playing, but the moon had set. It was rather dark outside. And a wee bit chilly—the temp was 22 degrees, and the windchill brought it down to five below zero. Sounded like a great day for a hike! Somehow my usual dress of shorts and tennis shoes seemed a little under-dressed—I added a pair of poly-pro underwear pants, and a fleece vest. Still not much, but when I do the kind of trail work that I would be doing today (hiking fast), I don't need too much. My goal was to hike 17 miles by 2pm. I had to wheel off the distance as I went, note any bad spots in the trail, and take pictures of all signs and places that needed heavy trail work.

As I drove away from the cabin there was a glow in the eastern sky, and no clouds anywhere to be seen. I did make my 17 miles by 2pm (1:45), and was rather chilled all day, but I made it just fine.

2/25/99 Emily and I had just made a shuttle for a four-day hike on the OHT, and made our way to the cabin to spend the night before our adventure. It was rather warm when we arrived late in the evening, in the 60's, and damp. No stars out. No moon.

There must have been a few big gusts prior to our visit—one of the bird feeders had been slung off of the spot where it was hanging, and it fell fifteen feet to the ground and crashed into about twenty pieces. Darn wind. Darn me for not having any duck tape at the cabin. I was going to tape down the hanging chain the last time that I was at the cabin, but didn't have the tape. I'll have to move the other feeder to a less violent spot (it had been knocked off of its hanger too, but didn't crash to the ground).

2/26-28/99 It was grey and dreary at dawn, just the way I like my days! We got up and ate a quick breakfast of Cloudland coffee and blueberry biscuits. There wasn't any big fire to stand in front of, since it was so warm. Although it felt a little chilly inside the cabin. It began to sprinkle as we drove away, but that would turn out to be the most precip that we would get on our 50-mile hike, even though they had forecast heavy rain for the next two days.

We drove to the Cherry Bend Trailhead, and headed out on a four-day hike on the OHT, ending at Ozone. It was glorious hiking weather the entire way. The first day was cloudy and damp, but no rain. It did get pretty darn cold when the wind blew. I only had shorts on. We stopped and peeked in the well at Hare Mountain—only about half full. Herrods Creek, our planned camp for the night, was low enough to cross dry, and since we had only done ten miles by 2pm we decided to hike on. And so we did.

Even Indian Creek was low enough for us to cross dry, which we did, and then made camp for the night nearby, a fourteen mile day. The trail was in pretty good condition. This stretch had been built by our OHTA volunteers way back in 1982—our first stretch of trail to build.

After dinner I drew out a pattern on the back of my bandanna, we gathered 48 little stones, and then we played our stones game. Emily won every game.

The sun came out the next day as we made our way through the Marinoni Scenic Area, but it was still breezy and a little nippy. There were deer everywhere—we saw singles, pairs, a group of about a dozen, and we even walked right up on three that were still in their beds—it took them about ten long seconds to figure out that they were no longer hidden, and then they were off in a flash. We saw wildlife all day, including a woodcock, and a woolly worm. There were also wildflowers popping up—trout lilies mainly, and they looked like they were glad to get out of the ground.

We only did nine miles the second day because we wanted to spend some time and the night at this wonderful campsite spot—three nice waterfalls and a wonderful bluffline with a spectacular view of the Little Mulberry River Valley. Emily took a dip in a pool below one of the waterfalls—yikes, it was cold! Then we laid out in the sunshine on the bluff and soaked up what was left of the day.

It was dry. Very dry out, and the wind was blowing, so we didn't build a fire. We gathered more rocks and played the stones game after dinner as we watched the sun slip down below the far ridge. All of the games this night were won by me, so we were now even.

I decided to call this spot Sunset Camp, Sunset Waterfalls, and Sunset Shelter, if we ever build one there. Nice place.

The sun was bright the next day, no wind, and it was a delightful fourteen miles to our next campsite (*lots* of waterfalls!). There were a couple of serviceberry trees that had popped out during the day, and the witch hazel was nearly overwhelming in some spots—lots and lots of it. It was clear and cold this night, and the bright moon kept us up for a while.

The last day was only twelve miles, and before lunch we had hiked more than ten of them. A few more serviceberry trees were out, but no more wildflowers. We were on auto pilot most of the day, and it felt great. It was good to get to the car though, mainly because we had a Mexican feast planned for dinner back in town!

February has been used up. And while I was able to spend many days in the woods, I didn't get to be at Cloudland nearly enough. It was a rather warm and dry month, with lots of wind!

MARCH 1999

3/7/99 It had been more than a week since I had been to the cabin—one of the longest stretches ever! I was thankful to find it had not been burned down or blown away. The weather station recorded a reading of 40mph winds a couple of days before, but not much rain. The floor on the main level and up in the loft was covered with wasp bodies. They must all be coming out and trying to fly into spring. Too bad for them—they should have taken refuge in a log somewhere else! So my first job was to vacuum up all of the crispy little things.

The sun was out some, but it was chilly—down in the 40's with the wind blowing. My legs were itching, so I had to go for a hike. At the edge of my meadow there were two serviceberry trees in full bloom—the first of the season at Cloudland. The river was so low that I could not hear its voice. I took the ladder trail down the steep hillside. Most everything was still in winter dress—lots of greys and browns. I was wearing lightweight shoes, and I kind of bound on down the hill from rock to rock and from bare spot to bare spot on the trail. My body just sort of flowed on down the hill effortlessly. It felt great.

About halfway down I stopped to admire a giant red oak that is right next to the trail. Much to my delight I found a tiny trout lily growing right in the middle of the trail and next to the big tree—this is the first official wildflower at Cloudland this year! Trout lilies are amazing little flowers, so named because of the patterns on their leaves. And that pattern is quite often much more remarkable than the flower itself. The delicate, often nearly white flower hangs upside down. This one was bowing to the immense tree creature growing at its side. They looked very funny together—the giant oak reaching high into the sky, and the tiny wildflower, with its head bent down in prayer. There were no other flowers around.

As I skipped on down the trail more of the lilies appeared (they are also called dog-tooth violets, after the shape of their bulbs), many of them preferring to pop up in the middle of the trail. Soon there were dozens and dozens of them, and I was glad to have their company.

The sky was overcast by the time I got to the bottom and it was easier to see the stones in the old root cellar. While I stopped to admire this historical structure a blur of color caught my eye—there were daffodils blooming nearby! I love these guys. They were often brought along by the early pioneers and planted around a cabin. This spot was a homesite no doubt, but I had never found the chimney or any remains of the cabin foundation. As I walked on over to the bright yellow flowers I was shocked to discover that they were growing in and around a pile, or actually a line of rocks that appeared to be—a fallen chimney!!! In fact, there looked to be two chimneys, one facing the other. The largest one had toppled over. I could see the outline of the cabin foundation too. And there was a dense field of wild iris framing the top of the big chimney, although none of them were in bloom yet. That would make one stunning picture—the iris and the daffodils and the cabin remains all together. And what was the most surprising to me was the fact that all of this was within a few feet of the trail—I had hiked right past it a hundred times!

I continued on down to the main chimney right next to Whitaker Creek. There were no flowers to be seen, and I wondered if the folks ever planted any, if they all died out, or if they were just late bloomers. This is a nice chimney, and I took a couple of pictures.

Down at the river I found clear water moving on downstream at a leisurely pace. The water level was quite low for this time of the year—more like summer flow. The rock bar right there was wonderful—full of polished stones of all shapes and colors. And all of the tiny sycamore sprouts that covered the rock bar were bare of all leaves—just a forest of single stalks about a foot tall. It looked a little odd, but beautiful just the same.

I headed on back up the trail, huffing and puffing and sweating all the way, but enjoying the exercise a great deal. When I got to the base of the bluff I turned and followed the bluff to the left. All of the times that I had taken this route before I was more or less just trying to get somewhere and wasn't really paying too much attention to the bluffline. But today I wanted to explore the bluffline, and had no timetable nor destination.

And explore I did. What a gorgeous rock formation this is! Much of the base of the bluff is overhung—little shelters here and there. And the shelters are filled with wind and leaf sculptures—piles of leaves carefully laid down by the wind in graceful curves. Some of the piles were several feet deep, and mostly undisturbed.

The bluff towered high overhead—up to 100 feet (I must measure it someday with the rope). And the color of the rock was amazing—blues and blacks and reds and oranges and greens. And there were different layers of rock, each having its own texture. Some layers were larger and smooth, others were thin and jagged and broken up. I walked along, and admired.

One stretch of bluffline had a middle level of grassy slopes, and one slope was absolutely covered with wildflowers, about twenty feet above the base of the bluff. I could tell that some of the flowers were trout lilies, but couldn't see the second variety well enough to ID. I hunted for, and found a way up to that level. It was like a second bluffline, and I could walk along the base for a couple of hundred feet. I had to drop down to get onto the wildflower slope. It was a lush grassy spot, covered with lilies and the other wildflowers (small white flowers, also bent down, growing five-six flowers to a stalk—I later ID'd them as toothworts). It was a marvelous little natural garden spot!

On the far end of my little world the two blufflines came together, and I had to retreat back to where I had come up to get back down. I continued on and soon came to another spot that I had wanted to investigate. There was a cave up there in the middle of the bluff, and a shelf. I hadn't been able to get up to it before, but I decided today was the day, and I found a spot to pull myself up the rock face and onto the ledge. The cave was pretty neat, a large opening, and it went back about 40 feet and then ended. It was about fifteen feet or so tall, with the classic fault line (crack) along the middle of the roof, and lots of breakdown on the floor. As I turned to exit the cave, I realized that it faced the southeast, and would catch the sunrise during the winter, and often the moonrise too. Hum, I wonder if an Indian had designed this cave?

I go up rock faces a lot easier than I go down them. Same goes for buildings and trees and such. The rock face where I came up to this spot was a bit of a stretch for me, so I wasn't looking forward to going down the same way. But there was this big tree that was laying right up against the bluff. I straddled it, and slid down. It was kind of fun, and I made it to the bottom lickety-split.

There was an area of big boulders along one level spot under the bluff, all of them covered with moss and leaves and such. Several spots looked like there were small caves underneath. I got down on all fours and crawled into one of them. It looked like the perfect spot for a bear den. I didn't have a flashlight or I would have gone in a little further. There wasn't any smell, so I figured no one was home.

The next stop was directly below Hawksbill Crag. This big chunk does loom out overhead as you would expect. It was good to find that there was almost no trash on the ground—only one Sprite can, and a couple of other odd bits. This is one of the most visited spots in wild Arkansas. Hikers are by and large good people and keep trash in their packs as they should.

There was another spot where the bluff was broken up some by grassy ledges and stuff, so I proceeded to investigate. As I got about a third of the way up, and was still climbing hand-over-fist, I peered under a ledge and came face to face with one of the most frightening critters in all of the wilderness. A bear? Nope. A cougar? Hardly. This dude was *really* scary, and strikes fear in even the toughest mountain man or woman. Within a foot of my face was the nose and beady little eyes of a SKUNK!!! Yikes! I nearly jumped off of the bluff. The skunk was a little shocked as well, but must have heard me scrambling up the bluff. He jumped up, turned around in mid-air, and scurried to the back of the ledge. He had been laying in a pile of leaves, and there was a depression where he had been. I got the heck out of there before any spraying began. Whew, I dodged a liquid bullet!

The sun broke back out just before dark as I got to the cabin. It was a wonderful hike, and it was great to be back at Cloudland!

The phone rang, and it was Milancy McNamara. I had to run up a book for her and a batch of books for Bill to autograph. While I was there a tiny donkey appeared in their yard. Apparently a neighbor of sorts has a bunch of farm animals at their cabin, and the animals run wild when the folks are not around, which is most of the time. The donkey likes to eat pretty bushes. The donkey was chased off, but I heard that it returned several times.

I returned to the cabin to the smell of fresh-baking bread. Ummmm, must be suppertime! I stoked up the fireplace, then sauteed some garlic, tomatoes and broccoli, and added a package of Mozzarella Garlic Tortelloni, then sat in my big leather chair and feasted to the sounds of Crosby, Stills and Nash, and the crackling of the fireplace. This was a wonderful dish, but the only problem was that I ate the entire pan—about four servings! I was stuffed, so much so that there was absolutely no room for the fresh 12-grain bread. Oh well, the night was still young.

I went out onto the back deck to see what stars were out. There were only a few of the brighter ones visible—the rest were obscured by a thin cloud cover. The wind had picked up, and was blowing pretty hard from the east. That is not normal, and often is a signal that something is about to happen. It was cold, but felt great outside. Especially knowing the fireplace was only a few feet away.

The computer was fired up and I typed on for a couple of hours. Just when it was time for bed I cut open one of the many small loaves of fresh bread that I had made, smothered it with honey and butter, and sat by the glowing embers and had my little dessert. As I looked around my little log cabin world, with my fat belly and my warm hearth, I wondered how in the world I could ever leave this place for very long. I had been gone much too long.

3/8/99 The wind howled and screamed all night—up to 40mph. When the wind blows like this it sucks more air out of the fireplace, which in turn burns the wood faster, so I had to make a couple of trips down to stoke the fireplace during the night. Just before daylight the pounding of heavy rain woke me up. Thank goodness—we really needed some rain! The fire was nearly out, and I got a little concerned when I realized that I had no more dry wood around! Oops. I crawled back into bed and snoozed a little longer, then got up for good as daylight, and thunder, filled the cabin.

The rain continued on—more than an inch already—and so did the wind, which was keeping up a 20-30mph pace. That easterly blow was doing its job. I don't mind the wind or the rain, in fact enjoy them both. But this wind brought the rain into the cabin. This had happened only once before, also during a big eastern blow—there were a couple of leaks under the loft floor by the back door. We have not been able to figure out where this leak is coming from, or how to fix it. It only happens when the wind and rain are just right. Otherwise, I continue to be amazed at how airtight this log structure is.

The wind was really thrashing about, which sent water, trees, bird feeder, and assorted deck furniture off in all directions.

I braved the driving wind and rain and went outside and gathered up some wet wood. My log stash is against the east side of the cabin, under the six-foot overhang, and is almost always dry. Only the storms from the east, like this one, ever get that wall wet. There was enough wood there to last for most of the day, but I would have to go down into the meadow to gather enough for tonight. I would wait and see if the storm let up to do this chore.

It was soon warm and toasty inside again, and I was busy working on the computer while the storm raged on outside. I had the classics on KUAF for company too. The clouds were not hanging low in the valley like they often are during storms like this one, but rather were on top of the ridges, which meant that I could see down into all of the valleys. There were a few cloud banks here and there, but mostly small ones that were swirling and dancing all over the place. And there were a few juncos out too, braving the weather for a few treats at the feeder. The temp was in the low 30's all night and throughout the morning—if it was only a few degrees colder there might be a foot of snow!

I enjoy being rustic and all that, but it sure is nice to have a computer and telephone out here at the cabin. That way I can stay here through my work day and not feel compelled to go back into the office in town. In fact I get some of my best written work done out here. I just don't do it enough. And the cold wind and rain just makes it all that much better. Of course, I must leave enough time available for naps too.

Part of the morning was spent designing a wall calendar that I am going to produce for the year 2000. I have never done a calendar before—it is just too cutthroat of a business, plus you only have three months to sell the calendars or they become worthless, and you must get a huge quantity printed in order to make the cost reasonable. At most of my programs someone always wants to know what my favorite picture is. After having shot well over a million images in my career, that is a difficult thing to say. But I have decided to take a crack at it, sort of. I will produce a wall calendar entitled "Arkansas Wilderness 2000—My Favorite Photographs." Well, there will be a dozen of my favorite photos anyway. It will be limited to a press run of only 2,000—most calendars have a minimum of 10,000 copies. This will be a nice calendar, and perhaps the only one that I ever do. We'll see.

While I put lunch on to cook I went outside and sat in the front porch swing and listened to the rain. The cabin is so well insulated that I can hardly hear the rain hitting the tin roof. But it was loud and clear on the front porch. The rain was really coming down, and making all kinds of music. I leaned over the log rail and watched the puddles in front gaining strength.

The drainage was not perfect. Ideally I want the rainwater to hit the ground and then run off, not sit around in puddles, which might leak into the basement. But there were puddles. And they were growing. So I decided to get dressed up and go out and play in the rain. I used to do this all the time as a kid—play in the rain, making and then destroying little dams of sticks and rocks and mud. This time I would be mostly getting rid of little dams, and digging out trenches for the water to flow through.

It was cold outside, and the rain was coming down pretty hard, but the work was fun, and immediately rewarding. It didn't take too much digging in the pools to create a waterway and free the rain. In the bottom of one of the pools there was still the faint impression of a bear track, leftover from last summer. Two bears stepped in the mud right next to each other. I had the tracks covered up for a long time to save them.

The rain was splattering on the roof, and the wind chimes were playing a lovely tune. Drainage accomplished. I went back inside, down through my new "mud room" in the basement. I haven't really done anything to it, but merely try to enter and exit there and take off my muddy boots before coming up into the living room. I have to put aspen boards up in the basement soon to finish it off somewhat, and I am having trouble trying to figure out exactly what to do with the remaining space there. I had originally planned on putting in another wall and creating a bedroom. So far I have left it open—except for the three rooms already in place. If I was going to build the wall, it would be a lot easier to do it before I do the aspen. With a little commercial carpet on the floor this space will become a really nice spot. I also plan to add a couple of beds, probably futons, and, *oh no*, a TV! No TV's are allowed up in the main cabin, but it would be nice to watch a video once in a while. Of course, there are always videos playing out at Cloudland—a different one out each window!

My chilled body was quickly warmed by both the fireplace as well as a heaping pile of hot veggies and rice. I got this new set of stoneware dishes from SAMS a couple of weeks ago, and one piece is this terrific shallow bowl, which is perfect for, well, for just about everything.

The wind has stopped blowing, and some fog is beginning to move in. I tried to lay down and take a nap, but the computer called me to it instead. Now the fog and rain are calling me to come out and play—it is 37 degrees and heavy rain. I try my best to obey the orders of nature, so I will go suit up and get out and soak up some of this wonderful day.

A driving rain hit me in the face when I stepped out the door. But it was OK—I was dressed for it. The fog was thick, and the forest was magical as I wandered up the lane towards the Faddis cabin. I could tell right away that there was a lot of color out—the browns of the leaf carpets and the greens of the moss-covered boulders were rich, very rich. All of the moisture in the air, and on the leaves and moss, created the lush hues.

The wind picked up as I passed through the Faddis Meadow, but it died down completely as I entered the woods once again. I made my way across a big flat of timbered land—never been to this spot before, although it was right off of the trail. A thick stand of tall pines and pesky greenbrier hid the entrance to the big flat. I was really surprised at how large and flat it was—well, relatively flat. It just went on and on. And a pileated woodpecker that flew about was the only resident that I could find.

The roar of Whitaker Creek below was loud and steady. And I was stunned to see a cascading waterfall coming down most of the hillside right in front of me—it must have been nearly 500 feet tall! Not a big "drop," but rather a long cascade as the torrent of water flew down the steep hillside. I had been here before during heavy rains, but never had seen anything like this! Wow, it was tremendous. All foaming whitewater. And there were several spots where the creek did a free-fall over a ledge. Very impressive.

And then I saw it, and it felt a little like being in Yosemite—way off down the valley, across the Buffalo River and up on the hillside, a *huge* waterfall. With the exception of Hemmed In Hollow Falls, I believe that this is the largest waterfall that I have seen in Arkansas—at least the next tallest anyway. This swollen river plunged over the big bluffline there, and then continued on in free-fall until it hit the steep forest floor below—a height of well over 100 feet. And this was no little trickle—it was large and impressive from even a mile away as I was. Just incredible! Then I realized that this giant of a waterfall was very close to my cabin. I was amazed.

I hurried down the trail back to the cabin—I wanted to get a closer look at this guy. I found that I could get a clear look at it from the lower corner of my meadow. What a sight! And from my spot there I could also see the cascading river that the falls created below, and it too was leaping from ledge to ledge and down the nearly vertical hillside. And then I saw yet *another* great waterfall— along the same bluffline, about a quarter-mile to the right. This one was massive too, although was less of a free-fall because it had more of a cascade at the top. I was proud to have these giants in my own back yard, if only for a few hours during a big rainstorm.

It was time to haul some wood, so I loaded up and spent about an hour climbing up from the meadow to the cabin with armfuls of wood. The river had come up some, but was still running clear. Whitaker Creek on the other hand was a bit muddy, and you could see it mixing with the Buffalo River waters far below. They both were making a lot of noise.

And then the sun began to burn a hole through the clouds. I never saw the actual sun, but was aware of its brightness in patterns on the floor of the meadow and later in the cabin. At the same time that the sun was trying to pop through the cloud bank got lower, and hung out at the tops of the ridges. You don't normally see the sun when the clouds are so low.

Once inside I dried off, served up a mug of Cloudland Cocoa (hot chocolate and Irish Cream), and sat down at the computer to write. I realized that not only were those big waterfalls in my own backyard, but that they were right outside my office window too! In fact, I could see them through the trees from every window on the east side of the cabin. Nice company to have. I had to close the blinds in order to concentrate on my work.

The wind had returned and was kicking up to 30mph. The temp had climbed up to 40 degrees, but the wind chill was still about 10 above. Those log walls and that big fireplace felt pretty darn nice.

As the day drew on I noticed that the Buffalo River had gotten muddy too. And it was high, probably high enough to float. The river and the creek made a constant loud noise. The big waterfalls continued to flow, although not nearly as much as early in the day. The rain never returned.

But the fog drew in close as the light faded. It was a little strange because the fog was so thick, yet the wind was still blowing 20-30mph. Usually a good wind will move the fog on out. I guess this wind just brought it in. The temp continued to climb, and was in the upper 40's by 8pm. By that time I had feasted on another bowl of veggies and rice (I like that stuff), spent a lot of time writing, and took a nap. The warm fog was so inviting that I wanted to go out

311

into the darkness for a walk. I don't like to hike with a flashlight though, so I stayed put and typed and listened to music and watched the fire. The rain total for the day was nearly two inches—we really needed it, plus a lot more.

Wouldn't ya know it, the fog finally got the best of me, and soon forced me out into it with my headlamp on. It was warm, but the driving wind made it seem a lot cooler. The fog was about as thick as I believe I had ever seen, or felt. My headlamp wasn't able to penetrate very much of the fog, and the walking was difficult. It was hard for me to even find the road. But it really felt great to be out in it and moving around, so I spent about an hour wandering—up to the Faddis cabin, then over to the East Meadow, then back down the hill through the woods to the cabin. That last part was slow going, and tough—I had to negotiate each and every footstep. This was *thick* fog!

As I got close to the cabin the glowing logs served as a welcome home beacon (I had turned on an outside spotlight). I didn't really get to see anything during my hike, except for lots of fog, and sometimes the ground at my feet, but it was a wonderful hour out in the foggy, nighttime forest, and I was glad that I went. After a little more computer work, I turned in for the night. The sun is supposed to come out tomorrow...darn.

3/9/99 Sometime during the night I got up to feed the fire and noticed these bright lights outside in the sky. Son of a gun, the fog and clouds had been blown away, and it was clear and sparkling out. And the temp had dropped 14 degrees. The wind was still blowing though, in fact making quite a racket. I had trouble getting back to sleep.

By early light a cloud cover had returned—no sunrise—but it was dead still out, not a wisp of breeze to be found. As I sipped my Cloudland Cocoa in front of the fireplace lots of birds gathered around the seed feeder, the peanut butter feeder (which I had just refilled), and in the trees around the cabin. It had been a while since I had seen this many birds here. They were mostly juncos and little woodpeckers, but there were lots of them, and they were hungry. I wonder if all the wind had been keeping them tucked away somewhere?

The rivers down below were no longer muddy, but were still up and making a lot of noise. The cloud cover seemed to be breaking up a little, and the sun popped through a little hole just for a minute. I had planned to drive over and hike into Sweden Falls and take a few pictures, but I couldn't do it if the sun was shining, so I got into high gear and packed up all my stuff, straightened up the cabin, and sped off in my truck.

The faster I drove the more the clouds disappeared. When I got to the parking spot for the waterfall the sun was shining brightly. But there were still a few clouds around, so I packed up my camera gear and my big tripod and headed down into the woods towards the Sweden Falls Natural Area.

This is a wonderful little spot, with tall painted bluffs, rich moss-covered boulders, and one giant waterfall. The falls were running pretty good when I got there, but the sun was blasting part of the scene with brilliant white light (waterfall pictures look best when shot on overcast days—mist or fog helps too!).

There is this neat little witch hazel tree growing right at the edge of the pool at the base of the falls, and the patterns of the branches have always intrigued me. I couldn't get the big waterfall shot that I had wanted (because of the harsh light), but I did spend a couple of hours there, taking pictures of the witch hazel tree, plus a couple of close-up shots of the waterfall.

3/12/99 An ice storm had hit Cloudland as Emily and I rolled/crawled down the hill late at night. We had shuttled our car at the far end of a 40-mile hike on the OHT that we are doing this weekend, and stopped by the cabin to spend the night. The ice was thick on the trees, and the old truck had to crawl through some of the low-hanging branches—probably scratched the hell out of my new Mercedes! The roads were OK though (except for the fact that there was one large tree down across the road at the top of the Boxley Valley hill—we had to drive around 30 miles to get here). It was cold in the cabin, but soon a roaring fire warmed everything up.

3/13/99 Daylight found us engulfed in more ice, and lots of fog. The radio said that we could expect *ten inches* of snow today! Yea!!! The only problem is that we will be out hiking in it instead of sitting in front of the fireplace. Oh well, I love to hike in the snow, so it will be wonderful. The birds are fighting to get to the only feeder that I have left here—it was blown off of its perch, and is sitting on the deck.

And all of the wooden bears outside are covered with thick ice, and have grown long teeth—the saber tooth bears have returned! The power is still on, but I'll bet it will be off before too long—the ice is getting really thick. We stopped at Bob's cabin on the way out to photograph the daffodils there which were covered with the ice. Bob had the cabin all warmed up, and was ready to stay put for a few days if the roads got bad. The trees on the way down to his place along the road were really hanging down low, at times nearly blocking off the road. But we pushed through, slowly.

There were more bent-over trees on the main road out to the highway, but it was not too bad. As we headed south towards the trailhead, the freeze line in the trees began to make its way up. It looked rather odd to see all of these frozen trees covered with ice, and then see the point where there was no ice, and the trees were all dark from that point on down to the ground.

By the time we reached the trailhead there was no ice, and it was drizzling. We hiked all day in that drizzle, which eventually turned to rain, then sleet, and finally into snow. The snow hiking was great! All of the rain though had brought the streams way up. We had to make six wet crossings (normally none on this stretch of trail), which got to be a little exciting as the snow got heavier. At one point we had our wading sandals on and were walking around in the snow (about 3" deep) trying to find a good crossing. While our little toes were about to freeze off, the snow did make the frigid creek waters feel *almost* warm!

We passed some of the tallest waterfalls along the Ozark Highlands Trail—they were wonderful! And flowing pretty good.

By the end of the day we were completely soaked, inside and out. I just happened to know of this great little bluff overhang near the trail where we could get out of the snow. It turned out to be one of the best little campsites that either of us had ever had. Not only were we out of the weather, but we could gather lots of dry firewood that had collected there, and a stream ran under the overhang at the far end so we could even pump water without getting wet! We spent several hours building up a nice fire and drying out all of our stuff. There was even a great level and soft spot to sleep, and we didn't need to put up the tent. When camping in snow, especially wet snow that was melting like this, it gets to be a pain when you have to pack up a wet tent in the morning. It snowed all night, but we were dry and toasty, and didn't have to pack any wet stuff!

3/14/99 It continued to snow all morning, but was warm (in the mid 30's), so there was no additional accumulation. We hiked past many great scenes of brilliant green moss-covered rocks sticking out through snow-covered ground. By the end of the day most of the snow had melted, but the streams and waterfalls were all running great. We finished up our hike in record time, and soon were back on the road again.

Emily headed back to town but I returned to the cabin. I quickly discovered that the main road off of the highway was blocked with trees, so I drove around and made my way to the cabin from the Boxley Valley end. The folks who live along this part of the road had kept the trees and limbs cut out, while no one really lives along the other end of the road to get the job done. There was a great deal more snow on Cave Mountain than we had seen on our hike, up to a foot in places, with more in the drifts.

As I drove down my little road to the cabin I was expecting to find lots of limbs blocking the way. But much to my surprise and delight, there wasn't even a single limb across my road! How could this be? But there was still lots of snow around in the woods, which is what I was hoping for. Some of it had melted for sure, but it appeared there was enough left for me to play in a little.

One of my main goals ever since I had built this cabin was to be able to go cross-country skiing right out the front door. The Ozarks are a great place to ski, and there are hundreds and hundreds of miles of terrific ski routes (old log roads make perfect ski trails, and we've got lots of them), but we seldom ever get enough snow. And this was the largest snowfall since the cabin was built.

It was late when I arrived, and I was tired and sore from the hike. I took a hot shower and built a big fire in the fireplace (the power was out, but there was enough water pressure, and hot water left in my great hot water heater, to take a good shower).

Snow outside, a fire inside, and me in my little log cabin. I was in heaven. But it was an early evening, especially after I broke out the wine. My only chore was to get the cross-country skis down from the wall, which took all of five minutes to complete. I was all set for an early morning ski, if the snow held out. And the lack of power didn't really bother me at all—there are lots of candles at the cabin now, and the fireplace for heat.

3/15/99 I was up early, and so was the sun. Clear blue skies, no wind, and a bit nippy outside—25 degrees. Still no power, but I didn't really need any. I hurriedly gulped down my Starbucks mocha, put on my skiing gear (same stuff as my hiking gear, only ski boots instead of hiking boots—the boots are about the same size, but the ski boots have an extended sole in front with three holes in them—to line up with the three pins in the bindings of the skis).

I didn't exactly get to ski right out the door, but there was enough snow on the ground about 50 feet away so I was happy. I have two pairs of cross-country skis at the cabin—my regular skis that I use in Colorado, and an old pair of "rock hoppers" that I use when the snow is thin and there is a chance of running over exposed rocks. These are the pair that I have hanging on the cabin wall, and they would work just great for my ski today. (Both pairs are waxless.)

As I got into the woods the snow was deeper, and a little crusty. I worked my away along the bench, heading to the north. I knew that the snow would be deeper over on the north side of the hill. Yippie! I was skiing at Cloudland!!! Kick, glide. Kick, glide. Stop and giggle a little. Kick, glide. It wasn't the best snow to ski on, but it was good enough for me.

I made my way around the little point that looks down into Dug Hollow—where the big flat is with that skewed tree. It was fabulous. Wonderful. Exciting. And peaceful. All at the same time. I glided silently through the forest, past my big tree friends, then turned around at the end of the big flat and skied back again. There wasn't enough snow to attempt some real serious skiing down the hill, which was fine with me because I probably would have buried myself into the hillside anyway, but I was quite happy just to glide back and forth across the flat. At last, skiing at Cloudland, mission accomplished!

3/19/99 The road from Hwy. 16 was all cleared out (by county workers—*thanks* guys!), but you could see the remains of lots and lots and lots of trees and large limbs that had been cut out of the way. As I unpacked my stuff at the cabin a feeling of excitement as well as calm swept over me—I was going to get to spend four days at Cloudland—the longest in a while. I needed the time here.

The only damage from the storm was a cedar tree downed in the meadow, plus a couple of limbs out of the pine trees down there. The power had been out for about three days, but it was back on now.

I had brought out a new toy, uh, er, tool today—a new chain saw, a small one, a Stihl with a 14 inch bar. I set out at once to cut down the multitudes of small stumps that were a foot or so tall down in the meadow. My other saw's 20 inch bar was too large for these smaller stumps. But they were bugging me. So I cut and I cut and I cut. And in a couple of hours the meadow's personality improved dramatically—it was looking more like a meadow now.

The new saw did great, although I did try to cut through a rock early on, and had to stop and spend some time putting an edge back on the blade.

It was kind of cool—in the low 50's, with a slight breeze, and it was about the perfect working weather. And cloudy. The river was running a little low for this time of the year, but the color of the water was just the perfect shade of blue/green, with some whitewater, and it was making a little noise. They had predicted rain all day the day before, but there was none, and the same forecast was out for today. I worked on.

Once I finished the little stumps I got out the big daddy saw and went after the larger stumps. None of the stumps had been cut off from when I first felled them nearly two years ago. Cutting the stumps down to ground level really improved the looks of things. Some of the stumps were over 20" in diameter at the base, and hardwood, but the old saw just ate right through them. It did chase after a rock or two as well, and I had to get out the round file.

As the afternoon drew on a red-tailed hawk came soaring by. His rust-colored tail feathers were about the brightest that I had ever seen—no need for binocs to ID this guy. I sat down and watched him for a little while. He would soar from one end of Whitaker Valley to the other, then fly back (doing a lot of flapping), then repeat. I guess there was a wind current going in one direction that he rode, but had to work some to get back.

And, oh yes, I found the first snake of the season! Well, it was almost a snake. Before I can cut off a stump, I have to move all of the rocks out from around the base of the stump. Sometimes this requires a little pulling and digging as the rocks are often firmly embedded in the tough Ozark soil. Anyway, there was a ringneck worm snake all coiled up under this one flat rock. I have always liked ring-necked snakes, ever since I found one in the front yard of my boyhood home. This guy was pretty large for a worm snake—nearly eight inches long when uncoiled, but only as big around as a pencil at his widest point. Ringnecks are very friendly. I moved this guy to under a nearby rock.

The first wildflowers of the meadow were out too—several delicate violets had popped up their heads. And there were these plants—we don't really know what they are yet, but we left them covering one section. They are single stalked, about two feet tall, growing thickly together. Anyway, they were all in bloom today—tiny yellow flowers covered their upper stalks. Not bright yellow, but yellow just the same. I will keep my eye on them as the season progresses. Glad we left them.

After a particularly tough stump I laid back in the meadow and stared up at the cloudy sky. As I took a deep breath I could smell rain—man, I love that aroma! Especially out here in the wild. Nothing else smells like it. The air was heavy, and sweet. Any time now.

I cut out a few more stumps, then the saw ran out of gas about halfway through a big stump. Then it began to rain. A good spot to stop. I admired the now-more-open meadow as I strolled up the trail to the cabin, sucking in as much of that wonderful wet air as I could with each step.

It wasn't a hard rain, but the drops were large. I didn't want to saw in the rain, but I did feel like walking in it. So I put a coat in my fanny pack and headed out. I hiked up the lane, silently, and listened to the raindrops as they made their way down through the tall trees around me, and landed on the forest floor with a soft splat. I didn't feel like wearing the coat. Sometimes you just want rain to hit you. This was one of those times.

There were a few little birds playing about in the Faddis Meadow as I walked through, and one squirrel took off like a shot out of a cannon when I came into view, but I didn't see any other critters out. Then I turned back towards the cabin. Once I arrived it was time for a nap. Since it was warm enough, and the rain was still coming down in large drops, but not too hard, a nap in the porch swing was in order.

Few things in life are as relaxing or as satisfying as kicking back in a porch swing at your log cabin in the woods and dozing off to the pit-a-pat of raindrops on a tin roof. The struggle of life continues.

The rain showed no signs of letting up, and I had a little more sawing to do. I got up from my swing nest and fired up the large chain saw. There was a pile of logs—each log 4-8 feet long—that I had wanted to cut up into firewood. That spot was mostly protected from the rain, so I spent an hour cutting up the wood. Now I had a good pile of wood under cover in case it got cold again.

As I stepped out of the hot shower my aching muscles reminded me that I had originally planned to put in a sauna downstairs, along with a shower and a hot tub. Hum. A sauna. Plans began to swirl in my head. A sauna in the corner of the tool room, and a shower, plus a mat and some exercise equipment (I already have a great cross-country ski machine at home just waiting to be moved to the cabin). A tired body could hang out in the sauna, then shower, then proceed to the hot tub outside. Hum, I need to get that hot tub soon. And I thought about painting the basement floor, then putting down some nice carpets, including two large indoor-outdoor carpets in the mud room and at the bottom of the stair, connected by a runner. Then a nice bed and stuff in the guest room, and two futons in the TV room (oops, I mean the other "open" room). That would do it for a while. If I could only get the rest of the aspen boards put up, the floor painted, and find a gold bar to pay for the other stuff!

After a tough day in the meadow I needed a good dinner. This trip to the cabin was carefully planned—I brought a lot of food. Good food. Some that I wanted to experiment with to see if it could be fed to others. I had three choices for dinner—smoked salmon and herbed Alfredo sauce over fresh pasta and broccoli, grilled sausage w/mustard from Switzerland (the best mustard I've ever had by far) with dried taters and onions, or the old standard Banff Pasta. It was a tough choice, but I decided to take them in the above order. So I broke out a slab of smoked salmon that I got for Christmas, and fired up the kitchen.

The salmon Alfredo pasta was good, very good, wonderful. Ahhhhh. With a little toasted homemade bread, a glass of wine, and a handful of dark chocolate mints. Yep, this wilderness living is tough.

And on the radio was ***Ozarks At Large***, and later the ***New Blues Show***, both shows on KUAF radio. It felt like a Friday night, and it was. Pure and simple. I don't normally like Friday's when I am in town, but somehow they take on a new meaning out here at the cabin.

3/20/99 Sometime during the night I got up and looked around—there were a million stars out. Quite a change from the cloudy and dreary daytime. An hour later I was awake and listening to the pounding of heavy rain. Quick change is a way of life, and often welcome. The water table is still very low in the Ozarks this year and so the more rain we get, the better. Once all of the trees begin leafing out available water will be sucked up in tremendous proportions. So we need to get a lot of water out there in the streams and in the waterfalls and in the ground, just to keep up with the oncoming spring.

By daylight the rain had quit. A veil of clouds hung low over the hills—not quite touching the tops of the ridges, but close. Steam clouds were forming and moving around, although there wasn't a bank of them down low like there often is. The temp was 42 degrees outside, and I built a fire in the fireplace—I had to have someplace to stand in front of and drink my Starbucks mocha.

Then the kitchen opened. I had been waiting all week to fix this egg dish that I found the recipe for in ***Sunset*** magazine. Thirty minutes later I sat down in front of the roaring fire with a plate of asparagus scrambled eggs (I tweaked the recipe just a tad, but the dish includes three different types of cheeses, green onions, fresh basil, and of course, asparagus). This was the best egg dish that I have ever eaten! I was impressed. And I wished that I had made more.

While I was in the kitchen working I looked out the window and saw a big fat wren sitting on the log rail in front of the swing. He seemed to be calling out to me to let him in. I just love wrens. They are one of the few birds that defy the normal bird body shape, with that turned-up tail and all. And they like to nest nearby. When I was growing up there was always a wren that lived outside in an old Singer sewing machine cabinet—in one of the little drawers. I was always sneaking a peak at the tiny eggs in the nest there. And the mom returned year after year. I never let the wren at the cabin in, nor did I share my egg dish with him. But I hoped he would find a suitable spot for a nest nearby. I guess if that happened then I would need to begin calling him a her!

As the morning drew on the cloud cover crept lower and closer. Soon the ridgetops were engulfed and more wisps of fog were born and danced around in the valleys below. The temp remained at 42 degrees for most of the morning. And no wind at all. There seemed to be a lot of little birds flying around—more so than usual. Perhaps they were all out awaiting the arrival of spring, which will come at 7:46pm tonight.

Several times fog banks would come blowing up from below the bluffline and disperse into the air above. I never know what causes such behavior.

After lunch and a short nap it was time for a hike. The temp was still 42 degrees and the wind still wasn't blowing, so it felt rather warm out. The first thing that I noticed as I made my way down the ladder trail was that there were no wildflowers out anywhere. The snow and ice had sent them back into the ground I figured. As I got lower, and down near the bottom, a few bloodroot flowers began to poke their heads out. The flowers were still all rolled up, but they were pointed up towards the sky, just waiting for a little sunshine.

There was this one branch that had fallen across the trail. It wasn't so much a branch as it was a moss and lichen factory. This little branch that was about a half-inch thick was covered with moss and lichen that was hanging down several inches. I looked close. Some of the lichens had solid stalks that appeared to be actual branches of the twig, and very solid. I pulled one off, only to discover that the fungi didn't penetrate the wood at all, but rather had grown a sheath completely around the branch. It was a miniature forest, thick and lush and several different shades of green. Wish I could get something like this to grow inside the cabin. Of course, I have the very same thing in the trees just outside anyway. Neat stuff.

I made it to the river and wandered around a little there. The water was up and making a lot of noise. Then I tried to figure out just exactly where to go next. The water was too high to cross the Buffalo River. I could go downstream and make my way up Dug Hollow, past all of the big waterfalls there. Or go up Whitaker Creek. Or climb up the old road through the bluffline and up on top of Beagle Point. Then I could follow the ridgetop way upstream, and drop down to Whitaker Creek and come around past the Crag that way. That sounded good to me.

The first order of business was to get across Whitaker Creek. The water was too high for me to cross near the old homesite where I usually do, so I went upstream. I was surprised to discover that I had to go upstream quite a ways before I found a suitable dry crossing, and even that spot was a little suspect, but I made it across OK.

I wandered across the flat and up the hillside, eventually coming to the old road trace that heads up the hillside. There were wildflowers on this hillside—in fact, zillions of them! Tons of trout lilies and bloodroot everywhere, although they weren't in bloom, just their flowers rolled up and hanging. There were several other species of wildflowers too. One species was in bloom, but the flowers were just *so* tiny, and a delicate shade of purple. I'd not seen them before.

When I reached the road trace I decided to follow it to the right instead of to the left (which goes up to the bluffline). The road actually went uphill just a little, then leveled off. It took me through some of the thickest brush that I have ever seen! In fact at one point it was impossible for me to stand anyplace without touching a bush or tree limb. All of this part of the hillside had been scraped clean by flocks of turkeys—they had scratched up practically all of the leaf-matter looking for bugs and worms and such.

I finally reached a point where I could not find any trace of a road. I really didn't know what I wanted to do next, so found myself sitting down next to a big tree. I was going to sit there until I came to some decision I guess. Since I enjoy sitting in the woods anyway, that became part of my hike. The ground was covered with many different kinds and shapes of leaves (no turkey scratching here). Beech, red oak, white oak, shagbark hickory, and dogwood. A solid matt of brown leaves.

And there were a million trees out there in front of me. I wondered just exactly how many I could see? What the heck, I might as well count them. So I did. I counted every visible tree trunk that I could see within my line of vision (everything that I could see from far left to far right). Four hundred and forty trees. It took a while to count them, but I was in no hurry. How many times have you sat on the forest floor and counted all of the trees that you could see? You should try it sometime. It is well worth your time.

Once my sitting and tree countin' was over I got up and just started to wander down the hillside. Then I found the old road trace again, or what I thought was it. There were about a dozen piles of rocks all in a row, heading up and across a hillside. I followed. Sure enough, eventually there was a road trace visible. It was heading up the Whitaker Creek drainage, just like someone had noted once in a short conversation that I had with an old timer last year. I'd never come across any road up this drainage before.

At one point I lost the road trace again. After milling around for a few minutes, it jumped out and slapped me in the face—right in front of me there was a plain road heading nearly straight up the hillside. Yikes, this was one steep road! I followed it up and up. Whitaker Creek was roaring down below and just out of sight. I guess the route had to climb this hill to avoid the creek, but it would have been a tough haul for man or beast.

Once the road leveled off I lost it again, or should I say that I came into a level spot that was so magical that I lost track of what I was doing. This spot was wonderful. Giant trees all over the place, and no underbrush at all, just a smooth floor of leaves. And most of the big trees were beeches. Tall and smooth and majestic. Most of the time when you see beeches this large they are all beat up and disfigured and ready to be blown over. But these guys were still in the prime of their lives—straight and strong and powerful. No rot or cracks that I could see.

I was drawn over to one of the larger beeches. As I walked closer, letters became visible. I had just been thinking about how wonderful it was to see such large beeches and no names scratched in them. But I was not displeased to see these letters. They were plain as day. And they were historical:

CLARENCE FADDIS—3/20/25

I had bought my land from this guy's son I believe, or perhaps his grandson (I will have to check on that). And he stood at that very same tree on the same day as today 74 years ago—first day of spring. I wondered what kind of man he was? Was he out on a hike too, having discovered this magical spot in the forest just as I had, or was this tree in his front yard? The letters were two to three inches tall. This was one giant beech tree, and it must have been large way back in 1925 too, or the tree would have grown so much that the letters would have been unreadable.

I looked up and out from my magical spot in the forest and noticed that I had come up the valley almost all the way to Hawksbill Crag, which was looming high above and just upstream. I could not locate the old road trace leaving this spot so I decided to head down to the creek. The creekbed was as lush as ever, all of the rocks being covered with bright green moss. And there was a lot of whitewater.

I found a spot to jump across (nearly fell in twice), then pointed my boots *up* the hillside. This was one *steep* spot. Hand-over-fist most of the way. And I slipped and did a face plant a couple of times. Of course, this was not any big deal since the hillside was so steep my face only fell about two feet before impacting the earth.

There wasn't a soul on the Crag. Guess the threat of rain kept folks in town. Don't know why—it was wonderful hiking. From the Crag I could see fresh tears in the forest canopy here and there—damage from the ice and snow storm. And then part of the opposite hillside got real light—looked like the sun was coming out, but the cloud cover was still pretty thick.

The threat of sunshine was enough to bring out some serviceberry trees. As I walked along the blufftop trail, I saw more than 20 of these trees in bloom. I had only seen four or five others this weekend that were out. They are the real first sign of spring, and the storms of last weekend certainly had knocked them back a week or two. But they were out today, and waiting for sunshine.

After a hot shower and a little liquid refreshment I sat out on the back deck for a spell. The sun did indeed find a hole in the clouds and came out for just a minute or two. And while it was out it began to rain lightly.

It was time for another nap, so I stoked the fire and got comfortable on the big couch. Just as I was about to doze off there came a knock on the front door. It was Bradley and Casey Woods and her dad, Bobby Young, who lives in nearby Swain. Casey and her family moved up here a couple of years ago from bayou country down in Louisiana. They all had a good look around, and I got to show off some more.

After my guests left there was quite a light show out back. The sun would pop out and light up one hillside at a time, and would move around. All of the rest of the hills and ridges were black. The scene changed every two or three minutes. I never get tired of this scene, and it is always different.

It was time for an early dinner so I fired up the grill and put on some chicken and apple sausages (sounds odd but tastes great!). Since it was about to be springtime I figured it was time for the BBQ. I also fried up some new potatoes and onions, topped off with cheddar cheese. Then I dug out my special mustard from Switzerland—man, that stuff made those sausages outstanding!

After such a heavy feast I strapped on my boots and headed out for another hike. It was still 42 degrees but it seemed a lot colder. The sun had gone down, but there was still plenty of daylight for an hour or so. I walked past one large maple tree that had been downed by the storm—such a waste. And there were several other trees down too, but not the wholesale damage that I had seen on other parts of the mountain.

I stood at the edge of the East Meadow and gazed up at the clouds. There were two layers of them. A lower layer of broken clouds was moving past at a pretty good clip. And an upper layer of solid clouds that were still. The lower layer was all lit up bright red and pink and orange, which looked really neat as they sailed past in front of the upper grey clouds. The light changed as I walked through the meadow, and by the time I had reached the far end, the lower clouds were grey, and the upper clouds were brilliant colors. It was all one moving visual serenade and a delight to the eye.

The little lane between the East and Faddis Meadows was blocked with a number of small trees and larger branches from the storm. I started moving the ones that I could out of the way, but there were just too many of them, and too large for me to handle. I vowed to come back tomorrow with the chain saw and cut them out. One of the larger trees down was a redbud, and it had just started to bloom. Wouldn't you know it, the only redbud that was blooming had been blown over! And then I found the wild peach tree in bloom—or at least I think it is the peach tree. It may be the tree next to it, but they looked like fruit blooms. I'll just have to wait and see what it turns out to be!

In the same area I found a wild plum in bloom. Actually my nose found it—what an incredible fragrance! It was as wonderful as witch hazel. Almost.

The far end of the East Meadow was covered with turkey poop. And I mean some really big stuff. You could hardly step without getting in it. Turkey poop is kind of khaki-colored, with a white tip. Lots of khaki out in the East Meadow.

It was about dark when I got back to the cabin. Felt good to walk off some of that heavy dinner. And to see the spectacular clouds. The cabin was warm inside and smelled like taters and onions. I took a seat at the computer and typed away the day's entries while folk music bounced off the log walls behind me. It had been a fine first day of spring. Well, actually I guess it isn't quite spring just yet. No wait a minute, yes it *is spring!* I just looked at the clock and spring happened just over an hour ago.

While we didn't have all that much snow here this past winter I enjoyed it immensely. Lots of warm days and rain and weather and just wonderful hiking and sitting around. Winter is great for chopping wood and sitting in front of the fireplace. But spring is something else altogether. My favorite season by far. I won't be able to get enough of it, but I will try to experience as much of it as I can, and I will pass some of the info on to you. YIPPIE, SPRING IS HERE!!!

I went outside to bring in another load of wood for the fire and was met with a black sky filled with stars. The clouds had all moved out once again. The big dipper was high above the cabin, and Orion was over in the western sky. And below Orion, about to slip below the horizon, was a delicate and beautiful orange sliver of a moon. Welcome back Mr. Moon—good to see ya.

3/21/99 Somebody was watching me again. It was 6:25 am. I opened my eyes and saw this incredible red ball sneaking up from behind the far hillside—the sun was rising. There was only a narrow gap between the horizon and a thick cloud bank. But the clouds had lifted just enough to allow the full ball of the sun to rise, then it was quickly engulfed by the clouds. The entire scene was shades of greys and blacks, except for that bright red ball. And then a pileated woodpecker landed and began to peck away at a tree just outside my window. It was all a wonderful sight. Though early, I just had to get up after that.

I walked out onto the back deck. It was chilly—in the upper 30's, but was very loud out. The river below was yelling up at me as usual. And the bushes and trees were filled with high-pitched squeaks and squawks—birds were everywhere! Hey, it must be spring. The first full day. I stoked the fire, and created another plate of breakfast, then took a seat on the deck and welcomed the day. The sun quickly burned off the clouds and soon the valleys were flooded with warm, yellow sunshine.

Today was going to be a work day—no fun hikes planned. But before I got started I noticed there were lots of juncos hanging around. I had given up on the only bird feeder that was left—will have to figure out a different spot for it and a new way to secure it. I tossed out a bowl full of seed on the ground and I swear I could see instant smiles on all their little faces.

First off, I made my way up my lane with the small chain saw, cutting out small trees here and there that had grown into the road corridor. Then I did the same thing with the loppers, getting the limbs and small brush, eventually heading back to the cabin to fill up with oil and gas (the saw, not me).

I headed back up the hill with the oil and gas and got the saw and worked on getting the road to the East Meadow opened up. There were a *lot* of trees and big branches down across it. I sawed and hauled brush away as best I could and got the road open, but there were still dozens of trees that were leaning over the road and would eventually have to be cut out. I wasn't up to the task today.

Next I went over to Bob's and cut out a major tree that had fallen across his little road to the North Meadow. Bob doesn't use this road much but the Woods boys do, and I didn't want them coming in late one night and find the mess waiting for them.

I hauled everything back to the cabin, and got out the big momma saw and returned to my little meadow and cut out more large stumps. It took me ten minutes to cut out one big guy. This was all a lot of work but the meadow sure was looking a lot better. The sun was out, it was warm, and I needed the exercise.

At one point I noticed several shadows moving across the ground. I looked up and saw a sky full of buzzards—17 of them—yikes! Just about that time the saw ran out of gas. I took it as a sign to stop and take a break.

There was a steady stream of folks out on the Crag—12 there at one time. It was a perfect spring day to be out in the woods. As I sat there drinking my diet Dr. Pepper I began to see a lot of soaring birds. They were everywhere. Not only in Whitaker Creek valley, but way upstream on the Buffalo River too. Some were weaving back and forth close by, others were high up, and there were many way, way up. At one point I counted over 50 birds.

But they weren't all buzzards. A lot of them were red-tailed hawks. And they were flying right in with the buzzards. I guess I should be calling them vultures—turkey vultures—since that is what they are. Anyway, it was great to see the hawks. There hadn't been too many around in a while. There were seven of them within my little area at the same time once. Don't recall ever seeing that many hawks here at one time before.

Since I realized that my chain saw must have been disturbing everyone over at the Crag, I decided to hold off for a while and do some different work. All of those stumps that I had been cutting down needed to be hauled off. So I got to work on that, and it turned out to be more work that I had thought. All of the stumps were still green and very heavy. A couple of them were so heavy that I couldn't pick them up, and had to roll them around.

Many of the stumps were just the right size for the fireplace, so I hauled them to the ever-growing pile of firewood (which needs to be brought up the hill!). But a lot of the stumps I didn't want to burn. I ended up putting most of them out in the woods off to the side of the cabin. They look a little funny. They all have lichen and stuff growing on them, even across the top, which had been cut nearly two years ago. So I stood them right-side up in the woods. And they all look like they had grown there and had been cut down some time ago. Some of the stumps are lined up next to each other, and considering the fact that the woods are already pretty full of trees, they just look very funny and out of place, but yet still natural. I guess you will just have to come by and see for yourself.

Since it was so warm out—in the 60's—and the work was very tough, and there were still all of those buzzards hanging around, I had to take a lot of breaks. I spent a lot of time with the binocs in my hands, watching the soaring birds, and looking around my little world.

And I discovered something that I hadn't seen before, right out there in front of me. Well, it was actually across the Buffalo River and up on the opposite hillside, but I should have seen it before—I've only looked at that hillside maybe ten thousand times. I guess the sun had to be just right. Anyway, I saw a road coming down from the top of the ridge, and it looked like it used to go all the way to the river. Another road, oh boy! I love finding old pioneer roads. One of these days I will have to go down and ford the river and see if I can find the road and follow it to the top, and to the bottom, and see where it goes. It's not on any maps. Oops, I take that back. I just looked at the topo map and there IS a road there. But it shows it ending right in the middle of the hillside. I'll bet it goes further down, probably all the way to the river. I'll see.

Something else that I spotted was a giant serviceberry tree in bloom. It was way up the valley beyond the Crag. At first I thought that the light was hitting the bluffline in a funny way and making it appear white. But when I put the telescope on it, I could see the blooms. By far the largest serviceberry tree I had ever seen—this dude was as tall as the bluffline, which was probably 80 feet tall, and the tree was covered with white blooms. A really big tree.

I returned to my chores down in the meadow and got most of the stumps hauled off. There is still one giant one that I couldn't deal with, but I'll get him next time.

While I know that it is probably too late for this year, I put up a second bluebird box at the edge of the meadow. I had them up last year too but the wind messed them up. This time I secured them pretty good and hoped they will be OK. As I was pounding in one of the aluminum poles a couple of folks came walking up the trail from the Crag that runs just below the meadow. We spoke for a moment, and then the lady asked me if they were going the right way. I said "that depends—where are you going?" They thought that they were headed back to the trailhead. Of course, they were going in the wrong direction! It turns out that I knew them—Susan and Larry Foley. We talked a spell and then I sent them off in the correct direction.

The sun began to get low in the western sky and the giant shadows of the ridges crossed the river and began to make their way up the opposite hillsides. It was time to quit for the day. I stowed my gear, brushed off my overalls, and headed to the kitchen. Another big plate of salmon/broccoli/Alfredo pasta out on the veranda. Good grub! And no finer spot on earth to sit and have dinner. The light show was spectacular. I think I'll have most of my meals out on the back now for a while—until next winter perhaps!

After I licked the plate I made a quick jaunt over to the Crag—hadn't had a fun hike all day. I was astonished to see how many more serviceberry trees were in bloom—nearly double from yesterday. These trees sure did know what day it was (the first full day of spring). I walked back silently in the dark, and stopped once to look up at the moon, which was nearly straight overhead. And one of the bright planets (Jupiter, Mercury, Saturn, or Venus—they are all in the western sky this month) was nearby and very bright too.

When I got back to the cabin I called and talked to Willie Faddis, the guy that I bought Cloudland from. He told me that Clarence Faddis (whose name I found on the beech tree) was his dad's first cousin. He said that his dad used to idolize old Clarence, and that he was as strong as an ox. Willie and his wife run a poultry operation and farm in NW Arkansas. In fact I think they sold this property to me in order to build a new chicken house—thank goodness that they did! They both seem to have a sense of history about this place and a love for the land, as I do. Willie said that his initials were on a beech tree or two in the area.

It's late in the evening now, the stars have pushed the little moon to the horizon, and the river is singing a low melody in the night. The dinner dishes are clean and stacked, my writing chores are done for the day, and I just had a cherry yogurt for a snack (there's no chocolate in the cabin!). I would say spring has begun on a fine note, and I look forward to the rest of the season.

3/22/99 The howling of nearby coyotes signaled the start of the new day. It was good to have them in the neighborhood again. The sun wasn't up yet but I had to get up and, well, you know. As I walked around little "crunch, crunches" could be heard. That reminded me that it was a warm day yesterday, and so there are many little wasp bodies on the floor. They have been coming out of the logs every day its been warm outside or the fire was big inside since last fall, when they swarmed and crawled into the cabin. I never mind crunching a wasp body or two, but unfortunately there are as many ladybugs as there are wasps, and I hate to see them—they always die upside down, with their tiny wings outstretched. They need to pick a different species to partner up with and follow in the fall than wasps.

Sunrise found me at the computer answering e-mail and working on my 2000 wilderness calendar. Since I didn't keep the fire going last night it was a bit cool in the cabin, at least downstairs. It was a beautiful sunrise, although the sun wasn't the red ball that it was yesterday. Not a cloud in the sky, and the wind was blowing. It is a little later now, and the temp is rising with the sun. I love to see the sunshine flooding the cabin, and watch the light work its way down the log walls.

It is 9am now and time to go home. The bright sunshine has been covered up with a solid bank of clouds, and it seems very cold outside. And the wind continues to blow, from the east—usually a sign that a storm is about to happen. The pressure is dropping. One of the big radio stations is predicting a 50/50 chance of showers later today. They are also saying that there is only a slight chance of rain. And they are giving the temp in Fayetteville at both 32 and 47 degrees.

3/25/99 It was a bright sunny day when I arrived back at the cabin. After spending some time sucking up dead wasps with the vacuum, guests began to arrive. First, Bob Hostler, from Richardson, Texas. He would soon be joined by a flock of ladies from the Hot Springs and NWA areas, all members of either the Ozark Highlands Trail Association, the Ouachita Mountain Hikers, or both. Six young ladies in all, plus Bob and I. What more could we ask for? (Erna, Betty, Paula, Ann, Sally, and LaQuita—all in their 50's and 60's.)

After getting things unloaded and stowed (the ladies brought at least several gallons of wine and tons of great food), we all took off down the ladder trail for an afternoon hike.

At first there wasn't a wildflower in sight. I was a little disappointed that my tiny friend at the base of the giant red oak wasn't even out. But soon after a brilliant white bloodroot appeared next to the trail. Then another, and another, and then dozens of them. As we walked along the display got more profuse. When we landed on the only level bench along the way there were many excited folks. Within the small area where we were all standing we found more than a *dozen* different species in bloom—good grief! Paula is an ID expert.

Here is a list of what we found in this spot, and along the rest of the hike:

Johnny-jump-up, trillium, violet wood sorrel, yellow violet, wood violet, bird's foot violet, bloodroot, pale coryoalis, toothwort, daffodils, wild comfrey, white trout lily, yellow trout lily, phlox, Dutchman's breeches, rue anemone, spring beauty, harbinger of spring, false garlic, and pussytoes. Others that we found that weren't quite in bloom yet, but whose leaves were there included: mayflower, cinquefoil, wild strawberry, day lilies, wild rose, Adam and Eve orchid, Jacob's ladder, and sweet anise. It was one incredible display to say the least!

We explored the old root cellar at the bottom of the hill, examined what they thought was gooseberry growing there, and discovered the old hand-dug well right next to the chimney—I had walked right past it many times, and never seen it. This one was unusual because it was square, not round. The water was about five feet from the top, and then about five feet deep—a ten foot deep well (no telling how much it had filled in over the years). The water looked good. The old chimney that had fallen down there was surrounded by a large patch of day lilies, not yet in bloom.

We wandered on down to the standing chimney where we found a large batch of yellow trout lilies that were just amazing—bright and big! Then we spent a few minutes on the banks of the Buffalo River admiring the rushing waters.

We crossed Whitaker Creek, which was still running pretty good (Bob wanted to try out the quick-drying qualities of his long pants, so he slipped and went in while helping someone across the creek). Then we climbed up the hillside where we identified the tiny flowers that I had found last week—they were harbinger of spring. They looked pretty amazing through a magnifier that one of the ladies had on hand! We all got down on hands and knees to have a look.

Next we wandered across a hillside just bursting with bloodroot—I had never seen such an incredible display of wildflowers in the Ozarks—the brilliant white and yellow blooms stretched up the hillside as far as we could see—splendid! And we kept seeing this little bush that was flowering with tiny yellow flowers. At first we thought it was sassafras, but after we cut open the roots of one small bush we decided it was not. There was a great deal of it around though, along with lots of gooseberry.

Eventually we made it to my new little magical beech forest bench area with the Faddis carvings on the one beech. It seemed like everyone was discovering new trees with words on them nearby, but the Faddis tree remained the best and clearest writings. We did figure out what one tree said: NOTICE: DEC 31, 1933. Another tree said: NOTICE ON THE OTHER SIDE. We couldn't read what was on the other side. Since there were so many of the carved trees along the old road trace, someone suggested that the area was where the Burma Shave people got the idea for their highway signs.

Oh yea, and we also found one small magnolia tree that had two modern tags in it—64NE one tag said. I thought it might be a camera point for the forest service since they have many of them in the area (they go back to the same

327

spot every 10 years or something like that and take pictures to see how/if the area is changing).

Up on top of one giant rock slab along the bench was a clump of tooth-wort—probably 50 flowers all together. Lots of cameras came out and snapped away.

Paula found a bunch of sweet anise. When mashed between your fingers this little plant has a strong smell of licorice. We saw lots of walking ferns on the moss-covered boulders, and beech drops here and there (a fungus that grows on the roots of beech trees and shoots up nearly a foot tall above the ground). Bob spotted this one grapevine that was about ten inches in diameter and growing high up into the canopy.

We also saw a couple of butterflies (saw them both up on the back deck before our hike, but also found them in the woods during the hike). They were zebra swallowtails and yellow swallowtails—the first real butterflies of the season. They looked wonderful. And there was this one poor dead tree that had been worked over by a pileated woodpecker—it had dug out a trench down one side of the tree, and there was a pile of wood chips at the base that would make great fire starter.

The climb back up the steep hill on the ladder trail wasn't too bad, and soon everyone was enjoying the view from the back deck. While we were talking about all that we had just seen a number of soaring birds put on a show out in front. There were lots of the usual buzzards, but also a pair of red-tailed hawks. And then a pair of bluebirds showed up—yea! The male sat on a limb right above one of the bluebird boxes and eyed it for the longest time. I do hope they take up residence this spring! There was also a pair of doves that hung around.

Before long it was time to get started on dinner. And man, what a dinner it was! Lots of great food, wine, conversation, and even homemade angel food cake with ice cream and strawberries! These ladies can come back anytime. After the feed the ladies talked of their past adventures all over the world, and told plans of new ones. They were a little concerned that they only had a few trips planned for this year—to France, China, and South Dakota.

By 10pm everyone was ready for bed. All of the ladies spread out on the living room floor in front of the fireplace, and Bob disappeared into his RV that was parked just outside. The moon and stars were out, and it was actually very bright outside, but no one was up for a night hike.

3/26/99 I heard noise downstairs. It was early, very early. No sun, but the eastern horizon was an orange glow. It was about 5:45am. Soon I could smell coffee, and hear lots of ladies working below, so I gave in and got up. Sally had put together some kind of wonderful breakfast dish, but it was covered with mushrooms (yuk!), which I can't eat. There was this great yeast roll dish, and we even had the juice of 24 fresh oranges, so I sat at the computer writing while feasting on the rolls and juice.

It had dipped down into the low 30's overnight, but it looked like it was going to be another bright and warm day. It got up into the 60's yesterday. Soon the breakfast dishes were put away, and we all packed up for a great hike.

It was cold, but the sunshine kept things pretty warm. We headed on up to the East Meadow where we found some tiny bluet wildflowers growing. I've seen these dudes for many years, but never knew what they were—only about a quarter inch across. Then we headed down into Dug Hollow, through Magnolia Canyon, which was lit up very nicely today—lots of brilliant green moss on the canyon walls.

As we followed along the base of the bluff, we saw a few alum root flowers and what was left of wild hydrangeas. There were lots of toothworts out, but not much else was blooming. There was quite a bit of damage from the ice storm—lots and lots of big trees and branches down, including several very large beeches. Too bad. There was one large beech that had fallen over that had a twin attached at the base—only the older part had fallen down several years ago and was rotting away.

Stairstep Falls was running pretty good, and so were all of the falls in Dug Hollow proper. We had a little trouble getting everyone up the bluff there, but after a few wet knees and a little help, we all were up.

As I was walking along a grey squirrel jumped up onto the lower part of the bluff and started running out in front of me. He didn't seem to really want to get away, but just to stay a little ways in front of me. When I stopped to look at something, he would stop. When I moved on, he did too. And once when I was stopped for several minutes, he turned and came hopping back towards me, then stopped and barked a little—trying to find out what was keeping me. He finally found a nice tree and scrambled up it and out of sight.

The ladies began to see some birds, including phoebes and pewees. I found out that a phoebe will sit on a branch and dip his tail—one way to identify these little birds. And there were a couple of tiny birds down along the creekbed that were singing away. They weren't identified, but I was told to be expecting an ID as soon as they figured out the bird call.

There was this giant grapevine at one point that was growing from the ground all the way up the sandstone bluff. I had walked within inches of it many times before but never noticed it.

From the falls area we headed up the steep hillside and visited the Woods cabin, Bob's cabin, and the Faddis cabin. Then we took the trail down to the Crag, where we found a large group of folks from Kansas who were staying at the Bible Camp down near Ponca. One of the leaders was holding the kids' legs (one kid at a time) as they would lie down and peer over the edge of the bluff.

Once we arrived back at the cabin I forced the group to put in ten minutes of hard labor, and we shuttled some of the big wood pile down in the meadow up the hill to the edge of the deck. That was a great help to me! After everyone had a bite to eat, goodbyes were said, and they all vanished in a flash. It was a terrific group, and I enjoyed their visit. I told them they must return when a new wave of wildflowers comes up to help me identify them.

3/27/99 My brother and his wife (Terry and Marsha) arrived during the night from Illinois for a weekend visit. I had gone into town to get my mom, and we arrived back at the cabin late morning. My sister and her husband (Dorcas and Corky Cecil) and their two kids (Matt and Sarah) also drove down from Illinois, and soon we had our entire Ernst/Cecil clan together. It was a mini-family reunion.

My mom was the star attraction, and we put her in the big over-stuffed leather chair right in front of the fireplace. While she wasn't exactly sure what all was going on, she seemed to be having a good time, and we all enjoyed having her in our midst (she was 81, with advancing Alzheimer's).

After lunch I took Matt and Sarah on a little hike. We went down the ladder trail to the river. That was the easy part. The flowers down there were blooming pretty good, and it was warming up. Then we headed back up the steep hillside. Since neither of my sister's kids are big outdoors people I didn't really expect them to bounce right on up the hill. But they did do a pretty darn good job. I know of many others their age (early 20's) that would have given out and been left for dead.

The rest of the afternoon was filled with visitors, phone calls, and lots of eating. The Pack Rat called out from Fayetteville with an urgent message for a hiker that was hiking on the OHT whose father had died. My brother, who hiked the entire trail in August many years ago, took off with his wife to try to track them down. I didn't give them much chance, but they did find a car near where the message said these folks might be, and he left a few notes. When you are out in the woods stuff continues to go on back in the real world. Sometimes you just have to wait until you get back to civilization to deal with such things.

Towards dark I struck out on my own for a short hike. It seemed like I had been hiking with lots and lots of folks the past few days, and I needed a few steps with just myself and the trees. I found that there were a dozen or more wild plums blooming right at the edge of my land where the East Meadow begins (ends). And then these five or six peach trees in full bloom jumped right out at me—most of them were very small trees, and I won't see any peaches soon, but the blooms were quite striking. And there was a redbud or two out blooming, finally.

We had a great feed for dinner, including BBQ ribs, chicken, and all kinds of fixings, and *Starbucks ice cream* for dessert! I had heard about this wonderful stuff but never had any. These Illinois family folks of mine sure know what good food is. They also brought nearly a case of fine wines. Some of those bottles didn't get consume and wound up in the Cloudland wine cellar.

3/28/99 There was another big feed for breakfast, and then everyone packed up and left. It was great to have family at the cabin, if only for a day or two. I must say that the cabin was extra clean when they left. That is pretty good after the last four or five days of company.

I spent the rest of the morning working on the OHTA newsletter. It had rained some during the night, and continued on. There were lots of low clouds swirling around down in the valleys and up on the ridgetops.

Most people would call it a gloomy day, a type of day that I normally love. But today there was a dark gloom hanging around me too. A couple of personal things had snuck up and were rearing their ugly heads right in front of me. I am usually a very happy guy, but today I was just in this funk. (Mom's Alzheimer's was getting worse, and it appeared that my girlfriend was being unfaithful.) Even the cabin and the rain and the clouds didn't help. I tried to nap, but those demons in my head kept me awake.

Outside, the rain kept on. It was one of those long, soaking rains—not too hard, but steady. After an hour or two of bouncing off of the walls (and doing a few odd cabin chores, like cleaning the oven), I decided there was nothing left to do but get dressed and go on a hike. Yikes, it is raining, foggy, and rather chilly, and I want to go on a hike? *Absolutely!* No finer medicine I know of.

I put on my rain gear and headed out, hardly noticing the rain. There were no sounds but the raindrops on the forest floor. I guess if you stood still and closed your eyes and just listened, the raindrops would put you fast asleep—until you fell over and hit the ground! The sound of raindrops is always soothing, and kind of like talking to a good friend.

Up ahead I could see a wall of fog. I was in the clear, and the brown forest floor and the black trees were all well defined. But behind the wall of fog everything was grey and a little blurred. It was pretty level all around. My pace quickened as I headed towards this wall of mist, which was blowing right towards me. I didn't really know what to expect when we collided, but I looked forward to the experience.

It got closer. I walked faster. Then finally we met. A blast of cool, white, thick air hit me in the face. Man, that was one wonderful blast! I closed my eyes for a minute and let the fog rush right through me. It was kind of weird to see everything turn from contrasty to blur. It was like walking into another world. I loved it.

The rain let up some, and there was intermittent fog as I walked through the forest. There was no one at the Crag, but the view was just incredible! Clouds playing all around, and the sound of Whitaker Creek down below. I followed the blufftop trail back towards the trailhead. There was one wonderful sight after another, as the clouds parted and allowed me to see out from the bluff deep into the wilderness.

I followed the trail out to the registration box, or where it used to be. There was only a post there now. Still no one on the trail. Here it was the first full weekend of spring, the weather and the scenery were just incredible, and I was alone on one of the most popular hiking trails in Arkansas. That was just fine with me!

My gloomy funk continued as I took the ladder trail down to the river. And so did the rain, only it was light. I found many of my little wildflowers to be all curled up and protecting themselves against the rain. It was funny to see all of the brilliant white bloodroot flowers wound up tight, with their wide single leaf spreading out at their base. They kind of reminded me of ballet dancers, all curled up and ready to spring into action. Our wildflowers certainly do put on a great dance.

I found that it was easier if I ran down the steep hill trail instead of just walking. I normally have to use my hands a lot to grab onto small trees to keep me from going down too fast. But I didn't want to get my hands wet today. Half of your efforts going down this trail are to slow yourself down. But when I jogged down, I didn't have to come to a near stop with every step—my momentum just kept right on going—so I didn't have to grab any trees. It was easier on my knees too. And it was a lot faster!

The river was singing a lively tune, but wasn't up too high, and was running clear. The polished rock bar along the near bank was wonderful, as always.

My head was still pounding with my silly little personal troubles as I headed up the hillside. I really leaned into the hill, and kept up a fast pace. I was thinking fast too. At the bottom of the hill the problems seemed insurmountable. The hill was just the hill. The further up I climbed the quicker my pace got, and the steeper the hill got. But my personal woes seemed less and less. I found myself transferring my mental energy from my personal problems to conquering the hill. I dug in deeper with each step. By the time I reached the bottom of the bluff my heart and lungs were pumping full blast. My brain had settled down and my problems seemed distant and small.

The wilderness continues to challenge and amaze me, and no doubt saves me from having to go see a shrink from time to time.

Back at the cabin I sat down on the back deck and cooled down from my heated climb. The rain was still coming down, but the wind was not blowing, and so all of the deck was dry, including the chairs. Since the wind blows so much here the rain often gets everything wet. I like to sit out on the back deck while cooling down, plus it gives me a chance to take in the view. The fog lifted somewhat, and revealed a stunning view of the river below.

Inside the cabin it was warm. Very warm. It was 74 degrees, which was about as hot as I'd ever seen it inside the cabin during the winter. I had to open a window or two and turn on a couple of ceiling fans. And the warm temps brought out many wasps—dead and dying wasps all over the cabin. I must return with some bug bombs soon.

I took the tablecloth off of the dining table to take home to wash, which I don't do very often. The natural wood of this wonderful table was shining bright. There was a clear glass bowl of water with fresh daffodils in it, which complemented the wood nicely.

After a hot shower I put on some music and sat back and relaxed a little. I realized that there were no less than *five* quarts of Starbucks Ice Cream in the freezer! I decided that I wasn't going to make a pig out of myself as I normally do, and limited my intake to a single scoop from one container. It was good, very good. Later I had some veggies and rice for dinner (life is uncertain—eat dessert first!), and worked on the computer for a few hours. The temp outside remained around 47 degrees, with light rain—about an inch total for the day.

3/31/99 I drove like hell to get to the cabin in time. The sky was blue, the sun was getting close to the western horizon. I had to make it to Cloudland by sunset. And I did. I knew it was close. I ran out onto the back deck, not even going inside the cabin. There it was, right on cue—a giant, beautiful, incredible, living BLUE MOON rising above the far hillside. The full moon always rises at sunset. This was the second full moon of the month—which is a blue moon—and the second blue moon this year. The last time that happened was 84 years ago.

Anyway, the moon was gorgeous, and it cleared the treetops in a hurry and climbed high in the sky. This thing has magic. It is magic. When the moonlight strikes your face, you are blessed. I know that everyone thinks that weird things happen during the full moon, but I think that *wonderful* things happen! All I had to do was to look around me and see that was the truth. The wilderness spread out before me was a marvel of nature.

The light quietly changed from white to yellow to "Ozarkglow" to soft moonlight, which highlighted the ridgetops. A haze hung in the air, and the scene did turn a little eerie. I remember one night when the big helicopter came by for a visit—it looked a lot like this. I sat in the swing and let the moon take me over...

The wind picked up and soon I had to retreat into the cabin. It was then that I realized that there were still five quarts of Starbucks ice cream in the freezer. I put on a long-sleeve shirt, scooped up a mug of the frozen cream, and returned to the swing. Heaven must be like this—great ice cream, a gentle breeze, and blue moon light across the wilderness. Now, where was that lady that I wanted to share it all with?

March had been one more terrific month at Cloudland. A bit of rain, plenty of wind, and even some ice and snow. Lots of great hikes, and good visits from friends and family. But I wasn't out here nearly long enough to suit me. I will have to work on that. March is always early spring, but April has always meant *spring* to me. So I look forward to this next terrific month, and the last full month of the Journal.

March rain was 4.3 inches, low 20 degrees, high 70 degrees, wind 40mph

APRIL 1999

4/1/99 Someone was singing a lullaby to me as my brain came to life. There was no sunrise outside my window, but there was a bird, perched on a nearby limb, singing his heart out. I think it was a bunting. Could he have been crying out for *food*, or just welcoming me back to the cabin? I took it as a sign to get up and see what April was all about. Oh yea, there was also a serviceberry tree in bloom a few feet from my head—brilliant white.

I had some yogurt and Grape Nuts and a banana for breakfast. It seemed warm as I stepped outside (63 degrees), but the wind was howling—up in the 30mph range—which made it a little chilly. I sat on my own little perch and marveled at all the movement out in the airspace in front of me. Even though it was just barely daylight, there were a dozen or more soaring birds out playing in the wind. Mostly buzzards, but there were a few hawks too. And little birds, several different species, darting back and forth in the meadow below.

Hey, there was a bluebird! And he flew right past one of the little houses and landed in a nearby tree. I got out the telescope and examined him. He had something in his mouth. I zoomed in close. He had either one of those green strands of something that grows on oak trees at this time of the year, or a caterpillar. And he kept tossing it up in the air and catching it, then tossing it back up again. He was very serious about this business. I wasn't sure what the heck he was doing. Every two or three tosses he would pause and look in my direction, as if to ask what the heck I was looking at.

He must have done this twenty or more times, and I eventually realized that whatever it was he was tossing was growing *longer!* What? Looked to be about two inches long. Then in one quick flip of his beak, and a big gulp that I swear I could hear, he tossed the object up in the air and inhaled the entire thing—it disappeared in a split second. I had to look twice to see that it was all gone. Sure enough. It had to have been a caterpillar. But why was he biting on it and tossing it up in the air? It remained in one piece. The only thing that I can think of is that he was tenderizing it, just like a piece of meat. Or trying to smash it down so that it wasn't so big around. At any rate, the entire scene was a treat for this porch-sitter to witness. Now, if he can only get his mate to take up residence in one of my houses—the caterpillar supply will be great.

I turned my attention to a very large red-tailed hawk that was soaring nearby. I watched him through the binocs, as he rode the wind currents with his outstretched arms. All he had to do was curve one of his wingtips just a little, and he went sailing off in a different direction. Such beauty. Such grace. Please let me be a hawk in the next life.

As I looked around I could see eleven serviceberry trees that were in bloom right in my little backyard. And some of the mature trees out in the wilderness were beginning to take an individual tree shape—budding out some. These were the first that I had noticed this year.

There were lots of clouds but the sun managed to break through every now and then, sending a shaft of light down into the forest. Moving clouds often create a real light show.

There were many chores on tap for me today but I decided to get out and walk around a little before I got too serious. Then I realized that I could do both. I grabbed a roll of flagging tape and headed on up towards the East Meadow. Since this is one of the routes that I use the most I need to get a trail built here soon. Within about ten minutes I had the route flagged all the way to the meadow. Nothing fancy, just a nice stroll through the woods. It will take a bit of work to construct, but that will be the fun part. There were about a hundred trout lilies along one stretch, but none of them were in bloom yet. In fact, there were very few wildflowers in bloom up this high.

Everywhere I walked there were birds. Lots of birds. Calling out into the woods, flying from tree to tree, soaring overhead. I counted about thirteen different species in twenty minutes, although I couldn't ID them all.

I went by the Faddis cabin and then Bob's, looking for a little digging tool. I found it in the little old log shed at Bob's, the one that the bear broke into last summer. There was this old homestead nearby that had a large patch of day lilies that I wanted to borrow a few of to plant at my place (on private land—can't dig wildflowers in the wilderness). On the way back to the cabin I stopped and got out a few clumps of the plants and loaded them up in my pack.

The wild plums and peaches were really coming out in full force. The peach blossoms were very colorful and striking. There seems to be lots of wild plums up here but I don't recall ever seeing any of the fruit. Now that I know the trees, I will keep my eyes open as summer approaches.

On the way back I found a nice redbud tree in full bloom that had been knocked over by another large tree as it fell from the ice storm. After about five minutes of heavy dragging and a bit of cursing I was able to remove the larger tree and free the redbud.

I took up my seat on the back deck again. Now the valley was full of smaller hawks—three of them all flying in formation. Round and round and up and up they went. Then they dove back down again.

I brought out a new addition to the cabin with me. Actually several. One thing was a 31 foot carpet runner, three feet wide. I unrolled it in the great room, and it stretched all the way from the front door to the back door. Now you can walk through the cabin without getting on the wood floor. Still no shoes allowed inside though!

My truck was packed with plants—thousand bucks worth, azaleas and rhododendrons mostly. I have tried to find someplace to buy wild azaleas to plant in the steeper areas of the meadow below the deck, but I was unable to find anybody who grew them. I know they are very difficult to transplant from the wild, plus I don't know of very many on private property. So we went with domestic varieties, but I think the colors will be good. The rhododendrons will add a bit of green color in the wintertime, plus some nice flowers in the spring.

I also brought out some bug bombs to slow down the wasps, which I set off upstairs in the loft. It would be four hours before I could re-enter the cabin, so I got a lot of little chores done outside.

One chore was to lay out the new deck that I am going to build to put the hot tub on. Once I figured out where the posts were going I had to get the heavy steel pry bar and move a few rather large boulders that were in the way. One of them went crashing down the hillside, but I managed to move the others out of the way without any further dramatics.

Come to think of it, I don't remember what any of the other chores were. Perhaps there weren't any in the morning, because I did head off soon for a little hike and then a trail maintenance work trip.

The hike took me down the ladder trail to the river. It didn't take me too long to skip down the steep slope. And you should have seen all of the blood-root flowers! They were *everywhere*, and just incredible! And dancing to the pulse of the wind. But they weren't the only flowers out. There seemed to be tiny blooms on this or that all around me. It was a fairy-tale hike for sure.

The sun was shining brightly when I reached the river. And it was getting rather warm. The river was running normal, and was this wonderful color. Let's see, last night was the blue moon, today is April 1st, the first real day of spring for me. It is warm, and there is this gorgeous river right at my feet. I don't know what came over me, but before I knew what was going on, I had stripped off my clothes and was screaming at the top of my lungs as I plunged my body into the *frigid* water! The first dip was downright painful. But I quickly got out, and then went right back in again. The second time is always better. I stayed in for maybe ten seconds this time. That was enough for me.

I got out and dried off as best as I could then turned towards the big hill and tried to make it to the top as fast as I could, nonstop, and taking large steps. I'm sure the cold water helped a little, and before I knew it I was sitting in one of my chairs on the back deck, panting heavily.

There were still lots of birds out, mostly little ones now. In fact there were a couple of pairs of very tiny birds that were chasing each other out over the meadow. I never could ID them, but they seemed to be having a great time. Once I rested up a little it was time for another hike.

I took a new route over towards the Crag. This area is one that I plan to put a trail through at some point, one that would connect my cabin with the Faddis Meadow. As I got to the end of the area, I discovered an old log road that went straight down the hillside. I followed it, and found that it joined another old road trace on the lower bench. I took this road on over through the maple grove near the Crag.

Right out in the middle of the woods there was a bright yellow balloon hanging from a limb. It must have gotten away from someone and floated all the way into the wilderness. It looked a little funny.

On the bench above the Crag there is a good campsite that is legal. It looked like a large group had used it lately—they rolled up a bunch of pretty good-sized boulders around a fire ring to use as backrests, seats and tables. It was a pretty nice looking campsite, and a much better spot to camp at than down right next to the Crag (which is illegal).

Along one stretch of the trail there were literally hundreds and hundreds of spring beauty wildflowers—the entire forest floor took on this pink/purple hue. What wonderful little fellows these tiny spring messengers are!

I found a little dead bird in the leaves—a downy woodpecker. Couldn't figure out what had happened. I guess they die of old age and other natural causes sometimes. It was a sad moment of the day. This little guy added so much beauty and music to the world during its short life, I hated to see it ended. Then I realized that I had certainly come a very long way since my childhood. I used to shoot and kill little birds like this one with my BB gun all the time. And now, here I was, nearly in tears. I guess I have walked many miles since those days.

As I walked on further I got to thinking about bears. There is a nice little bluffline right above the trail, and there are several very bear-looking holes in the base. These would be perfect dens for bears, and they are on the southern slope, and near the top of the ridge. Even though some of the bears caused a great deal of grief last summer, I feel like the last one that I saw became my friend of sorts, and I wondered how he had been all winter, and when I would get to wander around with him again? I looked forward to the next meeting.

I spotted one small black caterpillar crawling down on the trail. Hum—I wondered how long it would be before this guy became a bluebird snack?

Once I got to the trailhead I followed the road back. And I spotted what must have been a remarkable discovery—in fact, I thought that it was a brand new species of butterfly, because I had never seen anything like it before! It was black, and looked like it had two sets of wings, at right angles to each other. But it managed to fly through the air OK. Upon closer inspection I realized that my great discovery was merely two little black butterflies enjoying a spring afternoon together.

Then I made a real discovery. As I walked past a stand of wild plum—the fragrance was overwhelming, simply incredible—I spotted the skeleton of some large creature. My goodness, there aren't any cows around here, and elk never stray up this far. It was a large skeleton alright, that of an ancient tractor. There was something there sticking up that looked a lot like a set of rib bones. What struck me most about this old tractor was that the wheel had wooden spokes, like a wagon wheel. I heard later that this was typical of old tractors. It looked pretty neat, and I learned a little something about early Ozark life. And those plums were just, well, wonderful!

Also in the same general area (an old homestead) there was this flaming red flowering bush of something, and a large black and blue butterfly feeding on one of the brilliant blossoms. It was a stirring contrast of color indeed!

As I was kicking back on the deck once again I spotted more butterflies below. There were three or four large yellow ones flying around. I think it is going to be a very good year for butterflies.

Uh oh. A tick. First one of the season. Let's hope it wasn't an omen.

There has been a water leak down in the basement, actually in the main electric line coming into the cabin—water has been filling up the conduit and dripping out. I have never been able to figure out how or where this water is getting into the electric line (underground cable, so no problem). I tried a new technique to stop the leak, and it worked!

While I was fixing the leak I realized that I had a more serious water problem. There apparently is a leak in the main waterline coming into the cabin. I could tell because the water pressure drops a little over time, even though there were not faucets on or leaking toilets. That is not a good sign. I have no idea where the leak might be.

I vacuumed up a couple hundred dead wasps and ladybugs. And I had a spoonful or two of Starbucks ice cream for lunch.

It was time for one last hike, and I headed back down to the river just as the sun was beginning to set. I was soon without sunshine. When I got down to where the bloodroots were growing I found them all wound up tight. They looked like pure white tulips. I guess they had put in a long day and were in bed for the night.

I wanted to see what the yellow trout lilies were doing, but could hardly find any that were out—only two or three. Yet the flat ground where they were growing was literally covered with their distinctive leaves! I mean there were probably thousands of them there, but only a few with flowers out. There were other low-growing plants too, and the forest floor was nearly solid green—about ten different shades of it.

There were tons of phlox in bloom, and several other wildflower species too, including toothwort and dutchman's breeches. And I found a new one for this year—bellwort. Those are the yellow ones that hang their heads in shame, always looking like they are wilted. They could be such a pretty flower if they would only stand up and show themselves! There were also several tiny and tender wild iris coming out. I'll bet they bloom within a couple of weeks.

There was no way that I was going to jump in the river again today.

As I headed back up the hillside I realized that it got dark a lot sooner down there in the valley where all of the homesites were. Because of the tall ridges all around the sun got there late in the mornings too. I guess there would be maybe as much as an hour less daylight than up at the cabin. I wonder if that had any effect on the early pioneers who lived down there? Perhaps the extended darkness produced more children.

The owls were out, and hooting like crazy as I made my way up the steep hillside. In the dimming light I could see that there were lots of large trillium wildflowers beginning to take over long stretches of the trail. They weren't in bloom yet, but their distinctive leaves were everywhere.

It was a sweat climbing the hill again, but I knew there was ice cream waiting for me at the top, so I pressed on, trying to burn off enough calories to justify indulging more than my usual.

I slowed down as I walked through my little meadow. I got down and began to look closely (the sun was just now setting up at the cabin, so I still had plenty of light). There were all kinds of little plants coming up. I had no idea if they were some of the wildflowers that I had planted in February, or some from last year, or just weeds. I will be keeping an eye on them as spring progresses. One of these years I hope to be able to actually identify some of these plants before they flower.

And speaking of flowers, there were already six or eight different species of wildflowers blooming in the meadow, all small ones. The violets are about to take over one spot. I can't wait to witness the progression of color as the year goes on.

I spent ten minutes out on the "cooling down deck." The wind was still blowing hard, but it had shifted from the normal SW direction to the east—that usually means a change in the weather. It was blowing pretty good—up in the mid 30's. The barometric pressure was dropping too.

Someone told me recently that you can eat anything that you want within thirty minutes of serious exercise and your body will burn it up immediately. Hum. What a great deal! I have no idea if that is even remotely true or not, but just in case it was, I hurried to the freezer and scooped out a cupful of ice cream. I ate it slowly, back out on the deck, and enjoyed every single frozen drop.

I have this simple green and white checkered cotton table cloth for the dining table. It is now about one size too small—I took it home and washed it. Oops. Looks·like another trip to Wal-Mart.

After a well-deserved hot shower I had a plate of veggies and rice and a glass of wine, then sat down at the computer and spent several hours writing. It had been a great day, with lots of work done, and *four* hikes! Bob is up at his cabin for a few days, and I am going over to help him plant taters in the morning. I just stepped outside a few minutes ago to check on the progress of the rising moon, and discovered that not only was there no moon out, but it was misting. And still very warm.

4/2/99 A little lady named Robin woke me this morning. She was sitting on a limb right outside my bedroom window singing her heart out. It wasn't quite daylight yet. I could see a hazy yellow moon setting in the west out the other window. And to the east, the sky was getting light, although it was full of broken clouds. I laid back and rested a few more minutes.

I got up just before the sun rose and ate a quick bite. When I went outside to put my boots on I met a rabbit that was munching on some new green leaves near the edge of the carport. He didn't stick around long. By the way, we had a discussion about "rabbits" vs. "hares" the other night, and found out that a "hare" is born with hair, where a "rabbit" is born hairless. You would think that they would have spelled "hare" "hair."

Bob had already been working in the Faddis garden a while by the time I arrived. The sun wasn't quite up there yet. He had been tilling a spot in the corner of his big garden. I took over the tilling job while he cut up some seed potatoes. We put out three rows of them—about 120 in all. I plan to fry/bake/grill and otherwise eat as many of these spuds this summer as I can—I *love* potatoes!

Bob is in his 70's and still going strong. He is tall and slender, and you can usually find a smile on his face. There is a great deal of Ozark pioneer in his blood. He sat down on a pile of straw to survey the garden. The sun peeked over the trees far behind him and put a yellow rim of light on him. He said to me: "You know, working with the earth like this is very good for the soul."

I finished up the tilling of one end of the garden and then had to get back to the cabin. Bob was going to put out garlic, horseradish, rhubarb, lettuce, radish, kale, collards, English peas, and cabbage this weekend. Corn, green beans, tomatoes and a few other odds and ends would be added later. Summer is the best time to visit Cloudland because there is always *fresh* food in the skillet!

On the way back I plotted out another trail through the woods. This one dropped down from the garden through a small but colorful broken bluffline, then out across a wide bench that was covered with trout lilies, and finally along the edge of the bench where you can look down the steep hillside to the lower trail to the Crag below. I want to utilize this trail instead of walking down the road when going to the Faddis cabin, and to the garden.

Right out in the middle of the woods a bright yellow butterfly came floating by. He followed me nearly all the way back to the cabin. Nice company for a warm spring morning.

I like living out here at Cloudland. It seems like there is always something to look at, or feel or experience in some way. Right now as I am sitting in my office here typing away at the computer, there are butterfly shadows dancing across the mini-blinds. I guess they are trying to edit what I am writing about them. And I can hear little birds nearby, and the drumming of a woodpecker way off in the distance.

4/3/99 Lightning, thunder, *rain!* Lots of the above. That is what this Saturday was filled with. Must be April in the Ozarks. We sure did need the rain—could use some every week to keep the waterfalls and creeks up and running full tilt until summer.

I met with Bob and Dawna from Ft. Smith out on the Ozark Highlands Trail to hike in and take a look at some trail work that needed to be done. It had already rained quite a bit and all watercourses were swollen. After our little trail inspection we hiked on down into the Spirits Creek drainage. The very first thing that we found was this *incredible* waterfall! It was just below the main trail, but none of us had ever seen it before. It was multi-level and just went on forever, spilling down over moss-covered boulders.

And once we reached the main Spirits Creek gorge the wonderful water scenes just got better. This is one of the most scenic parts of the trail at any time of the year, but especially so with all of the water. There were also a lot of dogwoods beginning to blossom, although the flowers were coming out green at first instead of bright white. This area is only slightly south of Cloudland (and 50 miles to the west), but everything seemed about a week farther into spring, with many trees budding and/or leafing out.

And the forest floor was *covered* with wildflowers, although not all that many of them were blooming. We found one giant boulder that we climbed up on that was literally covered, every square inch of it, with trout lilies and a couple of other wildflowers, all rimmed with walking ferns.

Bob didn't have a raincoat with him. Mine was tucked into my daypack about a mile up the trail. As we continued exploring the creek the sky got very dark. I mean about as dark as you can get during the daytime. Then the sky opened up, and it began to pour buckets. Dawna had her rain gear on, of course. Bob and I headed straight up the steep hillside as the rain got heavier. I had on a pair of nylon shorts and a poly pro top. Thank goodness it wasn't too cold out. I enjoyed hiking in the rain, although I did have to hike about as fast as I could in order to stay warm. By the time I reached my daypack and my raincoat, I decided just to keep on going and keep the rain gear dry—I was soaked anyway.

On the way back up the hill we stopped and spent ten minutes building a very large waterbar across the trail. There was a great deal of water running down the trail—about six inches deep. I had never built a waterbar underwater before, but had to do most of the digging there. Before too long we had a decent ditch constructed and most of the water was running off of the trail. We will have to go back later and build a real waterbar there in the future.

On the way back from the trail we drove past dozens and dozens of waterfalls and cascades plunging down mountainsides. It was a great scenic driving tour for sure.

We had our spring hike-in scheduled at our hiking club's Williams Woods Nature Preserve this day, but the heavy downpour all day kept most away. I can't blame them. Hiking in the rain is one thing, but camping in it is quite another. Not too much fun, especially for novice hikers.

I got back to Cloudland just as the sky was breaking up a little and the daylight was fading. It had been one thunderous day outside, and I sat out on the back deck to wind down. Both the Buffalo River and Whitaker Creek were flooded and making a lot of noise. And just across the valley I could hear and see that pair of hundred foot waterfalls spilling over the big bluff—they were *awesome!*

The wind had topped out at 41mph, and we had 2.5 inches of rain. I suspect there was even more rain than that, but it was blowing horizontal and didn't get caught in the rain gauge.

But what really got me was the weird color and quality of the light. Weird, that pretty well describes it. It was a mixture of the warm colors of sunset through the clouds, and the green of the new trees budding out.

It was warm out, with a light breeze. Actually it was a pretty good breeze out in back, and so I spent some time sitting in the front porch swing. I like to do that sometimes. There isn't much of a view, but it was dark out so I didn't need a view. The rivers and the wind and the chimes and the stereo all combined to form a very relaxing tune. It was one of those top-ten moments at Cloudland. A glass of good wine sent to me by some new friends in California topped everything off. I sat and swayed back and forth and let my mind wander.

Here is a little tidbit that I learned about how lightning will stimulate plant growth. It seems that when conditions are just right, like they were this day, with spring rains and plants already about to bud out, a lightning storm will speed up the process. The lightning somehow changes the nitrogen in the atmosphere into a form that is more usable by plants. This gives the trees a jolt and makes them grow faster. I expected to see a lot of new growth the next day!

4/4/99 Easter. Even before it got light enough to see I could tell it was going to be one incredible morning. There was a sea of clouds down in the valley—one of the largest that I had ever seen. The nearly full moon was shining in one window of the loft. And there were stars out.

As the sun began to rise both the sun and the moon could be seen reflecting in the lamp beside the bed (through two different windows). Then sunlight spilled over the ridgetop and illuminated the sea of fog. Time to get up and greet the day!

I cooked up some asparagus eggs, garlic new potatoes, blueberry biscuits, and fresh ground coffee with that special Cloudland touch for breakfast (booze). Hey, it was a holiday. The incredible light and fog show was quite a treat to watch, even from inside the cabin. It was cool outside, and no wind at all. The clouds were going to hang around for a while.

And for a really special treat, those two big waterfalls across the way were still running. The top of the fog bank was hovering right about in the middle of the waterfalls—the waterfalls were spilling over this huge painted sandstone bluff right into the sea of fog! Gosh, it was just incredible.

But today was a work day so I got into work clothes and got to it. Plants. There were lots of plants to put in the ground. Emily came out from town to do the planting. I helped out some, but mostly tended to my own chores. She was in "hired hand" mode (I was paying her to do the plantings) and no longer in girlfriend mode. Bummer.

I moved on over to the other side of the big deck and worked on the hot tub site. There were more giant rocks to move and lots of dirt to dig up. I made a level spot to set the tub on (up on 6 x 6 posts). Once the hot tub gets here I will build a new deck around it, so it will be built in and sunken. The new deck won't be much larger than the hot tub though.

After much figuring and measuring I decided to orient the tub east-west. I plan on spending most of my time in the lounger, and from my seat I will be able to see under the big deck and will have a terrific view of the Buffalo River.

As the morning drew on the clouds eventually disappeared. It never got foggy at the cabin. I don't know what happens to the clouds—they just evaporate into the air I guess. But the sky was clear and blue and the sunshine felt great. And there were lots of birds out too. Including the bluebirds. We never actually saw them going into either birdhouse, but they were hanging around close. I'm keeping my fingers crossed that they nest soon.

And there were a pair of birds that were beginning a nest over near the hot tub site—up on top of the overhead light fixture.

An unusual bird landed on a nearby limb. It was about the size of a sparrow, but had very distinctive black and white stripes covering its entire body. Neither of us had ever seen a bird like this before. And we never could find it in the ID book. Someone help! This was one unusual feathered friend.

Roy and Norma came hiking by with friends. They were headed down to the bluff to do a little rappelling and waved as they went by. A few screams were heard coming from their direction later on—they were having fun.

It had been a hard morning but the work felt great. We took a break and had lunch on the deck. Just about the time we were finishing up a commotion broke out down below. Lizards. Two of them. And they were quite *large* lizards. Emily has a pet iguana, about five feet long, so she was especially interested in what these guys were up to. I had spent time on this deck looking through the binocs or the tele at birds, foxes, butterflies, people, but never lizards!

It seems they had a disagreement, or a territorial dispute or something. They were both up on a log down below that was covered with lichens. They faced each other and both started "pumping" (doing push-ups). This was funny to begin with. Then all of a sudden one jumped at the other, got him by the neck, and they twisted and flopped all around (no they weren't having sex— these dudes were fighting!). In fact they wrestled themselves right off of the log, and disappeared into the leaves.

We watched on, fascinated. They both climbed up onto a rock, pumped up some more, then went at each other again. At one point, they were down in the leaves thrashing around, and while they were actually out of sight, there was stuff being thrown up in the air by their fighting   it was a lot of fun watching them!

The reptile ID book that I had was of no use. Every time we thought we had a perfect match we discovered that particular lizard was only found in one county in California or something like that. They were large, not the normal lizards that you see in the Ozarks, and had bright green bellies.

The lizards moved on down the hillside and continued their argument. We went back to work and found that the trickle watering plan I had set up had completely drained the water well—this had not happened in over a year. That was not a good thing. Especially since we still had a lot of plants to get into the ground and to water. I couldn't get the well pump to pump any water, but there was still a little bit in the hose, so we just let a little water dribble into the plants and hoped that would be enough.

The sun began to beat down pretty good in the afternoon. It was in fact a little warm. Still felt great. We both were getting tired, dried out, and a little sunburned. But we finally did get the last of the big plants in the ground. I had finished with my leveling project and dug that last few holes while Emily did the planting. (She does plants as a part time job.)

Right before we quit for the day I tried to manually start the well pump once again, and it started up and filled up the water pressure tank in the basement. Yea, water again! We got the rest of the plants a good dose of the wet stuff, then shut everything down and packed up all the tools.

As Emily was leaving she spotted a rabbit out in front of the cabin. It wasn't afraid of her at all, and never ran off. It didn't dawn on me that it must have been the Easter Bunny!

Another terrific weekend at Cloudland. Spring is in full swing.

4/5/99 Sunrise never came today. It was dark, very dark. And the wind was blowing. No, *howling!* And then the rains came. The wet stuff was blowing horizontally, and so were many tree branches and other debris. Gale force winds topped out at 52mph. And about an inch of rain, which was great for all of the new plants in the neighborhood. This was a fitting beginning to my day as I had to get into town and go through a State Sales Tax audit. Not the most pleasant experience, but I did survive.

Everything was calm out at the cabin when I returned at night. No major damage, except for three chairs that had been blown from the lower deck way out into the front, and broken. Nothing on the upper decks was moved at all. Strange. And the well water was back to normal, thank goodness.

I got an e-mail from a Canadian journal reader who suggested an ID for the weird bird that we had seen over the weekend. While I was in town, I had picked up an Eastern US bird ID book, and son of a gun, her ID was correct— the black and white striped bird that we saw was a black and white warbler. The first warbler ID at Cloudland! The new book is a Peterson Field Guide, which I like a lot better than the Audubon guides. I'm sticking with Peterson's.

As I shut down the cabin and got ready for bed I spent a little time out on the back deck. It was calm out, and clear, with lots of stars. Out in the distance there were flashes of light—lots of them.

4/6/99 The flashes didn't produce anything, and a bright sun quickly filled the cabin and got me out of bed. Clear skies, no wind, 49 degrees. When I opened the back door to the deck I was met with throngs of bird songs—the trees and the ground and the sky were alive with motion and color! Lots of little birds especially, out playing in the trees.

There were bluebirds, juncos, sparrows, pewees, more of the warblers, red-tailed hawks, buzzards, crows, buntings, and both ends of the woodpecker spectrum—a couple of giant pileated ones and several tiny downy ones. I just sat and watched in amazement at all of the life outside my door.

The recent rains and sunshine were having an impact on the trees of the forest. Down below me I could see individual trees that had popped out and were green and taking on tree shapes. They were mostly down in the bottom of the valleys, a few up the hillsides, but none on the ridgetops. The side-lighting of the morning sun really brought out the green.

It was tough to tear myself away from the wonderful show outside. I spent most of the morning inside, down in the basement, getting the heavy wiring for the hot tub all set up and in place. It was actually easy, once I got about a dozen holes drilled in the floor joists. It took a chunk of 220 wire that weighs about 30 pounds to make the connection.

Then I moved outside and poured the concrete footing for the new deck post. There were a couple of birds that were a little annoyed while I was working in that spot. I later learned that they were pewees, and they were busy building a nest on top of one of the lower deck lights, right next to the future hot tub location. Oops. That was not a good place for them to nest.

Next on my list was to plant all of the daylilies (that I had dug up elsewhere in the forest). I put them along part of the drive out in front. It was getting a little hot by then, and gradually my clothes came off. I realized that I didn't have a pair of shorts out at the cabin—big mistake at this time of the year—so before long I was working in just my hiking boots, socks, and my underwear.

While I was taking a break on the back deck another new bird flew up and perched in the tree right in front of me. I even had my binocs at the ready, and studied him carefully. He looked just like the Black and White Warblers that were chasing each other around the meadow, although he had this brilliant yellow throat patch. A quick look in the new guidebook confirmed that it was a yellow-throated Warbler. I love these descriptive names. And I like all of the warblers around.

It would turn out to be a very long, hot, sunny, and productive afternoon. I spent most of it hauling wood up from the meadow, and clearing out logs from down there. I decided that this would be my last day of clearing down there. There were so many tiny new plants coming up in the meadow—wildflowers I hoped—that I didn't want to trample them any more. It was amazing just how many logs were left down there. Many of them were really too large for me to handle alone, but I did the best that I could.

Since it got pretty hot I decided to strip off what was left of my clothing and I spent the afternoon working in the buff. Good thing that I didn't have any visitors! Of course, if anyone had wandered by they wouldn't have seen much— probably would have had to use their binocs anyway. I did get a little worried about all of those birds flying around nearby though—after all, they were all out looking for little worms.

I also spent a lot of time taking breaks up on the back deck, and looking around at all the life. The valley below was filled with soaring birds—lots of hawks and even more buzzards. Curiously though they were all flying low, below the ridgetops. None were up in the sky. I don't know if it was the air temp, or currents, or what. At one point I looked up the Whitaker Creek drainage and there were about a dozen buzzards flying in formation right down the valley, weaving back and forth, but all remaining at about the same elevation. They looked like a squadron of jet fighters coming in for an attack.

Eventually the soaring birds did make their way up into the air. At one point there seemed to be two distinctly different groups of hawks flying around. There were several large red-tails circling high up, and a group of three or four smaller ones that mainly kept low in the valleys. It was like each bunch had its own territory, which was divided by elevation.

I watched one of the hawks through the binocs as he was doing his acrobatics. He would soar around a little, then dive down a hundred feet, then flare up into the wind and climb. He was backlit by the sun the whole time and I could see the brilliant rust-color in his tail plainly. Another hawk entered the valley at one end and sailed low all the way to the other end without flapping.

There were also a lot of butterflies soaring around down in the meadow. At first I just noticed a few here and there, then more came, and more. They were coming over the top of the cabin and spilling down into the meadow. Two kinds mostly—both zebra and yellow tiger swallowtails. Zebras and tigers oh my! I wondered how such gentle creatures could be named after ferocious animals? It was great to see the splash of color darting back and forth across the meadow. And I realized that it was nearly impossible to follow one of these butterflies through the binocs—they were just too fast and unpredictable.

One of the big lizards came out. He crawled out to the end of a log in the meadow and went through an exercise routine—doing push-ups. He appeared to be surveying his kingdom, and proclaiming himself as lizard king.

The rivers down below sang all day—there was a lot of water in them, although the color was normal. And at one point I heard a noise, and looked down just in time to see a kayak in the Buffalo. The "Hailstone" run from one end of the wilderness to the other—fifteen miles—is a float that I have been anxious to do, and I will get to it before this spring is out. For the experienced floater high water is best, and about the only time that it can be floated. But I'm not that good, and so will pick a more normal water flow, which means that I will probably have to get out and drag the canoe a lot, but I won't care. It will be a wonderful trip. I'll bet the floaters were having a great time today with all of the water.

As the afternoon drew on and it got warmer you could almost see the individual trees popping out below. I would say that the number of trees out doubled during the afternoon.

There didn't seem to be any dogwoods out though. They will often bloom before the rest of the forest leafs out. Some of the dogwoods down in the meadow appeared to be on the verge of popping out right before my eyes, but they held their buds tight. I did find one dogwood that had burst out though—the one right outside of the guest bath window. It had been heavily damaged by the cabin construction activities, but it seems to want to stand up and tell the world that it was still as beautiful as any tree in the forest—and it is! Great to see dogwood blooms again.

There was a small flock of juncos that were feeding on some seed that I had scattered on the ground. At first when I would walk near them they would all jump up into the air and take off, just like a group of pigeons in the park. As the day wore on, and I walked past them a lot, they got less and less afraid and eventually didn't pay me any attention and just kept right on eating.

The zillion tiny plants down in the meadow seemed to grow a little with each trip past them. The sun and that nitrogen were having quite an impact on the forest. I liked to think that my bare behind did too. Maybe that was what all of the chatter up in the trees was all about. Ha, ha, I'm sure the birds will talk about that for a while.

My friend, Ken Eastin, faxed me a design that he drew up for a little tower that I had to build for the big water tank that I wanted to install to catch rain water (to water plants with and fill the hot tub).

By the end of the day I was beat and sunburned all over. But it felt great to get so much work done. I was now ready for spring to happen down in the meadow. Perhaps I will plant a few more things—got some coneflowers all ready—but that may be about it until next year. Looks like the wild sunflowers will come on strong again this summer, and they have spread from last year. There will be an explosion of growth and color for several months ahead I bet. And all of that growth will bring many forms of life for all to watch and enjoy. Thank goodness for my meadow!

4/7/99 I arrived back at the cabin at mid-morning accompanied by Terry Fredrick. His truck was filled with long and heavy boards—treated 6 x 6 posts and 2 x 12's and stuff like that. And a 500 gallon water tank. It was time to get the cistern put up.

We unloaded everything and then I ran a shuttle for Terry, who was out to do a hike over in the Beech Creek drainage. I let him off down at the old Sassafras community. This was a woman's commune for many years back in the 70's—90's. There are 20 or so dwellings there, all abandoned. I heard that the last folks moved out a couple of years ago. Terry says that the long bench where the commune was located is one of the most incredible wildflower areas in the region. I vowed to return one day and see for myself, but I had work to do back at the cabin. (An *update*: Terry was met and run off by a woman, and he said that there was fresh construction going on, so I guess the community is alive and well once again—that means that we need to respect their rights and *not* trespass to get into the Beech Creek drainage. I have also since learned that someone else has purchased the property, and so it may not be the same community folks after all.)

And it was hard dirty work too. I dug holes and cut posts and poured concrete. The posts were so heavy that I could not even begin to pick one up, so I had to drag them around and muscle them into place. By the end of the day I had all four big posts cemented in the ground and the structure began to look a little like Ken's faxed design.

4/8/99 It was late morning when I got back to work and the wind was howling—up in the low 40's. It was in the low 70's temp wise. Lots of clouds. Ken Eastin came out to help with the final assembly of the water tower. We quickly got to work, sawing and drilling and hauling. The wind blew and blew all afternoon, but the rain held off.

We managed to solve all of the little problems that cropped up, and by the end of the day we had a finished rainwater catch system in place! I hadn't been able to get the rain gutter stuff that I wanted so we rigged up a temporary system that looked like some hillbilly contraption, with wires and hanging pipes and such. We had no idea if it would work. Or if the system would work at all. Or if the tower would hold the more than two ton weight of a full water tank. Now we needed some rain.

As we sat out on the back deck sipping a couple of beers a storm blew up. And I mean really *blew!* There was this one hawk that came flying through. He got up into the wind, which was blowing about 40mph. And you could tell that he was straining to keep from being blown away—his wings were tucked in close to his body as he made his way up the valley.

And in a fitting note Ken's pack of cigarettes blew right off of the deck and down into the woods—served him right for smoking. It was a funny sight to see this rain-soaked body trudging up the steep slope, clutching a pack of soggy cigarettes!

And then the rain got a little harder. We rushed to the guest bath window and stuck our heads out to see if we could hear any water running into the tank. And we could! It rained on, and the tank began to fill up. Within an hour it had rained about a quarter of an inch. I had no idea how much rain it would take to fill up the tank. We checked the tank and discovered, much to our great delight, that there was already over 100 gallons in the tank! And everything was working fine. Even our little hillbilly pipe contraption. Although we did have to shore it up in a spot or two with some rope.

We sat around and listened to the storm. The rain finally stopped, and stars came out. Just over one-half inch fell, and the tank had 300 gallons of water in it—yippie! What great timing. It may not rain again for a month. But I've got water, and the water tower was working fine. So it takes about an inch of rain to fill the tank completely. And I'm only using half the surface area of the roof—I could always add a second tank on the back side of the cabin if needed.

After Ken left and went home I sat out on the deck and watched one tremendous light show. There was still a bank of thunderheads on the horizon and it was filled with electricity. I think the lightning was just trying to match the brilliance of the sky full of stars above.

4/9/99 I got up in the middle of the night and realized that it was bright outside. A quarter moon was rising into the eastern sky. It was about 4am. I couldn't sleep so I got up and wrote for a couple of hours. It was warm and calm and loud outside—the rivers were really running! I had to strain to make out features in the wilderness in the dim light, but the river below was sparkling in the moonlight.

I returned to bed until the sun came up. When it did my eyes were flooded with green light from the budding trees outside my window. That wonderful bright spring green will soon cover the entire Ozarks. I've not seen anything to match that elsewhere in this country. New England may have its fall, the Rockies in the winter, but spring in the Ozarks is tops!

As the sun was climbing into the sky I took off down the ladder trail for a quick trip to the river and back. I just needed to work through some personal problems and didn't know of a better way to think. While there weren't all that many flowers out, cities of mayapples were popping up all over. No flowers on them yet, but they will be out soon. And there were tons of giant bloodroot leaves—some about the size of small elephant ears, but no blooms. The trillium were out in full force too, and blooming nicely.

Once I reached the river I found a raging torrent. The rock bar was completely under water with only the tops of the individual sycamore trees sticking up. Looked a little funny. Whitaker Creek was running high too, and there was no way that I could have crossed it dry. A half-inch of rain can sure send a lot of water!

The climb back up the hill was swift, and my brain was running on overdrive. I hardly even noticed the steepness of the hill at all. Really. That wasn't because I was in such great shape, but because my mental attention was elsewhere, on problems in my life.

Just as I made it to the top of the bluff I looked right out in front of me, and a few inches from my face was a lone shooting star wildflower, perched on a tiny ledge. Its whole purpose it seemed was to welcome me to the top, to let me know that I would always have the beauty of nature to make my heart soar. Thanks little buddy! When I reached the cabin I found tick #2 for the season.

Touches of green are beginning to climb up the hillsides now, and while most of the trees are still brown, the wilderness is taking on a green tint. And there are a few dogwoods here and there beginning to pop out, including several round the cabin. They are coming out with that yellow/green shade instead of pure white. They will eventually turn all white.

4/10/99 This Saturday was going to be a work day for me, mostly away from the cabin. I had to lead a group of folks to a couple of scenic areas, then a quick stop by the cabin, then a short hike into Dug Hollow, then into town for a little while, then back out to the cabin. A very long but wonderful spring day in the Ozarks.

We hiked into Kings River Falls first. There was lots of water in the river from the recent rains and the waterfall was as incredible as I had ever seen it— really spectacular! This is not a very tall waterfall, but it is wide, and has a great deal of personality. And the color of the water was this very rich green. There were a few wildflowers out there, but not nearly as many as usual at this time of the year. The redbuds and serviceberry were out in full force. And we saw two snakes along the trail—a copperhead and a big black snake, both still a little lethargic from a long winter rest.

Kings River Falls is one of those spots that you can go to at just about any time of the year and have a great hike. The water forms and rock sculptures are so wonderful there. And the vegetation is always lush. It is protected as a State Natural Area, just like Sweden Falls.

Next we drove on over and hiked down into the Glory Hole. It too was full of water and really pumping. There were a lot of other hikers on that trail. On the way out we saw and photographed a huge luna moth (aren't they all?) that was clinging to the trunk of a tree. The wind was whipping the poor guy around, and we were hardly able to take any pictures of him at all.

From there we visited the cabin, and spent some time lounging around on the back deck, munching on chocolate, sipping a little brew, and taking a few pictures. When it came time to move on I had trouble getting everyone up and going. I think they enjoyed the place.

I took one of the hikers down to Stairstep Falls while the rest of the group went down to the Crag. We visited the yellow lady slipper orchids, and found them to be just starting to come out of the ground—will probably be two to three weeks before any blooms. The waterfall was running pretty good, and the umbrella magnolia trees around it had begun to leaf out, but no blooms yet— another two to three weeks on them as well.

It was very late and dark when I returned to the cabin. The stars were shining brightly in the coal black sky. I was tired, and went straight up to bed.

4/11/99 I rested my head on the pillow and watched as the yellow ball eased up over the hillside, lighting up brilliant new green growth in the trees out my window. Sunshine filled the valleys one by one, and soon it was a bright green and blue kind of a day. And it was chilly out—in the low 50's with wind.

I didn't have any Starbucks, so I fixed up a Cloudland Cocoa and sipped it out on the deck and the light show went on. One thing that I noticed right away was that there weren't very many birds out. A few little ones playing in the treetops, but that was about it. I didn't see a single soaring bird of any kind.

There were a few inside chores to do, then I spent some time putting up the permanent gutter system to feed the cistern. I had to get out the chain saw and do a little alteration to the log carport in one spot. Yikes, I was cutting into my cabin with a chain saw! It turned out just fine, and no longer looked like a hillbilly setup. Probably won't work now.

As the morning went on the wilderness became greener with each passing hour. Most of the trees had some degree of green now. Some were with tiny leaves, others with those weird green things that grow on them first in the spring. And still no soaring birds. A single male bluebird spent a few minutes sitting in the top of one of the dogwoods down below.

Then a buzzard appeared way off in the distance. Just one guy. He took his time, and was just cruising down the valley. An old lonely buzzard. I guess we had a lot in common. Only my house is nicer than his. I think.

Some of the azaleas that we had planted last week were already blooming, and they were attracting a number of yellow tiger swallowtail butterflies. It was good to see the butterflies getting something to eat.

I tried out the new cistern, and while the water pressure was not very good, I was able to water a few plants with no problems, saving precious well water.

After another hour or two of chores I struck out for a hike. Did a quick trip out to the main trailhead and back. I passed a number of folks along the way, all couples. Not what I needed to see. Many folks don't like to do an out-and-back on the same trail—they would rather loop around and not see the same country twice. Well, I consider myself to be a pretty good spotter of things along the trails as I hike. On my way back down the very same trail I found gobs of wild-flowers that I hadn't even noticed just a few minutes before. And there were lots of firepink coming out. This is another one of those things that is not named correctly at all—they are bright *red*, not pink! But it was great to see them.

As I was crossing a level bench that was mostly void of wildflowers I came across a little oasis of color and movement. At the base of this large oak tree there were about fifty little spring beauty wildflowers, all clumped together. They were shimmering in the sunny wind.

I headed down the ladder trail, and passed a group of guys from Missouri that had spent the night down on the river. Their packs looked rather heavy, and they all appeared a little tired—could it have been our steep little hill?

Most of the wildflowers along the trail were at the bottom, although since the sun was out I didn't really have a good look deep into the forest. Both rivers were back down to normal spring-flow levels, and the color was nice. I stuck my head and shoulders into the Buffalo River and got a good cool-down.

The dogwoods along the river were out in full force—and blooming the typical bright white blooms too. It was great to see them—they were every-where! Looking up into a blue sky through backlit dogwood blossoms and new green growth was one stunning sight, and one that I never tire of.

The trip back up the hill didn't take too long, or hurt much. It felt good to stretch the leg muscles. As I wandered through the meadow I found that the huckleberry, wild sunflowers and polk salat were all coming out in great num-bers. I'm not sure about that polk salat—guess I need to learn how to cook it. Recipes anyone?

I spent some time down on the big low deck soaking up the bright sunshine and taking in the cooling breezes. I'm not normally a sun worshiper but today it felt just wonderful. Still no soaring birds out.

If I had to make a prediction I would say that next weekend will be the peak of spring around my little cabin. It will continue for several weeks for sure, but next weekend may be the best.

Later in the afternoon I took a nap in the back porch swing and had a cup of ice cream—two treats for getting all of my allotted chores done for the day.

While I was laying there I could hear the distant drumming of a woodcock over on Beagle Point. I had seen one near the cabin last month, but hadn't heard one until now. It was great to hear the sound waves echoing across the valley.

4/12/99 It was 3am when I got back to the cabin. It was clear and rather chilly out—down in the low 40's. It didn't take me long to drift off once I hit the pillow. But the early morning sky soon woke me up—lots of bright orange clouds over in the east—the best pre-sunrise that I had seen in a long time!

The sun soon followed all of the color and I had to get up and get to work. No breakfast or coffee or even hot chocolate for me today. I had a lot of work to do, and not much time to do it in. First thing I did was spend an hour or two cutting up all of the logs that I had brought up from the meadow the last couple of weeks. They were going to be in the way of the trailer that will be bringing in the hot tub, so I had to get them out of the way. I had been out of chain saw gas, but brought out a new gallon. The cutting was loud, but it went fast. By the time I had finished cutting and piled all the firewood up it was warm outside and I was ready for a break.

Just like the day before there were hardly any birds out. And no soaring birds at all. There were about a dozen or so little birds playing in the nearby treetops, but nothing else. Then a hawk flew in and landed in a tree at the lower edge of the meadow. Hawks seldom ever land here—they are always soaring overhead or through the meadow airspace. But this guy took a firm grip and stayed a while.

I hustled in and got the telescope and the bird book—he wasn't a red-tailed hawk for sure. As I studied the detail in his body and feathers he kept looking around him intently. Back and forth, rotating his head, pointing those piercing eyes down every little nook and cranny of the meadow. He was obviously hunting, but I wondered if he had seen some movement and stopped to check it out, or just thought that it would be a good spot to hunt.

Red-shouldered hawk, immature. That's what he looked like to me. A handsome devil for sure. I continued to study him through the scope. He continued his optical workout. The brightest color on him was his brilliant yellow beak, which was short and turned down and very sharp, and his yellow feet.

Then he got this weird look on his face, like he had spotted something, or something was approaching him. He tensed up and froze. Then ever so slowly, he arched his back a little, cocked his wings, and sprang to life. He dove the thirty or so feet down to the meadow below and landed. He pounced on something. I couldn't quite make it out, until he flapped his wings and got airborne again. A snake! He had grabbed a snake. I think it was a garden snake. And then he flew off and circled back around over the point and disappeared down the Buffalo River valley. I didn't know whether to feel sorry for the snake (a harmless and even helpful species), or applaud the patience and hunting savvy of the hawk. I settled instead on thinking how lucky I was to have been privy to such a raw act of nature right in my own back yard. Time to get back to work.

I spent the rest of the morning getting the big 6x6 treated post in place. This will form the corner post for the new deck that I'm going to build around the hot tub. I had to cut and level and attach a couple of ten foot long 2x8's to the post to keep it in place. Then I mounted a breaker box to the post. The big wire for the hot tub will come into this box, and then smaller wires will go into the hot tub itself to power everything. I also spent some time doing a little more leveling of the actual tub spot (which will be on solid ground, with the little deck built around it once the tub is in place). I continue to have trouble with the final placement of the tub (which direction it will face), but I think that I finally got that nailed down.

My only nourishment was the last cup of Starbucks ice cream. This stuff was simply wonderful, every last spoonful. And now it was all gone. It is a good thing that I have not been able to find a source for it in this area or I would put on a lot of weight. Speaking of weight, a combination of factors has contributed to me dropping 13 pounds in the past three weeks. It feels very good, and I hope to keep myself at or near this weight, at least through the summer. It is just like removing 13 pounds from your backpack (or getting to pack that much extra). I weighed in the low 180's all winter, and tipped the scale today at 169 (I'm about 6 foot, with a slender build).

The brilliant orange azaleas that are in bloom below the deck were covered with tiger swallowtails all morning, and their rich yellow color contrasted nicely with the deep orange blooms. Lots of dogwoods popping out all over. And the forest overall is getting greener and greener. Sometimes you just have to sit back and breathe deep and just try to take it all in.

4/13/99 It was another early arrival for me today and my truck was filled with concrete blocks. I spent the next couple of hours hauling the blocks to the hot tub site and putting them in place under the 6x6 timbers. All of this will form the base for the hot tub, which is supposed to arrive later in the week.

It was windy and cloudy all day, but warm. There weren't many birds out that I could see, but the mournful droning of mourning doves off in the distance echoed throughout the valley all day long. Kind of matched my general mood. Hum.

A *giant* hawk came soaring by near noon. I took a break and watched him through the binocs for a while. He was very animated as he toured the airways out in front. Back and forth he soared, looking left and right, dipping down and swooping up and turning to the left and then to the right. Every now and then he would glance over my direction and wink.

The dogwoods down in the meadow were beginning to bloom. Five of them in all were out, including both of the larger ones. It was *great* to see dogwoods in bloom in my little meadow!

I installed an electrical box on the new deck post, and finished the wiring for the tub. Lots of big wire was needed to feed this electrical hog. The company claims that it will only eat $15 worth of power a month. I'm skeptical.

A phone company truck arrived early in the afternoon and we spent a half hour going through every phone connection in the cabin looking for the reason why I could not receive any calls. Son of a gun, the guy found a bad cord in the guest room—it had just gone bad at some point. I had complete phone service again! The repairman was a turkey hunter, and made the comment that I must have to use ear plugs in the mornings here because the gobbling must be so loud. While I have seen literally hundreds of turkeys at Cloudland (some of them even in the woods), I have never heard a single gobble. One of these days I will have to do a little calling and see what happens.

4/14/99 It was late at night when I arrived at the cabin. It had rained a full inch, and I hurried out to see what the cistern was doing. It was full, and overflowing. I removed the supply pipe and rigged up an extension so that the water would run away from the cabin and out into the woods. Let's see, an inch of rain equals about 500 gallons for the cistern. It already had 300 gallons in it, so I figure that I wasted 300 gallons by not being able to catch the additional rainfall after the tank was full. If this system works out, and I need more water outside, I may add a second tank to catch the overflow. Plus, I'm only catching about half of the water that hits the roof anyway, so I could rig up even more tanks if needed. Of course, it doesn't always rain this much—about five inches so far this month already.

One of the little nagging problems that I have always had out here is a lack of a wine glass rack. I finally found one in town that I liked and installed it. Well, actually I had to cut it in two before I could put it where I wanted to. There is now a short rack on either side of the china cabinet, under the ends of the map bar. The racks only holds a total of 12 glasses, but they are in full view, and should accommodate most of the wine traffic. The glasses look like they belong under the map bar. I need to figure out how to store a few wine bottles in the same spot. I've got about a dozen more glasses, stashed inside the china cabinet.

The temp had dipped down into the 40's, and the wind was blowing. It was raining a little, but not much.

A couple of late night phone calls to and from a friend in Kansas helped lift my spirits, which have remained at a very low point now for three weeks. I'm not normally like this. It must be my version of a mid-life crisis. I have been unable to find much sympathy though. New car, new cabin, new hot tub, work when I want doing what I want, live in the most beautiful spot on earth, fame and fortune. Nope, not much sympathy. But, of course, there is one item missing from the above list, and I would trade all of the above for it in a second. Sorry, but I am a romantic, a hopeless one, and there is no romance at the moment at Cloudland.

4/15/99 It rained a little during the night, but not too much. It was very wet and dark and misty at daylight, and a little chilly—I had the heat pump on all night—I had taken all of the firewood out of the cabin and stored it down in the wood rack so I didn't build a fire. There were a number of small mist clouds dancing around down in the valleys below. The cloud cover was hanging low, right around the top of the ridgetops. And the wind was blowing quite a bit. Pretty much all of the trees are now beginning to leaf out, and that brilliant green now covers the entire wilderness—looks pretty darn nice!

While there is an overall dark cast outside the dogwoods around the cabin are very *bright* white, and just beaming out through the dim. This is what dogwoods were put here to do—shine the way through the forest. And these guys are working overtime.

The river below is singing a lively tune. And along the bank there is an old field or something that is almost completely covered with blooming dogwoods—looks like fifty or more of them. I must go down there and take a look soon—they are across the river, and it would be a bit of a swim today. Besides, I'm waiting for an important delivery this morning. There are birds singing outside too, all lined up in the treetops around the meadow. And some of those mist clouds were being blown straight up into the air from the valley below.

The new hot tub showed up right on time, and we actually managed to get all 650 pounds of it from the trailer, across the lower deck, and down onto the platform that I had built for it without any problems. A roller system that they brought out helped out a great deal—only took four of us. The last hot tub that I put in at my house (in Fayetteville) took about ten or twelve strong bodies to wrestle into place.

The tub looks good. It is sunken down into the deck, with about ten inches of it sticking up above the deck boards. There isn't too much room where the tub is sitting for deck around it—only 18 inches across two sides, but the other two sides will be open to the other decks.

We put about 100 gallons of water in the tub through the well—the cistern system did not have enough pressure to push water through a special pre-filter that came with the tub. After the well started burping, I decided to just fill the rest of the tub up without the filter, direct from the cistern (didn't run the well dry, but was probably close). Hey, it is pure Ozark rainwater, so what could be better than that?

The temp dropped to 40 degrees while we were out working on the tub, and with the wind and spitting rain, it got a little nasty. The windchill is in the upper teens. After being inside for 30 minutes now, my hands are still a little numb, and I am having trouble typing. Too bad the hot tub isn't filled and heated up already! I suspect it will take another hour or two to finish the filling—got lots of water in the cistern. The tub holds 355 gallons. Unless I have some problems, or a lot of drunks spill drinks into the tub, I will change out the water a couple of times a year, always timed with a full cistern.

While I waited for the tub to fill—a very slow process—I decided that conditions were right for pictures. I packed my camera gear up and headed over to Dug Hollow. It was raining a little, and the wind was blowing, but the forest was rich with deep colors of greens and browns. The North Meadow was alive with several large dogwoods, each full of sparkling white diamond blossoms.

I dropped on down to the waterfall area. Believe it or not I have never shot any serious pictures in Dug Hollow. Billy McNamara has made nearly 40 paintings of this area, but I've never taken a picture there. That was about to change, I hoped.

The very first waterfall was running full blast and making a lot of noise. I found a great spot on the side of a bluff that had a good angle, but discovered a large branch that had broken off of a tree and landed right at the top of the waterfall. Such things tend to mess up my pictures, so I try to clear them out when I can.

I made my way up around the little bluffline and on out to the edge of the creek by the branch. The rocks below my feet were very slick, and I tried to be careful. I had to step out into the water to get a hold of the branch. It was large, and very heavy. I couldn't budge it at first. I tried another position. Yea, I got a better grip, but still nothing. Then a third spot, which put me close to the edge of the falls. One big heave-ho and, OOPS!—my feet slid out from under me and I lunged towards the edge. I twisted myself around and grabbed for whatever I could get. My hands caught on the large limb, and it held in place, saving my butt from a nasty fall.

I pulled myself up to safety, and stood up and took a few deep breaths. Watch it buddy. While it might be a nice place to die, I have too much left to do to go right now! I was shaking a little as I returned to my chore, even more careful this time. I found out that I could roll the limb and it would move, so in a minute or two I was able to get the offending yet lifesaving branch out of the way of my picture. Deep breath.

When I got back to my perch on the side of the bluff I decided that I didn't want to take the picture after all. Sometimes it just happens like that. I was anxious to see what the other falls looked like.

The next waterfall was spectacular, and I got out the camera gear and shot away. The next waterfall was spectacular, and I got out the camera gear and shot away. The next waterfall was spectacular, and I got out the camera gear and shot away. I guess you get the picture. Sorry for that little pun. Wow, what a wonderful area in the rain!

I worked my way down through the cascades, crossing over a time or two for a different angle. I ended up deep in the back of the large overhang at the lower end of the falls area, finished up my third roll of film, and headed back. I couldn't pass up that very first waterfall, so I shot a few of it too. Dug Hollow is indeed one wonderful spot, perhaps one of the best little waterfall areas there is. So is Hubbard Hollow, Bowers Hollow, Hawk Hollow, Boen Gulf, Terrapin Branch, Indian Creek, and, well, you get the idea. I love waterfalls.

It felt *great* to get out and work behind a camera. I can't believe that sometimes I get paid to do this.

Two wonderful things happened to me on the hike back. First, I had a vision of my next book project, or should I say my next picture book project. Everyone has been asking what that was going to be, and I have not been able to give any answer. I won't go into details just yet, but let's just say that it will happen next spring, but it won't be just Buffalo River pics. All new stuff though. And a few essays. Yes, this book idea feels good, right from the very start. I will have to think about it and run it through my slow brain for a few months. But at least I now have a project in mind.

The other thing that happened was rather small, but made my heart soar anyway. As I made my way across a level bench I noticed a bright white spot up ahead. The rest of the forest floor was this rich brown color (wet leaves). The white really stuck out. As I got closer, I could make it out—it was a lone dogwood blossom, sitting all by itself on the forest floor. It was big and pure white and about as perfect a blossom as you will ever see. The middle was filled with those neat green things. The high winds must have torn it off from its tree, sent it flying through the woods, then gently set it down. I wondered what kind of sound it made when it landed? One little white dogwood blossom shining brightly in the forest. That's what life is all about, and I'm glad the waterfall didn't get me so that I could find it.

When I got back to the cabin I found the hot tub not only full, but over-filled a bit. I had to attach the drain hose and drop the level a couple of inches. Then everything was ready for the big test—did my electrical connection actually work? I flipped all three breakers, and sure enough, the tub fired right up and began doing its thing. The water temp was about 50 degrees so it would take a day to bring it up to a good sitting temp, but I was a little relieved that the power worked. Now I've got to get a deck built around it—the next project.

The outside temp hovered around 40 degrees the rest of the day. I worked in the cabin on the computer, then raced back to town to mail my taxes. I will return as soon as the water is hot.

I returned in a few hours to find a black sky full of brilliant stars, and *hot* water in the tub. It was getting nippy outside so I built a fire. It took a little extra work since I had already pretty much shut down the fireplace and removed all of the wood and kindling and stuff. Once the fire was roaring I poured a small glass of wild turkey liqueur, got down to the bare essentials, and slipped into the hot tub. This moment had been nearly two years in the making.

And it was worth the wait! The heated Cloudland rainwater felt wonderful, and the view up into the heavens was just about right. My seat is positioned so that I am looking straight out from the cabin right on over to Beagle Point. Directly above me there are trees to the left and right, but a good hole in the middle, which was filled tonight with a constellation that I need to look up. I guess that will be one measuring stick of how the stars are moving around—which stars are in the open slot above the tub. I could also see some bright planets shining through the trees—Venus in the west, and Mars rising in the east.

There was a breeze blowing and its coolness was a great contrast to the warmth below the water surface. That is what you are supposed to do in a hot tub—get all heated up and relaxed below, then be cooled off by spring breezes above. And then a shooting star broke out of the darkness and screamed across the sky out in front and over Beagle Point. Breathtaking! I laid back and counted my blessings.

Once I got back inside the crackling fire dried off all of the remaining drops that my robe missed. The fire felt great. Something about heat, no matter if it comes in the form of hot water, fire, or the touch of a loved one. It soothes the beast and levels out the bumps of life, if only for a little while.

As I climbed the staircase to the loft the entire cabin was lit by the dancing flames below. I absolutely love spring in the Ozarks, but it was nice to have a little bit of winter once again. The down comforter soon drove me off to sleep.

4/16/99 Fresh baking bread. Is there any more wonderful smell to wake up to? The aroma filled the cabin, and I was lured from my feather nest just as daylight creeped inside. Apple cinnamon bread with butter and honey. Hum, is that on my diet? It sure was this morning. I ate a big slab of it and stood in front of the fireplace. Then I realized that I had a date with a hot tub!

Most people only use these tubs at night, but I use mine more in the mornings, in fact every morning (I have one at my home in town too, and have had for nearly 20 years). The key is that you only are in long enough to wake up and stretch your muscles a little, not long enough to make you sleepy. I grabbed a Starbucks mocha from the fridge and hurried down the steps and into the hot water. Ahhhhh. Yes. That's it.

Up above there were clouds moving and coming from the west, not the usual south. Some of them were lit individually by the sun, which had not yet risen. The bright orange clouds streaked across the sky, racing each other. More and more of them lit up, and soon the sun appeared on the ridge way off yonder, and flooded my world with the same rays that had been lighting up the clouds. Man, this was one terrific light show! It looks like the sunrise will be visible from the hot tub most of the year, except in the middle of the summer. It will be interesting to track its path as it moves back and forth across the ridge.

The temp outside got down to about 34 degrees. There had been freeze warnings out all over but it didn't quite get that cold here. The breeze probably helped some, although it did drop the windchill down below 20. The temp in the tub was about 104. Ha, ha.

One more note about the hot tub. It is not intended to be a party tub, like many are. In fact it probably will be off limits during parties. Water is the main reason for this, or the lack of it. Everyone who goes into the tub must be *clean*, and have just taken a shower lately. There isn't enough water out here for many showers with a group of people. Also, I have found in the past that if the tub gets a great deal of use then the water needs to be changed out more often. There isn't enough water to fill the tub. Plus, the tub only holds about four folks at a time anyway. So its use will be more of a private thing, for me and a close friend or two or three. Of course, it is also a fact that any clothing worn in the hot tub, including swimsuits, adds detergent to the water, which causes foaming, so swimsuits are discouraged. Hey, its a hot tub in the wilderness, what do you expect? But there will be many wonderful moments happen while I am in the tub, and I will try to report them as I can.

The sun has climbed high into the sky now and the color is pure white. Many of the clouds have blown themselves away and it looks like I'm in for sunshine today. I've got to unload a bunch of heavy treated lumber from the trailer that I hauled out last night, and build the small deck around the hot tub. There is also a new queen mattress set for the downstairs guest room, and two futons—one of them a queen as well—for the TV room downstairs. Oops, did I say TV? Well, not yet.

The scene outside is one of soft, multi-colored hues of green and blue and white and grey. Sunlight is filtering through the clouds, and poking out directly through some of the holes, creating spots of light and different shades of green across the entire wilderness. Above, it is blue sky patches behind shaded clouds. Nothing very strong or brightly colored, but lots of different shades and patterns.

I spent the rest of the day building the narrow deck around the hot tub and got it all finished up except for two short boards that needed a little special attention. Now I can walk around the tub without getting all muddy. Rails will be added later, and perhaps even another bear post in the corner.

The sun played tag with me all day and never really came out for more than a few minutes at a time. There were lots of puffy clouds up there dancing around though, and scores of shadows moving across the green hillsides. The wind continued to blow all day, which made it cool at times. The temps stayed in the 40's.

One job left for me to do was to unload the futons and mattress set. The futons were no problem, but when it came to the queen mattress, I found that it was a little too heavy and cumbersome for me to handle. I tried every way, but just couldn't figure out a way to carry it. So I ended up using the turtle method. I got down on all fours, flipped the mattress onto my back, and sort of crawled around the end of the cabin and onto the lower back deck and into the basement. I'm sure it looked a little funny. In the process, of course, I hurt my back. Duh. Sometimes I find that there are things out here that must be done that I am just too weak to do, but I often end up having no choice but to go ahead and do them.

The clouds eventually cleared away and the nighttime was spectacular. As I sat in the tub near midnight soaking my weary bones another shooting star streaked across the sky. Down in the valley there was a narrow band of clouds hovering tight right over the Buffalo, but none up in Whitaker Creek. It was completely dark out since the moon was nowhere in sight (it is in a dark phase right now), but the white of the cloudbank shone through the darkness.

The temp was down in the 30's, with the wind blowing, and there was ice on the decks. It felt *great* to climb out of the hot tub and into the cold breeze—

this is when you know the water is at the right temperature—if you can stand and even enjoy the cold when you get out and are still wet.

Once I got back inside I spent some time in front of the roaring fire, sipping a little merlot and munching on fine dark chocolate. Another great Friday night, and the only thing missing was a female companion.

4/17/99 They had called for some snow during the night and temps down in the 20's, but it never even got to freezing at Cloudland. Although the decks were still frozen, which I suspect had something to do with the wind, which brought the windchill down into the teens.

I slept in late, then got up and slipped into the tub to survey my little world. I noticed that the water was a little dingy—we had to fill the tub with water from the cistern, unfiltered, and it looked like the hot tub filters hadn't been able to completely clean up the water, which was full of pollen and other stuff. I spent some time going from seat to seat rubbing dinginess from the sides of the tub. Each seat is a good one, with a wonderful view.

Before long there was solid cloud cover. It kind of looked and felt like a snow kind of a day, more like late October than mid-April. No matter, it felt very good.

A burst of sunshine broke through the clouds and lit up a couple of the dogwoods down in the meadow. As if on cue, a bright male bluebird flew across the meadow and landed right in the middle of all the white blossoms. What a delightful contrast—bright white dogwood flowers and blue and orange feathers, all beaming in the spring sunshine! What means *spring* more than dogwoods and bluebirds?

After a couple of hours of messing with the little hot tub deck I finally got it finished. All it needs now is a railing. I'm trying to decide if I should get another bear post or not for the corner of the new deck.

I also set up the queen-size futon frame, and the regular bed in the Aspen room. Hey, this new guest room is going to be pretty nice—I may have to move in down there. Need to get some little tables and lamps and stuff like that.

One of the continuing questions here is what I am going to put on the basement floor—paint the concrete and use a lot of throw rugs, or carpet the entire thing with that indoor/outdoor commercial carpet. I just can't make a choice. Right now it is cold, bare concrete.

I am taking a little break from cabin chores to write in the Journal, and munch on a bagel or two. A friend just called me from the top of a mountain over near Ponca—she was on the back of a horse moving down a trail. Cell phones are great, when they work. They don't work too well around here, but I do think the coverage is getting better.

Outside here it is still rather cloudy and grey, but the new forest that is emerging is putting out a wonderful green glow. Way off in the distance I can see a lone dogwood tree at the top of a bluff. It is just beaming white out over the valley.

And nearby the dogwood I can just barely see a giant sandstone block that has slipped off of the end of the bluffline on the other side of Hubbard Hollow. I've been looking at this block all winter long, wondering what it would be like to be sitting on top of it. I've also seen it on my hikes to the hollow, but have never actually went up to touch it. The block has been slowly disappearing behind the wall of new green. I've got to go see if I can climb it, and soon, before the view is completely obscured. Perhaps tomorrow.

And I hadn't noticed it until just now but the bluff over on Beagle Point is about to disappear as well. It's a layer of weathered sandstone, 50-80 feet thick, and covered with mosses and lichens and huckleberry. My gosh, that bluffline has been my constant companion out here ever since late October when the leaves fell off. I've watched it catch the first light in the morning, reflect moonbeams over to me, counted the blooms on the first serviceberry tree to bloom, and watched that tremendous cascade of whitewater leap from it. I have screamed cries of joy over to it as I discovered any one of dozens of new things, and even threw a few choice words that-a-way when things weren't going right for me. And now in a few days I will have to bid it farewell for the next six months. Have a grand summer my friend! Good grief, I am getting all sentimental about a *bluff!*

A single beam of sunshine swept across the forest. It paused when it lit up the batch of dogwoods down next to the river—it was as if the sunshine and dogwoods were having a contest to see who was the brightest. Or perhaps it was just the sun recharging the blossoms. The spotlight moved on, in search of more wonderful things to see.

The river below creates a blue stroke through the middle of all the green. I guess you could call it a "water" color scene.

Two young guys came walking down the road and knocked on the front door of the cabin. They introduced themselves, said they had been to one of my programs last fall, and then turned around and walked off back up the road. Kind of strange.

After I finished all of my cabin chores for the day I decided to make a quick trip down to the new spring in Dug Hollow and take a few pictures. I had never photographed it before, and the conditions seemed right for some good light and even better water.

I struck out up the hill along my new trail path. As I climbed up I could see four or five different mayapple forests down below. I wondered if all of the plants in each group are related, like aspen trees are? The groups were really dense, and I even found several flowers—white with yellow centers. Very nice.

Nothing in the East Meadow. Before too long there would be lots growing in the garden spot there, and probably a bear or two munching on corn or watermelons.

I dropped on down through the bluffline and stopped for a few minutes to admire a *huge* dogwood tree in full bloom that was guarding the entrance to Magnolia Canyon. I've not seen a larger or more full dogwood in bloom this year. The magnolias there were popping out, but no flowers yet. I have a feeling it is going to be a great magnolia year.

As I slipped and slid my way on down the steep hillside I went through some very lush areas covered with three or four different kinds of wildflowers, though none of them were in bloom. Then I passed through a stand of mayapples that were *huge!* I mean they were *taller* than my knees! And there were giant trillium, and some bloodroot leaves that were much larger than my hand. Something in the soil at this spot was really rich. It was tropical. A jungle. Spring in the Ozarks.

There were a few bellworts blooming and lots of rue anemone. Come to think of it, the rue anemone are about the only wildflowers that have continued to bloom through all of this cold weather. They have always been around. They are a small, delicate and nearly-white flower. Good to have them here.

The creek in Dug Hollow was running pretty good and I saw several nice little waterfalls, all dumping into emerald pools. I didn't linger there long and continued my quest towards the spring. I followed alongside the creek a little ways, walking through a couple of perfect flat benches that were also lush with wildflowers and other plants.

Soon I veered off towards the hillside where I hoped to find the spring. I went on and on, and on, and on. No spring. A little further. It must be here somewhere. My progress had taken me around the nose of the ridge, and I felt that this was just too far for the spring. So I reluctantly turned back, by way of climbing up to the bluff above, hoping to find the spring further upstream.

The hillside at this point was more like a tornado zone—you could hardly move because the underbrush was just so thick! Vines and plants and downed trees and rocks. Man, it was thick. Then I saw some orange paint. What? Out here in the middle of the wilderness? As I got closer I realized that it was not paint at all but rather some kind of bright orange fungus that was growing on several grape vines. It felt a little like thick Jello. And very bright orange. (One of my Canadian readers, Jeannette, sent an e-mail suggesting that this weird stuff is either Fairy Butter or Witches Butter—her ID book description sounded right on.)

As I made my way up onto a bench I came across a large chunk of sandstone that had obviously broken off of the bluff above. I climbed up onto the rock by way of a natural staircase and discovered a solid patch of spiderworts, many of them in bloom. Not only was this one incredible batch of wildflowers, and growing on top of solid rock, but these flowers were *white*, not the normal purple of most spiderworts. If you looked close you could maybe see just a hint of color in the blossom. I could hardly even step without getting some of them under my boot, so I backed away, admiring. Turns out they were Ozark spiderworts, a rare variety that grows in some of the hills around here.

Still no spring. But I did see a couple of turkeys. Two large toms flew across right in front of me, one at a time. I could see beards on them, but the beards weren't all that long.

I eventually made it back to the creek. Where had I gone wrong? It couldn't have been further upstream. I felt a little silly. So I decided once again to follow the stream down towards the Buffalo River and break off into the woods later. It was a tough hike down, not because the terrain was so rough, but because there seemed to be one incredible sight after another after another down on the creek—all beckoning me to come take their picture. I'll bet I could have taken a different picture every 25 feet. It was marvelous. And in addition to all of those little waterfalls and emerald pools, there were lots of dogwoods in bloom and magnolia, all hanging low over the water. Splendid!

Soon after I left the creek, sure enough, I came right to the spring, and it was well worth the trouble to find! My goodness, I knew it was nice, but I didn't remember it as being this nice. The spring comes out of the base of a small bluff, a bluff that I must have just walked above, not noticing the spring below. Then it spills down a steep hillside for a little ways, cascading down over moss-covered rocks, and creating a lot of whitewater. Once it hits a level bench below, it meanders its way through the woods, finally dumping into the creek, and then into the Buffalo River.

The light was perfect, the water white, and the moss green. I set up my tripod and began to fire away. I could never take enough pictures of beautiful things like this spring, no matter how many of them I had photographed before. And this one was special, not only because it is so close to my cabin, but because we discovered it quite by accident, and I have fond memories of every previous visit.

One roll shot. Then another. And another. I ended up shooting about 100 pictures, mostly from the same spot, although I did get a few different angles. Just as I packed up everything and was ready to leave I noticed this group of ferns growing right in the middle of it all. Out came the camera again, and I shot another roll. In all, I had spent about an hour there.

Photography oftentimes for me is something spiritual, very intense, and many times an emotional high. This was one of those moments. I plopped down beside the cascade, exhausted, emotionally drained, and thirsty. I got up and sucked down a few gulps of that cold water. It was *so sweet!* As I lay back on the forest floor I realized that the sun had broken through the clouds, and that it was getting late. Yikes, I had better get back up the hill!

So I bid my little spring farewell and returned to the creek. I crossed near an area where there were several house-sized boulders alongside the creek. Lots of moss, and white water, and dogwoods and magnolias.

I headed up the steep hillside, racing the light. About halfway up I found part of something that I had looked for many times—a section of the old Ryker to Mossville Trail. There it was, right under foot. I followed it for about a hundred yards. It wasn't nearly as wide as a road, but much wider than a deer path. It headed up the hill and into some very thick brush. Then I found this grapevine. No, it was a monster grapevine! I measured it, and it turned out to be a full twelve inches thick. That is one large grapevine.

As I looked around I could see many grapevines, much smaller ones, but lots and lots of them. I had lost the trail in the thick brush, so I continued my uphill struggle. There were many times when I was down on all fours, grabbing whatever I could to pull myself up. My feet weren't much help. This was *steep* country!

I finally made it to the top of the ridge, and as I popped up through the bluffline a blast of arctic air hit me. Since I was completely soaked with sweat from the climb the wind was quite chilly! But the low sunshine hit me in the face too. I felt a little like I had just been freeze-dried.

It was a great hike, and I hoped to have gotten a good picture or two, but the cabin was a warm sight and I was glad to be back. I sat out on the back deck to cool down, sipped on a glass of wine, and watched the light show of the setting sun. You see, since the sun is constantly moving, each and every sunrise and sunset is a little different. The shadows move around with the sun, creating different shapes and forms out there in the wilderness.

The river was talking a soothing line tonight.

After the sun went down there were several dark clouds over there in the west, illuminated from the fading rays of the sun. Out in front, up against one of those dark clouds, was the thinnest of all crescent moons. Even though it was small it shone brightly in the western sky. And that scene got me to think-ing. Clouds are always getting in front of and hiding the sun and moon, but I wondered, is it possible for the moon to ever get *in front* of a cloud? Hum. Looked like it did tonight. Sometimes things happen a little differently out at Cloudland.

And in the eastern sky a point of red light shone through the trees. I set up the tele and could see Mars rising. I've never really taken a close look at Mars, and its red glow, but it really is red. Being here at Cloudland I am able to look at and keep track of some of the things going on overhead at night. I need to get busy and learn all of the constellations—a good project for the summer months ahead.

The evening drew on with a good bowl of pasta, some great bluegrass music on the **Pickin' Post** on KUAF, and a fine fire.

And, of course, I spent some time in the hot tub. I suspect that I will take a dip every night and morning that I am here. The moon had gone down quickly, and was replaced by Venus, so bright and full of life, twinkling through the trees. And Mars had risen just enough to be exactly opposite of Venus. In the southwest, Orion stood tall and proud. I decided that whenever the sky is clear, I would stay in the tub until I saw a shooting star. They happen all year long, with many miniature showers and lots of really big ones, especially in the late summer. As I have always said, the more shooting stars you see, the more luck will come your way.

The owls were out late, and hooting and crying and talking to each other way up the valley. Sometimes it sounds like there is a party going on. I guess there is—an owl party!

I saw my shooting star, lingered a while longer, then went back inside to sit in front of the dying fire and listen to the **Folk Sampler** on the radio. Their theme was love songs, not what I really wanted to hear, but since I am still a hopeless romantic, I listened on. These radio shows on KUAF usually play some of the most interesting and unusual music, and tonight was no exception. Not the normal love songs for sure. They really dug up some great ones. A couple in particular were by Hal Bynum and by Lynn Miles ("Rust")—I must go out and try to find those two CD's—really nice stuff. I still fancy myself as a future writer of love songs. While I sold my wonderful maple guitar a few months ago, I do plan to get another one, probably a classical guitar with softer strings.

4/18/99 Clear blue skies, *no* wind, bright sunshine. Temps in the low 40's. I slept in a little, and missed sunrise from the tub. I did get to see it out the loft window though, then rolled over and went back to sleep. Looks like it is going to be a textbook spring day in the Ozarks. I'm headed out in a few minutes to hike over to Hubbard Hollow. Since the sun is out, I won't bother taking my big camera equipment—I really need overcast skies for good pictures. But I still want to see this boulder-choked hollow with good water in it. And I want to climb up to that large sandstone block that I can see from the cabin. Hiking in the spring here is part of my job, and I must get to work!

I wanted to travel light and fast so I only took a fanny pack with the little camera, a rope, bagel, a jug of water, and my note pad and pen. My feet got beat up from my hike the day before, so I put on my lightweight walking shoes, which I absolutely love anyway. *Walking* magazine sent them to me a couple of years ago to try out. They are made by Wilson, and are all leather. I've never had any problems with my feet while wearing them in the woods, although I have not used them with any weight.

As I headed out the door my little friend the bluebird landed in the dogwood tree again. I just couldn't pass this one up, so I hurried back into the cabin to get the real camera. It took me a minute to get my long lens all set up and everything on the tripod—looked like the little guy was going to keep posing for me. Just as I swung the camera around and pointed it at him, he flew off. Darn. Just a few more seconds and I would have had him!

I skipped on down the trail towards the river. Just below the bluffline I saw a phoebe. He acted nervous, like these birds always do, with his tail bobbing up and down, so I figured that he was building a nest under the bluff somewhere. There weren't many wildflowers out on this hillside, but it was lush. Towards the bottom of the hill though, large numbers of phlox and firepink were out.

Whitaker Creek was running pretty good, and instead of searching for a dry crossing upstream somewhere, I found a log jam down near the mouth of the creek that I crossed with great ease. There were two main logs spanning the split creek, with lots and lots of smaller logs all mingled together—I guess you would call them drift wood, since they had been drifting in the creek and got washed up here. I'd not seen the creek when the water was that high!

On the other side I found lots of wildflowers blooming—more phlox and firepink, bellwort, crested iris, and this plant that reminded me of arrow root, I guess because of the shape of the leaves, but it was not that.

My route took me along the Buffalo River, and I followed it upstream. Depending on the way the sunlight hit the water the pools would either be blue or green. Sometimes an upper pool in a scene was blue and the lower one was green, connected by thrashing whitewater. The water was perfect, just perfect.

In one stretch of level streamside there were many clumps of bloodroot wildflowers—no blooms, just large leaves, and 15-20 to a clump. I had always thought of bloodroot as individual plants before, not growing in groups. These guys were all very good friends I guess.

And then I came across this incredible forest of mayapples—as far as the eye could see, and growing so close together that you could not see the ground. The stand engulfed several trees, including one large beech. And they grew all the way to the river's edge. I just had to get a better look, so I got down on my hands and knees and then my belly and tried to crawl into the forest. Wow, it was wonderful! The earth was very soft. I could see into the forest a long ways, and found dozens and dozens of flowers under there, all of them bowing down to the ground a little. No way to photograph this, especially with my little camera. Oh to be two inches tall! I would love to be tiny and roam around in this forest, and sleep under the solid canopy. You know, you always see a smile on a lizard's face, and I wonder if it is because they get to hang out in places like this one? I loved it.

I walked through another stretch of flat ground that was completely covered with grasses, mayapples, trillium, violets, and bloodroot. I mean *solid* cover! It was so lush. And then up on another little hillside, yet another kind of vegetation, without blooms, but lush and covering the ground. These little plants swallowed up several moss-covered logs and rocks that were on the ground (where else would a rock be?). At first, I was afraid to walk through this dense undergrowth. But then when I did, I looked behind me and saw that the plants rebounded and completely covered up my passing.

Then I saw lots of yellow violets, and at least three white flowers that I could not identify. Plus several other wildflowers of different colors, all sticking their heads out from the ground cover. Are you getting the picture that this low land was one of extreme richness? I could have spent days here.

There were also several squirrels that were playing in this area. They seemed to be having a good time and enjoying the spring day, as was I.

As I headed up the steep hillside towards my little hollow I came across several Jack-in-the-Pulpits, perhaps the strangest plants in the forest. And they are tough to photograph too. I've tried. And there was this one large mayapple that had a sweet gum ball lodged right in the middle of the leaf. If I took a picture of it no one would believe that I found it that way.

When I got to the hollow where I was expecting to find thunderous waterfalls and giant moss-covered boulders, I was not disappointed. There were tremendous waterfalls everywhere! And house-sized boulders, all tossed about on the hillside like a giant had gone away and left all of his play toys.

Now let's see, should I explore up the creek or go around the side and climb around on all of the boulders? It was a tough decision. I did some of each. The waterfalls were great, mostly taller and narrower than those that I saw the day before. Some of the boulders were strewn across the creek, and there were often waterfalls inside the boulders, if you can imagine that.

I climbed up through one giant boulder, and when I came out on top, I recognized a spot where I had been before. The top edge of this boulder was covered with thick moss, and the rock drops off steeply to the stream below, and you can see several cascades flowing by. Up at that level there were tons of umbrella magnolia trees, all leafing out, plus dogwoods and even a few redbuds. I sat down at the same spot where my friend Emily and I had lunch back in December—it was our very first day together. I thought about the beauty of the wilderness, of the rocks and the trees and the water, and I thought about how wonderful it has been to spend some time with her. I have explored and discovered many things because of her. At this point our future is uncertain though, and so I may have to live with what has been with no future to look towards.

Oops, pardon me, back to earth. I continued up the magnolia-choked canyon and made my way around this big block that I knew had a secret passage way in it. Way in the back there was a hole that led up and out to the top of the rock. Only today I found that a number of logs had been washed into the hole, and so my passage was blocked. Good grief! The water must have been *really* high! I found another way around.

I finally made it to the top of the hollow and the big waterfall there, and sat down and took a quick break. This was a wider waterfall, splashing on the black rocks far below. There were ferns growing all around the base, but there was no pool of water like there normally is with waterfalls this size. I guess the water is in such a hurry to see the rest of the canyon. There was one surprise here—a small but brilliant rainbow arched across the base of the falls. Yep, mighty fine.

OK, I had seen the wonders of the canyon, now it was time to turn my attention to the object of my search—the giant block rock up on the bluffline. I began to make my way along the base of the bluff, but found the going very tough at first—like nearly a vertical dropoff and no handholds! I managed to get through the rough stuff, then things got a little easier.

There was a great deal of breakdown under this bluffline like you see all over, but I came across this one section of overhang that had no large breakdown under it. The floor was covered with tiny chunks of flat rocks, none larger than an inch or two across. And it was all very dry and smooth. There were a number of half-eaten acorns scattered there too.

One overhang had a band of water streaming off of it. Down below where the water hit, there was a band of green life about five feet wide that spanned the entire overhang. Where the water was not splashing, there was no life, only rocks.

And then all of a sudden, there it was—the huge block of sandstone that I could see from my cabin. It was big alright, about 40 feet tall, and maybe 75 feet square, and flat on top. But wait, there was a second block rock, about the same size, sitting right next to the main bluffline. An alley about ten feet wide separated the one block and the bluff, and there was space of about 30-40 feet between the two blocks. The blocks were about the same size as my cabin.

I was at once overjoyed to finally be standing next to these monsters, but yet a little disappointed because it was obvious that there would be no way for me to climb up either one of them. A climbing expert could probably run right up the side of either of them, but they would have to have rope to get back down with. Perhaps some day, when I learn to climb, I will attempt this.

From the side of one of the blocks there was a clear view of the cabin, about two miles away and at the same level. The old place looked pretty darn good! I sat down in the sunshine up against one of the rocks and had my bagel and gazed up into the blue sky.

This was one really nice spot. The little point of land where the blocks were stuck out into the main Buffalo River valley, and I could see both up and downstream. There was an especially good view of the river downstream, the blue waters cutting their way through all of the new green below. And I could hear the river, just like at the cabin. I wondered how many Indians or early pioneers had sat in the same spot and gazed out across the wilderness? This was one magical spot for sure. And I would be back.

I thought about spring for a moment—why it was such a wonderful time of the year. The air was fresh and clean, the sunshine seemed scrubbed, and all of the vegetation was new and glorious and brilliant green. And wildflowers coming up all over, and new critters being born. It is a time of renewal, of be-ginnings, of hope, and of joy for the future. Yes, spring is OK with me!

Just before I left I made one circle around both blocks. I discovered a way that I might be able to get to the top of one of the blocks, if I had the right equipment. I would be back!

I went over the edge and headed down towards the river. The hillside was about the steepest that I had ever gone down before! It was almost straight down, and there would have been no way that I could have climbed up it. At first there was no vegetation at all—just leaves on the ground. Then there were lots of little plants and trees growing all over. Thank goodness there were lots of regular trees too for me to hold on to. I did spend a few moments sliding on my butt too—there was simply no other way to do it. Right in the middle of the steepest part there was a deer trail running across the hillside.

This hillside and the sliding reminded me of a hike that I took once many years ago. My father-in-law (at the time) and I took an old road trace up to the top of this pointed mountain on some land that they owned along the Little Red River over near Clinton, Arkansas. It was very steep, but the road made the going easy. It had just snowed about two feet the night before. We decided to take the short way down—straight down. After a couple of steps it became obvious that there was no way we could proceed on our feet, so we just plopped down on our butts and slid all the way to the bottom—it was great fun!!!

Anyway, as I got near the bottom today, I landed on the top of a small bluffline that ran along the river. I could peer over and see the wonderful waters below, but could not get down. So I made my way on over to the mouth of Hubbard Hollow. Just upstream in the little hollow there was one last thunderous waterfall. A fitting end to a spectacular journey.

In the main river there was a giant boulder laying in the river bed, sticking up about ten feet in the air. It was kind of protecting the mouth of Hubbard Hollow. The pool that it was sitting in was a deep turquoise, with whitewater both above and below. I climbed up onto it and laid down and gazed at the sparkling water below, and the sunshine and blue sky above. This was a wonderful spot, one of the best that I knew about on the river. Yes, perhaps even the best swimming hole of all in summer. Then I realized that this very spot was the subject of one of Billy McNamara's paintings, and I had it as a two-page spread in my picture book. Hey, I was laying right in the middle of a painting!

It had been several days since I had seen any butterflies, but the sunshine had really brought them out today. There were about a dozen of them cruising along the river here. And one pair flying in close formation—one was a tiger swallowtail and one was a zebra swallowtail. It was good to see them.

A bird flew up and landed on the bank next to the river. It was some kind of sandpiper. He bobbed his tail up and down constantly, and kept pacing back and forth along the bank, often wading out into the water a few inches. He was feeding I guess. Every now and then he would stop his bobbing and turn and look directly up at me. It is nice to be noticed by a sandpiper.

I headed downstream along the river. Just as I was about to put my foot down into a batch of leaves a flash of white caught my eye, and just in time for me to alter the direction of my step. There was a cottonmouth snake coiled up tightly right in the middle of the pile of leaves that I was about to put my foot into! The white flash that I saw was the inside of the snake's mouth—he was trying to warn me of his presence, which *worked!* This guy was not all that sluggish either, like you might expect for this time of the year. I played with him for a minute, and he was very quick on the draw. I concentrated on where my feet were going a lot more after that. And I especially watched for white.

The rest of the trip downstream went pretty fast. I walked along the river, enjoying its every pool and whitewater run. It seemed that the river and I were one, in tune with each other, and with the earth. And we were both going the same direction, flowing downhill to the next exciting rapid and quiet pool.

Just before I reached Whitaker Creek I found a group of wild geraniums growing about a foot tall. The first really good wildflower picture that I ever took was of a wild geraniums over in Richland Creek nearly 20 years ago.

When I reached the ladder trail I went into overdrive. My feet went faster and faster with each step. The steepness of the hill didn't seem to bother me at all, and I kept accelerating all the way up. About the only thing that I remember about that climb was one bright batch of phlox beside the trail, with a yellow tiger swallowtail butterfly feeding on the flowers.

When I reached the top of the bluff I was greeted by my little wildflower buddy. He was almost in bloom. There will be three blooms, and I expect to see them sometime this week.

Wow, what a hike. What a day. What a place. What a great time of the year!

The wind picked up and blew all afternoon which kept the temps on the cool side. The sunshine called me out onto the back deck for an hour of nature worshiping, plus I cleaned off the big hot tub filters (the dingy water had already gotten the best of them). And I spent a couple of hours writing. Just another tough day at Cloudland.

4/19/99 There were two bluebirds sitting in the dogwood trees down in the meadow when I arrived back at the cabin around noon. Clear blue skies, lots of sunshine, temps in the low 70's, and a slight breeze. The forest has taken on this fluorescent green with all of the new growth. The world is so alive with great beauty!

I quickly unloaded the truck, strapped on my walking shoes, and headed out into the spring woods towards a secret little spot where I go sometimes to think, to reflect, and to cry. It is a small, comfortable spot, a canyon of sorts, with steep sandstone walls that are covered with thick green moss and ferns and wildflowers. There is a little trickle of water passing one end of it—this little creek eventually spills on down the hillside and runs directly into the Buffalo River. The floor is uncluttered and deep with brown leaves, with the exception of three chunks of rock that had been laid down from above. They too are covered with moss. One of them is up against the tallest wall, and it is there that I sit and lay back and exercise my mind and explore my soul. No one but me has been here that I know of—the entrance is hidden, and I steer my hikes away so as not to invite any company.

When I reached this spot today I found a dogwood in full bloom, leaning in close to hear my thoughts. There were crested iris blooming, a couple of spiderworts, and a group of mayapples down at the far end, five of them with large white blossoms. The sunshine was streaming down through an umbrella magnolia tree, casting shadows on the floor. I sat down, laid back, and looked up into the blue sky.

I came here today with a heavy heart and a bright soul (you might have guessed—Emily dumped me). Sitting here in my little secret canyon and tossing all of my pain and triumph back and forth in my head does seem to ease the pain a little, and bring me back down to earth. There is so much beauty everywhere that I look, and the world has been so great to me, I should have a permanent smile plastered on my face. And I do most of the time.

There is a little bird high up in the upper branches of a nearby hickory tree that is just singing his heart out. I don't have my binocs with me, and so I can't even get a close look at this little guy. He must be calling out to someone, maybe even to me. Perhaps he just wants to let me know, like that little shooting star at the top of the bluff, that everything is going to be OK. And it is. The moss beneath me is soft and brilliant, the breezes are creating a kaleidoscope of bright colors overhead as the new leaves dance across the blue patches of sky, and the little bird and the river below are singing a melody as pure and sweet as spring water. Speaking of spring water, I am thirsty, and I think I'll crawl on over to the tiny creek and take a sip. Yep, it is sweet indeed, just like my life out here at Cloudland!

I leave my little sanctuary and head back towards the cabin, following a yellow tiger swallowtail butterfly that passed through the canyon. I am a very lucky man, and I count my blessings. And I thank you, the reader, for taking the time to wade through all of this with me.

When I got back to the cabin I discovered that the swing out back had been neglected, and needed some company, so I got out a pillow and sat down for a good long swing and waited for a TV crew to arrive (they were going to shoot an *Ozarks Spirit* segment for the 10 o'clock news). The wind was playing music through the chimes in front, and there were many birds flying back and forth in the treetops. All at once I was engulfed with about twenty butterflies—they were everywhere! Mostly the big yellow ones, but there were several of the black and white zebra ones too, plus a couple of smaller ones that I could not ID. They were all flying in this mass formation of swirling color and light. They came close to me, under the overhang, then right past me and back out into space. Just for a moment, I thought that I could feel the beating of their wings. Is that possible?

I hear the TV truck approaching. Kelly Kemp (star reporter) and Larry Baker (ace videographer) actually made it from civilization out here to the wilds of Cloudland, and right on time too. After a quick tour of the cabin, we packed up and headed out for a hike. Packing up a huge TV camera and tripod and batteries takes a little more effort than just throwing a little still camera into a bag and taking off. But we managed OK, and soon were out in the woods shooting. We spent some time down at the Crag, and ran into several other hikers that were out enjoying a textbook spring day.

It was good to work with Larry, because he not only knew what he was doing, but was trying to get some interesting and unusual camera angles. I appreciate folks like that. Some people just let you wander around in front of the camera, without any direction, and whatever happens, happens. He tried to pre-visualize the scene, how I would walk through it, etc. One time he told me to "walk down the trail and put your *left* foot right *here*." I did, and I'll bet it looked good.

Once the filming was finished at the Crag we headed back to the cabin and spent about an hour out on the back deck talking and shooting a long interview, one of those sit-down-and-look-straight-into-the-camera kinds of things. Kelly Kemp is a great reporter, a TV personality really, since she has had her own noon news and talk show. We have done many shows together before, and so I was at ease with her. That is until she started asking some pretty tough questions! In fact, about half of the questions I had never been asked before. While I don't mind working from the cuff—which is what I always do anyway—I got a little choked up trying to answer a couple of them.

And the whole time we were doing the interview the aroma of fresh baking sourdough bread was pouring out of the cabin windows—it was tough to concentrate with that wonderful smell around!

We discovered a little bat, probably an eastern pip, sleeping up on the side of one of the porch lights. Kind of strange to see a bat, in the daylight, sitting on a light.

The light out in the wilderness from the late afternoon sun was just spectacular, but we couldn't include that scene in the background because the light where we were sitting was just too different. I think Larry got some good footage of it anyway, to be used elsewhere in the piece. He forced me to go sit in the swing and enjoy the view for a few minutes while he framed the back of the cabin with one of the dogwoods down in the meadow. Then he had me stand up and lean over the railing and gaze out into the wilderness. Hey, he was capturing some of what I really do out here!

Kelly had brought some special black Angus beef with her, and after a bit of grilling, we all sat down to one of the best cuts of beef that I had ever eaten, plus the homemade sourdough bread and giant baked potatoes. All three of us like our meat well done, so I slow-grilled it to perfection! Couldn't believe how tender it still was, even after all of that cooking. Hum, cooking s-l-o-w on the grill seems to work.

Once the dishes were cleared away we got down to some serious discussions. It was kind of funny, but we almost seemed to span three generations in our ages and experiences. I was the old guy, in my 40's. Kelly is in her early 30's, married to a guy that I went to high school with, and they have a young son. And Larry is in his 20's, married, and expecting his first child in a few weeks. We listened to a lot of music from the 70's (James Taylor, Carole King, America), talked about life, loves, and the pursuit of happiness. And we even talked about our favorite TV shows over the years. It was interesting to hear all of the comments from the three different decades.

We talked long into the night and it was nearly 1am before they went off to bed and I slipped into the hot tub. As I sat there in the darkness, surrounded by a million stars, I saw something that I could hardly believe—fireflies! At first I thought that I was seeing things, or some kind of reflections, but as I sat up and looked closer, sure enough, there were five or six lightning bugs flying about down in the woods at the far end of the meadow. Normally they would hang out in the open, but these guys were in the woods. And about a month early I would say.

I saw not one, but four shooting stars, then shut the cabin down and climbed up into the loft to bed.

4/20/99 It was early when I got up and made my way downstairs to put on coffee and blueberry biscuits and to start up a new loaf of 12-grain bread for lunch sandwiches. As I was typing away at the computer the sun peeked up over the ridge to the east. Then I noticed a strange shadow moving across the shade. A big shadow—good grief, what the heck was it? Had the warm temps brought a bear out from his hiding place in search of food? Na, it was just Larry, shooting some nice video of the sunrise through the dogwood blossoms.

The following quote was e-mailed to me by a Journal reader, and it applies quite well to my situation these days:

"Happiness is as a butterfly which, when pursued, is always beyond our grasp, but which if you will sit down quietly, may alight upon you."
—Nathaniel Hawthorne (1804-1864)

I put some new age Beatles nature music on the stereo and continued typing while Larry tried the porch swing on for size, and Kelly did her best to drain the well from inside the shower. Sunshine, blue skies, light breezes, warm temps, and lots of birds out.

We packed up all of the camera gear and hiked down into Dug Hollow and spent about three hours photographing the waterfalls there. Even though the light was terrible (that awful sunshine!), I think Larry got some good footage. Just as we were leaving I found a phoebe nest right next to one of the waterfalls. There were five eggs in it, and nervous birds flying around wanting for us to leave. We did.

We returned to the cabin and had some smokehouse sandwiches with the fresh bread, took a few more pictures, and then set a spell in the warm afternoon breezes. It had been a good visit, and I think they got enough video to do several stories. I look forward to seeing the finished product.

Those little breezes soon turned into high winds up in the 40mph range. The temp climbed to about 80 degrees—first time this year I think. I spent the rest of the afternoon writing and cleaning up and just messing around the cabin.

4/21/99 *Howling* would be an understatement! The wind woke up and began to race through the trees late in the afternoon, 47 miles per hour. And the wind was swirling, coming out of the south, then the east, then on over from the west. One of the deck chairs down below was blown across the deck, and landed on the west side. The BBQ grill blew out of its nest and lodged against the east railing. But there were several things that normally get blown away in medium winds that didn't even move at all. Funny wind.

And clouds were building up, some of them on the dark side. It is time for some rain, so the clouds were a welcome sight for me. Not only do the plants need the water, but so do any waterfalls that want to jump in front of my camera. Conditions are right this next week for some fine photography of the new spring growth and water features. But we need some of that rain. A couple inches would do.

I sat out on the back deck and watched a big hawk working between the cabin and the Crag. He would fly up into the current, bend his wings and tilt his body in just the right way, and then he would just hover there, not moving at all. He had to work a little in the high wind to stay put, but he could do so for ten or fifteen seconds at a time before being tossed on over to another spot.

And a little later another hawk came streaking by right over the meadow, wings tucked tight against his body. He looked like he was on an amusement park ride, as he flared up when he got out over the valley and peeled back—a little like a hot shot jet pilot that had flown by the cabin site.

The wind didn't seem to be bothering the hot tub cover—I had worried about it being blown off. It is buckled down to the tub, but probably should have some sort of heavy object on top of it for a little extra security.

The wind did move the big oak tree that is growing up through the lower deck—it swayed back and forth pretty good, but did not move enough to rub against the deck. On the upper deck the swing was a swinging, and the rockers were a rocking. Lots of wind.

As it got close to sundown I took off on a hike. I wanted to feel more of the wind, and see what it was doing to the forest. Actually, I wanted to go out and find this great tree to climb up in and do a trick like John Muir—to see how the tree feels in the high winds. I followed along the top of the bench to the west of the cabin, where I could look down onto the bench below—the woods are very open there, because of all the maples.

I was also looking for that mystery tree that we have been trying to identify all winter. It is time to figure out what the heck this species is. I looked many trees over good from above to see if any were the right tree, but I couldn't find a single one.

There were lots of squirrels out running around, more than I had seen since last fall. And they wouldn't just jump up into a tree and climb up and disappear. These guys all took off running along the ground, sometimes bouncing off of a tree here and there, but they would just keep going, and not go up into the trees.

As I made my way up the hillside I came across this wonderful large shag-bark hickory tree. I just love these trees, not only because their shaggy bark makes them so easy to identify, but because I think these trees have a great personality. Don't know why. As I stood there admiring this great plant I looked around and realized that I had never been to that spot before. And I wondered how much of my own little 40 acres I have not set foot on yet? Hum, I must make that a goal to see all of my property. Lay eyes on every tree. Walk up and touch all of the big rocks. Then I'll head for the 13,000 acre wilderness surrounding me. Guess I have some work to do.

I cut through the woods and got to the connecting lane between the East and Faddis Meadows. It was lined with dogwoods—everywhere! It was quite impressive. And at the end of the lane was that large dogwood tree that had been split over by the ice storm was in full bloom. There was hardly any tree attached to the base after the split, I couldn't believe that there was enough juice to create the bloom. And the flowers were large and bright and beautiful, as if to say "Look at me, I'm not going to die that easy!"

I hurried through the meadow and dropped down to the little lane that heads on over to Bob's cabin. Both sides were grown up with thick brush, since a lot of it had been logged in the last decade. Still lots of larger trees around, but enough holes in the canopy to allow lots of sunlight to reach the ground, a new forest to sprout up.

Then I came across this wonderful batch of wild iris in full bloom. They were very dark and rich colored, almost blue. It contrasted well with the green leaves. And there were so many of them together and in bloom. I would soon discover that there lots of these bunches of iris along this road, most of them growing right down the middle of the road. It's funny, but I remember all of these wildflowers from last spring, but once they quit blooming last year I forgot completely about them. I have been walking right over them all fall and winter and early spring, and now they have popped up to pronounce their beauty to the world.

One batch of iris was about seven feet long and four feet wide. Amazing! And one smaller batch was completely encircled with wild mint plants, growing at about the same height as the iris.

I turned onto another lane that dropped on down into the drainage. My eyes were pretty much glued to the ground in front of me, watching for the next batch of iris. Then all of a sudden the air changed. Something felt different. I looked up and saw this incredible open forest with large trees all around me and hardly any underbrush at all. And it was a long ways up into the canopy. Wow, this was a wonderful forest! Beeches, oaks, sweetgum.

And just then I found a copy of the mystery tree right next to the lane. I hum, those new leaves way up there sure did look a lot like the kind of tree that I think it is. I continue to play this guessing game about this tree, but it won't be long now before I will have proof.

But the overall forest was center stage. As I walked down the hill I veered off of the lane to take a look at some showy orchids. They were hidden in between three rather large oaks, just a few feet from a nice stream. The orchids were there alright, but hadn't bloomed yet. It looked like a few more days and something might happen.

Most of them were around the base of this one dark, giant tree. I wrapped my arms around it—didn't reach—and looked right straight up the nearly-black trunk. Way up there it went, high into the canopy. And it ended right at the base of a half moon, which was beaming down through a hole in the clouds. That was a neat scene, and I wish that I could have photographed it. Tough light to take a picture.

I wandered along the lane and across the creek and up the other side of the ravine, I heard a thrush sing out. Some kind of wood thrush I think. It sounded just wonderful, as it echoed through the open forest.

A little further down the lane I came across an umbrella magnolia tree that was in bloom—yea, they have returned! We had one terrific magnolia bloom last year, and I'm hoping for another good one this year. This poor magnolia was a lot like the dogwood up in the meadow—it had been knocked over by the ice storm and was barely alive, though had put out some remarkable big blooms.

And then I came to the yellow lady slipper orchids. Not all of them were up out of the ground yet, but a number of them were. And one had the very first bloom—a yellow ball all curled up inside some larger green leaves. If we had a little rain and a few days of sunshine, there would be yellow on these plants! Last year there were 17 blooms in this bunch.

It was getting rather dim out so I turned and hurried back down the lane and up the hill. The thrush continued to sing. It was a terrific little spot to hike.

As I walked I got to thinking about why sometimes you go out and hike and keep going and don't stop much, while on other hikes you stop and sit and watch for a while in a spot or two. Does the plan come from within—a desire to stop or keep walking—or from the outside—rocks and trees and flowers reaching out to you to stop, or hike further? Just wondered.

The clouds were lighting up as I crossed the meadow. And then a whippoorwill called out from the edge of the forest—What? This is April. Isn't that a summer bird? Gosh, it was great to hear him. A sure sign of long lazy summer nights ahead.

There was a big stand of mayapples growing right across the new trail route, and I had to be careful not to knock them down as I passed. I probably should get this trail built before too long. Perhaps after all of the apples bloom.

It was dark when I arrived back at the cabin. The wind was still blowing pretty hard—in the upper 30's. It was warm though, about 70 degrees.

As I sat down for a moment on the back deck another whippoorwill called out. Could it have been the same one from the East Meadow—did he follow me here? That would be an interesting thought, to have wildlife following you. Hum, how about a bear? Speaking of bears, their time is coming soon, and I would expect to see one anytime in the next few weeks. I am looking forward to seeing what they will be up to this year.

The wind continued to blow and howl and make music long into the night. This cabin is so tight that with all of the windows and doors closed you really can't even tell that the wind is blowing.

When I crawled into the hot tub I figured there might be white caps on the water. The wind just wasn't blowing into the tub much. But it was blowing up in the trees, and the moon was out and shining through the new growth on those waving trees, and, well, the night just had this incredible feeling to it.

I looked and looked and looked but never saw a shooting star. They were out tonight for sure, but were hiding behind the many dark clouds that were moving around up there. But I did see a single firefly, and it came up close to the tub. So I figured that was my shooting star for this night, and so I dried off, shut down the computer, and climbed up to the loft.

4/22/99 More wind at daylight. But it felt a little different. This wind was full of moisture—yea! It was misting a little when I crawled into the hot tub at first light. A warm mist—it was still in the 60's. Now, if it only will rain an inch or two today. There were lots of soaring birds around this morning early, which is unusual for them. Maybe they sense the weather change (duh, of course they do) and are out trying to get one last meal before the big storm. The valleys below are filled with the mist, and the bright greens of new growth are mixed and muted, although still very rich. Photographs are a lot better with this kind of air, so I hope it continues.

This is going to be a busy weekend for me, and so I may not be able to make another post until Monday, which is my normal weekly posting time anyway. Sometimes I just post more often because I can. Several folks are coming out to spend the weekend, with the main goal of going out and taking pictures. We will get up early, stay up late, and shoot a lot of film, if the rain comes and the clouds remain that is. See you soon...

Well, I got a spot of time, so I thought that I had better get up to date. It didn't rain much during the day, but did wet everything down just a little. As evening approached, a few dark clouds circled, and the light got really nice. No sunset though.

I grilled some salmon (very good) and eggplant, made up a batch of Banff Pasta, and generally made a pig out of myself for dinner. As the dishes were being washed off, the sky began to light up. In fact, when the lightning would strike, you could see the flash out of all the windows (must have been overhead). The wind blew, and the sky flashed, but not much of anything else happened. I elected to stay out of the hot tub.

It wasn't until after I went to bed that it began to rain. It didn't drop too much—less than a tenth of an inch. But the light show was very nice.

4/23/99 I got up just in time to see one of the most incredible sunrises ever—as I rolled over and looked out the window there was a giant red ball, flattened a bit, rising above the ridge. All of the colors were muted, from the greens of the half-leafed-out trees, to the red of the sun, to the shades of white in the clouds that were still hanging around. It was one terrific pastel scene indeed!

It didn't take me long to jump into the tub and continue to enjoy the wonderful morning. The wind had died down and there were lots and lots of birds out, playing in the treetops and singing for joy. I don't recall ever seeing so many different birds at the same time here before. Up in the big tree next to the tub there seemed to be a different bird on every branch. There was a big fat bluebird dude sitting on the lowest branch. Sitting there in the swirling warm waters surrounded by all of this beauty, well, it was very special.

Next I put on my shoes and headed on down the ladder trail towards the river. As I got lower and lower the sunrise pretty much stayed the same—one continuous sunrise all the way down. And the air got cooler with each bench that I went down. And the smells were tremendous—lots of plant smells that I can't really describe.

The forest was full of bird sounds, many different levels of them, from high-pitched squawks up close, to the purely musical tones of a thrush somewhere out there, to the deep bass of a woodpecker that echoed through the valley. Man, it was a spring morning in the Ozarks alright, all framed with the sound of the rivers running.

When I walked up to the river I startled a great blue heron that had been fishing along the bank. Darn, I should approach a little more carefully, just like you should do when coming into a meadow—you tend to see a lot more wildlife that way. The heron cleared the treetops in a hurry, and lumbered on upstream out of sight.

The climb out seemed very fast and I was breathing hard. As I was making my way up the two steepest benches my head was bent low to the ground and I was taking the earthy aromas deep into my lungs. Gosh, I don't know of too many better smells than earth and leaves and new plants. I'll bet it did my lungs a lot of good.

And when I reached the top of the bluff the shooting star wildflowers were blooming everywhere. My little flower friend at the very top of the bluff was standing tall and smiling. He knew it was a grand day as well.

While sitting on the cool-down deck I found tick #3, a big fellow. By the way, I don't plan to note each and every tick that snags a ride, but I always find it amusing to remember that there really aren't as many ticks out there in the woods as many people would have you believe. And when you find one, you simply pull it off, pinch its little head off, and go on about your day.

The sun disappeared behind the clouds and it got a little hazy, mostly from the fine mist that was hanging around. The humidity was 93%.

Birds continued to dominate the morning. One hummingbird—first I had seen this season—came by to check out the deck, to see if I had the feeder out yet, and almost invited himself into the cabin. Then a minute later a brilliant flash of red streaked by and landed in one of the dogwoods in the meadow. It was a *scarlet* tanager, a bird that lives up to his name! Smaller than a cardinal, it is easy to tell what this bird is. Always a delightful surprise to see one of these in the area.

No real rain yet, which we need for our waterfall photography, but the overcast skies are great. I would be happy if it would rain this afternoon and/or tonight, then be nice and cloudy and misty all day tomorrow and Sunday. Keep your fingers crossed for me. Thank you.

I had hired a cook to come out and spend the weekend and take care of the food chores for the photo workshop that was happening at the cabin—that was a good move. The cabin was soon filled with an aroma of my special homemade

Cloudland Chocolate-chip Oatmeal Cookies, and some sourdough bread that I was baking. She made a *lot* of the cookies—two pounds of butter in the batch! I had bought a mountain of food, some really great stuff, and we were going to eat our way through the weekend.

After a few hours of food prep the cook retired to the swing for a short nap, and I worked on my weekend workshop plan. Then I put together the last futon, which I put down in the tool/wine room—the cook's other assignment for the weekend was to sleep there and guard the wine rack. Kind of like getting the fox to guard the chicken house.

I also put up the hummingbird feeder out on the back deck. It wouldn't be long now before the little buggers would be buzzing around and fighting each other.

Three photographers arrived early in the evening. Ray Scott from Little Rock, a great photographer and a wonderful drummer for a rock and roll band; Mark Hardgrave from Knoxville, who had been to the McNeil Bear Preserve in Alaska and had some amazing grizzly images to show us; and Chuck Haralson (A.C.), who has been the official photographer for the Arkansas Department of Parks and Tourism for sixteen years (chances are that most any picture that you have ever seen advertising Arkansas was his). It was going to be one great weekend of shooting and talking nature photography with some pretty high-powered photographers. I was honored to have all three at Cloudland.

We snacked and munched and talked about each other's work and saw slides long into the night. The bear pictures from Alaska were really something! Mark had full-frame head shots of thousand pound grizzlies, which he shot from only several yards away. I ate about a dozen cookies. No new rain.

4/24/99 A *very* loud whippoorwill cracked the early morning silence, and soon it was daylight and everyone was up and moving around. No sunrise, but it looked like the heavy cloud cover was going to stick around all day—that was *perfect* shooting light for us!

The cook fixed one terrific breakfast, including a great egg dish, homemade herb biscuits, bacon, garlic taters, a big plate of fruit slices, and fresh-squeezed orange juice. I think everyone wanted to stick around and just keep eating, but we had work to do, so we packed up and took off for the woods.

We went down into one of my favorite waterfall areas. While the water was not nearly as high as it had been the week before, there was still plenty flowing. We spent many hours going from one waterfall to the next, each one of us picking different angles to shoot from. We spent a lot of time looking through each other's cameras to get their perspective—this is my most effective teaching tool. Besides all of the waterfalls, we had lots of shooting stars, wild iris, and umbrella magnolias to photograph.

At one point the sky opened up and it began to rain—yea! We just happened to be under this big overhang and there was a terrific scene from there that included a couple of waterfalls, so we just went right on shooting, and stayed dry. The rain didn't last too long, and we moved onto another waterfall area for more pics.

We visited the yellow lady slipper orchids and found one bright yellow boat just about fully out, but not enough so to take pictures of. Before anyone realized it the time was 3pm! Lunch was overdue, so we returned to the cabin.

We had left the cook at the cabin, and she had gone on a little adventure of her own. She took a hike down the ladder trail to the river. While she was near the old homesite there she came face to face with *a bear!* Not only was this the first bear sighting of the season out here, but it was also the very first time that anyone but me staying at Cloudland had seen one. What exciting news! She was pretty happy about it all too.

She got back in time to create this incredible Thai Salad that was simply out of this world. We teamed it with meats and cheeses from the Ozark Mountain Smokehouse for another feast. Everyone was a little slow moving by the time we finished, but we still had daylight left and pictures to shoot (the group was warned ahead of time that it would be long exhausting days).

We drove on over to Pearly Spring, one of my favorite shooting locations in the area, and spent a couple of hours there. One of my pictures of this spring appears on the label of "Arkansas Ale" beer.

Then we found these large rock slabs in the woods that were completely *covered* with wildflowers! And I mean that you could not step without getting a flower or two under foot. It was late in the day, we were all sort of mentally exhausted from all of the wonderful scenes that we had been photographing. There was something very special about all of us standing there, knee deep in wildflowers (Ozark spiderworts and wild hibiscus), with all of this rich color everywhere. We were all on the same plane, people who work at taking pictures of the natural world simply because we are drawn to the great beauty and want to share it with others through our photographs. I really enjoyed the moment. And the entire day.

It was dark by the time we returned to the cabin. We were greeted with an incredible smell when we opened the door—more great food! Our cook had been slaving away again and laid out a spread that included this wonderful dish of baked herb veggies, fresh French bread, and a salad that had about eight different varieties of greens in it. Plus we had my secret recipe of Cloudland Cajun Grilled Tuna, marinated in this special sauce and grilled to perfection. Oh yes, and for desert we had fresh cheese cake! What a tremendous dinner. Hey, just another typical feed at Cloudland.

We talked on again long into the night about the more serious side of photography—selling pictures. This was a workshop for advanced photographers, and the business discussions that we had all weekend were an important part.

4/25/99 It thundered and rained a little on and off during the night, but no real downpours like we had hoped. No matter, it looked like it was going to be another cloudy day, so we were all happy.

Breakfast was on the lighter/quicker side today, then we made sandwiches and packed everything up and headed out to another shooting location.

We had a long hike this morning to get to our scenic spot, but when we did arrive, there was a big round of oohs and aahs—I had taken them to the largest and most spectacular waterfall in the wilderness. And it was running pretty good. No problem finding something to take pictures of here! We all set up and fired away, roll after roll. Several times during the day the sky opened up and it really poured (*now* it rained!). A lot of the great scenes were right there from under this terrific bluff overhang, so we didn't mind the rain one bit. Spectacular! I'll bet we took more than 500 pictures of that waterfall today. There were also a lot of wonderful, lush ferns lining the banks of the creek for us to photograph, and a number of wild azaleas that were blooming—deep, rich color and this incredible aroma. All too soon it was time to hike out. And then a strange thing happened—it quit raining, and remained dry all the way out. Life isn't supposed to work out like that.

The cabin was engulfed with heavy fog when we got back—just Cloudland living up to its name. The rainfall had completely filled up the cistern. Soon the photographers were all packed up and headed back to civilization. It had been one fine weekend of natural beauty, great conversation, and five star cuisine. Some of the pictures taken by Chuck will probably end up as ads for the state of Arkansas in the years to come—we set up a few of them with a photographer or hiker standing in front of a gorgeous waterfall. It wasn't a stretch at all.

Night has fallen now and it is still really foggy outside, with a warm wind blowing the trees around. Everything is wet, soggy wet, and the air is full of moisture. The humidity is about 110%. I had wanted to go take a well-deserved long soak in the hot tub, but it has just now begun to rain again, heavily. I am tired, so I will put off my soak and go on up to bed. There is this great waterfall that I want to hike into and take pictures of in the morning.

4/26/99 There was thunder and lightning and some rain for several hours during the night, then calm. It had rained a little over an inch total yesterday. The forest really needed that to feed the tremendous appetite of all the new growth, while still maintaining good waterfall and river levels.

It was still foggy when I got up at daylight but it had lifted somewhat and I could see out into the wilderness. The hot tub felt great. There were birds out singing and playing all around me. It was warm—in the mid 60's, and hardly any wind. The Buffalo River was up and running pretty good, and so was Whitaker Creek. The waterfall that I want to go hike into and photograph this morning is the twin one. The second part of the falls only runs when there is good water, and it should be doing its thing this morning. After a little Starbucks mocha and some Journal editing (my sister sent me an e-mail correcting the spelling of "cistern," which I had spelled wrong eleven times already—took about ten minutes just to find and change all of them), I packed up my camera gear and headed out into the fog.

The first part of the hike was through a thick stand of mature pines. The ground was covered with pine needles and a layer of green—poison ivy! The ivy was solid as far as you could see. Thank goodness that I am not allergic to it. They say that my body chemistry will change some day and I might eventually become allergic to it. If that day ever does come my outdoor career will probably come to an end. In the meantime I will continue to snicker at the rest of the world, which I know will come back to haunt me some day.

Anyway, the heavy fog in the pines and the green ivy really made for an unusual scene, one of those that looked great while standing there, but impossible to put onto film—lots of environmental factors contributing to the whole thing, like the feel and smell and temperature of the fog. It was quiet as I walked, with only a distant bird call now and then, and the snap of a twig or two underfoot.

I left the pines behind and began to drop down a steep hillside, leaving the fog behind too. Soon I reached the creek and began to search for the waterfall. I had only been to this spot once before, on New Year's Day, when everything was ice and snow and blowing cold. I made my way downstream and finally came to a spot where the earth dropped away—what I was about to witness became a near religious experience for me.

The creek splits in two just before it leaps off of a 60-70 foot overhanging bluff, and both falls plunge into this incredible pool below. The forest around the bluffs above and the falls and below around the pool were filled with magnolia, dogwood, sassafras, redbud, hickory, oak, and a number of other trees that I could not identify. In a word—*lush!*

I made my way around to one side of the falls. I could feel that the light was about to change, and this was one remarkable scene, so I tried to hurry to find a suitable photo spot. At the same time where I was walking was close to the edge and very dangerous—one tiny little slip and I would be over the edge. But I had to stay close to the edge, for that is where I would find a picture spot. I had never photographed this falls before, and didn't even know if there was an open spot anywhere with a good view. But I had to try.

And then I found it, right at the edge. The trees opened up just enough to allow me an open view of the falls and the pool below. Holy Ansel Adams, I was stunned and brought nearly to tears at the incredible beauty that stood before me. And the light was perfect, the wind was not blowing, and the water was just fabulous. I tied myself and my tripod to a nearby tree, and got set up as quickly as possible.

Then I discovered a problem. It was *soooo* humid and wet out that my lens had fogged up. Wiping it off did no good. The thundering waterfalls were pushing even more moisture up into the air, and right onto my lens. Darn. No, *damn!* Here I was, finally at what I considered the most scenic of all waterfalls in the Ozarks, with perfect conditions, and I couldn't take a picture. This was one of those times in life when you learn something—today it was patience. All I could do was sit there and hope that everything would clear up.

And it did clear up. Prayers answered. I spent the next 30 minutes running roll after roll after roll of film through my camera. Probably got the picture with the very first shot, but the scene was so incredible that I just kept shooting. It was no use to look for another vantage point because I knew this was the only open spot. I shot some more. Then I zoomed out just a little, and a second shot showed up. A couple more rolls of film went through the camera. This scene will probably become the cover for my next picture book. It was that good.

The light was changing fast as the sun burned through the fog. I couldn't shoot with sun on the scene—just too dull. But I couldn't meter when the sun was out either, because the reading would be off when the sun went behind a cloud. So I had to wait until the sun was behind a cloud, meter, then wait for the next cloud to take any pictures. It was a bit frustrating at times, but I knew that I had to keep firing away to make sure that I had a good picture.

I had already taken about 350 pictures when disaster struck. As I leaned over to adjust the focus on the camera, I leaned a little too far, and my feet slipped out from under me. Within a split second both me and my camera/tripod had gone over the edge. I started roping myself up to a tree a year ago in situations just like this. The rope worked just fine the only other time that I had slipped and headed towards the edge. I normally leave just enough rope for me to move around, and to stop me from going over the edge. Something went very wrong today.

Either I hadn't measured correctly and left too much slack, or the knot slipped—I went over the edge of the cliff. I'm not exactly sure what happened next, but I think that when I went over the edge and the rope went tight, my body swung in under the lip and I smashed into the bluff. I hit my head, hard, and I'm not sure if I was knocked out or not. I do know that the next thing that I remember is a very tight feeling in my gut—I had only tied a slip knot around my waist (no web harness like I should have had), and it was *very* tight. In fact, it hurt like hell, and every time that I tried to move, it cinched up even tighter. So there I was, dangling in space about 60 feet from the rocks below, and I was slowly being cut in half by my own rope. Not a good situation at all.

The rope was thin and wet and slick, and my hands were wet, and I could not get a grip on the rope. Damn, I was in trouble. This was serious business, and I knew it. My head was throbbing. The earth kept moving around me. I was about to panic. That would have been it. The rope kept getting tighter and tighter. I had to get a hold of myself. I fought hard to concentrate on something, *anything.*

And then the noise of the waterfall suddenly entered my mind. I turned to look at it, and that is what got me back to earth. Yes, the waterfall, pictures of the waterfall. OK, my head was clearing. I turned my attention to the rope and the bluff in front of me. I dried my hands on my pants. I found a foothold that I could use to steady myself on and use to push off and up on. I knew that no one was going to come get me, I had to do this myself. I've always had terrible arm strength, but I knew that I had no choice but to grab the rope and pull

383

myself up. I tried to take a deep breath, but the rope around me wouldn't allow it. I took a slow breath, then wrapped my hands around the rope as tight as I could and gave it all I had.

As I got close to the top I reached out and grabbed onto the base of a small tree—I yanked it right out of the soft earth, and fell back part way over the bluff. The rope tightened even more. The next time I grabbed a larger tree—reached and stretched with all my might, and this one held, and I pulled myself up over the edge to safety. The rope was *sooo* tight that I could not get it loose. My camera bag was nearby and I was able to grab my Swiss Army knife and cut the darn thing free. What a *relief!* I could breathe again.

As I lay there gasping for air, tears were streaming down my face. I don't guess that I had ever come that close to death before. I drank my entire bottle of water, and tried to regain my composure. It wasn't easy. That waterfall was so beautiful though, and I know sitting right there looking at it had to have helped. Then I remembered my camera—smashed on the rocks below. No big deal—I've got another one.

OK, I was alive, now I had to go down and gather up the camera. I made my way back across the top of the waterfall, and down through the bluffline to the bottom and the creek. It was pretty slick going on the way down, and I couldn't believe that Emily and I had made this same descent when everything was covered with ice back in January. My legs were pretty weak, and I was shaking the entire time, but I was moving OK.

My poor camera. It was in about six or eight pieces, and the lens was shattered. But the tripod only had one broken leg. It is made of wood, really good wood, and has always withstood a lot. Now it survived a 60 foot fall. Well, almost survived.

I sat down at the base of the falls to rest before the trip out. I thought about how lucky I was to be alive, to have been spared. And I thought about how great my life was in general, to be able to go out pretty much whenever I want to and explore special places like this one, and spend my life in the wilderness. And to have survived many close calls. I don't know who was keeping an eye on me, but I thanked whoever it was.

Then my thoughts turned back to the waterfall. It needed a name. It reminded me of Punch Bowl Falls in Oregon, one of the most beautiful waterfalls that I had ever laid eyes on. I saw pictures of it made by the color master photographer David Muench, and then visited it myself. This waterfall was even better than that one. But it needed a different name than Punch Bowl. It was a twin falls, but there are already at least two Twin Falls in the Buffalo drainage, so that was out. Besides, the second part of the "twin" only runs when the water is good.

Then I thought about Neil Compton, and how much he had done for the region and for the world. He needed a waterfall named after him. So I decided the official name for this falls would be Neil Compton's Double Falls. Yes, that fit. A spectacular waterfall named after an incredible man.

Even if you are not dangling over the edge of the bluff trying to take pictures the area around this waterfall is really treacherous, and while the beauty is extreme, so is the danger, and I do not recommend this as a casual hiking trip for anyone but expert level. And even then extreme caution must be exercised. Don't be stupid like me.

As I left the falls area and headed up the steep slope I came across this little fountain of water that was coming out of a moss-covered boulder. Actually it was a very large slab of sandstone. What was most unusual about this fountain was that the water was actually *above* any surrounding ground level—the rock was sticking up above the forest floor. That meant that the fountain was actually a little artesian spring, being pushed uphill inside the rock by some force. I leaned over and took a good long drink.

The fog was gone and the sun was breaking up the sky as I drove back to the cabin. It was a terrific little hike, except for that one little mishap. My head was pounding, and there was a nice lump, but no broken skin or blood. I quickly packed up the truck with all of the weekend photo class stuff and rushed back to town to get the film processed and see if my cover picture actually turned out (and to get my backup camera and another tripod). It had been one incredible, splendid and grand weekend at Cloudland.

It was dark when I returned, late at night actually. The cabin seemed empty, yet warm and inviting. I slipped into the hot tub and laid back to survey the night sky. What I found was one spectacular light show going on.

First off, the heavy cloud cover was beginning to break up and beaming down from straight overhead was a two-thirds full moon. It lit up the wilderness with a soft glow. It also backlit the clouds, many of which were black, and the moonlight gave them a silver lining.

There were a few bright stars visible through the clouds, even a few formations. It was interesting to watch the clouds move across in front of the stars.

Over in the southern sky there was an amazing light show going on—lots and lots of flashes from a big thunderstorm that was raging somewhere. And every time that a flash happened it too created many silver linings in the black clouds. Lots of black clouds, and an equal number of silver linings. I guess that is a good lesson in life.

There were also smaller and thinner clouds floating around at a lower altitude. Every once in a while one would break away from the pack and come cruising by all by itself.

As I was sitting back enjoying the show and the hot bubbles I caught some movement out of the corner of my eye. Something was moving up the tree next to the tub. He stopped his progress for a moment and looked down right at me—a raccoon! I had seen them up near the gate before, but never at the cabin. He moved around from limb to limb for a while, then I lost track of him. It was an unusual sight with the bright moon and the lightning flashes and the black clouds and now this raccoon. I guess you never know what scene will happen at Cloudland.

No fireflies out tonight—guess the moon lit everything up well enough.

When I opened the window in the loft to get some fresh air to sleep by I could hear a few raindrops falling. One of my last thoughts before I fell asleep was how great it was to be alive.

4/27/99 The eastern horizon glowed orange early. I was sitting in the hot tub when the sun showed up. It was a very blue morning—blue jays, bluebirds, and blue skies! The trees were alive with the sounds and movements of dozens of birds of all types. There were at least twenty birds in this one flock of bluejays. A group of them would rise up together and fly across the meadow towards me, lit by the rising sun. Reminded me of the Blue Angels jet team.

And the few puffy clouds that were out were constantly changing color. First, they were their normal white. Within five minutes they turned pink, then dark grey, then back to white again.

There were cloud banks down in the valleys too. One main bank went all the way up the Buffalo River, then began to break up and the sun hit it. Several of the parts broke off and went up side canyons, while others moved down the main canyon, hanging low and scraping the treetops.

There was a single cloud hanging out below the Crag. It was round and fluffy, and looked like it had been placed there to catch someone who might jump off of the Crag to a soft landing.

There wasn't any wind at all, and it was a cool 52 degrees.

This was one of those mornings that you just had to spend some time sitting out on the back deck watching all that was going on. I took my place and munched on a toasted bagel.

One large bird took off from my area and headed out over the main valley. I wondered if he really knew what he was getting himself into? He soared and flapped a little and soared some more, heading towards the opposite hillside. It was almost a mile to the next tree. It took him a minute or even longer to find a landing spot.

And as if to defy the blue theme of the morning, a brilliant red scarlet tanager flew up and landed on a nearby limb. I don't really know all that much about complementary colors, but I do know that at Cloudland blue and green and red all go together quite well. Oh yes, and the pure white of the dogwoods down in the meadow, now at their peak, looked like they belonged too.

After an hour or so of lounging around on the deck I realized two things. First, this deck is about the best spot on earth to begin the day. And second, I was still in my bath robe, and I had better get dressed and get some work done!

One other thought crossed my mind. My old flame, Leslie, e-mailed me one of those "lists" yesterday—I get a lot of that stuff, most of which I simply delete. This list was entitled "Instructions for Life," and included a lot of things that I happen to agree with, so I saved it in my special quotes file. Anyway, I started thinking about other things to add to that list. The first one that I came up with was that you should drink a lot of water each day for sure, but you should also eat at least three cookies every day as well. And be awake and watch and listen and enjoy the first hour of every day.

I forgot to post the following recipe for "poke salat" that was e-mailed to me by Hilda Turner in Russellville recently:

Cook tender greens slightly. Drain well and chop. Cook bacon. Drain and crumble. Use a bit of bacon grease to saute green onions. Add crumbled bacon, chopped "poke," and lightly beaten eggs. Cook until eggs are done, stirring well.

The eggs, bacon, and onion do a good job of camouflaging the taste of "poke salat."

Sounds great! And there is getting to be a lot of poke down in the meadow—I need to pick and cook some before it gets too high and tough.

And I did get a lot of work done today. First I installed handles on all of the windows in the cabin—they are really tough to open, and the handles should help. Then I got up on the ladder and glued all of the joints together of the gutter system that leads to the cistern—it had been leaking. And I put up a bracket or two on some sagging gutters elsewhere. Then I built a stand to put the hot tub cover up on when it is removed. You can buy this same type of thing for a couple of hundred bucks, but I made mine out of scrap lumber—it only cost me about thirty minutes labor, and I am pretty cheap. I also planted some mint out in front (peppermint, spearmint and chocolate mint), and mulched all of the new larger plants with pine straw that I had collected.

While all of this work was going on I took several breaks—my head was still pounding a little from the bump the day before. The sky was blue and filled with puffy white clouds, the brilliant green of new spring growth was still dominant across the forest, and lots of birds played in the trees.

At one point there was a lot of chatter from the birds, and then a bluebird came and landed right on top of the large carved bear out back—looked pretty funny. I had set up my camera (the backup camera that I had at home) pointing towards the main dogwood tree down in the meadow, hoping to get a picture of that very bluebird sitting in it. Now he was standing on the bear right behind the camera.

Then a black and white warbler came flying up and landed in the tree nearby. Both birds were looking back behind them—they hesitated a moment, then flew off into the woods. Then I saw him—a large and very slow moving red-tailed hawk came gliding in over the meadow and landed in the big pine tree. Those birds must have seen him coming and got the heck out of there. I stepped over to the tele and zoomed in close on him—could count every feather on his body. His eyes were very intent, like he was looking for something very specific. He didn't stick around long, and soon jumped up and flew off.

As the day drew on I got to watching the pair of bluebirds that were hanging around. While they were always around somewhere close, I had never seen them land on or go into either one of the bluebird boxes. But today I noticed them around this snag down at the edge of the meadow a lot. It is located just a few feet away from one of the bluebird houses.

The bluebird would land on the top of the snag, sit there a while, then jump up and disappear behind the snag. Hum, something was up. I had to investigate. Son of a gun, an amazing discovery! These love birds had made their own little house in the snag—I found a hole just the right size, about seven feet off of the ground, and facing away from the cabin. It had to be their nest! I was *thrilled* to have bluebirds nesting at Cloudland! And to think that I almost cut down that old snag. Good lesson—snags are home to a lot of critters.

I had eaten too many chocolate chip oatmeal cookies during the day and decided that it was time for a hike to work them off. Besides, all of my chores were done and the day was perfect for hiking.

I headed down the ladder trail, crossed Whitaker Creek, and started up the steep slope towards Beagle Point. The hillside was lush, and the going was slow at times. When I got to the real steep part I found it to be covered with white violets—I mean thousands and thousands of them! I hated to even walk through them, but there was no place else to step. They were tall too. As I climbed up further the violets were replaced with spiderworts, also white ones, and a lot of maidenhair ferns. Towards the top of the slope the spiderworts turned from the pale ones to the darker purple ones.

The hillside was steep and I had to get down on all fours some of the time just to keep going, grabbing for anything solid that I could find. I sat down to take a breather and could see a splendid view of the river below through the trees.

I finally made it up to the base of the bluff. Tough climb. My goal was to make my way around the bluff to the spot where I had rescued those two deer dogs last fall, and get up on top of the bluff there. I started walking along the base of the bluff admiring tiny wildflowers. Just as I rounded the point of the bluff I looked up and got startled out of my wits—*a bear!* And only about twenty feet away—Yikes!!!

I'm not sure who was surprised more, or who jumped higher. He leapt into the sky, turned to his left, and hit the ground about ten feet down the slope and immediately disappeared. I literally was startled backwards and landed on my butt. The entire thing took maybe three seconds. I burst out laughing, uncontrollably, and laughed so hard that I started to cough. I'm sure my laughter could be heard throughout the wilderness. That bear had the funniest look on his face! I'm sure that I did too. He was a small bear, and perhaps the same one the cook had seen on Saturday. I had almost gotten used to seeing bears last summer but this one really took me by surprise. I wish that I could have seen him without startling him and watched to see what he was up to. Oh well, I suspect he won't be the last bear that I see this year.

I made it to the top of the bluff and went on out to the point and sat down and looked around a while. There was a great view of the river downstream, and of the cabin. I could hear the river just like over at my place. And a barred owl called out a couple of times—a little odd for the middle of the day. Well, actually it was late afternoon, so I guess he was entitled.

I climbed on up a little and followed a bench through open forest and past piles of stones left by pioneers. The deeper into the woods I traveled the larger the trees got. Beeches, oaks, hickories, and black gums—some of these dudes were *huge!* An entire forest of them, towering over everything else below. A wind storm had come through one section, and there were about a dozen of them big guys down on the ground, tossed about in all directions.

The bench that I was following was really nice and wide and flat and level. It was hard to believe that such a long stretch of fine level forest existed amidst all of this rough terrain. The bench followed along near the top of the bluffline, which I kept just in sight below. Every now and then there was an opening around the bluffline, and I wandered over and took a look at the view. One thing that I saw was the incredible red color in the sandstone of the bluff on the opposite side of the valley—looked a little like Utah redrock canyon country.

There were patches of wild azaleas in bloom along many parts of the bluff-top, and they smelled heavenly. And there were several old cedar trees lining the bluffs too—hadn't seen them in this area before.

The big trees gave way to an open spot ahead. It was a glade of sorts, covered with thick mosses and reindeer lichens and azaleas in bloom. Something was special here, I could feel it. And then I saw a waterfall leaping over the edge of the bluff—another twin falls, no it was a *triple* falls! And it wasn't just a pour-off from the recent rains either, but a real creek that came down the hillside and across the exposed rock of the blufftop.

I was careful not to get too close to the edge, ha, ha. The falls were backlit by the low sun and looked just spectacular. There was a giant cedar tree growing right on the edge and in between the falls. The bluff was really very large here, much larger than I had expected to find. Man oh man, this was one wonderful spot. But I could not find any good place to take a picture of it. I had my backup camera with me, and the other tripod, which was much smaller and lighter than my wood one. But no picture spot.

I could see that down below there was no pool like Compton falls—the water just splashed on black rocks and continued on down the slope. But the area below was filled with magnolias, and they appeared to be in full bloom. I had to find a way down.

Close by the bluff made an abrupt turn to the left, and son of a gun, there was a nice little path for me to go down. I hurried around the point and on over towards the falls. What I found was a wall of ferns, moss, Jack-In-The-Pulpits, and even small magnolia trees behind the waterfalls—it was really lush! And the fragrance of the magnolia blooms was overwhelming—reminded me of ripe pawpaws. I don't know what the height of these falls was—probably 60-70 feet—but they were very tall, and hit the rocks with a great deal of force.

But this place was more than just the waterfall. There were large sandstone boulders tossed about, many covered with moss and ferns and all surrounded by umbrella magnolias, their branches heavy with the white blossoms.

I set up the camera to take a picture, but had to wait for the sun to go behind a cloud and for the wind to stop. So I went exploring. I felt like a kid again, with a giant playhouse to run around in. There were lots of hiding places and neat little spots back in the rocks to peer into. And all of those blooms! It was one amazing little place. I thought that there might be something at this spot from looking at the map, but nothing as nice as it is.

The big cedar tree above was actually growing out away from the bluff and then straight up—I have no idea how it kept from falling. And down below it there was a little ledge that was filled with wild iris, most in bloom.

While I was playing in the rocks the sun went behind a cloud and the wind stopped—I missed my picture. But I got a few others, then realized that it was getting late, so I moved on. But before I left I went to the base of the falls and reached out into the falling water and filled my water bottle. I have heard that if you drink from such a place your travels will be blessed. I had a lot of traveling to do this week, and needed a little more blessing.

But the triple falls was not the only wonder in this little area. As I followed the water down the hill I came across not one, not two, not three, but *four* cascading waterfalls, each with a completely different shape and character. Then the water came to rest and flowed into Whitaker Creek.

The fragrance of the magnolia blooms followed me all the way down, and so did many more blooming trees. And I found one absolutely perfect blossom—open just right with all its petals, and the complete umbrella of giant leaves surrounding it. I sat down next to it and took the aroma deep into my lungs. And admired its beauty.

Whitaker Creek was flowing pretty good, but had a quiet personality most of the way. I followed it downstream, stopping every now and then to take a few pictures. It flowed past one area that was filled with giant sandstone blocks up on one side, all covered with moss. And many of the blocks had jagged edges and odd shapes.

The more I walked the more lush the forest got. I had never seen anything like the incredible display of blooming magnolias before. It is definitely tropical out there right now folks!

I had noticed that my exposures were getting longer, and when I looked up I saw pink clouds in the sky. Oops. It was about to get dark on me, and I was nowhere near home, or any trail that led to it. So I left the wonderful creek and headed up the hillside. It got very steep in a hurry, and sometimes it was difficult to suck in all the air that I needed for the climb because of the heavy magnolia blooms! I lead a cursed life don't I.

Before long I was at the base of those red sandstone bluffs that I had seen from across the way. And the evening light was really turning them *red*. I had no idea! Then I found my way to the top and took the trail back to the cabin, just as the last bit of daylight faded into the night.

Another terrific hike. A bear. A new spectacular waterfall. And I didn't fall off any bluffs. Hey, and I even got some work done around the cabin. Now that is what I call one fine day at Cloudland!

While I am sitting here writing this Journal entry tonight, I noticed the Ansel Adams wall calendar nearby. I have been x'ing out each day that I am out at the cabin, and see that April is almost full—I have been here every single day in April! I have never been here every day of any month since I have been keeping the Journal. Only three more days to go. And man have I got some adventures planned for those three days! And then the Journal will be finished, or at least over. Has it really been a year?

Time to go soak for a few minutes and see what the moon is up to.

4/28/99 Another classic, textbook morning at Cloudland. The sun appeared as a red ball on the horizon. The main Buffalo River valley was socked in with a low cloud bank. There were birds everywhere, already up and singing at the top of their lungs. Bluebirds, scarlet tanagers, warblers, hummingbirds at the feeder, doves, blue jays, and three or four others that flew by so fast I could not identify. The brilliant red tanagers seem to be hanging around more lately. Temp in the low 50's. Blue skies. The rivers below were singing too, calling out to me to come visit. I tried to get some work done at the computer, but the wonderful world outside kept dragging me away.

Speaking of the river, today is a day that I have been looking forward to for a very long time. I will go upstream and visit the river, get to know it intimately, and probably take a frigid bath or two in it along the way.

When I was a kid I used to spend a lot of time in a canoe. My dad built his own when he was young, and my older brother, Terry, was near expert level. All of the Ernst men knew how to drive a canoe. The last time that I had floated the upper Buffalo River there were more than 200 canoes waiting to put in. It was on that morning many years ago that I decided to quit floating and see the river from a different angle. Since then I have spent most of my time on trails, or bushwhacking, and have only floated the river a few times, mostly in the lower, calmer and less crowded stretches.

I had borrowed a friend's canoe last month and did a section of the middle river, kind of in preparation for this most upper section that I was about to attempt. It wasn't a special canoe, just a normal ABS canoe, but a little shorter than normal, so that a solo guy could handle it OK.

The "Hailstone" run has long been known as a stretch of the river that can only be run at flood stage, and only then for a few hours, perhaps even a full day, during and just after a lot of rainfall. I have heard that the name Hailstone comes from an attempt to keep folks from trying to float this stretch—trying to give it a name that just sounds bad. I have also seen this section called Hailstone Creek, and even seen the creek listed on maps. There is no Hailstone Creek. It is the Buffalo River and nothing else. It is one of the wildest and most remote floats in this part of the United States.

The upper put-in point is located at Dixon Ford, a forest road that connects Hwy. 16 near Fallsville with Cave Mountain Road near the Kapark Cemetery Trailhead. This road forms the upstream boundary of the Upper Buffalo River Wilderness Area. Once you put in your boat here there is no access whatsoever until you emerge from the wilderness area fifteen and a half miles downstream at the Hwy. 21 crossing of the Buffalo River in Boxley Valley. And if you get in trouble there is no way out, except the river, or to climb out of the Buffalo gorge, which is often a major problem in itself. The closest point of civilization along this entire stretch is CLOUDLAND.

The river was not at flood stage this day—I don't have anywhere near the skills to attempt such a thing. But it did have plenty of water in it, and I have also heard that you can float this stretch pretty much any time—the lower the water, the more dragging you had to do. No problem for me, I didn't mind a little dragging or portaging at all. I have spent a lot of time up in Canada with a canoe strapped to my back, and have done up to a mile portage at one time. I just wanted to get out and spend some time on the water, and see the river from within.

So I had a friend meet me at the Boxley bridge, where I left my truck. We got down to Dixon Ford via the rough forest road, and soon I was all suited up and ready to go. Just in case, we had outfitted the canoe with full flotation. What that means is that when the boat goes under, it probably will float instead of simply filling up entirely with water and sinking. Ha, ha. Even though it was pretty warm out—in the low 60's, I had put on my old wet suit from my scuba diving days. It wasn't a matter of if I was going to dump into the frigid waters, but when, and how many times. So I wanted to be prepared. And for the very first time, I wore a PFD—personal flotation device. In the past I had always just brought along a cushion and sat on it.

The river was running clear, and didn't look too tough at the put-in. I was traveling light, very light, so there wasn't much to load up, and soon I got in and pushed off. The sun was just beginning to burn off the fog in the valley, and there were rays peeking through here and there. The sun was a welcome sight.

There were a few anxious moments in the first mile or two of the river, but I managed to get through them OK, and mostly dry. There was this one spot where a giant boulder was sitting right in the middle of the river, splitting the waters. And there were several other places where rock ledges formed small waterfalls across most of the river. I could just imagine how these spots looked when the water was high. Today they were merely a little whitewater in between calm emerald pools. I did have to get out and carry around a couple of them, but I did run one or two just for fun.

Somewhere during the third mile or so of the run I attempted a fast little rapid. My heart sped up as I approached the opening "V" and put the bow into the whitewater. My dad always said that as long as I am moving faster than the water then I will have control. Go slower, and the river is in charge. So I paddled fast. No problem. Slosh and bump and scrape and oh, yea, it felt great!

Then at the far end of the rapid I hit a rock straight on and flipped right over. Dumb move. The rapid had been toying with me, allowing me to think that I was in charge, when in reality it had plans to get me wet all the time.

The canoe and I were spit out into a calm pool below the rapids. Once I got a hold of the boat and swam to the shore, I just had to sit down and laugh out loud a little. It really wasn't all that big of a rapid.

The water was very cold at first, but the wet suit soon warmed it up. I didn't have any gear to speak of—just my daypack, which was strapped into the canoe, and a throw rope. I flipped the canoe over and got all of the water out, then pointed it downstream and pushed on.

Then within an hour the sun had burned off all the fog and a spectacular spring day unfolded. Most of the float was gentle, one long pool after another, connected by short whitewater runs. The boat did drag a little, well, a lot, over some of the shallow stretches, and I spent a lot of time out of the canoe, dragging it along over the rocks. I only had to actually carry the canoe a couple of times. Much better than a mile portage up in Canada. And there were no mosquitoes here.

I dumped again. And then again. Stupid mistakes, nothing really dangerous or tough. The water seemed to get a little warmer each time. Good thing no one was watching though. Although there were a lot of folks watching—critters. I saw deer four different times, a couple of beavers working long pools, and a number of blue herons, fishing along the shallow banks. Plus there were literally hundreds of birds about. The forest was alive with bird activity, which seemed to increase when I dumped—can birds laugh? I'm sure they were today.

I floated past the mouth of Adkins Creek, where I had hiked down into in six inches of fresh snow twenty years ago. I remember nearly freezing on that trip—I didn't have a sleeping pad of any kind, nor did I bother to clear out a spot when I pitched the tent. All of the snow under me melted just a little, and turned to ice. So I slept on a bed of ice. I have this picture somewhere of me in front of a huge fire that first night—it is one of the best pictures of my early days, although the exposure is so long that I am blurred. The fire looks great though! And it was much needed. Come to think of it, that was the very first hike that I ever took into the upper Buffalo area. I have come a long way since that trip.

Next was Lovell Hollow. We spent the night on the river near there over Memorial Day Weekend last year. It rained and rained and rained. But it was a warm rain.

Then came Terrapin Branch. I have made a number of trips down into this incredible gorge from the top, but have never made it all the way to the river. It is a tough hike, but one of the most scenic that you will ever take. This was the very first time that I had seen this part of the river. More gorgeous pools, more rapids, but I managed to stay dry.

The tornado that swept through last year dipped down and got a lot of the trees along the river below Terrapin Branch. It continues to amaze me how much power the wind can have. Good thing I was on the river and not walking through that mess! Oops, I might have spoke a little soon—I plan to hike through this spot tomorrow!

Bowers Hollow was next, and the very first view of, of, *Cloudland!* I had to stop the canoe and get out and look close, but way off on top of a distant hill, surrounded by trees, I could see a tiny spec that was my little cabin, watching over the wilderness and all who pass through it. Some people have complained about this cabin, about the fact that you could actually see it from elsewhere in the wilderness. Regardless of what they might say, people *do* belong in wilderness (after all, they were there weren't they?). And what a better representation of man in wilderness than a log cabin? To me they go hand in hand. It was a painting on my grandparent's wall that I first saw when I was five years old that set my mind and my heart on a vision of wilderness—and on protecting wild places. There is a log cabin in that painting, a trail leading to it, and a lake, a snow-capped mountain, and a full moon. Yep, if you ask me, log cabins are OK in the wilderness.

I knew the route from that point on, and it got fun floating over and past many known spots along the way. Hubbard Hollow and the giant boulder in the river that I had sat on top of only last week. No one could guess what extreme beauty lay up this little drainage. Boen Gulf that comes into the river hidden behind another rock that I had slept on last summer. And I could feel the pull of Whitaker Creek. Another long pool, a set of rapids, and there it was! The one spot on the river that I visit several times a week. I got out and walked around and went over to the old homesite just to see what was going on.

I had come nine miles, and had almost seven to go. It was mid-afternoon, and I had the option of hiking up to the cabin and spending the night, then finishing up the float the next day. But since I had a full day planned tomorrow already I decided to continue on and make the float in one day. I pointed the bow downstream once again.

There was a large boulder in the river ahead, and the water went to both sides. Actually there were two boulders. I headed for the shoot of water that went between them. Probably a mistake. Just as the water hit the leading edge of the rock on the left the river turned sharply to the right. I didn't. The canoe smashed into the rock. I tried to push off, but it was no use. Plunk! Under the canoe went, and out into the water I went. This scene happened a few other times during the day too.

Downstream a ways the river bends to the left, goes through a set of rapids, then bends back to the right, emptying into one of the most gorgeous emerald pools on the entire river. The far bank is lined with a bluff, and a spring creates a waterfall that leaps out from the top of the bluff and over the entrance to a cave, then splashes in the deep pool. This is one of my favorite spots on the entire river. And just above the waterfall is my friend Yukon's grave. I got out and hiked up and spent a little time with my long lost friend. I know that no matter wherever I go in this wilderness, he is right there with me, just like old times.

Dug Hollow was next. And once again you would never guess what wild treasures lie upstream. And just downstream, Little Pine Hollow and Pine Hollow flow in. Well, sometimes they flow. I remembered the day when Emily and I explored this far side of the river looking for the bear cave. We finally found it, but didn't realize it until we had hiked back to the cabin. I've never returned. I wondered if I would ever would? Some things in life are left to be finished.

I had not been downstream from the cave area so the rest of the float would be all new to me. There were more rapids, and pools, and giant boulders in the middle of the river. And lush forest all around. I don't remember a spring as lush as this one. Perhaps I had spent more of it *out in* the woods than before.

Towards the end of the trip I passed cultivated fields on the right. We had shot part of the *Trailside* TV show in this field, and along the river there. They didn't use any of that footage but we had a good time shooting it. Then I heard the whining of a truck, one of those big ones coming off of the big hill on Hwy. 21 from Mossville. That, and the big fields, were a sign that the end was near. One more bluff. One more giant boulder. One more set of rapids. And then the highway bridge.

The river was terrific, the paddler was not too good, and his style a little sloppy. My arms were sore, and so were my legs—from being beat up by the boat and the rocks. I would have many bruises on my body tomorrow.

It was late in the day when I arrived, but only thirty minutes late. My friend was waiting to collect his boat, and to see if I actually had made it. Usually at the end of a wonderful float like this one there is a lot of quick talking and story telling and maybe a little stretch of the truth or two. But I didn't really have all that much to say. I guess that I had done this float for me, to see my wilderness, and to see if I could do it. Of course, it was also possible that I was quite literally worn down and exhausted from all the work of the day. My friend had been there before, and he understood. I thanked him and headed on up the road towards the cabin.

I ate a lot for dinner, but mostly good stuff like pasta and veggies. As I sat and soaked in the tub in the moonlight and sipped my wine, I thought about what a wonderful day it had been, and once again how lucky I was to not only be alive, but to be able to do things like float the "Hailstone" on my own time. The whippoorwills came out and welcomed me back to the cabin. It was good to be there. Only two days left. I was out before my head hit the pillow.

4/29/99 I was back in the hot tub before the sun came up. My upper body was a mess, tired and sore from all of the paddling. And I had a couple of pretty good blisters on my hands. No matter—it was a splendid morning at Cloudland, and I was joined by dozens of birds to welcome the new day.

It would be another big adventure for me today. For some reason I had been thinking that I needed to get out and do as much as I could this last week of April, and of the Journal. I sat down once and drew up a list of the top things that I had wanted to do this last week, places that I wanted to visit. I narrowed the list down to 38! Good grief. It was then that I realized that the wilderness would always be there, that I could never see it all in one year, and that no one expected me to. So I picked a few of the more important things that I wanted to do, which included the float, and the hike that I was going to do today.

I have always wanted to start at the very beginning of the Buffalo River and hike to the cabin. Lots of people ask me where the river begins. I think that many folks believe that there is this magical spot in the middle of the woods somewhere where the river just bubbles up and is full sized. I remember a cartoon that shows a big sign pointing to the beginning of the mighty Mississippi River—it is a faucet in someone's yard that is left on and is dripping. The White River actually does begin at one spot—at the base of an outhouse next to the highway at Boston. The flow increases with every flush.

Rivers are formed one raindrop at a time, falling on a wide area of watershed that all comes together and eventually forms a tiny creek. This creek joins with other small creeks, and gets larger with every one. Creeks from different drainages come together, and finally a river is born. The exact beginning point of the Buffalo River is impossible to determine. It begins in a million spots. But there are several points at the tops of drainages where one can say the river is born. It was at one of these points that I began my hike this morning.

I followed an old pioneer road that had become a four wheeler road. I don't mind four-wheelers (they can be a lot of fun) when they are used in their place, but they can be dangerous, and also tear up the land in a hurry.

The trail headed on down the drainage and soon came alongside a small creek, one of those that forms the headwaters of the Buffalo River. There was no fog this morning, only blue skies and lots of sunshine. It was going to be a long hike, with terrible light for pictures, so I didn't bother to bring along my camera gear, nor wanted to, because it was going to be a tough hike of sixteen miles. But the first part of the hike was really easy, thanks to the four wheeler trail.

The hillsides were lush with ferns and wildflowers. More ferns than I had seen anywhere else this spring. Entire hillsides of ferns! And I was glad to see the wildflowers out again—they had gone through a dull spell these last couple of weeks. The further I hiked, the more wildflowers came out.

And then I spotted three yellow lady slipper orchids, right in a row, and right next to the trail. I had heard stories about this incredible valley that was full of orchids. As many as a thousand orchids. Yea, right. Then I saw another patch of lady slippers. And another, and another. Each with bright yellow blooms. Nothing out here can match the flower of a lady slipper for pure beauty—they are just incredible!

As I walked on I passed more and more wild orchids. I started to count them. Twenty. Thirty. Forty. *Fifty!* I was amazed. And there were more and more other wildflowers too—at one point I counted twelve different kinds of wildflowers in bloom in one small area, all different colors. Wild iris, fire pink (*lots* of them!), phlox, spiderwort, wild geranium, buttercup, mayapple, and a ton of dewberries. Plus many that I didn't know. And the ground everywhere was lush with flowers and grasses and all kinds of vegetation. Sixty. Seventy. *Eighty* lady slippers! No kidding. These orchids weren't in big batches like the patch at Bob's, they were mostly single plants, or perhaps three or four in one area. They were really spread out.

I got into this rhythm, the trail was so easy, the weather very pleasant, and the miles just flew by. Before I knew it I was standing back at Dixon Ford, where I had begun my float trip the day before, and had already hiked seven miles. The lady slippers had played out a few miles back, and I hadn't seen any in a while. I counted over 100 blooms! There were certainly two or three times as many plants without blooms on them. And that was just within sight of the trail. Very impressive.

Wow, that first stretch had gone by so quickly, I would be back at the cabin by noon. I knew better. There had been a clear and wide trail the entire way so far (actually an old road), but I knew the next few miles would be tough going through that thick, lush, tropical environment, not to mention the lovely tornado area. My work was cut out for me. I plunged into the forest.

The first mile or two wasn't all that bad, as I followed an old pioneer road that more or less runs the entire length of the wilderness. Only it wasn't cleared out like the four-wheeler road was—no vehicles allowed in the wilderness. And the forest service had not allowed any type of trail along the route, so there has been no reason for anyone to clear anything out. I disagree with this policy, and believe that we should open up this old pioneer route along the river. It would make one of the greatest trails in the region. It would have to be a horse trail too, which would be fine, since the horses would not be tearing up a narrow hiking trail. The roadbed could stand the traffic quite well. One of these years perhaps.

Before long I came to a river crossing. That is one problem with this old pioneer road—it crosses the river a lot. Heck, I had been in the river lots of times the day before, so it should be a piece of cake. Hum. I took off my boots and waded across. The water seemed a bit *chilly* today! And I slipped on a rock and almost went in.

The old road bed continued along the river and crossed it a couple more times. One time I decided to not cross and just bushwhack my way along the bank. Big mistake. It was pretty easy going at first, then I realized why the pioneers had put the road on the other side—it was steep, nearly vertical down to the river, and choked with vines and boulders and just, well, it was *thick!* And the footing was tough. I'll bet it took me an hour to go one-half mile. No telling how many snakes I passed.

And speaking of snakes, I did see quite a few of them on this hike. Nearly stepped on a couple. I saw five copperheads and about a dozen cottonmouths. No rattlesnakes though. I know it is just a matter of time and bad luck before I get bit, which I have never had happen in my life, yet. And even though I know it is not a cure-all, I do carry my extractor kit with me for when that day comes.

I suspect that when I do get bit I will use the extractor, and then lay there in extreme pain for the rest of the day, perhaps will even have to spend the night in the woods. I don't carry extra food or shelter or anything like that with me on these dayhikes, but I do carry a lighter. I figure if I can get a fire going I can wait it out until I am well enough to walk/crawl out. I would just as soon that never happen. But you never know.

And then I came to the tornado area. Yikes! This was really a jungle. Trees down *everywhere*. Big ones, small ones, all twisted and woven together, and all right in my way. You never really appreciate a nice maintained hiking trail until you bushwhack through a tornado area. The forest was making the best of it though, and there was no shortage of new growth. There must have been a healthy crop of wild iris at the base of this one big tree before it got knocked over, but the new earth that was exposed had created a really rich environment for new flowers, and they had literally taken over. It was funny to see all of the flowers covering the root ball and crater.

And then I found the rock wall that I had heard so much about. This is without a doubt the most impressive pioneer rock wall in the Ozarks. It is something like six feet tall, and goes on forever. There is a picture of it in Ken Smith's book **Buffalo River Country**. Back then (in the 1960's) you could still drive the old road, and his white VW Beetle is parked on the road next to the wall in the photo. Oh how things have changed.

As I passed the mouth of Bowers Hollow I remembered that I had never been from the mouth up to the big waterfall before, and I wondered what treasures it held? There is so much to see in this country. I need a job where I can just get out and go hiking any time that I want to. Oh, I guess that is what I am doing.

Pretty soon I came to the mouth of Hubbard Hollow—one more crossing of the creek there, and I was home free. Good thing, because my legs were tired and I was all scratched up and needing a good soak in a hot tub. It was late afternoon, and the cabin way up there on the hill looked mighty good. Of course, I still had that big hill to climb, but I had a feeling it would be a piece of cake.

And it was. So *nice* to be on a cleared out trail again. The elevation just didn't seem to matter. As I sat out on the deck cooling down, the last rays of the sun shone on the wilderness, and the shadows stretched all the way across the valley. At last, I had walked through what I could see from that deck. From the beginning of the river to Cloudland, about sixteen miles. Let's see, now I have to continue on and walk to the mouth of the Buffalo River at the White River—it is only 137 miles! Perhaps next week.

I called a neighbor to come get me and run me back up to get the truck, then I had a good long soak in the tub. The moon was up and shining brightly on my wilderness world. Only one day left. Wow, it had been one incredible last month of the Journal, last week, last day! And now only one more day to go. I laid back in the water in the moonlight and wondered what I was going to do tomorrow.

4/30/99 Once again I was up and in the tub before the sun popped up. Another wonderful sunrise at the edge of the wilderness. There were so many things that I had wanted to do this day, there was no way that I could even begin to get them all done. So I decided to just kick back and enjoy the fabulous spring day and do whatever struck me at the time.

Part of the Cloudland experience is the great food. So I whipped up one terrific breakfast to go with the wonderful morning. Asparagus eggs, Cloudland hash, Cloudland coffee, and blueberry biscuits. I sat out on the back deck and savored every bite. It was a breakfast better than at any five star restaurant in the world. And the morning was golden.

Hey, how about a few pictures? I packed up my camera gear and headed down to the lady slipper patch at Bob's. The light was right for a few early pictures. And the flowers were simply gorgeous! I fired off about three rolls of film, then wandered on over to a magnolia tree that had some low branches in bloom. It was tough to concentrate on picture taking when the air was so heavy with the fragrance of these incredible blooms. A few more rolls went through the camera.

Then I stopped by the showy orchid plants nearby. There were five plants, all in different stages of bloom. One plant was in full bloom, and I shot another roll or two there—first pictures I had ever taken of these little wonders. And right next to one plant I found a morel mushroom. I took his picture too, even though I can't stand to eat mushrooms!

These orchids are growing around the base of this giant black gum tree. I still can't believe that everyone (including me) had been stumped all winter as to the identity of this mystery tree—they are growing all over the wilderness! Black gum. They are so *easy* to recognize now.

I saw Bob for a moment, and he told me that he had been down to my cabin the day before and found some fresh bear scat. I thought he was joking. But sure enough, about two hundred feet from the front door, and right in the middle of the road, was a small pile of bear scat. Hum.

I returned to the cabin and decided that a little work was in order. I started off by blowing out the route for the trail up to the East Meadow. I have this special backpack blower that puts out wind at 225 miles an hour. I use it for the first phase of trail construction, and while you have to work at it some, it does a great job of clearing out a nice walking path. That is just the first step, but it does give you an easy route to follow. That took me about two hours to do, and then I moved on to another chore.

Poison Ivy. There was lots of it sneaking around the lower decks and the meadow below. I spent the next couple of hours with a small spray can in hand, squirting Roundup on hundreds of the plants. I'm not allergic to the stuff but it seems that most others are, and so I wanted to try to get it under control for their sake.

While I was down close to the ground looking for the plants I found a lot of other plants growing in my little patch of heaven just below the lower decks.

Sassafras, wood sorrel in bloom, ferns, mosses, and six or eight plants that looked a lot like they would put forth flowers of some sort soon. I was thrilled to find such a variety of plant life down there. I continue to have trouble identifying plants, but am getting better at it. Someone recently called me a "naturalist" on a TV show. Well, I'm far from it. Perhaps I am a "Junior Naturalist." Yes, I could handle that title.

I spent the next hour watering the "domestic" plants that we had added to the scene. They were doing fine, but getting a little dried out from the lack of rain. The cistern setup worked great, and I drained about 75 gallons out of it. Let's see, 75 gallons a pop, I could water the plants six or seven times on one tank full. Surely it would rain by then and fill the tank. Well, maybe not this summer. I decided to water the plants whenever needed and just hope for the best.

After lunch the swing called me out and I spent an unknown amount of time there in deep conversation with my dreams. In order to take full advantage of Cloudland one must spend part of each day in the swing, napping.

A couple of weird things happened in the airspace out in front while I was hanging out on the back deck. First, I saw this object rising from the river valley below. It wasn't moving all that fast, but it was moving, and headed in my direction. And it had a funny color to it. I got out the binocs and tried to follow it. It kept coming up my way. And then it suddenly hit me what it was—a great blue heron! The darn thing came right on up the hill and landed in one of the big pines in the meadow. A heron, up at Cloudland! He really looked out of place, and I swear there was a confused look on his face. After a few moments he took off and flew on up Whitaker Creek.

And one time when I woke up I looked out and saw another strange shape in the air, only this object was just hovering there. I got up and put the binocs on him—it was a large red-tailed hawk riding the wind currents—only he was *facing* the cabin! That is why he looked so strange in the first place—I'm used to seeing them facing away from or to the side of the cabin. Then I realized that the wind was coming from the north, which it never does.

OK, enough of this lounging around, it was time to go hiking! One of the great hikes that I had been looking at all year but never set foot on, was the hillside and major bluffline right across the river from the cabin. Not even Billy McNamara had been over there. I wanted to go take a look at where those two giant waterfalls were, and see if I could climb up onto the big sandstone blocks that have their own contour lines on the map. Today was the day. It was sunny and warm, the river was low, and I needed to hike. So I packed up my gear and headed down the ladder trail.

The river was cool and inviting. I slipped off my shoes and waded across, then put on my long pants and headed *up* the hillside. Wow, this side of the hill was *lush!* My goodness, it was really tropical. There were places where I could not even see the ground for all of the flowers and plants growing there.

It didn't take long for the hill to get really steep. I didn't have any particular route in mind—I just wanted to go up until I got to the bluffline. And so I went up, and up and up. It was really steep, and I was often down on all fours, scrambling and reaching for anything to grab onto to get me a few feet higher.

And then I found some bear tracks, right there in the dirt. This dude was doing about the same thing that I was doing—climbing straight up the side of the hill. They looked to be at least a few hours old, perhaps even from the day before. I'm sure he wasn't having as tough a time as I was—especially since he had those claws to dig into the earth with.

As I climbed higher I came across his tracks again and again. I never did spot any logs that had been torn up, or big rocks turned over, or any scat. But lots of prints. He must have just been on his way up the hill, and not really foraging. After about a twenty minute climb I waded through a boulder field that was covered with grapevines and lots of other thick vegetation. Then I broke out into the open, and right up there above me was the bluffline. Whew, I had made it! The elevation gain was about the same as hiking from the river up the ladder trail to the bluffline, but since there was no clear and open trail to follow on this hill, the going was a little tougher. But I didn't mind at all, and it actually felt pretty good. Although I did lose my footing a couple of times and went tumbling back down the hillside on my rear. I'll bet the bear never did that!

OK, I was at the bluff, now what? It was a pretty solid bluff, about 50 feet thick. I decided to go to the south, along the base, until I found a spot where I could go up. And it didn't take me long to find a likely looking spot. A crack actually, with a few handholds here and there. After about a five minute struggle I made it to the top of the bluff. I'm not all that big on climbing you know.

Once on top I headed back towards the north to see what I could find. What I noticed right off the bat was that there wasn't a clear view over towards the cabin—lots and lots of big trees all around. But I kept going. The terrain on the bench above the bluff varied from completely flat, to mildly steep. And unlike the hillside below the bluff, there was hardly any ground cover at all.

I finally did get to a spot where I had a good view to the west towards the cabin. And much to my surprise, I couldn't see the cabin at all! I could see Hawksbill Crag just fine, and even the Buffalo Fire Tower, more than six miles away. I could see the real Whitaker Point—the lookout rock right down below the cabin. But no cabin. The trees had completely swallowed it up!

I started to look for a go-down spot, and found one in no time, so I slipped on back down to the base of the bluff. Now the real fun would begin. I followed the base of the bluff towards Little Pine Hollow, and towards those waterfalls and giant blocks. It was really lush in this area, with lots of wildflowers and magnolias in bloom. And the bluff itself was painted in different shades of reds and blacks. Some of the bluff was broken up and jagged like a lot of the bluffs in this area, but long stretches of it were very solid and sheer too—and thicker, more like 70-80 feet thick. It was a handsome bluff for sure!

And then I found the first waterfall, and it was running. It was surrounded by an umbrella magnolia in full bloom. The rocks around the base where the water was splashing were coal black, I guess from the minerals in the water that were released when the water hit them.

There were a number of overhangs in the bluff too, although since they faced west, I doubted that any were important bluff-dweller sites—they preferred southern exposure.

There were tons of ferns along this bluffline. Maidenhairs by the score, and three or four others that grew in bunches. All of them seemed to be happy to have company come along to talk to. They were in their prime, plump with fresh spring growth.

The second waterfall was right in the middle of the longest, straightest and thickest part of the bluffline. This one had more of a creek below it, which immediately leapt off of the hillside and went screaming down the steep pitch.

Then I came to a big crack in the bluff. You see these all the time, but this one looked different then most. I went up to it and found that I could actually walk right into the bluff. The crack was about three feet wide, and went all the way to the top of the bluff, some 60 feet or so. The floor was covered with leaves. I climbed right on in it.

The crevasse remained about two to three feet wide, and the floor headed downhill. I continued deeper into the bluff. It was pretty dark in there, but I swear that I could see daylight way down in the bottom. I went down about twenty feet, and finally bottomed out. Sure enough, there was daylight. The crevasse made a 90 degree turn, and although I had to squeeze past a block of rock in the way, I did manage to make the turn and continue on. I got a little uneasy poking around deep down in there, not knowing if I was about to put my foot on a rattlesnake's head or not.

I climbed on up and out towards the daylight, but just before I got to where I thought I could pop out of the bluff, there was another large rock blocking the way. Actually several of them. I could not go any further, so I turned around and went back. Wow, this crevasse really went far back into the bluff! It is an odd feeling of sorts to be so deep in, with all this tons of solid rock all around. I made it out OK, then went around to see where the crevasse came out. The rock blockage was only about twenty feet from the end—I almost made it. Neat spot for sure.

As I walked along the bluffline I found a couple of sandstone blocks, but they didn't seem large enough to be the ones that I was looking for. They were pretty large though, and I made a note to look for them after leaf-fall next winter. The bluff went on.

Then I found the real sandstone blocks—very large, but not quite as tall as the ones over near Hubbard Hollow. It was obvious where they had come from—there were large spots in the bluffline where these monsters used to rest. I would have loved to have been standing around a million years ago and seen them tumble off.

There were three blocks actually—I had only seen two from the cabin. And the middle one appeared to have a way up. So I set my mind to climbing up, and plotted the route. Real climbers would call this "bouldering," but I just call it trying to scramble up to the top for a view.

I got up the first few feet OK, then worked my way over to one side where I was able to climb up a lot farther, right on past a dewberry bush that was in full bloom. A few other moves brought me right on up to the top of the rock—hurrah! I had climbed up about 25-30 feet.

Oh my, what a view. It was stunning! I was looking down on a large pool in the river way below, and upstream to Hubbard and Bowers Hollows, and on up into Whitaker Creek—the Crag really stuck out—and I could even see up into Dug Hollow. Once again, no cabin. Didn't matter, I knew it was over there.

This was a really neat rock, and in fact there was another part of it that went up higher. At first, I could not find a way up on top. Then I found another crevasse that went into the rock, but the entrance was blocked with this most unusual chunk of vertical rock with sharp edges—only about six or eight feet tall. I looked farther, and discovered a second crevasse that I could walk right into. It wound around a little, and actually connected with the other crevasse that had the rock in it. And I was able to climb up and out of the crevasse and get up on top of the rock. My little camera couldn't take in all of the rock, but I did get a snapshot of where the two cracks came together. And once again, a great view.

OK, sandstone blocks done, now, how do I get down? Really. I had trouble finding the exact spot where I came up, and then I found the dewberry bush that I had climbed past on the way up—bingo. Climbing down is always the toughest for me anyway, but I did manage to make it down OK.

The third rock in the series was the largest, and I couldn't find a way up it. But I did find that this giant rock was split in two, right down the middle, and you could walk through the alley. It reminded me a little of this alley between two blocks over in Busby Hollow. Nice places, both.

I left the blocks and followed the bluffline on around the hill, then decided that I didn't have enough time to explore further, so I left the bluff behind and dropped on down the *steep* hillside, and landed in Little Pine Hollow.

This little hollow was a lot like Hubbard Hollow—filled with jagged boulders of all sizes, some of them very large, with a small stream leaping from rock to rock. It was steep, and rough going. And there were lots of magnolias drooping down over everything—very tropical indeed!

And then I came to this one neat spot. There was a giant boulder laying right across the creek, actually being held up at one end by a smaller boulder. And the creek had drilled a passageway right under the rock. I followed the creek inside, and eventually emerged on the other and lower side of the big block of rock. The creek spilled over a ledge and into a small pool, then formed another waterfall before leaving the darkness behind. I hate to keep doing this, but this was a miniature version of the cave over on Indian Creek that has the creek flowing through it. Once again, both are terrific places (Indian Creek is much larger though).

And I kept finding fossils. *Tons* of fossils. Sometimes entire rock beds of fossils. I got to thinking about this little drainage that hardly even shows up on a map. I was only seeing a small part of it—no doubt there were great waterfalls and boulders and glorious things higher up in the drainage. But I bet that I could shoot 100 rolls of film in just about any drainage in the upper Buffalo area. At least. Each and every one is so wonderful. And I haven't seen them all yet! But I am still young, and there are many years of exploration left.

I landed on the bank of the Buffalo River at a beautiful spot—I remembered this spot from my float—I had dumped there! The water was much lower today, and I was able to cross easily, but just had to stop a moment and laugh at how silly I must have looked going into the water from the canoe.

This Buffalo River is certainly one wonderful piece of water. It seems the more you look into it, the more color you see—greens, blues, silver and black. The texture of the water is great too. Often it will be calm, slick as glass, reflecting whatever is above. Then it will turn loud and rough and white and foamy as it plunges down a steep slope or around a rock. And sometimes there are a million tiny ripples in it from a light breeze.

One of my best memories of this river was when I slept on a rock out in the middle. There was this deep pool all around. I woke up early in the morning and gazed out across the smooth surface. A beaver was making his way across with a twig in his mouth. And trailing him were the most delicate waves going out in opposite directions. He made no sound, but eventually the ripples did make this gentle lapping noise as they came ashore. It was a calm, relaxing, serene wilderness scene. And then he saw me and slapped his tail against the water with a loud *crack!*, which nearly knocked me off of the rock.

Once across the river I bid it farewell and headed into the thick brush. Lots of briars along this part. Soon I passed about two dozen piles of stones—placed there last century by early pioneers who cleared the land to create fields. Then I passed the double chimneys of the old Sparks place. It won't be long now before one of them tumbles over, and a part of history will go along with it.

Then the real work began. I headed straight up the hillside through the lush vegetation. Up and up and up I went, no stopping. I had been this way many times before, but there was no trail, and my route was always just a few feet off from the last time. When I reached the base of the bluff I looked around and found a secret route up through it. Before long I was home again, and sitting on the back deck, gazing across at the big hill that I had just explored.

What a great hike! And it had been right there in front of me all year long. There are many more out there, just waiting. I'll get to them.

I spent a few minutes cooling down from the climb, shoveled in a few mouthfuls of this great trail mix that I found at SAMS (cashews, almonds, raisins, peanuts, and M & M's), then got ready for another hike. The shadows were getting long, and the sun was beginning to drop near the horizon. Tonight was a full moon, and I wanted to see it rise from the top of a bluff far up Whitaker Creek. It was clear, and was going to be one terrific moonrise!

To get to the bluff I went over to the Crag, then dropped down below the bluffline just beyond and made my way down into the bottom of the South Fork drainage. It was a steep climb up the other side, through lush magnolia blooms, to the base of the bluffs, then finally up through a break in the bluff to the top, where I found a spot with a grand vista of the Whitaker Creek drainage. The view included Hawksbill Crag and my cabin, way off over there on top of the point overlooking the Buffalo River. And just beyond the cabin was the big ridge that I see the sun and moon rise over.

It was nearly dark when I arrived on top of the bluff, and I laid back against a tree and next to an azalea bush in bloom and waited for the show. A full moon will always come up close to the same time as sunset, although since there are hills here, it would be a little later before the moon was actually visible. I didn't mind the wait at all. The fragrance of the azalea nearly put me to sleep. Or into some sort of dream state.

As the light faded I could hear whippoorwills and owls calling out way across the valley. There were a few little clouds hanging around overhead, and they lit up pink, then turned grey and faded into the night sky. Mars was the first object to show up, and it glowed red, as always. I could also see Venus up behind me—it was very bright. Then a single star came out—this is the one that I wished upon (the others were planets, so the wish doesn't work). Same wish as always.

And then a glow appeared behind the distant trees. It was an orange glow. Soon this huge, brilliant pumpkin appeared and rose slowly into the eastern sky. My God it was an incredible scene! I had witnessed many full moon rises before, but none the magnitude of color and power of this one. I sat there in stunned silence, overwhelmed by the great beauty and nearly in tears. The entire forest was silent as well—not a peep or hoot could be heard. I know that every other critter in the wilderness had to have been holding their breath too at this glorious scene. Wow, I never expected anything like this! And the moon remained that pumpkin color for a long while—it was just odd and beautiful and incredible to see that color rising into the sky. If I only had brought my camera.

The forest came back to life, and so did I. Now that I had a big lantern overhead it was time for me to hike back to the cabin. It was dark, and I had no flashlight, but the moonlight would lead me.

Instead of going back the same way that I had come I elected to follow the bluffline on up into the headwaters, where I could pick up the Crag trail and take it back to the cabin. It was pretty easy hiking, and the moonlight gave me plenty of illumination to go on.

Towards the end of the bluff it forms a horseshoe shape, with a big waterfall pouring off it. I made my way down through the bluffline and went under the thundering waterfall. The last time that I had been there, was when Emily and I took refuge there during a heavy thunderstorm.

There is this waterfall on the Daniel Boone Trail over in Kentucky that is called Moonbow Falls. When the moon is bright there you can actually see a "moonbow" created by the moonlight. I have always wondered if that just happened at that waterfall, or if you could see it at others. Since the moon was bright, and I was at the base of this large waterfall, I scrambled up behind it and took a look. Sure enough, if you stood in just the right spot and got the moonlight at just the right angle, there was a moonbow of sorts visible. It wasn't nearly as brightly colored like a rainbow is, but there definitely were a few bands of color from the moonlight. Wow, a moonbow falls right here in Arkansas!

As I climbed up the bluff on the far end, I passed a second waterfall in the main creek. OK, so I just had to go take a look. I slipped and slid on down to the base of this falls, and looked and looked all over from behind it, but I never could find the moonbow. One moonbow falls is enough.

It was an easy hike up from the falls area to the trail. And then a mostly level hike from there on over towards the cabin. Gosh, I could not think of a more fitting last hike of the journal year than one in the moonlight. My mind began to wander. What an incredible year I have had at Cloudland. *No* way to have imagined all of the great joy and discovery that has taken place.

I thought about all of the waterfalls that I had seen, most of them for the first time. And the moss-covered boulders and ferns and wildflowers and near tropical quality of the forest with its magnolia, dogwood and azalea blossoms. And all of those moonlit hikes last summer, up to the East Meadow to watch for shooting stars and drink champagne and listen to the winds. And the big trees that I have seen, my gosh, there are a lot of giants out here in the wilderness. And the weather. Winds up in the 50mph range several times. And standing and hiking in the pouring rain and loving it. And in the snow and the ice too, and laughing. And the incredible views, one after another after another after another. And the time that I got caught out in the dark and spent the night in my shorts and t-shirt, clinging to Yukon's grave with my shirt stuffed with leaves for warmth. And the wild critters that I have seen and heard and talked to. All of the colorful birds, the hawks and bluebirds and scarlet tanagers and turkeys, and the golden eagle that sat in the snag at the edge of the meadow by the cabin. And the wolf that broke the silence and woke up the wilderness and sent a chill down my spine. And, of course, all of the bears, the friends and the bad ones. I got to thinking about all of those bears a lot as I hiked on in the darkness. In fact, it seemed like I saw a bear in every black stump that I passed by. And there was that fresh bear scat right by the cabin. Hum. I walked on. The darkness didn't seem to bother me at all.

And I thought about all of the great food, the fresh veggies from Bob's garden, the salmon, the pasta, the *pizzas!* And all of the wonderful wine—very little of it from a box this year. And didn't we have a bushwhacker party or two? And the magnificent sunrises and sunsets, the brilliant clouds and thunderstorms and the couple of times that it snowed. I got to hike during every snow that we had this past year. But only one short cross-country ski—the snow just melted too fast! I thought about all of the work of the past year, the new aspen walls inside, clearing the meadow down below, the trail work, splitting all of that wood, and hey, how about all of those wonderful summer hikes down to the swimming hole at the river! And those lazy hours being underwater with a mask on, and all of the incredible color and *life* that I saw in the deep pools and shallow rapids. And that one time that I went fishing with my little fly rod, and caught the most beautiful and colorful fish that I had ever laid eyes on—and then I let him go. And I remember those tough climbs up from the river with great fondness. And that tiny shooting star wildflower at the top of the climb that always welcomed me when I was at my lowest and let me know everything was going to be OK.

And all of those textbook Cloudland mornings when the fog banks hung low in the valleys, and the sunlight spilled into the wilderness and created life. Gosh, mornings here are the best in the world!

I remembered the hundred or so fires that I had built at the cabin and sat in front of, warming, drying, letting my mind wander around by. And all of the terrific music that came from my little speakers. Especially the Friday and Saturday night blues and folk music on KUAF radio.

And I thought about the people of the past year. My old friends who have always been around and who came out to share in the joy and in the chores, and the new friends that I have made. There are so many, and I have appreciated meeting and spending time with them all. There have been a couple of very special friends, much more than just friends, and my experiences with them will live forever in my heart.

There was this one kiss, right there in front of the roaring fireplace, during the blue moon, that has to rank as the single most passionate moment of my entire life. I will never forget that moment.

And, of course, I have a lot of new friends that I have never met, but only know through e-mail. The Journal, while it has been a genuine chore to keep up at times, has been a giant blessing to me.

I know that each and every person that I have been around or met or corresponded with has added a great deal to my life, and for each one of them, I am a little better person for having known them.

Gosh, what a wonderful year. And it was coming closer to an end with each step towards the cabin that I took. None of the bears that I had imagined turned out to be real on this hike, but I kept watching for them just the same. It was a most comfortable hike for me, moving through the darkness. If this past year has taught me anything, it is that I am one with the wilderness, a part of it, and that I belong here as much as any.

Regrets? Sure, there are many. Probably a million things that I didn't get to do—but there would be plenty of time in the next twenty or thirty of years to get to them. I did do and experience about a million things that I never had even thought about, so I guess it all evens out.

There actually are three regrets. First, and it doesn't have anything to do with Cloudland, but with the year, is that I didn't get to spend enough time with my mom. She can't really get out and around much anymore, and I was so pre-occupied with Cloudland that I failed to spend enough time with her. That will haunt me for a long time to come. Secondly, I didn't spend enough time at Cloudland. That is a simple one—I could have easily spent every single day out here and loved every minute of it. I will try to fix that in years to come. And lastly, that soul mate of mine never stepped out of the clouds and into my arms. Another year ended without love. I must say that I did come pretty close though, and while my heart has a hole in it right now, I am still hopeful, only now just looking for a companion to share my life with, and theirs with mine, and the future will build itself, if there is one.

OK, enough of the past year, back to the present. I arrived safely at the cabin and realized that in my hurry to do the full moon hike, I had forgotten to eat! I fired up the grill, and worked up one last, terrific feast for myself. Grilled salmon, fresh corn on the cob, and assortment of fresh veggies, warm sourdough bread, and the best bottle of wine in the house. No meal had ever tasted better. (It took seven pots and pans and eight utensils—all for one serving!) I sat out on the back deck, filled to the brim, and listened to a new CD.

I had heard a song from this CD on the **Folk Sampler** radio show a couple of weeks ago, and finally found the CD in the rock department of a local music store. Oh my gosh, this lady, her music, this CD, is one terrific piece of work! Her name is Lynn Miles, and the CD is **Night In A Strange Town**. I bought it for the one incredible song at the end, but the entire CD is just wonderful (it ranks right on up there with the **Hard Days Night** album by the Beatles). It really spoke to me, and much of the music played right along with my emotions and feelings of the past year that continued to swirl through my mind.

But the last song on the CD, **"Rust,"** is perhaps the most powerful and wonderful piece of music that I had ever heard. I sat there in the swing in the moonlight and felt a huge wave of joy and sadness come over me. And I broke down, and I cried.

Part of the tears were from the joy of knowing my mom, who the song reminded me of a lot. She has been the most important person in my life for a very long time. There have been so many great times with her. But she is slipping away, and I am losing her to Alzheimer's.

The rest of the tears are selfish ones, because I end this year alone, and lonely. My heart has been ripped apart, and it aches. I will find my lifemate at some point, I know. And until then I will continue to howl at the moon.

The day and the year were about to end. So I dried my tears, poured a little more wine and headed down to the tub to soak in the moonlight. Few things in life are as satisfying as slipping into a hot tub under a full moon. The wilderness was all lit up, almost like daylight. I kept the bubbles off because I wanted to hear the sounds of the night. And it didn't take long for a conversation between two owls to strike up. In fact, a third one joined in, and then a fourth owl started talking! And they went back and forth for ten minutes. One of them was very close. I could really hear the grittiness in his voice. And then they got silent, and all I could hear was the wind and the hush of the river below.

I leaned over the side of the tub to survey my little world below, and spotted some movement down in the meadow. My first thought was a bear. Yea, right, there was a big bear that had come visiting in the middle of the night. Dream on bud. My eyes focused, and right there, as plain as day, *was* a bear! He was crossing the meadow, looking around and not in any big hurry. He stopped a couple of times to sniff the air. It was so bright out, he was easy to see. Not a big bear, but certainly not a little cub either.

What he did next must have really shocked me, because I immediately jumped up out of the tub, and went running down the trail towards this bear, in the moonlight, screaming at the top of my lungs. I was out there in the dark in the middle of the night chasing a bear, and I was naked. I told you it was a good bottle of wine! What the bear did that provoked such a knee-jerk response from me was that he went for the snag that the bluebirds were nesting in—no damn bear was going to eat my bluebirds!

I'm sure the bear took off at the first sound of my voice, but I ran down through the meadow anyway, just to make sure that he knew he was not welcome to eat my bluebirds. I had done a lot of comical things out here this last year, but I suspect this one would have topped them all. It didn't bother me so much that I was out there naked in the moonlight, or dripping wet, but the fact that I had *no shoes* on became a painful fact. I didn't feel a thing while I was running after the bear, but as I started back up the trail, every step hurt! What a wimp.

Needless to say it took a while for my heart to stop pounding. I need to get paid money if I am to go chasing bears in the middle of the night. I sat there in the bubbles and laughed at myself. But also patted myself on the back for saving those little baby bluebirds. At least they are safe for now. Every year the bears tear up the bluebird houses at Bob's cabin—I don't know why the birds keep coming back. I was bound and determined to keep that from happening at Cloudland. I suspect that there will be many more bear encounters this year than last. I only hope most of them are friendly!

Anyway, the bubbles did finally calm me down, and the stroke of midnight found me in a relaxed bliss, and not a care in the world. It had been one extra fine year at Cloudland. My mind had been swept clear and I was ready for the next year to begin. Words cannot express my heartfelt gratitude to all of you who have faithfully read this online Journal. Thanks for wading through it all with me. I hope to meet each and every one of you in the woods someday...

RECIPES

CLOUDLAND PIZZA

1 box bread machine mix (I use Olive & Herb, but most anything will do)
handful of flour, any kind
olive oil
sun-dried tomatoes (in oil, or if dry, soften first), sliced into thin strips
Greek olives, pitted and sliced into thin strips
artichoke hearts, sliced
onion, thinly sliced
feta cheese, crumbled
grated parmesan cheese
shredded Mexican cheese mixture (any)
fresh tomatoes, thinly sliced
very cold beer in frosted mug

Process bread mix in bread maker on dough cycle. Roll out on floured surface into whatever size pizzas you want (I make six small ones from each box). Place on greased pizza pans. Coat top with olive oil. Bake at 350 degrees until just beginning to turn light brown. Remove from oven and add all ingredients except tomatoes and beer, adding shredded cheese last to bind everything together. Continue baking until just about done (another ten minutes or until the cheese melts well), then add sliced tomatoes, and cook five minutes more. Sit out on the back deck and serve with cold beer.

CLOUDLAND VEGGIE CHILI

1 large onion, coarsely chopped
1 can (28 ounces) whole tomatoes, undrained, coarsely chopped
2/3 cup picante sauce
1.5 tsps. salt
1/2 tsp. basil leaves
1 can black beans
1 green pepper, cut into 3/4 inch pieces
1 red bell pepper, cut into 3/4 inch pieces
1 large yellow squash/zucchini, cut into 1/2 inch chunks
Toppings:
hot cooked rice
sour cream
shredded cheddar cheese
chopped fresh cilantro

Add all ingredients to a large saucepan and cook until veggies are tender, then ladle into bowls and add toppings.

CLOUDLAND BANFF PASTA

4-6 cloves garlic, thinly sliced
olive oil
3/4 cup sun-dried tomatoes (softened), sliced into thin strips
3/4 cup Greek olives, pitted and sliced into thin strips
green onions, a bundle or two, cut up
3/4 cup feta cheese, crumbled
one package fresh linguini pasta
1/2 cup of red wine (any)

Cook garlic in oil a minute or two, then add the tomatoes and olives. Continue to cook over low heat, and stir once in a while. Meanwhile, prepare the pasta as directed. While it is cooking, add the onions to the tomatoes and olives. Add some wine to the veggie mix. Drain pasta, and add to veggie mix. Turn off heat, cover, and let sit 5-10 minutes. Cut up pasta, toss to mix everything, and serve, topped with feta cheese and ground pepper. Serve with a good bottle of wine.

CLOUDLAND CAJUN GRILLED TUNA

tuna filets (2)
2-4 cloves minced garlic
1/2 cup balsamic vinegar
1/2 cup wine (any will do)
2 tbls fresh lemon juice
2 tbls Cajun Grill seasoning mix (or any grilling mix)
1 tbls cracked black pepper
1 tbls dehydrated orange peel
Basting sauce:
1/2 stick butter
1/3 cup olive oil
1/3 cup soy sauce
1/2 tsp. Rosemary
1/2 tsp. oregano
1/2 tsp. basil
1/2 tsp. garlic powder
1/2 tsp. thyme

Put the tuna into a zip-lock bag, add the first batch of stuff, and refrigerate for 3-4 hours. Grill fish over low heat for a few minutes while you melt some butter in a pan and then add the oil, soy sauce and spices. Turn the fish and baste. Turn once more and baste. Don't overcook, but do cook enough to let the basting sauce do its thing.

CLOUDLAND SALAD
package of "Spring Green" salad mix, or fresh greens of your choice
crumbled feta cheese
fresh green onion, sliced
handful of red grapes
ranch dressing (or another of your choice)
Mix everything together, drizzle on a little bit of dressing (not too much—this is *healthy* you know!). This is best enjoyed while sitting on the back deck enjoying the view, with a glass of fine wine (or like mine, out of a box), and a slice of garlic Texas toast.

CLOUDLAND HASH
shredded potatoes
chopped onion
chopped green pepper
a little garlic
little smokies
veggie oil
shredded cheddar cheese
scrambled egg mixture (optional)
1 or 2 small *fresh* tomatoes (*not* from the store)
salt and pepper to taste
Fry all ingredients in oil (but eggs, cheese and tomatoes), add eggs at last minute and turn until done, top with melted cheese and mix, then add chopped tomatoes (these must homegrown and fresh or don't bother).

CLOUDLAND APPETIZERS
box of black olive and herb bread mix
16 oz. package little smokie links
3/4 cup Greek olives, sliced
small jar of artichoke hearts, sliced
3/4 cup sun-dried tomatoes, softened and sliced
parmesan cheese
feta cheese, crumbled
shredded Mexican cheese mix
olive oil
Prepare bread mix as dough, roll out on floured surface, cut into triangles. Sprinkle Parmesan cheese over dough pieces. Microwave little smokie links a bit and drain. Place one link on each triangle piece. Add a slice or two of Greek olive, artichoke heart, and sun-dried tomato to each triangle. Add a few crumbled bits of feta cheese to each. Sprinkle Mexican cheese over each. Roll up each link inside triangle dough, being sure to wrap all ingredients inside and seal the edges. Place on oiled baking pan and brush with olive oil. Bake at 350 degrees until done.

CLOUDLAND OATMEAL CHOCOLATE-CHIP COOKIES
2 cups all-purpose flower
1 tsp. baking soda
1 tsp. salt
1 cup (2 sticks) butter, softened
1 cup granulated sugar
1 cup packed brown sugar
2 tsp. vanilla extract
2 eggs
2 cups (12 ozs.) chocolate chips
2 cups old fashioned Quaker oats
dash of cinnamon and nutmeg

Mix flour, baking soda, cinnamon, nutmeg, and salt in a small bowl. Mix butter, granulated sugar, brown sugar, and vanilla in a large bowl, then add eggs, one at a time, and mix until blended. Add the flower mixture and blend well. Add the chips and oatmeal and blend well. Spoon out mounds to your liking on an ungreased cookie sheet and bake at 350 degrees until done. Put on a cooling rack to cool, and watch out for anyone grabbing a hot one!

CLOUDLAND COFFEE or COCOA
any brewed coffee or hot chocolate
Bailey's Irish Cream to taste

CLOUDLAND BUSHWHACKERS
1 part vodka
1 part chocolate milk
1 part Tia Maria
1 part Khalua
1/3 can Creme da Cocoa

Fill blender with all ingredients, add crushed ice and blend until smooth. Repeat as needed until no one is left standing.

CUP OF CLOUDS
Fill a cup with reddiwhip or real whipped cream, and add chilled Bailey's Irish Cream to taste. Heavenly.

ANIMAL TRACKS

All of these mammals were either seen, heard (wolf), or talked about (cougar) at Cloudland during this first year.

Deer

Armadillo

Black bear

Rabbit

Opossum

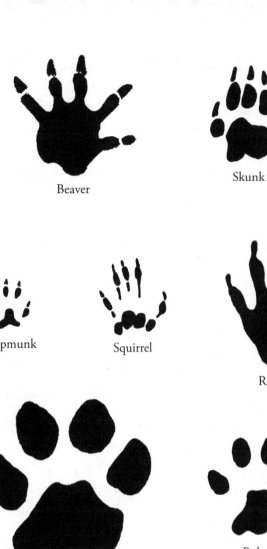

Beaver

Skunk

Chipmunk

Squirrel

Raccoon

Cougar

Bobcat

Fox

Coyote

Wolf

CLOUDLAND AREA—1998

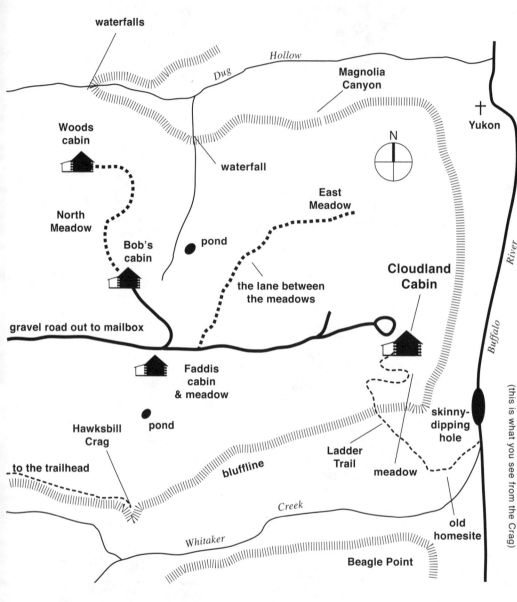

waterfalls

Hollow

Dug

Magnolia
Canyon

Yukon

N

Woods
cabin

waterfall

East
Meadow

North
Meadow

Bob's
cabin

pond

Cloudland
Cabin

the lane between
the meadows

River

gravel road out to mailbox

Buffalo

Faddis
cabin
& meadow

skinny-
dipping
hole

Hawksbill
Crag

pond

to the trailhead

bluffline

Ladder
Trail

meadow

Creek

Whitaker

old
homesite

Beagle Point

This map represents an area of about four square miles and shows the lay of the land in 1998 that contains many relevant features described in this Journal. Note that most of the area around the Cloudland Cabin is private property that belongs to many different land owners—please respect their rights and obey *no trespassing* signs. There is no public access to this area from Hawksbill Crag, nor can you see the Cloudland Cabin from there. The open field and buildings you can see from the Crag are actually at the edge of Mossville, a small community that is across the river on top of the ridge.